X WINDOW SYSTEM TOOLKIT

The Complete Programmer's Guide and Specification

WMO

Digital Press X and Motif Series

Motif Programming

The Essentials . . . and More

Marshall Brain

X Window System Toolkit

The Complete Programmer's Guide and Specification

Paul J. Asente and Ralph R. Swick

X and Motif Quick Reference Guide

Randi J. Rost

X Window System

The Complete Reference to Xlib, X Protocol, ICCCM, XLFD
Third Edition

Robert W. Scheifler and James Gettys
With Jim Flowers, David Rosenthal

X WINDOW SYSTEM TOOLKIT

The Complete Programmer's Guide and Specification

X Version 11, Release 4

Paul J. Asente   Ralph R. Swick

With Joel McCormack

Digital Press

digital™

9 8 7 6 5 4 3

Order number EY-E757E-DP

DECnet, the Digital logo, and Ultrix are trademarks of Digital Equipment Corporation. POSIX is a trademark of The Institute of Electrical and Electronics Engineers. UNIX is a registered trademark of AT&T Bell Laboratories. X Window System is a trademark of The Massachusetts Institute of Technology.

Design: David Ford
Manuscript editor: Alice Cheyer
Production coordinator: Editorial Inc.
Index: Rosemary Simpson
Compositor: Paul Asente and Chiron, Inc.
Printer: The Maple-Vail Book Manufacturing Group

Library of Congress Cataloging-in-Publication Data

Asente, Paul J., 1957-
    X Window system toolkit: the complete programmer's guide and specification /
  Paul J. Asente, Ralph R. Swick, with Joel McCormack.
        p.   cm. — (Digital Press X-motif series)
    Includes index.
    ISBN 1-55558-051-3
    1. X Window System (Computer system)   I. Swick, Ralph R., 1955-
    II. McCormack, J.   III. Title.   IV. Series
QA76.76.W56A74   1990
.005.4'3—dc20   90-40750
                                            CIP

Contents

Chapter 2. Widget Instantiation   660

Chapter 12. Nonwidget Objects   861

List of Figures

List of Examples

List of Tables

PART II SPECIFICATION 627

Acknowledgments

The design and development of the X Toolkit Intrinsics has most definitely been a team effort, but if we could single out one person as deserving credit for the present form of the Intrinsics, it would be Joel McCormack of Digital Equipment Corporation's Western Research Lab (WRL). It was Joel who took the initial X Version of 11 Toolkit architecture proposal, which had data abstraction and data hiding but lacked classes, and turned it into the present classing model. Joel also did some crucial performance analyses and wrote the first document describing the classing implementation of the X Toolkit. We who follow Joel's well-marked path are enormously indebted to him for the solid structure he established.

Much of the motivation for the class-oriented restructuring of the earlier design was provided by X protocol usage analysis done by Mike Chow of Digital's Western Software Lab (WSL). Working with Joel, Mike uncovered many performance problems in the previous version of the toolkit and was also a major contributor to the design.

The person responsible for many of the remaining components of the X Toolkit is Charles Haynes, also of Digital WSL. In particular, the design of the resource and translation management facilities is his work.

Several group managers provided strong leadership—first among them, Smokey Wallace, then of WSL, who was influential in several areas during the early history of X. Primarily through his efforts, Digital decided to make the prototype toolkit built by his group for X Version 10 nonproprietary, thereby creating a nucleus around which multivendor collaboration for the X11

Toolkit formed. The other members of the X10 Toolkit team were Charles Haynes, Terry Weissman, and Phil Karlton, all of WSL.

The responsibility for turning the WSL toolkit into a commercial product was assigned to Ron Kita of Digital's Ultrix Engineering Group (UEG). Working under Ron were Ram Rao, Mary Larson, Kathleen Langone, and Mike Gancarz.

A crucial point in the history of the X Toolkit occurred in the fall of 1986, when Smokey Wallace, Ron Kita, and Ralph Swick were contacted by Frank Hall of Hewlett-Packard's Corvallis Workstation Operation. Frank was the manager of the team that had developed a very different user interface toolkit with different design considerations, called the X-ray toolkit. A four-way collaboration between Frank Hall's group, the two Digital groups and Project Athena at the Massachusetts Institute of Technology (MIT) provided the real birthing ground of what has become the present X Toolkit Intrinsics. The other members of the Corvallis team were Ed Lee, Fred Taft, Rick Mackay, and Tom Houser. Phil Gust, then of HP Labs, and Ted Wilson, also of HP Labs, provided important early support while the collaboration was being established.

As the X11 Toolkit progressed to a usable state, Mark Ackerman, Ron Newman, and, later, Chris Peterson at Project Athena provided helpful feedback and joined the core team to develop the sample widget set. Chris's perseverence in the face of numerous changes in the Intrinsics and the widgets was no trivial matter, and his comments were of considerable benefit to the developers. The support of Dan Geer, manager of the Systems Development Group at Project Athena, was especially appreciated. Also helping to port widgets from the X10 architecture to the new architecture were Mary Larson (UEG) and Loretta Guarino-Reid (WSL). Loretta assisted the development team in numerous ways, including supervising it for much of the time and writing the selection manager. Rich Hyde (WSL) worked on the Shell widget implementation. Additional contributions to the design or implementation were made by Susan Angebranndt (WSL), Mark Manasse and Jim Gettys, both of Digital's Systems Research Center, and Bob Scheifler (MIT Laboratory for Computer Science). Leo Treggiari of Digital's Software Development Technology group played an important role uncovering flaws in both the design and the implementation. John Ousterhaut of the University of California,

Berkeley, reviewed several drafts of the specification prior to Release 1 and gave us useful feedback on the design.

The X Consortium architecture team that hammered out the final specification, ratified as an X Consortium standard in time for X11 Release 3 was composed of most of those mentioned above plus Steve Pitschke (Stellar), Doug Blewett (AT&T), Bob Miller (HP), David Schiferl (Tektronix), Michael Squires (Sequent), Marcel Meth (AT&T), Jim Fulton (MIT), Kerry Kimbrough (Texas Instruments), Mike Collins and Scott McGregor, both of Digital, Julian Payne (ESS), Jacques Davy (Bull), Gabriel Beged-Dov, then of SPC, and Glenn Widener (Tektronix).

Contributing to the architecture team after Release 3 were Don Alecci (AT&T), Ellis Cohen (Open Software Foundation), Donna Converse (MIT), Clive Feather (IXI), Nayeem Islam, Richard Probst, and Larry Cable, all of Sun Microsystems, Dana Laursen (HP), and Keith Packard (MIT). Thanks go to all the architecture team members for the countless hours spent reading and responding to electronic mail and reviewing drafts and code.

We are enormously indebted to Al Mento of Digital's Ultrix Documentation Group for assistance in producing the first several versions of the specification.

We would also like to thank Mark Ackerman, Joel Bartlett (WRL), Gene Dykes (Cornell), Joel McCormack, Howard Trickey (AT&T Bell Labs), and Terry Weissman for reviewing Part I of this book. Thanks, too, to Terry for sending mail.

Very special thanks go to Richard Swan and the entire staff of WRL, without whose support this book could not have been finished.

Finally, we must again thank Bob Scheifler and Jim Gettys for the opportunity that made it all work.

Paul J. Asente

Digital Equipment Corporation

Ralph Swick

External Research Group, Digital Equipment Corporation
and
Project Athena, Massachusetts Institute of Technology

July 1990

Introduction

The X Toolkit is a software module that simplifies writing applications for the X Window System. The user interface code for a toolkit application is typically about one-fifth as large as it would be in an equivalent program that used the lower-level X library directly.

A program written to the X library must code its user interface in terms of windows and input events. A toolkit program, instead, deals with higher-level abstractions called *widgets*. A widget is a user interface component like a menu, a scrollbar, a text entry field, a label, or a pushbutton. The X Toolkit allows an application to take existing widgets and put them together into a user interface. It also provides support for writing new widgets.

This book is a comprehensive guide both for programmers using the X Toolkit to write applications and for programmers writing new widgets. Application programmers should not be put off by the size of this book; well over half its contents is targeted toward widget writers. The X Toolkit contains advanced features that some programs need but many do not, and a long book is necessary to cover all available options exhaustively.

The X Toolkit has gone through several revisions, and this book describes the toolkit as specified in Release 4 of the X Window System. Since at publication time many released versions of the toolkit are still based upon the Release 3 specification, the programmer's guide notes all differences between Release 4 and Release 3. Wherever possible, the programmer's guide suggests work-arounds to achieve similar results when using Release 3; however, in most cases the changes for Release 4 represent new functionality not available in earlier releases.

This book is not an introduction to the X Window System; it assumes you have a basic understanding of the X architecture. Several excellent books are available that provide overviews of X, and you should read one if you are not familiar with how X works. Using the X Toolkit requires an understanding of the X architecture, but it does not require a thorough understanding of the X library interface.

Nor is this book a guide to any particular set of widgets, since each widget set has its own capabilities, quirks, and restrictions. The functionality described in this book applies to writing applications with any set of widgets whatsoever; programmers using a particular set of widgets need documentation on that widget set. All programming examples in the programmer's guide use the widget set developed in the widget writer's part of the programmer's guide.

What You Need to Know about X

This book is a companion volume to *X Window System—C Library and Protocol Reference* by Robert W. Scheifler, James Gettys, and Ron Newman. There are many cross-references to that book, which will hereafter be called simply *Xlib*. Like *Xlib*, this book assumes a knowledge of the C programming language.

Application programmers should have an understanding of X equivalent to that given in the Introduction and Chapter 1 of *Xlib*. Beyond that, application programmers need to understand some X concepts before using some of the capabilities of the X Toolkit, and this book refers to appropriate sections in *Xlib* when discussing these capabilities. It is not necessary to understand the intricacies of the X library interface to write toolkit applications; avoiding these details is the principal reason for using the X Toolkit in the first place.

Widget programmers, however, do need to use X library calls to implement a widget, particularly to display the contents of a widget on the user's screen. The X Toolkit provides assistance by calling widget-specific procedures whenever the contents of a widget need to be updated, but it is ultimately the implementation's responsibility to get the appropriate bits on the screen. Displaying a widget's contents requires knowing the X graphics context model and the X graphics interface as described in Section 5.3 and Chapter 6 of *Xlib*. Widget programmers also need a greater understanding of the X input model and the structure of X events than application programmers do, but they do not need to understand the X library event-handling procedures in detail, since the X Toolkit provides a higher-level interface.

Once you have a basic understanding of how X works, your easiest course is to start reading this book, using *Xlib* as a reference when you encounter a topic that requires a deeper understanding of some X concept.

History and Design Goals

From the beginning the primary goals of the X Toolkit have been to make it simpler to write applications and to make it possible to create user interface components that are reusable across applications. Writing to the X library layer is somewhat akin to using direct system calls to perform I/O—the level of abstraction is too low, requiring applications to be aware of too many irrelevant details. By making it possible to create a library of reusable interface components, the X Toolkit also encourages consistent behavior across different applications. Like the rest of the X Window System, the X Toolkit must be policy-free. It supplies mechanisms to create the user interface components but does not define what the components are, what they look like, or how they behave.

Consistent behavior has multiple meanings. The appearance and behavior (look and feel) of a full user interface toolkit is a design domain explicitly reserved to vendors; there is (deliberately) no standard X look and feel. Several common characteristics of most user interface toolkits can, however, be extracted independent of the look and feel, and an additional goal of the X Toolkit design was to standardize as much as possible without specifying appearance or behavior.

The first version of the X Toolkit was built for X Version 10 at the Digital Western Software Laboratory, with Smokey Wallace as the principal architect. The X10 Toolkit was based on the idea that "a window is the coin of the realm." The identifier for a widget was the widget's window; all routines manipulating widgets used windows as parameters.

Most of the fundamental facilities present in the current toolkit design were implemented in this first version. Resource management, flexible event-to-procedure bindings, the callback paradigm, and geometry flow of control were all present. Many of these ideas had also been implemented in other earlier toolkits by the same and other people.

The X10 Toolkit tried to take a fairly minimalist approach. Its basic structure was a loosely coupled set of modules that used a hash table to associate widget data with the widget's window. Each kind of widget defined what information it wanted associated with the window, and the hash table was indexed with (*window, kind of information*) pairs. There were no standard data representations; each kind of widget defined its own data structures stored in the hash table and retrieved the data structures itself whenever it needed them.

There were also no standard widget interfaces. An application had to keep track of each widget's type and call procedures appropriate to that type to manipulate the widget. The X10 Toolkit thus provided data abstraction by hiding the details of data representations from applications, but it was not object-oriented.

The X10 Toolkit met its design goals fairly well, but experience with it revealed that its goals were not ambitious enough. In the current toolkit, applications identify widget attributes with strings. In the X10 Toolkit, applications had to use unique identifiers for the attributes, and these identifiers were computed at runtime. Thus an application programmer had to write a considerable amount of code to fetch and keep track of these attribute identifiers.

Since there were no standard data representations, there was no consistency across widget implementations. Each type of widget used its own idiosyncratic data formats, so code maintenance was difficult. Worse, programmers would write a new type of widget by taking the implementation of some existing type and editing it to make the new type. This meant that the derived implementation automatically inherited all the bugs in the original, but when a bug was fixed, the fix was not propagated to the derived implementations. The resulting widget implementations contained lots of code that was similar, but not quite identical, to code in the implementations of other widgets. Some of this code implemented common bookkeeping functions like adding a child widget to a parent's list of children. Other code implemented behavior that was common to a set of widgets, like displaying the text in a simple label and in a pushbutton. Because there was no special provision for a developer to augment a widget set by specializing an existing widget, a developer wanting to write a new pushbutton type, for example, needed full source code to the existing widget in order to implement a consistent extension.

Finally, there were substantial performance problems. Using a window as a widget identifier meant that the window had to be created when the application created the widget. However, in general, the size and position of the window could not be determined until after other widgets existed. This, combined with widget implementations that performed their layout algorithms every time the application added a new child, led to most of the windows having their sizes and positions changed many times before the window even appeared on the screen. For each individual widget these changes did not amount to many requests to the X server, but an application with many widgets ended up issuing thousands of pointless server requests.

Another problem was that the authoritative size and position for the window resided only in the X server, not in the toolkit. Whenever this information was needed for some operation, such as geometry layout, the application or widget implementation would query the server. The X Window System manages to avoid most of the overhead of context switching between the application and the X server by batching requests and sending them asynchronously. These individual queries made the batching ineffective, however, since no more requests could be issued until the server's response arrived. In contrast to normal requests that incur only a small fraction of a millisecond's overhead, these round-trip requests required several milliseconds apiece to complete. Some widget implementations tried to avoid this overhead by caching the information themselves, but they had to rely upon server notifications to keep the cached values correct, adding additional server traffic.

In the months just prior to the final release of Version 10 of X from MIT, a second toolkit development group became involved through the coordination of MIT. This group, from Hewlett-Packard's Corvallis Workstation Operation and led by Frank Hall, had independently developed another toolkit that they retargeted for X Version 10 and named the X-ray toolkit. The WSL, CWO, and MIT groups quickly recognized and agreed upon the desireability of a common toolkit foundation for the benefit of application developers and developers wanting to write their own specialized user interface components. While independently releasing their existing work, the three groups agreed to work together on defining a common architecture and set of interfaces that was referred to as the *Intrinsics*.

In the very first joint meeting of the DEC, HP, and MIT teams, the question of naming the components that implement look and feel was addressed. All agreed that the term *tool* used by Digital was too generic, as was the term *object*. The term used by Hewlett-Packard, *field editor*, was thought to be too specific and a little unwieldy. Finally, the members adopted the nonpartisan term *widget*, and X usurped yet another generic word for a specific usage.[1]

The Digital Western Software Laboratory took advantage of the change from Version 10 to Version 11 of X to completely redesign the X Toolkit, maintaining the functional separation and modularity of the architecture agreed upon by the DEC/HP/MIT collaboration. This effort was led by Joel McCormack, Charles Haynes, and Mike Chow. The redesign added several new goals to the architecture:

- To enable applications to treat widgets more uniformly and avoid the effort of generating the unique identifiers used for widget attributes.

- To enable code sharing among widget implementations and to make the implementations more uniform, making it easier to write and maintain widget implementations.

- To improve application efficiency by reducing server traffic and eliminating round trips.

The resulting design is described in this book. The first prototype implementation was included with Release 1 of X Version 11 along with a request for comments and a set of widgets that duplicated the functionality of WSL's Version 10 toolkit. Ralph Swick represented MIT, was the X Consortium liaison during the design, and was responsible for the example widget set that became know as the Athena widgets. Paul Asente joined the design team shortly after this first limited release.

From the start, it was a priority goal that the toolkit be callable from languages other than C. This greatly influenced the C language bindings, as it was recognized that the work to produce other language bindings could be reduced if certain choices (such as not relying on variable argument procedures and uniformly passing arguments to application-supplied procedures by reference rather than by value) were made early in the design.

---

[1] Precisely who coined the term is a somewhat contentious point that will probably remain shrouded in obscurity.

The first widespread release of the new toolkit was a preliminary version included in Release 2 of X Version 11 early in 1988. The design was expanded and refined under the leadership of Paul Asente, and the result was accepted by the X Consortium as a nonexclusive standard for inclusion as part of Release 3 in October 1988. At this point, Ralph Swick took over the role of principal architect.

Experience with the Release 3 Toolkit exposed areas that required additional work. The design was again expanded and refined for Release 4; major areas of work included extending the toolkit's object management facilities to work on things besides widgets, improving resource management to support long-running applications, and complying with the new Inter-Client Communication Conventions Manual.

The overriding goal in the Release 4 design was compatibility. The result is fully source-compatible for applications written in the C language; all they need to do is recompile. (Programmers using languages with more stringent parameter-passing rules must modify a few procedures that added additional parameters.) With one small exception, the result is also binary-compatible; applications and widget implementations for the Release 3 toolkit can relink and run with the Release 4 toolkit.[2]

The Organization of This Book

This book contains two parts, a programmer's guide and a specification. The programmer's guide describes how to use the X Toolkit to write applications and widgets, and includes many examples. The specification describes the capabilities more succinctly and precisely, with a level of detail sufficient to enable a programmer to create a new implementation of the X Toolkit.

Each chapter in the programmer's guide contains two parts, an application writer's section and a widget writer's section. Application programmers need only read the widget writer's sections if they are curious about what is going on behind the scenes; widget programmers need to read both sections. All functions described in the application writer's sections are available to widget writers as well, so widget writers should generally add a silent "or widget implementations" wherever they encounter the word *applications*.

---

[2] The exception is widget implementations that are subclasses of the Shell widget class.

A few pieces of functionality are most often used by widget writers but are also incorporated into an occasional application. In these cases, the functionality is described in the widget writer's section and a reference is included in the application writer's section. Application writers who need to read one of these sections should generally add a silent "or applications" wherever they encounter *widget implementations.*

The programmer's guide is entirely self-contained; it contains implementations of all the widgets used in its code examples. Chapter 10 of the guide describes the interfaces to these widgets in its application writer's section and gives the implementations in its widget writer's section.

Cross-references in the guide (Part I) and in the specification (Part II) refer to chapters and sections within that part unless explicit reference is made to the other part or to an external source.

The programmer's guide contains ten chapters:

Chapter 1   A general introduction to the X Toolkit and how to write applications that use it.

Chapter 2   A closer look at widgets.

Chapter 3   How to use and define a widget's attributes.

Chapter 4   Using and writing widgets that hold other widgets.

Chapter 5   The interface between toolkit applications and window managers, and how to create pop-up widgets.

Chapter 6   The X Toolkit event-handling architecture.

Chapter 7   Translations, a higher-level event interface.

Chapter 8   Using the X Toolkit for nonwidget objects.

Chapter 9   Things that don't fit anywhere else.

Chapter 10   Descriptions and implementations of the widgets used in the guide, and some sample applications.

The specification is derived from the official X Toolkit specification distributed by MIT. Should there be inconsistencies between the programmer's guide and the specification, the specification is the final authority. Differences between the specification in this book and the official specification are limited to clarifications, elaborations, editorial improvements, corrections of minor errors, and the elimination of some introductory material covered more fully in the programmer's guide.

The appendices and index apply to both parts of the book.

Conventions Used in This Book

Most toolkit-defined names and types and all file names are printed in `this special font`. Names and types defined by the widget implementations in the book are printed in the normal font to distinguish them from toolkit definitions. Procedure arguments, field names, and variables are printed in *italics*. Within the programmer's guide, resource identifiers and toolkit constants are not distinguished typographically but are capitalized and easily identifiable in their context. The specification, with its more formal requirements, uses `this special font` for toolkit constants.

Some places in the programmer's guide contain a pointing hand in the margin. The hand indicates material that is particularly subtle, tricky, or easy to miss; the pointed-to material is a good place to start when you are looking for explanations of why your code is not working.

This book uses the ANSI C convention of including parameter types within the definitions of procedure types and follows the type definition with sample parameters. For example,

```
typedef Boolean (*XtAcceptFocusProc) (Widget, Time *)
    Widget w,
    Time *time,
```

means that the type `XtAcceptFocusProc` is a pointer to a procedure, and the procedure that it points to takes two parameters, one of type `Widget` and one of type `Time*`. The declarations of *w* and *time* just give names to the parameters for use within the text. A procedure that could be assigned to a variable or field of type `XtAcceptFocusProc` might begin

```
Boolean AcceptFocus(w, time)
    Widget w;
    Time *time;
{
    ...
```

The X Toolkit follows the X library naming conventions for procedures and structures, with appropriate modifications:

- All X Toolkit functions and macros begin with the characters "Xt" in that capitalization.

- Functions, global variables, macros, types, and structure names use mixed capitalization with capital letters to distinguish words.

- Parameters and structure elements use all lower-case with an underscore (_) to separate words.

- Parameters that return values to the caller always end with the characters _*return*.

- Parameters that pass values both into and out of a routine always end with the characters _*in_out*.

In addition, all nonwidget parameters to procedures that an application or widget implementation provides are passed by reference. Because of the way the toolkit lays out widget data structures (each widget contains a pointer to itself in its first word) widget parameters can be passed by value to procedures that expect them to be passed by reference. These conventions support programmers using languages that support only reference parameters; programmers can write procedures directly without needing to provide C wrappers. Languages that cannot call C routines directly still require a library of wrapper procedures to call into the toolkit, but this library should be provided with the language.

Note that this parameter-passing convention is in contrast to the normal C language convention of passing parameters by reference only to procedures that are permitted to modify them. The description of each of the X Toolkit interfaces specifies whether the called procedure is expected or permitted to modify its arguments.

PART I. PROGRAMMER'S GUIDE

Paul J. Asente

Chapter 1

Applications

Writing Applications

1.1   Structure of Toolkit Applications

The X Toolkit is an example of a layered software architecture. An application consists of several distinct code modules communicating with each other through well-defined interfaces. The structure of the modules presents successively higher-level abstractions through the module interfaces.

Figure 1.1 shows the structure of a toolkit application. At the lowest level is the X library Xlib, which communicates directly with an X server. The Xlib

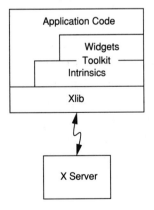

Figure 1.1. The structure of a toolkit application

abstractions include *windows* and *input events*; windows are areas of display screen space, and input events are notifications of user interactions like moving the pointer (usually a mouse), pressing a button, typing a key, or uncovering part of a window.

A toolkit sits on top of Xlib and replaces windows and input events with more abstract concepts; instead of dealing directly with windows and input events, a toolkit application deals with *widgets* and *callback procedures*. Widgets are user interface components like menus, pushbuttons, and text input areas. Callback procedures are procedures in an application that notify it that the user has interacted with a widget, for example, by selecting a menu entry, activating a pushbutton, or typing in a text area.

Most applications do not interact directly with Xlib. This is important enough that it is worth restating: *you do not need to know how to use Xlib to write toolkit applications.* Xlib is available for use if necessary, but even complicated programs rarely use it.[1]

The toolkit itself in turn contains two components, the *widget set* and the *Intrinsics.* The Intrinsics are a software module that defines the structure of widgets, provides the glue necessary to assemble widgets into a user interface, and dispatches input events to the correct widgets. The widgets in turn take these input events and call the appropriate callback procedures. Finally, the Intrinsics provide common bookkeeping functions for widgets, freeing the widget programmer from having to reimplement these functions for every widget.

The X Toolkit is another name for the Intrinsics. This is a potential source of confusion. When you talk about a particular vendor's toolkit you are referring both to a set of widgets and to the Intrinsics that they are built upon. When you talk about the X Toolkit you are referring to the Intrinsics. This book also uses "the" toolkit to refer to the X Toolkit.

There are, in addition, toolkits available that are not built upon the X Toolkit. These toolkits may or may not be based upon their own Intrinsics-like module. This book does not talk about these toolkits at all; assume that all references to toolkits apply to Intrinsics-based toolkits.

---

[1] The xmh mail-handling program included in the X distribution is a very large application, and it contains only two calls to Xlib—one of them to ring the workstation bell.

While there is only one set of Intrinsics, there are many sets of widgets. The Intrinsics do not define any particular user interface policy; rather, they make it possible to create a coordinated widget set that implements the policies defined by the user interface designer. Almost all application interactions with widgets take place through the Intrinsics, and this book provides the information necessary to use the Intrinsics to write toolkit applications. Since each widget set is slightly different, programmers also need a reference describing the details of the widgets they are using.

Although each widget set is different, there are substantial similarities among them. Most sets provide text areas, scrollbars, labels, pushbuttons, menus, and so forth. The actual names may be different, but the functionalities are similar. The widgets used in this guide, fully described in Chapter 10,[2] support a simple, useful subset of the capabilities commonly found in widget sets. While you might not use them to write actual applications (although you could), understanding them will give you a head start in understanding other widget sets in all their complexity.

1.2   What Is a Widget?

Just what a widget is depends upon whether you are a user, an application writer, or a widget writer.

To a user, a widget is an area on the screen. It displays some information and makes some action take place in the application when the user interacts with it using the pointer or keyboard. Each widget has some attributes that can be customized by adding entries to a user customization file.

To an application writer, a widget is an opaque value of some abstract data type. The application interacts with the widget by calling procedures; the interior structure of the widget is invisible. For example, to destroy a widget the application calls the `XtDestroyWidget` procedure, passing it the widget to destroy.

To a widget writer, a widget is an instantiation of a structure type. The Intrinsics define some fields in this structure, and the widget writer defines other fields to provide the functions specific to the particular kind of widget.

---

[2] All cross-references in the programmer's guide are to chapters or sections within the guide unless an explicit reference is made to the specification (Part II) or another source.

1.3   Object-Oriented Programming

The X Toolkit is an object-oriented programming system. If you know about object-oriented systems, knowing that widgets are objects in a single-inheritance class hierarchy will be helpful. Much of the Intrinsics is dedicated to implementing this classing system in C.

If you are not familiar with object-oriented programming, just think of it as a way of organizing data structures. The Intrinsics use a lot of the terminology of object-oriented systems, but this book describes the terms and concepts as they occur.

The important thing to understand about object-oriented systems is that, just as in any programming system, everything a program operates upon has a type and the allowable operations on a thing are determined by its type. In the C language certain things are integers, declared as type `int`. The operations defined on an integer include addition, subtraction, comparisons, and assignment. Other operations in the language, such as pointer dereferencing and procedure calling, are not defined for integers. In the toolkit, some things are widgets, declared as type `Widget`. Operations like creation, deletion, and moving are defined on widgets, while operations like addition and comparisons are not. Since the type `Widget` is not built into the C language, the Intrinsics implement operations upon widgets with procedure calls that take widgets as parameters.

Object is just another term for "thing," and the objects the toolkit deals with are represented by C data structures. Just as the C language must do different things when a program adds two integers than when a program adds two floating-point numbers, so the toolkit must do different things when creating a Menu widget than when creating a Scrollbar widget. C programmers add two integers the same way they add two floating-point numbers, by specifying +, but the compiler must execute different routines to generate the correct code. Similarly, toolkit programmers create a Menu widget and a Scrollbar widget the same way, by calling `XtCreateManagedWidget`, but the Intrinsics must call different procedures to create the correct widget. The type of an object is called that object's *class*, and the widget implementations store the information the Intrinsics use to operate upon objects of a particular class in data structures called *class records*.

The Intrinsics also use the term *Object* (capitalized) in a slightly different but related sense: it is a specific data type for things that use a subset of the widget functionality. Chapter 8 is devoted to an explanation of this data type. For now, assume that all uses of *object* refer to the general definition given in the previous paragraph and not to the specific meaning given in Chapter 8.

1.4 Terminology

This book uses many terms, often in a very specific sense. Some of these terms are specific to the toolkit, and others refer to concepts in object-oriented programming. The following is a list of basic concepts that are important to understand:

Application   A program that uses the toolkit.

User interface   The part of an application that interacts with the user.

Application   The part of an application that implements its underlying
functionality   capabilities. For example, the application functionality of a mail-handling program creates mail messages, displays incoming mail, and so forth.

Widget   A component in the user interface; also called a widget instance. Typical widgets include pop-up menus, pushbuttons, text fields, and scrollbars.

Callback   A procedure in the application that implements a part of the ap-
procedure   plication functionality. Applications register callback procedures with widgets, and the widgets invoke the procedures when the user interacts with the widgets. Callback procedures are often called *callbacks* for short.

Widget class   The type of a widget. For example, all pushbuttons in this book are of the class Pushbutton. The widget class defines the complete set of attributes and operations supported for a particular widget instance.

Widget set   A coordinated group of widget classes that present a consistent interaction style and appearance to a user.

Intrinsics   The glue that supports writing widget classes, creating a user interface, binding the interface to the application functionality, and translating user actions in the interface to callbacks in the application functionality.

Resource   A named, settable attribute, usually of a widget. For example, a Pushbutton widget has resources for the text string to display in the pushbutton and the font to display it in.

Name	A string that is associated with some object. Each widget instance in the user interface has a name, and so does each resource of a widget.
User	A person who interacts with an application to accomplish some task. In this book, users are always male.
Application programmer	A person who uses the toolkit and a widget set to write an application. In this book, application programmers are always female.
Widget programmer	A person who uses the toolkit to implement widgets. In this book, widget programmers are always female.
Object	A piece of data defined by the operations that can be performed upon it. The Intrinsics represent an object internally as a pointer to a dynamically allocated data structure. The principal objects the toolkit supports are widgets.
Class	The type of some object. All objects of the same type are of the same class. The class of an object defines the operations that can be performed on that object.
Subclass	A class that is defined by specializing another class. The subclass typically adds features to the other class, called the superclass, or uses the facilities of the superclass to implement a more specific set of interfaces.
Class hierarchy	The tree-structured organization of classes. A widget class in this tree always supports all the operations supported by the classes closer to the root of the tree, but might support them with different implementations and might also add new operations.
Superclass	A class closer to the root of the class hierarchy than another class. Some of the interfaces defined by a class are usually implemented by and inherited from the class's superclasses.
Instance	The same thing as an object. Instance is used to emphasize that a particular object is being discussed, rather than the class of the object.
Method	A procedure implementing one of the operations supported by an object class.
Inheritance	Using the same method to implement an operation as the immediate superclass in the class hierarchy. Inheritance greatly simplifies defining new object classes and is one of the main reasons for organizing classes into a hierarchy.

1.5 Intrinsics Data Types

The Intrinsics define a number of basic data types that applications use:

```
typedef char Boolean;                          /* implementation-specific */
typedef unsigned char XtEnum;                  /* implementation-specific */
typedef unsigned int Cardinal;                 /* implementation-specific */
typedef long XtPointer;                        /* implementation-specific */
typedef long XtArgVal;                         /* implementation-specific */
typedef unsigned short Dimension;              /* implementation-specific */
typedef short Position;                        /* implementation-specific */
typedef char *String;
typedef unsigned long Pixel;
typedef struct _WidgetRec *Widget;             /* opaque */
typedef Widget *WidgetList;
typedef struct _XtAppStruct *XtAppContext;     /* opaque */
typedef struct _TranslationData *XtTranslations;   /* opaque */
typedef struct _TranslationData *XtAccelerators;   /* opaque */
#define FALSE 0
#define TRUE 1
```

Types labeled with an "implementation-specific" comment can have different definitions in different implementations of the Intrinsics. Types labeled with an "opaque" comment refer to data structures whose contents cannot be directly read or written by programmers.

These data types have the following uses and restrictions:

Boolean
A Boolean value. Must be able to hold TRUE and FALSE.

XtEnum
A value of various enumerations. Must be able to hold at least 128 different values, including TRUE and FALSE.[3]

Cardinal
The number of entries in a list or the size of something. Must be unsigned and at least 16 bits.

XtPointer
A pointer to unspecified data. Must be able to hold a pointer to a character, pointer to an integer, function pointer, structure pointer, and long integer. In ANSI C implementations of the toolkit, `XtPointer` is normally defined as `void*`.[4]

XtArgVal
A widget resource. Must be able to hold data of type `XtPointer`, `Cardinal`, `Dimension`, and `Position`.

[3] All data of type `XtEnum` are of type `Boolean` in Intrinsics implementations that conform to specifications earlier than Release 4.

[4] All data of type `XtPointer` are of type `caddr_t` in Intrinsics implementations that conform to specifications earlier than Release 4.

Dimension	A horizontal or vertical size of a widget or other object. Must be unsigned and at least 16 bits.
Position	A horizontal or vertical position of a widget or other object. Must be signed and at least 16 bits.
String	A NULL-terminated character string.
Pixel	An index into a colormap, representing a color. Xlib uses `unsigned long` to refer to data of this type.
Widget	A widget. The type `Widget` is opaque to application programmers but not to widget programmers.
WidgetList	An array of widgets.
XtAppContext	An application context; used to identify the application in toolkit calls. See Section 1.10.
XtTranslations	A compiled description of how a widget reacts to X events in its window. See Chapter 7.
XtAccelerators	A compiled description of how a widget reacts to X events in other windows. See Chapter 7.

Be careful when doing arithmetic with `Dimension` and `Cardinal` values: they are unsigned, so incorrect values can result when subtracting them. For example, in the code

```
Position p = 1;
Dimension d = 3;

if (p - d < 0) ...      /* Bug! */
```

The condition is never true since the C compiler promotes signed values to unsigned values before combining them with unsigned values in arithmetic expressions. Always cast `Dimension` values into integers before doing anything more complicated than adding them to another value.

Be similarly careful with `Cardinal` values. The code

```
Cardinal count;
for (count = 10; count >= 0; count--) ...      /* Bug! */
```

produces an infinite loop since unsigned variables never become negative. It is best to avoid `Cardinal` values in computations whenever possible.

1.6   The Callback Model

Most applications for character-cell terminals have *modal* user interfaces. With a modal interface, the meaning of user interactions depends upon the current state, or *mode*, of the program. The program often indicates the current mode through the current input prompt.

Many electronic mail programs provide good examples of modal interfaces. If a user is at the top-level command interface and types an *r*, it means to *read* a new mail message. If he is reading messages and types the same *r*, it means to *reply* to the current mail message. And if he is replying to a message and types another *r*, the mail program inserts the character *r* into the current reply.

Conventional programming methodologies make it easy to write modal programs. The application is in some mode and asks for some input from the user. Depending upon the input, it performs some action, possibly enters another mode, and asks for some more input. Whenever the program gets input, it uses criteria specific to the current mode to decide how to proceed.

The problem with modal interfaces is that the user frequently gets caught in an inconvenient mode. If, while composing a message, he needs to consult some messages that he has stored away, he must first exit message composition mode and enter a command mode that allows him to look at his stored messages. After consulting them, he has to return to composition mode to continue writing his message. At best, this mode navigation is inconvenient; at worst, incomplete, prohibiting the user from fully exploiting the power of the application.

With window-based applications, using separate windows for the different types of functionality eliminates many of the modes. By directing keystrokes to different areas of the screen, the user gives commands to different parts of the application; the meaning of each command is determined by the window with which the user is interacting. In the mail example, the user consults his other messages by redirecting his attention to a message browser window and causing it to bring up the desired mail in a message-reading window. After consulting the messages he directs the keyboard back to the composition window and continues writing. In effect, the user switches modes by switching input to a different window, logically suspending the previous window.

How does an application implement this kind of *modeless* operation? If the mail program is in a state asking for characters to insert into a message and instead receives a command in a different part of the interface, it must somehow transfer control to another part of the program and interpret the input in this new context. This leads to convoluted program logic that is difficult to implement and maintain.

The problem lies with letting the application ask for input in the first place. The X Toolkit encourages a different style of programming—more of a "don't call us, we'll call you" organization.

Instead of writing code that asks for input directly, the application programmer structures a toolkit application as a set of procedures for the toolkit to invoke when the user interacts with the interface. In the mail example, the programmer provides a procedure that takes a character and inserts it into the current message. When the user types a character into the message window, the toolkit calls this procedure, passing it the typed character, and the application incorporates it into the message. Alternative procedures associated with other windows invoke the read and reply functions of the mail handler; see Figure 1.2.

These procedures are called *callback* procedures since the toolkit "calls back" into the application program in response to user actions. Typical toolkit applications never ask for input directly but instead call a toolkit input-handling procedure responsible for getting input from the user and dispatching it to the appropriate callback procedures. Each callback procedure responds to the input and then returns to the toolkit so that another input event can be processed.

Applications need not respond to every input event; some widgets handle most events themselves and only invoke callbacks after the user has performed some specific action. A text editor might have a widget for getting the name of

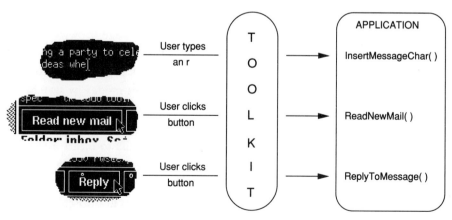

Figure 1.2. Mapping user actions to application functions

the file to be edited. The widget handles most keyboard input events itself, only calling the application after the user types an entire file name.

Modeless applications are generally easier to use than modal ones. Sometimes, though, modality is desirable. If the user asks a text editor to load a new file without saving changes to the current one, the editor might ask the user for confirmation before proceeding and suspend the rest of the application until the confirmation arrives. The toolkit allows the application to activate *modal* widgets in these situations. When there is an active modal widget in the interface, the user cannot interact with the rest of the application until the application deactivates the modal widget in response to the user's actions. While most programs activate modal widgets by popping them up on the screen, the toolkit allows the application to make other widgets modal if the interface requires it.

Besides being simpler to use, modeless applications are often easier to write and maintain. Callback procedures are precisely the short, single-function, independent routines encouraged by modular programming practices.

1.7   Error Handling

The toolkit detects a large number of different types of errors. Section 9.6 gives full details on error handling, but an overview will help in understanding the examples.

Because even seemingly simple toolkit calls can uncover complex error situations, the toolkit handles most error conditions internally rather than by returning a success or failure code on each call. Errors are divided into two classes. Fatal errors, called simply *errors*, occur whenever it is unlikely that useful results will be obtained by continuing in the same code path. Nonfatal errors, called *warnings*, occur when it is likely that continued operation will still be possible. By default, the toolkit prints a message in an operating-system-specific place and exits on errors, and prints a message and continues on warnings. On Unix systems, the error and warning messages are written to the `stderr` file. An application can install its own error or warning handlers to modify this behavior: it can print the message in a different place or format, or can invoke additional cleanup procedures before exiting.

In some cases the toolkit reports an error condition to the application as a reserved return value (often NULL) from a toolkit procedure. These special cases are clearly described in the description of these procedures in this book.

1.8   The Application User Interface

The X Window System organizes all windows on a screen into a hierarchical tree structure. There is one window, called the *root window,* that covers the entire screen. Other windows on the screen are either children of the root window or children of some other window that is in turn either a direct or indirect child of the root window. If a child window extends beyond the boundaries of its parent, the areas of the child outside the parent are never visible.

The toolkit organizes an application's widgets into a tree structure that mirrors the tree structure of the windows representing the widgets. An application user interface consists of a tree of widgets, the root of which has a window that is a child of the root window of the display. All other widgets have windows that are part of the window tree beneath the window for the base widget.

Figure 1.3 shows a simple application consisting of two simple widgets enclosed in a box and the widget tree corresponding to this application.

There are three main kinds of widgets in a widget tree. The leaves of the tree are *primitive* widgets that have no children. Pushbuttons, labels, menu items, and text entry fields are typical primitive widgets.

Composite widgets form the internal nodes in the tree. They usually do not display any information themselves but instead act as containers for other widgets to group them together in the user interface. A composite widget is responsible for determining the positions and sizes of its children, and different kinds of composite widgets enforce different layout policies. A Box widget allows the application to specify the positions and sizes of its child widgets directly, while a Menu widget forces all its children to be the same width and stacks them up in a vertical row. Another type of composite widget, the Pane widget, allocates all its interior space to its children but allows the

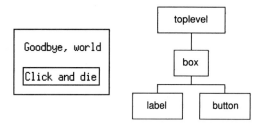

Figure 1.3. A sample application's interface and its widget tree

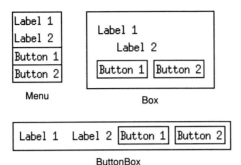

Figure 1.4. Layout policies of various composite widgets

user to dynamically change the proportion of the space given to each child, and still another type, a ButtonBox widget, packs its children into horizontal rows.[5] Figure 1.4 shows the same widgets being held by various types of composite widgets. Composite widgets can also provide other functionality besides layout, for example, controlling how keyboard input gets delivered to their children.

The root of the widget tree is a special kind of widget called a *shell* widget. To be part of a properly conforming X application, the top-level window for any program must obey certain conventions that allow the application to communicate correctly with the external window manager. These conventions allow the program to request that its window be moved or resized, define the way the program must react if the user moves or resizes the window himself, and so forth. The Intrinsics provide shell widgets that know how to participate in these conventions, thereby sparing the application writer from worrying about them herself. A shell widget always has exactly one visible child that it "shrink-wraps," completely filling the interior of the shell with the child's window.

Many applications have several widget trees. Some applications have more than one independent window, and some create temporary subsidiary windows like confirmation boxes and pop-up menus. Normally these other windows should not be clipped by the application window; the widgets for these windows exist in their own window trees, each complete with its own shell widget. These subsidiary shells are called *pop-up* shells since their primary use

---

[5] These composite widget types are found in many widget sets but are not part of the Intrinsics.

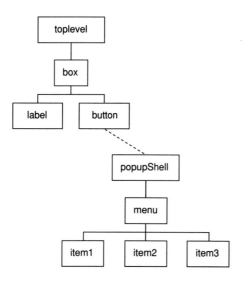

Figure 1.5. The widgets in the sample application with a pop-up

is to support pop-up menus and pop-up dialog boxes, and any widget in the user interface can have pop-up shells associated with it. Figure 1.5 shows a widget tree that allows the application shown in Figure 1.3 to pop up a menu when the user activates the pushbutton.

Some widgets appear to an application to be primitive but actually consist of several cooperating widgets. A common example is a Scrollbar widget that contains pushbuttons to activate the scrolling.

1.9   A Simple Application—"Goodbye, world"

The "Hello, world" program has earned a beloved place in the hearts of many C and Unix programmers. Something slightly more sophisticated is required to illustrate the capabilities of the toolkit, so this section presents "Goodbye, world." It creates a label displaying "Goodbye, world" and a button labeled "Click and die," which the user activates to terminate the program.

"Goodbye, world" illustrates the major parts found in all toolkit applications:

• A set of callback procedures implements the application's functionality.

• A call to XtAppInitialize initializes the toolkit and opens a display connection to an X server.

- The application creates a tree of widgets for the user interface and associates the callback procedures with the widgets.

- The application *realizes* its widgets to make them appear on the screen.

- An event-dispatching loop gathers X events from the display connection and sends them to the widgets for processing.

Example 1.1 shows "Goodbye, world." The first lines include the standard header files. The file `<X11/Intrinsic.h>` contains declarations of the data types and procedures necessary for applications to use the toolkit. The file `<X11/StringDefs.h>` contains definitions of the strings used in argument lists.

Every widget class has a set of definitions that an application needs to use the widget. Usually each class provides a header file containing its definitions, and the next three lines include the header files for the three classes of widget this application uses.

Goodbye is this application's single callback procedure. The toolkit calls Goodbye when the user activates the quit button in the user interface. All callback procedures take three parameters: the widget that triggered the callback, a piece of data that the application specifies when it associates the callback procedure with a particular widget, and a piece of data defined by the class of widget that activates the callback. This simple callback procedure ignores its arguments and just terminates the program.

Each class of widget has a large number of attributes that an application can specify. Each attribute has a default value, and the application only needs to specify the attributes that require nondefault values. The declarations of *labelArgs* and *buttonArgs* give values for the x, y, and label attributes for the Label and Pushbutton widgets in this application's user interface. XtNx, XtNy, and XtNlabel are defined in the `<X11/StringDefs.h>` header file. All other attributes take on their default values. Some attributes, like the border width, text font, and text color, have fixed default values; others, like width and height, have default values that the widget computes based upon its contents. Other ways to specify attribute values exist in the toolkit, usually preferable to specifying them this way; but this method is the simplest and most self-contained.

The main program defines `Widget` variables *toplevel, label, button,* and *box* for the four widgets it creates in its interface and an `XtAppContext` variable to hold its *application context.* The application passes this context to Intrinsics

```
#include <X11/Intrinsic.h>        /* Standard include files */
#include <X11/StringDefs.h>
#include "Box.h"                  /* Widget include files */
#include "Label.h"
#include "Pushbutton.h"

void Goodbye(widget, clientData, callData)   /* Callback procedure */
    Widget widget;
    XtPointer clientData, callData;
{
    exit(0);
}

Arg labelArgs[] = {      /* The arguments to the label widget */
    {XtNx,      10},
    {XtNy,      10},
    {XtNlabel,  "Goodbye, world"}};

Arg buttonArgs[] = {     /* The arguments to the button widget */
    {XtNx,      10},
    {XtNy,      40},
    {XtNlabel,  "Click and die"}};

int main(argc, argv)
    unsigned int argc;
    char **argv;
{
    Widget toplevel, label, button, box;
    XtAppContext app;

    toplevel = XtAppInitialize(&app, "Goodbye",
            (XrmOptionDescList) NULL, 0, &argc, argv,
            (String *) NULL, (ArgList) NULL, 0);

    box = XtCreateManagedWidget("box", boxWidgetClass,
            toplevel, (Arg *) NULL, 0);

    label = XtCreateManagedWidget("label", labelWidgetClass,
            box, labelArgs, XtNumber(labelArgs));

    button = XtCreateManagedWidget("button", pushbuttonWidgetClass,
            box, buttonArgs, XtNumber(buttonArgs));
    XtAddCallback(button, XtNcallback, Goodbye, NULL);

    XtRealizeWidget(toplevel);
    XtAppMainLoop(app);
}
```

Example 1.1. The "Goodbye, world" program

routines that do not take widget parameters; it tells the Intrinsics which application is issuing the call.

`XtAppInitialize` performs several functions: it initializes the internal state of the toolkit, creates an application context, parses the command line, opens a display connection to an X server, and returns a shell widget for the application to use. The first parameter returns the application context, and the second is a string called the *application class*, which the toolkit uses to fetch user customizations and certain auxiliary files for the application. The next two parameters give a pointer to and a count of the definitions for application-specific command line options. This application has no command line options beyond the defaults provided by the toolkit, so it passes in NULL and zero. The application passes the command line in the next two parameters so that `XtAppInitialize` can parse any options specified there. Even if an application has no command line options of its own, it should pass *argc* and *argv* to `XtAppInitialize` so that the toolkit can parse any predefined options that the user specified on the command line. The next argument is one of the alternative ways to specify attributes; this is NULL since this application does not use this method. Finally the last two arguments specify override values for the shell widget's attributes; no override values are specified here. `XtApp-Initialize` returns a shell widget to hold the application's user interface, which this program assigns to the variable *toplevel.*

The next three statements create the other widgets in the interface with `XtCreateManagedWidget`. This procedure takes a string that is the name for the widget, the class of the widget to create, the widget to use for the parent, the list of attribute values for this widget, and the number of elements in the attribute list. These attribute values override any default attributes for the widget specified by the user or by the widget implementation.

A Box widget is a simple container that holds the other two widgets in the interface. The program creates one inside the shell widget returned by `XtAppInitialize` and specifies no override values.

The application creates its Label and Pushbutton widgets inside the Box widget. The calls to `XtCreateManagedWidget` specify the *labelArgs* and *buttonArgs* lists specified earlier and use the macro `XtNumber` to calculate the number of elements in these lists.

After creating the widgets, the application associates the Goodbye callback procedure with the Pushbutton widget using `XtAddCallback`. Its parameters are the widget to which to attach the callback, the name of the callback, the callback procedure, and the client data. The name is needed since a widget can have different types of callback procedures that it invokes under different circumstances. The client data argument is passed uninterpreted as the *clientData* parameter of the callback procedure and is usually the address of a data structure upon which the callback procedure operates. This application needs no client data and so passes NULL.

The program calls XtRealizeWidget to make all the widgets appear on the user's screen.

The last statement calls XtAppMainLoop. This routine gathers input events from the X server and dispatches them to widgets, eventually calling the application's callback procedures. XtAppMainLoop never returns—it simply loops forever, waiting for input events and dispatching them.

The "Goodbye, world" program contains eight executable statements. Writing a similar application using Xlib calls directly would require close to 100 executable statements. As you will see later, the toolkit version automatically includes many user customization features. Adding these features to the equivalent Xlib application would increase its size by another order of magnitude.

1.10   Application Contexts

An *application context* is a pointer to an opaque data structure that contains all the information the toolkit maintains for one application. All calls to the Intrinsics take an application context, either explicitly through an application context parameter or implicitly through a widget or other object. The Intrinsics' internal data structures contain enough state to go from a display, widget, or similar object to the application context with which the object is associated. Application contexts enable shared library implementations of the toolkit to share some toolkit data structures among different applications while keeping other information separate. Every application needs an application context, which is of type XtAppContext, and almost all applications use exactly one of them.

The primary component of an application context is a list of displays that the application is using; each display connection belongs to exactly one application context. While most applications use only a single display, many applications create windows on more than one display. Examples include an application that creates windows on many workstations to remind people of a meeting, or a distributed whiteboard that allows people to look at and modify a drawing while they are talking on the telephone. Multiple-display applications make these possible. The Intrinsics automatically gather events from all the displays in an application context, making multiple-display applications as simple to write as single-display ones.

The toolkit maintains a default application context, maintained as a global variable, to support applications that were written before application contexts existed. Most of the routines that take an explicit application context parameter have alternative versions without this parameter; these alternative versions operate upon the default application context. For a description of these compatibility routines see Appendix C. Programs that use the default application context are not as portable as those that use an explicit application context since some shared library implementations of the toolkit cannot support the necessary global state.

The only applications that require more than one application context are those implementing multiple independent logical applications within a single address space. While application contexts were designed to support this organization, there is limited experience with it and its use may well expose toolkit deficiencies.

To find which application context is associated with a widget or a display, use `XtWidgetToApplicationContext` or `XtDisplayToApplication-Context`.

XtAppContext XtWidgetToApplicationContext(*w*)
    Widget *w*;
    w   Specifies the widget to find the application context for.

`XtWidgetToApplicationContext` returns the application context that contains the display on which the widget's window was or will be created.

XtAppContext XtDisplayToApplicationContext(*display*)
    Display **display*;
    display   Specifies the display to find the application context for.

`XtDisplayToApplicationContext` returns the application context that contains the display. A display connection, and therefore a widget instance, can only belong to one application context.

1.11   Initializing the Toolkit

These routines set things up at the beginning of an application. They initialize the toolkit, create application contexts, open displays, and create shell widgets. A single application never uses all these routines; different applications use various combinations according to the degree of control required over the initialization process. Most applications use XtAppInitialize, as shown in the "Goodbye, world" example and described at the end of this section. XtAppInitialize calls each of the required basic initialization routines, passing a default set of parameters appropriate to most applications. The following five routines are all packaged within XtAppInitialize.

To initialize the toolkit, use XtToolkitInitialize.

void XtToolkitInitialize()

XtToolkitInitialize performs all the one-time initialization in the Intrinsics. Applications must call it, either directly or indirectly by calling XtAppInitialize, before calling any other toolkit routines. The effects of calling XtToolkitInitialize more than once are undefined.

To create an application context, use XtCreateApplicationContext.

XtAppContext XtCreateApplicationContext()

XtCreateApplicationContext returns an application context with no open displays. Applications must have an application context before creating any widgets, but they can install an already opened display connection into a new application context. The contents of an application context are private to the Intrinsics and are not directly visible to an application.

To open a display connection and install it in an application context, use XtOpenDisplay.

Display *XtOpenDisplay(*app_context, display_string, application_name, application_class,*
                        options, num_options, argc, argv)
    XtAppContext *app_context*;
    String *display_string*;
    String *application_name*;
    String *application_class*;
    XrmOptionDescRec *options*;
    Cardinal *num_options*;
    Cardinal *argc*;
    String *argv*;

app_context	Specifies the application context to add the display to.
display_string	Specifies the display string, or NULL.
application_name	Specifies the name of the application instance, usually NULL.
application_class	Specifies the class of the application.
options	Specifies how to parse the command line for any application-specific resources.
num_options	Specifies the number of entries in the options list.
argc	Specifies a pointer to the number of command line parameters.
argv	Specifies the command line parameters.

XtOpenDisplay opens a display connection to the X server specified in *display_string* and adds it to the specified application context. The display string is in the same format used by XOpenDisplay; on Unix systems this is usually *hostname:display-number.screen-number.* For example, to open display 0 connected to the host *penzance* and make screen 2 the default screen, specify *penzance:0.2.* The screen number is useful only when a display supports more than one screen and omitting it uses the server-defined default screen. Omitting the host name opens a display on the current host. Other syntaxes may be used on other systems or to specify different connection protocols; for example, using two colons instead of one specifies a DECNET connection on systems that support DECNET. For a full description of the process of opening a display see Section 2.1 in *Xlib.* For a full description of the permitted syntax for the display string refer to a document specific to the operating system being used.

If *display_string* is NULL, XtOpenDisplay gets the display from the command line as passed in the *argv* parameter, or from the user's environment (the DISPLAY environment variable on Unix systems). Specifying NULL for *display_string* is almost always the right thing to do; very few applications should specify a display explicitly. The only common use is in applications that use more than one display, and then the application usually gets the display string from a configuration file.

XtOpenDisplay is responsible for determining the name of the application. It checks the following possibilities, in order:

• If the command line passed in *argv* contains a –name entry, the entry following –name is the application name.

• Otherwise, if the *application_name* parameter is not NULL, its value is the application name.

- Otherwise, if the environment variable RESOURCE_NAME is set, its value is the application name.

- Otherwise, if the name used to invoke the program, found in *argv*[0], is present and is not NULL, it is stripped of any directory and file type components and the resulting value is the application name.

- Otherwise, the name is the constant string "main".

The remaining parameters are involved in parsing the command line and fetching resources; they are described in Chapter 3. Most programs specify *application_name* as NULL so that users can specify it using RESOURCE_NAME or as the program name. XtOpenDisplay modifies the *argc* and *argv* parameters to contain only the command line entries not matched when parsing the command line. Applications are responsible for saving a copy of the original *argc* and *argv* contents so that they can be specified as attributes to XtAppCreateShell; see the example at the end of this section. Saving the contents also allows applications that open more than one display to pass the same command line in each call to XtOpenDisplay.

XtOpenDisplay returns the newly opened display, or NULL if the display could not be opened. An application that calls XtOpenDisplay directly must check the return value for NULL and take appropriate diagnostic action, usually issuing an error message. Applications using XtAppInitialize automatically exit with an error message if the display cannot be opened.

After opening the display, XtOpenDisplay adds it to an application context by calling XtDisplayInitialize. Applications can add an already opened display, usually obtained by calling XOpenDisplay, to an application context by calling XtDisplayInitialize directly.

void XtDisplayInitialize(*app_context, display, application_name, application_class, options, num_options, argc, argv*)

    XtAppContext *app_context*;
    Display **display*;
    String *application_name*;
    String *application_class*;
    XrmOptionDescRec **options*;
    Cardinal *num_options*;
    Cardinal **argc*;
    String **argv*;

app_context   Specifies the application context to add the display to.

display	Specifies the display to initialize.
application_name	Specifies the name of the application instance.
application_class	Specifies the class of this application.
options	Specifies how to parse the command line for any application-specific resources.
num_options	Specifies the number of entries in the options list.
argc	Specifies a pointer to the number of command line parameters.
argv	Specifies the command line parameters.

Very few applications use `XtDisplayInitialize` directly. It is the same as `XtOpenDisplay` but instead of a display string takes a display that is already open. All other parameters are the same. A single display connection can be installed in only one application context. Applications must install a display in an application context before creating any widgets on the display.

To create an initial shell widget for an application's user interface, use `XtAppCreateShell`.

Widget XtAppCreateShell(*application_name, application_class, widget_class,*
　　　　　　　　　　　　display, args, num_args)
　　　String *application_name*;
　　　String *application_class*;
　　　WidgetClass *widget_class*;
　　　Display **display*;
　　　ArgList *args*;
　　　Cardinal *num_args*;

application_name	Specifies the name of the application instance; this should be the same as the name passed to `XtOpenDisplay`.
application_class	Specifies the class of the application; this should be the same as the class passed to `XtOpenDisplay`.
widget_class	Specifies the widget class that the application top-level widget should be.
display	Specifies the display to get the resources from.
args	Specifies the argument list to use in creation.
num_args	Specifies the number of arguments in the argument list.

`XtAppCreateShell` returns a shell widget of the specified class; this is almost always `applicationShellWidgetClass`. Every application must have a shell widget before creating additional nonshell widgets. For complete information on shell widgets and `XtAppCreateShell` see Chapter 5.

Very few applications need the flexibility provided by the preceding routines. Most applications initialize the toolkit, create an application context, open a display, and get a shell in one call by using `XtAppInitialize`.[6]

Widget XtAppInitialize(*app_context_return, application_class, options, num_options, argc,*
                          argv, fallback_resources, args, num_args)
    XtAppContext *app_context_return*;
    String *application_class*;
    XrmOptionDescRec *options*[ ];
    Cardinal *num_options*;
    Cardinal *argc*;
    String *argv*;
    String *fallback_resources*;
    ArgList *args*;
    Cardinal *num_args*;

app_context_return	Returns the application context.
application_class	Specifies the class name of this application.
options	Specifies how to parse the command line for any application-specific resources.
num_options	Specifies the number of entries in the options list.
argc	Specifies a pointer to the number of command line parameters.
argv	Specifies the command line parameters.
fallback_resources	Specifies resource values to be used if the Intrinsics cannot open the application defaults file, or NULL.
args	Specifies resource values to override any other specifications for the created shell widget.
num_args	Specifies the number of entries in the *args* parameter.

`XtAppInitialize` calls `XtToolkitInitialize` to initialize the toolkit and sets *app_context_return* to point to a new application context. If *fallback_resources* is not NULL, `XtAppInitialize` calls `XtAppSetFallback-Resources` with its value; see Section 3.5. `XtAppInitialize` then calls `XtOpenDisplay` to open the display specified on the command line or in the user's environment, calls `XtAppCreateShell`, and returns the resulting shell widget. This shell widget is always of class `applicationShell-WidgetClass`; see Chapter 5.

Failing to open the display terminates the application with an appropriate error message. `XtAppInitialize` modifies *argc* and *argv* as `XtOpen-Display` does.

---

[6] `XtAppInitialize` and `XtVaAppInitialize` are not supported by Intrinsics implementations that conform to specifications earlier than Release 4. Applications using such an implementation must perform all initialization steps individually or use `XtInitialize`, which creates the default application context.

An alternative version of XtAppInitialize, called XtVaApp-
Initialize, is identical except that a varargs list replaces the argument list
and count.

Widget XtVaAppInitialize(*app_context_return, application_class, options, num_options, argc,*
argv, fallback_resources, . . .)
    XtAppContext **app_context_return*;
    String *application_class*;
    XrmOptionDescRec *options*[ ];
    Cardinal *num_options*;
    Cardinal **argc*;
    String **argv*;
    String **fallback_resources*;

app_context_return	Returns the application context.
application_class	Specifies the class name of this application.
options	Specifies how to parse the command line for any application-specific resources.
num_options	Specifies the number of entries in the options list.
argc	Specifies a pointer to the number of command line parameters.
argv	Specifies the command line parameters.
fallback_resources	Specifies resource values to be used if the Intrinsics cannot open the application defaults file, or NULL.
. . .	Specifies the override resources for the shell.

Section 3.9 describes how to use varargs lists.

Example 1.2 shows the main program for "Goodbye, world" doing all the
steps in initialization explicitly. The callback procedure and the code to create
the widgets are unchanged. This version first initializes the toolkit using
XtToolkitInitialize and then creates an application context. It creates
copies of *argc* and *argv* since the call to XtOpenDisplay modifies them, but
they must be specified as attributes to XtAppCreateShell with their
original values. Next it uses XtOpenDisplay to open the default display and
then creates a shell on that display, specifying the saved *argc* and *argv* as
resources. The rest of the code, starting with the creation of the Box widget, is
unchanged.

1.12   Exiting Applications

The easiest way to terminate an application is just to exit the program using
whatever mechanism is appropriate for your system. On Unix systems, this is

```
int main(argc, argv)
    unsigned int argc;
    char **argv;
{
    Widget toplevel, label, button, box;
    XtAppContext app;
    Display *dpy;
    Arg args[2];
    int n;
    unsigned_int saved_argc;
    char **saved_argv;

    XtToolkitInitialize();                  /* Initialize the toolkit */

    app = XtCreateApplicationContext(); /* Create an app context */

    /* Copy argc and argv */
    saved_argc = argc;
    saved_argv = XtMalloc(argc * sizeof(char *));
    bcopy(argv, saved_argv, argc * sizeof(char *));

    /* Open the default display */
    dpy = XtOpenDisplay(app, NULL, NULL, "Goodbye",
            NULL, 0, &argc, argv);

    if (dpy == NULL) {
        fprintf(stderr, "Couldn't open display connection\n");
        exit(1);
    }

    /* Create a shell */
    n = 0;
    XtSetArg(args[n], XtNargc, saved_argc);      n++;
    XtSetArg(args[n], XtNargv, saved_argv);      n++;

    toplevel = XtAppCreateShell(NULL, "Goodbye",
            applicationShellWidgetClass, dpy, args, n);

    /* The rest of the code is identical */
}
```

Example 1.2. "Goodbye, world" using explicit initialization

the `exit` procedure. Deactivating the application image frees all application resources and breaks the connection to the X server, causing the server to free its resources and destroy the application's windows.

If a program needs to continue after closing its displays, it uses `XtDestroyApplicationContext` or `XtCloseDisplay`.

void XtDestroyApplicationContext(*app_context*)
    XtAppContext *app_context*;
app_context   Specifies the application context to destroy.

`XtDestroyApplicationContext` closes all the displays in the application context, causing any queued requests to be sent to the server before the connection is broken. It then frees all data structures associated directly with the application context. Since applications can continue after destroying the application context, the actual destruction is delayed until any event dispatching currently being executed is complete. This prevents the application context data structures from vanishing from beneath the event-dispatching mechanism, making it safe to call `XtDestroyApplicationContext` from anywhere in an application. Applications that need to make their windows disappear immediately do so by unmapping their top-level widgets using `XtUnmapWidget` if this delay is unacceptable.

To close a display without destroying its associated application context, use `XtCloseDisplay`.

void XtCloseDisplay(*display*)
    Display **display*;
display   Specifies the display to close.

Like `XtDestroyApplicationContext`, `XtCloseDisplay` delays the actual closing until any pending event dispatches are complete. While closing a display makes the windows used by an application's widgets disappear, it does not destroy the widget data structures in the application program. Since the widgets typically serve no useful function without their windows, applications should call `XtDestroyWidget` with the top-level shell widget on the display before closing the display. Attempting to destroy widgets after closing the display on which they were created will usually result in unpredictable runtime errors.

1.13   Writing Applications

All toolkit applications must include two header files.

`<X11/Intrinsic.h>`   This file includes definitions of all types and data structures the application needs for toolkit calls and many Xlib calls and includes declarations for all toolkit procedures applications use.

`<X11/StringDefs.h>`   This file includes definitions of literal strings used to specify common widget attributes.

Applications also need widget-class-specific information. This is usually included in a separate header file for each widget class and includes string definitions for widget attributes, the widget class variable for use with `XtCreateManagedWidget`, and declarations for any special procedures this widget implements. Applications must include the header file for each widget class they use.

If you are using an installed widget set, the header files are normally in a subdirectory of `/usr/include/X11` on Unix systems. If you are using a non-installed widget set, you may need to specify a `-I` option when compiling your application.

The creator of a widget set may instead provide a single header file that contains the combined information for all widgets in the widget set. If this is the case, applications only include this one file. The combined header may also include `<X11/Intrinsic.h>` and `<X11/StringDefs.h>`; check the documentation for the widgets your application is using.

The method used for linking a toolkit application depends both on the operating system and on the widget set. The specific instructions here are for Unix systems, but analogous procedures apply for other operating systems. Most widget sets provide a library; for example, you link the Athena widgets provided with the X distribution from MIT into an image by specifying −lXaw.

Some widget sets require additional libraries; refer to the specific instructions for your widget set for further details. Applications that use the Athena widget set must link in the MIT miscellaneous utility library by specifying −lXmu.

You can also link in individual widget modules. This is most useful when linking application-specific widgets or when developing a widget set. If you link in a widget module, you must also link in the modules for any non-Intrinsics superclasses of the widget.

You always need to link in the Intrinsics library by specifying –lXt and the X library by specifying –lX11. Some widget sets may include the Intrinsics library with the widget library; again, consult your widget set documentation.

The normal order to specify modules in linking is

1. All application modules.

2. All widget modules.

3. The widget library.

4. Any auxiliary libraries.

5. The Intrinsics library.

6. The X library.

On Unix systems, to link a program named `program.c` that uses the Athena widget set, specify

```
cc -o program program.o -lXaw -lXmu -lXt -lX11
```

To link the same program with another widget set, –lXwid, that includes the Intrinsics library with the widget library and has no extra library, specify

```
cc -o program program.o -lXwid -lX11
```

To link the program with an additional widget MyWidget and the Athena widgets, specify

```
cc -o program program.o MyWidget.o -lXaw -lXmu -lXt -lX11
```

1.14 Writing a New Widget

A well-designed widget set includes enough widgets to write many useful programs. The time will come, however, when an application writer needs a user interface component not found in the set. A programmer writing a graphics editor is not likely to find a graphics editor widget that she can just drop into her application; she must provide the functionality herself. She has two choices as to how to do this.

If the new component is not likely to be useful in other applications, the programmer can create an instance of some appropriate widget class and then use its window as a raw X window, using Xlib drawing routines. She modifies the event handling of the widget to send the events to the application for appropriate handling. Section 7.18 describes how to do this. This is relatively straightforward but has some disadvantages.

Most important, the component is not available for other applications to use. You may think that no other program would need this component, but this has a way of coming back to haunt you at a later date. Recoding the functionality in another program can be a substantial task.

Also, allowing user customization of the component's attributes requires duplication of much of the resource handling that the Intrinsics do automatically. Failing to provide for this results in an application that disallows many of the customizations that users expect.

Writing a new widget class is usually a better approach. This involves more work for the programmer initially, but the effort pays off in code reusability and often a better final program.

Writing a new widget class should not be regarded as a Herculean task. First, browse through the widget writer's parts of this book, especially the first three chapters. Then, take some existing class like Label, shown in Chapter 10, and study it to understand the various parts of a widget implementation. Next, try to find some existing widget class that implements a similar functionality; if such a class exists, make the new widget a subclass of this widget. In this case you only need to implement the additional functionality of the new widget.

In a well-designed widget set, it is not necessary to have source code for an existing widget to create a subclass that inherits its behavior. While sources may make the task appear easier, the X Toolkit was designed to allow widget subclassing without sources. Not looking at private implementation details of the superclass is also much better object-oriented programming style. Of course, all this depends on the behavior of the superclass being extremely well documented, something that is all too rarely true.

If no appropriate widget class exists, the new class must be a subclass of one of the Intrinsics-defined classes, normally Core for simple widgets and either Composite or Constraint for widgets that hold other widgets.

In any case, the easiest way to implement the new widget is to take the implementation of an existing class and edit; the Label or Box widget in this book or the Template widget in the Athena widget set are good places to start. In the entire history of the X Toolkit probably fewer than ten widgets have been implemented completely from scratch; all others were derived by editing other widgets.[7] Editing an existing implementation is especially useful for writing header files and declaring class records; a lot of the effort here is quite

---

[7] Even ten may be generous.

mechanical. Some tools are available that construct skeleton files for a new widget implementation.

1.15   Debugging Toolkit Applications

There is a certain amount of black art to debugging toolkit applications. Whenever you are dealing with a system that uses data hiding, it is difficult to find out just what went wrong when your application does not work.

One helpful technique is to install new Xlib and Intrinsics error handlers that call the Unix `abort` function, divide by zero, or dereference an invalid pointer after reporting the error. If you run your application under a debugger, this allows you to get a stack trace when the error occurs; the standard error handlers just print out a message and terminate, so by the time you find out about the error it is too late to find out what the stack is. Alternatively, you can insert a breakpoint in the standard error handlers, or on Unix systems, in `exit`.

If an application generates Xlib errors, running it with the –synchronous switch can help isolate them. This makes the application run considerably more slowly but makes the error messages occur during the offending Xlib call rather than at some future time. If –synchronous is not specified, errors from Xlib are almost never related in any meaningful way to the stack at the time of the message.

It is often helpful to be able to look at the values stored in a widget instance to see whether the fields have the values you expect them to have. If the application is linked with a toolkit library that was compiled with debugging turned on, you just dereference the widget value in the debugger. If this option is not available, you can change the include files your application uses to the private header files so that the data structure definitions become available to the debugger. Instead of writing

```
#include <X11/Intrinsic.h>
#include "Label.h"
```

write

```
#include <X11/IntrinsicP.h>
#include "LabelP.h"
```

and the debugger should be able to print out the widget records. Casting widget values into the most specific type before printing them out is helpful; this makes the debugger print out all the fields in the widget instance. Section 2.13 describes widget data structures.

1.16   Procedures and Macros

An implementation of the toolkit can implement some routines as macros with arguments. Any such macro must behave exactly like a procedure call, evaluating its arguments exactly once and using parentheses to protect its arguments and return value, if any. If an implementation provides such macros, it must also provide actual procedures with the same name. A program that needs an actual procedure, most often to assign the routine name to a procedure pointer variable, makes sure that no macro is defined using

```
#undef routine
```

before using the routine name.

Implementations are not required to provide procedure versions of `XtCheckSubclass`, `XtNew`, `XtNewString`, `XtNumber`, `XtOffsetOf`, `XtOffset`, or `XtSetArg`.

1.17   Procedure Types

The Intrinsics define many procedure pointer types for which programmers provide values, both in data structures and as parameters to Intrinsics routines. For example, a callback procedure is a procedure returning `void` (that is, returning nothing) that takes three parameters, one of type `Widget` and two of type `XtPointer`. This book defines procedure pointer types using ANSI C style typedefs.

typedef void (*XtCallbackProc)(Widget, XtPointer, XtPointer);
    Widget *w*;
    XtPointer *client_data*;
    XtPointer *call_data*;

w	Specifies the widget that the callback is registered for.
client_data	Specifies a piece of data defined by the application.
call_data	Specifies a piece of data defined by the widget class.

The Intrinsics routines and data structures have parameters and fields that use these procedure pointer types.

void XtAddCallback(*w, callback_name, callback, client_data*)
    Widget *w*;
    String *callback_name*;
    XtCallbackProc *callback*;
    XtPointer *client_data*;

w	Specifies the widget to add the callback procedure to.
callback_name	Specifies the callback list to add the procedure to.
callback	Specifies the callback procedure.
client_data	Specifies the value passed to the callback procedure in the *client_data* parameter, or NULL.

Thus the type of a callback procedure is `XtCallbackProc`, which is the same as a function of three arguments returning nothing. If you declare a variable that holds a pointer to a callback procedure, you declare the variable as an `XtCallbackProc`:

```
XtCallbackProc callback;
```

However, the procedure itself has return type `void`:

```
void Callback(w, clientData, callData)
    Widget w;
    XtPointer clientData, callData;
```

Declaring the callback procedure as an `XtCallbackProc` would incorrectly mean that the procedure returns a pointer to a callback procedure.

Do not interpret the phrase "the type of the whatever procedure is `XtWhateverProc`" in this programmer's guide as meaning "a whatever procedure returns data of type `XtWhateverProc`." The return type of the procedure is always described in the function prototype definition, and the simpler phrasing is used instead of the more formally correct "the type of a whatever variable or argument is `XtWhateverProc`."

Writing Widgets

If you don't need to know how to write widgets, skip to Chapter 2.

1.18   More on Header Files

Widget implementations include header files also but need access to more of the Intrinsics than applications do. Instead of including the header file `<X11/Intrinsic.h>`, widget implementations include the header file `<X11/IntrinsicP.h>`; this contains all the information included in `<X11/Intrinsic.h>` and some extra information for writing widgets. This file name follows the Intrinsics convention of naming header files for widget implementations with a trailing "P" (for private). `<X11/StringDefs.h>` defines strings used for widget attributes. The widget implementation also includes a private header file for the class, which contains all the information in the public header file plus information describing the implementation in more detail. Subclasses also use this private header file. As with the public header files, the information that could be in individual private header files for the widgets can be combined into a single header file for widgets in a widget set.[8]

1.19   Designing Widget Sets

When creating a widget set the designer must decide upon the organization of widget header files and the widget library.

For header files, a widget set can provide either individual header files for each widget or one combined header file for all widgets. The main trade-off here is programmer convenience against flexibility. If the header files are merged, the application programmer only needs to include one header. The programmer does not need to update a list of include files to use an additional widget. Difficulties occur, however, if she wants to mix widgets from different sets in her application or to replace a widget in the widget set with her own version; the header files may have conflicting definitions making this impossible (although if implementors scrupulously follow the naming conventions, this is less likely to happen).

An additional problem with combined header files is that they include an external class reference for every widget in the set. This makes most linkers pull every widget in the widget library into the program image, leading to very large binaries for even simple programs. This problem, however, usually does not occur with shared library implementations of widget sets. Conversely, if the program is using a user interface management system, the actual widget classes the application uses might not be known until runtime, so all potential widgets must be available. In this case a combined header file is the preferred solution.

The best solution is to provide both a combined header file and individual header files. The combined file can be as simple as a list of includes for the individual files.

A similar trade-off exists when deciding whether to include the Intrinsics library with the widget library. If the libraries are combined, programmers only specify a single library when linking the program. It makes things dif-

---

[8] Programmers familiar with the C++ programming language can think of the private header files as containing the "protected" information.

ficult, however, for a programmer who wants to combine widget sets since the separate libraries are not available. Providing both options is possible here, too, although the amount of disk space needed to hold two copies of the libraries can be substantial.

Chapter 2

Widgets

Writing Applications

2.1   Common Widget Classes

Some widget classes are commonly found in many widget sets in one form or another. Several discussed in this book are

Label	A simple text label on the screen. Some Label implementations allow pictures instead of or in addition to text. Labels are output-only; the user cannot interactively enter text into a Label widget.
Pushbutton	A widget that acts as a button to activate some application functionality; the user clicks a pointer button in the Pushbutton widget to invoke the function. Pushbutton widgets are also called Command widgets since activating them sends a command from the user to the application.
Toggle	A Button widget that switches back and forth between two states each time it is activated, much like a light switch or a shift lock key on a keyboard. Toggle buttons are also called Boolean buttons since they have two states.
ButtonBox	A widget that holds other widgets, often pushbuttons or toggle buttons, and packs them closely together to fill the available space.
Menu	A widget that holds other widgets, often pushbuttons, and arranges them into a vertical row, all having the same width.
Scrollbar	A widget that allows the user to select the portion of a data space that is visible on the screen.

ScrollingWidget   A widget that holds another widget and one or more scrollbars to control what is visible in that widget. Scrolling widgets are also called Viewport widgets.

VerticalPane   A widget that organizes its children into a vertical column and allows the user to interactively change how much vertical space is allocated to each child.

Box   A widget that holds other widgets, relying upon the application to specify all the layout information. Box widgets are also called dialog boxes.

MinMax   A widget similar to a simple box except that it also allows the application to specify minimum and maximum sizes for the widgets. If its size changes, a MinMax box resizes its children within these constraints.

Confirm   A pop-up widget that requests confirmation of some action. A Confirm widget usually suspends the execution of the rest of the application until the user responds.

TextField   A widget that allows the user to enter a text string.

2.2 The Class Hierarchy

The classes that widgets belong to are arranged into a hierarchical tree structure called the *class hierarchy*. The root of the tree is usually visualized as being at the top and the leaves of the tree at the bottom, leading to references to a class being above or below another class in the hierarchy. A widget that belongs to one class also belongs to all classes further up (i.e., closer to the root) in the hierarchy. Widget classes that are above a particular class along the path to the root of the tree are said to be *superclasses* of that class, and widget classes that are below it are *subclasses* of that class. Classes that are directly above or below a particular class are called *direct* superclasses or subclasses; references to "the" superclass of a class mean the direct superclass, while references to "a" superclass mean any superclass. If a widget class is a direct subclass of another class, it is said to be *derived* from that class.

A widget of a particular class supports all the attributes of all its superclasses and so can be used anywhere a widget of any of its superclasses can. Since a widget of a class also belongs to its superclasses, when this book says "a widget of class Whatever" it refers both to widgets whose class is Whatever and to widgets whose class is a subclass of Whatever.

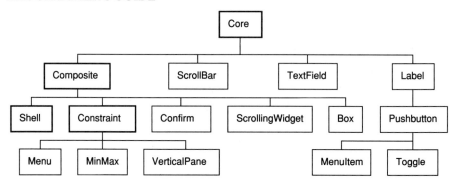

Figure 2.1. An example widget class hierarchy

Figure 2.1 shows a sample hierarchy of widgets found in many widget sets. Classes shown with thick borders are defined by the Intrinsics; all other classes are particular to the widget set. The Toggle widget class in this figure is a subclass of Pushbutton, Label, and Core, and the Box widget class is a subclass of Composite and Core. This means that an application can pass Toggle widgets to procedures expecting Toggle, Pushbutton, Label, or Core widgets, and can pass Box widgets to procedures expecting Box, Composite, or Core widgets.

Be careful not to confuse the widget class hierarchy with the widget instance tree. The class hierarchy is a static property of the widget set that the application is using. It defines the relationships between the classes of the widgets available to the application. The instance tree describes the organization of the widget instances in a particular application's user interface. This programmer's guide always uses *hierarchy* to refer to the class organization and *tree* to refer to the widget instance organization. In addition, illustrations showing a class hierarchy always capitalize the names of the classes (Figure 2.1) and illustrations showing a widget tree always begin the names of the widget instances with a lower-case letter (Figure 1.3).

There are two major reasons for arranging classes into a hierarchy. The first is that a particular class defines uniform protocols for manipulating widgets of that class and all its subclasses. This is most important for classes near the root of the hierarchy; the Core class defines operations to create, destroy, and otherwise manipulate widgets of any class at all, and the Composite class defines operations to add and delete children, used by widgets that contain other widgets.

The class hierarchy also makes it easier to define and create a new widget class. If a new widget class is similar to another class, it is much easier to derive the new class from the existing one than to create the new class from scratch. A Pushbutton widget is very similar to a Label widget: both display their contents in almost the same way and have similar attributes, like the text string to display and the font and color to display it in. They also share algorithms such as computing the size needed to display their string. The widget programmer derives the Pushbutton class from the Label class, only worrying about new attributes like the application callback procedure and new operations like calling this procedure.

A new widget class shares code and declarations with its superclass. Earlier versions of the toolkit had no class hierarchy; programmers derived one class from another by editing one class implementation into another. In this scheme, widget implementations inherited all the bugs in the class they were derived from but none of the bug fixes—if you fixed a bug in one class you had to track down all derived classes and fix the bug there as well. The code sharing allowed by subclassing leads to a significant reduction in code maintenance effort.

2.3   Initializing Widget Classes

A widget implementation contains procedures the Intrinsics execute to initialize the widget class. The Intrinsics call these procedures automatically just before creating the first widget of a particular class, but some applications need facilities provided by the class before creating any widgets of the class. To initialize the class explicitly, use XtInitializeWidgetClass.[1]

void XtInitializeWidgetClass(*widget_class*)
    WidgetClass *widget_class*;
widget_class   Specifies the class to initialize.

An application uses XtInitializeWidgetClass if it needs to call a procedure the class supplies or to use type conversions the class registers before creating any widgets of the class. See Section 3.7 for information on type conversions. Calling XtInitializeWidgetClass in other cases is harmless but unnecessary.

[1] XtInitializeWidgetClass is not supported by Intrinsics implementations that conform to specifications earlier than Release 4.

2.4   Widget Naming Conventions

Naming conventions make it easier for the application programmer to write programs. She need not remember whether the external reference to the Label widget class is named labelWidgetClass, labelClass, or label_widget_class, or whether resource for the border width is named XtNborderWidth, borderWidth, or border_width.

Each widget implementation provides a header file containing public definitions for that widget. The name of the header file is the same as the name of the widget class followed by ".h"; long class names are truncated to ten characters in header file names. The header files for an installed widget set are typically in a subdirectory of /usr/include/X11. If the header information for the widgets has been combined into a single file, the application just includes the one file.

The widget header file for each widget class defines a C type for widget instances, formed by concatenating the capitalized class name with the string "Widget". For example, the Label widget header file Label.h defines the type LabelWidget and the Menu header file defines MenuWidget. These type names may be preceded with a prefix that specifies the widget set to which this widget belongs. Applications that just use Intrinsics interfaces do not need to use these types; they declare all widgets to be the predefined type Widget. Some widget classes, however, define interfaces specific to widgets of that class, so widgets passed into these procedures should be cast to the correct type. Alternatively, an application declares its widgets using more specific types and casts them to type Widget when passing them to Intrinsics routines.

Each widget header file also declares an external reference of type WidgetClass to the widget class structure, named by concatenating the uncapitalized class name with the string "WidgetClass". For example, the Label header file declares the external variable *labelWidgetClass* and the Menu header file declares *menuWidgetClass*. Again, these may be preceded with a prefix specifying the widget set. Applications pass this value to the widget creation functions to specify which class of widget to create, and the XtClass function, used to find a widget's class, returns one of these values. In brief,

Header file	Label.h	Menu.h
Type	LabelWidget	MenuWidget
Class name	*labelWidgetClass*	*menuWidgetClass*

2.5   Widget Resources

Each widget class declares a list of *resources* for instances of the widget class. The toolkit uses the term *resource* with a very specific meaning: a resource is a piece of data in the widget instance that is accessible to the application and usually customizable by the user. The widget attributes described in the "Goodbye, world" program in Chapter 1 are examples of resources. Chapter 3 discusses widget resources in detail; this section only briefly introduces them. Section 3.2 describes in detail the naming conventions used with resources.

Resource values can be shared with other widget instances or can be private to a single instance. Their initial values can be specified in the application or can originate from a variety of external sources. The widget class specifies a default value for each resource; resources take their default value in the absence of any other specification. In most cases, resource values are automatically shared between widget instances and are specified externally to the application program.

A uniform set of Intrinsics interfaces allow applications to set, query, and modify resources. Any resource a class defines is automatically defined for any subclass of that class, though subclasses can provide different default values.

Each resource is identified by two strings, a resource name and a resource class. For example, the resource controlling a widget's border width is identified with the name string "borderWidth" and the class string "BorderWidth". The resource name uniquely defines this resource within the widget class, and the class groups resources together, allowing the user or application to provide values for similar resources in one place. Note that a resource class is not the same thing as a widget class. To facilitate application and widget development, particularly debugging, the Intrinsics define identifiers (usually macros) for each string constant that defines resource names and classes, and widget libraries are expected to do likewise. These identifiers permit the compiler to notice spelling errors that would otherwise go undetected within a string constant.

The identifier for a resource name string is the string prefixed with the characters "XtN", and the identifier for a resource class string is the string prefixed with "XtC". The border width resource has the name identifier XtNborderWidth and the class identifier XtCBorderWidth. This book always uses the identifier for a resource name or class.

Each resource also has a representation type which, like its name and class, has a string constant. The type has an associated identifier that is the value of the string, prefixed with "XtR". The border width resource is of type Dimension; it has the type string "Dimension" and the type identifier XtRDimension. The Intrinsics use the representation type to convert a value of one type to the appropriate representation type used by the widget class. This book usually gives resource types as the actual C data type that the resource type represents. Chapter 3 lists the corresponding string constants and identifiers.

2.6   The Base Widget Classes

The Intrinsics define several widget classes that are present in every widget class hierarchy. Applications rarely create widgets of these classes; they exist primarily to define resources and fundamental operations for other widget classes. These classes are implemented as subclasses of simpler classes still, but these simpler classes are not visible to application writers who use only widgets.[2]

The base widget classes are Core, Composite, and Constraint. The Intrinsics also define several varieties of shell widgets, described in Chapter 5.

2.6.1   The Core Widget and Its Resources

The Core class is the root of the widget class hierarchy, so all widgets belong to class Core. There are two synonymous types defined for core widgets, Widget and CoreWidget. Applications rarely need to create core widgets, but if they do they pass either widgetClass or coreWidgetClass to the widget creation routine.[3] Section 7.18 describes one way that an application might use a core widget directly.

Resources defined for core widgets apply to all widgets.

Name	Class	Type	Default
XtNdestroyCallback	XtCCallback	XtCallbackList	NULL
XtNx	XtCPosition	Position	0

[2] The simpler classes are not supported by Intrinsics implementations that conform to specifications earlier than Release 4.

[3] The symbols CoreWidget and coreWidgetClass are not supported by Intrinsics implementations that conform to specifications earlier than Release 4.

Name	Class	Type	Default
XtNy	XtCPosition	Position	0
XtNwidth	XtCWidth	Dimension	0
XtNheight	XtCHeight	Dimension	0
XtNborderWidth	XtCBorderWidth	Dimension	1
XtNsensitive	XtCSensitive	Boolean	TRUE
XtNancestorSensitive	XtCSensitive	Boolean	special
XtNscreen	XtCScreen	Screen *[4]	special
XtNdepth	XtCDepth	Cardinal	special
XtNcolormap	XtCColormap	Colormap	special
XtNbackground	XtCBackground	Pixel	special
XtNbackgroundPixmap	XtCPixmap	Pixmap	special
XtNborderColor	XtCBorderColor	Pixel	special
XtNborderPixmap	XtCPixmap	Pixmap	special
XtNmappedWhenManaged	XtCMappedWhenManaged	Boolean	TRUE
XtNtranslations	XtCTranslations	XtTranslations	special
XtNaccelerators	XtCAccelerators	XtAccelerators	none

Resources have default values for a reason; application programmers rarely specify resources other than the position, size, border, background, translations, and accelerators. All these resources are described more completely in later chapters.

XtNdestroyCallback is a list of callback procedures that the Intrinsics invoke when the widget is destroyed. Applications rarely use this.

XtNx, XtNy, XtNwidth, XtNheight, and XtNborderWidth are collectively called a widget's *geometry* resources. They determine the position, size, and border width of the widget's window.

XtNsensitive and XtNancestorSensitive determine whether a widget reacts to user input. Applications never manipulate XtNancestorSensitive and specify XtNsensitive directly only when creating a widget. To change sensitivity, applications use the `XtSetSensitive` routine. See Section 6.14 for more information.

XtNscreen determines which screen the widget appears on. This can only be specified for shell widgets; all other widgets appear on the same screen as their parent. Its default value is the screen of the widget's parent or, for top-level shell widgets, the default screen of the display. Note that this resource is

[4] An asterisk (*) in this column of a resource table indicates a pointer, not a footnote.

a pointer to an Xlib `Screen` data structure and not a screen number; see Section 2.2 of *Xlib* for more information.

XtNdepth determines the number of bits stored for each pixel in the widget's window. Its default value is the depth of the widget's parent or, for top-level shell widgets, the default depth of the screen. Applications only specify XtNdepth when creating a widget; attempts to change it later are ignored. Specifying a depth that the screen does not support results in a `BadMatch` error from the X server when the Intrinsics create a window for the widget. Allowable window depths are also a function of the window's visual; see Section 2.7.

XtNcolormap determines the colormap used for drawing in the widget's window. Its default value is the colormap of the parent widget or, for top-level shell widgets, the default colormap of the screen. Specifying a colormap that is not valid for the widget's screen and visual results in a `BadMatch` error from the X server when the Intrinsics resolve color names; see Section 2.7.

XtNbackground and XtNbackgroundPixmap determine the background of the window; the background is used when the background pixmap is not specified. Applications needing to set the background set XtNbackground to a pixel value or set XtNbackgroundPixmap to either a pixmap value or one of the special values ParentRelative, which means to use the same background as the widget's parent; None, which means that the window has no background; or XtUnspecifiedPixmap, which means to use XtNbackground for the background. The default value for XtNbackground is XtDefaultBackground, which usually corresponds to the `WhitePixel` value for the widget's screen, and the default value for XtNbackgroundPixmap is XtUnspecifiedPixmap.[5]

XtNborderColor and XtNborderPixmap determine the border of the window; XtNborderColor is used when XtNborderPixmap is not specified. Applications needing to set the border set XtNborderColor to a pixel value or set XtNborderPixmap to either a pixmap value or one of the special values CopyFromParent, which means to use the same border pixmap as the widget's parent, or XtUnspecifiedPixmap, which means to use XtNborderColor for the border. The default value for XtNborderColor is XtDefaultForeground, which

---

[5] XtUnspecifiedPixmap is not available to applications that use Intrinsics implementations that conform to specifications earlier than Release 4. XtNbackgroundPixmap and XtNborderPixmap take default values with the same effect as XtUnspecifiedPixmap, but applications cannot change these resources back to the default value after giving them a different one.

usually corresponds to the `BlackPixel` value for the widget's screen, and the default value for XtNborderPixmap is XtUnspecifiedPixmap.

XtNmappedWhenManaged determines whether the widget appears on the screen when it is managed. A managed widget is one that is allocated screen space by its parent. See Sections 4.3 and 4.4.

XtNtranslations defines how the widget maps input events from the X server to widget and application functions. Translations specify the keystrokes and pointer actions the user uses to manipulate the widget. Its default value is specified by the widget programmer for all widgets of a particular class. Chapter 7 describes translations.

XtNaccelerators defines how the user can invoke this widget's functionality from other widgets in the user interface. Accelerators allow, for example, a user to invoke a menu item's functionality from keystrokes in the application's main window. Section 7.15 describes accelerators.

2.6.2 The Composite Widget and Its Resources

The Composite class is a direct subclass of Core, and defines resources and routines common to all widgets that contain child widgets. Widgets whose class is Composite or a subclass of Composite are called composite widgets. Composite exists only to be a superclass for other classes, so applications never create widgets of class Composite.

The type for composite widgets is `CompositeWidget`. Composite defines three resources beyond those defined by Core.

Name	Class	Type	Default
XtNinsertPosition	XtCInsertPosition	XtOrderProc	InsertAtEnd
XtNchildren	XtCReadOnly	Widget *	special
XtNnumChildren	XtCReadOnly	Cardinal	special

Applications rarely use any of these resources.

XtNinsertPosition specifies a procedure that returns where a new child goes in the list of existing children. The default procedure always inserts the new child at the end of the list.

XtNchildren and XtNnumChildren supply the list of children of the composite widget and are primarily intended to be used within insert position procedures.[6] Both of these resources are read-only resources; programs should never attempt to set or modify them. Similarly, programs must never modify the list of children obtained with the XtNchildren resource. Their classes are XtCReadOnly as a reminder; the only time resource classes are used is to specify resource values.

See Chapter 4 for full details on composite widgets.

2.6.3   The Constraint Widget

The Constraint class is a direct subclass of Composite and allows widgets to associate extra information with each of their children for their own exclusive use. An example is MinMax, a class that allows the application to specify a minimum and maximum size for each child. Widgets whose class is Constraint or a subclass of Constraint are called constraint widgets. Constraint exists only to be a superclass for other classes, so applications never create widgets of class Constraint.

The type for constraint widgets is `ConstraintWidget`; Constraint defines no resources beyond those defined by Composite. Section 4.6 describes constraint widgets.

2.7   Visuals, Colormaps, and Window Depths

The X server communicates the color capabilities of its display to applications by providing a list of *visual* types it supports for each screen. Different visual types indicate monochrome, gray scale, and several kinds of color screens. A single screen can support several visual types, so a color screen might also support being treated as a gray scale or monochrome screen. Different windows in an application can use different visual types.

Visuals, colormaps, and window depths are closely related. The set of depths that are valid for a window is a function of the window's visual type, and the set of valid colormaps is a function of the visual type and depth. Sections 3.1, 5.1, and 10.8 of *Xlib* describe visuals and colormaps.

Most applications do not need to worry about visuals, colormaps, or window depths. The Intrinsics provide default handling appropriate for most applications.

---

[6] XtNchildren and XtNnumChildren are not supported by Intrinsics implementations that conform to specifications earlier than Release 4.

Some widget classes override the Intrinsics' defaults to provide needed functionality, most commonly to support imaging, complex graphical editing, or sophisticated rendering. Widget classes that do this should document what an application has to do to use them.

The most frequent override that a user or application may make is to specify an alternative visual type on a display that supports multiple types. For example, an application might wish to always have gray scale windows even if it is running on a color display. Setting the XtNvisual resource on the application's top-level shell accomplishes this; see Section 5.2.

Because visuals, colormaps, and depths are so closely related, an application that overrides the default value for any of them needs to be aware of all three. For example, an application that sets the XtNvisual resource on its shell may also need to set its colormap and depth.

The most common thing an application must do is to set its colormap windows; see Section 9.7.

2.8 Creating Widget Instances

Creating a user interface is actually a two-phase process for an application. In the first phase the application creates a number of widgets. This phase allocates the widget data structures and collects the required resource values but does not yet create any windows. The application then executes the second phase, creating a window for each widget in the tree. This two-phase process allows the toolkit to minimize the total number of requests sent to the X server when the application starts.

When an application creates a widget, it can override the values for some of the widget's resources. This is done with an *argument list* of name-value pairs. Argument lists are discussed fully in Chapter 3; to create them, declare an `ArgList`.

```
typedef something XtArgVal;
typedef struct {
    String      name;
    XtArgVal    value;
} Arg, *ArgList;
```

Something is an implementation-dependent data type of a specified minimum size; see Chapter 3. The name field is a string specifying the resource's name and the value field contains the override value. A sample argument list for creating a Label widget is

```
Arg labelArgs[] = {
    {XtNx,      10},
    {XtNy,      10},
    {XtNlabel,  "Goodbye, world"}
};
```

This specifies values for the XtNx, XtNy, and XtNlabel resources. Applications use the XtNumber macro to find the number of entries in an argument list.

Some resource values, called *reference* resources, are actually pointers, and the application must make sure that the data pointed to by any such resources last as long as the widget does. Widgets typically allocate their own copy of some reference resources, so for these the application can safely use the address of transient information like local variables. Widgets expect other reference resources to be permanent, so the application must not let the real data go away while the widget exists. The documentation for a widget class indicates into which category each reference resource falls. The most common case is for widgets to copy string resources and to expect other reference resources to be permanent; in the absence of an explicit statement, application programmers can usually assume this behavior.

Any Intrinsics routine that takes an argument list also has an alternative version that takes a variable parameter list; these are called *varargs* routines. Section 3.9 describes how to use the varargs interfaces.

It is important to understand that an application does not have to use arglists or varargs parameters to specify resources. In most cases the same information can be specified in other ways that allow users to customize the application and developers to change the resources without recompiling the application. Chapter 3 describes the various options available for specifying resources.

Applications normally create widgets using XtCreateManagedWidget.

Widget XtCreateManagedWidget(*name, widget_class, parent, args, num_args*)
    String *name*;
    WidgetClass *widget_class*;
    Widget *parent*;
    ArgList *args*;
    Cardinal *num_args*;
  name   Specifies the name of this widget instance. This name should normally be unique for all children of a single parent.

widget_class	Specifies the class of widget to create.
parent	Specifies the parent widget.
args	Specifies the argument list of override resource values for this instance.
num_args	Specifies the number of entries in the argument list.

The *widget_class* parameter determines what kind of widget XtCreate-ManagedWidget creates. XtCreateManagedWidget returns a reference to the new widget.

The name of a widget serves several purposes. Most important, it identifies the widget so that its resources can be specified from outside the application code itself. One such outside source is a user defaults file containing the user's desired customizations. The Intrinsics also allow an application to find a widget in the interface given its name. Widget names need not be unique within the application, but they should be unique among the children of each parent. They consist of letters and numbers, and by convention begin with a lower-case letter.

It is up to the application programmer to ensure that the parent is willing to accept children. Most widgets willing to accept children are composite, but the Intrinsics do not require this. Noncomposite parents always define some additional steps the application must go through to add the child, and these steps should be described in the widget documentation. Adding a child to a noncomposite parent and not following the widget class's instructions does not generate an error, but the child never appears on the screen.

To create a widget using the varargs interface, use XtVaCreate-ManagedWidget.[7]

Widget XtVaCreateManagedWidget(*name, widget_class, parent,* . . .)
    String *name*;
    WidgetClass *widget_class*;
    Widget *parent*;

name	Specifies the name of this widget instance. This name should normally be unique for all children of a single parent.
widget_class	Specifies the class of widget to create.
parent	Specifies the parent widget.
. . .	Specifies the override resources for this instance.

See Section 3.9 for more information.

---

[7] XtVaCreateManagedWidget and XtVaCreateWidget are not supported by Intrinsics implementations that conform to specifications earlier than Release 4.

Applications can also create widgets that are not initially allocated screen space within their parent and are therefore not initially visible. These widgets are said to be *unmanaged*; Section 4.3 gives full details. `XtCreateWidget` creates such a widget.

Widget XtCreateWidget(*name, widget_class, parent, args, num_args*)
    String *name*;
    WidgetClass *widget_class*;
    Widget *parent*;
    ArgList *args*;
    Cardinal *num_args*;

name	Specifies the name of this widget instance. This name should normally be unique for all children of a single parent.
widget_class	Specifies the class of widget to create.
parent	Specifies the parent widget.
args	Specifies the argument list of override resource values for this instance.
num_args	Specifies the number of entries in the argument list.

`XtCreateWidget` is identical to `XtCreateManagedWidget` except that the created widget is flagged so that its parent ignores it when allocating screen space.

To create a widget with no initial screen space using the varargs interface, use `XtVaCreateWidget`.

Widget XtVaCreateWidget(*name, widget_class, parent, . . .*)
    String *name*;
    WidgetClass *widget_class*;
    Widget *parent*;

name	Specifies the name of this widget instance. This name should normally be unique for all children of a single parent.
widget_class	Specifies the class of widget to create.
parent	Specifies the parent widget.
. . .	Specifies the override resources for this instance.

2.9   Realizing Widgets

Realizing a widget means creating a window for the widget. This is a separate action from creating a widget in order to reduce the amount of communication with the server at application startup.

Consider the case of a Menu widget, which acts as a vertical container for the items that appear in the menu. A menu cannot compute its height until the application has added all the items in the menu. Further, the menu forces all the menu items to have the width of the widest item, and the menu cannot determine this width until all menu items are present.

If the toolkit initially created a window for the menu, it would have to change the size of the window as the application added the menu items. The menu item windows would also have their sizes updated once the menu had determined its width. These size changes do not amount to much for a single widget, but in an application containing hundreds of widgets the number of server requests would be considerable. It is better, then, to delay creating a widget's window until the widget has a final size.[8]

To realize a widget tree, use `XtRealizeWidget`.

void XtRealizeWidget(*w*)
    Widget *w*;
    w   Specifies the widget to realize.

`XtRealizeWidget` creates a window for the specified widget and then, if it is a composite widget, recursively realizes all the widget's managed children. `XtRealizeWidget` also maps the windows of managed widgets (those created using `XtCreateManagedWidget` or managed with `XtManage-Child`) whose XtNmappedWhenManaged resource is TRUE. Mapping a widget makes it appear on the user's screen if all its ancestors are also mapped and if the user's window manager agrees to give the application some screen space. Most applications call `XtRealizeWidget` only once, for the application's top-level widget, to create windows for all widgets in the user interface. `XtRealizeWidget` returns without doing anything if called with a widget that is already realized and generates an error if called with a widget with an unrealized parent. As described above, realizing a widget is likely to cause size changes for the widget and its descendants because their actual sizes are not computed until then.

Because of the buffered nature of Xlib, the actual creation of the windows may be delayed until the application enters an event-dispatching loop. Further, the contents of the widgets will not appear until the toolkit processes the

---

[8] This performance improvement is not hypothetical—earlier versions of the toolkit did not have a separate realization step, and it was a major performance bottleneck.

exposure events that the X server generates. These effects are not normally noticeable in simple applications that create their user interfaces initially, but some applications require special steps to make their interfaces appear. See Section 6.10.

To test whether a widget is realized, use `XtIsRealized`.

Boolean XtIsRealized(*w*)
    Widget *w*;
w   Specifies the widget to test.

`XtIsRealized` returns a Boolean value indicating whether the specified widget is currently realized.

2.10   Unrealizing Widgets

Applications can reduce server memory usage by destroying the windows for widgets that do not currently appear on the screen. This might be appropriate for menus and pop-up dialog boxes that have been displayed once but are in general rarely used; if the application needs to display them again, it realizes them again. Destroying the windows, called *unrealizing,* should be used sparingly since making the widget reappear again later involves creating a new window, which takes time. The performance gains of unrealizing widgets have become much smaller with new X servers that use smaller data structures; you should only use unrealizing when server memory usage becomes a noticeable problem.

To unrealize a widget tree, use `XtUnrealizeWidget`.

void XtUnrealizeWidget(*w*)
    Widget *w*;
w   Specifies the widget to unrealize.

`XtUnrealizeWidget` recursively unrealizes all the children of the specified widget if the widget is composite. It then unrealizes the specified widget. If the widget is not currently realized, `XtUnrealizeWidget` returns without doing anything.

When the Intrinsics unrealize a widget, they check if the widget has any callbacks named XtNunrealizeCallback, and execute these callback procedures if so. This procedure allows the widget or application to note any special actions that might be needed in the future if the widget is realized again.

An unrealized widget remains invisibly sensitive and active even though it does not have a window. It receives events if the widget has accelerators that are installed on another realized widget; see Section 7.15 for more details.

2.11 Destroying Widgets

There are many places where an application wants to destroy a widget, but doing so would make the toolkit lose the context of its current operations. Consider a pop-up dialog box containing a pushbutton to dismiss the box. If the application does not anticipate needing the dialog box again, it makes the "dismiss" button destroy the dialog box and all its children. The Intrinsics, however, are using data structures in the Pushbutton widget to dispatch the event that triggered the pushbutton, and deallocating these data structures would leave the Intrinsics with dangling references.

Rather than copying data structures on the chance that a widget will be destroyed and the original data freed, the Intrinsics use a two-phase destroy process. Destroying a widget simply marks the widget and its children as being destroyed and adds the widget to a list of widgets awaiting destruction. When the Intrinsics no longer have references to destroyed widget data, the second phase of the destroy process actually deallocates the widget storage. It is therefore safe to destroy a widget from any place in an application.

As an application writer, you need not be particularly aware of this two-phase process except to understand that destroying a widget does not always happen immediately. This is usually only noticeable when debugging; unless you are single-stepping through an application, you are unlikely to notice the delay.

To initiate widget destruction, use `XtDestroyWidget`.

void XtDestroyWidget(*w*)
    Widget *w*;
  w   Specifies the widget to destroy.

`XtDestroyWidget` is the only way to destroy a widget; this includes widgets that destroy themselves. It automatically destroys any descendants of the specified widget as well.

If the specified widget is already marked as being destroyed, `XtDestroy-Widget` simply returns. Otherwise, it marks the widget and all its pop-up and normal children as being destroyed and puts them on a list.

The second phase of destruction occurs when the Intrinsics determine that deallocating the widgets is safe, possibly immediately.

Every widget has a destroy callback list to send notifications of the widget's impending demise. The Intrinsics invoke callbacks on this list at the beginning of phase 2 in postorder; that is, the callbacks for child widgets are called before their parents' callbacks. See Chapter 3 for a full discussion of callback procedures. After calling the destroy callbacks, the Intrinsics destroy the widget's window and deallocate the widget's storage.

Since destroying a widget destroys the widget's window, it is never necessary to explicitly unrealize a widget before destroying it. The Intrinsics do not call any XtNunrealizeCallback callback lists in the widget instances; instead they call the destroy callbacks.

To add a callback procedure to a widget's destroy callback list, an application calls `XtAddCallback` specifying XtNdestroyCallback as the callback name.

2.12   Widget Information Functions

The Intrinsics provide several functions to find out information about a widget. These procedures can also be implemented as macros, especially when used in a widget implementation, but are always functions for application use. To find out information about a widget use `XtDisplay`, `XtScreen`, `XtParent`, `XtWindow`, `XtName`, `XtClass`, and `XtIsSubclass`.

```
Display *XtDisplay(w)
    Widget w;
```
w   Specifies the widget to get the display for.

`XtDisplay` returns the specified widget's display pointer.

```
Screen *XtScreen(w)
    Widget w;
```
w   Specifies the widget to get the screen for.

`XtScreen` returns the specified widget's screen pointer. Note that the screen pointer is not the same as the screen number used in some Xlib calls.

```
Widget XtParent(w)
    Widget w;
```
w   Specifies the widget to get the parent for.

`XtParent` returns the specified widget's parent.

Window XtWindow(*w*)
    Widget *w*;
   w   Specifies the widget to get the window for.

`XtWindow` returns the specified widget's window.

String XtName(*w*)
    Widget *w*;
   w   Specifies the widget to get the name for.

`XtName` returns the specified widget's name. The application must treat the returned string as read-only; modifying or freeing this string will cause obscure errors.[9]

WidgetClass XtClass(*w*)
    Widget *w*;
   w   Specifies the widget to get the class for.

`XtClass` returns the specified widget's class.

Boolean XtIsSubclass(*w*, *widget_class*)
    Widget *w*;
    WidgetClass *widget_class*;
   w   Specifies the widget to test.
   widget_class   Specifies the widget class to test against.

`XtIsSubclass` returns TRUE if the widget is of the specified class or any subclass thereof.

Every widget class defined by the Intrinsics comes with a routine to check if a widget is a member of that class or a subclass. Each is equivalent to calling `XtIsSubclass` with the appropriate widget class variable, but may be more efficient.[10]

Boolean XtIsWidget(*w*)
Boolean XtIsComposite(*w*)
Boolean XtIsConstraint(*w*)
Boolean XtIsShell(*w*)

---

[9] `XtName` is not supported by Intrinsics implementations that conform to specifications earlier than Release 4.

[10] None of these routines except `XtIsComposite` are supported by Intrinsics implementations that conform to specifications earlier than Release 4.

Boolean XtIsOverrideShell(w)
Boolean XtIsWMShell(w)
Boolean XtIsVendorShell(w)
Boolean XtIsTransientShell(w)
Boolean XtIsTopLevelShell(w)
Boolean XtIsApplicationShell(w)
    Widget w;

w Specifies the widget to check.

Applications rarely use any of these routines.

Writing Widgets

The widget writer's parts of this programmer's guide present pieces of the implementations of several simple widgets. The complete implementations, with annotations, are in Chapter 10. These widgets make up a simple but useful widget set that exercises most of the capabilities of the toolkit. They illustrate many of the functions found in many widget sets and should integrate smoothly with the Athena widgets included in the MIT X distribution.

Most of the examples are drawn from Label and Pushbutton. The Label class is a direct subclass of Core that adds several resources to those Core defines.

XtNlabel   The string to display in the label. If this is not specified, the label widget uses its name as the default.

XtNfont   The font to use to display the text. The font structure is assumed to be a static resource; the widget does not create its own copy.

XtNforeground   The pixel value to use to display the text.

XtNjustify   Whether the label centers, left justifies, or right justifies its text in its window.

XtNspace   The extra space to leave around the text string.

XtNloseSelection A callback to execute if the label loses the selection. It passes the selection identifier in the call_data.

Selections are fully described in Section 9.13; at this point you only need to know that they are a means of communicating data between applications. An application can make data available as a selection, and other applications can request the data. At a later time another application can take ownership of the selection, making the previous owner lose the selection.

Label modifies the default window border width so that labels by default appear with no border, and if no height and width are specified Label calculates a size sufficient to hold the label's text in its font. Label provides one new class method.

LabelSelectText   Asks the label to select or unselect its text string, returning whether it succeeded.

The Pushbutton widget is a direct subclass of Label, inheriting all its resources and adding several more.

XtNcallback   The callback procedure list to execute when the widget is activated.

XtNinsensitiveForeground
                  The pixel value to use for the foreground when the widget is insensitive.

XtNinsensitivePixmap
                  The pixmap to use as the foreground when the widget is insensitive.

XtNhighlightBorder
                  The width of the line drawn inside the border of the widget when it is highlighted.

XtNacceleratorString
                  The string to use to represent the widget's accelerator.

Pushbutton modifies the default window border width back to 1, and provides no new class methods; however, as a subclass of Label it supports the LabelSelectText method.

2.13   Widget Data Structures

Widget data structures are linked together in a predefined fashion that allows the Intrinsics to manipulate them. Each widget class defines a class record containing a pointer to its superclass, and each widget class defines a widget instance record containing a pointer to its class record. Each widget class has only one class record but can have many instance records.[11]

---

[11] Programmers familiar with the C++ programming language may think of these data structures as separating all static class members into a separate data structure that the Intrinsics call the class record.

Figure 2.2 shows an example. The two Pushbutton widget instances have pointers to the Pushbutton class record, and the two Label widget instances have pointers to the Label class record. The Pushbutton class record has a pointer to the Label class record since Pushbutton is a direct subclass of Label, and the Label class record has a pointer to the Core class record since Label is a direct subclass of Core.

Widget instance records have links to form the widget instance tree. Each widget contains a pointer to its parent, and each composite widget contains a list of pointers to its children. Figure 2.3 shows this structure for the widgets in the "Goodbye, world" program described in Chapter 1.

The semantics of the Intrinsics require that anywhere a widget class or instance record is needed the class or instance record of any subclass can be used instead. To enforce this, the initial segments of the subclass records match the records for their superclass. For example, the beginning of the Label class record is identical to the class record for its superclass, Core, and the beginning of the Label instance record is identical to the instance record for Core. A subclass always adds any additional fields after the fields of its superclass.

One way to implement this matching rule would be to actually include the superclass's record in the definition of the subclass record. For example, Label is a subclass of Core and Pushbutton is a subclass of Label, so the structures could be declared like this:

```
typedef struct _LabelRec {
    CoreRec core;
    ...additional fields defined here...
} LabelRec;

typedef struct _PushbuttonRec {
    LabelRec label;
    ...additional fields defined here...
} PushbuttonRec;
```

and similarly for the class records. This approach leads to unwieldy field references in the widget implementation. The Pushbutton implementation refers to a field in its part of a Pushbutton widget simply as *widget->field*, but it refers to a field in the Core part as *widget->label.core.field*. As the subclass hierarchy grows, so does the qualification necessary to access the field. Worse, if the class hierarchy above the class is ever rearranged or has an additional class inserted, all field references must change.

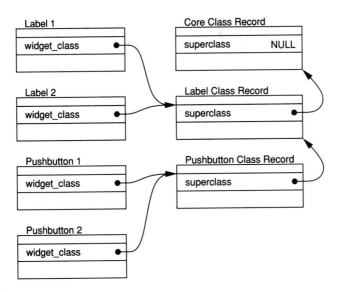

Figure 2.2. The class linkage of several widgets

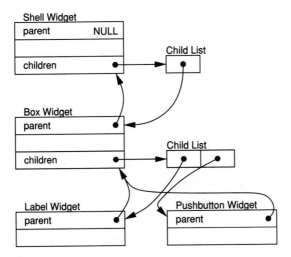

Figure 2.3. The instance linkage of several widgets

To avoid this problem, widget data structures are defined as a series of substructures, called *part records,* one for each class. Thus for Label and Pushbutton the declarations look like this:

```
typedef struct _LabelPart {
    ...new fields defined here...
} LabelPart;

typedef struct _LabelRec {
    CorePart    core;
    LabelPart   label;
} LabelRec;

typedef struct _PushbuttonPart {
    ...new fields defined here...
} PushbuttonPart;

typedef struct _PushbuttonRec {
    CorePart        core;
    LabelPart       label;
    PushbuttonPart  pushbutton;
} PushbuttonRec;
```

and similarly for the class records. With this scheme every field reference always has exactly one structure qualification: a field in the Core part is always *widget–>core.field* no matter how many superclasses the widget class has. This means that every widget instance has a Core part, and every widget class has a Core class part.

 Always remember the distinction between parts and records. Each class of widget contains a Core class part in its class record, but the values of the fields in this part apply to the particular class and not to the Core class. Similarly, each widget instance record contains a Core instance part, no matter what class the widget actually belongs to.

Widgets should never rely upon the fields in any of the instance class parts for Intrinsics classes being in any particular order. Intrinsics implementations are free to reorder the fields in instance part data structure definitions to improve space efficiency or for any other reason.

By convention the last field in each class part record is a pointer named *extension;* for many class parts this is the only field. If future revisions of a widget class add new fields to its class part record, recompilation of previously written subclasses can be avoided by defining the new field in an extension record. Any implementation of a subclass that wants to provide a value for the new field declares an extension record and places a pointer to it in the extension field of the class part. Section 2.21 gives a complete description of extension records.

Since the C language does not permit empty structure declarations, a subclass that adds no new fields to its superclass must declare a dummy field when it defines its part data structures. For example, the MenuItem widget defined in Chapter 10 defines its instance part this way:

```
typedef struct {
    int     empty;       /* No empty structures allowed */
} MenuItemPart;
```

This applies to the class part declaration as well, though the *extension* field normally satisfies the requirement.

2.14   Structure Naming Conventions

The names of various structures follow a rigid naming convention to ensure uniformity, making the programmer's life easier. She does not need to remember different naming conventions that different widgets may use. For a new widget class AbcXyz, the implementation must define certain names:

• A widget part structure type named AbcXyzPart. Fields in this structure are all lower-case and use an underscore (_) to separate words.

• A widget instance structure type named AbcXyzRec and struct _AbcXyzRec. The fields in this structure are named by the uncapitalized widget name; for example the AbcXyzPart is named abcXyz.

• A widget class part structure type named AbcXyzClassPart. Fields in this structure are all lower-case and use an underscore (_) to separate words.

• A widget class structure type named AbcXyzClassRec and struct _AbcXyzClassRec. The fields in this structure are named by the uncapitalized widget name followed by "_class"; for example, the AbcXyzClassPart is named abcXyz_class.

• A type declaration for AbcXyz widgets named AbcXyzWidget. This is defined to be a pointer to an AbcXyzRec.

• A widget class structure named abcXyzClassRec.

• A global pointer to the abcXyzClassRec structure named abcXyzWidgetClass.

Constraint widgets use additional conventions; see Chapter 4. The implementations of the Label and Pushbutton widgets later in this chapter give concrete examples of the naming conventions.

2.15   Writing Header Files

Every widget class implementation creates a private header file used by the implementations of the widget and of its subclasses and a public header file used by applications. It may also create an internal header file used only by its implementation.

To accommodate operating systems with file name restrictions, the widget class names used to construct the header file are truncated so that the resulting file names are no more than 12 characters long. For example, the file names for a widget class Verylongname are `Verylongna.h` and `VerylongnP.h`.

The conventions described here are specific to the C language; equivalent conventions allow using widgets in other languages and even subclassing them if the language's structure layout conventions are compatible with C conventions.

2.15.1   Writing Private Header Files

Every widget class needs some of the declarations of its superclass, so its superclass puts these declarations into a private header file. By convention this file is named with the first nine letters of the capitalized widget class name followed by a "P" (for private); for example, the private header file for the label widget is named `LabelP.h`.

This header file contains the following information:

• Directives to prevent the preprocessor from including the contents of this file more than once.

• An #include directive for the public header file for this widget class.

• An #include directive for the private header file for this class's superclass. If this class is a direct subclass of an Intrinsics base class, this include is not needed since these classes are defined in `<X11/IntrinsicP.h>`.

• Type definitions for any new internal types in the widget instance record. New types for widget resources should be in the public file since applications use them to declare variables.

• A part structure type containing the new fields for instances of this class. Some of these fields are resource fields and some are internal fields.

• A complete widget instance structure type containing the instance part structures for all superclasses, in order, followed by the instance part structure for this class.

- If the widget is a subclass of Constraint, some fields defining the constraint structure as described in Chapter 4.

- Type definitions for any new types used in the class record. These are often procedure types.

- A part structure type containing the new fields for the class record.

- A complete widget class structure type containing the class part structures for all superclasses, in order, followed by the class part structure for this class.

- A type declaration of the standard extension record, if the class has one. See Section 2.21.

- An external definition for a declared class structure. Any direct subclasses of this widget store the address of this structure in their superclass field.

- An inherit value for each new field in this widget's class structure. This is used by subclasses that inherit the superclass value for the field; see Section 2.27.

- Declarations for any internal routines that may be used by subclasses of this class.

- The end of the preprocessor directives that make it safe to include the header file multiple times.

Example 2.1 shows the private header file for the sample Label class. It shows most of the parts found in private header files.

2.15.2 Writing Public Header Files

Applications need a limited amount of information provided by the widget implementation, and this information is in a public header file. By convention this file is named with the first ten letters of the capitalized widget class name; for example the public header file for the Label widget is named `Label.h`.

This header file contains the following information:

- Directives to prevent the preprocessor from including the contents of this file more than once.

- An #include directive for the public header file for this class's superclass. If this class is a direct subclass of an Intrinsics base class, this include is not needed since these classes are defined in `<X11/Intrinsic.h>`.

- Definitions for names, classes, and types of resources for this widget, if no suitable definitions exist in `<X11/StringDefs.h>`.

- Data types used for resources in this widget.

- An external reference to the class record pointer for this class. This variable points to the class record declared in the private header file.

```
/* Make it safe to include this file more than once. */
#ifndef LABELP_H
#define LABELP_H

/* Include the public header file for Label */
#include "Label.h"

/* Label is derived from Core, so no need to include the superclass
   private header file.  No internal types need to be defined. */

/* Define the Label instance part */
typedef struct {
  /* New resource fields */
    String         label;            /* Text to display */
    Pixel          foreground;       /* Foreground pixel value */
    XFontStruct    *font;            /* Font to display in */
    Justify        justify;          /* The justification value */
    Dimension      space;            /* Inner padding value */
    XtCallbackList lose_selection;   /* Notify app. of lost selection */

  /* New internal fields */
    GC             gc;               /* Graphics context for displaying */
    Dimension      label_width;      /* The calculated width */
    Dimension      label_height;     /* The calculated height */
    Cardinal       label_len;        /* The length of the text string */
    Boolean        size_computed;    /* Whether the size was computed */
    Dimension      desired_width;    /* The width the widget wants to be */
    Dimension      desired_height;   /* The height the widget wants to be */
    String         accel_string;     /* Accelerator string */
    GC             current_gc;       /* GC we are currently using */
} LabelPart;

/* Define the full instance record */
typedef struct _LabelRec {
    CorePart    core;
    LabelPart   label;
} LabelRec;

/* Define new type for the class method */
typedef Boolean (*LabelSelectionProc)();
    /* Widget    w;              */
    /* Atom      selection;      */
    /* Boolean   own;            */
```

(continued)

Example 2.1. The Label private header file

```
/* Define class part structure */
typedef struct {
    LabelSelectionProc  select;
    XtPointer           extension;
} LabelClassPart;

/* Define the full class record */
typedef struct _LabelClassRec {
    CoreClassPart       core_class;
    LabelClassPart      label_class;
} LabelClassRec, *LabelWidgetClass;

/* External definition for class record */
extern LabelClassRec labelClassRec;

/* Inheritance constant for select_text method */
#define InheritSelectText ((LabelSelectionProc) _XtInherit)

/* End of preprocessor directives */
#endif /* LABELP_H */
```

Example 2.1. The Label private header file

- A type definition to use for widgets of this class. This is defined as a pointer to the instance record defined in the private header file.

- Declarations of functions that implement new class methods.

- The end of the preprocessor directives that make it safe to include the header file multiple times.

The definitions for resource names, classes, and types have a single space between the macro name and the value and should not contain any trailing spaces, tabs, or comments after the value. This allows an application to include different public header files that define the same macros without generating warning messages from the C preprocessor, as any redefinitions of the macros are identical.

Example 2.2 shows the public header file for the sample Label widget.

2.15.3 Internal Header Files

Some widget implementations define an additional header file for their own use, especially if the implementation is split into several files. The content of this file is completely up to the widget programmer; however, the Intrinsics suggest that the file be named with the first nine letters of the capitalized widget class name followed by "I" (for internal); for example, if the Label widget needed an internal file, it would be named LabelI.h.

```
/* Make it safe to include this file more than once. */
#ifndef LABEL_H
#define LABEL_H

/* Label is derived from Core, so no need to include the superclass
   public header file.  */

/* New resource */

#define XtNloseSelection "loseSelection"
#define XtCLoseSelection "LoseSelection"

/* New type for justification */
typedef enum { Center, Left, Right } Justify;

/* External reference to the class record pointer */
extern WidgetClass labelWidgetClass;

/* Type definition for label widgets */
typedef struct _LabelRec *LabelWidget;

/* Method declaration */
extern Boolean LabelSelectText();
    /* Widget   w;          */
    /* Atom      selection; */
    /* Boolean  select;     */

/* End of preprocessor directives */
#endif /* LABEL_H */
```

Example 2.2. The Label public header file

2.16   The Base Widget Classes

The Intrinsics define three base classes: Core, Composite, and Constraint.
This section shows the data definitions for all structures used in their class and
instance definitions.

2.16.1   The Core Class Structure

Core's class part record defines fields common to all widget class records.
Every widget implementation provides a single global instance of its class
record, and this record consists of subparts defined by the class and all its
superclasses. Since all widget classes are subclasses of Core, either directly or
indirectly, all widget class records contain a Core class part. The widget implementation fills in this class part with values that apply to the class. For

example, the Core class part contains the field *cla*
class implementation fills in this field in its class
name. Section 2.17 shows the class record declaratio

```
typedef struct {
    WidgetClass              superclass;
    String                   class_name;
    Cardinal                 widget_size;
    XtProc                   class_initialize;
    XtWidgetClassProc        class_part_initialize;
    XtEnum                   class_inited;
    XtInitProc               initialize;
    XtArgsProc               initialize_hook;
    XtRealizeProc            realize;
    XtActionList             actions;
    Cardinal                 num_actions;
    XtResourceList           resources;
    Cardinal                 num_resources;
    XrmClass                 xrm_class;
    Boolean                  compress_motion;
    XtEnum                   compress_exposure;
    Boolean                  compress_enterleave;
    Boolean                  visible_interest;
    XtWidgetProc             destroy;
    XtWidgetProc             resize;
    XtExposeProc             expose;
    XtSetValuesFunc          set_values;
    XtArgsFunc               set_values_hook;
    XtAlmostProc             set_values_almost;
    XtArgsProc               get_values_hook;
    XtAcceptFocusProc        accept_focus;
    XtVersionType            version;
    XtPointer                callback_private;
    String                   tm_table;
    XtGeometryHandler        query_geometry;
    XtStringProc             display_accelerator;
    XtPointer                extension;
} CoreClassPart;
```

The fields in this record have the following meanings; most of these descriptions are elaborated upon elsewhere in this book.

superclass   A pointer to the class record of this class's superclass.

class_name   The string name for this widget class.

widget_size   The size in bytes of the instance record for widgets of this class. Most widget implementations specify this by applying the `sizeof` operator to the widget instance record.

class_initialize   A procedure called once before any widgets of this class are created. Described in Section 2.20.

class_part_initialize

                   A procedure called to initialize the class records of this class and any subclasses of this class. Described in Section 2.20.

class_inited   An XtEnum value that indicates whether this class has yet been initialized. It should be initialized to FALSE; only the Intrinsics change it. After a class has been initialized, *class_inited* will have some nonzero value that is not necessarily TRUE.[12]

initialize   A procedure called to initialize instances of widgets of this class. Described in Section 2.23.

initialize_hook   Another procedure called to initialize widget instances. Described in Section 2.23.

realize   A procedure called to create the windows for widgets of this class. Described in Section 2.24.

actions   A list of the action procedures defined by this widget class. Described in Section 7.20.

num_actions   The number of entries in the action list.

resources   A list of new resources for this class. Described in Section 3.17.

num_resources   The number of entries in the resource list.

xrm_class   A private variable containing an encoded identifier for this class. It should be initialized to NULLQUARK; only the Intrinsics use it.

compress_motion   Whether to compress multiple adjacent pointer motion events into a single event when reporting them to widgets of this class. Described in Section 6.15; usually set to TRUE.

---

[12] *Class_inited* is a Boolean field in Intrinsics implementations that conform to specifications earlier than Release 4.

compress_exposure How to compress multiple exposure events into a single event when reporting them to widgets of this class. Described in Section 6.15; usually set to XtExposeCompressMultiple for simple widgets.[13]

compress_enterleave Whether to eliminate events when the pointer enters and leaves a widget of this class with no other events in between. Described in Section 6.15; usually TRUE.

visible_interest Whether to keep the *visible* field in widgets of this class up-to-date. Described in Section 6.17; usually FALSE for simple widgets.

destroy A procedure called to destroy widgets of this class. Described in Section 2.25.

resize A procedure called to inform widgets of this class that their width or height has changed. Described in Section 4.16.

expose A procedure called when widgets of this class get exposure events. Described in Section 6.16.

set_values A procedure called when the values of resources for widgets of this class are changed. Described in Section 3.24.

set_values_hook Another procedure called to set widget resource values. Described in Section 3.24.

set_values_almost A procedure called when changing resource values would result in a geometry change, but this change is not allowed without modification. Described in Section 4.13.

get_values_hook A procedure called when the values of resources for widgets of this class are queried. Described in Section 3.23.

accept_focus A procedure called to notify a widget of this class that it should take the input focus if it wants to. Described in Section 6.19.

version The implementation version of the Intrinsics this widget class was compiled with. This should either be the constant XtVersion or, if the widget class believes it can cope with future Intrinsics changes with no recompilation, XtVersionDontCare. XtVersion changes with each release of the toolkit specification that requires widgets to be recompiled.

callback_private A private variable containing information about callbacks. It should be initialized to NULL; only the Intrinsics use it.

---

[13] *Compress_exposure* is a Boolean field in Intrinsics implementations that conform to specifications earlier than Release 4; the usual value is TRUE.

tm_table	The default set of translations for widgets of this class. Described in Section 7.20.
query_geometry	A procedure called to find the preferred geometry of a widget of this class. Described in Section 4.17.
display_accelerator	A procedure called to notify a widget of this class that its accelerators have been installed on some other widget, so it can modify its appearance. Described in Section 7.21.
extension	A pointer to an extension record holding additional class fields for CoreClassPart, usually NULL. See Section 2.21 for more information on extension records.

The full class record for widgets of the Core class is `WidgetClassRec`.[14]

```
typedef struct _WidgetClassRec {
    CoreClassPart    core_class;
} WidgetClassRec, *WidgetClass, CoreClassRec, *CoreWidgetClass;
```

2.16.2   The Core Instance Structure

Core's instance part record defines fields common to all widget instances. Each widget class defines an instance structure type; the Intrinsics allocate values of this type as widget instances. This instance structure contains subparts defined by the class and by all its superclasses; since all widget classes are subclasses of Core, either directly or indirectly, all widget instances contain a Core instance part. The fields in this part apply to the particular instance, no matter what the instance's class may be. For example, the Core instance part contains the *widget_class* field that in each widget instance points to the class record for that instance's class.

In general, widget implementations should not directly set or modify fields in the Core instance part or indeed in the instance parts of any of their superclasses. For example, a widget implementation should not try to manage a widget by setting its *managed* field or try to change its background by modifying its *background_pixel* field. The correct way to affect superclass fields is normally to use the same routines that an application writer would use, calling `XtManageChild` or `XtSetValues` in the above examples. This guide describes exceptions to this rule as they occur; the most important of these are

---

[14] The types `CoreClassRec` and `CoreWidgetClass` are not supported by Intrinsics implementations that conform to specifications earlier than Release 4.

- A widget implementation can modify the *x, y, width, height,* and *border_width* Core fields in its set_values and initialize procedures. It modifies them elsewhere using `XtMakeGeometryRequest` instead of the `XtSetValues` call applications use.

- A widget implementation sets the *window* Core field in its realize procedure.

- A widget implementation modifies the *children, num_children,* and *num_slots* Composite fields in its insert_child and delete_child procedures.

The Core instance part record is

```
typedef struct _CorePart {
    Widget              self;
    WidgetClass         widget_class;
    Widget              parent;
    XrmName             xrm_name;
    Boolean             being_destroyed;
    XtCallbackList      destroy_callbacks;
    XtPointer           constraints;
    Position            x, y;
    Dimension           width, height;
    Dimension           border_width;
    Boolean             managed;
    Boolean             sensitive;
    Boolean             ancestor_sensitive;
    XtEventTable        event_table;
    XtTMRec             tm;
    XtTranslations      accelerators;
    Pixel               border_pixel;
    Pixmap              border_pixmap;
    WidgetList          popup_list;
    Cardinal            num_popups;
    String              name;
    Screen              *screen;
    Colormap            colormap;
    Window              window;
    Cardinal            depth;
    Pixel               background_pixel;
    Pixmap              background_pixmap;
    Boolean             visible;
    Boolean             mapped_when_managed;
} CorePart;
```

The fields in this record have the following meanings:

self	A pointer to the widget instance. This should never be modified.
widget_class	A pointer to the widget class record. This should never be modified.
parent	A pointer to the parent of this widget. This should never be modified.
xrm_name	The encoded name of this widget. This should never be modified and is rarely useful to widget implementations.
being_destroyed	Whether this widget has been marked for destruction. This should never be modified.
destroy_callbacks	The value of the XtNdestroyCallbacks resource.
constraints	A pointer to the constraint record for this widget. Described in Section 4.18.
x	The value of the XtNx resource.
y	The value of the XtNy resource.
width	The value of the XtNwidth resource.
height	The value of the XtNheight resource.
border_width	The value of the XtNborderWidth resource.
managed	Whether this widget's parent should give the widget screen space. Described in Section 4.3.
sensitive	The value of the XtNsensitive resource.
ancestor_sensitive	The value of the XtNancestorSensitive resource.
event_table	A private variable used by the event dispatcher. This should never be read or modified.
tm	A private variable used by the translation manager. This should never be read or modified.
accelerators	The value of the XtNaccelerators resource.
border_pixel	The value of the XtNborderColor resource. Note that this field does not follow the resource naming conventions for historical reasons.
border_pixmap	The value of the XtNborderPixmap resource.
popup_list	A list of the pop-up children of this widget. Described in Section 5.7.
num_popups	The number of entries in the pop-up list.
name	The name of this widget as a string.

screen   The value of the XtNscreen resource.

colormap   The value of the XtNcolormap resource.

window   The widget's window. Has the value None before the widget is realized.

depth   The value of the XtNdepth resource.

background_pixel   The value of the XtNbackground resource.

background_pixmap

                  The value of the XtNbackgroundPixmap resource.

visible   Whether this widget's window is currently visible. Described in Section 6.17.

mapped_when_managed

                  The value of the XtNmappedWhenManaged resource.

The full instance record for widgets of the Core class is `WidgetRec`:[15]

```
typedef struct _WidgetRec {
    CorePart    core;
} WidgetRec, *Widget, CoreRec, *CoreWidget;
```

2.16.3 The Composite Class Structure

Composite's class part record defines additional fields common to all subclasses of Composite.

```
typedef struct {
    XtGeometryHandler    geometry_manager;
    XtWidgetProc         change_managed;
    XtWidgetProc         insert_child;
    XtWidgetProc         delete_child;
    XtPointer            extension;
} CompositeClassPart;
```

The fields in this record have the following meanings; all are fully described in Chapter 4.

geometry_manager   A procedure that is called to resolve geometry change requests from children of widgets of this class.

---

[15] The types `CoreRec` and `CoreWidget` are not supported by Intrinsics implementations that conform to specifications earlier than Release 4.

change_managed   A procedure called to inform widgets of this class that their set of managed children has changed.

insert_child   A procedure called to add a child widget to a widget of this class.

delete_child   A procedure called to delete a child widget from a widget of this class.

extension   A pointer to an extension record holding additional class fields for `CompositeClassPart`.

The standard extension record for Composite is `CompositeClass-ExtensionRec`.[16]

```
typedef struct {
    XtPointer     next_extension;
    XrmQuark      record_type;
    long          version;
    Cardinal      record_size;
    Boolean       accepts_objects;
} CompositeClassExtensionRec, *CompositeClassExtension;
```

The first four fields are the standard extension header; see Section 2.21. The remaining field has the following meaning:

accepts_objects   Whether this widget class is capable of handling children that are not widgets. Nonwidget objects are covered in Chapter 8. If a composite subclass supplies no extension record, the Intrinsics assume *accepts_objects* is FALSE.

The full class record for widgets of the Composite class is `Composite-ClassRec`.

```
typedef struct _CompositeClassRec {
    CoreClassPart         core_class;
    CompositeClassPart    composite_class;
} CompositeClassRec, *CompositeWidgetClass;
```

2.16.4   The Composite Instance Structure

Composite's instance part record defines additional fields common to all widget instances for subclasses of Composite.

---

[16] There is no Composite extension record in Intrinsics implementations that conform to specifications earlier than Release 4. The *extension* field should be NULL in earlier versions.

```
typedef struct {
    WidgetList      children;
    Cardinal        num_children;
    Cardinal        num_slots;
    XtOrderProc     insert_position;
} CompositePart;
```

The fields in this record have the following meanings; all are fully described in Chapter 4.

children   The value of the XtNchildren resource.

num_children   The value of the XtNnumChildren resource.

num_slots   The number of spaces in the child list.

insert_position   The value of the XtNinsertPosition resource.

The full instance record for widgets of the Composite class is `CompositeRec`.

```
typedef struct _CompositeRec {
    CorePart        core;
    CompositePart   composite;
} CompositeRec, *CompositeWidget;
```

2.16.5   The Constraint Class Structure

Constraint's class part record defines additional fields common to all sub-classes of Constraint.

```
typedef struct {
    XtResourceList      resources;
    Cardinal            num_resources;
    Cardinal            constraint_size;
    XtInitProc          initialize;
    XtWidgetProc        destroy;
    XtSetValuesFunc     set_values;
    XtPointer           extension;
} ConstraintClassPart;
```

The fields in this record have the following meanings; all are fully described in Chapter 4.

resources   A list of all additional resources that widgets of this class support for their children.

num_resources   The number of entries in the resource list.

constraint_size   The size of the constraint record for children of widgets of this class.

initialize   A procedure to initialize the constraint record of children of widgets of this class.

destroy   A procedure called when children of widgets of this class are destroyed.

set_values   A procedure called when the values of resources for children of widgets of this class are changed.

extension   A pointer to an extension record holding additional class fields for `ConstraintClassPart`.

The standard extension record for widgets of the Constraint class is `ConstraintClassExtensionRec`.[17]

```
typedef struct {
    XtPointer      next_extension;
    XrmQuark       record_type;
    long           version;
    Cardinal       record_size;
    XtArgsProc     get_values_hook;
} ConstraintClassExtensionRec, *ConstraintClassExtension;
```

The first four fields are the standard extension header; see Section 2.21. The remaining field has the following meaning:

get_values_hook   A procedure called when the values of resources for children of widgets of this class are queried. If a class supplies no extension record, the Intrinsics assume get_values_hook is NULL.

The full class record for widgets of the Constraint class is `Constraint-ClassRec`.

```
typedef struct _ConstraintClassRec {
    CoreClassPart           core_class;
    CompositeClassPart      composite_class;
    ConstraintClassPart     constraint_class;
} ConstraintClassRec, *ConstraintWidgetClass;
```

---

[17] There is no Constraint extension record in Intrinsics implementations that conform to specifications earlier than Release 4. The *extension* field should be NULL in earlier versions.

2.16.6   The Constraint Instance Structure

There are no additional fields common to all widget instances for subclasses of Constraint. However, the instance part record still exists, so that if this changes in the future, subclasses of Constraint will not have to change.

```
typedef struct {
    int     empty;
} ConstraintPart;
```

The field in this record has the following (non)meaning:

empty   The C compiler does not allow structures with no fields, so this field exists.

The full instance record for widgets of the Constraint class is `Constraint-Rec`.

```
typedef struct _ConstraintRec {
    CorePart          core;
    CompositePart     composite;
    ConstraintPart    constraint;
} ConstraintRec, *ConstraintWidget;
```

2.17   Declaring the Class Record

As stated before, there is exactly one copy of the class record for each widget class. Widget implementations declare the class record and name it with the uncapitalized widget class name followed by "ClassRec"; for example, the Label widget class record is named *labelClassRec*. Implementations declare a variable pointing to the class record, named with the uncapitalized widget name followed by "WidgetClass"; for example, *labelWidgetClass*. This pointer is of type `WidgetClass` and an external reference to it appears in the public header file.

Example 2.3 shows the static declaration of the widget class records for the sample Label widget class.

The Intrinsics header file `<X11/Intrinsic.h>` contains external definitions for the class records for Core, Composite, and Constraint.[18]

---

[18] The names `coreClassRec` and `coreWidgetClass` are not supported by Intrinsics implementations that conform to specifications earlier than Release 4.

```
/* Forward declarations */

static void ClassInitialize(), ClassPartInitialize(), Initialize(),
        Redisplay(), Destroy(), Resize(), LoseSelection();
static Boolean SetValues(), SelectText();
static XtGeometryResult QueryGeometry();

/* Class record declaration */

LabelClassRec labelClassRec = {
    /* Core class part */
  {
    /* superclass             */ (WidgetClass) &widgetClassRec,
    /* class_name             */ "Label",
    /* widget_size            */ sizeof(LabelRec),
    /* class_initialize       */ ClassInitialize,
    /* class_part_initialize  */ ClassPartInitialize,
    /* class_inited           */ FALSE,
    /* initialize             */ Initialize,
    /* initialize_hook        */ NULL,
    /* realize                */ XtInheritRealize,
    /* actions                */ NULL,
    /* num_actions            */ 0,
    /* resources              */ resources,
    /* num_resources          */ XtNumber(resources),
    /* xrm_class              */ NULLQUARK,
    /* compress_motion        */ TRUE,
    /* compress_exposure      */ XtExposeCompressMultiple,
    /* compress_enterleave    */ TRUE,
    /* visible_interest       */ FALSE,
    /* destroy                */ Destroy,
    /* resize                 */ Resize,
    /* expose                 */ Redisplay,
    /* set_values             */ SetValues,
    /* set_values_hook        */ NULL,
    /* set_values_almost      */ XtInheritSetValuesAlmost,
    /* get_values_hook        */ NULL,
    /* accept_focus           */ NULL,
    /* version                */ XtVersion,
    /* callback offsets       */ NULL,
    /* tm_table               */ NULL,
    /* query_geometry         */ QueryGeometry,
    /* display_accelerator    */ NULL,
    /* extension              */ NULL
  },
```

(continued)

Example 2.3.   The Label class record declaration

```
      /* Label class part */
    {
      /* select                 */ SelectText,
      /* extension              */ NULL
    }
};

/* Class record pointer */

WidgetClass labelWidgetClass = (WidgetClass) &labelClassRec;
```
Example 2.3. The Label class record declaration

/* Declarations for the Core class */
extern WidgetClassRec widgetClassRec;
#define coreClassRec widgetClassRec
extern WidgetClass widgetClass, coreWidgetClass;

/* Declarations for the Composite class */
extern CompositeClassRec compositeClassRec;
extern WidgetClass compositeWidgetClass;

/* Declarations for the Constraint class */
extern ConstraintClassRec constraintClassRec;
extern WidgetClass constraintWidgetClass;

2.18 Class Methods

The procedures stored in the class record are called *methods* for the class. The Intrinsics support two kinds of methods: *regular* and *chained*. Some of the methods of the Intrinsics widget classes are regular and some are chained; most methods of non-Intrinsics classes are regular methods.

The Intrinsics call regular class methods indirectly through the class structure. Often a widget class can use the same procedure to implement a regular method as its superclass does. For example, Composite defines the insert_child method that the Intrinsics call to add a new child to a parent's list of children. Composite also provides a procedure that implements this method and stores a pointer to the procedure in the Composite class record. Many subclasses of Composite do not need to reimplement this procedure; they *inherit* the superclass's implementation. To allow subclasses to inherit a method implementation, widget implementations provide *inheritance constants* for each regular class method. If a subclass stores the inheritance constant in the method field of its class record, it means that the subclass wants to inherit its superclass's implementation of the method. Widget classes can also inherit nonprocedure fields; inheriting a data field means using the superclass's value for the field.

The Intrinsics define the following inheritance constants for methods in the predefined classes:

For Core:	XtInheritTranslations
	XtInheritRealize
	XtInheritResize
	XtInheritExpose
	XtInheritSetValuesAlmost
	XtInheritAcceptFocus
	XtInheritQueryGeometry
	XtInheritDisplayAccelerator
For Composite:	XtInheritGeometryManager
	XtInheritChangeManaged
	XtInheritInsertChild
	XtInheritDeleteChild
For Shell:	XtInheritRootGeometryManager

The most commonly inherited operations are XtInheritRealize, XtInheritSet-ValuesAlmost, XtInheritInsertChild, XtInheritDeleteChild, and XtInherit-RootGeometryManager.

Sometimes a widget class cannot inherit its superclass's method because it needs to do a little bit of extra work either before or after the superclass's operations. In this case the subclass method calls the superclass's method directly. For example, if a widget class Xyz only draws a little bit more than its superclass when asked to redisplay, it writes its expose procedure this way:

```
void Redisplay(w, event, region)
    Widget w;
    XEvent *event;
    Region region;
{
    (*xyzClassRec.core_class.superclass->core_class.expose)
            (w, event, region);
    /* ...do the extra drawing... */
}
```

This technique is called *enveloping* the superclass method. Sometimes the call to the superclass method occurs before the extra operations, sometimes after, and sometimes in the middle; the semantics of each individual case determine where the call goes.

You *must* use the superclass from the class record of the class being implemented. A common mistake is to use the superclass of the passed widget, but the passed widget might actually belong to a subclass of Xyz. The superclass of the passed widget could be a subclass of Xyz or even Xyz itself; calling this would invoke the wrong procedure, leading to an infinite loop if Xyz's method gets called again.

Enveloping is always desired for methods like initialize. A widget contains all fields defined by its superclasses, but it is not particularly interested in initializing or maintaining the contents of these fields. The class delegates such responsibilities to its superclass. The superclass, in turn, only initializes the fields that it declares and delegates responsibility for the fields its own superclass declared.

The Intrinsics enforce such cases by defining some methods as *chained* methods, meaning that the Intrinsics always envelop the superclass's method. If a widget class Xyz is a subclass of Composite and therefore indirectly Core, the Intrinsics initialize an Xyz widget instance by passing it to the initialize procedures for Core, Composite, and Xyz, in that order. The widget implementation never calls chained superclass methods itself; the Intrinsics handle calling such methods automatically.

The Intrinsics chain most methods in superclass-to-subclass order; that is, they call the procedures for all superclasses starting at Core and working down to the class itself. The destroy methods are chained in the opposite order, starting with the class and going upwards to Core. Chained methods have no inheritance constants; if a widget class does nothing beyond what its superclass does, it just specifies NULL for the method.

Nonprocedure fields can be chained as well; this means that the values in a subclass record augment the data in their superclasses' records rather than replacing them. The Intrinsics chain the Core *resource* and *actions* fields and the Constraint *resource* field.

The following table shows which methods are regular and which are chained. For regular methods it shows whether the method is allowed to be NULL, meaning to do nothing, or if a real procedure is required. For chained methods it shows whether the chaining is superclass-to-subclass or subclass-to-superclass.

Class	Method	Can be NULL?	Chained?	Direction
Core	class_initialize	Yes	No	
	class_part_initialize	Yes	Yes	Super-to-sub
	initialize	Yes	Yes	Super-to-sub
	initialize_hook	Yes	Yes	Super-to-sub
	realize	No	No	
	destroy	Yes	Yes	Sub-to-super
	resize	Yes	No	
	expose	Yes	No	
	set_values	Yes	Yes	Super-to-sub
	set_values_hook	Yes	Yes	Super-to-sub
	set_values_almost	No	No	
	get_values_hook	Yes	Yes	Super-to-sub
	accept_focus	Yes	No	
	query_geometry	Yes	No	
	display_accelerator	Yes	No	
Composite	geometry_manager	No	No	
	change_managed	No	No	
	insert_child	No	No	
	delete_child	No	No	
Constraint	initialize	Yes	Yes	Super-to-sub
	destroy	Yes	Yes	Sub-to-super
	set_values	Yes	Yes	Super-to-sub
	get_values_hook	Yes	Yes	Super-to-sub
Shell	root_geometry_manager	No	No	

The Intrinsics define inheritance constants for all nonchained methods.

To summarize the difference between regular and chained methods, regular methods are completely responsible for some action. If they want to use their superclass's implementation, they invoke it directly using enveloping. Chained methods are responsible only for the fields defined in their class's part records.

Normally the same method implementation applies to all instances of a widget class: a widget class uses the same expose procedure for all its widgets. Sometimes it is useful to have a method with a different implementation for each instance of the widget. You can provide for this by storing a procedure pointer in the widget instance and having the class method call this procedure.

2.19 Class Information Functions

These routines return information about the class of a widget. For widget writers they are usually macros. Also see the widget information functions in Section 2.12.

To find the superclass of a widget, use XtSuperclass.

WidgetClass XtSuperclass(*w*)
    Widget *w*;
    w   Specifies the widget to get the superclass of.

To verify the class of a widget and issue an error message if it is the wrong class, use XtCheckSubclass.

void XtCheckSubclass(*w, widget_class, message*)
    Widget *w*;
    WidgetClass *widget_class*;
    String *message*;
    w   Specifies the widget to check the subclass of.
    widget_class   Specifies the class to check against.
    message   Specifies the error message.

XtCheckSubclass checks if the widget is of the specified class. If not, XtCheckSubclass constructs an error message out of the widget's actual class, the specified class, and the specified message, then calls XtErrorMsg. The default error message is "Widget class *actual* found when subclass of *widget-class* expected: *message*."

Procedures that implement new class methods should use XtCheck-Subclass to verify that the application passed in a valid widget. XtCheckSubclass is a macro that executes only if the widget was compiled with the preprocessor symbol DEBUG defined. Otherwise, the macro expands to nothing and XtCheckSubclass has no effect.

2.20 Class Initialization

Each widget class must be initialized before creating any widgets of a class. The Intrinsics support three types of class initialization: static initialization, one-time initialization, and class part initialization.

Static initialization refers to declaring a class record and filling it in with values appropriate to the particular widget class at compile/link time. Widget programmers do this by statically declaring an instance of the class record and initializing the fields to the desired values. Example 2.3 in Section 2.17 shows Label's static initialization.

One-time initialization refers to any dynamic one-time initialization the class needs to do at runtime. The Intrinsics call the class_initialize procedure, which is of type XtProc, exactly once before creating any widgets of the class.

```
typedef void (*XtProc) (void);
```

The most common one-time initializations are registering type converters for new types used by the class and registering grab actions for some of the class's actions; see Chapter 3 and Section 7.10. If a class needs no dynamic initialization, it specifies NULL in its *class_initialize* field.

Example 2.4 shows the Label widget's class_initialize procedure, which registers the new type converter for the class.

The final type of initialization is class part initialization, which gives a widget class the chance to modify fields in its class record or in the class records of its subclasses. Class part initialization is primarily used to implement inheritance but can also do things like compile data structures in the class record into an internal form. Section 2.27 describes the details of using class part initialization to resolve inheritance.

Widget classes do class part initialization on their subclasses by providing a class_part_initialize procedure of type XtWidgetClassProc.

```
typedef void (*XtWidgetClassProc) (WidgetClass);
      WidgetClass widgetClass;
widgetClass       Specifies the widget class to initialize.
```

The class_part_initialize procedure is chained from superclass to subclass. When the Intrinsics initialize a class, they pass its class record to the class part initialization procedures of all that class's superclasses and of the class itself, in order, starting with Core and proceeding to the class. Each class's procedure is

```
static void ClassInitialize()
{
    /* Register a converter for string to justification */

    XtSetTypeConverter(XtRString, XtRJustify, CvtStringToJustify,
            (XtConvertArgList) NULL, 0,
            XtCacheAll, (XtDestructor) NULL);
}
```

Example 2.4.   The Label class initialization procedure

responsible for any necessary modifications to that class's part of the class record. For example, consider a class C that is a subclass of classes Core, Composite, A, and B. At class initialization time, the Intrinsics pass C's class record to Core's class part initialization procedure. This resolves inherited methods and compiles data structures in the Core part of C's class record. Next the Intrinsics pass C's class record to Composite's class part initialization procedure to resolve any inherited methods in the Composite part, and then to the class part initialization procedures for A, B, and C. If a widget class implements no new methods and has no need for any other class part initialization, *class_part_initialize* is NULL.

Label's class part initialization procedure only makes sense in the context of handling new class methods and so is discussed in Section 2.27.

The Intrinsics initialize a class before creating the first widget of that class or when an application explicitly requests class initialization by calling `XtInitializeWidgetClass`. Before initializing a class, the Intrinsics make sure that all its superclasses have also been initialized, initializing them if necessary in superclass-to-subclass order.

2.21 Extension Records

As time goes by, it is sometimes necessary to add new class fields to the class part records of preexisting widget classes. This happened with the Release 4 versions of the Composite, Constraint, and Shell classes, and can happen as well with widgets in a widget set. If new fields were added to the class part structures, all subclasses of the changing class would have to be recompiled, since class fields that follow the new field would have incorrect offsets.

In many environments, requiring recompilation of the subclasses presents no problems. If this is the case, new fields can be added to the ends of the class parts with impunity, and recompilation automatically incorporates the new fields. If the style for static class declarations demonstrated in this book is followed, carefully using curly braces to delimit the class parts, the C compiler will initialize the missing fields in the class structure declaration to zero. Code that uses the new field should treat zero in some default way (often meaning to inherit the superclass's value).

Other environments make recompilation difficult. To accommodate these and to allow the use of nonstandard extensions, all class parts end with an XtPointer field called extension. Rather than adding new fields to the class part, widget programmers define a new structure, an *extension record*; widget classes that use the new field declare an instance of the extension record and place a pointer to it in the extension field. To allow additional fields to be added to the extension record without requiring further indirection, all extension records contain version information.

Since all environments use the Intrinsics base classes, any changes to these classes take place through the extension record mechanism and not by modifying the class parts. Before deciding to use extensions in a widget set, you should carefully consider whether defining new subclasses would achieve the same results more directly; see Section 2.22.

☞ Code *must not* assume that a field in an extension record exists. Programs must check that the extension field is non-NULL and that the version of the extension record contains the desired field; if the field is not present, the program must take some appropriate default action.

There are two types of extension records, standard extensions and nonstandard extensions. The owner of the class definition defines standard extensions; the owner of all Intrinsics-defined classes is the Intrinsics specification, and the owner of any derived class is the individual or organization that defined the class. If a future revision of this book were to define new class fields for its implementation of the Label widget, it would define a standard extension for the Label class part. Standard extensions become part of the definition of a widget class.

Nonstandard extensions allow libraries or widget sets to add their own fields to classes they do not own. For example, a widget set designer might decide that every widget class needs a new method, query_minimum_size, that returns the desired minimum size of a widget of the class. This method could be added to all widget classes by defining a nonstandard extension to Core. A library of drawing functions for widget writers might define a nonstandard Core extension containing procedures that the widget writer provides, and any widget class that used the library would have an extension record with these procedures. Nonstandard extensions allow code modules to associate arbitrary data with any class part.

Any particular widget class can have multiple extensions for each of its class parts. At most one extension for each part is a standard extension; the others are nonstandard extensions.

All extension records must start with the following four fields:

```
typedef struct {
    XtPointer       next_extension;
    XrmQuark        record_type;
    long            version;
    Cardinal        record_size;
    . . .additional fields. . .
};
```

The fields in this header have the following meanings:

next_extension   Allows multiple extension records to be chained together for one class.

record_type   Identifies the extension. For a standard extension, should be NULLQUARK.

version   A private field indicating the version of the extension record.

record_size   Must be set to the size of the extension record, usually with `sizeof`.

The widget set defining the query_minimum_size method defines this extension record with the new field:

```
typedef struct {
    XtPointer           next_extension;
    XrmQuark            record_type;
    long                version;
    Cardinal            record_size;
    MinimumSizeProc     query_minimum_size;
} MyCoreClassExtensionRec, *MyCoreClassExtension;
```

The *version* field of an extension record is privately owned by the definer of the extension. The owner can define any value it wishes to be stored in the field, but the value should change with each revision of the extension record so that code can check the version in any particular extension record to see if a needed field is present. If new fields are always added at the end of the record, the *record_size* field provides an alternative way of checking this information.

The Intrinsics provide a symbolic constant for each Intrinsics-defined class with a standard extension, named Xt*class*ExtensionVersion. The currently defined extension versions are XtCompositeExtensionVersion, XtConstraintExtensionVersion, and XtShellExtensionVersion.

Classes that use standard extensions usually declare an extension record statically the same way they declare a class record and store a pointer to the extension record in the extension field of the appropriate class part. A class that needs the *get_values_hook* in the Constraint extension record declares the following structure:

```
ConstraintClassExtensionRec constraintClassExtensionRec = {
    /* next_extension   */      NULL,
    /* record_type      */      NULLQUARK,
    /* version          */      XtConstraintExtensionVersion,
    /* record_size      */      sizeof(ConstraintClassExtensionRec),
    /* get_values_hook  */      GetValuesHook
};
```

and initializes the *extension* field of the ConstraintClassPart of its class record to &*constraintClassExtensionRec.*

Widget sets or libraries that provide nonstandard extensions should provide a subroutine interface to handle the extension record. The widget set with the query_minimum_size extension should provide a new procedure, named something like MyDefineQueryMinimumSize, that takes a class record and a MinimumSizeProc as parameters. This procedure looks for the appropriate extension record in the chain of extension records pointed to by the Core extension field, creating one if none is found, and sets the *query_minimum_size* field according to its parameter. See Example 2.5.

The string constant whose quark identifies the extension can be any string that does not begin with the two characters "XT"; names beginning this way are reserved for the Intrinsics. The string must uniquely identify the extension. The X Consortium maintains a registry of extension names; see Appendix H.

Defining a procedural interface to nonstandard extension records is not strictly necessary, but it does make things much easier for programmers using the extension. Nonstandard extension records cannot be fully declared statically since the *record_type* field must be filled in with the result of a function call, so requiring programmers to declare the extension record themselves just creates more opportunities for mistakes.

Just as with class and instance structures, conventions exist for standard extensions. A widget class AbcXyz that defines a standard extension defines the following names in its private header file:

```
void MyDefineQueryMinimumSize(widget_class, proc)
    WidgetClass widget_class;
    MinimumSizeProc proc;
{
    static Quark myWidgetSet = NULLQUARK;
    MyCoreClassExtension extension;

    if (myWidgetSet == NULLQUARK) {
        myWidgetSet = XrmStringToQuark("MY_WIDGET_SET");
    }

    for (extension = widget_class->core_class.extension;
            extension != NULL && extension->record_type != myWidgetSet;
            extension = extension->next_extension) {}

    if (extension == NULL) {
        extension = XtNew(MyCoreClassExtensionRec);
        extension->next_extension = widget_class->core_class.extension;
        widget_class->core_class.extension = extension;
        extension->record_type = myWidgetSet;
        extension->version = something;
        extension->record_size = sizeof(MyCoreClassExtensionRec);
    }

    extension->query_minimum_size = proc;
}
```

Example 2.5. A sample extension initialization routine

• An extension record type named AbcXyzClassExtensionRec.

• A type that points to an AbcXyzClassExtensionRec named AbcXyzClassExtension.

• A version constant named AbcXyzExtensionVersion.

Every change to the extension record should be accompanied with a new value for AbcXyzExtensionVersion. A widget that recompiles with the new version of the header file automatically gets a new extension record with the new fields. This imposes the following constraints:

• All new fields to an extension record should be at the end so that static initialization of the extension record does not have to change.

• If the program does not declare a value for the new field, the C compiler initializes it to zero. Code must treat a value of zero in the new field the same way it treats having no extension record or having an extension record with a version that does not have the field.

Restating the last constraint, code must not treat an extension field containing zero differently than a missing extension field. For example, you cannot define a method in an extension record with "inherit parent's value" as the default action when no method is present and with NULL meaning to do nothing; NULL must also mean to inherit the parent's value. In cases like this you might define an additional symbolic constant, NoQueryMinimumSize for example, that widget implementations specify to disable the default action.

2.22   Anticipating Subclassing

Often it is possible to anticipate the needs of subclasses when designing a widget class, making the class implementation slightly more complex but the implementation of the subclasses much simpler. Of course, it is much easier to do this when the same person is designing the class and the subclasses!

The Label class demonstrates this with the *current_gc* and *accel_string* fields. Label itself does not need them, but by making the redisplay procedure use these fields Pushbutton becomes simpler. Pushbuttons sometimes alter their appearance, becoming insensitive or inverted. By updating the *current_gc* field, the Pushbutton implementation makes Label's expose procedure draw the pushbutton differently.

The *accel_string* field holds a string that tells the user what the widget's accelerators are. Label never stores anything into this field but Pushbutton updates it when an application installs the pushbutton's accelerators. See Section 7.21 for information on displaying accelerators.

Taking this to an extreme leads to creating a widget class whose only purpose is to support other classes. If many classes use a set of common resource or class fields, the widget set designer creates a class that declares and maintains these fields. Other classes need not worry about the fields; they just make themselves subclasses of the support class. Resources like a foreground color or a window cursor fall into this category. Support classes like these, often called something like Common or Simple, occur in many widget sets.

Resist the temptation, however, to make superbig support classes. Only put fields in a support class instance if most subclasses actually use the fields. Support class fields that are not widely used lead to unnecessarily large widget instances, degrading application performance. (Remember this when you find yourself wondering, and you almost certainly will, "Why didn't the Intrinsics designers include the *whatever* resource in Core?")

Nonstandard extensions provide an alternative way of defining new class fields. If a widget set designer wants to add a new method to all widget classes, she either defines a nonstandard extension, as described in Section 2.21, or defines a support class that provides this method.

Defining an extension has the advantage that the new method is available to all subclasses of the extended class. A Core extension can be used by any widget in the widget set, regardless of whether the widget is composite. If the new method were declared in a support subclass of Core, Composite sub-classes would need their own support subclass—the designer cannot insert the new class between Core and Composite.

Defining a new support class has the advantage of being easier for widget programmers to deal with and being more efficient. Code must look up methods in extension records whenever it uses the method; methods in class records are immediately available. Checking for an extension record with the appropriate version and a correctly specified field is more complicated than simply checking for a non-NULL field in the class record.

2.23   Initializing Widgets

Applications create new instances of a widget by passing the widget class pointer to `XtCreateManagedWidget` or a similar routine. The Intrinsics allocate a copy of the widget instance record and do most of the work to initialize the instance by filling in all the widget resource fields and such non-resource fields as *widget_class*, *parent*, and *name*. Most widget classes must do extra initialization on their own to copy data, check consistency, or compute derived fields. A class initializes new widgets by providing a widget instance initialization procedure of type `XtInitProc` in the *initialize* field of its class record.[19]

```
typedef void (*XtInitProc) (Widget, Widget, ArgList, Cardinal *);
    Widget request;
    Widget new;
    ArgList args;
    Cardinal *num_args;
```

request   Specifies a copy of the widget with resource fields initialized to the requested values.

---

[19] The *args* and *num_args* parameters are not supported by Intrinsics implementations that conform to specifications earlier than Release 4.

new   Specifies the widget with the new values that are actually allowed by
                   the superclass.

args   Specifies the argument list passed to the widget creation routine.

num_args   Specifies the number of entries in the argument list.

The initialize procedure takes two widget parameters, *request* and *new*. The *request* parameter specifies a copy of the widget as it existed after filling in all its resource values but before the Intrinsics called the initialize procedures for any superclasses. Initialize procedures never modify this widget. The *new* widget is the widget that the Intrinsics will return from the create call, so any modifications are to this widget, and if the initialize procedure calls any routines that take a widget parameter, the parameter is the *new* widget.

The *args* and *num_args* parameters are described at the end of this section.

Initialize is a superclass-to-subclass chained procedure, so by the time the Intrinsics call the initialize procedure for a widget class they have already called the initialize procedures for all the class's superclasses. This means that the procedure usually does not worry about dealing with fields in the part structures belonging to the superclasses; the superclasses' initialize procedures have already initialized those data.

There are four types of operations typically done by initialize procedures:

• Copying some resources that are referred to by address.

• Computing values for unspecified resource fields.

• Computing values for nonresource fields.

• Checking fields for internal consistency.

A widget must copy resource values that are specified by address unless it requires the application to maintain the pointed-to data in permanent storage. The most commonly copied resources are strings. String resources are defined as pointers, and the application may have stored the data they point to in temporary memory like the stack. To avoid pointers to data that no longer exist, the initialize procedure copies the pointed-to data into allocated memory; the routines XtNew and XtNewString, described in Section 9.4, are particularly useful for this.

The widget designer must decide which reference resources the implementation copies and which it relies upon the application to keep. Doing this sensibly requires an understanding of the resource conversion and caching mechanisms described in Chapter 3.

Briefly, the Intrinsics take care of conversions between the resource representations used in external files, usually strings, and the resource representations used in widget instances. To save the cost of converting the same values multiple times, the results of the conversions are usually stored in a resource cache. Copying reference resources that usually come from the conversion cache makes things simpler for the occasional application that specifies them directly but wastes large amounts of space in the normal case. Font structures, for example, almost always come from converting a font name string to a font structure. In this case the font structure is already in permanent memory in the conversion cache, so there is no point in copying it again. A text label, however, almost never comes from a conversion, so widgets copy it. The widget documentation must specify which reference resources the widget does not copy so that the application can make sure their values remain permanently.

Widget implementations never copy callback lists; the Intrinsics automatically copy them while converting them into an internal form.

Resource lists allow a widget implementation to provide default values for resources. Some resources have no one correct default value. Consider the height and width of a Label widget: if the application does not specify them directly, the default is a size big enough to contain the label's text. If there are resources of this type, the initialize procedure must check if their values are the same as the default values specified in the resource list and, if so, compute reasonable defaults. (This assumes that the resource list default is not one that an application would ever specify, such as a zero height or width.) Label's initialize procedure, shown later this section, computes default values for the label text, the height, and the width. Another way to address this problem is with resource default procedures; see Section 3.17.

Often a widget instance part contains internal bookkeeping fields derived from resource fields. For example, Label keeps track of the width and height of the text string when rendered in the label's font rather than recomputing them all the time. Another common use for derived fields is for graphics contexts; Label uses the specified font and foreground colors to create a graphics context for drawing the text. It is easy to overdo derived fields, though—remember that each derived field exists for each copy of the widget. Avoid saving fields that are simple to recalculate when needed.

Finally, the initialize procedure checks fields for consistency. A text widget might allow the application to use different resources to specify the widget's height either in pixel units or in lines of text; if the application specifies both and they do not agree, the initialize procedure issues a warning, chooses which to use, and sets the other to the corresponding value.

One type of operation that is rarely necessary for any but the most paranoid widget implementations is checking resource fields for basic validity, for example, checking that a font structure pointer actually points to a font structure. For simple resources like width and height every possible value that the resource field can take is valid. For other resources there is often no way of distinguishing valid values from invalid ones—there is no good way, for example, to tell if a pointer value is valid without actually dereferencing it. Complex resources like pixel values and font structure pointers usually come from resource conversions, and the conversions are responsible for always producing valid values. However, if a widget class uses resources that it expects the application to provide directly and which are straightforward to check, it should by all means check them.

There are a few occasions where a subclass must modify the values set by its superclass; these are usually geometry calculations. For example, one might want a pushbutton to be larger than a label so that there is space to give the button a three-dimensional appearance. (The Pushbutton class in this book does not do this.) Such a pushbutton adds some extra space to the height and width fields, but only if the fields had their values calculated by the Label class. If the application specified the height or width directly, Pushbutton must make do with the dimensions as they are.

The initialize procedure uses the *request* widget to determine whether the resource values were specified by the application or computed by a superclass. The *request* parameter is a copy of the widget after the Intrinsics have filled in all the resources but before calling any of the initialize procedures. If the fields in *request* still have the default values, either the application did not specify them or they were specified to their default values. In this case the Pushbutton initialize procedure can safely modify them. If they do not have the default values, the application specified them, so they should be left alone. Again, all modifications are to the *new* widget; initialize procedures must not modify *request*.

If a widget class does not need any initialization code for the fields in its instance part, it specifies NULL for its *initialize* procedure.

Some widget classes have resources that are not stored in the widget; their only use is to derive values. Other classes store resources in some data structure other than the widget instance record. The *args* and *num_args* parameters, together with the routine XtGetSubresources, support this functionality; they are described in Section 3.25. Both of these uses are rather rare; most initialize procedures ignore their *args* and *num_args* parameters. Note that *num_args* is passed by reference, but the initialize procedure must not modify its value.

If the application created the widget with a varargs interface, the Intrinsics convert the variable argument list into an argument list before calling any initialize procedures and pass the argument list in the *args* parameter.

The *args* and *num_args* parameters are new to the Intrinsics with Release 4. Earlier versions had a special procedure, the initialize hook, that provided this functionality. Initialize hooks still exist to support widgets that use them, and are of type XtArgsProc.

```
typedef void (*XtArgsProc) (Widget, ArgList, Cardinal *);
     Widget w;
     ArgList args;
     Cardinal *num_args;
 w                 Specifies the widget.
 args              Specifies the argument list passed to the creation procedure.
 num_args          Specifies the number of arguments in the argument list.
```

If a class has an initialize hook procedure, the Intrinsics call it immediately after the initialize procedure, or in its place if the initialize procedure is NULL. The initialize hook gets passed the widget being initialized (the *new* parameter to the initialize procedure) and the argument list or converted varargs list specified in the create call.

Examples 2.6 and 2.7 show Label's initialize procedure along with the two internal procedures it uses; Label does not have an initialize hook. These procedures take the *accel_string* field into consideration, concatenating it to the label. *Accel_string* is a field Label provides to assist subclasses but does not use itself, so *accel_string* is always NULL for labels. Subclass instances with installed accelerators set *accel_string* to some other value to show the user which accelerator is installed; see Sections 2.22 and 7.21.

```
static void SetTextWidthAndHeight(lw)
    register LabelWidget lw;
{
    register XFontStruct *fs = lw->label.font;
    int accel_len;

    lw->label.label_len = strlen(lw->label.label);
    lw->label.label_width =
            XTextWidth(fs, lw->label.label, lw->label.label_len);
    lw->label.label_height =
            fs->max_bounds.ascent + fs->max_bounds.descent;

    if (lw->label.accel_string != NULL) {
        accel_len = strlen(lw->label.accel_string);
        lw->label.label_len += accel_len;
        lw->label.label_width +=
                XTextWidth(fs, lw->label.accel_string, accel_len);
    }
}

static GC GetNormalGC(lw)
    LabelWidget lw;
{
    XGCValues    values;

    /* Allocate a graphics context with the foreground and font */

    values.foreground = lw->label.foreground;
    values.font = lw->label.font->fid;
    return XtGetGC((Widget) lw, GCForeground | GCFont, &values);
}
```

Example 2.6. Utility procedures for the Label initialize procedure

The SetTextWidthAndHeight routine computes the dimensions of the text string and stores them in the widget instance. GetNormalGC allocates a graphics context for the widget; the XtGetGC routine is described in Section 9.11.

Label's initialize procedure does not use the *request*, *args*, or *num_args* parameters but does, of course, use *new* and casts it into a Label widget instance for convenience. If the application specified no label text string, Label uses the widget's name as the default. Initialize allocates a copy of the label string since this resource is unlikely to come from a resource conversion. *Accel_string* is not in Label's resource list, so Initialize sets it to NULL—the Intrinsics do not initialize nonresource fields in non-Intrinsics instance parts.

```
static void Initialize(request, new, args, num_args)
    Widget request, new;
    ArgList args;
    Cardinal *num_args;
{
    LabelWidget lw = (LabelWidget) new;

    /* If no label is specified, use the name */
    if (lw->label.label == NULL) lw->label.label = lw->core.name;

    /* Copy the label */
    lw->label.label = XtNewString(lw->label.label);

    /* Clear accelerator string */
    lw->label.accel_string = NULL;

    /* Compute the text dimensions and get a graphics context. */
    SetTextWidthAndHeight(lw);
    lw->label.gc = lw->label.current_gc = GetNormalGC(lw);

    /* If no size specified, compute one */
    lw->label.size_computed =
            (lw->core.width == 0) && (lw->core.height == 0);

    if (lw->core.width == 0) {
        lw->core.width = lw->label.label_width + 2 * lw->label.space;
    }
    if (lw->core.height == 0) {
        lw->core.height = lw->label.label_height + 2 * lw->label.space;
    }

    lw->label.desired_width = lw->core.width;
    lw->label.desired_height = lw->core.height;
}
```

Example 2.7. The Label initialize procedure

Initialize then calculates the text dimensions and gets a new graphics context. The *current_gc* field of the widget contains a copy of this context; *current_gc* is the context Label uses to draw into the window later on. Duplicating the context makes Label slightly more complex, but it simplifies the implementation of the Pushbutton subclass by allowing Pushbutton to store different contexts in *current_gc* when the widget is in states that require a different appearance. This allows the Label display procedure to handle all types of redisplay. This is described in more detail in Section 2.22 and when discussing the expose procedure in Section 6.16.

Finally Initialize decides whether it needs to compute a size and computes the dimensions if necessary. Other procedures in the Label implementation use the *size_computed* field to decide whether to resize the label's window if the text or font changes: if the application specified the dimension, the size does not change, but if the widget calculated the dimensions, the size does. This could be made slightly more sophisticated by storing separate flags for the width and height, but in practice an application almost never specifies one and not the other. The label's parent might at a later time force the label to be a different size, so Initialize copies the widget's height and width into the *desired_height* and *desired_width* fields so that these dimensions can be returned later on if the widget's preferred size is queried.

2.24   Realizing Widgets

The realize procedure is called by the Intrinsics to actually create a window for the widget. It is of type XtRealizeProc and cannot be NULL, although it is often inherited.

typedef unsigned long XtValueMask;

typedef void (*XtRealizeProc)(Widget, XtValueMask *, XSetWindowAttributes *);
    Widget *w*;
    XtValueMask *value_mask*;
    XSetWindowAttributes *attributes*;

w	Specifies the widget to be realized.
value_mask	Specifies the fields in the attributes structure to use.
attributes	Specifies the window attributes to use in the XCreateWindow call.

The Intrinsics always call the realize procedure of a parent widget before calling the realize procedures of any of its children.

The Intrinsics fill in certain fields of the *attributes* parameter and *value_mask* before calling the realize procedure; this structure is described fully in Section 3.2 of *Xlib*.

• If the *background_pixmap* field of the Core part is not XtUnspecifiedPixmap, the Intrinsics copy it into the *attributes* structure. If it is XtUnspecifiedPixmap, the *background_pixel* field is copied instead.

• If the *border_pixmap* field of the Core part is not XtUnspecifiedPixmap, the Intrinsics copy it into the *attributes* structure. If it is XtUnspecifiedPixmap, the *border_pixel* field is copied instead.

• The Intrinsics fill in the *event_mask* field based upon the event handlers registered for the widget, the translations that are specified, whether the expose procedure is non-NULL, and whether the *visible_interest* field is TRUE. See Chapter 6 for more information on events.

• The Intrinsics set the *bit_gravity* field to NorthWestGravity if the widget class's expose field is NULL.

• The Intrinsics set the *colormap* field from the widget's *colormap* field.

The Intrinsics set bits in the *value_mask* parameter to reflect which fields of *attributes* have been filled in. The realize procedure is free to fill in more fields or modify those already filled in; it must set the bits in *value_mask* accordingly before actually creating the window. Since realize is not a chained procedure, the realize procedure is obliged to take the data in all its non-Core super-classes into account when filling in the fields. A widget class that modifies the attributes can provide a routine for its subclasses to call from their own realize procedures; enveloping a call to the superclass's realize procedure is also help-ful. After creating the window, the realize procedure must store the window identifier in the widget's *window* field before returning.

The realize procedure is almost always inherited, ultimately from Core. Core's procedure just passes the *attributes* parameter into the XtCreate-Window routine, specifying CopyFromParent for the *window_class* and *visual* parameters. The sample Label widget inherits its realize procedure.

There are three common cases when a widget class needs its own realize procedure. First, it can modify the attributes, most often the *bit_gravity*, *visual*, or *backing_store* fields. Second, a composite widget can realize its children in a particular order, usually to control their stacking positions, by calling XtRealizeWidget for each child, starting with the bottom one and proceeding to the top. Finally a widget can have private subwidgets that it must realize explicitly. Subwidgets are described in Section 4.7.

The XCreateWindow procedure is complicated and has many parameters. Most realize procedures instead use the Intrinsics procedure XtCreate-Window to create a window.

```
void XtCreateWindow(w, window_class, visual, value_mask, attributes)
    Widget w;
    unsigned int window_class;
    Visual *visual;
```

XtValueMask *value_mask*;

XSetWindowAttributes **attributes*;

w	Specifies the widget to create a window for.
window_class	Specifies the Xlib window class (`InputOutput`, `InputOnly`, or `CopyFromParent`).
visual	Specifies the visual type (usually `CopyFromParent`).
value_mask	Specifies which attribute fields to use.
attributes	Specifies the values for the attribute fields.

`XtCreateWindow` calls the Xlib `XCreateWindow` routine with the passed parameters and relevant fields from the widget data structure: *depth, screen, parent−>core.window, x, y, width, height,* and *border_width.* It assigns the created window to the widget's *window* field.

2.25   Destroying Widgets

As described in Section 2.11, widget destruction is a two-phase process. After calling the destroy callbacks, the Intrinsics call the destroy procedures for all widgets marked for destruction. This procedure is of type `XtWidgetProc`.

typedef void (*XtWidgetProc)(Widget);

Widget *w*;

w	Specifies the widget.

The destroy procedure is a subclass-to-superclass chained procedure: the Intrinsics call the class's destroy procedure first, then the superclass's, and so forth up to Core. A destroy procedure must free any storage pointed to by fields in its instance part. Some of the types of deallocation needed are (don't expect to understand all of these yet):

- Calling `XtFree` for storage allocated with `XtMalloc`, `XtCalloc`, `XtRealloc`, `XtNew`, and `XtNewString`.

- Calling `XFreePixmap` for pixmaps created with Xlib calls.

- Calling `XtReleaseGC` for graphics contexts allocated with `XtGetGC`.

- Calling `XFreeGC` for graphics contexts allocated with Xlib calls.

- Calling `XtRemoveEventHandler` for event handlers added to other widgets with `XtAddEventHandler`.

- Calling `XtRemoveTimeOut` for timers created with `XtAppAddTimeOut`.

- Calling `XtDestroyWidget` for each subwidget the widget has.

```
static void Destroy(w)
    Widget w;
{
    LabelWidget lw = (LabelWidget) w;

    XtFree((char *) lw->label.label);
    XtReleaseGC(w, lw->label.gc);
}
```

Example 2.8. The Label destroy procedure

Two types of deallocation that are not necessary are freeing callback lists and freeing normal children; see Section 4.7 for the difference between sub-widgets and normal children.

Example 2.8 shows the destroy procedures for the Label widget.

2.26 Designing Class Methods

Deciding when to add a new class method can be rather complex. In most object-oriented systems, class methods are needed to obtain and set the values of fields in the instance record. This is not necessary for the toolkit since the Intrinsics provide generic routines to set and get resource values. A method to set or get a resource is only appropriate if the Intrinsics interface is deemed too cumbersome for this particular resource.

New class methods are most appropriate for defining new operations on widgets of the class, usually to request a widget to perform some action. In the Label widget, the new method instructs the label to take or to relinquish the selection. This could also be implemented by having a resource that the application sets and having the implementation do the action when the resource value changes, but this leads to rather contrived code. Class methods are the preferred solution if a widget designer finds herself adding resources whose only purpose is to get the widget instance to do something and which do not really reflect an actual attribute of the widget.

2.27 New Widget Methods

Once a designer has decided on new methods for a class, the programmer must implement them. Every external entry point the widget class provides should call a procedure stored in the class record; classes should never implement functionality directly in these external functions since subclasses may want to implement the functionality differently.[20]

There are no agreed-upon conventions for naming these external functions. The scheme that seems to be gaining popularity is to make the function name begin with the widget class name, possibly preceded by some prefix indicating the widget set. Using this convention, an Athena Label class providing a new method would specify an external function with a name beginning "XawLabel".

There are several steps to implementing a new class method.

First, the implementation must provide an external function to allow applications to use this method. The external function calls the corresponding procedure field in the widget class record. A widget class implements a chained method by having this external function call the procedures for the class of the passed widget and for all superclasses up to the class defining the new method. This can be either in superclass-to-subclass order or in subclass-to-superclass order.

Next, the implementation provides a procedure that actually implements the new method for this class and stores a pointer to this procedure in the widget class record.

Example 2.9 shows the implementation of Label's new method to select the text in the label. The external function LabelSelectText checks that the passed widget is actually a Label widget and if so calls the select method from the widget class. SelectText is the implementation of the new method that Label stores in its class record. SelectText uses the Intrinsics selection routines to own or disown the selection. See Section 9.13 for information on selections.

Finally, the class provides an inheritance constant and resolves the inheritance in the class part initialization procedure.

The inheritance constant is usually the value _XtInherit cast to the appropriate type for that field. _XtInherit is a special internal function that issues an error message if it is ever called, indicating that the inheritance resolution for that method was incorrectly implemented. If the class defines new nonprocedure fields in its class part, it often provides inheritance constants for them, too, but _XtInherit is usually not an appropriate value for

---

[20] Consult the Athena widget implementations for many examples of the wrong way of doing this—subclassing these widgets in a way that overrides the implementations of the external entry points is impossible.

```
Boolean LabelSelectText(w, selection, own)
    Widget w;
    Atom selection;
    Boolean own;
{
    /* Check that we're in Label or a subclass */

    XtCheckSubclass(w, labelWidgetClass, NULL);

    /* Call the class method */

    return (*((LabelWidgetClass) XtClass(w))->label_class.select)
           (w, selection, own);
}

/* Label's select implementation */

static Boolean SelectText(w, selection, own)
    Widget w;
    Atom selection;
    Boolean own;
{
    LabelWidget lw = (LabelWidget) w;

    if (own) {
        return XtOwnSelection(w, selection,
                XtLastTimestampProcessed(XtDisplay(w)),
                DeliverSelection, LoseSelection,
                (XtSelectionDoneProc) NULL);
    } else {
        XtDisownSelection(w, selection,
                XtLastTimestampProcessed(XtDisplay(w)));
        return TRUE;
    }
}
```

Example 2.9. The Label select text method

this. The inheritance constant should be some special tag value that is otherwise invalid for the field.

Example 2.10 shows the class part initialization procedure for Label. The Intrinsics will pass the class records for any subclasses of Label to ClassPartInitialize when initializing these subclasses, and ClassPartInitialize must resolve any inheritance in Label's class part. ClassPartInitialize compares the value of the *select* field with its declared inheritance constant, and if they are equal, ClassPartInitialize copies the value out of the widget's superclass. Most class part initialization procedures that implement inheritance are similar.

```
static void ClassPartInitialize(widget_class)
    WidgetClass widget_class;
{
    register LabelWidgetClass wc = (LabelWidgetClass) widget_class;
    LabelWidgetClass super =
            (LabelWidgetClass) wc->core_class.superclass;

    if (wc->label_class.select == InheritSelectText) {
        wc->label_class.select = super->label_class.select;
    }
}
```

Example 2.10. The Label class part initialization procedure

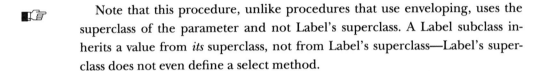

Note that this procedure, unlike procedures that use enveloping, uses the superclass of the parameter and not Label's superclass. A Label subclass inherits a value from *its* superclass, not from Label's superclass—Label's superclass does not even define a select method.

Chapter 3

Resources and Callbacks

Writing Applications

3.1 What Is a Resource?

A *resource* is a named, settable piece of data in some data structure. Most resources are part of widget instances, but they can be in any data structure at all.

Unfortunately this use of the term *resource* conflicts with its usage in the X protocol and Xlib. There, *resource* refers to an object like a window, pixmap, cursor, font, graphics context, or colormap that the server allocates and for which the application has a corresponding identifier. In the best of all possible worlds these very different concepts would have different names, but both uses are now sufficiently entrenched that changing either of them would cause more problems than it would solve. In this book any use of the term in the protocol meaning is always qualified as a *server resource*. Of course toolkit resources can, and often do, take server resources as values, but not all toolkit resources are server resources.

Widget attributes are the most common resources. Applications can also declare their own resources for fields stored in their own data structures. A text editor might have resources to control whether it does backups, what name to give the backup files, whether the user is an expert, or whether the editor allows the user to change the file being edited.

Resources serve two major purposes:

- They provide a uniform interface to setting and querying widget attributes.
- They allow software installers and users to customize applications.

Uniform interfaces allow applications to treat all classes of widgets the same. To create a widget, an application calls `XtCreateManagedWidget` or a similar procedure, passing widget attributes as resources in an argument list or variable parameter list. To change a widget's attributes, an application passes resource values to `XtSetValues`. To query a widget's attributes, an application specifies resource names to `XtGetValues`.

Customization is equally important. Up to now, examples in this book showed resource values only in argument lists. Applications can also specify initial resources in an application defaults file, so called because users can override resources stored there; the resources are the application's default values. Users cannot override resources specified in the application directly, so specifying resources in the defaults file gives users more flexibility.

The application defaults file also gives software installers the ability to make sitewide customizations. If an application stores its text strings and font names in its defaults file, the application can be translated into another language like French by installing a different defaults file containing text strings in that language and fonts appropriate for displaying that language.

Further, users often provide their own files of resources to customize colors, fonts, labels, and even keyboard bindings. A user of the text editor described above could give a TRUE value to the "expert" application resource, telling the editor to always treat him as an expert.

The Intrinsics create a database of resource specifications for each display an application uses. This database contains resources from the application defaults file and the user customization files, modified by resources the user specified on the command line.

Each display opened by an application has a different database, allowing users to customize widgets differently on different displays. A meeting reminder application creates windows on many users' displays; since each display has a different database, each user's window reflects his own personal customizations.

Besides having a name, each resource has a class. Resource classes are not the same thing as widget classes. A resource class is a name for a group of resources that all have similar functions; resource databases can specify values for all resources within the group by specifying a value for the resource class. For example, a Clock widget might have different resources for the foreground colors it uses to draw the clock's hands, the numbers on the face, and the tick marks around the perimeter. These colors can all be different, but a user with more subdued tastes might prefer to have them all be the same. If all three resources have the same resource class, the user can set them all to the same color by specifying a value for this class. Similarly, widgets often use different fonts for different purposes, but if all fonts have the same class, the user can specify them all at once.

When the toolkit creates a widget it looks in three places for the widget's resources:

• If the resource is named in the argument list or a varargs parameter to the creation routine, the resource takes this value.

• Otherwise, the Intrinsics consult the resource database for the display the widget is being created on, and if the database specifies a value for the resource, the resource takes that value.

• If neither of these places specifies the resource, the resource takes the widget class's default value for the resource.

The resource also takes the default value if the argument list or the resource database incorrectly specifies the resource. This could happen if the resource name is spelled incorrectly—in which case it actually specifies a different, non-existent resource. This also happens if the Intrinsics cannot convert the specified resource value to the correct type, as with a misspelled font or color name.

The widget class documentation should clearly describe the resources supported by a widget class. Remember that a widget class automatically inherits all resources defined for superclasses of the widget.

`XtDatabase` returns the resource database associated with a display.

XrmDatabase XtDatabase(*display*)
    Display **display*;
    display   Specifies the display to get the database from.

An application can query or modify this database using the Xlib resource manager routines in Section 10.11 of *Xlib*. Very few applications need to do this. The Intrinsics only use the resource database to supply resource values when creating widgets and to supply application resources. Applications that create all their widgets initially can call `XrmDestroyDatabase` to reclaim the database storage after creating all their widgets and fetching their application resources. Applications that call `XtCloseDisplay` or `XtDestroy-ApplicationContext` should not do this, however; these routines also free the database and the Xlib specification does not define the effect of freeing the same database twice.

3.2   Resource Naming Conventions

The Intrinsics use text strings to name resources. The header file `<X11/StringDefs.h>` contains definitions for all resources for Core and Composite as well as definitions for resources commonly found in many widgets. Appendix E lists the contents of this file.

Resource names follow rigid naming conventions to allow programmers to use resources without worrying about exactly how a particular widget names them.

The string for a resource name starts with a lower-case letter and uses capitalization to distinguish words. The field that it refers to is in all lower-case and uses underscores to separate words; this is the same convention used by the Xlib field definitions. A symbolic name, usually a macro, for each resource has the characters "XtN" added to the beginning of the name string. Hence the border width resource is named "borderWidth"; its field is *border_width*, and its symbolic name is XtNborderWidth. Using symbolic names instead of the actual string allows the compiler to catch spelling mistakes that would otherwise go undetected.

Resource classes use the same conventions as resource names except that they have an initial capital letter. Their symbolic names start with the characters "XtC", so the class for the border width resource is named "BorderWidth" and has the symbolic name XtCBorderWidth. Resource classes do not, in general, have any special relationship with field names, but the usual convention is to use the field name when no other general grouping seems appropriate.

Each resource also has a representation type, and the type has an associated string that begins with a capital letter and a symbolic name that begins with "XtR". For example, the C type `char*` has the string name "String" and the symbolic name XtRString.

Do not define resource name, class, or type strings that begin with the two characters "xt" in any capitalization; the Intrinsics reserve strings beginning this way for internal use. This only applies to the strings themselves, not the symbolic names—the symbolic names always begin with "Xt".

3.3   Resource Types

Applications must know the types of resources, since the values stored in argument lists must be of the correct type. The documentation for a widget class should list all the class's resources and the type for each one.

`<X11/StringDefs.h>` defines several type names. The following table indicates what type the name refers to and where the type is defined.[1]

Name	Type	Where defined
XtRAcceleratorTable	XtAccelerators	Intrinsics
XtRAtom	Atom	Xlib
XtRBitmap	Pixmap	Xlib
XtRBoolean	Boolean	Intrinsics
XtRBool	Bool	Xlib
XtRCallback	XtCallbackList	Intrinsics
XtRCardinal	Cardinal	Intrinsics
XtRColor	XColor	Xlib
XtRColormap	Colormap	Xlib
XtRCursor	Cursor	Xlib
XtRDimension	Dimension	Intrinsics
XtRDisplay	Display *	Xlib
XtREnum	XtEnum	Intrinsics
XtRFile	FILE *	<stdio.h>
XtRFloat	float	C language
XtRFont	Font	Xlib
XtRFontStruct	XFontStruct *	Xlib
XtRFunction	(*) ()	C language
XtRGeometry	String	Intrinsics
XtRInitialState	int	ICCCM
XtRInt	int	C language
XtRLongBoolean	long	C language

[1] The resource types XtRAtom, XtRBitmap, XtRCardinal, XtRColormap, XtREnum XtRGeometry, XtRInitialState, XtRObject, XtRScreen, XtRStringArray, XtRVisual, XtRWidget-Class, and XtRWidgetList are not supported by Intrinsics implementations that conform to specifications earlier than Release 4.

Name	Type	Where defined
XtRObject	Object	Intrinsics
XtRPixel	Pixel	Xlib
XtRPixmap	Pixmap	Xlib
XtRPointer	XtPointer	Intrinsics
XtRPosition	Position	Intrinsics
XtRScreen	Screen *	Xlib
XtRShort	short	C language
XtRString	String	Intrinsics
XtRStringArray	String *	Intrinsics
XtRStringTable	String *	Intrinsics
XtRTranslationTable	XtTranslations	Intrinsics
XtRUnsignedChar	unsigned char	C language
XtRVisual	Visual *	Xlib
XtRWidget	Widget	Intrinsics
XtRWidgetClass	WidgetClass	Intrinsics
XtRWidgetList	WidgetList	Intrinsics
XtRWindow	Window	Xlib

Some of these types require additional explanation:

XtRBitmap The pixmap must be of depth 1.

XtRBool This resource type is for Boolean values stored in Xlib structures. Xlib defines the type Bool to be 32 bits, which is usually larger than the Intrinsics type Boolean.

XtRFunction This is a pointer to a procedure.

XtRGeometry The string must be in the format expected by `XParseGeometry` and `XWMGeometry`. See Section 10.3 of *Xlib*.

XtRInitialState The only legal values are 1 and 3 as defined by the ICCCM; see Section 5.2.

XtRLongBoolean This is an obsolete synonym for XtRBool.

XtRStringArray Generally used for counted lists of Strings; the count is normally a separate resource.

XtRStringTable Generally used for NULL-terminated lists of strings.

The Intrinsics also define the three resource types XtREditMode, XtRJustify, and XtROrientation for the convenience of widget writers, but these types have no standard representations.

3.4 Resource Specifications

When the Intrinsics initialize a display, they construct a resource database for it. Most of the information in this database comes from resource specification files. Some of these resource files are provided by the application writer and some by the user.

A resource specification consists of a list of widget names followed by the name of the resource, with periods separating the names. The list of widget names contains the names of all the ancestor widgets of the widget being specified, starting with the name of the application's shell widget and ending with the widget itself. The name of the shell widget is the same as the name of the application. After the resource name the line contains a colon followed by the value for the resource.

Assume a program named "test" has a main widget named "main" that contains a pushbutton named "exit", and the resource file contains the value "blue" for the "background" resource of the pushbutton. The resource specification for this is

```
test.main.exit.background : blue
```

A specification does not actually have to name all the widgets on the path to the widget being specified; an asterisk separating two components on the list matches any number of intervening widgets, including none. In this example one need not specify that the exit pushbutton is directly contained in the main widget; it could sometime later be moved into a menu or a button box. A specification for the resource without the intermediate widget is

```
test*exit.background : blue
```

Using an asterisk, called *wildcarding*, is not limited to intermediate widgets. A specification that starts with an asterisk applies to all programs. A specification to set the background color for all widgets named "exit", no matter what the application, is

```
*exit.background : blue
```

The widget is also optional, so a specification to set the background color for all widgets in the test application is

```
test*background : blue
```

You can even specify a value for all widgets in all applications.

```
*background : blue
```

For a further level of flexibility, the names of applications, widgets, and resources can be replaced by their classes. The class of an application is a more generic name for the application. The name of the application is usually the program name specified on the command line, but the class is an application-defined string. This allows users to customize different instances of an application differently and still be able to specify some customizations that apply to all instances.

Assume an application normally invoked as "xeditor" has the class "XEditor". To specify a font and background color that applies by default to all instances of the application, write

```
XEditor*font : fixed
XEditor*background : blue
```

However, you can override the resources for specific instances by writing

```
importantEditor*background : red
anotherEditor*font : TimesRoman12
```

To give these instances their specific names, specify –name on the command line or create a link with another name to the xeditor application. The font for the "importantEditor" instance and the background color for the "anothereditor" instance still come from the specifications for application class "XEditor".

The class name of a widget is a capitalized string specifying the widget's class, for example "Label", "Pushbutton", or "Menu". Specifying a resource by widget class specifies values for all widgets of that class, so to give all Pushbutton widgets in the test application a blue background write

```
test*Pushbutton.background : blue
```

and to specify a blue background for all Pushbutton widgets in all applications write

```
*Pushbutton.background : blue
```

Using a resource class in place of a resource name specifies all resources of that class. For the Clock widget example discussed previously, a user specifies different colors for the hands, numbers, and tick marks as

```
*Clock.handColor : blue
*Clock.numberColor : red
*Clock.tickColor : green
```

A different user gives all three resources the same color by writing

```
*Clock.Foreground : blue
```

assuming that the three color resources were all of the class XtCForeground.

In general, specific resource specifications override general ones. Resources specified with less wildcarding override those specified with more, and resources specified with names override those specified with classes. See Section 10.11.1 in *Xlib* for the exact precedence rules.

Since specifications by name override specifications by class, you can combine them. Assume the exit widget is a pushbutton; then

```
*Pushbutton.background : blue
*exit.background : red
```

makes the exit pushbutton's background red and all other pushbutton backgrounds blue.

The Intrinsics quietly ignore a specification for a nonexistent resource. If a resource specification does not seem to have any effect, check that the resource name is spelled correctly, that the class actually has the resource, and that the resource value is spelled correctly.

A resource specification that specifies an improper or unavailable value usually generates a warning message. The most common examples are font or color names that the particular X server does not support. In these cases the resource normally takes the widget class's defined default value.

3.5   Resource Files

The Intrinsics merge four files and the parameters on the command line to get the initial resource database. The next section describes command line parsing; the four files are the application defaults file, the per-user application defaults file, the user defaults file, and the user's per-host defaults file. These four files are processed in that order, so if resource specifications in two files conflict, the specification in the latter file overrides the one in the former.

The application defaults file provides the application's default values for its widget's resources. Section 1.9 showed a version of "Goodbye, world" that specifies widget resources in the application. Example 3.1 shows the main program for a version that uses a defaults file, and Example 3.2 shows the defaults file. The main program is similar to the original version except that the calls to XtCreateManagedWidget specify NULL and zero as the argument list and count. This version of "Goodbye, world" is more flexible than the original one since it allows all its resources to be customized. The sample applications in Chapter 10 provide other examples of application defaults files. The application writer provides the application defaults file, but applications do not modify it dynamically.

The per-user application defaults file allows applications to store customization information for the user. If the application has customization menus, dialog boxes, or property sheets, it stores the results of user customizations in

```
int main(argc, argv)
    unsigned int argc;
    char **argv;
{
    Widget toplevel, label, button, box;
    XtAppContext app;

    toplevel = XtAppInitialize(&app, "Goodbye",
            (XrmOptionDescList) NULL, 0, &argc, argv,
            (String *) NULL, (ArgList) NULL, 0);

    box = XtCreateManagedWidget("box", boxWidgetClass,
            toplevel, (Arg *) NULL, 0);

    label = XtCreateManagedWidget("label", labelWidgetClass,
            box, (Arg *) NULL, 0);

    button = XtCreateManagedWidget("button", pushbuttonWidgetClass,
            box, (Arg *) NULL, 0);
    XtAddCallback(button, XtNcallback, Goodbye, NULL);

    XtRealizeWidget(toplevel);
    XtAppMainLoop(app);
}
```

Example 3.1. "Goodbye, world" using a defaults file


```
*label.x: 10
*label.y: 10
*label.label: Goodbye, world
*button.x: 10
*button.y: 40
*button.label: Click and die
```

Example 3.2. The "Goodbye, world" defaults file

this file. Future invocations of the application will start up with the user's changes. Users can also store customizations in this defaults file, so applications should maintain any entries that they are not overriding.

The user defaults file contains user customizations. Customizations that apply to all applications are here, and many users also use this file for application-specific customizations in preference to the per-user application defaults file. Applications should not modify the user defaults file.

The per-host defaults file supplies user customizations based upon the computer on which the application is running. This supports per-host customization in networked environments that share the user's home directory among different computers. Applications should not modify the per-host defaults file.

The name of the application defaults file is site-specific and depends upon the language specified for the application; see Section 9.8.

The name of the per-user application defaults file depends upon the values of several environment variables and on the language specified for the application; see Section 9.8.

The Intrinsics usually get the contents of the user defaults file from the RESOURCE_MANAGER property on the root window of the display. This property comes from the user's `.Xdefaults` file on Unix systems and is set up automatically by the user's session manager or explicitly through the user running `xrdb` or a similar utility. If the RESOURCE_MANAGER property does not exist, the Intrinsics use the file `.Xdefaults` in the user's home directory.

On Unix systems, the name of the per-host defaults file is in the XENVIRONMENT environment variable if it exists. If not, the name of the file is `.Xdefaults-`*host* in the user's home directory, where *host* is the name of the computer on which the application is running.

Applications normally list most of their widget resources in their application defaults file. If this file is not present, many programs will not run correctly—widgets have the wrong sizes and positions, buttons and menu items are missing their labels, and so forth. Installing the defaults file sometimes presents problems since the directory where it resides is a public directory that developers or users importing applications might not have access to. There are two solutions to this problem.

The easiest solution is to tell the user to set his XFILESEARCHPATH environment variable to point to the directory containing the application defaults file; see Section 9.8. If `dir` is the directory with the file, the appropriate value for XFILESEARCHPATH is "`dir/%N%S`". A special case, especially useful when developing a new application, is to have the defaults file in the current directory and to set XFILESEARCHPATH to "`:`".

This works well when only one person uses the application but becomes awkward when an application is to be used by several people. In this case the programmer can specify the contents of the defaults file as an array of strings in the application and use `XtAppSetFallbackResources`.[2]

---

[2] Fallback resources are not supported by Intrinsics implementations that conform to specifications earlier than Release 4.

void XtAppSetFallbackResources(*app_context, specification_list*)
    XtAppContext *app_context*;
    String **specification_list*;
app_context   Specifies the application context.
specification_list   Specifies a NULL-terminated list of resource specifications.

Applications call `XtAppSetFallbackResources` after creating an application context but before opening any displays on that context. If `XtDisplayInitialize` cannot open the application defaults file, the Intrinsics load the strings pointed to by *specification_list* into the database instead. Each string in *specification_list* is a string terminated by a null byte containing a single resource specification. The strings and the array must be allocated in storage that will remain uncorrupted until the application opens its displays.

Calling `XtAppSetFallbackResources` more than once replaces the old fallback resources with those in the new call, and passing it NULL as *specification_list* removes the fallback resources completely.

Applications can also specify fallback resources with the *fallback_resources* parameter to `XtAppInitialize`. Example 3.3 shows code to set fallback resources in the "Goodbye, world" program. The rest of the main program is identical to the "Goodbye, world" program using an application defaults file in Example 3.1.

3.6   Parsing the Command Line

Resource files eliminate many occasions when users need to specify command line options to a program. Users permanently store their preferred options in their user defaults file. The Intrinsics support command line options that override values in the database, allowing users to provide customizations for just one invocation. Most toolkit programs let the Intrinsics do all their option handling, only looking in the command line for things like file names.

After the Intrinsics construct a resource database from the resource files, they modify this database with information specified on the command line when invoking the program. The *argc* and *argv* parameters passed to `XtOpenDisplay`, `XtDisplayInitialize`, or `XtAppInitialize` specify the command line. These routines modify the argument values and count to contain only the values that do not match any of the recognized options; the returned arguments include the first entry in the command line, usually the

```
String fallback_resources[] = {
    "*label.x: 10",
    "*label.y: 10",
    "*label.label: Goodbye, world",
    "*button.x: 10",
    "*button.y: 40",
    "*button.label: Click and die",
    NULL
};

int main(argc, argv)
    unsigned int argc;
    char **argv;
{
    Widget toplevel, label, button, box;
    XtAppContext app;

    toplevel = XtAppInitialize(&app, "Goodbye",
        (XrmOptionDescList) NULL, 0, &argc, argv,
        fallback_resources, (ArgList) NULL, 0);

    ...
}
```

Example 3.3. Fallback resources for "Goodbye, world"

program name. An application like a text editor might interpret any remaining values in *argv* as text files to edit, while other applications might print an error message reporting unrecognized options.

The following table lists the predefined options the Intrinsics recognize. The first column specifies the option. The second column specifies the resource specification that the Intrinsics add to the resource database if the command line specifies that option; the resource is prefixed by the name of the program and takes the value specified by the final column. Thus, if the user invokes a test program by typing

```
test -bw 3
```

the Intrinsics add the line

```
test.borderWidth : 3
```

to the resource database. Resources that begin with a period apply only to the top-level shell of the application; those that begin with an asterisk apply to all widgets. Any unique abbreviation of an option is acceptable, but an application can define additional options that may conflict with the abbreviations.

Option	Resource Name	Resource Value
–background	*background	next argument
–bg	*background	next argument
–bordercolor	*borderColor	next argument
–bd	*borderColor	next argument
–borderwidth	.borderWidth	next argument
–bw	.borderWidth	next argument
–display	.display	next argument
–foreground	*foreground	next argument
–fg	*foreground	next argument
–font	*font	next argument
–fn	*font	next argument
–geometry	.geometry	next argument
–iconic	.iconic	"on"
–name	.name	next argument
–reverse	.reverseVideo	"on"
–rv	.reverseVideo	"on"
+rv	.reverseVideo	"off"
–selectionTimeout	.selectionTimeout	next argument
–synchronous	.synchronous	"on"
+synchronous	.synchronous	"off"
–title	.title	next argument
–xnllanguage	.xnlLanguage	next argument
–xrm	next argument	next argument

Several of these options are special. The –xrm option allows a user to specify any resource from the command line; the value of the option is the line to add to the database. Thus the following two command lines do exactly the same thing:

```
test -background blue
test -xrm "*background : blue"
```

Always quote the resource specification as appropriate to the command shell being used to prevent the shell from expanding any asterisks or breaking the specification into separate words.

The reverse video, selection timeout, synchronous, and xnlLanguage resources modify application resources; rather than applying to any particular widget they modify the execution environment of the entire application. Section 3.11 describes these resources.

Application writers add additional command line options to this list by passing option tables to `XtOpenDisplay`, `XtDisplayInitialize`, or `XtAppInitialize`. See Section 10.11.4 of *Xlib* for the format of these option tables. To make the "Goodbye, world" program of Example 3.1 or 3.3 accept the command line options –label to specify its label text and –button to specify the pushbutton text, declare the option table

```
static XrmOptionDescRec options[] = {
    {"-label", "*label.label", XrmoptionSepArg, NULL},
    {"-button", "*button.label", XrmoptionSepArg, NULL}
};
```

and pass this table to `XtAppInitialize`. With these options, invoking "Goodbye, world" as

```
goodbye -label "Ta-ta for now" -button "Click here"
```

adds the lines

```
goodbye*label.label : Ta-ta for now
goodbye*button.label : Click here
```

to the resource database, and the application appears as in Figure 3.1.

Figure 3.1. "Goodbye, world" with customizations

3.7   Resource Conversions

The Intrinsics convert resource values from one representation type to another. This mechanism is mostly used to convert resource values specified as strings in the database to the types used by the widgets, but applications can directly invoke it as well. The examples of resource specifications in Section 3.4 specified colors as the string "blue". Widgets do not deal with colors as strings; they represent colors as pixel values. The Intrinsics automatically convert the string value "blue" into the appropriate pixel value. Another example is fonts—resource files specify fonts by name, but widgets use font structures. Widget classes define the resource type for each of their resources.

The Intrinsics automatically support the following conversions:

From XtRString to:

> XtRAcceleratorTable, XtRAtom, XtRBoolean, XtRBool, XtRCursor, XtRDimension, XtRDisplay, XtRFile, XtRFloat, XtRFont, XtRFontStruct, XtRInitialState, XtRInt, XtRPixel, XtRPosition, XtRShort, XtRTranslationTable, XtRUnsignedChar, and XtRVisual.

From XtRInt to: XtRBoolean, XtRBool, XtRColor, XtRDimension, XtRFloat, XtRFont, XtRPixel, XtRPixmap, XtRPosition, XtRShort, and XtRUnsignedChar.

From XtRColor to XtRPixel.

From XtRPixel to XtRColor.

Many of the conversions are straightforward. The following are not:

XtRString to XtRAtom
> Calls XInternAtom for the string.

XtRString to XtRAcceleratorTable and XtRTranslationTable
> Converts the table from its external representation, a string, into the opaque internal representation stored in widgets.

XtRString to XtRBoolean and XtRBool
> Converts the strings "true", "on", and "yes", in any capitalization, to TRUE, and the strings "false", "off", and "no" to FALSE.

XtRString to XtRCursor
> Converts the name for the cursor, listed in the include file ⟨X11/cursorfont.h⟩, to a cursor. The string does not include the initial "XC_" characters. See Appendix B of *Xlib*.

XtRString to XtRDisplay
> Opens the display specified by the string and returns a pointer to the display structure. The string uses the same format as XtOpenDisplay; see Section 1.11.

XtRString to XtRFile
> Uses the standard I/O library to open the file for reading, and returns a pointer to a FILE structure.

XtRString to XtRFont
> Loads the font with the given name and returns the font identifier; the server defines the valid font names. There is a special source value, XtDefaultFont, that converts to a default font; see Section 3.11.

XtRString to XtRFontStruct

> Loads and queries the font with the given name and returns a pointer to the font structure. Also recognizes XtDefaultFont.

XtRString to XtRInitialState

> Converts the strings "NormalState" and "IconicState" to the integers 1 and 3, respectively. See Section 5.2.

XtRString to XtRPixel

> If the string begins with a #, parses the string as an RGB value using `XParseColor` and allocates the result using `XAllocColor`. If not, allocates the named color using `XAllocNamedColor`. There are two special source values, XtDefaultForeground and XtDefault-Background, that correspond to the black and white pixels for the display; see Section 3.11 for more information.

XtRString to XtRVisual

> Calls `XMatchVisualInfo` to find a Visual for the widgets screen and depth that matches the string type and returns the first matching Visual returned. The allowed string values are "StaticGray", "StaticColor", "TrueColor", "GrayScale", "PseudoColor", and "DirectColor". Visuals affect how the server interprets pixel values; see Section 3.1 of *Xlib* for more details. Few applications need to worry about Visuals.

XtRInt or XtRPixel to XtRColor

> Queries the display for the color value.

XtRInt to anything else besides XtRFloat

> No conversion is performed; the source is just cast to the new type.

Widgets can define new type conversions; for example, the Label widget defines a converter from strings to justification types to allow a resource file to specify that a label is to left-justify, center, or right-justify its text. The end result of the conversion is the value of an enumerated type.

Applications use type converters since the values they store into argument lists must be of the correct type. This is very important to remember—the Intrinsics do not convert the values in argument lists. Forgetting this is one of the most common errors that application writers make. Don't write

```
Arg colorArgs[] = {
    {XtNbackground, "blue"}      /* Wrong, wrong, wrong */
};
```

This is wrong since XtNbackground is a pixel-valued resource, not a string-valued resource. Instead write

```
Arg colorArgs[] = {
    {XtNbackground, NULL}
};
Pixel blue;
...
/* Convert the string "blue" to a pixel value in the variable
   blue.  The code to do this is on the next page. */
...
colorArgs[0].value = blue;
```

Applications convert values from one type to another by calling XtConvert-AndStore.[3]

```
typedef struct {
    unsigned int    size;
    caddr_t         addr;
} XrmValue, *XrmValuePtr;
```

Boolean XtConvertAndStore(*w, from_type, from, to_type, to_in_out*)
    Widget *w*;
    String *from_type*;
    XrmValuePtr *from*;
    String *to_type*;
    XrmValuePtr *to_in_out*;

w	Specifies the widget to use for additional arguments, if any.
from_type	Specifies the type being converted from.
from	Specifies the value to be converted.
to_type	Specifies the type being converted to.
to_in_out	Specifies a descriptor for a location to store the converted value into.

The widget parameter is present since some conversions require extra information from the widget. For example, to convert from a string to a pixel value, the conversion procedure asks the display to allocate a pixel value from a colormap, looks up the string in the display's color table, assigns the color to the pixel value, and returns the pixel value. The conversion procedure thus needs the display and the colormap from the widget. When an application converts to a value for inclusion in the argument list to XtCreateManaged-Widget or a similar creation routine, the specified widget is usually the parent of the new widget.

---

[3] XtConvertAndStore is not supported by Intrinsics implementations that conform to specifications earlier than Release 4.

The caller of XtConvertAndStore must fill in the source address and size with the value to convert. If the source type is XtRString, the size is the length of the string, including the trailing null byte, not the size of a character pointer. There are two options possible with the destination value.

If *to_in_out->addr* is NULL, XtConvertAndStore replaces it with a pointer to the converted value and sets *to_in_out->size* to the size of the converted value. The caller must copy the data immediately before executing any other toolkit functions (the toolkit memory allocation functions are safe to use for this) and must not modify the pointed-to data in any way. This option exists mainly for compatibility with earlier code.

If *to_in_out->addr* is not NULL, XtConvertAndStore assumes it points to storage to hold the converted value and that *to_in_out->size* specifies the size of the destination storage. If the destination storage is large enough to hold the converted value, XtConvertAndStore stores the converted value there and sets *to_in_out->size* to the actual size of the converted value. This option is more portable since it presents fewer problems with shared libraries and multiple threads.

XtConvertAndStore returns TRUE if the conversion succeeded. Possible reasons for failure include trying to convert between types with no registered converters, trying to convert an illegal source value, and not specifying enough storage to hold the converted value. In the last case XtConvertAndStore updates *to_in_out->size* to the needed size.

This code fragment converts from the string "blue" to a pixel value:

```
XrmValue source, dest;
Pixel blue;

source.size = strlen("blue")+1;
source.addr = "blue";
dest.size = sizeof(Pixel);
dest.addr = &blue;

if (!XtConvertAndStore(w, XtRString, &source, XtRPixel, &dest)) {
    /* Unknown color, do appropriate thing */
}

/* The variable blue now contains the pixel value */
```

This code does not worry about insufficient destination storage since Pixel values are always the same size.

Applications should use `XtConvertAndStore` rather than directly computing the resource value, especially if the computation involves calling Xlib routines. The Intrinsics may have already performed the same conversion and saved the value, and if so `XtConvertAndStore` returns this saved value immediately. Even if this is the first time for this conversion, using `XtConvertAndStore` makes the result available for future conversions.

Applications can implicitly request conversions by using the varargs versions of the Intrinsics routines taking argument lists. See Section 3.9.

A possible problem exists converting resources for the first widget created of a particular class. Widget classes register new type conversions when the class is initialized, and this does not normally happen until the application creates the first widget of the class or of a subclass. This means that the Intrinsics do not know about the type conversion before the creation of the first widget. If an application needs to invoke a widget-defined conversion in order to create the first widget of a class, it must first explicitly initialize the class by calling `XtInitializeWidgetClass`; see Section 2.3.

`XtConvertAndStore` is new to the Intrinsics with Release 4. A different routine, `XtConvert`, was used in earlier versions and still exists for backward compatibility. Appendix C describes `XtConvert`.

3.8   Argument Lists

Whenever an application specifies resources, whether to create a widget, set a widget's resource values, or query a widget's resource values, the application provides an argument list describing the resources. An argument list is an array of `Arg` structures.

```
typedef something XtArgVal;
typedef struct {
    String      name;
    XtArgVal    value;
} Arg, *ArgList;
```

The `XtArgVal` type is an implementation-specific type that is large enough to hold a `long`, an `int*`, a `char*`, an `XtPointer`, or a pointer to a function. If the value field is large enough to hold the resource value, the application stores the resource value in the value field directly. Otherwise the application stores a pointer to the resource value in the value field. This creates an unfortunate portability issue, in that an application must know when to directly store resources and when to store a pointer, but in practice this is not usually a problem.

A problem exists with storing `float` values into an argument list; the application must jump through hoops to keep the C compiler from casting the `float` value to an integer. The most reliable way to do this is to declare a union type:

```
union {
    float f;
    int i;
} hack;
```

Assign the `float` value to *hack.f* and store *hack.i* into the argument list. If the resource is defined as a pointer to a `float` value, however, this problem does not occur.

Argument lists can be declared statically or dynamically. For a static declaration the application defines and initializes the resource in an array and usually uses the `XtNumber` macro to calculate the number of elements in the array:

```
Arg labelArgs[] = {
    {XtNx,      10},
    {XtNy,      10},
    {XtNlabel,  "Goodbye, world"}
};
...
label = XtCreateManagedWidget(..., labelArgs, XtNumber(labelArgs));
```

This incurs less execution time since the argument list does not need to be set up at runtime, but works only awkwardly if the application must calculate some of the resource values at runtime. The programmer must know which argument list entry to update with the computed value and must remember to change this in the code if she ever modifies the order of entries in the argument list.

For a dynamic declaration, the application declares an empty argument list and fills in the fields at runtime, usually using `XtSetArg`.

void XtSetArg(*arg, name, value*)
    Arg *arg*;
    String *name*;
    XtArgVal *value*;
  arg   Specifies the name-value pair to set.

name   Specifies the name of the resource.

value   Specifies the value of the resource if it fits in an XtArgVal or the
                       address if not.

XtSetArg can be implemented as a macro that uses its first argument more
than once, so never specify a first argument that has side effects. In particular,
do not increment or decrement an array index in this argument.

Applications usually use XtSetArg in a highly stylized manner that minimizes the probability of making a mistake when adding or deleting a resource
specification:

```
Arg args[10];
int n;
...
n = 0;
XtSetArg(args[n], XtNx, 10);                      n++;
XtSetArg(args[n], XtNy, 10);                      n++;
XtSetArg(args[n], XtNlabel, "Goodbye, world");    n++;

label = XtCreateManagedWidget(..., args, n);
```

This costs a little additional execution time to set up the argument list, but the
application can reuse the same argument list for different widgets and places
the code that specifies the resources closer to the code that uses them. Most
important, it frees the programmer from having to worry about which argument list entry to update with resource values computed at runtime.

Programmers must be aware of the declared size of the argument list; setting too many resources is a common cause of hard-to-find bugs. Forgetting to
increment the argument counter is another common mistake.

The Intrinsics quietly ignore an argument list entry for a nonexistent
resource. If an argument does not seem to have any effect, make sure that the
resource name is spelled correctly and actually exists for the appropriate
widget type.

To merge two argument lists, use XtMergeArgLists.

ArgList XtMergeArgLists(*args1*, *num_args1*, *args2*, *num_args2*)
    ArgList *args1*;
    Cardinal *num_args1*;
    ArgList *args2*;
    Cardinal *num_args2*;

args1   Specifies the first argument list.

num_args1   Specifies the number of entries in the first argument list.

args2	Specifies the second argument list.
num_args2	Specifies the number of entries in the second argument list.

`XtMergeArgLists` creates a new argument list large enough to hold the two specified ones and copies them into it. It does not check for duplicate entries. When the returned argument list is no longer needed, free it using `XtFree`. Merging argument lists is useful when the application design requires different code modules to specify resources for a single widget, but this is rather rare.

3.9 Variable Argument Procedures

All Intrinsics routines that take argument lists have alternative versions that allow the resource specifications to occur directly as the parameters to the routines. These are called *varargs* routines since they take variable argument lists.[4] *Variable* applies to the parameters of the routine, and not to an Intrinsics argument list; calling them variable parameter lists might be less confusing, but the terminology predates the Intrinsics.

Any varargs routine has the same name as the corresponding argument list routine with the characters "Va" inserted after "Xt"; for example, the varargs version of `XtCreateManagedWidget` is `XtVaCreateManagedWidget`. The argument list and count parameters are replaced by alternating resource names and values, terminated by the value NULL.

Programmers using the C language can use the argument list routines and the varargs routines interchangeably according to personal preference. This programmer's guide uses argument lists for all its examples; any references to resources in argument lists apply equally to resources specified through a varargs interface.

Here again is the argument list version of creating the Label widget in "Goodbye, world":

```
Arg args[10];
int n;
...
n = 0;
XtSetArg(args[n], XtNx, 10);                 n++;
XtSetArg(args[n], XtNy, 10);                 n++;
XtSetArg(args[n], XtNlabel, "Goodbye, world"); n++;
```

---

[4] Varargs routines are not supported by Intrinsics implementations that conform to specifications earlier than Release 4.

```
label = XtCreateManagedWidget("label", labelWidgetClass, box,
    args, n);
```

And here is the varargs version:

```
label = XtVaCreateManagedWidget("label", labelWidgetClass, box,
    XtNx, (XtArgVal) 10,
    XtNy, (XtArgVal) 10,
    XtNlabel, (XtArgVal) "Goodbye, world",
    NULL);
```

It is important not to forget the trailing NULL; omitting it will at best result in runtime errors and at worst in using random memory locations as resource values.

The rules for the resource value are the same in varargs routines as in argument list routines: if the resource value fits in an XtArgVal, the parameter list includes it directly, and if the resource value does not fit, the parameter list includes a pointer to the value.

Varargs routines provide one bit of functionality not available in argument list routines—automatic type conversions. Rather than converting a resource value explicitly using XtConvertAndStore, programmers specify the conversion in the variable argument list by replacing the resource name with the special value XtVaTypedArg.

XtVaTypedArg must be followed by four arguments giving the resource name, the source type, the source value, and the size of the source value. Usually the source type is XtRString, and in this case the source value is a pointer to a character string and the size is the number of bytes in the string, including the trailing null byte. If the source type is not XtRString, the source value is either the value itself cast to an XtArgVal or a pointer to the value, depending upon its size, and the size is the size of the data.

To create a widget with a blue background, a programmer either directly converts the string "blue" to a pixel value as shown in Section 3.7, or requests a conversion in a variable argument list this way:

```
widget = XtVaCreateManagedWidget(...,
        XtVaTypedArg, XtNbackground, XtRString,
                      "blue", strlen("blue")+1,
        NULL);
```

If a type conversion in a variable argument list fails, the Intrinsics issue a warning message and skip the resource. Be sure to always specify four more arguments after XtVaTypedArg; specifying the wrong number will result in runtime errors or invalid resources.

To create a variable argument list for inclusion in other variable argument lists, use `XtVaCreateArgsList`.

typedef XtPointer XtVarArgsList;

XtVarArgsList XtVaCreateArgsList(*unused*, . . .)
    XtPointer *unused*;
unused   Must be NULL.
. . .   Specifies resource names and values.

The *unused* argument exists to support variable argument implementations that require at least one fixed argument before the variable arguments. The variable arguments follow the same rules as other variable argument lists; they must alternate names and values and must end with NULL. Any type conversions specified in the parameters with XtVaTypedArg will be delayed until the variable argument list is used in a call other than `XtVaCreateArgsList`. `XtVaCreateArgsList` copies its parameters but not the values any of them might be pointing to, so indirect data must be stable enough to last as long as the variable argument list does.

A variable argument list returned by `XtVaCreateArgsList` is included in another argument list by preceding it with the special value XtVaNestedList. For example,

```
XtVarArgsList varargs;

varargs = XtVaCreateArgsList(NULL,
        ...                           /* name-value pairs */
        NULL);

widget = XtVaCreateManagedWidget(...,
        XtVaNestedList, (XtArgVal) varargs,
        ...                           /* other resources */
        NULL);
```

The effect is as if the resources in the nested list were included in the variable argument list at the place where XtVaNestedList occurs. Variable argument lists can be nested arbitrarily deep by including XtVaNestedList in the arguments to `XtVaCreateArgsList`.

When a variable argument list is no longer useful, free it using `XtFree`. Since `XtVaCreateArgsList` does not copy any nested lists, you cannot free a nested list until after freeing any lists that include it. Nested variable argument lists are useful in the same cases as merging argument lists.

3.10   Resource Files versus Argument Lists

An application specifies initial resources for widgets either in an application defaults file or in argument lists. Usually the defaults file is preferable, but there are exceptions.

The Intrinsics initialize widget resources by checking in the following places, in this order, using the first value found:

• The argument list to the create routine.

• The resource database, consisting of
  — The options specified on the command line.

  — The user's per-host defaults file.

  — The user's defaults file.

  — The per-user application defaults file.

  — The application defaults file.

• The widget class's default value for the resource.

Therefore, a user cannot override resources that came from argument lists, either on the command line or in his resource files. A user can override resources specified in the application defaults file. Each application designer must make a policy decision whether to specify a resource in the defaults file, allowing user customization, or in an argument list, prohibiting it.

Using the defaults file is usually better, since the user can customize as he wishes. Software installers can make site-specific customizations in the defaults file instead of by modifying the code. Foreign language translations require only modifying the defaults file, not the application. Finally, most implementations of the Intrinsics fetch resources from the database more efficiently than from argument lists.

There are several reasons to use an argument list. If a resource value can only be determined at runtime, it is impossible to specify it in the defaults file (though the dynamic value can be stored into the resource database explicitly before creating the widgets). The application designer might decide that some resources are not customizable in order to guarantee a certain level of consistency across different users' invocations. Finally, the program might be just a simple throw-away application for which it is easier not to bother with defaults files.

Resource files are often appropriate even in these cases. Applications can often handle resources that must be calculated at runtime by having the Intrinsics invoke clever type conversions. Designers should think carefully before prohibiting a potential customization, since users accustomed to customizing their applications become frustrated when forbidden to do so. And throw-away applications have an annoying tendency not to be thrown away and often end up being used by other people who may want to customize them. In general, defaults files are the preferred way to set resources.

Programmers specify resources in application defaults files as generically as possible to allow users the most customizing flexibility. Remember that specific resource specifications override general ones, and that the Intrinsics merge all the resource files together into one database before doing any lookups. This merge only eliminates lines that have exactly matching left-hand sides. So if the defaults file for a test program specifies

```
test.main.exit.label: Exit
```

and the user defaults file specifies

```
test*exit.label: Quit
```

the Intrinsics ignore the user's customization since a more specific resource specification exists. The application defaults file should use as much wild-carding as possible. The test program probably contains only one widget named "exit" and its application defaults file will only be used for the one application, so the specification

```
*exit.label: Exit
```

suffices to specify the resource uniquely. In particular, application defaults files should never specify the application name or class since this prohibits the user from making customizations that apply across all applications.

Application programmers should describe the widget tree in the application documentation so that users can customize the application without digging through program listings to find the widget names.

3.11   Application Resources

Certain resources do not apply to any particular widget but instead to the application as a whole. These are called *application resources*.

The Intrinsics define the application resources XtNreverseVideo, XtNxtDefaultFont, XtNxnlLanguage, XtNmultiClickTime, XtNsynchronous, and XtNselectionTimeout.[5] Applications are free to define additional ones.

---

[5] The default font, language, and multi-click timeout resources are not supported by Intrinsics implementations that conform to specifications earlier than Release 4.

Reverse video switches the default foreground and background values for the application. Each screen defines two color values `BlackPixel` and `WhitePixel`; these colors may not actually be black and white but are supposed to be different from each other. If the user and application specify no other colors, most widgets use `BlackPixel` for their foreground and border and `WhitePixel` for their background. If the reverse video resource is set, these are switched: the foreground and border are `WhitePixel` and the background is `BlackPixel`. The Intrinsics swap colors by exchanging the pixel values that the string-to-pixel converter returns for the strings "XtDefaultForeground" and "XtDefaultBackground". Specifying reverse video has no effect beyond this; in particular it does not modify colors specified by any names other than "XtDefaultForeground" and "XtDefaultBackground". Don't expect reverse video to work if you have resources in your defaults file like

```
*Foreground: green
*Background: violet
```

Reverse video is only effective for simple monochrome applications that specify no color resources. The name of the reverse video resource is "reverseVideo", its class is "ReverseVideo", the command line option –rv turns it on, +rv turns it off, and it is a Boolean value that defaults to FALSE.

The default font is the font that the string-to-font and string-to-fontstructure converters return when passed the string "XtDefaultFont". There is no command line option to specify the default font directly; it must come from the resource database or from an –xrm command line option:

```
myprogram -xrm "xtDefaultFont : TimesRoman12"
```

The default font must be specified with name "xtDefaultFont" or class "XtDefaultFont" unqualified by any application or widget names or classes. In other words, the specification must just contain "xtDefaultFont" or "XtDefaultFont" followed by a colon and a font name, for example

```
xtDefaultFont : fixed
```

If the resource database does not contain a specification for "xtDefaultFont" or if the Intrinsics cannot fetch the specified font from the server, the font converters return an implementation-dependent font that uses the ISO Latin-1 encoding (i.e., it is an appropriate font for displaying text in most Western European languages, including English).

The language resource affects where the Intrinsics look for the application defaults file and the per-user application defaults file. It allows having multiple installed defaults files on a system that provide an application's text in different languages. Section 9.8 describes how the Intrinsics use the language resource. Its name is "xnlLanguage", its class is "XnlLanguage", the command line option –xnllanguage specifies it, and it defaults to the value of the LANG variable in the user's environment, or to NULL if LANG is not set.

The multi-click timeout specifies how close in time multiple pointer button events must come for the Intrinsics to consider them part of a multi-click sequence. See Section 7.2 for full details. The name of this resource is "multiClickTime", its class is "MultiClickTime", and it is an integer value specifying the timeout in milliseconds that defaults to 200. There is no direct command line option to set this resource, but it can be specified by using the –xrm option:

```
myprogram -xrm "*multiClickTime : 500"
```

Setting the synchronous resource makes all display connections operate in synchronous mode. Running this way is considerably slower, but it makes debugging easier since Xlib reports errors from the server immediately after the request that caused them. The name of this resource is "synchronous", its class is "Synchronous", the command line option –synchronous turns it on, +synchronous turns it off, and it is a Boolean value that defaults to FALSE. You usually set this resource by specifying –synchronous on the command line during a debugging session, but you can put it into a resource file to avoid specifying it every time during extensive debugging.

The selection timeout resource controls how long the Intrinsics wait for a selection transfer before concluding that the other process involved is not going to respond; see Section 9.16 for more details. Few applications are concerned with this. The name of this resource is "selectionTimeout", its class is "SelectionTimeout", the command line option –selectionTimeout specifies it, and it is an integer value specifying the time in milliseconds, defaulting to 5000.

Applications define their own application resources with a resource list. Section 3.17 in the widget writer's part of this chapter describes resource lists since it is primarily widgets that use them. If you need to define application resources, read Section 3.17 before reading the rest of this section.

Applications fetch their application resources by using `XtGet-ApplicationResources` or `XtVaGetApplicationResources`.[6]

void XtGetApplicationResources(*w, base, resources, num_resources, args, num_args*)
    Widget *w*;
    XtPointer *base*;
    XtResourceList *resources*;
    Cardinal *num_resources*;
    ArgList *args*;
    Cardinal *num_args*;

w	Specifies the widget used to find the resources.
base	Specifies the base address of the data structure to store the resource values into.
resources	Specifies the list of resources to fetch.
num_resources	Specifies the number of entries in the resource list.
args	Specifies the argument list of values to override those in the resource database.
num_args	Specifies the number of entries in the argument list.

The Intrinsics fetch resources from the resource database as if they were specified as resources for the specified widget, and the database used for the search is the one associated with the widget's display. This widget is usually the application's top-level shell since this shell has the same name and class as the application.

The Intrinsics compile the resource list into an efficient internal form, so applications cannot read or modify the resource list after passing it to `XtGetApplicationResources`.

`XtGetApplicationResources` assigns the fields described in the resource list the values of the corresponding resources from the database and argument list. All application resources should be declared as structure fields, with the offsets in the resource list being the offsets of the fields in the structure and the address of the structure being the base parameter to `XtGetApplicationResources`. Resist the temptation to put the actual addresses of the fields into the resource list and pass zero as the base, since this practice is not portable—there is no guarantee that an address will fit into a `Cardinal` field.

---

[6] `XtVaGetApplicationResources` is not supported by Intrinsics implementations that conform to specifications earlier than Release 4.

The varargs interface to fetching application resources is `XtVaGet-ApplicationResources`.

void XtVaGetApplicationResources(*w, base, resources, num_resources, . . .*)
    Widget *w*;
    XtPointer *base*;
    XtResourceList *resources*;
    Cardinal *num_resources*;

w	Specifies the widget used to find the resources.
base	Specifies the base address of the data structure to store the resource values into.
resources	Specifies the list of resources to fetch.
num_resources	Specifies the number of entries in the resource list.
. . .	Specifies the resource specifications to override those in the resource database.

Example 3.4 shows the code to fetch application resources in the mail notifier program shown in Chapter 10. The *options* structure and the *resources* array specify the five resources "quiet", "mailFile", "interval", "defaultMessage", and "fromMessage". OptionDesc defines command line options that allow the user to set three of these resources when executing the program; the main program passes this array to `XtAppInitialize` to tell the Intrinsics how to parse the three options. `XtGetApplicationResources` fetches resources from the resource database and stores them into the *options* structure.

3.12   Finding Out about a Widget's Resources

Applications like interactive user interface editors need to know the list of resources a widget class supports. Most applications, however, do not need to do this (the programmer needs to know the resources, but the application does not); you can probably skip this section.

To find a widget class's resource list, call `XtGetResourceList`.

void XtGetResourceList(*class, resources_return, num_resources_return*) ;
    WidgetClass *class*;
    XtResourceList **resources_return*;
    Cardinal **num_resources_return*;

class	Specifies the widget class to fetch the resource list from.
resources_return	Returns the resource list.
num_resources_return	Returns the number of entries in the resource list.

```
typedef struct {
    Boolean quiet;
    String mail_file;
    int timeout;
    String default_message;
    String from_message;
} OptionsRec;

OptionsRec options;

#define Offset(field) XtOffsetOf(OptionsRec, field)

XtResource resources[] = {
    {"quiet", "Quiet", XtRBoolean, sizeof(Boolean),
        Offset(quiet), XtRImmediate, (XtPointer) FALSE},
    {"mailFile", "MailFile", XtRString, sizeof(String),
        Offset(mail_file), XtRImmediate, (XtPointer) NULL},
    {"interval", "Interval", XtRInt, sizeof(int),
        Offset(timeout), XtRImmediate, (XtPointer) 60},
    {"defaultMessage", "DefaultMessage", XtRString, sizeof(String),
        Offset(default_message), XtRString, "New mail from someone"},
    {"fromMessage", "FromMessage", XtRString, sizeof(String),
        Offset(from_message), XtRString, "New mail from %s"}
};

#undef Offset

XrmOptionDescRec optionDesc[] = {
    {"-quiet", "*quiet", XrmoptionNoArg, (XtPointer) "on"},
    {"-file", "*mailFile", XrmoptionSepArg, (XtPointer) NULL},
    {"-interval", "*interval", XrmoptionSepArg, (XtPointer) NULL}
};

main(argc, argv)
    int argc;
    char *argv[];
{
    toplevel = XtAppInitialize(&app, "DemoBiff",
            optionDesc, XtNumber(optionDesc), &argc, argv,
            (String *) NULL, (ArgList) NULL, 0);

    XtGetApplicationResources(toplevel, (XtPointer) &options,
            resources, XtNumber(resources), (Arg *) NULL, 0);

    /* Rest of main program omitted */
}
```

Example 3.4. Fetching application resources

XtGetResourceList returns a copy of the resource list for the specified widget class. The caller must not modify this list or any values pointed to by list entries, and should free the returned list using XtFree when it is no longer useful. If an application calls XtGetResourceList before the specified class has been initialized, XtGetResourceList returns a resource list with just the resources this class defines, and if an application calls it after the class has been initialized, it returns a fully merged list containing the resources for the widget class and all its superclasses. Section 3.17 describes resource lists. The list XtGetResourceList returns does not contain any resources that the widget class implements as subresources; see Section 3.25 for more details. The Intrinsics compile resource lists into an opaque internal form, but the list XtGetResourceList returns always has the external form.

Widget classes that are subclasses of Constraint have an additional set of resources called constraint resources that apply to child widgets. Section 4.6 describes this in detail. To get the list of constraint resources for a class, call XtGetConstraintResourceList.[7]

void XtGetConstraintResourceList(*class, resources_return, num_resources_return*);
    WidgetClass *class*;
    XtResourceList *resources_return*;
    Cardinal *num_resources_return*;
class   Specifies the widget class to fetch the resource list from.
resources_return   Returns the constraint resource list.
num_resources_return
                Returns the number of entries in the resource list.

The same restrictions on the list returned by XtGetResourceList apply to the list returned by XtGetConstraintResourceList. If the widget class is not a subclass of Constraint, XtGetConstraintResourceList sets *resources_return* to NULL.

3.13 Resources at Widget Creation

When an application creates a widget, the Intrinsics initialize all the widget's resources with the values in the widget class defaults, the resource database and the values specified in the call to the creation routine. The Intrinsics

---

[7] XtGetConstraintResourceList is not supported by Intrinsics implementations that conform to specifications earlier than Release 4.

automatically convert any resources from the class defaults or the resource database to the appropriate type for the widget.

Most applications destroy few or no widgets during their execution; most of their widgets remain until the program exits. A few applications create and destroy widgets many times, and the Intrinsics allow these applications to enable reference counting for their resources. If all widgets that use a particular reference-counted resource are destroyed, the Intrinsics free the resource and reclaim its storage.

An example would be an application that repeatedly creates and destroys widgets with different background colors. If the resources were not reference-counted, the application would rapidly use up the entire colormap. If the resources are reference-counted, the Intrinsics can free colormap entries that are no longer being used.

Applications enable reference counting using the XtNinitialResources-Persistent resource.[8] Maintaining the reference counts requires additional storage and computation, and for simple applications that do not destroy many widgets the overhead is unnecessary. XtNinitialResourcesPersistent defaults to TRUE, which disables reference counting. An application that needs reference counting for a widget must specify XtNinitialResourcesPersistent FALSE for the widget in the resource database or the argument list. XtNinitialResourcesPersistent is a Boolean resource; its string name is "initialResourcesPersistent" and its class is "InitialResourcesPersistent".

3.14   Getting Widget Resources

Applications obtain the values of a widget's resources by using `XtGetValues`.

```
void XtGetValues(w, args, num_args)
    Widget w;
    ArgList args;
    Cardinal num_args;
```

w	Specifies the widget whose resources are being obtained.
args	Specifies the resources to obtain.
num_args	Specifies the number of entries in the argument list.

---

[8] Reference counting and XtNinitialResourcesPersistent are not supported by Intrinsics implementations that conform to specifications earlier than Release 4.

The argument list contains the names of the resources needed and pointers to variables to store these values into. For example, to get a widget's border width, the correct code is

```
Dimension borderWidth;
Arg args[10];
int n;

n = 0;
XtSetArg(args[n], XtNborderWidth, &borderWidth);        n++;

XtGetValues(widget, args, n);
```

After the call to `XtGetValues`, the *borderWidth* variable contains the resource value. `XtGetValues` does not return the resource value in the argument list; there is always a level of indirection. Early versions of the toolkit stored values directly into the list, so you might encounter some old code that counts on versions of the Intrinsics that support this old behavior, but there is no guarantee that this will continue to work.

It is very important that the variable pointed to in the argument list is of the proper type for the resource; for example, XtNborderWidth must be fetched into a `Dimension` variable. The Intrinsics always write exactly as many bytes as are taken up by the data. If the variable is of the wrong type, the Intrinsics may write more or fewer bytes than the application expects, leading to memory corruption or variables with old data left in some of the bytes.

One potential source of confusion exists with resources of type String. This type is a pointer to a character, so the result of doing `XtGetValues` for a string resource is a pointer to the actual characters and not the characters themselves. Whenever an application fetches a resource that is a pointer value, it must treat the pointed-to data as read-only. Modifying the data is likely to corrupt memory and confuse widget implementations. The pointed-to data are only guaranteed to be valid until the next Intrinsics call; if the application needs the data longer, it makes a copy. The Intrinsics' memory allocation routines are safe to use for this.

The varargs version of `XtGetValues` is `XtVaGetValues`.[9]

void XtVaGetValues(*w*, . . .)
    Widget *w*;

---

[9] `XtVaGetValues` is not supported by Intrinsics implementations that conform to specifications earlier than Release 4.

w	Specifies the widget whose resources are being obtained.
...	Specifies the resource to obtain.

The values in the variable argument list must be pointers to variables to hold the fetched values. If the variable argument list specifies XtVaTypedArg, XtVaTypedArg must be followed by the resource name, the type to convert it to, the address to store the converted value into, and the size of the destination storage. If the conversion fails for any reason, including the destination storage not being large enough, the Intrinsics issue a warning message and do not update the destination.

For example, to retrieve a widget's background color as an XColor, write

```
XColor color;
```

```
XtVaGetValues(widget,
    XtVaTypedArg, XtNbackground, XtRColor, &color, sizeof(color),
    NULL);
```

Type conversions in XtVaGetValues are of limited usefulness since the Intrinsics do not define many "backward" type converters—for example, there is a string-to-font converter but no font-to-string converter. Widget sets may, however, define additional converters.

3.15   Setting Widget Resources

Applications modify a widget's resources with XtSetValues.

void XtSetValues(*w, args, num_args*)
    Widget *w*;
    ArgList *args*;
    Cardinal *num_args*;

w	Specifies the widget whose values are being set.
args	Specifies the resources to set and the new values.
num_args	Specifies the number of entries in the argument list.

The argument list passed to XtSetValues uses a format identical to that for create routines: the value field contains the value for the resource if it fits into an XtArgVal and a pointer to the resource if not. Values must have the correct types since the Intrinsics do no type conversion with the arguments; forgetting this and expecting type conversion is a common error. The information on setting up argument lists for widget creation routines applies equally to XtSetValues; see Section 3.7.

Issuing an `XtSetValues` call is a request and not an order; widget implementations are free to ignore or modify the resource values. XtNscreen is a good example—the X protocol does not allow a window to be moved to a different screen, so attempts to modify the XtNscreen resource are ignored. Changes to a widget's size and position in particular should be viewed as requests since the widget's parent has the final authority over the child's geometry.

The varargs version of `XtSetValues` is `XtVaSetValues`.[10]

void XtVaSetValues(*w*, . . .)
    Widget *w*;
w   Specifies the widget whose values are being set.
. . .   Specifies the resources to set and the new values.

3.16   Callback Procedures

Callback procedures allow widgets to inform applications that something of interest happened. Typical callbacks indicate that the user activated a pushbutton, selected a menu item, filled in a text field, or moved a scrollbar.

All callback procedures are of type `XtCallbackProc`.

typedef void (*XtCallbackProc)(Widget, XtPointer, XtPointer);
    Widget *w*;
    XtPointer *client_data*;
    XtPointer *call_data*;
w   Specifies the widget that the callback is registered for.
client_data   Specifies a piece of data defined by the application.
call_data   Specifies a piece of data defined by the widget class.

The data pointed to by the *call_data* parameter are defined by the widget invoking the callback procedure. For example, a callback to indicate that the user filled in a text field passes the address of the string in this parameter, and a scrollbar passes a structure describing the new position of the slider. Simple widgets like Pushbutton usually pass NULL; the widget parameter uniquely indicates which button the user activated so no additional information is needed. Consult the widget to find out what the widget passes as the call data for each callback resource.

---

[10] `XtVaSetValues` is not supported by Intrinsics implementations that conform to specifications earlier than Release 4.

Applications can either use the same callback procedure for multiple widgets and within the callback test the widget parameter to determine which widget was activated, or can use different procedures for different widgets. The latter organization often leads to a more modular program structure. Any callback procedure that does an "if" test on its widget should probably be broken up into separate callbacks.

The application specifies the *client_data* parameter when it associates the callback procedure with a widget; this is usually the address of a data structure the application uses to maintain some state or to convey some information to the callback procedure. If the needed data fit into an XtPointer, applications can pass the data directly in *client_data*. For example, an application could have two global flags, indicating whether the user is a novice or an expert, and whether the user wants verbose or terse messages. The application includes two Toggle buttons in its user interface to allow the user to switch the settings; it uses the same callback procedure for both buttons by passing the address of the flag to modify in the *client_data* parameter.

Assuming that Toggle passes the new Boolean value of the toggle in *call_data*, the callback procedure to set the flag looks like this:

```
void SetToggle(w, client_data, call_data)
    Widget w;                    /* Not used */
    XtPointer client_data;       /* Pointer to flag */
    XtPointer call_data;         /* New flag value */
{
    *(Boolean *) client_data = (Boolean) call_data;
}
```

The application adds the callback for the two flags by specifying

```
XtAddCallback(expertToggleWidget, XtNcallback,
        SetToggle, &expertFlag);
XtAddCallback(verboseToggleWidget, XtNcallback,
        SetToggle, &verboseFlag);
```

The calculator program in Chapter 10 provides another example; it uses the same callback procedure for all the digit buttons on the calculator, passing the digit to the callback in *client_data*.

The Intrinsics do not interpret the client data; they pass the value to the callback procedure exactly as the application specified when registering the callback. If an application does not need to use *client_data* for a particular callback, it specifies NULL when registering the callback.

Callbacks are identified by resource names. Widgets can have more than one callback resource; for example a Scrollbar widget might execute one callback when the user clicks a pointer button in one of the stepping buttons and a different callback when the user moves the slider. A Toggle button might have two callbacks, one for when the user sets the button and one for when the user clears it. The widget designer decides whether to have one callback and use *call_data* to indicate what happened or to have multiple callbacks. Application writers must consult the widget documentation to determine what a particular widget class does. The only callback resources defined by the Intrinsics are the XtNdestroyCallback resource of the Core class and the XtNpopupCallback and XtNpopdownCallback resources of the Shell class. These callbacks pass NULL as *call_data.*

Each callback resource actually refers to a list of callback procedures. This feature is most useful to an application that dynamically changes what it does in response to a callback. Rather than having one callback that checks some state variables to decide just what to do, the application uses multiple simple callbacks that perform one action apiece. The application modifies the list of callbacks to reflect the current semantics from anywhere in the application; there is no need to centrally maintain the list. The order in which the Intrinsics call the callback procedures is undefined.

The easiest way to specify callbacks is to use `XtAddCallback`, described shortly. The most general way is by giving a value to a callback resource when creating the widget or calling `XtSetValues`. The type of all callback resources is a pointer to a NULL-terminated list of `XtCallbackRec` structures.[11]

```
typedef struct {
    XtCallbackProc      callback;
    XtPointer           closure;
} XtCallbackRec, *XtCallbackList;
```

The *closure* field is the value that the Intrinsics pass to the callback procedure in the *client_data* parameter. To specify that a widget should call the two procedures A and B and pass them the client data values *clientDataA* and *clientDataB*, respectively, write

[11] The *closure* field should really have been named *client_data.*

```
static XtCallbackRec callbacks[] = {
    {A, (XtPointer) clientDataA},
    {B, (XtPointer) clientDataB},
    {NULL, NULL}
};
...
XtSetArg(args[n], XtNsomeCallback, callbacks);  n++;
```

and pass the argument list to a widget creation procedure or to
`XtSetValues`.

If a procedure appears in a callback list more than once, the Intrinsics call
it as many times as it appears.

Passing a callback resource to `XtSetValues` completely replaces the exist-
ing callback list. To selectively add and remove callbacks, use `XtAdd-
Callback`, `XtAddCallbacks`, `XtRemoveCallback`, and `XtRemove-
Callbacks`.

void XtAddCallback(*w, callback_name, callback, client_data*)
    Widget *w*;
    String *callback_name*;
    XtCallbackProc *callback*;
    XtPointer *client_data*;

w	Specifies the widget to add the callback procedure to.
callback_name	Specifies the callback list to add the procedure to.
callback	Specifies the callback procedure.
client_data	Specifies the value passed to the callback procedure in the *client_data* parameter, or NULL.

`XtAddCallback` adds the callback procedure to the specified callback list for
the widget. When creating a widget, it is usually easier to use
`XtAddCallback` than to declare an `XtCallbackRec` and specify a resource.

void XtAddCallbacks(*w, callback_name, callbacks*)
    Widget *w*;
    String *callback_name*;
    XtCallbackList *callbacks*;

w	Specifies the widget to add the callback procedures to.
callback_name	Specifies the callback list to add the procedures to.
callbacks	Specifies a NULL-terminated list of callback procedures with their corresponding client data.

`XtAddCallbacks` adds the list of callback procedures to the specified callback list for the widget.

void XtRemoveCallback(*w, callback_name, callback, client_data*)
    Widget *w*;
    String *callback_name*;
    XtCallbackProc *callback*;
    XtPointer *client_data*;

w	Specifies the widget to remove the callback procedure from.
callback_name	Specifies the callback list to remove the procedure from.
callback	Specifies the procedure to remove from the callback list.
client_data	Specifies the client data to match to remove the procedure.

`XtRemoveCallback` removes the callback procedure from the specified callback list for the widget. Both the procedure and client data must match for `XtRemoveCallback` to remove the procedure.

void XtRemoveCallbacks(*w, callback_name, callbacks*)
    Widget *w*;
    String *callback_name*;
    XtCallbackList *callbacks*;

w	Specifies the widget to remove the callback procedures from.
callback_name	Specifies the callback list to remove the procedures from.
callbacks	Specifies a NULL-terminated list of callback procedures with their corresponding client data.

`XtRemoveCallbacks` removes each of the listed callback procedures from the specified callback list for the widget. Both the procedure and client data must match for a procedure for `XtRemoveCallbacks` to remove it.

To remove all the callback procedures from a callback list, call `XtRemoveAllCallbacks`.

void XtRemoveAllCallbacks(*w, callback_name*)
    Widget *w*;
    String *callback_name*;

w	Specifies the widget to remove the callbacks from.
callback_name	Specifies the callback list to be removed.

All these procedures issue a warning message and do nothing if the specified callback list does not exist for the specified widget. To check the status of a callback list, use `XtHasCallbacks`.

typedef enum {XtCallbackNoList, XtCallbackHasNone, XtCallbackHasSome}
    XtCallbackStatus;

XtCallbackStatus XtHasCallbacks(*w, callback_name*)
    Widget *w*;
    String *callback_name*;
w   Specifies the widget to check.
callback_name   Specifies the callback list to check.

`XtHasCallbacks` returns XtCallbackNoList if the widget does not have the specified callback list. It returns XtCallbackHasNone if the callback list exists but has no callback procedures, and XtCallbackHasSome if the callback list exists and has at least one callback procedure. Applications that want more details about the callback list use `XtGetValues` to fetch the value of the callback resource; this returns a pointer to a NULL-terminated list of `XtCallbackRec` structures.

Writing Widgets

3.17   Resource Lists

A widget implementation or an application with application resources must inform the Intrinsics which resources the widget or application supports. This lets the Intrinsics initialize resource fields when creating a widget or in `XtGetApplicationResources`, modify resource fields in `XtSetValues`, and fetch resource fields in `XtGetValues`. The implementation does this by filling the *resources* field of the widget class structure with a pointer to a resource list.

When they initialize a class, the Intrinsics merge the class's resource list with the resource lists of all superclasses. A resource list can provide a new default value for a resource a superclass defines by redefining that resource.

The order of entries in a resource list is significant; the Intrinsics fetch resources from the database in the order in which the resources first appear in the superclasses' or widget class's resource lists. All entries in the superclasses' resource lists come before resources in the current class's list, even if redefined. Ordering is important for resource conversions and for writing resource default procedures, described later in this section.

Entries in a resource list are of type `XtResource`.

```
typedef struct {
    String          resource_name;
```

```
String          resource_class;
String          resource_type;
Cardinal        resource_size;
Cardinal        resource_offset;
String          default_type;
XtPointer       default_addr;
} XtResource, *XtResourceList;
```

The *resource_name* and *resource_class* fields define the name and class for this resource. The *resource_type* field describes the resource's representation type so that the Intrinsics can invoke an appropriate type conversion to fill in the resource at widget creation time.

The *resource_size* and *resource_offset* fields define where the Intrinsics should store the resource value in the widget instance. Implementations normally use sizeof(*type*) for *resource_size* and XtOffsetOf for *resource_offset* so that the compiler correctly calculates the size and offset.[12]

Cardinal XtOffsetOf(*stucture_type, field_name*)
    type structure_type;
    field field_name;
structure_type   Specifies a type that is declared as a structure.
field_name   Specifies the name of the field for which to calculate the byte offset.

XtOffsetOf is a macro that returns the offset in bytes of the field within the structure type. For example, if the structure type Test is

```
typedef struct {
    int a;
    int b;
} Test;
```

XtOffsetOf(Test, a) returns the offset of *a*, which is zero, and XtOffsetOf(Test, b) returns the offset of *b*, normally the size of an int variable plus whatever padding the compiler inserts between the two fields.[13]

Intrinsics versions before Release 4 use a different macro, XtOffset, to calculate byte offsets. XtOffset differs from XtOffsetOf in that its first

---

[12] XtOffsetOf is not supported by Intrinsics implementations that conform to specifications earlier than Release 4.

[13] For the terminally curious, XtOffsetOf casts the NULL pointer to point to the specified structure, dereferences the pointer, selects the field, and returns the address of this expression. Some compilers are justifiably picky about things like this; if your compiler complains about XtOffsetOf, talk to a compiler expert. ANSI C compilers should be able to define XtOffsetOf simply as offsetof.

argument is a pointer type rather than a structure type. XtOffsetOf is implementable in more C compilers than XtOffset and is thus the preferred macro, but XtOffset exists for backward compatibility.

The *default_type* and *default_addr* fields define the default value for this resource.[14] *Default_addr* points to a storage location containing the default value, and *default_type* indicates what type this value is. For efficiency, this type should be the same as the type of the resource whenever possible; if it is not, the Intrinsics invoke a type conversion procedure to convert the value from the default type to the resource type. To redefine a superclass resource, giving it a new default value, you must give the same values as the superclass for all resource fields besides *default_type* and *default_addr*.

Default resource values must be valid—if a resource conversion fails here, the Intrinsics have no value to use when initializing the resource field. This is no problem for numeric or string resources; there are plenty of values available that work for these. Resources that the X server provides require care since there is usually no value that always works. For example, there is no guarantee that any particular font name works for a particular server, so font defaults present problems. Pixel resources are equally problematic since there are no color names that a server must recognize. To avoid these problems, the string-to-font, string-to-font-structure, and string-to-pixel converters know about three special string values.

• XtDefaultFont is a special name that the string-to-font and -font-structure converters recognize. It evaluates to an implementation-dependent font as determined by the "xtDefaultFont" application resource; see Section 3.11.

• XtDefaultForeground is a special name recognized by the string-to-pixel converter. It evaluates to the server-defined black pixel for the widget's screen if the application is not running in reverse video, and to the white pixel if it is (see Section 3.11). This color may actually not be black or white but normally contrasts with the value specified by XtDefaultBackground.

• XtDefaultBackground is a special name recognized by the string-to-pixel converter. It evaluates to the server-defined white pixel for the widget's screen if the application is not running in reverse video, and to the black pixel if it is (see Section 3.11). This color may actually not be white or black but normally contrasts with the value specified by XtDefaultForeground.

---

[14] *Default_addr* is called *default_address* in Intrinsics implementations that conform to specifications earlier than Release 4, but no known implementations complied with this.

There are three special default types, XtRString, XtRImmediate, and XtRCall-Proc. The type XtRString eliminates a level of indirection: the *default_addr* field contains the address of the string rather than the address of the address of the string. (Recall that the XtRString type is a pointer to a character; if the Intrinsics did not treat XtRString specially, the default address would point to the address of the string.) This special case lets you include string values directly in the resource list.

If the *default_type* is XtRImmediate, the *default_addr* field contains the value for the default rather than its address. The type must be the same as the representation type; the Intrinsics perform no type conversion. This allows you to include simple defaults in the list without an additional level of indirection.

If the *default_type* is XtRCallProc, the Intrinsics use *default_addr* as a pointer to a procedure that returns the default value. This procedure can assume that all resources specified in earlier list entries and all resources specified in superclasses' resource lists have already been filled in, and is of type XtResourceDefaultProc.

```
typedef void (*XtResourceDefaultProc) (Widget, int, XrmValue *);
    Widget w;
    int offset;
    XrmValue *value;
```

w	Specifies the widget whose default resource is being obtained.
offset	Specifies the offset of the resource field in the widget record.
value	Specifies a resource value descriptor that the default procedure fills in.

The resource default procedure fills in *value->addr* with a pointer to a computed default value in its correct type. This pointer cannot refer to a local variable in the default procedure since its data might be overwritten before the Intrinsics can make a copy. The offset parameter contains the offset of the field being initialized; this lets the same default procedure be used for more than one resource.

Default procedures slow down widget creation and so should be used only when necessary. It is often better to specify a tag value as the default and have the initialize procedure check for this value and compute a reasonable default. Default procedures are most useful for resources that other resources depend on. The default value for the XtNcolormap resource, for example, is whatever colormap the widget's parent uses. Making the XtNcolormap be NULL and having Core's initialize procedure copy the colormap from the widget's parent does not work. The colormap must be in place before the Intrinsics can convert strings to pixels for pixel-valued resources, and this conversion occurs before the Intrinsics call Core's initialize procedure.

The Intrinsics compile resource lists into an efficient internal form before using them. Programs should not read or modify resource lists after compilation; this takes place just before class initialization for widget resource lists and immediately upon the first use of any other resource lists.

Example 3.5 shows the resource list for Label. It contains one entry for each resource that Label defines. The first entry describes the XtNlabel resource, a string with the default value of NULL. This is an example of specifying a tag default in the resource list; if the label field is NULL, Label's initialize procedure fills it in with the widget's name. An application cannot force the value to be NULL; if it wants an empty label, it must specify the empty string.

The XtNfont resource has a default value of `XtDefaultFont` and the XtNforeground resource has a default value of `XtDefaultForeground`.

```
#define Offset(field) XtOffsetOf(LabelRec, label.field)

static XtResource resources[] = {
    {XtNlabel, XtCLabel, XtRString, sizeof(String),
        Offset(label), XtRString, (XtPointer) NULL},
    {XtNfont,  XtCFont, XtRFontStruct, sizeof(XFontStruct *),
        Offset(font), XtRString, (XtPointer) XtDefaultFont},
    {XtNforeground, XtCForeground, XtRPixel, sizeof(Pixel),
        Offset(foreground), XtRString,
        (XtPointer) XtDefaultForeground},
    {XtNjustify, XtCJustify, XtRJustify, sizeof(Justify),
        Offset(justify), XtRImmediate, (XtPointer) Left},
    {XtNspace, XtCSpace, XtRDimension, sizeof(Dimension),
        Offset(space), XtRImmediate, (XtPointer) 2},
    {XtNloseSelection, XtCLoseSelection, XtRCallback,
        sizeof(XtCallbackList), Offset(lose_selection),
        XtRCallback, (XtPointer) NULL},
    {XtNborderWidth, XtCBorderWidth, XtRDimension, sizeof(Dimension),
        XtOffsetOf(LabelRec, core.border_width),
        XtRImmediate, (XtPointer) 0},
};
#undef Offset
```

Example 3.5. The Label resource list

Both specify the default as a string; the Intrinsics convert the string to a font structure or a pixel automatically.

The next two resources specify the XtNjustify and XtNspace resources. Since the default values for these fit within the *default_addr* field and need no type conversion, the list specifies them using XtRImmediate.

XtNloseSelection is a callback resource that takes NULL as its default.

The last resource shows how to redefine a superclass resource to give it a new default value. It redefines XtNborderWidth, giving it a default value of zero.

Example 3.6 shows Pushbutton's resource list. The things to note here are the use of default procedures for the XtNinsensitiveForeground and XtNinsensitivePixmap resources and the resource specification for the *use_insens_pixel* field. Note also that the last resource redefines XtNborder-Width once again, giving it a default value of 1.

Pushbutton allows an application to specify the insensitive foreground either as a pixel or as a pixmap. If the application specifies neither, Pushbutton constructs a default pixmap consisting of the normal foreground stippled to half intensity. The problem lies in knowing when the insensitive pixel foreground has its default value so that the implementation knows to use the insensitive pixmap—all possible values from 0 to $2^{32} - 1$ are legal pixel values; there is no tag value Pushbutton can safely use the way that Label uses NULL as a tag in its XtNlabel resource.

Pushbutton solves the problem by specifying a default procedure for XtNinsensitiveForeground. The default procedure sets the *use_insens_pixel* field FALSE; if *use_insens_pixel* is FALSE, the rest of the implementation knows that the the pixel value came from the default procedure and not from the application.

An additional snag comes in ensuring that *use_insens_pixel* is TRUE if the Intrinsics do not call the default procedure. The initial contents of widget fields that are not resources are undefined, and by the time the Intrinsics call Pushbutton's initialize procedure it is too late. The initialize procedure has no way to know whether *use_insens_pixel* is FALSE because it just happened to start that way or because the XtNinsensitiveForeground default procedure gave it that value.

The solution lies in a resource list entry that makes *use_insens_pixel* default to TRUE. This entry must precede the XtNinsensitiveForeground entry so that

```
static void InsPixel(), InsPixmap();

#define Offset(field) XtOffsetOf(PushbuttonRec, pushbutton.field)

static XtResource resources[] = {
    {XtNcallback, XtCCallback, XtRCallback, sizeof(XtCallbackList),
        Offset(callback), XtRCallback, (XtPointer) NULL},
    {"pri.vate", "Pri.vate", XtRBoolean, sizeof(Boolean),
        Offset(use_insens_pixel), XtRImmediate, (XtPointer) TRUE},
    {XtNinsensitiveForeground, XtCForeground, XtRPixel, sizeof(Pixel),
        Offset(insensitive_foreground),
        XtRCallProc, (XtPointer) InsPixel},
    {XtNinsensitivePixmap, XtCPixmap, XtRPixmap, sizeof(Pixmap),
        Offset(insensitive_pixmap),
        XtRCallProc, (XtPointer) InsPixmap},
    {XtNhighlightBorder, XtCBorderWidth,
        XtRDimension, sizeof(Dimension),
        Offset(highlight_border), XtRImmediate, (XtPointer) 1},
    {XtNaccelString, XtCAccelString, XtRString, sizeof(String),
        XtOffsetOf(PushbuttonRec, label.accel_string),
        XtRString, NULL},
    {XtNacceleratorString, XtCAcceleratorString,
        XtRString, sizeof(String),
        Offset(accelerator_string), XtRString, NULL},
    {XtNborderWidth, XtCBorderWidth,
        XtRDimension, sizeof(Dimension),
        XtOffsetOf(PushbuttonRec, core.border_width),
        XtRImmediate, (XtPointer) 1},
};

#undef Offset

static void InsPixel(w, offset, value)
    Widget w;
    int offset;          /* Not used */
    XrmValue *value;
{
    PushbuttonWidget p = (PushbuttonWidget) w;

    /* Any value will work; it won't be used */
    value->addr = (caddr_t) &p->label.foreground;
    p->pushbutton.use_insens_pixel = FALSE;
}
```

(continued)

Example 3.6.   The Pushbutton resource list

```
/* Return a 2x2 pixmap with the foreground at 50% */

static Pixmap GetPixmap(pw)
    PushbuttonWidget pw;
{
    static char bits[] = {0x01, 0x02};

    return XCreatePixmapFromBitmapData(XtDisplay(pw),
        RootWindowOfScreen(XtScreen(pw)), bits, 2, 2,
        pw->label.foreground, pw->core.background_pixel,
        pw->core.depth);
}

static void InsPixmap(w, offset, value)
    Widget w;
    int offset;             /* Not used */
    XrmValue *value;
{
    PushbuttonWidget pw = (PushbuttonWidget) w;
    static Pixmap pixmap;

    if (pw->pushbutton.use_insens_pixel) pixmap = None;
    else pixmap = GetPixmap(pw);

    value->addr = (caddr_t) &pixmap;
}
```

Example 3.6. The Pushbutton resource list

the Intrinsics fill in *use_insens_pixel* before fetching the XtNinsensitive-Foreground resource. The resource name and class contain periods, making it impossible to accidentally specify this as a resource in a defaults file.

The XtNinsensitivePixmap default procedure tests *use_insens_pixel* to decide whether to construct the half-intensity stippled pixmap.

The net result is that if the application specifies an insensitive foreground pixel, Pushbutton uses it; if not, Pushbutton uses the insensitive pixmap, either as the application specified it or as the XtNinsensitivePixmap default procedure constructed it.

3.18   Designing Resources

When you design a widget class, you should provide enough resources so that applications and users can configure widget instances as needed. Be careful, though, of configurability overkill: every widget instance stores each resource, so specifying resources that are unlikely to be used wastes a lot of memory. The Label widget provides one resource, XtNspace, to control the amount of extra space it leaves around the label text. You may want to define two resources, one for the horizontal space and one for the vertical space. You do not want to define four resources, one for each side—how many applications need this level of configurability? If a particular application needs this functionality, it can always subclass Label and define the resources itself. Don't include a resource just because it is theoretically possible to use it.

When adding a new resource, stop to think whether the user might want to group this resource with another in his customizations. If so, make the resources have the same class. Resource names provide the means to uniquely specify a resource; if all resources have different classes, the resource classes become useless.

If you declare new pointer resources, declare new resource types as well. While using XtRPointer as the resource type works, it does not give enough information to applications like user interface editors that query the resource list.

Because of the difficulties in specifying `float` values in argument lists (see Section 3.8) it is best to avoid them as widget resources whenever possible. One option is to replace the `float` resource with a pair of integer ones and compute the floating-point value in the widget; another is to define the resource to be a pointer to a `float` instead of a `float` directly.

3.19   The Conversion Cache

Starting up a substantial application can require hundreds, if not thousands, of resource conversions. A simple resource specification like
```
*background : blue
```
applies to every widget in an application, and each conversion requires a round trip to the server to find the pixel value that corresponds to "blue". To cut down the number of necessary conversions, the Intrinsics save the results of conversions in a conversion cache. If the same conversion is requested a second time, the Intrinsics return the converted value directly from the cache instead of calling the converter.

The Intrinsics store failed conversions in the cache as well to avoid multiple conversion warnings. If the resource database contained the misspelling
```
*background : bluee
```

a warning message would result the first time the Intrinsics tried to convert "bluee" to a pixel, but subsequent requests for conversion would fail without a warning.

The conversion cache helps efficiency in other ways besides eliminating round trips and warning messages. Since the conversion cache must store the converted value, widget instances can share the converted value to avoid multiple copies of the data. The potential savings here depend upon the size of the destination data. A pixel value takes just one word, so no savings would occur if widgets contained a pointer to the cached value instead of the pixel itself. A font structure, however, can take many thousands of bytes, so having widgets contain a pointer to the cached font structure instead of the font structure itself can save a huge amount of storage.

The conversion cache also eliminates repeated calculations. Even conversions that do not involve a round trip can involve a fair amount of computation, and by caching the converted value the computation only needs to be done once.

While many resource conversions rely only upon the source value, others need additional data. The pixel value resulting from a string-to-pixel conversion relies not only on the color name but also on the widget's screen and colormap. Converting a color name will yield different pixel values for widgets on different screens and with different colormaps. The Intrinsics copy any additional data the conversion relies upon into the conversion cache along with the source value, and both the source and the additional data must match for a cache hit to occur.

Entries in the conversion cache become stale if their additional data become invalid. If an application closes a display, any cache entries containing that display or screens on that display are no longer useful. This would not be much of a problem (other than wasting some storage) if it were not the case that another display the application opens later could end up with the same display value. Conversions for the new display would incorrectly result in cache hits since the Intrinsics cannot distinguish between the new and the old displays.

This is not as unlikely an occurrence as one might think; in fact, it tends to happen with most applications that open and close displays serially. Typically the last thing an application does when closing the display is to free the display data structure, and if the application does not allocate any additional data before opening the next display, the new display data structure will often end up using the same storage as the previous one.

To eliminate this problem, the Intrinsics mark conversions that depend upon the display so that when the application closes the display all cache entries for that display can be invalidated.

Some conversions depend upon volatile data that are not display-specific. The next section describes a string-to-widget converter that takes a widget as additional data and returns a child of that widget whose name is the specified string. If the widget the conversion depended on were destroyed later on, the cache entries would become stale.

The types of volatile data that can be used in a conversion are diverse enough, and the uses for non-display-specific conversion data are rare enough, that the Intrinsics provide no general cache-invalidating mechanism. Instead, conversions relying upon volatile, non-display-specific data never appear in the conversion cache at all; they are called *uncached* conversions.

Uncached conversions can also be used to avoid cache records for trivial conversions. For example, a Boolean-to-integer conversion only needs to cast the source value to an integer and return it; performing the conversion each time is faster than looking for the appropriate cache record. Conversions can also be uncached if the programmer thinks it unlikely that the same conversion would ever be requested more than once; a conversion to a type only used in a single application resource might fall into this category.

The Intrinsics also support reference-counted cache records, freeing them when their value is no longer being used in any widget.

The entire type conversion mechanism was extensively redesigned for Release 4 of the Intrinsics. Earlier versions used a simpler interface that did not support invalidating stale conversion cache data. The procedure type XtConverter and the routines XtConvert, XtDirectConvert, and XtAddConverter have been retained for compatibility; see Appendix C.

3.20   Resource Converters

Sometimes a widget class defines a new resource type. It should also define new type conversion procedures to convert values of appropriate types to and from the new type; the definition of appropriate depends upon the resource but normally includes at least a converter from a string so that defaults files can hold the resource values.

Type converters use pointers to `XrmValue` structures, defined in the Xlib header file `<X11/Xresource.h>`, for their input and output values:

```
typedef struct {
    unsigned int    size;
    caddr_t         addr;
} XrmValue, *XrmValuePtr;
```

A type converter is a procedure of type `XtTypeConverter`.[15]

```
typedef Boolean (*XtTypeConverter) (Display *, XrmValuePtr, Cardinal *,
                            XrmValuePtr, XrmValuePtr, XtPointer *)
        Display *display;
        XrmValuePtr args;
        Cardinal *num_args;
        XrmValuePtr from;
        XrmValuePtr to;
        XtPointer *converter_data;
```

display	Specifies the display connection for this conversion.
args	Specifies a list of additional arguments needed for the conversion, or NULL.
num_args	Specifies the number of additional arguments, or zero.
from	Specifies the value to convert.
to	Specifies a descriptor to store the converted data into.
converter_data	Specifies a location the converter can fill with conversion-specific information.

Converters typically use the *display* parameter only to find an application context for issuing a warning or error message; it must *not* be used as a substitute for a conversion argument since the Intrinsics do not enter it into the conversion cache record.

The additional conversion arguments provide extra data necessary for the conversion; their contents are defined when the converter is registered. The Intrinsics automatically set up the conversion arguments before calling the converter. Most simple converters require no additional arguments.

The *from* value is the value to convert, and the *to* value specifies the storage for the converted value. *Converter_data* is useful for communication with type destructor procedures, described later in this section.

---

[15] `XtTypeConverter` is not supported by Intrinsics implementations that conform to specifications earlier than Release 4.

Converters should do the following actions:

- Do a consistency check to make sure the number of additional arguments is correct and issue an error message if not. Having the wrong number of additional arguments indicates a programming error.

- Attempt the type conversion.

- If the conversion succeeded and *to–>addr* is NULL, fill in the *to* value with the converted result. Set *to–>addr* to point to the converted result, *to–>size* to the size of the converted result, and return TRUE. The converted result must persist after the conversion procedure returns; it must not be a dynamic local variable that might change. The Intrinsics will copy the returned value before calling the converter again, so a static variable suffices.

- If the conversion succeeded and *to–>addr* is not NULL, copy the converted value to the address in *to–>addr* after verifying that *to–>size* is large enough to hold the value. If *to–>size* is large enough, update it to the actual size and return TRUE; if it is not large enough, update it to the required size and return FALSE.

- If the conversion failed, issue a warning message and return FALSE without updating any fields in the *to* parameter. The failure usually reflects a misspelled resource file entry; a warning is appropriate since the Intrinsics then use the default resource value in this case.

The Label widget uses a simple converter to convert strings into justification values. Example 3.7 shows this procedure. It first checks that the number of additional arguments is zero and issues an error if not. Then it converts the passed value to lower-case since it is appropriate for this conversion to be case-insensitive. The LowerCase procedure, not shown here, copies the string in its first argument into the second, converting characters to lower-case as it goes. It returns TRUE if the source string is too long to fit into the destination, using its third argument as the destination length. See the complete Label implementation in Chapter 10 for the LowerCase code.

If the string is too long to fit into the lower-case buffer, it cannot possibly be a valid value, so CvtStringToJustify only tests for valid values if the entire string was successfully copied. CvtStringToJustify compares the lower-cased value against the three possible valid string values and sets the static variable *j* accordingly. If no match was found or the string was too long, CvtStringToJustify issues a warning message; otherwise it fills in the *to* parameter with the converted value. The statements in the final "if" cover the various options for returning the converted value depending upon *to–>addr*.

```
Boolean CvtStringToJustify(dpy, args, num_args, from, to, data)
    Display *dpy;
    XrmValuePtr args;
    Cardinal *num_args;
    XrmValuePtr from, to;
    XtPointer *data;
{
#define LOWER_SIZE 10
    char lower[LOWER_SIZE];      /* Lower-cased string value */
    register int i;
    Boolean badConvert;
    static Justify j;

    if (*num_args != 0) {        /* Check for correct number */
        XtAppErrorMsg(XtDisplayToApplicationContext(dpy),
                "cvtStringToJustify", "wrongParameters",
                "XtToolkitError",
                "String to justify conversion needs no extra arguments",
                (String *) NULL, (Cardinal *) NULL);
    }

    /* Lower case the value */
    badConvert = LowerCase(from->addr, lower, LOWER_SIZE);

    /* Try to convert if a short enough string specified */
    if (!badConvert) {
        if (strcmp(lower, "left") == 0) j = Left;
        else if (strcmp(lower, "center") == 0) j = Center;
        else if (strcmp(lower, "right") == 0) j = Right;
        else badConvert = TRUE;
    }

    /* String too long or unknown value -- issue warning */
    if (badConvert) {
        XtDisplayStringConversionWarning(dpy, from->addr, "Justify");
    } else {
        if (to->addr == NULL) to->addr = (caddr_t) &j;
        else if (to->size < sizeof(Justify)) badConvert = TRUE;
        else *(Justify *) to->addr = j;

        to->size = sizeof(Justify);
    }
    return !badConvert;
#undef LOWER_SIZE
}
```

Example 3.7. The string-to-justification converter

```
Boolean CvtStringToJustify(dpy, args, num_args, from, to, data)
    Display *dpy;
    XrmValuePtr args;
    Cardinal *num_args;
    XrmValuePtr from, to;
    XtPointer *data;
{
#define LOWER_SIZE 10
    char lower[LOWER_SIZE];      /* Lower-cased string value */
    register int i;
    Boolean badConvert;
    XrmQuark q;
    static Justify j;
    static XrmQuark Qleft, Qcenter, Qright;
    static Boolean haveQuarks = FALSE;

    if (*num_args != 0) {        /* Check for correct number */
        XtAppErrorMsg(XtDisplayToApplicationContext(dpy),
                "cvtStringToJustify", "wrongParameters",
                "XtToolkitError",
                "String to justify conversion needs no extra arguments",
                (String *) NULL, (Cardinal *) NULL);
    }

    if (!haveQuarks) {
        Qleft   = XrmStringToQuark("left");
        Qcenter = XrmStringToQuark("center");
        Qright  = XrmStringToQuark("right");
        haveQuarks = TRUE;
    }

    badConvert = LowerCase(from->addr, lower, LOWER_SIZE);

    /* Try to convert if a short enough string specified */

    if (!badConvert) {
        q = XrmStringToQuark(lower);
        if (q == Qleft) j = Left;
        else if (q == Qcenter) j = Center;
        else if (q == Qright) j = Right;
        else badConvert = TRUE;
    }
```

(continued)

Example 3.8.   The string-to-justification converter using quarks

```
        /* String too long or unknown value -- issue warning */

    if (badConvert) {
        XtDisplayStringConversionWarning(dpy, from->addr, "Justify");
    } else {
        if (to->addr == NULL) to->addr = (caddr_t) &j;
        else if (to->size < sizeof(Justify)) badConvert = TRUE;
        else *(Justify *) to->addr = j;

        to->size = sizeof(Justify);
    }
    return !badConvert;
#undef LOWER_SIZE
}
```

Example 3.8. The string-to-justification converter using quarks

Some type converters must perform many string comparisons. This is not as much of a problem as it might be since the Intrinsics only call the converter once for each source value encountered, with the conversion cache providing the value in the case of duplicates. However, if the comparisons do impact performance (there might be many valid values to compare against), the *quark* routines provided by Xlib's resource manager can help.

A quark is a unique identifier for a string; any two different strings always have different quarks, and multiple occurrences of the same string always have the same quark. The conversion procedure can get quark values for all the possible valid source values the first time it is called. On each call, it converts the source to a quark and compares the quarkified source against the valid quarks. To decide whether the trade-off is worthwhile, in most implementations turning a string into a quark takes approximately twice as long as a string comparison. The cost of initially turning the valid source values into quarks must be amortized over the lifetime of the conversion procedure. Using quarks is more efficient when there are more than eight valid source values or, possibly, when writing an uncached converter.

Example 3.8 shows a version of the string-to-justification converter that uses quarks. For more information about quarks, see Section 10.11 of *Xlib*.

Though CvtStringToJustify needs no additional conversion arguments, consider a converter that turns a widget name into a widget value. This would allow users control over where to insert a widget into a menu by allowing the user to specify an existing widget that the new widget should precede; see the

```
static Boolean CvtStringToWidget(dpy, args, num_args, from, to, data)
    Display *dpy;
    XrmValuePtr args;
    Cardinal *num_args;
    XrmValuePtr from, to;
    XtPointer *data;
{
    static Widget w;
    Widget parent;
    Boolean badConvert;

    if (*num_args != 1) {
        XtAppErrorMsg(XtDisplayToApplicationContext(dpy),
                "wrongParameters", "cvtStringToWidget",
                "XtToolkitError",
                "StringToWidget conversion needs parent arg",
                (String *) NULL, (Cardinal *) NULL);
    }

    /* Convert first arg into parent */

    parent = *(Widget*) args[0].addr;

    w = XtNameToWidget(parent, (String) from->addr);
    badConvert = (w == NULL);

    if (badConvert) {
        XtDisplayStringConversionWarning(dpy, from->addr, "Widget");
    } else {
        if (to->addr == NULL) to->addr = (caddr_t) &w;
        else if (to->size < sizeof(Widget)) badConvert = TRUE;
        else *(Widget *) to->addr = w;

        to->size = sizeof(Widget);
    }
    return !badConvert;
}
```

Example 3.9. The string-to-widget converter

Menu implementation in Chapter 10 for more details. In order to search for a matching widget, the converter needs the widget's parent.

Example 3.9 shows a conversion procedure to convert strings to widgets. How the converter gets the parent is described in the next section; for the moment just accept that *args*[0] contains the parent. CvtStringToWidget makes sure it has the correct number of arguments and then casts the first argument into a widget. XtNameToWidget, described in Chapter 9, takes a widget and a string and returns a child of the widget whose name matches the string. If `XtNameToWidget` succeeds, the converter returns the child; otherwise the converter issues a warning message.

`XtDisplayStringConversionWarning` is a convenience routine for resource converters that convert from a string to some other type.[16]

> void XtDisplayStringConversionWarning(*display, src, dst_type*)
>   Display **display*;
>   String *src, dst_type*;
> *display*   Specifies the display to use to find the warning handler.
> *src*   Specifies the string that could not be converted.
> *dst_type*   Specifies the name of the type that could not be converted into.

This function issues a warning message with name "conversionError", type "string", class "XtToolkitError", and the default message string "Cannot convert "*src*" to type *dst_type*." For more information on warning messages, see Section 9.6. Previous versions of the Intrinsics supplied a different procedure, `XtStringConversionWarning`, which still remains for compatibility. See Appendix C.

Under certain circumstances, described in the next section, the Intrinsics will remove a cached entry from the conversion cache. For many types of resources nothing special needs to be done to free the resource value; just freeing the value is enough. Other resource types, particularly those that are pointers, require some additional processing.

Consider the string-to-font-structure converter. The type XtRFontStruct is actually a pointer to a font structure; to completely reclaim the storage the Intrinsics must call `XFreeFont`. The Intrinsics support this by allowing a destructor function to be associated with any type converter; this is of type `XtDestructor`.[17]

> typedef void (*XtDestructor) (XtAppContext, XrmValuePtr, XtPointer, XrmValuePtr,
>   Cardinal *)
>   XtAppContext *app_context*;
>   XrmValuePtr *to*;
>   XtPointer *converter_data*;

---

[16] `XtDisplayStringConversionWarning` is not supported by Intrinsics implementations that conform to specifications earlier than Release 4.

[17] Destructor functions are not supported by Intrinsics implementations that conform to specifications earlier than Release 4.

       XrmValuePtr *args*;
       Cardinal **num_args*;

app_context	Specifies the application context in which the resource is being freed.
to	Specifies the resource being freed as returned by the type converter.
converter_data	Specifies the *converter_data* returned by the type converter.
args	Specifies the additional converter arguments as passed to the type converter when the conversion was performed.
num_args	Specifies the number of additional converter arguments.

The destructor is responsible for freeing any auxiliary storage associated with the resource conversion. It should not free the storage directly in the *to* argument or in any of the additional converter arguments; the Intrinsics free this storage themselves after calling the destructor.

Any type converter that needs to pass extra information to its destructor can store it in its *converter_data* parameter before returning; the Intrinsics pass *converter_data* uninterpreted to the destructor. If the type converter needs to pass more than a single word of information, it should allocate a data structure and put its address in *converter_data*; the destructor must free this structure after using the information in it.

Example 3.10 shows a converter that converts a string containing embedded newlines into a NULL-terminated list of the substrings. Its return value is a pointer to the string list. Both the string list and the substrings are in allocated storage.

Example 3.11 shows the corresponding destructor, which frees all the storage allocated by the converter. This pair of procedures does not need to use *converter_data* to communicate.

Type converters can call other type converters with `XtCallConverter`. Besides eliminating duplicated code, this can improve efficiency if several converters that convert to the same type use a common intermediate result, since the intermediate result is entered in the conversion cache and returned immediately if used again.[18]

typedef long XtCacheRef;

Boolean XtCallConverter(*display, converter, args, num_args, from, to_in_out,*
                            cache_ref_return)

---

[18] `XtCallConverter` is not supported by Intrinsics implementations that conform to specifications earlier than Release 4.

```
static Boolean CvtStringToStringList(dpy, args, num_args,
        from, to, data)
    Display *dpy;
    XrmValuePtr args;
    Cardinal *num_args;
    XrmValuePtr from, to;
    XtPointer *data;
{
    register int i, count = 1;
    register char *ch, *start = from->addr;
    static String *list;
    int len;

    if (*num_args != 0) {
        XtAppErrorMsg(XtDisplayToApplicationContext(dpy),
            "cvtStringToStringList", "wrongParameters",
            "XtToolkitError",
            "String to string list conversion needs no extra arguments",
            (String *) NULL, (Cardinal *) NULL);
    }
    if (to->addr != NULL && to->size < sizeof(String *)) {
        to->size = sizeof(String *);
        return FALSE;
    }
    if (start == NULL || *start == '\0') list = NULL;
    else {
        for (ch = start; *ch != '\0'; ch++) {     /* Count strings */
            if (*ch == '\n') count++;
        }
        list = (String *) XtCalloc(count+1, sizeof(String));

        for (i = 0; i < count; i++) {
            for (ch = start; *ch != '\n' && *ch != '\0'; ch++) {}
            len = ch - start;
            list[i] = XtMalloc(len + 1);
            (void) strncpy(list[i], start, len);
            list[i][len] = '\0';
            start = ch + 1;
        }
    }
    if (to->addr == NULL) to->addr = (caddr_t) &list;
    else *(String **) to->addr = list;
    to->size = sizeof(String *);
    return TRUE;
}
```

Example 3.10. The string-to-string-list converter

```
static void StringListDestructor(app, to, converter_data,
        args, num_args)
    XtAppContext app;
    XrmValuePtr to;
    XtPointer converter_data;
    XrmValuePtr args;
    Cardinal *num_args;
{

    String *list = (String *) to->addr;
    register String *entry;

    if (list == NULL) return;

    for (entry = list; entry != NULL; entry++) {
        XtFree((XtPointer) entry);
    }

    XtFree((XtPointer) list);
}
```

Example 3.11. The string-to-string-list destructor

Display *display*;
XtTypeConverter *converter*;
XrmValuePtr *args*;
Cardinal *num_args*;
XrmValuePtr *from*;
XrmValuePtr *to_in_out*;
XtCacheRef *cache_ref_return*;

display	Specifies the display to pass to the type converter.
converter	Specifies the conversion procedure to call.
args	Specifies the argument list containing the additional arguments needed to perform the conversion, or NULL.
num_args	Specifies the number of entries in the argument list (often zero).
from	Specifies the value to be converted.
to_in_out	Specifies a descriptor for a location to store the converted value into.
cache_ref_return	Returns a cache id, or NULL.

If *to_in_out->addr* is NULL, the type converter replaces it with a pointer to the converted value and sets *to_in_out->size* to the size of the converted value. The caller must copy the data before executing any other toolkit functions and must not modify the pointed-to data in any way.

If *to_in_out->addr* is not NULL, the type converter assumes it points to storage to hold the converted value and that *to_in_out->size* specifies the size of the destination storage. If the destination storage is large enough to hold the converted value, the type converter stores the converted value there and sets *to_in_out–>size* to the actual size of the converted value.

XtCallConverter returns TRUE if the conversion succeeded. Possible reasons for failure include trying to convert an illegal source value or not specifying enough storage to hold the converted value. In the last case the type converter updates *to_in_out–>size* to the needed size.

If the type converter was registered as a cached conversion, XtCallConverter stores the result in the conversion cache. If the type converter was registered as a reference-counted conversion, *cache_ref_return* returns a cache id. If the caller of XtCallConverter is not able or willing to store the cache id, *cache_ref_return* should be NULL. The next two sections include information on reference counting.

As an example of when XtCallConverter is useful, assume type converters are needed to convert from source types S1 and S2 to destination type D, and that the code to convert from S2 is a subset of the code to convert from S1. The converter for S1 first converts the value to type S2 and then calls the S2-to-D converter to do the final conversion. Besides eliminating duplicate code, this has the advantage that the resource cache ends up containing entries for both source types, so that a later call to convert from S2 would find the conversion already cached.

3.21   Adding New Type Converters

To inform the Intrinsics about a new type converter, use XtSetType-Converter or XtAppSetTypeConverter.[19]

typedef int XtCacheType;

void XtSetTypeConverter(*from_type, to_type, converter, convert_args, num_args, cache_type,*
      destructor)
 String *from_type*;
 String *to_type*;
 XtTypeConverter *converter*;
 XtConvertArgList *convert_args*;
 Cardinal *num_args*;
 XtCacheType *cache_type*;

---

[19] XtSetTypeConverter and XtAppSetTypeConverter are not supported by Intrinsics implementations that conform to specifications earlier than Release 4.

XtDestructor *destructor*;

from_type	Specifies the source type.
to_type	Specifies the destination type.
converter	Specifies the type conversion procedure.
convert_args	Specifies the additional conversion arguments, or NULL.
num_args	Specifies the number of additional conversion arguments, or zero.
cache_type	Specifies how values resulting from this conversion should be cached.
destructor	Specifies a destructor for values resulting from this conversion, or NULL.

Registering a type converter with the same source and destination types as an already registered one replaces the old type converter with the new one. The additional conversion arguments do not have to match in the new and old converters.

`XtSetTypeConverter` makes the specified type converter available in all application contexts, both those currently present and those created in the future by the same process. To make a converter available to just one application context, use `XtAppSetTypeConverter`.

void XtAppSetTypeConverter(*app_context, from_type, to_type, converter, convert_args, num_args, cache_type, destructor*)

XtAppContext *app_context*;
String *from_type*;
String *to_type*;
XtTypeConverter *converter*;
XtConvertArgList *convert_args*;
Cardinal *num_args*;
XtCacheType *cache_type*;
XtDestructor *destructor*;

app_context	Specifies the application context.
from_type	Specifies the source type.
to_type	Specifies the destination type.
converter	Specifies the type conversion procedure.
convert_args	Specifies the additional conversion arguments, or NULL.
num_args	Specifies the number of additional conversion arguments, or zero.
cache_type	Specifies how values resulting from this conversion should be cached.
destructor	Specifies a destructor for values resulting from this conversion, or NULL.

Using `XtAppSetTypeConverter` is quite rare, and this function exists primarily for backward compatibility. Most converters are added during widget class initialization, and since widget classes are global to all application contexts, their type converters need to be global also.

Many type converters need no additional arguments, so `XtSetType-Converter` can specify NULL as the converter argument. Converters like CvtStringToWidget in the previous section need additional information from the widget in order to perform the conversion, and the programmer must tell the Intrinsics how to supply this extra information.

Additional conversion arguments are described in records of type `XtConvertArgRec`.

```
typedef enum {XtAddress, XtBaseOffset, XtImmediate, XtResourceString,
              XtResourceQuark, XtWidgetBaseOffset, XtProcedureArg}
          XtAddressMode;
typedef struct {
    XtAddressMode      address_mode;
    XtPointer          address_id;
    Cardinal           size;
} XtConvertArgRec, *XtConvertArgList;
```

Each XtConvertArgRec describes one additional argument for the converter. The *address_mode* field determines how to interpret the *address_id* field to find the data passed to the type converter.

XtBaseOffset   The *address_id* is an offset the Intrinsics add to the address of the widget to obtain the address of the data.

XtWidgetBaseOffset

  The *address_id* is an offset the Intrinsics add to the address of the widget to obtain the address of the data. If the widget is not a subclass of Core, the Intrinsics add the offset to the address of the closest ancestor that is a widget to obtain the address of the data. See Chapter 8 for information on nonwidget objects.[20]

XtResourceString The *address_id* is the name of a resource that the Intrinsics look up in the widget, and the value of the resource's field is the data.

XtResourceQuark

  The *address_id* is a quarkified version of an XtResourceString.

---

[20] `XtWidgetBaseOffset` is not supported by Intrinsics implementations that conform to specifications earlier than Release 4.

XtAddress   The *address_id* is the address of variable data.

XtImmediate   The *address_id* is the data.

XtProcedureArg The *address_id* is a pointer to a procedure that returns the data.

XtBaseOffset allows converters to use fields in the widget being converted for. XtWidgetBaseOffset is similar to XtBaseOffset, but allows conversions for non-widget objects to depend upon window and display fields in their closest widget ancestor. It is the most commonly used address mode.

XtResourceString and XtResourceQuark are similar to XtBaseOffset but allow conversions to depend upon widget fields that exist in different places in different widget classes. XtBaseOffset only works if the field is always in the same place, usually because it is a Core field.

XtImmediate is useful for passing constant information to a converter. A string-to-bitmap converter might treat the source string as a file name that contains the bitmap information and use an XtImmediate argument to pass in a directory name that contains the bitmap file. This directory name would most likely be an application resource.

XtAddress is similar to XtImmediate, but *address_id* points to data that can change over time. The Intrinsics copy all the data into the conversion cache for each conversion.

XtProcedureArg provides an escape if none of the other argument types suffice. *Address_id* should point to a procedure of type `XtConvertArgProc`.

```
typedef void (*XtConvertArgProc) (Widget, Cardinal *, XrmValue *)
      Widget w;
      Cardinal *size;
      XrmValue *value;
```
w   Specifies the widget the resource is being converted for, or NULL if the conversion is from `XtCallConverter`.
size   Specifies the size from the `XtConvertArgRec`.
value   Specifies a descriptor the procedure stores the data into.

The Intrinsics call this procedure before calling the converter. It should fill in the *value* parameter with the conversion argument. The returned value must last as long as the widget does. Using an XtProcedureArg argument should be considered the last resort; usually some other type is better.

In all cases the *size* field should contain the size of the additional data.

This code adds the string-to-widget converter:

```
static XtConvertArgRec parentConvertArgs[] = {
    {XtBaseOffset, (XtPointer) XtOffsetOf(WidgetRec, core.parent),
        sizeof(Widget)},
};

XtSetTypeConverter(XtRString, XtRWidget, CvtStringToWidget,
    parentConvertArgs, XtNumber(parentConvertArgs), XtCacheNone,
    (XtDestructor) NULL);
```

The *address_mode* field specifies that the Intrinsics should add the *address_id* field (the offset of the *parent* field in the widget) to the address of the widget to obtain the address of the additional argument. The size of this argument is the size of a `Widget` value. The conversion argument will thus be the value of the widget's parent.

Many conversions depend upon the screen or colormap. Converters that make server calls like `XCreatePixmap` or `XLoadFont` need the screen, and anything that converts into a pixel value needs the colormap. The Intrinsics define two sets of conversion arguments, `screenConvertArg` and `colorConvertArgs`, for these uses. With `screenConvertArg` the widget's screen is in the first argument, and with `colorConvertArgs` the widget's screen is in the first argument and the widget's colormap in the second argument.

```
XtConvertArgRec screenConvertArg[ ] = {
    {XtWidgetBaseOffset, (XtPointer) XtOffsetOf(WidgetRec, core.screen),
        sizeof(Screen *)}
};

XtConvertArgRec colorConvertArgs[ ] = {
    {XtWidgetBaseOffset, (XtPointer) XtOffsetOf(WidgetRec, core.screen),
        sizeof(Screen *)},
    {XtWidgetBaseOffset, (XtPointer) XtOffsetOf(WidgetRec, core.colormap),
        sizeof(Colormap)}
};
```

The *address_mode* of the arguments is XtWidgetBaseOffset arguments so that conversions for a nonwidget object use the screen and colormap from the nearest widget ancestor.

The *cache_type* parameter to `XtSetTypeConverter` should use the following values:

```
#define XtCacheAll 0x001
#define XtCacheNone 0x002
#define XtCacheByDisplay 0x003
#define XtCacheRefCount 0x100
```

These values have the following meanings:

XtCacheAll   Enter all values resulting from calling this type converter into the
                conversion cache.

XtCacheNone   Never enter values resulting from calling this type converter into the
                conversion cache.

XtCacheByDisplay
                Enter values resulting from calling this type converter into the con-
                version cache marked so that they can be invalidated if the display is
                closed with XtCloseDisplay.

XtCacheRefCount
                If this value is OR'ed together with one of the other values, the
                Intrinsics reference-count entries in the conversion cache resulting
                from calling this type converter. If all widgets that use a value get
                destroyed, the Intrinsics invalidate and free the cache entry. Specify-
                ing XtCacheRefCount with XtCacheNone is not meaningful.

Specify XtCacheAll for converters that do not rely on the display, screen, or
any other volatile data to perform the conversion. The string-to-justification
value converter should be registered with XtCacheAll.

Specify XtCacheNone for converters that rely upon volatile data other than
the display or screen, for converters that perform trivial conversions, or for
conversions that are not expected to be used more than once. Examples are
the string-to-widget converter (the widget conversion argument could become
invalid) and the Boolean-to-integer converter (so simple that it is faster to
convert each time than to look up the cached value).

Specify XtCacheByDisplay for converters that rely upon the display or
screen so that the Intrinsics can invalidate the cache elements when the display is closed. The built-in string-to-pixel, string-to-font, and string-to-font-
structure converters are registered with XtCacheByDisplay.

Specifying XtCacheRefCount trades off space used by the conversion cache
for time to do the conversions. When an application destroys the last widget
using a reference-counted resource, the Intrinsics invalidate the conversion

cache entry and reclaim the storage used by the converted value. If the same conversion is necessary later on for a new widget, the Intrinsics perform it again since the cached value is no longer available.

Which predefined conversions are reference-counted is implementation-specific; the following guidelines can help decide when reference counting is appropriate:

• To minimize the amount of space taken up by the conversion cache, reference-count many resource conversions.

• To minimize the amount of time used in resource conversion, reference-count few resource conversions.

• Reference counting incurs some space overhead. To optimize the Intrinsics for applications that do not destroy many widgets, reference-count few resource conversions.

• To optimize the Intrinsics for long-running applications that create and destroy many widgets, reference-count many resource conversions.

• Reference counting conversions that use server resources saves space in the server. A long-running application that does not reference-count pixel values could end up using the entire colormap.

• Reference counting conversions with large source or destination values or many or large converter arguments saves the most space.

• Not reference counting conversions that require a round trip to the server saves the most time. A server round trip typically takes several milliseconds.

• Applications can control reference counting by using the XtNinitialResourcesPersistent resource, but they cannot enable it for conversions that were not registered as reference-counted. Reference counting many resource conversions gives the application writer the most flexibility.

If a destructor procedure is specified with the type converter, the Intrinsics will call it before freeing the storage in the cache record. Only converters that need to do extra work to reclaim the storage used by the converted value need to specify a destructor procedure; of the sample converters in the previous section only the string-to-string-list converter requires a destructor. To register this converter with reference counting, specify

```
XtSetTypeConverter(XtRString, XtRStringTable,
    CvtStringToStringList, (XtConvertArgList) NULL, 0,
    XtCacheAll | XtCacheRefCount, StringListDestructor);
```

3.22   Reference Counting

If a resource converter was registered with reference counting, the Intrinsics count uses of resource values resulting from the converter. The reference count is initialized to 1 when the converter returns the value, and the Intrinsics increment the count any time they return the value directly from the conversion cache.

Almost all resource conversions are associated with some widget. The routines that create widgets (XtCreateWidget, XtCreateManaged-Widget, XtCreatePopupShell, XtAppCreateShell, and their varargs versions) associate the conversion with the widget being created. XtGet-ApplicationResources, XtGetSubresources, their varargs versions, and XtConvertAndStore associate the conversion with the widget parameter to the routine. The Intrinsics associate any resource conversions implicitly requested through XtVaTypedArg parameters in a variable argument list with the widget being created or with the widget parameter to the varargs routine. When the Intrinsics destroy a widget, they decrement the reference count of all conversions associated with the widget. If the count reaches zero, the Intrinsics invalidate the cache entry and reclaim its storage, calling the destructor procedure associated with the converter if one exists.

When a widget implementation or a type converter uses XtCall-Converter directly, the Intrinsics do not have a widget to associate the conversion with and so return a cache identifier along with the converted result. It is the responsibility of the calling code to decrement the reference count itself by using XtAppReleaseCacheRefs.[21]

void XtAppReleaseCacheRefs(*app_context, refs*)
    XtAppContext *app_context*;
    XtCacheRef *refs*;

app_context   Specifies the application context.
refs   Specifies a NULL-terminated list of cache ids to decrement.

XtAppReleaseCacheRefs decrements the reference count for all conversions with the specified cache identifiers and frees the cache entry if the reference count reaches zero.

---

[21] XtAppReleaseCacheRefs and its associated callback routines are not supported by Intrinsics implementations that conform to specifications earlier than Release 4.

Code calling `XtCallConverter` must call `XtAppReleaseCacheRefs` with the cache identifier returned from the call when no further references to the converted value are possible. If a type converter calls `XtCallConverter`, it typically passes the cache identifier to its corresponding destructor using the *converter_data* parameter, and the destructor calls `XtAppRelease-CacheRefs`.

When a widget implementation calls `XtCallConverter` it usually stores the converted value in a widget record, so the reference count should be decremented when the widget gets destroyed. The easiest way to do this is to add `XtCallbackReleaseCacheRef` or `XtCallbackReleaseCache-RefList` to the widget's destroy callback list.

void XtCallbackReleaseCacheRef(*w, client_data, call_data*)
    Widget *w*;
    XtPointer *client_data, call_data*;
w   Specifies the widget, which is used to find the application context.
client_data   Specifies a cache identifier.
call_data   Ignored for this callback.

`XtCallbackReleaseCacheRef` calls `XtAppReleaseCacheRefs` specifying its client data as the cache identifier. When a procedure adds `XtCallbackReleaseCacheRef` to a callback list, it must specify a cache identifier as the *client_data*.

void XtCallbackReleaseCacheRefList(*w, client_data, call_data*)
    Widget *w*;
    XtPointer *client_data, call_data*;
w   Specifies the widget, which is used to find the application context.
client_data   Specifies a pointer to a NULL-terminated list of cache identifiers.
call_data   Ignored for this callback.

`XtCallbackReleaseCacheRefList` is just like `XtCallbackRelease-CacheRef`, but it treats its client data as a pointer to a NULL-terminated list of cache identifiers. Code adding `XtCallbackReleaseCacheRefList` must specify the *client_data* accordingly.

If neither of the two preceding cases apply, the code must keep track of the cache identifier somehow and release it when the converted value will no longer be used. If keeping track of the identifier is impossible, the code should specify NULL as its *cache_ref_return* parameter; this disables reference counting for this particular resource value since there is no way for the Intrinsics to know when it is safe to reclaim the storage.

3.23   Providing Resource Values

When an application calls `XtGetValues`, the Intrinsics copy the requested resources into the storage pointed to by the argument list entries. The widget's resource list provides all the information the Intrinsics need to find the data; the widget implementation does not need to be involved.

Occasionally a widget has to do something extra for an `XtGetValues` request. Some widget resources could be expensive to compute or to keep correct, and an implementation may choose to do lazy evaluation, updating these fields only when they are actually needed. Similarly, some widgets provide resources that applications can query but that are not stored at all; the widget computes them only when they are requested.

A widget implementation can intervene in an `XtGetValues` request by providing a get_values_hook procedure, which is of type `XtArgsProc`.

typedef void (*XtArgsProc) (Widget, ArgList, Cardinal *);
    Widget *w*;
    ArgList *args*;
    Cardinal **num_args*;

w	Specifies the widget.
args	Specifies the argument list passed to the creation procedure or to `XtGetValues`.
num_args	Specifies the number of arguments in the argument list.

Get_values_hook is a superclass-to-subclass chained procedure, so the Intrinsics call the get_values_hook procedures for a widget class after calling those for all superclasses. Before calling any hooks, the Intrinsics fill in the values in the argument list for resources specified in the resource lists of this widget class or its superclasses. The hook procedure looks in the argument list for any resources that need special processing and fills in the appropriate value. The value field of the argument list points to the location to store the resource into; if the resource is of type *type*, the correct code to assign the value is

    `*` (*type* `*`) (`args[i].value`) `=` *resource-value*;

The get_values_hook procedure can also provide values for resources stored in data structures other than the widget structure; see Section 3.25. Both uses are rather rare; most widget implementations specify NULL for *get_values_hook*.

3.24   Setting Resource Values

When an application tries to set the values of widget resources using `XtSetValues` the widget implementation must react to these changes. Ways that it can react include

- Accepting a change as made.

- Informing the server of a changed value.

- Creating private copies of resources specified by address.

- Updating derived fields like graphics contexts to reflect the changes.

- Denying a change. For example, the Core class denies attempts to change the widget's screen since the X Window System does not support moving a window to another screen.

- Checking fields for consistency.

The set_values procedure in the widget implementation is responsible for reacting to the change request. This is a superclass-to-subclass chained procedure of type `XtSetValuesFunc`.[22]

```
typedef Boolean (*XtSetValuesFunc)(Widget, Widget, Widget, Arglist, Cardinal *);
    Widget old;
    Widget request;
    Widget new;
    ArgList args;
    Cardinal *num_args;
```

old	Specifies a copy of the widget as it was before the `XtSetValues` call.
request	Specifies a copy of the widget with all values changed as asked for in the `XtSetValues` call but before any class set_values procedures have been called.
new	Specifies the widget with the changes asked for in the `XtSetValues` call, modified by calls to superclass set_values procedures.
args	Specifies the argument list passed to `XtSetValues`.
num_args	Specifies the number of arguments.

    The *new* parameter points to the real widget; *old* and *request* point to copies. All changes should be made to the *new* widget—never modify *old* or *request*—and if the set_values procedure calls any procedures that take a widget parameter, it should specify *new* as the widget.

---

[22] The *args* and *num_args* parameters are not supported by Intrinsics implementations that conform to specifications earlier than Release 4.

The *args* and *num_args* parameters are described at the end of this section.

Set_values procedures can tell if the application changed a resource by comparing the field values in the *old* and the *new* widgets. A set_values procedure is like a widget initialize procedure in many ways, and the set_values and initialize procedures for a widget class usually look similar. Like the initialize procedure, the set_values procedure deals mostly with fields in its widget's instance part, leaving fields in the superclasses' instance parts to the superclasses' set_values procedures.

As with initialization, sometimes the set_values procedure needs to know whether the value in a changed field in a superclass's part came from the application or from some superclass's own set_values procedure. The Label and Pushbutton classes again provide the canonical example here; many implementations (including the one in this book) of Label react to having their width and height set to zero by recalculating the width and height based upon the size of the label's text string. The Pushbutton class might want to make these larger to make room for graphics to give the button a three-dimensional appearance, but it should only do this if the Label set_values procedure computed the dimensions. If the application specified the values directly, Pushbutton should make do with the space allowed.

The *request* parameter provides the needed information to resolve these cases just as with initialize procedures. It is a copy of the widget with the changes requested by `XtSetValues` before the Intrinsics invoked any superclass set_values procedures. If the field in the *request* parameter has a special value like zero indicating that the widget should recompute the resource, the set_values procedure can safely modify it; if the field has a valid value, it should be left alone.

Just as with initialize, the set_values procedures must copy some reference resources. The same resources must be copied here as were copied in initialize. Since these resources were also copied by the initialize procedure (or by an earlier invocation of the set_values procedure), the old allocated memory must be freed. The appropriate field in the *old* parameter contains the pointer to the old memory.

A set_values procedure must also do the same consistency checking for mutually dependent fields as the initialize procedure does.

A set_values procedure returns a Boolean value to indicate whether the widget needs to be redisplayed based upon the changes. Since a subclass

☞ set_values procedure might modify or disallow the changes, set_values procedures should never redisplay their widget directly. Instead they return TRUE when redisplay is needed. If any of the set_values procedures for a widget returned TRUE, the Intrinsics clear the widget's window to its background, causing the server to generate an expose event that in turn invokes the widget's expose procedure.

☞ Similarly, a set_values procedure should never react to changes to the geometry (size or position) or request a new geometry. Subclasses can modify geometry fields, and the widget's parent has the final authority to determine the widget's geometry. Instead, the set_values procedure should store (or leave) any desired changes in the geometry fields. After calling all set_values procedures, the Intrinsics consult the parent to resolve any geometry changes and, if the parent permits the changes, call the widget's resize procedure. This takes place before redisplaying the widget.

If a widget class does not need to do anything in response to an XtSetValues call, it specifies NULL in the *set_values* field of its class record.

If the widget class has resources that are not stored in the widget, it can use the *args* and *num_args* parameters and the routine XtSetSubvalues to set their values. This is described in Section 3.25; its uses are rather rare.

Like initialize, set_values still has a hook procedure to support widgets that used it before the *args* and *num_args* parameters to the set_values procedure existed. It is of type XtArgsFunc.

```
typedef Boolean (*XtArgsFunc) (Widget, ArgList, Cardinal *);
    Widget w;
    ArgList args;
    Cardinal *num_args;
w               Specifies the widget.
args            Specifies the argument list passed to XtSetValues.
num_args        Specifies the number of arguments in the argument list.
```

The Intrinsics call this procedure, if present, immediately after the set_values procedure for the widget class. Its return value indicates whether the widget instance needs to be redisplayed as a result of the changes. The widget parameter is the same as the *new* parameter to the set_values procedure.

Example 3.12 shows the Label widget's set_values procedure. Compare it with Label's initialize procedure in Section 2.23 to see how set_values procedures parallel initialize procedures.

```
static Boolean SetValues(old, request, new, args, num_args)
    Widget   old, request, new;
    ArgList args;
    Cardinal *num_args;
{
    LabelWidget oldlw = (LabelWidget) old;
    LabelWidget newlw = (LabelWidget) new;
    Boolean redisplay = FALSE;

#define NE(field) (oldlw->field != newlw->field)

    /* If the label has been reset to NULL, change to the name */

    if (newlw->label.label == NULL) {
        newlw->label.label = newlw->core.name;
    }

    /* Decide whether to compute the size */

    if (newlw->core.width == 0 && newlw->core.height == 0) {
        newlw->label.size_computed = TRUE;
    } else if (NE(core.width) || NE(core.height)) {
        newlw->label.size_computed = FALSE;
        if (NE(core.width)) {
            newlw->label.desired_width = newlw->core.width;
        }
        if (NE(core.height)) {
            newlw->label.desired_height = newlw->core.height;
        }
    } /* else leave the same */

    /* If label, font, or accelerator string has changed,
       compute size and recopy */

    if (NE(label.label) || NE(label.font) || NE(label.accel_string)) {
        SetTextWidthAndHeight(newlw);
        redisplay = TRUE;

        if (NE(label.label)) {
            XtFree((char *) oldlw->label.label);
            newlw->label.label = XtNewString(newlw->label.label);
        }
        if (NE(label.accel_string)) {
            XtFree((char *) oldlw->label.accel_string);
            newlw->label.accel_string =
                    XtNewString(newlw->label.accel_string);
        }
    }
```

(continued)

Example 3.12.   The Label set_values procedure

```
/* Compute the size if necessary */

if ((newlw->label.size_computed && redisplay) ||
        newlw->core.width == 0) {
    newlw->label.desired_width = newlw->core.width =
            newlw->label.label_width + 2 * newlw->label.space;
}
if ((newlw->label.size_computed && redisplay) ||
        newlw->core.height == 0) {
    newlw->label.desired_height = newlw->core.height =
            newlw->label.label_height + 2 * newlw->label.space;
}

/* If foreground or font has changed, update GC */

if (NE(label.foreground) || NE(label.font->fid)) {
    XtReleaseGC(newlw, oldlw->label.gc);
    newlw->label.gc = GetNormalGC(newlw);

    if (newlw->label.current_gc == oldlw->label.gc) {
        newlw->label.current_gc = newlw->label.gc;
        redisplay = TRUE;
    }
}

return redisplay || NE(label.space) || NE(label.justify);
#undef NE
}
```

Example 3.12. The Label set_values procedure

It first checks if the new label is NULL and uses the widget's name if so. Then it decides whether to reset the *size_computed* flag that it uses to decide whether to resize the widget when its contents change. If the application set the width and height to zero, it means that the application wants the label to compute a size, so *size_computed* is set to force recomputation. If either width or height has a new, nonzero value, the label will stop recomputing its size when its contents change and remain this size. If neither is the case, *size_computed* retains its previous value.

If the text string, accelerator string, or the font structure changed, the saved text dimensions are no longer valid, so SetValues calls SetTextWidthAndHeight to recalculate them. If either string changed, it frees the old copy and creates a new copy.

If *size_computed* is TRUE, meaning that the label should resize itself in response to changed resources, and *redisplay* is TRUE, meaning that the text or font has changed, SetValues computes a new size. It also computes a new size if the corresponding field is now zero. Both checks are needed since the application can change one dimension field but leave the other one the same. This size computation incorporates any change to the internal space resource into the widget size.

Finally it checks if it needs to update the graphics context, releasing the old one and creating a new one if so. If *current_gc* matches the old graphics context, it means that the old context was the one being used for drawing, so SetValues updates *current_gc* to the new value. The procedure returns that the widget needs to be redisplayed if the label, the accelerator string, the font, the foreground, the background, the internal space, or the justification is different.

3.25   Subresources

Sometimes a widget class stores resources in a data structure other than its widget structure. A class might have a set of resources that are useful only for some instances of the widget, and to conserve space it could define a substructure that it allocates and points to in the widget data structure for those instances that use the resources. Another example would be a widget that contains other widgets as part of its interface but hides this internal structure from applications. An acknowledgment dialog box might include a Label widget to display a message and a pushbutton for the user to click in to dismiss the dialog; as far as the application is concerned, the message and the pushbutton callback belong to the acknowledgment widget.

Other widgets have resources that do not actually need to be stored anywhere; they exist only to derive other resources. An example would be a widget that allows the application to specify its height and width in millimeters rather than in pixel units. Such a widget defines two new resources, XtNheightMM and XtNwidthMM; if the application specifies a value for either, the widget converts the value into pixel units for storage in the widget instance record.

The toolkit allows widgets to fetch, query, and set resources that are not stored in the widget instance by using the argument list passed to the initialize, get_values_hook, and set_values procedures. These resources are called *subresources.*

```
typedef struct {
    int width_mm;
    int height_mm;
} mmDimensions;

static XtResource subresources[] = {
    {XtNwidthMM, XtCWidthMM, XtRInt, sizeof(int),
        XtOffsetOf(mmDimensions, width_mm),
        XtRImmediate, (XtPointer) -1},
    {XtNheightMM, XtCHeightMM, XtRInt, sizeof(int),
        XtOffsetOf(mmDimensions, height_mm),
        XtRImmediate, (XtPointer) -1}
};
```

Example 3.13. Subresources for millimeter dimension resources

If a widget has substructures, each substructure requires a resource list describing all the resources in that structure. If a widget has nonstored resources, the implementation defines a data structure to temporarily hold the resource values and defines a resource list defining the resources there. These resource lists are of the same format as a widget resource list; the Intrinsics compile them into an internal form the first time they are passed to a routine that manipulates subresources.

There are no simple examples to show subresources in substructures; these subresources are useful only in large, complicated widgets. This section shows sample implementations of subresources for the millimeter width and height resources.

Example 3.13 shows the structure definition and the subresources for these resources. The resource list differs from a widget resource list only in that the offsets are offsets into the mmDimensions structure instead of into a widget instance.

A class with subresources should initialize them by calling `XtGet-Subresources` in its initialize procedure, passing it the *args* and *num_args* parameters.

void XtGetSubresources(*w, base, name, class, resources, num_resources, args, num_args*)
    Widget *w*;
    XtPointer *base*;
    String *name*;
    String *class*;
    XtResourceList *resources*;

        Cardinal *num_resources*;
        ArgList *args*;
        Cardinal *num_args*;

w	Specifies the widget that wants subresources.
base	Specifies the address of the data structure that the resources should be stored into.
name	Specifies the name of the subpart.
class	Specifies the class of the subpart.
resources	Specifies the resource list for the subpart.
num_resources	Specifies the number of entries in the subresource list.
args	Specifies the argument list to override resources found in the resource database.
num_args	Specifies the number of entries in the argument list.

XtGetSubresources fills in the resource fields in the structure based on the argument list, the resource database, and the default values in the resource list. XtGetSubresources fetches resources from the database as if they were specified for a child of the widget with the specified name and class; these can be NULL to fetch resources for the widget itself.

A class that calls XtGetSubresources anywhere besides its initialize or initialize_hook procedure should document when it fetches resources from the database. Applications using these widgets must be careful about freeing the resource database.

Example 3.14 shows the code from the initialize procedure to deal with the subresources. The call to XtGetSubresources stores values into

```
{
    mmDimensions dim;

    XtGetSubresources(new, &dim, (String) NULL, (String) NULL,
        subresources, XtNumber(subresources), args, num_args);

    if (dim.width_mm != -1) {
        new->core.width = dim.width_mm * WidthOfScreen(XtScreen(new)) /
            WidthMMOfScreen(XtScreen(new));
    }
    if (dim.height_mm != -1) {
        new->core.height = dim.height_mm *
                HeightOfScreen(XtScreen(new)) /
                HeightMMOfScreen(XtScreen(new));
    }
}
```

Example 3.14. Initializing the subresources

dim.width_mm and *dim.height_mm* if the XtNwidthMM or XtNheightMM resources were specified in the argument list or in the resource database, or sets them to their default −1 if not. If either was specified, the procedure converts from millimeters to pixels and stores the value in the corresponding field in the widget instance structure.

A class with subresources should provide access to their values by calling XtGetSubvalues in its get_values_hook procedure, passing the argument list passed to the hook.

void XtGetSubvalues(*base, resources, num_resources, args, num_args*)
    XtPointer *base*;
    XtResourceList *resources*;
    Cardinal *num_resources*;
    ArgList *args*;
    Cardinal *num_args*;

base	Specifies the address of the data structure the resources are retrieved from.
resources	Specifies the subresource list.
num_resources	Specifies the number of entries in the subresource list.
args	Specifies the argument list with the resources to retrieve.
num_args	Specifies the number of entries in the argument list.

XtGetSubvalues stores the values of any resources specified in both the subresource list and the argument list into the storage pointed to by the value fields of the argument list entry.

Section 3.23 describes another way of providing subresources; its method is most appropriate when the subresources are expensive to compute since it allows lazy evaluation.

Example 3.15 shows the code from the get_values_hook procedure to provide the millimeter subresources. Note that the resource values must be computed each time, whether or not they were requested; this is why XtGetSubvalues is not useful for lazy evaluation.

A class with subresources should modify their values by calling XtSetSubvalues in its set_values procedure, passing the argument list passed to the procedure.

void XtSetSubvalues(*base, resources, num_resources, args, num_args*)
    XtPointer *base*;
    XtResourceList *resources*;

```
{
    mmDimensions dim;

    dim.width_mm = w->core.width * WidthMMOfScreen(XtScreen(w)) /
            WidthOfScreen(XtScreen(w));
    dim.height_mm = w->core.height * HeightMMOfScreen(XtScreen(w)) /
            HeightOfScreen(XtScreen(w));

    XtGetSubvalues(&dim, subresources, XtNumber(subresources),
            args, num_args);
}
```

Example 3.15. Providing subresource values

        Cardinal *num_resources*;
        ArgList *args*;
        Cardinal *num_args*;

base	Specifies the address of the data structure that the resources will be stored into.
resources	Specifies the subresource list.
num_resources	Specifies the number of entries in the subresource list.
args	Specifies the argument list specifying the resources to modify.
num_args	Specifies the number of entries in the argument list.

XtSetSubvalues updates the data structure with any resources specified in both the subresource list and the argument list. Any fields not specified in both are unchanged.

Example 3.16 shows the code from the set_values procedure that handles the subresources. Since XtSetSubvalues does not modify any fields not specified in the argument list, the code first initializes the fields to −1 and then checks to see if they have been changed.

Varargs interfaces to XtGetSubresources, XtGetSubvalues, and XtSetSubvalues also exist.[23]

void XtVaGetSubresources(*w, base, name, class, resources, num_resources, . . .*)
        Widget *w*;
        XtPointer *base*;
        String *name*;
        String *class*;
        XtResourceList *resources*;

---

[23] These interfaces are not supported by Intrinsics implementations that conform to specifications earlier than Release 4.

```
{
    static mmDimensions dim = {-1, -1};

    XtSetSubvalues(&dim, subresources, XtNumber(subresources),
            args, num_args);

    if (dim.width_mm != -1) {
        new->core.width = dim.width_mm * WidthOfScreen(XtScreen(new)) /
            WidthMMOfScreen(XtScreen(new));
    }
    if (dim.height_mm != -1) {
        new->core.height = dim.height_mm *
            HeightOfScreen(XtScreen(new)) /
            HeightMMOfScreen(XtScreen(new));
    }
}
```

Example 3.16. Modifying subresource values

Cardinal *num_resources*;

w	Specifies the widget that wants resources for a subpart.
base	Specifies the address of the subpart data structure that the resources should be stored into.
name	Specifies the name of the subpart.
class	Specifies the class of the subpart.
resources	Specifies the resource list for the subpart.
num_resources	Specifies the number of entries in the resource list.
. . .	Specifies the resource values to override resources found in the resource database.

void XtVaGetSubvalues(*base, resources, num_resources, . . .*)
    XtPointer *base*;
    XtResourceList *resources*;
    Cardinal *num_resources*;

base	Specifies the address of the data structure the resources are retrieved from.
resources	Specifies the subresource list.
num_resources	Specifies the number of entries in the resource list.
. . .	Specifies the resources to retrieve.

void XtVaSetSubvalues(*base, resources, num_resources, . . .*)
    XtPointer *base*;
    XtResourceList *resources*;
    Cardinal *num_resources*;

base	Specifies the address of the data structure that the resources will be stored into.
resources	Specifies the subresource list.
num_resources	Specifies the number of entries in the resource list.
...	Specifies the resources to modify.

These procedures are not very useful since the resource specifications always come to the initialize, get_values_hook, or set_values procedure as an argument list.

3.26   Callbacks

A widget implementation informs an application that something has happened by executing the procedures in a callback list. Callback lists are resources with representation type XtRCallback, and callbacks cannot be declared in subresource lists.

The Intrinsics compile callback lists into an internal form at widget creation time and translate to and from this form if the application modifies or fetches the callback resource using `XtSetValues` or `XtGetValues`. Widget implementations must treat all callback resources as opaque values and not look at or modify them directly.

A widget designer decides whether the widget should have one or many callbacks. Consider a Scrollbar widget; it might have multiple callbacks to indicate that the user wants to scroll up or down by one unit, scroll up or down by one page, or has moved the slider to a new location. An application that uses this widget must provide five callback procedures, one for each action. Alternatively, the widget can define a single callback that passes information in the *call_data* parameter indicating how the visible portion of the total available information changed as a result of the scrollbar interaction.

The Toggle widget provides another example. It could have two callbacks, one for when the user sets the toggle and one for when he resets it. Alternatively Toggle could have one callback that passes the toggle state in *call_data.*

Callbacks should make the application interface to the widget as simple as possible. Having five scrollbar callback procedures forces the application to determine how the scrolled region has changed and react appropriately. If the widget can do the calculations, the application code becomes much simpler, but the application must pass more information to the widget so that the widget can calculate how much to scroll. If the different callbacks perform variations on the same action, they should be combined into a single callback; if they perform different actions, they should be left separate.

In both the Scrollbar and the Toggle examples, applications become simpler if there is only one callback. An example of multiple callbacks occurs in the Pushbutton widget example in Chapter 10. It defines the XtNcallback resource, used when the user activates the pushbutton, and inherits the XtNloseSelection resource from Label, used when the widget loses the selection.

Occasionally a widget uses a callback procedure to get some data from the application. The widget passes a pointer to a data structure as the call data, and the application's callback procedure fills in the data structure.

The Intrinsics do not define the order in which they invoke callback procedures. Sometimes ordering is useful; for example, a text entry field might allow the application to validate the field before passing it to the callback that handles the data. This makes the application simpler since the validation code and the text-handling code are separate. To implement this the widget class defines two different callbacks that the widget invokes upon completion of the field. The validation callback has a field in its *call_data* parameter that the application sets to indicate whether the widget should invoke the text-handling callback. Sample code that implements this is

```
typedef struct {              /* This goes in the public header */
    String      string;       /* file so applications can use it*/
    Boolean     valid;
} ValidationStruct;

ValidationStruct v = {string, TRUE};
XtCallCallbackList(w, w->part.validation_callback,
        (XtPointer) &v);

if (v.valid) XtCallCallbackList(w, w->part.callback,
        (XtPointer) string);
```

An application that needs to do validation provides a validation callback:

```
void Callback(w, clientData, callData)
    Widget w;
    XtPointer clientData, callData;
{
    ValidationStruct *v = (ValidationStruct *) callData;

    if (/* v->string is invalid */) v->valid = FALSE;
}
```

Widgets usually invoke callback procedures as a result of user interactions; how to do this is described in Chapter 7. To invoke a callback the implementation uses `XtCallCallbackList`.[24]

void XtCallCallbackList(*w, callbacks, call_data*)
    Widget *w*;
    XtCallbackList *callbacks*;
    XtPointer *call_data*;

w	Specifies the widget whose callbacks are called.
callbacks	Specifies the address of a callback list in the widget.
call_data	Specifies the callback-specific data to pass to each of the callback procedures in the callback list.

The *callbacks* parameter must be a callback list in the widget, and the Intrinsics call all the procedures in the callback list in an undefined order. The widget documentation should describe the data in the *call_data* parameter; if no data are needed, *call_data* can be NULL. Simple callbacks like the one Pushbutton uses to notify the application that the user activated the button typically need no call data.

    `XtCallCallbackList` is new to the Intrinsics with Release 4; earlier versions used `XtCallCallbacks`, which specifies the callback list by its resource name.

void XtCallCallbacks(*w, callback_name, call_data*)
    Widget *w*;
    String *callback_name*;
    XtPointer *call_data*;

w	Specifies the widget whose callbacks are called.
callback_name	Specifies the name of the callback list to call.
call_data	Specifies the callback-specific data to pass to each of the callback procedures in the callback list.

Widget implementations should generally use `XtCallCallbackList` instead of `XtCallCallbacks` for efficiency. `XtCallCallbacks` exists for backward compatibility and for the few cases where code other than that in a widget implementation needs to call callbacks.

---

[24] `XtCallCallbackList` is not supported by Intrinsics implementations that conform to specifications earlier than Release 4.

Chapter 4

Composite Widgets and Geometry Management

Writing Applications

4.1 **Geometry**

A widget's *geometry* is its size, position on the screen, border width, and stacking position. The XtNx, XtNy, XtNwidth, XtNheight, and XtNborderWidth resources of a widget are called its geometry resources.

A widget's parent is responsible for allocating its space among its children and so always has the final say in deciding what the widget's geometry is. Applications request changes, but the parent gets to decide whether or not to grant the request. Different classes of composite widgets use different layout algorithms and thus use different criteria for deciding on whether to grant an application's request. Some parent widgets are very strict about geometry; a Menu widget, for example, forces all of its children to have the same width as the widest menu item. If an application asks to make one of the children narrower than this width, the menu denies the request unless the changing widget is the widest entry. If an application asks to make one of the children wider than this width, the menu changes all its children to have the new width. The menu denies any requested changes to the child's position, since its layout algorithm completely controls the position of menu entries.

Other parents are quite lenient. A Box widget allows any changes requested for its children, possibly reconfiguring itself if a child grows larger to ensure that the entire child remains visible.

The only way for an application to request a geometry change for a widget is to issue an `XtSetValues` call setting some of the geometry resources. This is very important to remember. Other methods of changing geometry exist in the toolkit, but they are for use either by parents to change the geometry of their children or for a widget instance to request a change in its own geometry. Unfortunately, the Intrinsics cannot enforce this. If you ever find yourself using anything other than `XtSetValues` to control a widget's geometry from within an application, you have made a programming error, and the widgets are likely to become corrupted.

If it is important to find out whether a requested geometry change took place, an application can call `XtGetValues` on the appropriate geometry resources after calling `XtSetValues` and compare their values with the requested ones. If they do not match, the application is free to ask again, but it should not expect any more success the second time than the first.

The parent is allowed to change other geometry resources than the requested ones; for example, it might be able to grant a size request only if it moved the widget to a new position. Similarly, the parent can change a child's geometry at any time without warning. In the Menu widget, changing one entry's width also changes the widths of all other entries. Sometimes the change is completely outside the application's control; if the user resizes the application's top-level window, many of the application's widgets are likely to change their sizes as a result.

Requests can even be partially granted. If the application asks to make the widest menu entry narrower than the second-widest one, the Menu widget changes the width of all the children to that of the previously second-widest and now widest entry.

The widget itself can deny a change before its parent even gets a chance to participate in the geometry decision. Some widgets disallow changes to make them smaller than some minimal useful size. The Menu widget itself wants to be exactly the size needed to enclose all its menu entries; if the application tries to modify this size, it will fail.

Many widgets have some default size they take if no other size is specified. A Label or Pushbutton widget's default size is just large enough to contain the widget's text surrounded by a small border; a Box widget's default is large enough to contain all the children plus some appropriate margin. Many widgets assume their default size if the application sets the width and height resources of the widget to zero, so applications request the default size this way. This is sometimes called *shrink-wrapping* if the widget is composite since the widget changes to a size just large enough to hold all the children. Application writers should consult the widget documentation to see if a widget class supports this behavior.

The first chance a parent gets to look at its children's geometries is just before the parent gets realized. If the application modifies a widget's geometry before its parent is realized, the Intrinsics allow the request unless the widget itself denies the change. Just before realization the Intrinsics notify the parent of its children's geometries; the parent can modify them according to its own layout policy if necessary.

There is one big deficiency in the Intrinsics' handling of geometry, and that is with stacking order requests. There is no `XtSetValues` call an application can issue to make the stacking order of the widgets change and no way at all to change the stacking order prior to realization. Unless the documentation for the parent states that the parent stacks its children in some other way, the default stacking order is the order of the children within the parent, with the first child on top and the last child on the bottom. This order is controlled by the XtNinsertPosition resource of the parent; see Section 4.2 for more information. Usually the default value for this resource inserts new children at the end of the child list, causing them to initially appear below any intersecting children.

If an application absolutely has to change the stacking order after realization, it uses `XtMakeGeometryRequest`, described in the second part of this chapter. This is the only valid use for `XtMakeGeometryRequest` in an application, and the application uses it to change only the stacking order and never any other geometry fields.

4.2 Order of Children

An application controls the order of the children in a particular composite widget by providing a value for the widget's XtNinsertPosition resource. The default value for this resource inserts new children at the end of the child list.

XtNinsertPosition takes a procedure pointer as a value, and the procedure is of type `XtOrderProc`:

typedef Cardinal (*XtOrderProc) (Widget)
    Widget *w*;
   w   Specifies the widget being added.

This procedure returns the number of children that should precede the new widget in the widget list. Use `XtParent` to find the widget's parent, and `XtGetValues` on the XtNchildren and XtNnumChildren resources of the parent to get the list of existing children. Returning zero means to add the new child at the beginning, and returning the value of the parent's XtNnum-Children resource means to add the new child at the end.

Possible uses for this procedure would be for an application that keeps a set of pushbuttons grouped by function or a set of widgets representing file names in alphabetical order.

4.3   Managed and Unmanaged Widgets

It is often useful to allow a composite widget to have children that do not currently show up on the screen. An application might contain a button box containing Pushbutton widgets to invoke various parts of the application functionality, not all of which are appropriate at all times. The application can make some of the widgets disappear when their functionality is withdrawn and make them reappear later when the functionality is again appropriate. Another example is an application that has a text command entry area at the bottom of its main window. When the application needs to get a command it makes the Text widget appear, and when it does not need the widget it removes it to give the space to the main application work area.

Managed widgets are taken into consideration in the parent's layout procedure; *unmanaged* widgets are not. The parent ignores all unmanaged widgets when allocating space to its children, so they do not appear. Managing and unmanaging widgets to add and withdraw application functionality should be used with discretion; its overuse leads to user interfaces that are unpleasantly flashy—the changing display is distracting to the user. Often it is more appropriate to add and withdraw functionality by changing the sensitivity of the widgets in the interface; see Chapter 6.

Widgets are initially managed if the application created them using

XtCreateManagedWidget and initially unmanaged if created with
XtCreateWidget. XtManageChild, XtManageChildren, XtUnmanage-
Child, and XtUnmanageChildren change the managed state of widgets.

void XtManageChild(*child*)
    Widget *child*;
child   Specifies the widget to manage.

XtManageChild manages one widget. If the widget is already managed, it
has no effect.

void XtManageChildren(*children, num_children*)
    WidgetList *children*;
    Cardinal *num_children*;
children   Specifies a list of widgets to manage.
num_children   Specifies the number of widgets in the list.

XtManageChildren manages a list of widgets, all of which must be children
of the same parent.

void XtUnmanageChild(*child*)
    Widget *child*;
child   Specifies the widget to unmanage.

XtUnmanageChild unmanages one widget. If the widget is already unmanaged, it has no effect.

void XtUnmanageChildren(*children, num_children*)
    WidgetList *children*;
    Cardinal *num_children*;
children   Specifies a list of widgets to unmanage.
num_children   Specifies the number of widgets in the list.

XtUnmanageChildren unmanages a list of widgets, all of which must be
children of the same parent.

If the child's parent is realized, XtManageChild and XtManage-
Children automatically realize any widgets passed to them that are not currently realized, causing the creation of their windows. However, you should
explicitly realize a composite child of a realized widget before managing the
child to ensure that the child appears with its correct size. This is an unfortunate side effect of the way the Intrinsics order the size calculations; see
Sections 4.10 and 4.11 if you want to know the details.

If the widgets being managed or unmanaged are children of a realized parent, it is much more efficient to use `XtManageChildren` or `Xt-UnmanageChildren` than to repeatedly call `XtManageChild` or `XtUnmanageChild` for each widget. A realized parent lays out its children any time their managed state changes, so repeated calls to `XtManageChild` or `XtUnmanageChild` cause multiple layouts, resulting in distracting and potentially slow screen changes. If the parent is not realized, it makes no difference which routines are used since the Intrinsics delay calling the parent's layout routine until just before the parent gets realized.

Applications and widgets check whether or not a widget is managed by using `XtIsManaged`.

Boolean XtIsManaged(*w*)
    Widget *w*;
  w   Specifies the widget to test the managed state of.

`XtIsManaged` is often implemented as a macro, especially for widget implementors.

4.4   Mapping and Unmapping

Some styles of user interfaces call for widgets not to appear on the screen but to still take up space within the parent. An application might wish to make a menu in a menu bar disappear if none of the items in the menu are currently active, but not want the other menus to move into the inactive menu's space since users rapidly become accustomed to always finding interface objects in the same place. A widget is said to be *mapped* if the server is displaying the widget's window on the screen and *unmapped* if the server is not. Normally managed widgets are mapped to the screen and unmanaged widgets are unmapped, but it is possible to have widgets that take up space but are unmapped by using the `XtSetMappedWhenManaged` procedure.

void XtSetMappedWhenManaged(*w, map_when_managed*)
    Widget *w*;
    Boolean *map_when_managed*;
  w   Specifies the widget to set *mapped_when_managed* for.
map_when_managed
                Specifies whether to set the *mapped_when_managed* flag for the widget to TRUE or to FALSE.

If the widget is realized and managed, and the new value of *mapped_when_managed* is TRUE, the Intrinsics map the widget's window. Conversely, if the widget is realized and managed and the new value of *mapped_when_managed* is FALSE, the Intrinsics unmap the widget's window. If the widget is unmanaged or unrealized, the new value is stored away, and later when the widget becomes realized and managed the Intrinsics will honor the value. Unmanaged windows by definition never take up any screen space, so they are not mapped.

Figure 4.1 shows three buttons in a button box. In the first picture the first widget is managed and mapped, in the second it is managed but unmapped, and in the third it is unmanaged. As long as the first widget is managed it takes up space, regardless of whether or not it is mapped. When the first widget is unmanaged, it receives no space.

Applications also can control a widget's mapped-when-managed state by setting the XtNmappedWhenManaged resource at widget creation time or with `XtSetValues`, and they can query it using `XtGetValues`. The default value is TRUE.

The mapped-when-managed state of a top-level application shell widget is used slightly differently; see Section 5.3 for a description of its effect.

An alternative method to control the mapped state of a widget is to set the XtNmappedWhenManaged resource to FALSE and to map and unmap the widget using `XtMapWidget` and `XtUnmapWidget`. If the application uses this scheme, it must keep track itself of whether the widget is mapped.

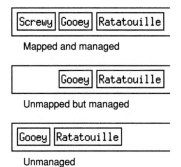

Mapped and managed

Unmapped but managed

Unmanaged

Figure 4.1. Managed, mapped, and unmanaged widgets

void XtMapWidget(*w*)
    Widget *w*;
    w   Specifies the widget to map.

`XtMapWidget` maps the widget's window. Calling this for an unrealized widget generates an error, and calling it for an unmanaged widget results in a muddled layout since the widget's parent has not allocated space for it.

void XtUnmapWidget(*w*)
    Widget *w*;
    w   Specifies the widget to unmap.

`XtUnmapWidget` unmaps the widget's window.

As with managing and unmanaging widgets to add and withdraw application functionality, mapping and unmapping widgets should be used sparingly to avoid flashy user interfaces. Controlling a widget's sensitivity is usually a better choice.

4.5   Realized, Unrealized, Managed, and Unmanaged Widgets

The Intrinsics maintain two invariants for the widgets in the widget tree:

- If a widget is realized, then all its managed children are also realized.
- If a widget is realized, then all its managed children that have their *mapped_when_managed* flag set to TRUE are mapped.

The first invariant implies that whenever a widget gets realized, all its managed children also get realized. It also implies that if an application uses `XtCreateManagedWidget` to add a widget to a realized parent, the Intrinsics automatically realize the new widget. If the application adds the widget using `XtCreateWidget` and later manages it with `XtManageChild` or `XtManageChildren`, the widget is realized when it becomes managed.

4.6   Using Constraint Widgets

If a composite widget's size changes, it has to decide what to do with the new extra space or how to manage with the new smaller space. The simplest approach would be to just leave the new extra space empty or to truncate the contained widgets to the new smaller space, but this is not likely to make the user very happy. Usually he resizes a window to make the work space of his application larger or smaller, not just to make more or less of the work space visible, and he will become upset at the uncooperative program and curse the software designer.

More helpful composite widgets resize their children to make optimal use of the new space, but they often need extra information to do this effectively. A drawing program gives any new space it gets to the drawing canvas, not to the palette of drawing commands. A program that has an area devoted to displaying messages to the user allows this area to shrink but always to remain large enough to hold one line.

An application must tell the composite parent how best to allocate its space, but where should this information go? It cannot be specified as resources for the parent without resorting to awkward and limited schemes like defining XtNfirstChildInfo, XtNsecondChildInfo, and so forth for each possible child. It cannot be stored in the child widgets; the child widget has no idea what sort of parent will contain it, and different instances of the child might well be contained in different sorts of parents, each requiring a different kind of information.

The solution involves a subclass of composite widgets called constraint widgets. Constraint widgets define a new set of resources that the application specifies for each child, and the Intrinsics take care of storing the information. The parent defines and uses the resources, but the application specifies them for the child just like any other child resources.

A simple useful example would be a parent that associates desired maximum and minimum sizes with each child. The drawing program specifies the resources for the palette and canvas widgets this way:

```
i = 0;
XtSetArg(arg[i], XtNx, 0);            i++;
XtSetArg(arg[i], XtNwidth, 100);      i++;
XtSetArg(arg[i], XtNminWidth, 100);   i++;
XtSetArg(arg[i], XtNmaxWidth, 100);   i++;
...set other resources and create the palette widget...

i = 0;
XtSetArg(arg[i], XtNx, 100);          i++;
XtSetArg(arg[i], XtNwidth, 500);      i++;
XtSetArg(arg[i], XtNminWidth, 10);    i++;
...set other resources and create the canvas widget...
```

This indicates that the palette has a fixed width of 100. Making it any wider is pointless, and making it any narrower makes it useless. The canvas, however, has no maximum size, so it can be made to be as large as necessary.

The program with the message area specifies the resources for the message widget like this:

```
i = 0;
XtSetArg(arg[i], XtNheight, 45);        i++;
XtSetArg(arg[i], XtNmaxHeight, 75);     i++;
XtSetArg(arg[i], XtNminHeight, 15);     i++;
...set other resources and create the message widget...
```

Assuming that each message line is 15 pixels high, this states that the initial height is three lines, the maximum useful height is five lines, and the minimum useful height is one line. Note that in both these examples the application specifies the resources that the parent defined, XtNmaxWidth, XtNminWidth, XtNmaxHeight, and XtNminHeight, just like the resources the widget defined, such as XtNx, XtNwidth, and XtNheight.

Resources defined by the parent but specified for the child are called *constraint* resources since their most common use is to constrain the child's geometry. Any parent that defines constraint resources documents their names, classes, types, and default values just as for any other resource. The application treats them like normal resources; it specifies them through argument lists or resource files, modifies them using XtSetValues, and queries them using XtGetValues. Always do these for the child widget, not the parent widget—unless, of course, the parent is in turn the child of another constraint widget.

Of course, the application cannot insist that the widgets always satisfy the constraints any more than it can insist that the application always have a particular size. The user can shrink the application so that there is no room for all the widgets, even at their minimum size, or can enlarge the application, giving it more room than the widgets can use even at their maximum sizes. In these cases the parent typically does its best, either shrinking widgets as much as possible and clipping what still does not fit or enlarging widgets as much as possible and leaving empty space.

Writing Widgets

This chapter contains examples from Box, a very simple composite widget. It has only one resource:

XtNmargin   Additional space to leave on the right and bottom when computing an ideal size to hold its children.

It always attempts to be large enough to hold its children with their specified positions and sizes, and allows the children's geometries to change freely. If it cannot be large enough to hold its children, it clips them.

4.7   Composite Widgets

Composite widgets are widgets to which an application can add other widgets. They generally have two axes of complexity:

- Their layout procedure—some composites do almost no layout for their children, relying upon the application to specify the sizes and locations, while others make all the layout decisions themselves.

- Their added functionality—some composites act simply as containers, adding no functionality to their children, while others allow the user sophisticated controls over the children's sizes, positions, or contents.

The simplest composite widget is a box that just places the children with the geometries set by the application. Button boxes and menus are widgets with more sophisticated layouts; button boxes pack their children closely together to fill the available space, and menus line their children up vertically, making them all the same width. A scrolling widget has a simple layout, usually putting the scrollbars and the widget being scrolled in fixed positions, but the user can manipulate the scrollbars to control what part of the scrolled widget is visible. Finally, a vertical pane lines up all its children in one column, making them all have the same width, and allows the user to dynamically change how the pane's space is allocated to the children; this has both a sophisticated layout and considerable added functionality.

Often a widget contains other widgets not added by the application; for example, the scrolling widget creates one or more scrollbars to accompany the application's widget. Other widgets appear to be one simple widget but actually contain other widgets. A scrollbar might include pushbuttons that allow the user to scroll by just one unit. A widget set can include very complex widgets like confirmation dialogs, file selection widgets, and help widgets that contain dozens of labels, pushbuttons, text entry fields, and other simple widgets.

When implementing one of these complex widgets the programmer must decide whether to make the widget a composite. The Intrinsics know about composites and maintain a list of their children, giving a lot of support for adding, deleting, and realizing widgets. This support is very general, and widgets that want to do all the bookkeeping themselves can save some space by handling their children themselves. These special children, called *subwidgets*, are not entered into the general child list; in fact, a widget cannot contain subwidgets if it is a subclass of Composite. Whenever this book uses the term *normal children* it refers to children of composite widgets that are in the child list; if a description applies to both normal children and subwidgets, both are always mentioned.

Consider an example to understand the difference between normal children and subwidgets. A confirmation dialog box might contain two other widgets, a label displaying some message and an OK pushbutton for the user to click to indicate that he has seen the message. The implementor creates the two child widgets either as normal children or as subwidgets. Chapter 10 contains two implementations of a confirmation box, one using normal children and one using subwidgets.

In either instance the confirmation box creates the two internal widgets in its initialize procedure. If implemented as a composite, it knows that the first entry in its child list is the label and the second entry the pushbutton. The class method to add a new child makes sure that the confirmation box never has more than two children to prevent the application from trying to add its own widgets to this box. If a third child is added, the procedure generates an error message. On the other hand, if the confirmation box is willing to do some extra layout, it could allow the application to add additional widgets to display some extra information or to give the user other choices besides simply acknowledging that he has seen the box.

Alternatively, the implementor might not make the confirmation box a composite at all. It creates its two children as subwidgets and stores them in fields in the widget instance record. The application cannot add any children since there is no child list to add the children to.

A widget with subwidgets is responsible for doing what the Intrinsics do for normal children:

- It must realize and map all its subwidgets in its realize method.
- It must destroy all its subwidgets in its destroy method.

Composite widgets are always the answer when the application adds the child widgets to the container or when the children may need to change their geometries. Subwidgets are appropriate when the widget adds the children itself if the implementation is willing to handle the subwidgets and if the geometries of the subwidgets never change except when the widget changes them itself.

Whenever an application or a widget adds a child to a composite parent, the Intrinsics make sure the new widget ends up on the parent's child list. When a subwidget is added to a noncomposite parent, the implementor is responsible for making sure that the widget identifier gets stored where it will not get lost. If a noncomposite widget wants to allow the application to add additional subwidgets to it, it must define a way for the application to notify it of the subwidgets.

4.8   Inserting and Deleting Children

The Composite widget class defines four new class methods. Two of them, insert_child and delete_child, handle adding and removing children from the child list, and both are of type `XtWidgetProc`.

```
typedef void (*XtWidgetProc)(Widget);
     Widget w;
w                 Specifies the widget.
```

These methods are often inherited from Composite. Composite's insert_child method calls the insert_position procedure for the parent and adds the widget to the child list at the appropriate place. Composite's delete_child procedure removes the child from the child list and moves all widgets that occur after the deleted child one space towards the front of the list.

New insert_child and delete_child procedures find the parent of the widget being added or removed by calling `XtParent` with the widget parameter. The most common reasons to have a new insert_child procedure are to limit the number or classes of children being added to the parent, to create companion widgets to the newly added widget, or to modify the newly added widget. In most cases it is still convenient to use the superclass's method by enveloping a call; see Section 2.18. If the new insert_child method verifies the child, it calls the superclass's method to actually insert the child after checking that the child should be added. If it creates a companion widget or modifies the child, it calls the superclass's method before doing the extra work.

Similarly, the delete_child method must delete any companion widgets created by the insert_child method. Enveloping is useful here also.

If a widget class provides a completely new insert_child procedure, it must make sure that there is enough room in the child list for the new widget. Composite provides three fields for maintaining the list, *children*, *num_children*, and *num_slots*. The *children* field must always point to an array of widgets containing at least *num_children* entries, and the *num_slots* field allows the insert_child method to allocate extra entries to avoid excessive calls to memory management routines.

Similarly, the delete_child method can copy the child list into a smaller area of memory if it decides that there are too many unused slots at the end. Both procedures must maintain the *num_slots* and *num_children* fields to indicate the number of entries allocated to the child list and the number of entries currently occupied by children. The occupied entries must be contiguous and at the beginning of the list.

If an insert_child method decides that the new child should not be added for whatever reason, it should issue an error or warning message since this usually indicates a programming error in the application.

Modifying the child and adding companion widgets are most useful when the composite gives the user interactive control over the widget layout. Consider a widget that allows the user to reposition the children. It has two alternatives. First, it could add some additional translations to the child that allow the user to press a pointer button in the child and move it to a new location; Chapter 7 gives information on translations. The other way is to create one or more additional widgets that act as handles; when the user interacts with the handles, usually by dragging them to a new location, the position of the child follows. Either way is appropriate in some user interface styles; and in both cases the insert_child procedure is the appropriate place to do the work. If the insert_child procedure creates companion widgets, it has to make sure that it is reentrant since it will be called to insert the new child, and it also must distinguish the companion widgets by class or by some static state so that it does not try to create companion widgets for them also.

4.9   Data Caching

The geometry information stored in the widget record is a copy of the information stored in the server for the widget's window. Why is it stored in the widget at all?

Earlier versions of the toolkit relied upon the server to maintain the geometry. This turned out to be a major performance bottleneck. A composite widget had to query the server for its children's geometries at each layout. Since the X protocol is asynchronous, normal requests to the server get buffered and transported in blocks; this allows the overhead of interprocess communication and context switching to be amortized among requests and results in considerable performance improvements. A request that returns information makes this batching break down; the application can issue no further requests until the answer to the query comes back.

Caching the geometry in the widget record eliminates these server round trips. The Intrinsics make sure that the geometry information is always correct so that composites can use the local geometry fields. The only time round trips are necessary is when some requested geometry change would result in the application's top-level window changing its geometry; then the user and his window manager are responsible for deciding whether to allow the change. Composite widget implementations can always assume that the geometry fields are correct.

4.10   Notification of Managed Set Changing

At any particular time, each of the composite's children is either managed or unmanaged. The managed children comprise the composite's *managed set*. When the composite widget considers its children for layout it checks each child to see if it is managed by calling `XtIsManaged`; the composite must completely ignore any unmanaged children during layout.

Composite widgets get notified that their managed set has changed through their change_managed method. This is of type `XtWidgetProc`.

```
typedef void (*XtWidgetProc)(Widget);
    Widget w;
    w                Specifies the widget.
```

The widget passed to the change_managed method is the composite widget itself; this procedure is responsible for laying out the children in this widget's managed set. Information about which children have been added to or removed from the managed set is not available; the change_managed procedure just performs a new layout of the managed children each time it gets called.

```
static void ChangeManaged(w)
    Widget w;
{
    BoxWidget box = (BoxWidget) w;
    XtWidgetGeometry request;
    XtGeometryResult result;

    CalculateNewSize(box, &request.width, &request.height);

    if (request.width != box->core.width ||
            request.height != box->core.height) {
        request.request_mode = CWWidth | CWHeight;
        do {
            result = XtMakeGeometryRequest(w, &request, &request);
        } while (result == XtGeometryAlmost);
    }
}
```

Example 4.1. The Box change_managed procedure

The Intrinsics do not invoke the change_managed procedure for an unreal-ized composite widget until just before realizing the widget. This avoids repeated layouts with the addition of each new managed child; it is better to delay the first layout until the initial managed set is completely known. Calls to manage or unmanage children for widgets with unrealized parents just mark the managed bit for the child without invoking the change_managed proce-dure.

Once the parent has been realized, each call to XtCreateManaged-Widget, XtManageChild, XtManageChildren, XtUnmanageChild, and XtUnmanageChildren results in a call to the parent's change_managed routine so that the parent can perform a new layout.

Example 4.1 shows the change_managed procedure for the Box widget. It calls CalculateNewSize to compute a new size based upon the new managed set and then, if this new size is different from its current size, asks to become the new size. If the box's parent offers a compromise size, ChangeManaged just accepts it. See Section 4.13 for information on XtMakeGeometry-Request.

4.11   Control Flow for Widget Creation

All the pieces of the Intrinsics' actions at widget creation time have now been presented. Here's a recap.

Whenever an application creates a widget of a particular class, the Intrinsics first check if that class has been initialized yet. If not, the Intrinsics initialize the class, performing the following steps:

• If the class's superclass has not yet been initialized, the Intrinsics initialize it using these same steps. This recursively initializes that class's superclass if necessary, and so forth on up through the superclasses until the Intrinsics encounter an already initialized class or until there are no more superclasses.

• The Intrinsics invoke the class's class_initialize procedure, if any.

• The Intrinsics resolve class method inheritance by passing the class record to the class_part_initialize procedures for the class and all its superclasses, starting with Core and proceeding through the classes, ending with the procedure for the class itself.

The Intrinsics next allocate a widget instance record and fill in nonresource fields like *parent* and *self.* The argument list, the resource database, and the widget class's resource list supply values for the widget's resource fields. The Intrinsics then initialize the widget by passing the widget record to the initialize and initialize_hook procedures for the class and all its superclasses, starting with Core and proceeding to the class itself.

If the parent of the widget is a constraint widget, the Intrinsics allocate a constraint record and initialize its resource fields from the argument list, the resource database, and the parent's constraint resources. The Intrinsics then pass the widget to the constraint initialize procedures for the parent's class and all its superclasses, starting with Constraint and proceeding to the parent's class. See Section 4.18 for more information.

Next, if the parent of the widget is a composite widget, the Intrinsics call the parent's insert_child method to add the new widget to its parent's child list.

If the new widget is unmanaged, no further processing occurs. If the new widget is managed and the widget's parent is not realized, which is the usual case when initially creating the application's user interface, the Intrinsics just mark the widget as managed and no further processing occurs. If the new widget is managed and its parent is realized, the Intrinsics realize the new widget and call the parent's change_managed procedure to inform the parent that its managed set has changed.

After a series of calls to create widgets, the application has a tree of unrealized widgets, some of which are managed and some unmanaged. None of the composite widgets have had their layout routines called yet. The application realizes these widgets by calling `XtRealizeWidget` on the root of the widget tree.

When a composite widget is realized, either explicitly through an application call to `XtRealizeWidget` or implicitly through managing a previously unrealized child of a realized parent, widget layouts occur. The Intrinsics recursively invoke the layout routines for the composite widget and its composite children before creating windows for the widgets in the tree.

First the Intrinsics call the change_managed procedures for all composite widgets with any managed children. This is performed recursively in post-order; the Intrinsics call the change_managed procedures for all children of each composite widget before calling change_managed for the composite. Layout thus starts at the composite widgets nearest the leaves of the widget tree and proceeds upward toward the root; this lets the layout algorithms know the preferred sizes for all the children. The layout for a particular widget often changes the sizes of some of its children, and if the child is another composite, this causes a new layout for the child's children. These size changes ripple up and down the tree, but a widget is not allowed to request a new geometry as a result of being resized, so the process is guaranteed to terminate. However, programming errors, in particular a widget that requests a new size when it is resized, can cause this process to loop.

Consider realizing the widget tree in Figure 4.2. The Intrinsics first call the change_managed procedures for the two children of the top widget, which makes them lay out their children and calculate a desired size. Next the top widget's change_managed procedure lays out its two children. If this layout changes the size of either child, the layout procedure resizes the child. This

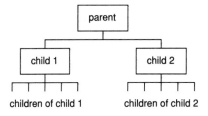

Figure 4.2. Geometry propagation at realization

resize makes the child do a new layout of its children, but the child must accept the new size; it cannot ask for a different one.

Eventually all the widgets in the tree have their correct sizes and positions, and the Intrinsics realize the widgets. Realizing makes a second pass through the tree, this time from the top to the bottom. The Intrinsics first create a window for the widget being realized by calling its realize method, then recursively realize each of its managed children. The Intrinsics also map all managed children that have their *mapped_when_managed* flag TRUE. If the widget being realized is the application's top-level shell and it also has its *mapped_when_managed* flag TRUE, the Intrinsics map the widget's window to the screen, thereby causing the entire widget tree to appear.

4.12   Geometry Changes

Geometry information flows both upward and downward through the widget tree. Before the initial layout that is done just before realizing the widgets, no restrictions are placed upon widget geometry changes. Widget routines can set geometry fields with impunity, and the application can change them freely through `XtSetValues`. This geometry propagates upward from leaf widgets toward the shell root when the initial layout occurs.

After the widgets are realized, however, the parent has absolute authority over the geometries of its children. Any widget that wants a new geometry must ask its parent, and if the parent denies the geometry request, the widget must accept the parent's decision and make do with the space allotted to it. The Intrinsics make these requests if an `XtSetValues` call results in new values for any geometry fields. A widget implementation can also issue geometry requests directly if the widget needs a new size. These direct requests are often a result of a widget's layout procedure deciding that it needs additional space to hold its widgets.

Parent widgets can change the geometries of their children at any time, and the children must accept the new geometry. A considerate parent often queries its children to find their preferred geometries and tries to accommodate them, but it is under no obligation to do so.

Thus there is a bidirectional flow of geometry information. Geometry requests and the results of geometry queries go from children to parents, geometry changes go from parents to children, and either can propagate through several layers of the tree. A child's geometry request can in turn result in the parent's asking its parent for more space to grant the child's request, and a parent's direct change can result in the child's changing the geometries of its children as a result of the new size. At times the information flow proceeds in both directions through different branches of the tree; a child's request can make the parent change the geometries of some of the child's siblings in order to grant the request.

Consider Figure 4.2 again. If a child of the left widget makes a geometry request, the left widget might have to ask the top widget for more space. The top widget might grant this request by resizing the right widget, and the right widget might in turn resize its children.

4.13   Making Geometry Requests

A widget's initialize procedure changes the widget's geometry directly by writing whatever values it needs into the widget's geometry fields. After the widget is realized, however, the widget must ask its parent for a geometry change using XtMakeGeometryRequest.

typedef enum {XtGeometryYes, XtGeometryNo, XtGeometryAlmost,
        XtGeometryDone} XtGeometryResult;

XtGeometryResult XtMakeGeometryRequest(*w, request, reply_return*)
        Widget *w*;
        XtWidgetGeometry **request*;
        XtWidgetGeometry **reply_return*;
w   Specifies the widget making the request.
request   Specifies the desired widget geometry.
reply_return   Returns the allowed widget geometry; may be NULL if the requesting
                         widget is not interested in handling XtGeometryAlmost.

The return value from XtMakeGeometryRequest indicates the status of the request. A return of XtGeometryYes means that the parent granted the request, and that XtMakeGeometryRequest updated the widget's geometry fields and reconfigured the widget's window, if any. A return of XtGeometryNo means that the parent denied the request. A return of XtGeometryAlmost means that the parent denied the request, but would grant some other request that it considers similar, and *reply_return* gives this compromise geometry. If the requesting widget is not interested in any compromise geometry, it specifies NULL as the *reply_return* parameter. It is legal to specify the same data structure for both the *request* and *reply_return* parameters; this often makes code to accept the compromise simpler. XtMakeGeometry-Request never returns XtGeometryDone.

If the child is unmanaged, its parent is unrealized, or its parent is not a composite widget, XtMakeGeometryRequest always makes the requested changes and returns XtGeometryYes. If all the requested changes match the values currently in the widget record, XtMakeGeometryRequest returns XtGeometryYes without making any changes. If the widget is marked as being destroyed, XtMakeGeometryRequest always returns XtGeometryNo. Otherwise XtMakeGeometryRequest consults the parent widget to decide on whether to allow the request.

If XtMakeGeometryRequest returns XtGeometryAlmost, the widget determines whether the returned compromise geometry is acceptable and if so issues another geometry request using this geometry. Parents must grant a geometry returned with XtGeometryAlmost as long as the new request comes immediately after the previous one. The only exception to this occurs when granting the compromise geometry would involve changing the size of the application's top-level window—the top-level widget may not be able to tell whether the user's window manager would grant the change. A widget can also react to an XtGeometryAlmost or an XtGeometryNo by making a completely different geometry request.

An XtWidgetGeometry structure is similar but not identical to an Xlib XWindowChanges structure:

typedef unsigned long XtGeometryMask;

```
typedef struct {
    XtGeometryMask    request_mode;
    Position          x, y;
    Dimension         width, height;
    Dimension         border_width;
    Widget            sibling;
    int               stack_mode;
} XtWidgetGeometry;
```

A requesting widget fills in all the fields in the request structure that it cares about, including fields that it wants changed and fields that it wants the parent to maintain at their present values. It fills in the *request_mode* field with an OR'ed set of flags indicating which fields it set:

```
#define CWX              (1<<0)
#define CWY              (1<<1)
#define CWWidth          (1<<2)
#define CWHeight         (1<<3)
#define CWBorderWidth    (1<<4)
#define CWSibling        (1<<5)
#define CWStackMode      (1<<6)
#define XtCWQueryOnly    (1<<7)
```

All these flags except for XtCWQueryOnly indicate that the widget set the corresponding field in the request structure. Widgets set XtCWQueryOnly to indicate that the geometry request is just a query to find out what the answer would be if the request were really executed; this is most useful in geometry manager procedures and is discussed in Section 4.14.

If the widget cares about stacking, it sets the *stack_mode* field to one of the following values:

```
#define Above           0
#define Below           1
#define TopIf           2
#define BottomIf        3
#define Opposite        4
#define XtSMDontChange  5
```

Each of these values except for XtSMDontChange has the same meaning as the flags to the XConfigureWindow Xlib call. If a widget also specifies a sibling, the widget's window is restacked as follows:

Above   The window is placed just above the sibling's window.

Below   The window is placed just below the sibling's window.

TopIf   If the sibling's window occludes the window, the window is placed at the top of the stack.

BottomIf   If the sibling's window occludes the window, the window is placed at the bottom of the stack.

Opposite   If the sibling's window occludes the window, the window is placed at the top of the stack. If the window occludes the sibling's window, the window is placed at the bottom of the stack.

If no sibling is specified, the widget's window is restacked as follows:

Above	The window is placed at the top of the stack.
Below	The window is placed at the bottom of the stack.
TopIf	If any sibling's window occludes the window, the window is placed at the top of the stack.
BottomIf	If any sibling's window occludes the window, the window is placed at the bottom of the stack.
Opposite	If any sibling's window occludes the window, the window is placed at the top of the stack. If the window occludes any sibling's window, the window is placed at the bottom of the stack.

Specifying XtSMDontChange indicates that the widget wants its current stacking position maintained; not setting the *stack_mode* field and flag indicates that the child does not care about its stacking position.

After a successful geometry request, that is, one that returned XtGeometryYes, the widget's geometry fields have their new values and its window has been reconfigured. The widget's resize procedure, described in Section 4.16, may or may not have been called depending upon how the parent handled the geometry request. The resize procedure is responsible for reacting to a size change, usually by doing a new layout and redisplaying the widget's contents with the new size.

If the resize procedure was not called, the requesting widget usually calls it directly when it receives an XtGeometryYes. The designer of a widget set must decide whether the composite widgets in the set call the resize procedure for a widget making a geometry request, and documents this behavior in the widget set documentation. The decision should be made uniformly across the widget set. Failing to follow the same policy uniformly requires each widget either to pessimistically assume that its resize procedure has not been called and always to call it, leading to multiple redisplays, or to go through inconvenient bookkeeping to avoid the extra redisplay. Section 4.14 discusses the trade-offs between the two schemes.

If a widget writer wants to make sure the widget works correctly no matter what the parent does, it sets a flag in the widget record before issuing the geometry request, has the resize procedure reset the flag, and then tests the flag after the request to decide whether to call the resize procedure. This flag must be in the widget instance since the geometry request can result in calling the resize procedure for other widgets of the same class as the requesting one; a global flag would indicate only that the resize procedure was called, not that it was called for the requesting widget.

A simpler interface to making a geometry request is provided by XtMake-ResizeRequest.

XtGeometryResult XtMakeResizeRequest(*w, width, height, width_return, height_return*)
    Widget *w*;
    Dimension *width, height*;
    Dimension **width_return, *height_return*

w	Specifies the widget making the request.
width	Specifies the desired width.
height	Specifies the desired height.
width_return	Returns the allowed width; may be NULL.
height_return	Returns the allowed height; may be NULL.

Most widgets only really care about their size and are willing to let their parent do whatever it wishes with their position and stacking order. XtMakeResizeRequest takes its parameters and issues a geometry request to make the widget's width and height take the new values. If the request returns XtGeometryAlmost, XtMakeResizeRequest stores the width and height from the reply into *width_return* and *height_return* unless these fields are NULL. The *width_return* and *height_return* parameters are allowed to point to variables passed in the *width* and *height* parameters.

Set_values procedures can update the widget's geometry fields freely, and after calling all set_values procedures the Intrinsics reset the geometry fields to their original values and make a geometry request. If this request results in a return of XtGeometryAlmost or XtGeometryNo, the Intrinsics call the widget's set_values_almost procedure to decide what to do.[1] This procedure is of type XtAlmostProc.

typedef void (*XtAlmostProc)(Widget, Widget, XtWidgetGeometry *,
                            XtWidgetGeometry *)
    Widget *old*;
    Widget *new*;
    XtWidgetGeometry **request_in_out*;
    XtWidgetGeometry **reply*;

---

[1] The Intrinsics do not call set_values_almost after XtGeometryNo in Intrinsics implementations that conform to specifications earlier than Release 4.

old	Specifies a copy of the widget as it was before the `XtSetValues` call.
new	Specifies the widget.
request_in_out	Specifies the geometry request sent to the geometry manager.
reply	Specifies the compromise geometry from the geometry manager.

The *old* widget is a copy of the widget as it existed before the call to `XtSetValues`, and the *new* widget is the final version except with all geometry fields reset to their values in the *old* widget. If the geometry handler returned XtGeometryNo, *reply–>request_mode* contains zero; otherwise the *reply* parameter contains the compromise geometry.

This procedure must update *request_in_out* to reflect the new desired geometry. To accept the compromise, it copies the *reply* geometry into *request_in_out*. To try a different geometry, it stores the new geometry in *request_in_out*. To terminate geometry negotiations and make do with the original geometry, it sets *request_in_out–>request_mode* to zero. Most widget classes inherit their set_values_almost procedure, ultimately from Core; Core's procedure accepts the suggested compromise.

If *request_in_out–>request_mode* is not zero after calling the set_values_almost procedure, the Intrinsics issue another geometry request with the geometry in *request_in_out*. If this request returns XtGeometryAlmost or XtGeometryNo, the Intrinsics call the set_values_almost procedure again for another round.

Specifications of the Intrinsics before Release 4 had a different set of requirements for the set_values_almost procedure, but no known implementations of the Intrinsics followed these requirements. The Release 4 specification conforms to the earlier implementations.

Set_values procedures should, in general, not assume that any geometry changes they encounter or make will actually occur. If the parent allows the change, the Intrinsics call the widget's resize procedure to inform it of its new geometry. An alternative organization is to have the set_values procedure act on the geometry changes, assuming they will be granted, and to have a set_values_almost procedure that, if the geometry changes are refused, undoes any changes the set_values procedure made.

The following summarizes the Intrinsics' actions relating to geometry when an application calls `XtSetValues`:

1. `XtSetValues` calls the set_values and set_values_hook procedures for the widget's class and all superclasses, starting with Core and proceeding to the widget class. None of these procedures can assume that geometry changes in the widget actually take place unless the class also provides a set_values_almost procedure that handles the XtGeometryNo case.

2. After calling all procedures, `XtSetValues` compares the geometry fields in the widget with their original values.

3. If no geometry fields differ, skip to step 8.

4. If any geometry fields differ, `XtSetValues` creates a geometry request from the differing fields and resets these fields to their original values.

5. `XtSetValues` calls `XtMakeGeometryRequest` with the request.

6. If `XtMakeGeometryRequest` returns XtGeometryNo or XtGeometryAlmost, `XtSetValues` calls the set_values_almost procedure. Go to step 5 if set_values_almost returns a new geometry, or to step 8 if set_values_almost accepts the original geometry.

7. If `XtMakeGeometryRequest` returns XtGeometryYes, `XtSetValues` calls the resize procedure.

8. If any of the set_values or set_values_hook procedures returned TRUE, indicating that the widget needs to be redisplayed, `XtSetValues` redisplays the widget.

4.14   Geometry Managers

When a widget issues a geometry request, either directly or as a result of an `XtSetValues` call's changing geometry fields, `XtMakeGeometryRequest` calls the geometry_manager method for the widget's parent. This procedure is of type `XtGeometryHandler`.

```
typedef XtGeometryResult (*XtGeometryHandler) (Widget, XtWidgetGeometry *,
                                               XtWidgetGeometry *);
        Widget w;
        XtWidgetGeometry *request;
        XtWidgetGeometry *geometry_return;
    w                Specifies the widget making the geometry request.
    request          Specifies the requested geometry changes.
    geometry_return  Returns the compromise geometry, if any.
```

The geometry_manager procedure finds the composite widget it is being called for by calling `XtParent` with the widget parameter. It must not assume that the *request* and *geometry_return* parameters point to different areas of storage; the caller is allowed to use the same structure for both parameters, so the geometry manager must allocate its own temporary storage if necessary.

If the *request–>request_mode* specifies XtCWQueryOnly, the geometry manager returns what its answer would be in response to this geometry request, but must not change the geometries of any widgets. The rest of the description here assumes that XtCWQueryOnly was not specified in the request mode.

A bit set to zero in the *request_mode* field means that the requesting widget does not care about that particular geometry field, and that the parent can change this field as it wishes. A bit set to 1 means that the requestor wants that geometry field changed to the value in the corresponding field of request, or wants that geometry field maintained at its current value if this is the same as the value in *request*. Consult Section 4.13 for the meanings of the *stack_mode* and *sibling* fields.

If the geometry manager cannot grant the request and has not suggested compromise geometry, it returns XtGeometryNo without changing any widget geometries. If it cannot grant the request but would grant a geometry that it considers similar to the request, it puts that compromise geometry into the *geometry_return* parameter and returns XtGeometryAlmost, again without changing any widget geometries.

If the geometry manager decides to grant the geometry request, it returns either XtGeometryYes or XtGeometryDone, depending upon the widget set policy. XtGeometryYes means that the geometry manager grants the request but is leaving it up to `XtMakeGeometryRequest` to actually make the changes. XtGeometryDone means that the geometry manager grants the request and has actually made the changes. If the geometry manager returns XtGeometryDone, `XtMakeGeometryRequest` transforms this reply to XtGeometryYes before returning it to the requesting widget; `XtMake-GeometryRequest` never returns XtGeometryDone.

If a programmer decides to use XtGeometryYes, the geometry manager updates the requesting widget's geometry fields to reflect the new geometry and returns XtGeometryYes; `XtMakeGeometryRequest` then reconfigures the requesting widget before returning.

Often granting a geometry request involves changing the geometries of other children of the composite widget. It is often easier to treat the requesting widget the same as any other child and reconfigure it directly. In this case it returns XtGeometryDone to indicate that the reconfiguration has already taken place and that `XtMakeGeometryRequest` does not need to do it.

A widget set designer should decide whether the composite widgets in the set return XtGeometryYes or XtGeometryDone, implement this uniformly across the widgets, and document it thoroughly. `XtMakeGeometryRequest` never calls the requesting widget's resize procedure before returning, whether it reconfigures the widget or not. A geometry manager returning XtGeometry-Done indicates that it used `XtResizeWidget` or `XtConfigureWidget` to make any size changes to the requesting widget, and these procedures *do* call the resize procedure. Widgets making geometry requests need to know whether they need to call their resize procedures themselves upon a successful geometry request, and widget code is simplified immensely if requesting widgets can always assume their parents all do the same thing. This problem resulted from the interface to `XtMakeGeometryRequest` being frozen too early in the development of the toolkit.

If you are designing a new widget set, it is usually easier on widget programmers to use the XtGeometryDone policy. Many widget implementations predate XtGeometryDone, and if you are writing widgets to fit into a set that uses XtGeometryYes, you should use it also. All the widgets presented in this book return XtGeometryYes and not XtGeometryDone.

Geometry managers are free to change any unflagged geometry fields when returning XtGeometryYes or XtGeometryDone. For example, if a child requests a size change but does not set the x or y flags in *request->request_mode*, the geometry manager can move the child to find room for it with its new size. The geometry manager does not return XtGeometryAlmost in this case; if the child cared about its position, it would have set the position flags.

Sometimes the geometry manager cannot grant the request fully but could grant some other request that it considers similar. It might be able to grant some subset of the requests, for example, size but not position, or it might be able to grant a similar but lesser request, for example, allowing the widget to grow larger than it currently is but not to become as large as the widget requested. In such cases the geometry manager updates the *geometry_return* parameter with the compromise geometry, including the *request_mode*, and returns XtGeometryAlmost. The widget geometry in *geometry_return* must exactly describe the geometry request that would be granted so that the requesting widget can use this request for another call to `XtMakeGeometry-`

Request if it decides that the compromise is acceptable. More bits can be set in the *geometry_return->request_mode* than were set in the initial request if the geometry manager would change these geometry fields to grant the compromise.

If the requesting widget immediately makes another geometry request passing in the compromise geometry, the geometry manager must grant this geometry if at all possible. In other words, the geometry returned with XtGeometryAlmost must be a geometry that the geometry manager is willing to grant—it must not just be a guess at something that the manager thinks it might accept. The only time that a geometry manager can break this rule is when granting the request would make the application's top-level shell window change its size. The user's window manager has the ultimate authority to grant or deny changes to this window, and there are no standard protocols the shell can use to find out if a potential change would be granted. Further, window managers are ultimately capricious; they can grant a request at one time and then refuse to grant it immediately afterward. In practice this does not occur very often, so the times when a widget requests the compromise and does not get it should be very few.

A further wrinkle in generating XtGeometryAlmost replies occurs if the composite widget needs to ask its own parent for a geometry change in order to satisfy the request. If the composite has decided to grant the request, it calculates the geometry change it needs to grant the request and issues an XtMakeGeometryRequest to its parent. If the parent grants this request, the composite then grants the original request, and if the parent denies the request or suggests a compromise, the composite decides whether or not to grant the request or generate an almost reply based upon this knowledge.

If, however, it initially decides to generate an XtGeometryAlmost, it might still need to consult its parent. It should not issue a regular geometry request since the original requestor could decide not to accept the compromise and make do with its current geometry—but the composite's parent has already changed the composite. On the other hand, it cannot just return XtGeometry-Almost hoping that the parent will grant the request later since, if the composite's parent denies the change, the composite will not be able to grant the compromise geometry that it promised.

The solution lies in the XtCWQueryOnly bit. The composite asks its parent what its response to the needed change would be without actually asking for the change by specifying XtCWQueryOnly in its *request_mode*.

The composite widget must ensure that if it gets called again with the suggested compromise, it will make exactly the same geometry request to its parent as it did earlier; otherwise it might find itself unable to grant the promised geometry. It can be helpful to cache the intermediate request so that the composite can be sure to issue exactly the same one later. A similar case arises if the composite had planned to return XtGeometryYes, but the request to the composite's parent returned XtGeometryAlmost and as a result the composite itself returns XtGeometryAlmost; the compromise offered by the composite's parent can be cached so that the composite can issue it later. In both of these cases the composite only needs to save one geometry since the composite only guarantees to grant its compromise for the next geometry request.

Example 4.2 shows the geometry manager for the Box widget. This is a very simple geometry manager that always grants any request. If the request requires the box to change size to accommodate the child, the geometry manager tries to make the box the new size. If this fails, the geometry manager still grants the request. An uncooperative parent makes the box clip its children or leave extra unused space.

If the query-only bit is set, GeometryManager immediately returns XtGeometryYes since it always grants all geometry requests. Otherwise, it updates all geometry fields in the child widget with their newly requested values and calls CalculateNewSize to compute the size the box needs to hold its children. If this is different from its current size, GeometryManager asks for the new size, accepting any compromise its parent makes. Regardless of whether its resize succeeded, it returns XtGeometryYes.

GeometryManager implicitly grants stacking requests, requiring no code to do so. Since it returns XtGeometryYes, `XtMakeGeometryRequest` will perform any stacking requests it finds in the geometry request. This is typical of geometry managers that return XtGeometryYes; the only thing they usually do with stacking is to check for a stacking request when deciding whether to grant the geometry request. Geometry managers that return XtGeometryDone are responsible for performing any requested stacking changes, usually by calling `XConfigureWindow`. See Section 3.7 of *Xlib* for more information.

Example 4.3 shows a more complex geometry manager for Box. It denies geometry requests that would require the box to change size if the box's parent disallows the change. First it saves the child's geometry fields and up-

```
static XtGeometryResult GeometryManager(w, desired, allowed)
    Widget w;
    XtWidgetGeometry *desired, *allowed;
{
    BoxWidget box = (BoxWidget) XtParent(w);
    XtWidgetGeometry request;
    XtGeometryResult result;

#define Wants(flag) (desired->request_mode & flag)

    if (Wants(XtCWQueryOnly)) return XtGeometryYes;

    if (Wants(CWWidth)) w->core.width = desired->width;
    if (Wants(CWHeight)) w->core.height = desired->height;
    if (Wants(CWX)) w->core.x = desired->x;
    if (Wants(CWY)) w->core.y = desired->y;
    if (Wants(CWBorderWidth)) {
        w->core.border_width = desired->border_width;
    }

    CalculateNewSize(box, &request.width, &request.height);

    if (request.width != box->core.width ||
            request.height != box->core.height) {
        request.request_mode = CWWidth | CWHeight;
        do {
            result = XtMakeGeometryRequest((Widget) box,
                    &request, &request);
        } while (result == XtGeometryAlmost);
    }

    return XtGeometryYes;

#undef Wants
}
```

Example 4.2. The Box geometry manager

dates them with the desired changes, then calculates the size the box would be with these changes.

If granting the child's request would not require the box to change size, GeometryManager returns XtGeometryYes, first restoring the child's geometry fields to their original values if this was a query-only request.

If this new size is not the same as the current size, GeometryManager makes a geometry request to the box's parent, making it a query-only request if the child's request was query-only. GeometryManager treats XtGeometryAlmost

```
static XtGeometryResult GeometryManager(w, desired, allowed)
    Widget w;
    XtWidgetGeometry *desired, *allowed;
{
    BoxWidget box = (BoxWidget) XtParent(w);
    XtWidgetGeometry request;
    XtGeometryResult result;
    Dimension save_width, save_height, save_border_width;
    Position save_x, save_y;

#define Wants(flag) (desired->request_mode & flag)

    save_width = w->core.width;
    save_height = w->core.height;
    save_border_width = w->core.border_width;
    save_x = w->core.x;
    save_y = w->core.y;

    if (Wants(CWWidth)) w->core.width = desired->width;
    if (Wants(CWHeight)) w->core.height = desired->height;
    if (Wants(CWX)) w->core.x = desired->x;
    if (Wants(CWY)) w->core.y = desired->y;
    if (Wants(CWBorderWidth)) {
        w->core.border_width = desired->border_width;
    }

    CalculateNewSize(box, &request.width, &request.height);

    if (request.width == box->core.width &&
            request.height == box->core.height) {
        if (Wants(XtCWQueryOnly)) {
            w->core.width = save_width;
            w->core.height = save_height;
            w->core.border_width = save_border_width;
            w->core.x = save_x;
            w->core.y = save_y;
        }
        return XtGeometryYes;
    }

    request.request_mode = CWWidth | CWHeight;
    if (Wants(XtCWQueryOnly)) request.request_mode |= XtCWQueryOnly;

    result = XtMakeGeometryRequest((Widget) box, &request,
            (XtGeometryRequest *) NULL);
    if (result == XtGeometryAlmost) result = XtGeometryNo;
```

(continued)

Example 4.3. A complex Box geometry manager

```
        if (result == XtGeometryNo || Wants(XtCWQueryOnly)) {
            w->core.width = save_width;
            w->core.height = save_height;
            w->core.border_width = save_border_width;
            w->core.x = save_x;
            w->core.y = save_y;
        }
        return result;

#undef Wants
}
```

Example 4.3. A complex Box geometry manager

from the request to the parent the same as XtGeometryNo; in either case the box cannot become big enough to hold its children, so GeometryManager denies the request. If the parent denies the change or if the initial request was query-only, GeometryManager restores the child geometry fields to their original values. Finally, the result of the parent geometry request is returned to the child.

For a very complex example, consult the geometry manager for the Menu widget in Chapter 10. This generates XtGeometryAlmost replies for changes that could be partially granted.

4.15 Changing Geometry from Above

When a composite does a widget layout, it uses `XtMoveWidget`, `XtResize-Widget`, and `XtConfigureWidget` to reconfigure its children.

void XtMoveWidget(*w*, *x*, *y*)
    Widget *w*;
    Position *x*;
    Position *y*;

w	Specifies the widget to move.
x	Specifies the new x position for the widget.
y	Specifies the new y position for the widget.

If the new x and y positions match those already in the widget record, `XtMoveWidget` returns immediately. Otherwise, it updates the widget's fields and calls `XMoveWindow` on the widget's window if the widget is realized.

void XtResizeWidget(*w, width, height, border_width*)
       Widget *w*;
       Dimension *width*;
       Dimension *height*;
       Dimension *border_width*;

w	Specifies the widget to resize.
width	Specifies the new width for the widget.
height	Specifies the new height for the widget.
border_width	Specifies the new border width for the widget.

If the new width, height, and border width match those already in the widget, `XtResizeWidget` returns immediately. Otherwise it updates the widget's fields and calls `XConfigureWindow` on the widget's window if the widget is realized. If the new width or height differ from the original values, `XtResizeWidget` calls the widget's resize procedure to inform it of the size change.

void XtConfigureWidget(*w, x, y, width, height, border_width*)
       Widget *w*;
       Position *x*;
       Position *y*;
       Dimension *width*;
       Dimension *height*;
       Dimension *border_width*;

w	Specifies the widget to configure.
x	Specifies the new x position for the widget.
y	Specifies the new y position for the widget.
width	Specifies the new width for the widget.
height	Specifies the new height for the widget.
border_width	Specifies the new border width for the widget.

If all new geometry fields match those already in the widget, `XtConfigureWidget` returns immediately. Otherwise it updates the widget's fields and calls `XConfigureWindow` on the widget's window if the widget is realized. If the new width or height differ from the original values, `XtConfigureWidget` calls the widget's resize procedure to inform it of the size change.

4.16   Responding to Geometry Changes

The configuration procedures call the widget's resize procedure if they change the widget's size. This procedure is of type `XtWidgetProc`.

typedef void (*XtWidgetProc) (Widget);
    Widget *w*;
w   Specifies the widget.

If a particular widget class does not need to recalculate its layout in response to being resized, it specifies NULL as the resize procedure in its class method. Classes that can do this are rather rare and are limited to those with very trivial display semantics. The widget passed to the resize procedure has the new width and height already stored in it; if a class's resize procedure needs to know what the old width and height were in order to react to the reconfiguration, it must manage to have these values stored elsewhere in the widget record.

The resize procedure does any layout necessary with the new size. The Label widget, for example, needs to reposition the text in the label if the application requested centered or right-justified text, and most composite widgets need to layout their children anew in response to the new size. Resize procedures must be able to act on both realized and unrealized widgets; they must check if their widget is realized before doing anything that requires a window.

If the resize procedure redisplays the widget's contents, it may wish to coordinate with the expose procedure to avoid unnecessary redisplays as a result of `XtSetValues`. See Section 6.16 for full details.

The resize procedure must treat being resized as a command and not as a request. In particular, it cannot try to get a new size by making a geometry request or by any other method. If the new size is too small for the widget to fully display its contents, it must do the best that it can, even if this means that some of the widget's contents are lost. Breaking this rule can lead to infinite loops in the widget layout process.

Example 4.4 shows Label's resize procedure. It just clears the window and calls the widget's expose procedure. This results in an unnecessary redisplay if a left-justified label becomes smaller, but the complexity of the bookkeeping code necessary to avoid this outweighs the advantage of avoiding it.

```
static void Resize(w)
    Widget w;
{
    /* If widget is realized, clear and redisplay */

    if (XtIsRealized(w)) {
        XClearWindow(XtDisplay(w), XtWindow(w));
        (*(XtClass(w)->core_class.expose))(w,
                (XEvent *) NULL, (Region) NULL);
    }
}
```

Example 4.4. The Label resize procedure

4.17   Querying Geometry

When a composite widget lays out its children, it should pay as much attention to its children's desired sizes as possible. During the first call to the change_managed procedure, the composite can assume that the children's geometry fields reflect the desired geometries, but later this may not be the case because intermediate layouts might have forced the children to sizes they do not really prefer.

Consider two examples. A scrolling widget holds one scrolled child and one or more scrollbars to control what part of the child is visible. The most convenient way to control the visible part of the scrolled child is to create an auxiliary widget that acts as a clipping window and reparent the scrolled child's window to be a child of the clipping window. The scrolling widget controls what part of the scrolled child is visible by moving the child around beneath the clipping window. The maximum size of the clipping window is the size of the scrolling widget, less any space needed for the scrollbars, but its size should never be larger than the scrolled child's preferred size. If the scrolling widget grows, usually because the user made the application larger, it is better to have some extra blank background space than to make the scrolled child larger than it wants to be.

Another example occurs with the VerticalPane widget. This composite arranges all its children in a vertical row with all their widths equal. The preferred width for the vertical pane is the width of the widest child, but the pane's parent or the user's window manager may force a different width. Some of the children of the pane might be willing to make height/width trade-offs. A button box child does not care exactly what its dimensions are, as long as it has enough area to display all its buttons. After the pane determines a width, it consults the button box to find its preferred height for this width.

A composite widget finds out the preferred geometry of a child by calling `XtQueryGeometry`.

XtGeometryResult XtQueryGeometry(*w, intended, preferred_return*)
    Widget *w*;
    XtWidgetGeometry **intended, *preferred_return*;
w   Specifies the widget being queried.
intended   Specifies any changes the parent plans to make to the widget's geometry, or NULL.
preferred_return   Returns the child's preferred geometry.

Composite widgets should use `XtQueryGeometry` whenever they think the information is likely to be useful. Some widget classes' layout policies have no room for flexibility; implementations of these classes are not obligated to query the preferred geometry when they are not able to use the result.

To find out the child's preferred geometry with no constraints, call `XtQueryGeometry`, specifying NULL as the *intended* geometry. To find the child's response to changing some of the fields, store the proposed new geometry in the *intended* parameter and set bits in *intended–>request_mode* corresponding to fields whose values are not negotiable; this includes fields whose values are changing and fields whose values cannot change.

Upon return from `XtQueryGeometry`, the *preferred_return* parameter has all geometry fields except perhaps *sibling* filled in. If the bit corresponding to a field is set in *preferred_return–>request_mode*, it means that the child set the corresponding field and cares about this particular geometry element; if the bit is not set, it means that the child expressed no preference for the field and that `XtQueryGeometry` filled in the field from the child's current geometry values.

The return values have different meanings depending upon whether the *intended* parameter is NULL; however, no matter what, *preferred_return* contains the widget's preferred geometry and *preferred_return–>request_mode* indicates which geometry fields the child cares about.

When *intended* is NULL, a return of XtGeometryYes means that the child does not have a preferred geometry and that any geometry change is acceptable. A return of XtGeometryAlmost means that *preferred_return* contains the child's preferred geometry and that at least one of the child's geometry fields currently differs from its preferred geometry. A return of XtGeometryNo means that *preferred_return* contains the child's preferred geometry and that this is the same as its current geometry.

If *intended* is not NULL, a return of XtGeometryYes means that the child either does not have a preferred geometry or would be happy with the geometry described in the intended parameter. A return of XtGeometryNo means that the proposed changes are not acceptable to the child and that the child prefers to retain its current geometry. A return of XtGeometryAlmost means that some change is acceptable, and the caller must examine the contents of *preferred_return* to find out what the preferred change is. If all the fields that were flagged in *intended* have the same values in *preferred_return*, XtGeometryAlmost means that changes in the proposed geometry are acceptable but that the child wants some additional changes made to other fields. If the fields have different values, it means that the child wants these fields changed but not to the proposed values. In both cases the flagged fields in *preferred_return* hold the child's preferred values.

 Programs should not expect `XtQueryGeometry` to reflect any geometry requests currently executing. Geometry managers use the requested geometry instead of calling `XtQueryGeometry`.

Examples 4.5 and 4.6 show how the Menu widget uses `XtQueryGeometry` to calculate its size. Menu queries its children to find which one has the widest preferred width and uses this width as the menu's width. It then queries each child to find out what the child's preferred height is given the menu's width, adds together these heights, and uses this sum as the menu's height.

The procedure WidestDesiredSize queries each child to find the child that desires the widest width. If Menu calls this procedure with a non-NULL *initiator* parameter, the parameter is a widget currently making a geometry request. WidestDesiredSize uses its width directly instead of calling `XtQuery-Geometry`.

CalculateDesiredSizes finds out what the desired height and border width are given a particular width. Again, the *initiator* widget is treated specially.

A child returns its preferred geometry by specifying a query_geometry procedure. If it does not have a preferred geometry, it specifies NULL, and `XtQueryGeometry` always returns XtGeometryYes to any queries. The query_geometry procedure is of type `XtGeometryHandler`.

```
static int WidestDesiredSize(menu, initiator)
    MenuWidget menu;
    Widget initiator;
{
    register int i, width = 0;
    register Widget child;
    XtWidgetGeometry desired;

    for (i = 0; i < menu->composite.num_children; i++) {
        child = menu->composite.children[i];
        if (!XtIsManaged(child)) continue;

        if (child == initiator) {
            if (child->core.width > width) {
                width = child->core.width;
            }
        } else {
            (void) XtQueryGeometry(child, NULL, &desired);
            if (desired.width > width) width = desired.width;
        }
    }

    if (width <= 0) return 1;
    else return width;
}
```

Example 4.5. A sample use of XtQueryGeometry

typedef XtGeometryResult (*XtGeometryHandler)(Widget, XtWidgetGeometry *,
                                              XtWidgetGeometry *);
    Widget *w*;
    XtWidgetGeometry *intended*;
    XtWidgetGeometry *preferred_return*;
w   Specifies the widget being queried.
intended   Specifies the proposed geometry changes.
preferred_return   Returns the preferred geometry.

This procedure is called with the parameters passed to XtQueryGeometry,
except that if the *intended* parameter is NULL, XtQueryGeometry replaces it
with a geometry specification with no bits set in *request_mode*. The
query_geometry procedure is responsible for filling in the fields it cares about
in *preferred_return*, setting the bits in *preferred_return->request_mode* to indicate
these fields, and returning the appropriate value as described in XtQuery-
Geometry. If the proposed geometry is acceptable, the query_geometry procedure returns XtGeometryYes. If the widget prefers to remain with its current

```
static void CalculateDesiredSizes(menu, width, initiator)
    MenuWidget menu;
    Dimension width;
    Widget initiator;
{
    XtWidgetGeometry proposed, desired;
    register Widget child;
    MenuConstraint mc;
    register int i;

    for (i = 0; i < menu->composite.num_children; i++) {
        child = menu->composite.children[i];
        if (!XtIsManaged(child)) continue;
        mc = (MenuConstraint) child->core.constraints;

        if (child == initiator) {
            mc->menu.desired_height = child->core.height;
            mc->menu.desired_border_width =
                    child->core.border_width;
        } else {
            proposed.width = width;
            proposed.request_mode = CWWidth;
            (void) XtQueryGeometry(child, &proposed, &desired);

            mc->menu.desired_height = desired.height;
            mc->menu.desired_border_width = desired.border_width;
        }
    }
}
```

Example 4.6.   Another use of XtQueryGeometry

geometry, the procedure returns XtGeometryNo. If the changes in the proposed geometry are acceptable as long as some other geometry changes are made as well, or if the widget prefers values for any of the changed fields that are different from both the proposed new value and the widget's current value, the procedure returns XtGeometryAlmost. In other words, the query_geometry procedure returns XtGeometryAlmost whenever it sets a bit in *preferred_return* that was not set in *intended* or whenever a flagged field in *preferred_return* has a value that is different from the one in *intended*.

Example 4.7 shows Label's query_geometry procedure. Label cares about the width and height and is willing to accept any x, y, border width, and stacking position. If the proposed geometry has a width and a height that match the desired dimensions, and the parent intends to use these values (i.e., CWWidth and CWHeight are set in *proposed–>request_mode*) QueryGeometry

```
static XtGeometryResult QueryGeometry(w, proposed, desired)
    Widget w;
    XtWidgetGeometry *proposed, *desired;
{
    LabelWidget lw = (LabelWidget) w;
#define Set(bit) (proposed->request_mode & bit)

    desired->width = lw->label.desired_width;
    desired->height = lw->label.desired_height;
    desired->request_mode = CWWidth | CWHeight;

    if (Set(CWWidth) && proposed->width == desired->width &&
            Set(CWHeight) && proposed->height == desired->height) {
        return XtGeometryYes;
    }

    if (desired->width == lw->core.width &&
            desired->height == lw->core.height) {
        return XtGeometryNo;
    }
    return XtGeometryAlmost;
#undef Set
}
```

Example 4.7. The Label query_geometry procedure

returns XtGeometryYes. Otherwise, the parent intends to use values for width and height that differ from the desired size. QueryGeometry returns XtGeometryNo if the desired size is equal to the current size or XtGeometry-Almost if the desired size is different from the current size.

4.18   Writing Constraint Widgets

Section 4.6 described why a composite widget might associate extra resources with its children. This section describes how to go about doing this.

The Intrinsics store a pointer to a constraint data structure in the *core.constraints* field of each widget instance. If the widget's parent is a normal composite widget or is not a composite at all, this field is NULL. If it is a subclass of Constraint, however, this field points to a data structure defined by the constraint parent.

When an application creates a widget and specifies a parent that is a sub-class of Constraint, the Intrinsics allocate a structure whose size is given by the *constraint.constraint_size* field in the parent's class record. They then use the parent's constraint resource list, specified by the *constraint.resources* and

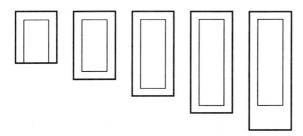

Figure 4.3. The same MinMax widget at different sizes

constraint.num_resources fields, to fill in all the resource fields in this structure using the resource database and the creation argument list. The Intrinsics fill in this structure exactly the same way as they fill in the widget instance record.

An example will make this more concrete. Consider MinMax, a constraint widget that associates a minimum and maximum size for each child. If a MinMax widget becomes smaller, it shrinks each child widget that would otherwise extend beyond the boundaries of the parent until that widget reaches its minimum size. If it becomes larger, it expands each child widget up to the maximum size for the child. Figure 4.3 shows a MinMax widget with one child at different sizes. In the first picture the MinMax widget is short enough that its child would have to be smaller than its minimum height to fit, so the MinMax widget clips the child. In the last picture the MinMax widget is so tall that its child would have to be larger than its maximum height to fill it up, so there is unused space.

The first step is to define the data structure that holds the constraints. Widgets declare these structures analogously to the way they declare widget data structures, in parts, in the widget private header file. This allows subclasses of the constraint widget to add further constraint fields the same way normal subclasses add additional fields to the widget instance record.

Example 4.8 shows part of the private header file for MinMax. The definition for MinMaxConstraintRec contains the part structure MinMaxConstraintPart. A subclass would define its own part structure containing its own constraint fields and define a constraint record that contains both MinMaxConstraintPart and its own constraint part.

Example 4.9 shows the public header file for MinMax. It defines the resource names XtNminWidth, XtNmaxWidth, XtNminHeight, and XtNmax-

```
/* Define constraint part structure */

typedef struct {
  /* New resource fields */
    short               min_width;
    short               max_width;
    short               min_height;
    short               max_height;
} MinMaxConstraintPart;

/* Define the full constraint record */

typedef struct _MinMaxConstraintRec {
    MinMaxConstraintPart minMax;
} MinMaxConstraintRec, *MinMaxConstraint;
```

Example 4.8. Part of the MinMax private header file

```
/* Make it safe to include this file more than once. */
#ifndef MINMAX_H
#define MINMAX_H

/* MinMax is derived from Constraint, so no need to include the
   superclass public header file.   */

/* Define the new resources that MinMax uses */

#define XtNmargin "margin"
#define XtNminWidth "minWidth"
#define XtNmaxWidth "maxWidth"
#define XtNminHeight "minHeight"
#define XtNmaxHeight "maxHeight"
#define XtCMinWidth "MinWidth"
#define XtCMaxWidth "MaxWidth"
#define XtCMinHeight "MinHeight"
#define XtCMaxHeight "MaxHeight"

/* External reference to the class record pointer */
extern WidgetClass minMaxWidgetClass;

/* Type definition for minMax widgets */
typedef struct _MinMaxRec *MinMaxWidget;

/* End of preprocessor directives */
#endif /* MINMAX_H */
```

Example 4.9. The MinMax public header file

```
#define Offset(field) XtOffsetOf(MinMaxConstraintRec, field)

static XtResource constraintResources[] = {
    {XtNminWidth, XtCMinWidth, XtRShort, sizeof(short),
        Offset(minMax.min_width), XtRImmediate, (XtPointer) -1},
    {XtNmaxWidth, XtCMaxWidth, XtRShort, sizeof(short),
        Offset(minMax.max_width), XtRImmediate, (XtPointer) -1},
    {XtNminHeight, XtCMinHeight, XtRShort, sizeof(short),
        Offset(minMax.min_height), XtRImmediate, (XtPointer) -1},
    {XtNmaxHeight, XtCMaxHeight, XtRShort, sizeof(short),
        Offset(minMax.max_height), XtRImmediate, (XtPointer) -1},
};
#undef Offset
```

Example 4.10. The MinMax constraint resources

Height and the resource classes XtCMinWidth, XtCMaxWidth, XtCMin-Height, and XtCMaxHeight for use in specifying resources for children of a MinMax widget.

The implementation of a constraint widget must provide a resource list for resources stored in the constraint structure. This is exactly the same as a normal widget resource list except that the offsets specified are offsets into the constraint structure. Note that a constraint widget must provide two resource lists, one for the resources of the widget itself and one for the resources in the constraint structure. Example 4.10 shows the resource list for MinMax's constraint resources.

Next the implementation fills in the ConstraintClassPart of its static widget class record initialization with a pointer to the constraint resource list, the number of entries in this list, the size of the constraint record, and methods for initializing, setting values, and destroying children. The *constraint_size*, *resources*, and *num_resources* fields allow the Intrinsics to allocate the constraint record for children of a constraint widget and fill in its resource fields. Example 4.11 shows part of MinMax's class record initialization.

When the Intrinsics create a child of a constraint widget, they fill in the resource fields in the widget and the constraint record and proceed as with a child of a nonconstraint widget. They call the initialize methods for the child's class and all its superclasses and call the parent's insert_child procedure. After this, however, things change. The Intrinsics call the constraint initialize methods for the parent's class and all its constraint superclasses, starting with Constraint and proceeding down to the parent's class.

```
    /* Composite class part */
    {
      /* geometry_manager        */ GeometryManager,
      /* change_managed          */ ChangeManaged,
      /* insert_child            */ InsertChild,
      /* delete_child            */ DeleteChild,
      /* extension               */ (XtPointer) &compositeExtension,
    },
      /* Constraint class part */
    {
      /* resources               */ constraintResources,
      /* num_resources           */ XtNumber(constraintResources),
      /* constraint_size         */ sizeof(MinMaxConstraintRec),
      /* initialize              */ ConstraintInitialize,
      /* destroy                 */ NULL,
      /* set_values              */ ConstraintSetValues,
      /* extension               */ NULL
    },
      /* MinMax class part */
    {
      /* extension               */ NULL,
    }
};

WidgetClass minMaxWidgetClass = (WidgetClass) &minMaxClassRec;
```

Example 4.11.   Part of the MinMax class declaration

These methods do the same sorts of initialization for the constraint fields as the normal initialize procedures do for the widget fields. If the constraint structure contains derived nonresource fields, the constraint initialize method fills them in, and it can check the constraints and the widget fields for consistency.

Sometimes this initialization requires a geometry change for the child. For example, a child of a MinMax widget might have an initial size that does not fall within the desired minimum and maximum limits. If the constraint initialize procedure needs to change the child's geometry, it calls XtMoveWidget, XtResizeWidget, or XtConfigureWidget on the child.

Example 4.12 shows MinMax's constraint initialize procedure and its utility procedures. If the application set neither minimum nor maximum for a dimension, ConstraintInitialize sets them both to the current size. If one size is set but not the other, ConstraintInitialize sets the unspecified one to either the minimum or maximum value the dimension could take. Next Constraint-Initialize checks that the minimum sizes are not greater than the maximum

```
static void CheckConstraint(w, smaller, larger, which)
    Widget w;
    short *smaller, *larger;
    String which;
{
    String params[3];
    Cardinal num_params;

    if (*smaller > *larger) {
        params[0] = params[1] = which;
        params[2] = XtName(w);
        num_params = 3;
        XtAppWarningMsg(XtWidgetToApplicationContext(w),
                "constraintError",
                "width", "WidgetError",
                "Min %s greater than max %s for widget %s",
                params, &num_params);
        *smaller = *larger;
    }
}

static void ResizeWithinConstraints(w, width, height)
    Widget w;
    Dimension *width, *height;
{
    register MinMaxConstraint mmc =
            (MinMaxConstraint) w->core.constraints;

    if (*width < mmc->minMax.min_width) {
        *width = mmc->minMax.min_width;
    } else if (*width > mmc->minMax.max_width) {
        *width = mmc->minMax.max_width;
    }

    if (*height < mmc->minMax.min_height) {
        *height = mmc->minMax.min_height;
    } else if (*height > mmc->minMax.max_height) {
        *height = mmc->minMax.max_height;
    }
}
```

(continued)

Example 4.12.   The MinMax constraint initialize procedure

```
static void ConstraintInitialize(req, new, args, num_args)
    Widget req, new;
    ArgList args;
    Cardinal *num_args;
{
    MinMaxConstraint mmc = (MinMaxConstraint) new->core.constraints;
    Dimension width = new->core.width, height = new->core.height;
#define MAXDIM 32768

    if (mmc->minMax.min_width == -1 && mmc->minMax.max_width == -1) {
        mmc->minMax.min_width = mmc->minMax.max_width = width;
    }
    if (mmc->minMax.min_height == -1 && mmc->minMax.max_height == -1) {
        mmc->minMax.min_height = mmc->minMax.max_height = height;
    }

    if (mmc->minMax.min_width == -1) mmc->minMax.min_width = 1;
    if (mmc->minMax.max_width == -1) mmc->minMax.max_width = MAXDIM;
    if (mmc->minMax.min_height == -1) mmc->minMax.min_height = 1;
    if (mmc->minMax.max_height == -1) mmc->minMax.max_height = MAXDIM;

    CheckConstraint(new, &mmc->minMax.min_width,
            &mmc->minMax.max_width, "width");
    CheckConstraint(new, &mmc->minMax.min_height,
            &mmc->minMax.max_height, "height");
    ResizeWithinConstraints(new, &width, &height);

    if (width != new->core.width || height != new->core.height) {
        XtResizeWidget(new, width, height);
    }
#undef MAXDIM
}
```

Example 4.12. The MinMax constraint initialize procedure

sizes; if they are, it resets the maximum to be the minimum, issuing a warning message. Finally it checks that the child's size is within the limits in the constraints and resizes the child if necessary.

The set_values method for constraints acts similarly. When an application calls XtSetValues for a child of a constraint widget, the Intrinsics call the set_values procedure for the widget's class and all its superclasses, just as usual. Then, however, they call the constraint set_values procedures for the parent's class and all its constraint superclasses, starting with Constraint and proceeding to the parent's class. Like regular set_values procedures, the return value from a constraint set_values procedure indicates whether the child widget needs to be redisplayed. The constraint records pointed to within the three widgets passed to the constraint set_values procedure have the same semantics as those for the widget records themselves; the old and request widgets have pointers to copies of the constraint record as it was before the `XtSetValues` and after modifying the fields according to the argument list, respectively.

A difficulty occurs when a constraint resource changing its value requires a new widget size or position. Just as with the normal set_values procedure, the constraint set_values procedure cannot assume that the change to the constraint will actually occur since a subclass might disallow or modify the change. It should wait for the geometry request generated at the end of `XtSet-Values` to actually act upon the new constraint value. The problem is that `XtSetValues` only issues the request if a geometry field in the child is different; it has no idea whether a changed constraint field requires a geometry request.

If a changed constraint requires a new geometry, the constraint set_values procedure needs to change at least one geometry field in the child widget. It may be possible to change the value to what it will be in the new geometry, but sometimes computing this involves going through the complete layout process just to compute this one value, and then doing it again when the geometry request actually occurs. To avoid this the constraint set_values procedure makes a completely arbitrary change to a geometry field, just to cause the geometry request. An example is to copy the child's border width into a field in the parent's widget instance record and then to change it to a different value. When `XtSetValues` calls the geometry manager, the geometry manager checks for this special case, replaces the border width, and then does the layout. Any widget that does something like this should document it thoroughly so that subclasses understand what is going on and cooperate. For an example, see the Menu widget implementation in Chapter 10.

Fortunately, MinMax does not need to go through these contortions; if a constraint changes so that the widget's current size lies outside the new values, it is easy to calculate the appropriate new size. Example 4.13 shows the constraint set_values procedure for this widget class.

Constraint widgets provide subresource values or values for resources that do not exist in the constraint resource list by providing a get_values_hook procedure.[2] This procedure must be specified in an extension record; see

---

[2] The constraint get_values_hook procedure is not supported by Intrinsics implementations that conform to specifications earlier than Release 4.

```
static Boolean ConstraintSetValues(old, req, new, args, num_args)
    Widget old, req;
    ArgList args;
    Cardinal *num_args;
    register Widget new;
{
    register MinMaxConstraint mmc =
            (MinMaxConstraint) new->core.constraints;

    CheckConstraint(new, &mmc->minMax.min_width,
            &mmc->minMax.max_width, "width");
    CheckConstraint(new, &mmc->minMax.min_height,
            &mmc->minMax.max_height, "height");
    ResizeWithinConstraints(new, &new->core.width, &new->core.height);

    return FALSE;
}
```

Example 4.13. The MinMax constraint set_values procedure

Section 2.21 for a sample specification. MinMax needs no get_values_hook and so supplies no extension record for its Constraint part.

The final new method for constraint widgets is the constraint destroy method. The Intrinsics call this method for the parent's widget class and its superclasses after calling the parent's delete_child procedure and before calling the normal destroy procedures for the widget's class and its superclasses. Like the normal destroy procedure, the constraint destroy procedure is responsible for freeing any data pointed to by fields in this class's part of the constraint record; it is chained from subclass to superclass so the Intrinsics call the procedures starting with the parent's class and proceeding to the Constraint class. The constraint destroy procedure should not free the actual constraint record; the Intrinsics to this automatically. If nothing special needs to be done when the child is destroyed, this procedure is NULL; this is the case with MinMax.

Chapter 10 contains the complete implementation of MinMax.

Chapter 5

Shell Widgets and Pop-Ups

Writing Applications

5.1 Shell Widgets

A shell widget acts as an interface between the internal, self-consistent world of a toolkit application and the external, asynchronous world of window managers. The name *shell* derives from its functionality: it holds a toolkit application much like an eggshell holds an egg.

Users do not normally see shell widgets. A shell displays one child widget; the shell's size and the child's position are such that the child's interior completely fills the shell's interior and the shell's border appears to be the child's border.

Widgets within an application negotiate their geometries through a set of toolkit interfaces. The root of the widget tree, however, must negotiate its geometry with the user's window manager or with the X server. Rather than requiring every widget that might be at the root of the tree to include the logic necessary do these negotiations, the toolkit provides shell widgets that understand these protocols and other conventions for dealing with the "outside world." The protocols and conventions are described in a document called the *Inter-Client Communications Convention Manual,* or more often, the ICCCM.[1] The ICCCM is available in the MIT X distribution and in the second edition of *Xlib.*

---

[1] Or sometimes, the dread ICCCM.

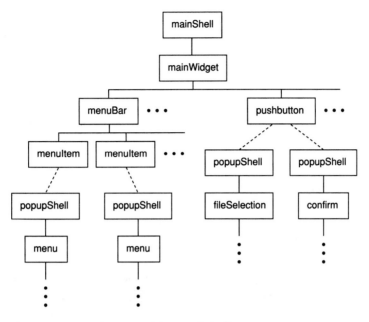

Figure 5.1. A widget tree with several shells

Each independent window of an application requires a shell widget. Every application with a window therefore needs at least one shell, and if the application creates additional top-level windows, pop-up dialog boxes, or pop-up menus, it requires additional shells for each additional independent window. The shell widget that is at the root of the application's window tree is called the *main* shell, and the shell widgets that hold other windows are called *pop-up* shells. Figure 5.1 shows a widget tree for an application that contains menus and dialog boxes; the widget at the root of the tree is the main shell and the widgets at the root of the subtrees are pop-up shells.

Applications that create widget trees on multiple displays have a main shell on each display; this is the only time an application has more than one main shell.

Any widget in the user interface can be the parent for a pop-up shell. This parenthood is not like being a regular parent; the pop-up shell's window is not a child of the widget's window but rather a child of the root window. Parents of pop-up shells are rarely even aware that the pop-up child exists. The pop-up shell's parent really just serves to give the pop-up widget tree a place to be linked into the main widget tree; the Intrinsics construct the list of widgets used to look up resources for widgets within a pop-up shell tree as if the pop-up shell were a normal child of its parent.

Consider an application named "program" that within its principal widget named "box" has a pushbutton named "options" that pops up a menu. The menu's pop-up shell is named "menuPopup"; it contains a Menu widget named "menu" that contains a menu item named "quit". To set the background for the menu item to red, specify

```
program.box.options.menuPopup.menu.quit.background : red
```

Of course, wildcarding would normally be used to eliminate some levels of qualification; a user would probably specify this as something like

```
program*options*quit.background : red
```

caring only that the "quit" widget is somewhere in the tree below the "options" widget. It is not necessary for the pop-up shell to be a pop-up child of the widget that pops it up; widgets can pop up shells that exist anywhere in the widget tree. Having it be a child of the widget that activates it, however, creates a more intuitive widget tree, making things easier both for the programmer and for the user who is trying to customize the program.

Pop-up shells differ from regular widgets in that they never appear on the screen automatically, even if they are realized. Instead there is a set of routines including XtPopup and XtPopdown that controls when pop-up widget trees appear and disappear. The managed flag and XtNmappedWhenManaged resource for a pop-up shell have no meaning and do not control whether the shell is visible or not.

The Intrinsics support four classes of shells for applications:

OverrideShell Used to hold extremely transient widgets; the shell's window bypasses the user's window manager completely. Pop-up menus are usually held by override shells. The class pointer for override shells is overrideShellWidgetClass.

TransientShell Used to hold widgets that are subsidiary to a main widget. Many window managers treat these windows differently from main windows, perhaps providing fewer manipulation options to the user and automatically unmapping and mapping the window when the user iconifies or deiconifies the main window. A transient shell is said to be a transient for the shell widget to which it is subsidiary, and this widget is found in the transient shell's XtNtransientFor resource.

Pop-up dialog boxes are usually held by transient shells. The class pointer for transient shells is `transientShellWidgetClass`.

TopLevelShell　　Used to hold relatively permanent widgets. If an application has multiple independent windows, each is held by a top-level shell. The class pointer for top-level shells is `topLevelShellWidgetClass`.

ApplicationShell　Used to hold the application's main widget. The difference between application shells and top-level shells is that application shells appear as applications to the user's session manager; application shells understand the protocols that permit a user to suspend and restart his session. The application's main shell is usually an application shell, and each application normally has exactly one application shell. The class pointer for application shells is `applicationShell-WidgetClass`.

Applications that do anything more complicated with shells than just using the one returned by `XtAppInitialize` need to include `<X11/Shell.h>` for the necessary declarations and resource definitions.

A few applications only display windows on the user's display intermittently; most of the time no window is visible even as an icon. Applications like this may never realize their main shell, which exists only to provide a root in the widget tree.

Shell widgets can have subclasses just like any other widgets; widget sets often subclass one or more of these shells to provide additional functionality to applications. Consult the widget set documentation to see if applications using the widget set should use a subclass of one of these shells instead of the shell listed here.

The toolkit tries to make shells as invisible as possible. Applications must create shells, but after that there are only a few times when an application must worry about them:

• An application realizes its widget tree by passing its main shell to `XtRealizeWidget`.

• To move its window tree elsewhere on the screen, an application uses `XtSetValues` on the XtNx and XtNy resources of the shell. Most user interface styles discourage this; the user normally controls window positions.

• To make a subsidiary window appear in a specific location relative to the main window, the application finds the screen coordinates of this location using `XtTranslate-Coords` and sets the XtNx and XtNy resources of the subsidiary shell to the appropriate coordinates before popping it up. See Section 5.6 for more information.

- An application can ask the window manager to iconify or deiconify a widget tree by setting the XtNiconic resource of the shell widget. Most user interface styles discourage this; the user normally controls which windows are icons.

- To make a widget tree like a pop-up menu or a dialog box appear or disappear, an application passes its shell to certain toolkit procedures. See Section 5.6 for more information.

Applications, for the most part, ignore their shell widgets the rest of the time. In particular, they never resize their shells; instead they resize the widget inside the shell.

5.2   Shell Widget Resources

Shells define many resources, and for most applications their default values provide the appropriate functionality. You should feel free to skim or even skip most of this section on your first reading. The most commonly used shell resources are XtNallowShellResize, defined for all shells, XtNtitle, XtNinput, and XtNiconPixmap, defined for nonoverride shells, and XtNiconName, defined for top-level and application shells. However, applications that rely upon certain shell resources having their default values should generally set these values explicitly, since Intrinsics implementations are allowed to change some shell resource defaults.

All shell widgets are subclasses of Composite. They therefore support all resources defined by Core and Composite as well as these extra resources:

Name	Class	Type	Default
XtNallowShellResize	XtCAllowShellResize	Boolean	FALSE
XtNgeometry	XtCGeometry	String	NULL
XtNsaveUnder	XtCSaveUnder	Boolean	special
XtNoverrideRedirect	XtCOverrideRedirect	Boolean	special
XtNvisual	XtCVisual	Visual *	special
XtNcreatePopupChildProc	XtCCreatePopupChildProc	see text	NULL
XtNpopupCallback	XtCCallback	XtCallbackList	NULL
XtNpopdownCallback	XtCCallback	XtCallbackList	NULL

XtNallowShellResize controls whether children of the shell are allowed to resize themselves. If it is FALSE, the shell, as parent of its child, always refuses any resize request. Many user interface styles specify that applications should not change their sizes on their own; only the user is allowed to change the

☞ size. If an application needs to change its size, it sets this resource to TRUE; a common programming error is forgetting about this resource and subsequently wondering why code to change the size has no effect.

XtNgeometry specifies the initial size of the shell, and this size propagates to its managed child. Changing it after the shell is realized has no effect. Its format is a geometry specification as accepted by the `XParseGeometry` Xlib call; see Section 10.3 of *Xlib*. If a value for this resource is specified, the shell forces its child to this size and sets flags to tell the window manager that the user specified the application's geometry. If XtNgeometry has its default value, the shell takes its child's size and sets flags to tell the window manager that the application specified the application's geometry. Window managers often interact with the user to request a size and position when presented with an application that specified its geometry itself. Applications therefore never specify XtNgeometry in the application or in the application defaults file; to create an initial size they specify a size for the shell's child. The geometry resource usually comes from the user's defaults or from the command line.

XtNsaveUnder controls whether the shell asks the server to preserve the contents of the screen that are obscured by the shell's window. It should be TRUE for shells that the application expects to be on the screen for only a short time. The default value is TRUE if the shell is an override or transient shell and FALSE if the shell is a top-level or application shell.[2]

XtNoverrideRedirect controls whether the shell instructs the server to bypass the user's window manager when dealing with the shell's window. See Section 3.2.8 of *Xlib* for more information on override-redirect. XtNoverride-Redirect should be TRUE only for shells holding extremely transient widgets such as pop-up menus. The default value is TRUE if the shell is an override shell and FALSE otherwise.

XtNvisual controls which type of visual is used for widgets within this shell's tree.[3] Its default value is the value of XtNvisual for the shell holding this shell's parent, or the default visual for the screen if the shell is the top-level widget in the tree. The easiest way to get a visual value is to use the string-to-visual converter supplied by the Intrinsics; see Section 3.7. Most programmers do not need to worry about visuals; see Section 2.7 for more details.

---

[2] Remember that a widget that belongs to a class also belongs to all its superclasses, so these defaults apply to widgets that are subclasses of these classes as well.

[3] XtNvisual is not supported by Intrinsics implementations that conform to specifications earlier than Release 4.

XtNcreatePopupChildProc is of type `XtCreatePopupChildProc`. If it is not NULL, the Intrinsics call it automatically before mapping the shell to the screen. This allows applications to delay creating widgets in pop-up shells until just before the shell appears. It is described in Section 5.6.

XtNpopupCallback allows applications to make last-minute changes before mapping the pop-up shell. It is described in Section 5.9.

XtNpopdownCallback allows applications to make changes after the Intrinsics unmap the shell. It is described in Section 5.9.

Override shells have no additional resources, but the default values for the XtNsaveUnder and XtNoverrideRedirect resources are TRUE.

Transient, top-level, and application shells support the following additional resources:

Name	Class	Type	Default
XtNtitle	XtCTitle	String	special
XtNtitleEncoding	XtCTitleEncoding	Atom	XA_STRING
XtNwmTimeout	XtCWmTimeout	int	5000 milliseconds
XtNwaitForWm	XtCWaitForWm	Boolean	TRUE
XtNtransient	XtCTransient	Boolean	special
XtNminWidth	XtCMinWidth	int	XtUnspecifiedShellInt
XtNminHeight	XtCMinHeight	int	XtUnspecifiedShellInt
XtNmaxWidth	XtCMaxWidth	int	XtUnspecifiedShellInt
XtNmaxHeight	XtCMaxHeight	int	XtUnspecifiedShellInt
XtNwidthInc	XtCWidthInc	int	XtUnspecifiedShellInt
XtNheightInc	XtCHeightInc	int	XtUnspecifiedShellInt
XtNbaseWidth	XtCBaseWidth	int	XtUnspecifiedShellInt
XtNbaseHeight	XtCBaseHeight	int	XtUnspecifiedShellInt
XtNminAspectX	XtCMinAspectX	int	XtUnspecifiedShellInt
XtNminAspectY	XtCMinAspectY	int	XtUnspecifiedShellInt
XtNmaxAspectX	XtCMaxAspectX	int	XtUnspecifiedShellInt
XtNmaxAspectY	XtCMaxAspectY	int	XtUnspecifiedShellInt
XtNwinGravity	XtCWinGravity	int	special
XtNinput	XtCInput	Bool	FALSE
XtNinitalState	XtCInitialState	int	NormalState
XtNiconPixmap	XtCIconPixmap	Pixmap	None
XtNiconMask	XtCIconMask	Pixmap	None
XtNiconWindow	XtCIconWindow	Window	None

Name	Class	Type	Default
XtNiconX	XtCIconX	int	XtUnspecifiedShellInt
XtNiconY	XtCIconY	int	XtUnspecifiedShellInt
XtNwindowGroup	XtCWindowGroup	Window	XtUnspecifiedWindow

XtNtitle gives a string for the window manager to use as the application's title. If the shell's class is TopLevelShell or ApplicationShell and its XtNiconName resource is not NULL, the default value for XtNtitle is the value of XtNicon-Name. Otherwise, the default value is the shell's name.

XtNtitleEncoding specifies the character set used in the title resource.[4] The ICCCM only defines one standard value for this, XA_STRING, which means that the title is a string of characters in the ISO Latin-1 character set used for Western European languages. Individual window managers define other valid values for this resource.

Since window managers operate asynchronously, the shell widget must wait for an answer to any requests it makes involving the window manager. XtNwm-Timeout controls how long the shell waits, in milliseconds, before deciding that the window manager is not reacting properly or has gone away.

XtNwaitForWm controls whether the shell's geometry manager waits for the window manager to respond to a request. If this is FALSE, the shell acts very pessimistically: it assumes that any requests will not be granted and im-mediately denies any geometry requests. It still makes the request, however, and if the request succeeds, the shell asynchronously notifies the application and widgets of the change exactly as if the user had moved or resized the window. Setting XtNwaitForWm FALSE is appropriate if the application is run-ning across a network with long delays to avoid having the application freeze while it waits for window manager responses. The shell implementation will reset XtNwaitForWm if the window manager responds or fails to respond within the XtNwmTimeout interval.

If XtNtransient is TRUE, the shell sets a property to inform the window manager that this shell's window is a transient for another window. If the shell is a transient shell, the other window is the value of the XtNtransientFor resource. Otherwise, the other window is specified by the XtNwindowGroup resource unless the window group is the special value XtUnspecified-

---

[4] XtNtitleEncoding is not supported by Intrinsics implementations that conform to specifica-tions earlier than Release 4.

WindowGroup; if XtNwindowGroup has this value, the Intrinsics do not specify the property. The transient resource defaults to TRUE if the shell is a transient shell and FALSE otherwise. Consult the ICCCM and Section 9.1.9 of *Xlib* for more information on transients.

The next set of resources specify size information to the user's window manager. Consult the ICCCM and Section 9.1.6 of *Xlib* for more information. For all these resources, the default value XtUnspecifiedShellInt means not to specify the resource to the window manager.

XtNminWidth, XtNminHeight, XtNmaxWidth, and XtNmaxHeight specify the minimum and maximum useful sizes for the application's window. XtNwidthInc and XtNheightInc specify resizing increments, and XtNbase-Width and XtNbaseHeight specify the base value that the size increments get added to.[5] XtNminAspectX, XtNminAspectY, XtNmaxAspectX, and XtNmax-AspectY allow the application to specify a range of aspect ratios that it prefers.

XtNwinGravity allows an application to specify which corner of its window is critical for placement.[6] If the window manager decides to place the shell's window where the application asked, it places the position on the shell window border named by the XtNwinGravity where the shell window would have been placed in the absence of any window manager decorations. If XtNgeometry is not NULL, the default value for XtNwinGravity is the gravity implied by the geometry string. If XtNgeometry is NULL, the default value is NorthWest-Gravity. Consult the ICCCM for more details on top-level window gravity.

The remaining resources control fields in the window manager hint structure. Consult the ICCCM and Section 9.1.5 of *Xlib* for more information.

XtNinput controls whether the application expects the window manager to give the input focus to the application. If XtNinput is FALSE, the window manager never assigns input focus. This is appropriate for applications that never need the focus and for applications that take the focus themselves when the user interacts with the application. If XtNinput is TRUE, the window manager gives input focus under circumstances that it defines. This is appropriate for applications that expect the window manager to handle all their focus management and for applications that redirect the focus within them-

---

[5] XtNbaseWidth and XtNbaseHeight are not supported by Intrinsics implementations that conform to specifications earlier than Release 4.

[6] XtNwinGravity is not supported by Intrinsics implementations that conform to specifications earlier than Release 4.

☞ selves when the window manager assigns it. Note that the type of this resource is `Bool`, defined by Xlib, and not `Boolean`, defined by the toolkit. For a full discussion of handling input focus in toolkit applications, see Section 6.7.

XtNinitialState controls how the window appears initially. It is an integer value with resource type XtRInitialState, so resource files specify the strings "NormalState" or "IconicState" and have the string converted to the appropriate value by the string-to-initial-state converter. Applications normally use the macro names defined in `<X11/Xutil.h>`; the possible values are

NormalState   The application wants to start as a normal window.

IconicState   The application wants to start as an icon.

XtNiconPixmap and XtNiconMask give bitmaps for the window manager to use as the application's icon. If the icon mask is specified, the window manager may display only the bits in the icon pixmap corresponding to 1 bits in the icon mask, allowing nonrectangular icons, but this behavior is optional. Both of these values must be bitmaps (pixmaps of depth 1), and window managers can put restrictions upon the sizes of icon bitmaps they accept.

XtNiconWindow provides a window for the window manager to use as an icon. Window managers can restrict icon windows to be a particular size.

XtNiconX and XtNiconY give an initial position for the application's icon. Window managers can ignore these values.

XtNwindowGroup specifies the window group to the window manager and also, if the transient resource is set and the shell is not a transient shell, specifies which window this shell is a transient for. The shell replaces its default value, XtUnspecifiedWindow, with the window of the application's main shell. To disable setting this hint, give the window group resource the special value XtUnspecifiedWindowGroup.[7]

Particular implementations of the Intrinsics may additionally define some extra resources for transient, top-level, and application shells to support private window manager protocols; these resources should be described in the implementation documentation. Typical uses are to tell the window manager not to put a title bar on this shell's window, to ask the window manager what font it uses to display a title, or to handle the WM_TAKE_FOCUS client message (see Section 6.7). Be very careful about these resources; applications that use

---

[7] XtUnspecifiedWindowGroup is not supported by Intrinsics implementations that conform to specifications earlier than Release 4.

them can be difficult to port to other implementations of the Intrinsics or might find that the user's window manager does not support the private protocols to deal with these resources. Be especially careful when doing an XtGetValues on these resources since, if the window manager does not support the protocols, nonsense values are likely to be returned. To check if the implementation of the Intrinsics supports a particular resource, store a known, invalid value in the variable that XtGetValues will fetch the resource into and check for this value after XtGetValues returns.

Transient shells have one additional resource, and the defaults for the XtNtransient, XtNsaveUnder, and XtNoverrideRedirect resources are TRUE.

Name	Class	Type	Default
XtNtransientFor	XtCTransientFor	Widget	NULL

XtNtransientFor defines the widget that the shell is a transient for if the shell has the XtNtransient resource TRUE and is a transient shell.[8] If XtNtransient is TRUE and XtNtransientFor is NULL, the shell uses the value of the window group resource instead.

Top-level and application shells support the following additional resources:

Name	Class	Type	Default
XtNiconName	XtCIconName	String	special
XtNiconNameEncoding	XtCIconNameEncoding	Atom	XA_STRING
XtNiconic	XtCIconic	Boolean	FALSE

XtNiconName gives a text string for the window manager to use in the application's icon. Its default value is the name of the shell.

XtNiconNameEncoding specifies the character set used in the icon name resource.[9] The ICCCM only defines one standard value for this, XA_STRING, which means that the icon name is a string of characters in the ISO Latin-1 character set. Individual window managers define other valid values for this resource.

---

[8] XtNtransientFor is not supported by Intrinsics implementations that conform to specifications earlier than Release 4; they always use the window group resource for this purpose.

[9] XtNiconNameEncoding is not supported by Intrinsics implementations that conform to specifications earlier than Release 4.

XtNiconic allows the application to iconify or deiconify a widget tree and also provides an alternative way of setting the XtNinitialState resource. Changing XtNiconic through `XtSetValues` changes the iconic state; setting it to FALSE for a shell that is not already popped up calls `XtPopup` on the shell with *grab_kind* equal to XtGrabNone.

Application shells support the following additional resources:

Name	Class	Type	Default
XtNargc	XtCArgc	int	0
XtNargv	XtCArgv	String *	NULL

The application shell uses XtNargc and XtNargv to set the WM_COMMAND property that specifies the command line used to invoke the program. If an application uses `XtAppInitialize`, the Intrinsics automatically set these resources to the values of *argc* and *argv* passed to `XtAppInitialize`. If an application creates a shell directly with `XtAppCreateShell`, the application must set these resources itself.

5.3 Shells and Geometry

Like any other widget, a shell must react to geometry requests from below and geometry changes from above. However, in the case of shells, *above* means from the user's window manager. If the window manager changes a shell's position, the server moves the shell's child along to the new position; this is entirely transparent to the application. The shell attempts to keep its XtNx and XtNy resources up-to-date with the shell's current position on the screen. If the user is using a reparenting window manager, these coordinates are not actually the coordinates of the shell's window within its parent window but are instead the position of the shell within the root window—the coordinates the shell's window would have if the window manager were not reparenting. Some older window managers do not provide the information the shell needs to keep these fields correct.

If the window manager resizes the shell's window, the shell reacts by resizing its child to be the new size. The shell's child window always completely fills the interior of the shell.

Shells react to geometry requests from below by asking the window manager for the new geometry if the shell's XtNallowShellResize resource is TRUE. Applications never resize their shells directly; instead they call XtSetValues on the XtNwidth and XtNheight resources of the shell's child. The only time an application deals directly with a shell's geometry is to set its XtNx and XtNy resources to move it to a new location.

The XtNmappedWhenManaged resource acts differently for main shells than for other widgets; being managed or unmanaged is meaningless for them since they have no parent. Instead, when the Intrinsics realize the shell they check this resource and only map the shell's window to the screen if the resource is TRUE. This is useful for when an application bases the shell's position upon its size, for example, to center the shell on the screen, since the initial sizes of the widgets in the widget tree are not known until the tree is realized. This means that the application cannot do the calculation to determine the position before realization. By setting XtNmappedWhenManaged to FALSE before realizing the shell, the application prevents the shell from appearing upon the screen. It then calculates the correct position, moves the shell to this position by doing XtSetValues on its XtNx and XtNy resources, maps the shell by calling XtMapWidget, and optionally calls XtSetMapped-WhenManaged on the shell to reset the flag to TRUE. The Intrinsics specification does not require XtSetMappedWhenManaged to map top-level shells when changing their XtNmappedWhenManaged resource.

5.4   Children of Shells

Shells always have at most one managed child. They can, however, have other unmanaged children. An application that is extremely space-conscious can save on memory by sharing a shell among pop-up widget trees that never appear on the screen simultaneously. To pop up a particular widget tree, the application manages the appropriate child of the shell and pops up the shell. When the widgets are no longer needed on the screen the application pops down the shell and unmanages the child.

Some widget sets take this even a step further, providing special subclasses of shells that automatically pop themselves up and down whenever a child is managed or unmanaged. Consult the widget set documentation to see if this is the recommended way of doing pop-ups for your widget set.

5.5   Creating a New Widget Tree

To create a main shell widget for an application, use XtAppCreateShell.

Widget XtAppCreateShell(*application_name, application_class, widget_class,*
                                    display, args, num_args)
       String *application_name*;
       String *application_class*;
       WidgetClass *widget_class*;
       Display **display*;
       ArgList *args*;
       Cardinal *num_args*;

application_name	Specifies the name of the application instance; this should be the same as the name passed to XtOpenDisplay.
application_class	Specifies the class of the application; this should be the same as the class passed to XtOpenDisplay.
widget_class	Specifies the widget class that the application top-level widget should be.
display	Specifies the display to get the resources from.
args	Specifies the argument list to use in creation.
num_args	Specifies the number of arguments in the argument list.

Many applications do not need to call XtAppCreateShell directly; XtAppInitialize calls it automatically and returns the created shell.

The name and class should be the same as those passed to XtOpen-Display or XtDisplayInitialize; normally the name is NULL, meaning to use the name as determined by XtOpenDisplay. When the Intrinsics look up resources for widgets in the shell's widget tree, these strings act as the leftmost components for the database queries.

The created shell widget is of the class specified in the call; normally this is applicationShellWidgetClass or a subclass of it.

The *display* parameter describes which display's database the Intrinsics use to fetch resources. If the shell's XtNscreen resource is NULL, XtAppCreate-Shell creates the shell on the default screen for *display*. If it is not NULL, XtAppCreateShell creates the shell on that screen and *display* is used only for resource lookup. XtNscreen can refer to a screen on any display in the application context; it does not have to be a screen of the display passed to XtAppCreateShell.

XtVaAppCreateShell is the varargs version of XtAppCreateShell.

Widget XtVaAppCreateShell(*application_name, application_class, widget_class, display, ...*)
    String *application_name*;
    String *application_class*;
    WidgetClass *widget_class*;
    Display **display*;

application_name	Specifies the name of the application instance.
application_class	Specifies the class name of this application.
widget_class	Specifies the widget class that the application top-level widget should be.
display	Specifies the display to get the resources from.
...	Specifies the resources for the shell.

5.6   Pop-Up Shells and Pop-Up Children

Every pop-up tree of widgets must have a pop-up shell at its root. The shell and the widgets within it are collectively called a *pop-up*. All toolkit routines that manipulate pop-ups take the pop-up shell as a parameter.

An application must decide when to create its pop-ups; it has three choices:

- At startup time—this leads to very fast response when the user activates the pop-up.

- At pop-up time—this leads to faster application startup at the cost of slower response the first time a pop-up is activated, and saves memory if some pop-ups are never used.

- In the background—this leads to faster application startup and fast response unless the background processing has not created the pop-up by the time it is needed, but leads to more complicated code. Chapter 6 describes how to use background procedures.

A particular application can choose to use a combination of all three methods. It creates any pop-ups it expects the user to interact with immediately at startup time, creates other pop-ups that it expects are commonly used in the background, and delays creating others that it expects might never be used until pop-up time.

The XtNcreatePopupChildProc resource provides the hook needed to delay creating pop-up widget trees.

typedef void (*XtCreatePopupChildProc)(Widget);
    Widget *w*;

w	Specifies the pop-up shell.

The Intrinsics call this procedure just before they pop up the shell, and the pop-up shell is its single parameter. An application using delayed creation creates the pop-up shell at startup time and specifies a procedure that creates the widgets within the pop-up widget tree as the XtNcreatePopupChildProc resource of the pop-up shell. Usually the last thing this procedure does is reset XtNcreatePopupChildProc to NULL using `XtSetValues`. This prevents future pop-ups from calling the procedure. If memory is very tight and the pop-up is unlikely to be used again, the application can destroy the children of the pop-up after popping the shell down and recreate them each time.

5.7   Creating Pop-Up Shells

To create a pop-up shell, use `XtCreatePopupShell`.

Widget XtCreatePopupShell(*name, widget_class, parent, args, num_args*)
    String *name*;
    WidgetClass *widget_class*;
    Widget *parent*;
    ArgList *args*;
    Cardinal *num_args*;

name	Specifies the name for the created pop-up shell widget.
widget_class	Specifies the class of widget to create.
parent	Specifies the parent for the new shell.
args	Specifies the argument list to override the resource defaults.
num_args	Specifies the number of arguments in the argument list.

`XtCreatePopupShell` creates pop-up shells to hold pop-up menus, pop-up dialog boxes, and subsidiary windows.

`XtVaCreatePopupShell` is the varargs version of `XtCreatePopup-Shell`.

Widget XtVaCreatePopupShell(*name, widget_class, parent, ...*)
    String *name*;
    WidgetClass *widget_class*;
    Widget *parent*;

name	Specifies the name for the created pop-up shell widget.
widget_class	Specifies the class of widget to create.
parent	Specifies the parent for the new shell.
...	Specifies the resources to override the defaults.

When an application creates a shell for a pop-up menu, the widget class is usually `overrideShellWidgetClass`; when creating a shell for a dialog box the widget class is usually `transientShellWidgetClass` or `topLevelShellWidgetClass`, and when creating a shell for a subsidiary window the widget class is usually `topLevelShellWidgetClass`.

Pop-up dialog boxes use either transient or top-level shells, depending upon whether the dialog box is useful without the main application window. Many window managers automatically iconify dialog boxes contained in transient shells when the user iconifies the main window, and some give the user fewer options for manipulating the window. If it makes sense to let the user treat the dialog box like any other window, a top-level shell is the answer.

Some window managers may not allow the user to move pop-up dialog boxes that are in transient shells. If the user is likely to need to consult information in the main window to interact with the dialog box, the application should either be careful about the position it gives the dialog box or should create the dialog box in a top-level shell.

Consider a text editor that creates a dialog box to prompt for a search string. If the model is to create the box when the user requests a search, get the search string, and then have the box go away, a transient shell is the answer. If, however, the model is to create a permanent search box that the user can move and iconify separately from the editor, a top-level shell is appropriate.

Applications treat subsidiary windows the same way they treat permanent dialog boxes; in fact, to the toolkit they are exactly the same thing. Just because the shell is called a pop-up shell does not mean it has to pop up and down like a jack-in-the-box—applications can pop the shell up and leave it on the screen indefinitely.

For example, a mail program might have one window displaying message headers, another showing the current message, and another to hold a message that the user is creating. Each independent window has its own pop-up shell, and each appears as an independent window to the user.

If there is a clear choice as to which of an application's independent shells is the main one, the best organization is to have the subsidiary shells be pop-up children of the main shell. If the header window of the mail application is the main window, the read and compose windows are subsidiaries. Making the read and compose shells be pop-up children of the main shell leads to resource specifications like this:

```
mail.geometry : ...
mail.read.geometry : ...
mail.compose.geometry : ...
```

The first line specifies the geometry resource for the main window and the second and third specify geometries for the read and compose shells.

In other applications there is no one window that qualifies as the main window. To the user of the mail program the header window, read window, and compose window all appear equal. In situations like this the resource specifications can be made more uniform by making the three shells all be pop-up children of the main shell and never realizing the main shell. In this case the only purpose of the main shell is to act as a root for the widget hierarchy; it never has any normal children and never appears on the screen. This scheme leads to more uniform resource specifications:

```
mail.headers.geometry : ...
mail.read.geometry : ...
mail.compose.geometry : ...
```

Each line specifies the geometry for one child; nothing is specified for the main shell since it never appears. If an application creates its shells this way, it picks one of them to be an application shell and specifies the XtNargv and XtNargc resources for it; this guarantees that the WM_COMMAND property gets set for the application. It does not matter which shell the application chooses for this purpose as long as the shell appears when the application starts up.

The resource specifications are the only difference between these two schemes. Applications should choose whichever leads to more natural resource specifications for the user.

5.8 Types of Pop-Up Widgets

There are three different types of pop-up widgets: modeless, modal, and spring-loaded.

Modeless pop-ups appear to the user as normal windows; they are visible to the window manager, which treats them like any other window. The user is free to switch between the modeless pop-up and other windows in the application. The message composition window of the mail application is an example of a modeless pop-up; while composing a message the user is free to go back and consult other messages.

A *modal* pop-up suspends the operation of the rest of the application while the pop-up is on the screen. These pop-ups are used when there is nothing the application can do until the user finishes interacting with the pop-up. The toolkit ignores any input to other parts of the application, but the user can continue to interact with other applications. A text editor uses a modal pop-up to get the name of a file to be edited or to request user confirmation before reading a file into a buffer that has unsaved modifications. Use modal pop-ups with discretion—they are appropriate only when you are absolutely sure that the input to the rest of the application must be suspended. Modal pop-ups may or may not be visible to the window manager depending upon the application user interface style.

A *spring-loaded* pop-up is a type of modal pop-up that is activated by a pointer button press and deactivated by the button release. They often block out input to any window except those within the pop-up; this includes other applications' windows. Pop-up and pull-down menus are the only spring-loaded pop-ups most users ever see, although certain user interface styles have other pop-ups that behave this way. Spring-loaded pop-ups are almost never visible to the window manager.

Any pop-up can, in turn, pop up other pop-ups. A pop-up dialog box can have pop-up menus or other pop-up dialog boxes, or a menu can have sub-menus activated by moving the pointer into a special area of the menu. The set of modal pop-ups currently active is called the *modal cascade*. A widget can be on the modal cascade *exclusively*, meaning that the user can no longer interact with other widgets on the cascade, or *nonexclusively*, meaning that the user can continue to interact with other widgets on the cascade back to the most recent exclusive pop-up. Exclusive pop-ups are useful for the same kinds of things modal pop-ups are useful for; a file selection dialog box in a text editor might create an exclusive pop-up dialog box to inform the user that the file selected is read-only. Nonexclusive pop-ups are useful for things like cascading menus when the user can continue to interact with the widget that popped up the nonexclusive widget. Exclusive and nonexclusive pop-ups are both modal pop-ups.

5.9   Controlling Pop-Ups

Pop-up shells never appear on the screen automatically, even if they are realized. Instead the application makes them appear by using XtPopup or a routine that calls XtPopup.

void XtPopup(*popup_shell, grab_kind*)
    Widget *popup_shell*;

XtGrabKind *grab_kind*;

popup_shell   Specifies the shell to pop up.

grab_kind   Specifies how input events should be constrained.

XtPopup first checks to make sure that its *popup_shell* is actually a shell, generating an error if not, and that it is not already popped up. It then calls the callback procedures in the shell's XtNpopupCallback resource, specifying the shell as the widget and NULL as the *call_data* parameter. Then, if the create child procedure in the shell's XtNcreatePopupChildProc is not NULL, XtPopup calls it with the shell as its single parameter. If the shell is not already realized, XtPopup calls XtRealizeWidget to realize it, and finally the shell is mapped to the screen. Pop-ups are always mapped raised; they are never obscured by other windows on the screen when they are first popped up, although they could be later.

The *grab_kind* parameter is of type XtGrabKind.

typedef enum {XtGrabNone, XtGrabNonexclusive, XtGrabExclusive} XtGrabKind;

This defines how user input is constrained. If *grab_kind* is XtGrabNone, this is a modeless pop-up; user input is not restricted at all. If it is XtGrabExclusive, this is an exclusive modal pop-up; user input is restricted to this shell's widget tree. If it is XtGrabNonexclusive, this is a nonexclusive modal pop-up; input is restricted to this shell's tree and to other widgets that are on the modal cascade back through the most recent exclusive widget.

The pop-up callback list can make last-minute changes to the widgets in the pop-up widget tree or modify widgets elsewhere in the application's user interface. When an application has to dynamically modify the data displayed in a pop-up, setting the sensitivity of menu items, for example, it can either always keep the pop-up widgets correct or it can wait and only update the widgets before popping them up. If it chooses the latter scheme, it adds one or more pop-up callbacks to update the widgets. The most common example of modifying the rest of the interface is to indicate that the rest of the application is inactive when popping up a modal widget. Pop-up callbacks should be used with discretion, since they make it take longer for the pop-up to appear.

An application that uses pop-up callbacks to modify the pop-up widget tree and the create pop-up child procedure to delay creating the widgets has to coordinate between these since XtPopup calls the pop-up callbacks before calling the create pop-up child procedure. Probably the easiest way is to have the pop-up callbacks check to be sure that the widgets they modify actually exist and to return without doing anything if not, and to have the create pop-up child procedure invoke the callbacks after it has created the pop-up widgets by calling

```
XtCallCallbacks(widget, XtNpopupCallback, NULL);
```

where *widget* is the pop-up shell.

When a pop-up widget is no longer needed, the application removes it from the screen by calling XtPopdown.

void XtPopdown (*popup_shell*)
    Widget *popup_shell*;
popup_shell   Specifies the shell to pop down.

XtPopdown unmaps the pop-up shell and, if it is a modal pop-up (i.e., it was popped up with an exclusive or nonexclusive grab), removes it from the modal cascade. It then calls the shell's pop-down callback, specifying NULL as the *call_data*.

Popping down a modal pop-up removes it from the modal cascade and also removes any other widgets from the cascade that were added after the widget being popped down. This does not pop these widgets down, however, and when the application does pop them down the Intrinsics generate a warning message when attempting to remove them from the modal cascade but finding they are already gone. To avoid this message, an application should always pop down modal pop-ups in the reverse order from which it popped them up.

Pop-down callbacks can reset any changes to the application's interface performed by the pop-up callbacks, if this is appropriate. They can also unrealize or even destroy the widgets in the pop-up widget tree if the application believes the pop-up is unlikely to be used again, but applications should be careful about doing this since it slows down subsequent pop-ups.

Another use for pop-up and pop-down callbacks is to simulate save-unders when the X server does not support them. The application enables and disables backing store for some of its windows that are time-consuming to redraw and that will be obscured by the pop-up. This avoids the server memory overhead of having backing store always enabled, but the window refreshes more quickly after the pop-up goes away. See Section 3.2.4 of *Xlib* for more information on backing store.

Often an application pops up a widget in a callback procedure; for example, clicking in a button might make a dialog box appear. If popping up a widget is the only thing the callback procedure does, the application can specify one of the pop-up convenience routines as the callback procedure. These three routines, XtCallbackNone, XtCallbackExclusive, and XtCallbackNonexclusive, differ only in the value they specify as the *grab_kind* parameter.

void XtCallbackNone(*w, client_data, call_data*)
    Widget *w*;
    XtPointer *client_data*;
    XtPointer *call_data*;

w	Specifies the widget that activated the pop-up.
client_data	Specifies the shell to pop up.
call_data	Specifies the call data; this parameter is ignored by this procedure.

void XtCallbackExclusive(*w, client_data, call_data*)
    Widget *w*;
    XtPointer *client_data*;
    XtPointer *call_data*;

w	Specifies the widget that activated the pop-up.
client_data	Specifies the shell to pop up.
call_data	Specifies the call data; this paramaeter is ignored by this procedure.

void XtCallbackNonexclusive(*w, client_data, call_data*)
    Widget *w*;
    XtPointer *client_data*;
    XtPointer *call_data*;

w	Specifies the widget that activated the pop-up.
client_data	Specifies the shell to pop up.
call_data	Specifies the call data; this parameter is ignored by this procedure.

An application specifies one of these procedures exactly the same way it specifies any callback procedure, in an argument list or through XtAddCallback or XtAddCallbacks. In any case, the application must specify the shell to pop up as the client data for the callback; for example, to pop up a modeless shell called *dialogShell* when the user activates the Pushbutton widget *button,* write

```
XtAddCallback(button, XtNcallback, XtCallbackNone,
        (XtPointer) dialogShell);
```

to add the callback.

Each of these callback procedures calls XtPopup for the shell specified in the *client_data* parameter, specifying *grab_kind* as appropriate to the name of the procedure. They then make the invoking widget insensitive by calling XtSetSensitive so that it will not respond to any further input events. If an application needs to do anything else in its callback procedure or does not want to make the invoking widget insensitive, it must write its own callback procedure.

Similarly, the Intrinsics provide a callback procedure XtCallback-Popdown, which pops a shell down.

void XtCallbackPopdown(*w, client_data, call_data*)
    Widget *w*;
    XtPointer *client_data*;
    XtPointer *call_data*;
w   Specifies the widget that activated the pop-down.
client_data   Specifies an XtPopdownID structure.
call_data   Specifies the call data; this parameter is ignored by this procedure.

The client data for this callback must be set to an XtPopdownID structure indicating the widget to pop down and a widget that is to become sensitive. XtPopdownID is defined as

typedef struct {
    Widget   shell_widget;
    Widget   enable_widget;
} XtPopdownIDRec, *XtPopdownID;

The *shell_widget* field must be set to the widget to pop down, and the *enable_widget* field is normally the widget that originally made the shell pop up. Continuing the example above, assume the dialog box within *dialogShell* has a button called *dismissButton* that makes the shell pop down. To add the callback, write

```
static XtPopdownIDRec popdown = {
    dialogShell,    /* shell_widget */
    button          /* enable_widget */
};

XtAddCallback(dismissButton, XtNcallback, XtCallbackPopdown,
    (XtPointer) &popdown);
```

XtCallbackPopdown calls XtPopdown on the *shell_widget* and makes the enabling widget sensitive again by calling XtSetSensitive on it.

Note that `XtCallbackNone`, `XtCallbackExclusive`, `XtCallback-Nonexclusive`, and `XtCallbackPopdown` have nothing to do with the shell pop-up and pop-down callbacks and are rarely, if ever, appropriate values to specify for these resources.

Shells popped up with `XtPopup` or one of the pop-up callback procedures are never spring-loaded. To pop up a shell in response to a pointer button press and have it popped down by the button release no matter where the release occurs, an application uses one of the two built-in action procedures `XtMenuPopup` and `XtMenuPopdown`, described in Chapter 7, or `XtPopup-SpringLoaded`.[10]

void XtPopupSpringLoaded(*popup_shell*)
    Widget *popup_shell*;
popup_shell   Specifies the shell to pop up.

In general, it is much easier for an application to use `XtMenuPopup` and `XtMenuPopdown` actions than to call `XtPopupSpringLoaded` directly. Applications and widgets normally use `XtPopupSpringLoaded` only from within custom action procedures that substitute for `XtMenuPopup` and that are intended to be bound to button events. See Chapter 7 for information on action procedures.

`XtPopupSpringLoaded` is identical to `XtPopup` except that it marks the pop-up as spring-loaded and the *grab_kind* is always XtGrabExclusive. Applications use `XtPopupSpringLoaded` only in response to receiving a button press event, for example, in the callback for a Pushbutton widget, and only if the documentation for the pop-up shell or the pop-up child specifies that it can be used as a spring-loaded pop-up. None of the Intrinsics-defined shell classes can be popped up spring-loaded without additional help from their child, although a shell subclass specific to a widget set might be. Of the widgets in this book, only the Menu widget can be popped up spring-loaded. This is typical of many widget sets; menus are usually the only spring-loaded widgets.

A widget popped up with `XtPopupSpringLoaded` is popped down with `XtPopdown` as usual.

---

[10] `XtPopupSpringLoaded` is not supported by Intrinsics implementations that conform to specifications earlier than Release 4.

Writing Widgets

There are very few occasions for programmers to need to know the internals of shells; the shell classes provided by the Intrinsics fill the needs of most applications. Occasionally a user interface style requires a shell subclass, and some widget sets include special shell resources to implement private window manager protocols.

5.10   The Shell Class Hierarchy

The Intrinsics define seven classes of shells. Besides the override, transient, top-level, and application shell classes visible to applications, there are three internal classes, shell, window manager shell, and vendor shell, that serve as places to hold resources common to various shell subclasses.

Figure 5.2 shows the class hierarchy for shell classes. The different shell classes are

Shell   The root of the shell hierarchy; has fields and algorithms common
                     to all shells. A direct subclass of Composite.

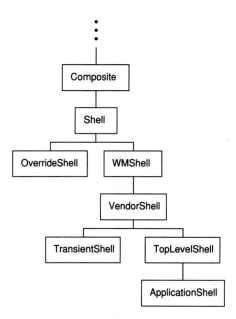

Figure 5.2.   The shell class hierarchy

OverrideShell	A subclass of Shell with no new fields but different default values for some resources; used for shells that bypass the user's window manager.
WMShell	An internal subclass of Shell with fields and algorithms common to all shells that are visible to the window manager.
VendorShell	An internal subclass of WMShell with fields and algorithms to support private window manager protocols.
TransientShell	A subclass of VendorShell with fields and algorithms for shells that are transients for other shells.
TopLevelShell	A subclass of VendorShell with fields and algorithms for shells that the window manager treats as independent windows.
ApplicationShell	A subclass of TopLevelShell with fields and algorithms for shells that appear as applications to the user's session manager.

You should view WMShell and VendorShell as one logical class; there should never be subclasses of WMShell that are not also subclasses of VendorShell. VendorShell is a separate class to isolate programmers implementing private window manager protocols from the complexity of the standard window manager interactions, and to simplify linking a specific implementation of VendorShell into the toolkit library.

The declarations needed to subclass shells are in the header files `<X11/ShellP.h>` and `<X11/VendorP.h>`.

No shell classes define any new fields in their class parts, so the class part records for all shell classes consist only of the extension field:

```
typedef struct {
    XtPointer    extension;
} ShellClassPart, OverrideShellClassPart, WMShellClassPart, VendorShellClassPart,
  TransientShellClassPart, TopLevelShellClassPart, ApplicationShellClassPart;
```

The definition of `VendorShellClassPart` can be different for a particular implementation of the vendor shell. No standard extensions exist for any shell class except Shell.

The full class records for each shell class consist of the appropriate shell class parts following the Core and Composite parts:

```
typedef struct _ShellClassRec {
    CoreClassPart            core_class;
    CompositeClassPart       composite_class;
```

```
        ShellClassPart              shell_class;
} ShellClassRec;


typedef struct _OverrideShellClassRec {
        CoreClassPart               core_class;
        CompositeClassPart          composite_class;
        ShellClassPart              shell_class;
        OverrideShellClassPart      override_shell_class;
} OverrideShellClassRec;


typedef struct _WMShellClassRec {
        CoreClassPart               core_class;
        CompositeClassPart          composite_class;
        ShellClassPart              shell_class;
        WMShellClassPart            wm_shell_class;
} WMShellClassRec;


typedef struct _VendorShellClassRec {
        CoreClassPart               core_class;
        CompositeClassPart          composite_class;
        ShellClassPart              shell_class;
        WMShellClassPart            wm_shell_class;
        VendorShellClassPart        vendor_shell_class;
} TransientShellClassRec;


typedef struct _TransientShellClassRec {
        CoreClassPart               core_class;
        CompositeClassPart          composite_class;
        ShellClassPart              shell_class;
        WMShellClassPart            wm_shell_class;
        VendorShellClassPart        vendor_shell_class;
        TransientShellClassPart     transient_shell_class;
} TransientShellClassRec;


typedef struct _TopLevelShellClassRec {
        CoreClassPart               core_class;
        CompositeClassPart          composite_class;
        ShellClassPart              shell_class;
        WMShellClassPart            wm_shell_class;
        VendorShellClassPart        vendor_shell_class;
        TopLevelShellClassPart      top_level_shell_class;
```

```
} TopLevelShellClassRec;

typedef struct _ApplicationShellClassRec {
        CoreClassPart                   core_class;
        CompositeClassPart              composite_class;
        ShellClassPart                  shell_class;
        WMShellClassPart                wm_shell_class;
        VendorShellClassPart            vendor_shell_class;
        TopLevelShellClassPart          top_level_shell_class;
        ApplicationShellClassPart       application_shell_class;
} ApplicationShellClassRec;
```

5.10.1   The Shell Widget

The Shell class defines a standard extension record with one method.[11]

```
typedef struct {
        XtPointer               next_extension;
        XrmQuark                record_type;
        long                    version;
        Cardinal                record_size;
        XtGeometryHandler       root_geometry_manager;
} ShellClassExtensionRec, *ShellClassExtension;
```

The first four fields are the standard extension header; see Section 2.21. The remaining field has the following meaning:

root_geometry_manager

> Resolves geometry requests for shell widgets; described in Section 5.11. If a class supplies no extension record, the Intrinsics assume *root_geometry_manager* has the value XtInheritRootGeometryManager.

Shell's instance part record defines fields common to all shell widgets.[12]

```
typedef struct {
        char                    *geometry;
        XtCreatePopupChildProc  create_popup_child_proc;
        XtGrabKind              grab_kind;
        Boolean                 spring_loaded;
```

---

[11] There is no extension record in Intrinsics implementations that conform to specifications earlier than Release 4. The extension field in ShellClassPart should be NULL in earlier versions.

[12] There is no *visual* field in Intrinsics implementations that conform to specifications earlier than Release 4.

```
        Boolean                    popped_up;
        Boolean                    allow_shell_resize;
        Boolean                    save_under;
        Boolean                    override_redirect;
        XtCallbackList             popup_callback;
        XtCallbackList             popdown_callback;
        Visual                     *visual;
} ShellPart;
```

The fields in this record have the following meanings:

geometry   The value of the XtNgeometry resource.

create_popup_child_proc
                    The value of the XtNcreatePopupChildProc resource.

grab_kind   An internal variable set to the grab kind that was specified when this widget was popped up; only the Intrinsics modify it.

spring_loaded   An internal variable set to whether the shell was popped up as a spring-loaded pop-up; only the Intrinsics modify it.

popped_up   An internal variable set to whether this shell is currently popped up; only the Intrinsics modify it.

allow_shell_resize The value of the XtNallowShellResize resource.

save_under   The value of the XtNsaveUnder resource.

override_redirect The value of the XtNoverrideRedirect resource.

popup_callback   The value of the XtNpopupCallback resource.

popdown_callback The value of the XtNpopdownCallback resource.

visual   The value of the XtNvisual resource.

The full instance record for widgets of the Shell class is `ShellRec`.

```
typedef struct {
    CorePart          core;
    CompositePart     composite;
    ShellPart         shell;
} ShellRec, *ShellWidget;
```

5.10.2 The Override Shell Widget

There are no additional fields in the OverrideShell instance part, but the instance part record still exists so that if this changes in the future, subclasses of OverrideShell will not have to change.

```
typedef struct {
    int    empty;
} OverrideShellPart;
```

The field in this record has the following (non)meaning:

empty　　　　The C compiler does not allow structures with no fields, so this field exists.

The full instance record for OverrideShell widgets is `OverrideShellRec`.

```
typedef struct {
    CorePart            core;
    CompositePart       composite;
    ShellPart           shell;
    OverrideShellPart   override;
} OverrideShellRec, *OverrideShellWidget;
```

5.10.3 The Window Manager Shell Widget

The WMShell instance part record defines fields common to transient, top-level, and application shells.[13]

```
typedef struct {
    String          title;
    int             wm_timeout;
    Boolean         wait_for_wm;
    Boolean         transient;
    Atom            wm_configure_denied;
    Atom            wm_moved;
    struct _OldXSizeHints {
        long            flags;
        int             x, y;
        int             width, height;
        int             min_width, min_height;
```

---

[13] There are no *base_width, base_height, win_gravity*, or *title_encoding* fields in Intrinsics implementations that conform to specifications earlier than Release 4.

```
        int              max_width, max_height;
        int              width_inc, height_inc;
        struct {
              int       x, y;
        } min_aspect, max_aspect;
    } size_hints;
    XWMHints          wm_hints;
    int              base_width, base_height;
    int              win_gravity;
    Atom             title_encoding;
} WMShellPart;
```

The fields in this record have the following meanings:

title   The value of the XtNtitle resource.

wm_timeout   The value of the XtNwmTimeout resource.

wait_for_wm   The value of the XtNwaitForWm resource.

transient   The value of the XtNtransient resource.

wm_configure_denied
                     An obsolete field that is not officially part of the Intrinsics. However, many implementations still have it. Do not set or modify this field.

wm_moved   An obsolete field that is not officially part of the Intrinsics. However, many implementations still have it. Do not set or modify this field.

size_hints   The values of various size hint resources.

wm_hints   The values of various window manager hint resources.

base_width   The value of the XtNbaseWidth resource.

base_height   The value of the XtNbaseHeight resource.

win_gravity   The value of the XtNwinGravity resource.

title_encoding   The value of the XtNtitleEncoding resource.

The rather odd part declaration stems from providing compatibility with earlier versions of the Intrinsics. Between Release 3 and Release 4 the XSizeHints structure added three new fields, *base_width*, *base_height*, and *win_gravity*. Updating the *size_hints* field to use the new type would have added new fields to the middle of the part record, breaking backward compatibility for WMShell subclasses. Instead, the Intrinsics redefined *size_hints* to be a structure that is a copy of the old XSizeHints structure and added the new fields to the end of the `WMShellPart` record. The Intrinsics construct a new `XSizeHints` structure out of *size_hints* and the new fields.

The full instance record for WMShell widgets is `WMShellRec`.

```
typedef struct {
    CorePart        core;
    CompositePart   composite;
    ShellPart       shell;
    WMShellPart     wm;
} WMShellRec, *WMShellWidget;
```

5.10.4 The Vendor Shell Widget

Each implementation of the toolkit can have different fields in the Vendor-Shell instance part. The version as distributed from MIT has no meaningful fields.

```
typedef struct {
    int     vendor_specific;
} VendorShellPart;
```

The fields in this structure have meanings defined by the implementor of the toolkit. The full instance record for VendorShell widgets is `Vendor-ShellRec`.

```
typedef struct {
    CorePart        core;
    CompositePart   composite;
    ShellPart       shell;
    WMShellPart     wm;
    VendorShellPart vendor;
} VendorShellRec, *VendorShellWidget;
```

See Section 5.12 for information on how to extend the vendor shell.

5.10.5 The Transient Shell Widget

The TransientShell instance part record defines fields in the transient shell widget.[14]

---

[14] The *transient_for* field is not supported by Intrinsics implementations that conform to specifications earlier than Release 4.

```
typedef struct {
    Widget      transient_for;
} TransientShellPart;
```

The field in this record has the following meaning:

transient_for   The value of the XtNtransientFor resource.

The full instance record for TransientShell widgets is `TransientShellRec`.

```
typedef struct {
    CorePart            core;
    CompositePart       composite;
    ShellPart           shell;
    WMShellPart         wm;
    VendorShellPart     vendor;
    TransientShellPart  transient;
} TransientShellRec, *TransientShellWidget;
```

See the ICCCM for full information on windows that set the transient properties.

5.10.6   The Top-Level Shell Widget

The TopLevelShell instance part record defines fields common to top-level and application shells.[15]

```
typedef struct {
    char        *icon_name;
    Boolean     iconic;
    Atom        icon_name_encoding;
} TopLevelShellPart;
```

The fields in this record have the following meanings:

icon_name   The value of the XtNiconName resource.

iconic   The value of the XtNiconic resource.

icon_name_encoding
        The value of the XtNiconNameEncoding resource.

The full instance record for TopLevelShell widgets is `TopLevelShellRec`.

---

[15] The *icon_name_encoding* field is not supported by Intrinsics implementations that conform to specifications earlier than Release 4.

```
typedef struct {
    CorePart            core;
    CompositePart       composite;
    ShellPart           shell;
    WMShellPart         wm;
    VendorShellPart     vendor;
    TopLevelShellPart   topLevel;
} TopLevelShellRec, *TopLevelShellWidget;
```

5.10.7 The Application Shell Widget

The ApplicationShell widget instance part record defines fields for the application shell.

```
typedef struct {
    char        *class;
    XrmClass    xrm_class;
    int         argc;
    char        **argv;
} ApplicationShellPart;
```

The fields in this record have the following meaning:

class   Internal field that stores the application's class.

xrm_class   Internal field that stores the application's class as a quark.

argc   The value of the XtNargc resource.

argv   The value of the XtNargv resource.

The full instance record for ApplicationShell widgets is `Application-ShellRec`.

```
typedef struct {
    CorePart                core;
    CompositePart           composite;
    ShellPart               shell;
    WMShellPart             wm;
    VendorShellPart         vendor;
    TopLevelShellPart       topLevel;
    ApplicationShellPart    application;
} ApplicationShellRec, *ApplicationShellWidget;
```

5.11   What Shells Do

Shells are responsible for performing many interactions between the application and the outside world of window and session managers. These interactions include

- Setting all properties to inform the window and session manager of the application's name, class, command line, and so forth.
- Interacting with the window manager to achieve application-directed iconification and deiconification.
- Performing the protocols necessary to achieve size and position changes.
- Understanding how to react to external size and position changes.
- Setting size hints and window manager hints.

Shells leave some interactions to the application:

- Specifying the WM_PROTOCOLS the application understands.
- Handling the WM_TAKE_FOCUS, WM_SAVE_YOURSELF, and WM_DELETE_WINDOW client messages.
- Setting the WM_COLORMAP property.

See Sections 6.6 and 9.7 for how to handle these in an application.

5.11.1   Setting Properties

Window manager shells set the following properties on their windows; consult the ICCCM and Section 9.1 of *Xlib* for more information:

- The shell sets the WM_NAME property to the value of the shell's XtNtitle resource. Its property type is specified by the XtNtitleEncoding resource. The Intrinsics only support property types that use eight-bit encodings with the title value terminated by a null byte; other encodings can be supported by vendor shell implementations.
- If the XtNtransient resource is TRUE, the shell sets the WM_TRANSIENT_FOR property to the value of the XtNtransientFor resource if the shell is a transient shell or the value of the XtNwindowGroup resource if not.
- The shell sets the WM_CLASS property to specify the window's name and class. The name is the name of the shell widget, and the class is the class name supplied when creating the application's main shell.
- The shell sets the WM_CLIENT_MACHINE property to the name of the machine running the application.

- The shell sets the WM_HINTS and WM_NORMAL_HINTS properties as described in Section 5.11.5.

Top-level shells set this additional property:

- The shell sets the WM_ICON_NAME property to the value of the shell's XtNiconName resource. Its property type is specified by the XtNiconNameEncoding resource. The Intrinsics only support property types that use eight-bit encodings with the icon name value terminated by a null byte; other encodings can be supported by vendor shell implementations.

Application shells set this additional property:

- The shell sets the WM_COMMAND property to the value of the XtNargv and XtNargc resources. These resources get set automatically if the application uses `XtApp-Initialize`.

5.11.2   Iconification and Deiconification

Shells perform the necessary protocols to iconify or deiconify their window if their XtNiconic resource changes. Changing XtNiconic to FALSE for a pop-up shell makes the Intrinsics call `XtPopup` on the shell with *grab_kind* XtGrabNone if the shell is not already popped up.

5.11.3   Changing Size and Position

When an internal widget in an application makes a geometry request, its parent's geometry manager decides on whether to allow the change. When a shell makes a geometry request, the shell's root_geometry_manager procedure decides on whether to allow the change. Shell geometry requests can stem from a position change to the shell or from a size change to the shell's managed child.

The root_geometry_manager procedure supplied for Shell handles the complex interactions required to negotiate the geometry change with the server and the user's window manager. The term *complex* is not used lightly—think twice (at least) before deciding to provide a new implementation of this method. Describing the intricacies of these negotiations is beyond the scope of this book; study the implementation in the toolkit sources if you dare.[16]

Specifying XtInheritRootGeometryManager is highly recommended. At the very minimum, a subclass should envelop the root_geometry_manager and not try to replace it.

---

[16] "If you think you understand it, you don't, so look again." —James Gosling

5.11.4   External Geometry Changes

Shells react to ConfigureNotify events that specify a new size by propagating the change to their managed child with XtResizeWidget.

The *core.x* and *core.y* fields in a shell widget always hold the x and y position of the shell's window on the screen, irrespective of any reparenting that the user's window manager may do. Do not expect a shell's position fields to be the same as the position of the shell's window within its parent. A Configure-Notify event that specifies a new position updates the widget fields so that `XtTranslateCoords` can translate into screen coordinates without requiring a round trip to the server.

5.11.5   Size and Window Manager Hints

Window manager shells set the WM_NORMAL_HINTS property according to the resources XtNminWidth, XtNminHeight, XtNmaxWidth, XtNmaxHeight, XtNwidthInc, XtNheightInc, XtNbaseWidth, XtNbaseHeight, XtNmin-AspectX, XtNminAspectY, XtNmaxAspectX, XtNmaxAspectY, and XtNwin-Gravity. They set the WM_HINTS property according to the resources XtNinput, XtNinitalState, XtNiconPixmap, XtNiconMask, XtNiconWindow, XtNiconX, XtNiconY, and XtNwindowGroup.

If a resource has the value XtUnspecifiedShellInt, None, or XtUnspecifiedWindowGroup (depending upon the resource) the shell does not set the corresponding field in the hint. If the shell has a value for XtNgeometry that specifies a size, the shell sets USSize in the normal size hints; otherwise it sets PSize, and similarly for USPosition and PPosition. The shell always sets the input and initial state fields in the window manager hints according to the XtNinput and XtNinitialState resources.

Many of the fields in the size and window manager hint structures come in either width/height or x/y pairs. Each pair has only a single flag bit, so if one field in the pair has a nondefault value, the shell must give the other a sensible value also. Shells use the following values to fill in an unspecified resource that is part of a pair:

Resource	Value
XtNiconX, XtNiconY	−1
XtNbaseWidth, XtNbaseHeight	0

Resource	Value
XtNwidthInc, XtNheightInc	1
XtNmaxWidth, XtNmaxHeight	32767
XtNminWidth, XtNminHeight	1
XtNminAspectX, XtNminAspectY, XtNmaxAspectX, XtNmaxAspectY	−1

The aspect ratio fields actually form a quartet; one flag bit controls all four fields.

5.12 Vendor Shells

Some window managers implement private protocols to extend the functionality defined by the ICCCM. The VendorShell class provides a place to implement these protocols in the toolkit. It is expected that each window manager that implements private protocols will provide a vendor shell implementation that supports its protocols.

Vendor shells can also implement additional types for the XtNtitle and XtNiconName properties. The window manager shell assumes that the strings are eight-bit, NULL-terminated values; if other types are needed, the vendor shell can call `XSetWMName` and `XSetWMIconName` with different values to replace the ones set by the window manager shell.

Window managers provide no standard way to query whether they will grant a geometry request, so the default root_geometry_manager never responds XtGeometryAlmost. If a particular window manager supports this function, the vendor shell can provide a different, more sophisticated implementation of the root_geometry_manager method.

The sample implementation of the toolkit separates the vendor shell implementation out into the files `Vendor.c`, `Vendor.h`, and `VendorP.h`, and other implementations are encouraged to do so also. To supply a new implementation of the vendor shell, create new versions of these three files and recompile the Intrinsics to form a new Intrinsics library. Recompiling is necessary since some code modules use fields in shell instance and class records that occur in parts that follow the vendor instance and class parts; the offsets of the fields will change if the vendor parts change.

This section describes a sample implementation of a vendor shell that supports two private window manager protocols:

- If the shell sets the MY_WM_NO_TITLE property on a window, the window manager provides no title bar for that window.
- The window manager stores the property MY_WM_TITLE_FONT containing the font identifier used to display text in the title bar on the root window of the screen.

The vendor shell implementation supports two new resources, XtNnoTitle, a Boolean value that determines whether the shell sets MY_WM_NO_TITLE, and XtNtitleFont, the window manager's title font.

The first step is to provide versions of `<X11/Vendor.h>` and `<X11/VendorP.h>` that support the resources. Examples 5.1 and 5.2 show these files.

The `Vendor.h` file defines the new resources for the widget and includes the class constants just as for any other widget class. `VendorP.h` defines the class and instance part records and full class and instance definitions.

The implementation of the vendor shell looks just like the implementation of any other widget. It is easiest to start with the skeleton definition of `Vendor.c` provided with the Intrinsics and modify it as necessary; the file as distributed is essentially a null class that inherits all its methods.

Example 5.3 shows the resource list for the sample implementation. It contains entries for the two new resources.

```
#ifndef VENDOR_H
#define VENDOR_H

#define XtNnoTitle "noTitle"
#define XtNtitleFont "titleFont"

#define XtCNoTitle "NoTitle"
#define XtCTitleFont "TitleFont"

/* Class record constants */

typedef struct _VendorShellClassRec *VendorShellWidgetClass;

extern WidgetClass vendorShellWidgetClass;

#endif /* VENDOR_H */
```

Example 5.1. The sample `Vendor.h` header file

```
#ifndef  VENDORP_H
#define VENDORP_H

/* New fields for the VendorShell widget class record */

typedef struct {
    XtPointer extension;
} VendorShellClassPart;

typedef struct _VendorShellClassRec {
    CoreClassPart        core_class;
    CompositeClassPart  composite_class;
    ShellClassPart       shell_class;
    WMShellClassPart     wm_shell_class;
    VendorShellClassPart vendor_shell_class;
} VendorShellClassRec;

extern VendorShellClassRec vendorShellClassRec;

/* New fields for the vendor shell widget. */

typedef struct {
    Boolean     no_title;
    Font        title_font;
} VendorShellPart;

typedef struct {
    CorePart            core;
    CompositePart       composite;
    ShellPart           shell;
    WMShellPart         wm;
    VendorShellPart     vendor;
} VendorShellRec, *VendorShellWidget;

#endif  /* VENDORP_H */
```

Example 5.2. The sample `VendorP.h` header file

```
#define Offset(field) XtOffsetOf(VendorShellWidgetRec, vendor.field)

static XtResource resources[] = {
    {XtNnoTitle, XtCNoTitle, XtRBoolean, sizeof(Boolean),
        Offset(no_title), XtRImmediate, (XtPointer) FALSE},
    {XtNtitleFont, XtCTitleFont, XtRFont, sizeof(Font),
        Offset(title_font), XtRImmediate, (XtPointer) None}
};

#undef Offset
```

Example 5.3. The sample vendor shell resources

Supporting these resources requires new realize, initialize, and set_values procedures. These use the FetchAtom procedure in Example 5.4, which uses the predefined string-to-atom converter to get an appropriate atom. This saves time since the resource cache provides atom values that are requested more than once, for example, for multiple shells. Details of using atoms and properties are in Sections 4.2 and 4.3 of *Xlib*.

Example 5.5 shows the realize procedure. It calls the superclass realize procedure to actually create the window and then, if the widget's window should have no title bar, places the MY_WM_NO_TITLE property on the window.

Example 5.6 shows the initialize procedure. Note that since atom values are display-specific, it would be an error to declare the local variable *my_wm_title_font* to be static and to evaluate it only once. Doing so would prevent a multi-display application from using this class.

Finally, Example 5.7 shows the set_values procedure. If the widget is realized and the value of the XtNnoTitle resource has changed, the procedure either sets or deletes the property as appropriate. Next, since the title font resource is a read-only resource, any change made is disallowed. The procedure returns FALSE to indicate that nothing it has done requires a redisplay of the widget.

```
static Atom FetchAtom(w, name)
    Widget w;
    String name;
{
    Atom a;
    XrmValue source, dest;

    source.size = strlen(name)+1;
    source.addr = name;
    dest.size = sizeof(Atom);
    dest.addr = (caddr_t) &a;

    (void) XtConvertAndStore(w, XtRString, &source, XtRAtom, &dest);
    return a;
}
```

Example 5.4.   Fetching an atom using type conversion

```
static void VendorShellRealize(w, mask, attr)
        Widget w;
        XtValueMask *mask;
        XSetWindowAttributes *attr;
{
        VendorShellWidget v = (VendorShellWidget) w;
        Atom my_wm_no_title = FetchAtom(w, "MY_WM_NO_TITLE");

        /* Make my superclass do all the dirty work */

        (*wmShellWidgetClass->core_class.realize) (w, mask, attr);

        if (v->vendor.no_title) {
            XChangeProperty(XtDisplay(w), XtWindow(w),
                    my_wm_no_title, my_wm_no_title,
                    8, PropModeReplace, NULL, 0);
        }
}
```

Example 5.5. The sample vendor shell realize procedure

```
static void VendorShellInitialize(req, new, args, num_args)
    Widget req, new;
    ArgList args;
    Cardinal *num_args;
{
    VendorShellWidget v = (VendorShellWidget) new;
    Atom my_wm_title_font, actual_type;
    int actual_format;
    unsigned long nitems, bytes_after;
    unsigned char *data;

    my_wm_title_font = FetchAtom(new, "MY_WM_TITLE_FONT");

    if (XGetWindowProperty(XtDisplay(v),
                RootWindowOfScreen(XtScreen(v)),
                my_wm_title_font, 0L, 1L, False, my_wm_title_font,
                &actual_type, &actual_format, &nitems,
                &bytes_after, &data) == Success &&
            actual_type == my_wm_title_font &&
            actual_format == 32) {
        v->vendor.title_font = (Font) *data;
    } else v->vendor.title_font = None;

    if (data != NULL) XFree((char *) data);
}
```

Example 5.6. The sample vendor shell initialize procedure

```
static Boolean VendorShellSetValues(old, ref, new, args, num_args)
    Widget old, req, new;
    ArgList args;
    Cardinal *num_args;
{
    VendorShellWidget ov = (VendorShellWidget) old;
    VendorShellWidget nv = (VendorShellWidget) new;
    Atom my_wm_no_title;

    if (XtIsRealized(new)) {
        if (ov->vendor.no_title != nv->vendor.no_title) {
            my_wm_no_title = FetchAtom(new, "MY_WM_NO_TITLE");

            if (nv->vendor.no_title) {
                XChangeProperty(XtDisplay(new), XtWindow(new),
                        my_wm_no_title, my_wm_no_title,
                        8, PropModeReplace, NULL, 0);
            } else {
                XDeleteProperty(XtDisplay(new), XtWindow(new),
                        my_wm_no_title);
            }
        }
    }

    nv->vendor.title_font = ov->vendor.title_font;
    return FALSE;
}
```

Example 5.7. The sample vendor shell set_values procedure

Chapter 6

Event Handling

Writing Applications

Most toolkit applications are event-driven. Events arrive from various sources and the application acts upon the events. While most of the events an application has to deal with are X events from one or more X servers, some applications must also process timers and other input sources. It is seldom acceptable for an application that has multiple sources of input to process any one source for a long period of time while ignoring the others. The toolkit multiplexes various event sources together into a consistent event-handling strategy, unifying X events, files, and timers into a single "call a procedure when an event source is ready" scheme.

6.1   X Events

The X server delivers events to an application when the user interacts with the pointer or keyboard, when the configuration of the screen changes, and when some state in the server like the current owner of the selection changes. Some descriptions in this programmer's guide refer to X *input* events; these are events that result from the user interacting with the keyboard or the pointing device (usually a mouse). The X input events are KeyPress, KeyRelease, ButtonPress, ButtonRelease, PointerMotion, EnterNotify, and LeaveNotify.

There are three ways that applications can gain control when an X event occurs:

• They can register callback procedures with widgets in their user interface and rely upon the toolkit and the widgets to call these procedures when appropriate events occur. This is the most common case, and completely frees the application from needing to be aware of X events. Using callback procedures leaves it up to the widget designer to decide how the application functionality is invoked when the events arrive. Only applications that need to augment their widgets' capabilities need to use any method besides callback procedures.

• They can write new *action procedures*, which are procedures that are called when an event or sequence of events occurs. Each widget has a resource XtNtranslations, called the widget's *translations*, that defines which action procedures the Intrinsics invoke when events arrive for that widget's window. Since the binding from events to action procedures is controlled by a resource, it is customizable. Action procedures are the right solution for an application that needs to add a way to gain control beyond the ways supplied by the widget classes it uses. Chapter 7 describes action tables and the XtNtranslations resource.

• Finally, they can write new event-handling procedures that the Intrinsics invoke when an event arrives. Event handlers define directly which event types trigger them; the binding between events and event handlers is not customizable. Applications almost never use event handlers since action procedures provide their functionality in a more customizable way. Section 6.22 in the widget writer's part of this chapter describes event handlers.

Figure 6.1 summarizes the toolkit's handling of X events. The events arrive and are dispatched to one or more event handlers. One of these event handlers is the Intrinsics translation manager that uses the widget translations to decide which action procedures to call. Some of these action procedures in turn invoke callback procedures. Event handlers are usually supplied by the Intrinsics, sometimes by widget implementations, and occasionally by applications. Action procedures are usually supplied by the widget implementations, sometimes by applications, and sometimes by the Intrinsics. Callback procedures are usually supplied by the application, sometimes by widget implementations (when one widget needs to react to events in another widget), and sometimes by the Intrinsics.

6.2   The Application Main Loop

After an application creates and realizes its user interface, it must go into a loop that gathers events from all the various sources and dispatches them to the widgets in the interface. Most applications can use `XtAppMainLoop` for this.

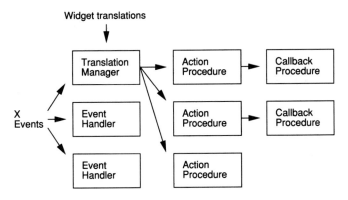

Figure 6.1. Toolkit event handling

void XtAppMainLoop(*app_context*)
    XtAppContext *app_context*;
app_context   Specifies the application context.

`XtAppMainLoop` never returns; it is simply an infinite loop that waits for input and dispatches it to the appropriate place.

The rest of this chapter covers relatively advanced topics, and you may wish to skim or skip it on your first reading.

6.3   Alternate Input Sources

Some applications must process other types of input. Often the application handles the other input sources just as any non-toolkit application does, by opening a file and reading the contents using routines appropriate to the operating system. Other applications must block waiting for input.

Consider a terminal emulator. It must deal with two sources of input, the user and the application running in the emulator. The user sends input by typing characters to send to the running application, and the application generates text to display in the window. The emulator must block waiting on both sources of input and respond to whichever source generates the input first.

The Intrinsics support this need by allowing an application to register input sources with the toolkit. When input becomes available, the Intrinsics call input callback routines in the application to notify it that input is available.

These routines can also block on output streams and exceptional file conditions, although these uses are more rare. In Unix operating systems, writing to a pipe blocks if the buffers become full. An application that sends potentially blocking output registers the output file descriptor with the Intrinsics and has a callback procedure invoked to resume output.

Applications should not use the toolkit event handling to read or write to normal files. Since these operations never block, the Intrinsics would call the callback procedure continually. Regardless of whether a file is open for reading or for writing the toolkit refers to it as an alternate input source, recognizing the most common case.

To register an alternate input source with the toolkit, use `XtAppAddInput`.

```
typedef unsigned long XtInputId;
```

```
XtInputId XtAppAddInput(app_context, source, condition, proc, client_data)
    XtAppContext app_context;
    int source;
    XtPointer condition;
    XtInputCallbackProc proc;
    XtPointer client_data;
```

app_context	Specifies the application context.
source	Specifies the file descriptor for the alternate input source.
condition	Specifies the condition the Intrinsics should wait for.
proc	Specifies the procedure to call when the file can be read from or written to.
client_data	Specifies a piece of data passed to the input procedure.

The *source* is a file descriptor. On Unix systems, this is the result of an `open` call or, if using the standard I/O package, the value of `fileno(fd)` where *fd* is the file descriptor returned from `fopen`. The legal values for *condition* are operating-system-specific; on Unix systems this is some subset of XtInputReadMask, XtInputWriteMask, and XtInputExceptMask OR'ed together.

The callback procedure is of type `XtInputCallbackProc`.

```
typedef void (*XtInputCallbackProc) (XtPointer, int *, XtInputId *);
    XtPointer client_data;
    int *source;
    XtInputId *id;
```

client_data	Specifies the client data passed to `XtAppAddInput`.
source	Specifies the file descriptor for the input.
id	Specifies the identifier returned from `XtAppAddInput`.

Note that the *source* and *id* parameters are passed by reference to support languages that do not permit parameter passing by value.

The Intrinsics call the input callback when a condition specified in the *condition* parameter becomes true. The callback does whatever is appropriate with the file descriptor, possibly nothing. If more input is available after the procedure returns, the Intrinsics will call it again at some future time.

The application removes an alternate input source by calling `XtRemove-Input`.

```
void XtRemoveInput(id)
    XtInputId id;
```
id	Specifies the input id to remove.

The *id* parameter is the value returned from the `XtAppAddInput` call that added the file descriptor.

6.4 Timers

Some applications need timers to make some action happen at a future time. A terminal emulator might blink the text cursor every second when it is idle, and a clock program might update the displayed time every minute. The toolkit allows applications to register a procedure that will be called after a specified time interval.

To register a timer, call `XtAppAddTimeOut`.

```
typedef unsigned long XtIntervalId;

XtIntervalId XtAppAddTimeOut(app_context, interval, proc, client_data)
    XtAppContext app_context;
    unsigned long interval;
    XtTimerCallbackProc proc;
    XtPointer client_data;
```
app_context	Specifies the application context.
interval	Specifies the time interval in milliseconds.
proc	Specifies the procedure to call after the specified interval.
client_data	Specifies a piece of data to pass to the timer callback procedure.

The Intrinsics will call the specified procedure at some future time that is at least as much later as specified by the interval (in milliseconds); it may be called later than specified if intervening events keep the toolkit busy. This is not an asynchronous timer—only Intrinsics event-handling routines like `XtAppNextEvent` and `XtAppMainLoop` call timer callbacks. If the application requires truly asynchronous timers that go off irrespective of what else is happening in the application, it must provide them itself.

The timer procedure is of type `XtTimerCallbackProc`.

typedef void (*XtTimerCallbackProc) (XtPointer, XtIntervalId *);
    XtPointer *client_data*;
    XtIntervalId **id*;

client_data   Specifies the client data passed to `XtAppAddTimeOut`.
id   Specifies the identifier returned from `XtAppAddTimeOut`.

Note that the *id* parameter is passed by reference to support languages that do not permit parameter passing by value.

After calling the timer callback, the Intrinsics remove the timer. To create a recurring timer the timer callback adds a new timer before returning.

Applications remove a timer that has not yet triggered by calling `XtRemoveTimeOut`.

void XtRemoveTimeOut(*timer*)
    XtIntervalId *timer*;
timer   Specifies the timer to remove.

It is an error to remove a timer that has already gone off; unfortunately the Intrinsics cannot always detect this condition in `XtRemoveTimeOut`. Applications must take care not to remove expired timers; the *client_data* parameter helps with this if difficulties arise keeping track of which timers have fired. The application passes the address of a flag that the timer callback resets and the application tests this flag before removing the timer. Some implementations of the Intrinsics keep track of some expired timers, but timer identifiers can be reused and removing an expired timer can inadvertently remove a more recently added timer instead.

A timer callback procedure never removes its timer explicitly; the Intrinsics do this automatically.

6.5 The Grab List

An application restricts which of its widgets receive X input events by putting widgets on a special list, called the *grab list*, maintained by the Intrinsics. The act of putting a widget on the grab list is called a *toolkit grab*, or simply a *grab* for short. These toolkit grabs should not be confused with the key and button grabs provided by the X protocol, which are called *server grabs* in this book. In X parlance, a grab refers to taking exclusive control of something. A server grab allows an application to take exclusive control of the keyboard or pointer, locking out other applications. A toolkit grab, somewhat analogously, allows a widget to take exclusive control of the user, locking out other widgets in the application.

When the grab list is nonempty, X input events are only distributed to the widgets on the list. A widget on this list can either be there *exclusively*, meaning that only it and its descendants receive input events, or *nonexclusively*, meaning that events are also delivered to other widgets on the list back to the most recently added exclusive widget. The set of widgets on the list from the most recently added exclusive widget onward is called the *active set* of the grab list.

Putting a widget on the grab list makes it a *modal* widget for as long as it remains on the list. Modal widgets allow an application to suspend the rest of its interface until the user interacts with the modal widget in some specified way.

This description should look familiar from the discussion of pop-ups in Section 5.8. A modal pop-up is one whose shell is on the grab list; an exclusive pop-up has its shell on the grab list exclusively and a nonexclusive pop-up has its shell on the grab list nonexclusively.

Consider a text editor that informs the user that the file he selected to edit cannot be modified. The editor pops up a modal dialog box that says the file is read-only and does not proceed until the user clicks an "Acknowledged" button. To do this the editor just pops up the dialog as a modal pop-up and has for the button's callback a procedure that pops the dialog down. Because the dialog is modal, the user cannot interact with the rest of the application until he acknowledges the pop-up.

A more complicated example is an application that detects a possibly erroneous condition during some computation and asks the user if the computation should continue. A dialog box that offers the user two buttons, "Abort" and "Continue", is useful here. The code at the decision point looks like this:

```
if (erroneous_condition) {
    /* Pop up dialog box */
} else {
    /* Call procedure to do the rest of the computation */
}
return;
```

The callback for the abort pushbutton in the dialog just pops down the dialog box. The callback for the continue pushbutton pops down the dialog box and then calls the procedure to complete the computation.

As these two examples show, most user interfaces with modal widgets pop them up on the screen. The pop-up routines described in Section 5.9 automatically take care of updating the grab list when widgets are popped up or down. However, any widget can be made modal by using XtAddGrab.

void XtAddGrab(*w, exclusive, spring_loaded*)
    Widget *w*;
    Boolean *exclusive*;
    Boolean *spring_loaded*;

w	Specifies the widget to add to the grab list.
exclusive	Specifies whether the grab should be exclusive or nonexclusive.
spring_loaded	Specifies whether the grab was activated by a pointer event and activated a pop-up.

The *spring_loaded* parameter must be FALSE for grabs handled directly by the application; only grabs added by XtPopupSpringLoaded have *spring_loaded* TRUE.

One use for non-pop-up grabs is in an application with a message area always on the screen. If the user must respond to a message before the application continues, the application adds the message area to the grab list before asking for the response. It is often a good idea for such an application to change its appearance somehow to make sure the user notices that a response is required.

To remove a modal widget from the grab list, use XtRemoveGrab.

void XtRemoveGrab(*w*)
    Widget *w*;

w	Specifies the widget to remove from the grab list.

XtRemoveGrab removes the specified widget and any other widgets added to the grab list more recently than the specified widget from the grab list.

6.6   Setting Window Manager Protocols

The ICCCM defines several protocols in which an application can participate. The next section describes the WM_TAKE_FOCUS protocol; the full details of the WM_SAVE_YOURSELF and WM_DELETE_WINDOW protocols are beyond the scope of this book. Consult the ICCCM for full details.

An application that uses the WM_TAKE_FOCUS and WM_SAVE_YOURSELF protocols executes the code in Example 6.1. To participate in any of these protocols, the application must set the WM_PROTOCOLS property on its main shell by calling `XSetWMProtocols`. `XSetWMProtocols` is a new function and is not in the first edition of *Xlib*.

Status XSetWMProtocols(*dpy, w, protocols, count*)
    Display **dpy*;

```
/* Make these global, we'll need them later.  If this is a multi-
   display application, these must be kept for each display. */
Atom wm_take_focus, wm_save_yourself;

static Atom FetchAtom(w, name)
    Widget w;
    String name;
{
    Atom a;
    XrmValue source, dest;

    source.size = strlen(name)+1;
    source.addr = name;
    dest.size = sizeof(Atom);
    dest.addr = &a;

    (void) XtConvertAndStore(w, XtRString, &source, XtRAtom, &dest);
    return a;
}

/* Time to set the protocols */
Atom protocolList[2];

wm_take_focus = FetchAtom(shell, "WM_TAKE_FOCUS");
wm_save_yourself = FetchAtom(shell, "WM_SAVE_YOURSELF");
protocolList[0] = wm_take_focus;
protocolList[1] = wm_save_yourself;

(void) XSetWMProtocols(XtDisplay(shell), XtWindow(shell),
        protocolList, XtNumber(protocolList));
```

Example 6.1. Setting the window manager protocols

```
Window w;
Atom *protocols;
int count;
```

dpy	Specifies the application's display.
w	Specifies window of the application's top-level shell.
protocols	Specifies the protocols the application uses.
count	Specifies the number of protocols.

The application must handle the protocol messages, usually by adding a new translation to the shell widget. See Example 6.2 for sample code (although you will not be able to understand all the details of it until you read Chapter 7).

6.7   Handling Focus

Dealing with the keyboard focus in toolkit applications is one of the more complicated tasks since there are so many different ways to do it. This section

```
static void WMProtocolAction(w, event, params, num_params)
    Widget w;
    XEvent *event;
    String *params;              /* unused */
    Cardinal *num_params;        /* unused */
{
    Atom protocol = (Atom) event->xclient.data.l[0];

    if (event->type != ClientMessage) return;

    /* Use atom values we got earlier */
    if (protocol == wm_take_focus) {
        Time t = (Time) event->xclient.data.l[1];
        (void) XtCallAcceptFocus(mainWidget, &t);
    } else if (protocol == wm_save_yourself) {
        /* Save application state */
    }
}

static char *shellTrans =
        "<ClientMessage> WM_PROTOCOLS : WMProtocolAction()";
static XtActionsRec actions[] = {
        {"WMProtocolAction", WMProtocolAction}
};

XtAppAddActions(app, actions, XtNumber(actions));
XtAugmentTranslations(shell, XtParseTranslationTable(shellTrans));
```

Example 6.2. Responding to window manager protocols

describes the various things an application can do to affect the focus and then gives some suggestions as to how best to use these to achieve various interfaces.

The XtNinput resource of a shell tells the user's window manager whether the window expects the window manager to assign focus to the shell's window. If it is FALSE, it means that either the window never wants the input focus or that it takes the focus on its own. If it is TRUE, it means that it wants to receive keyboard events and expects the window manager to assign the focus to its shell window under conditions that the window manager defines. Window managers only set the input focus to shell widgets and never to widgets within the shell. An application that cares about the XtNinput resource should set it explicitly, since different implementations of the Intrinsics have different default values for XtNinput.

The application also has the option of setting the WM_TAKE_FOCUS atom in the WM_PROTOCOLS property on their root window. Applications are responsible for setting this up and responding to it themselves; see Section 6.6. If this atom is present, the window manager sends a special ClientMessage event to the application's shell when the user asks the window manager to give focus to the application.

The decision as to when to assign focus directly to a window that specified XtNinput TRUE and when to send the client message to a window that specified the WM_TAKE_FOCUS atom is up to the individual window manager. One possibility is a window manager that assigns focus directly when the user clicks a pointer button in the window and sends the client message when the user clicks in the title bar or deiconifies the window. The client message approach supports applications that take the focus at some times but not others, or only take the focus if the user interacts with a particular part of the interface. Assigning focus supports applications that never want to worry about taking the focus themselves.

The toolkit allows the application to tell the Intrinsics to redirect keyboard events that arrive in a particular widget subtree to a widget within the subtree. To redirect the keyboard events, use `XtSetKeyboardFocus`.

```
void XtSetKeyboardFocus(subtree, destination)
    Widget subtree;
    Widget destination;
```

subtree	Specifies the root of the widget subtree that keyboard events are being redirected for.
destination	Specifies the widget within the subtree that will receive the keyboard events, or NULL.

The *subtree* parameter is any widget in the application's interface, and *destination* is any widget that has *subtree* as an ancestor. If a keyboard event arrives for *subtree* or a widget that is a descendant of *subtree*, and this widget is not also a descendant of the *destination* widget, the Intrinsics deliver the event to the *destination* widget. If the event arrives for a widget that is a descendant of the *destination* widget or for a widget that is not a descendant of the *subtree* widget, the Intrinsics deliver it normally.

In the widget subtree in Figure 6.2, widget 3 has redirected keyboard events to widget 5. Here's what happens if a keyboard event arrives for each of the widgets in the tree:

Widget 1 or 2	This widget is not a descendant of any widget that has redirected the keyboard, so the event goes to the widget it occurred in.
Widget 3	Widget 3 has redirected the keyboard to widget 5, so the event goes to widget 5.
Widget 4 or 5	This widget is a descendant of widget 3, so the event goes to widget 5.
Widget 6	Widget 6 is a descendant of the destination, so the event goes to widget 6.

Calling XtSetKeyboardFocus for the same *subtree* widget as an earlier call but a different *destination* replaces the earlier redirection with the new one,

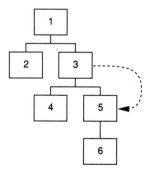

Figure 6.2. Focus redirection

and calling it with NULL as *destination* removes any earlier redirection for subtree. The toolkit sets up redirection for each shell to redirect any keyboard events delivered to the shell to its managed child.

Multiple keyboard redirections can operate at once, and they can be chained. If a widget A has redirected the input to a widget B, and B has in turn redirected it to a widget C, the Intrinsics deliver keyboard events in A's subtree to C.

If the grab list is nonempty, redirection occurs as usual, but the Intrinsics discard the event unless the *destination* widget or some ancestor of the *destination* widget is in the active set of the grab list. Keyboard grabs also affect redirection, but this is normally invisible to applications.

An application asks a widget to take the focus by calling `XtCall-AcceptFocus`.

Boolean XtCallAcceptFocus(*w, time*)
    Widget *w*;
    Time **time*;

w	Specifies the widget to accept the input focus.
time	Specifies a timestamp from the event that initiated the focus assignment.

The Boolean return value indicates whether the widget accepted the focus. Widgets should document what they do when asked to take the focus. Most composite widgets call `XtCallAcceptFocus` for each child until they find one that accepts the focus and `XtCallAcceptFocus` returns TRUE if any child accepted the focus. `XtCallAcceptFocus` always returns FALSE for widgets like Pushbutton that have no use for keyboard input. Widgets like the text field that expect keyboard input typically assign the X input focus to their window and `XtCallAcceptFocus` returns TRUE.

The *time* parameter is a timestamp from the X event that triggered the focus change. If the application does not have this event, it can use `XtLast-TimestampProcessed`; see Section 9.10. Note that *time* is passed by reference.

Applications can use `XtCallAcceptFocus` to redirect the input focus within themselves. If, for example, a user activates a "Create new message" function in a mail program, the mail program might ask the composition window to take the input focus. However, directly playing with the focus is considered antisocial by users who use "real-estate driven" input focus; that is, rather than designating a window to have the focus they have characters sent to whichever window contains the pointer. Consider having an application resource that controls whether the application manipulates the focus.

Now for some examples. These all refer to an application but apply equally well to a subsidiary window or a pop-up widget of a more complex application.

The simplest case is an application that never expects keyboard events; it sets XtNinput for its shell to FALSE, does not set the WM_TAKE_FOCUS atom, and never worries about the focus.

Next in complexity is an application that only has one widget that expects keyboard events. It sets XtNinput to TRUE and sets up WM_TAKE_FOCUS as described in Section 6.6.

The most common example is an application that lets the user interact with some of its widgets without setting the input focus. A text editor often lets the user scroll the displayed text with a scrollbar or interact with its menus without transferring the focus to the editor. Such an application sets XtNinput FALSE, telling the window manager not to assign focus just because the user interacted with the window, but sets up WM_TAKE_FOCUS. The widget displaying the text is responsible for setting the focus to itself under the appropriate circumstances, usually receiving a pointer button click.

If the application has more than one widget that accepts text input, it relies upon its composite widgets to handle transferring the focus among the widgets. The application treats this case the same as whichever of the two previous cases is appropriate for the user interface.

6.8   Getting Events

There are three routines an application uses to check the status of X input events, XtAppPending, XtAppPeekEvent, and XtAppNextEvent.

XtAppPending checks whether input is present without processing it.

typedef unsigned long XtInputMask;

XtInputMask XtAppPending(*app_context*)
    XtAppContext *app_context*;
app_context   Specifies the application context to check for X events.

If there are no X events available on any of the application context's displays, no alternate input sources with input available, and no timers ready to go off,

XtAppPending returns zero. Otherwise it returns a bit mask that has some subset of the flags XtIMXEvent, XtIMTimer, and XtIMAlternateInput OR'ed together to indicate which event sources are ready. If there are no X events pending, XtAppPending flushes the output buffers of all displays in the application context, sending any queued requests to the servers.

XtAppPeekEvent returns an X event from one of an application's display connections without removing it from the event queue.

Boolean XtAppPeekEvent(*app_context, event_return*)
    XtAppContext *app_context*;
    XEvent **event_return*;
app_context   Specifies the application context.
event_return   Returns the event.

The *event_return* parameter must be the address of an XEvent structure; XtAppPeekEvent does not allocate the storage for the event itself.

If any display in the application context has events pending, XtAppPeek-Event chooses one and copies the first event into the *event_return* parameter and returns TRUE. The order in which XtAppPeekEvent checks the displays is not defined. If there are no events pending, XtAppPeekEvent flushes the output buffers for all displays in the application context, sending any queued requests to the servers.

If some alternate input source is ready, XtAppPeekEvent returns FALSE after calling any timer callbacks whose intervals have already passed.

Otherwise, XtAppPeekEvent blocks until either an X event is available or some alternate input source is ready for processing, calling timer callbacks as their intervals pass. If an X event arrives first, XtAppPeekEvent copies it into the *event_return* parameter and returns TRUE; if an alternate input source becomes ready, XtAppPeekEvent returns FALSE.

In short, a TRUE result means that there is a valid X event in *event_return* and a FALSE result means that no X events are available but some alternate input source is ready.

XtAppNextEvent returns an X event from a display connection, removing it from the event queue.

void XtAppNextEvent(*app_context, event_return*)
    XtAppContext *app_context*;
    XEvent **event_return*;

| *app_context* | Specifies the application context. |
| *event_return* | Returns the event. |

The *event_return* parameter must be the address of an XEvent structure; XtAppNextEvent does not allocate the storage for the event itself.

If there is an X event available on one of the displays in the application context, XtAppNextEvent removes the event from the display's event queue and copies it into *event_return*. If no X events are available, XtAppNextEvent flushes the output buffers to the displays in the application context, sending any queued requests to the servers, and blocks waiting for an event.

If any timers or alternate input sources become ready, XtAppNextEvent calls their callback procedures. XtAppNextEvent never returns until it obtains an X event.

The order in which XtAppNextEvent checks the displays is undefined; however, it does guarantee that no display connection can be starved by a steady stream of events on another connection. Similarly, it is undefined whether XtAppNextEvent checks timers and alternate input sources for a particular call that finds X events already in the event queue, but it does guarantee that they will be processed eventually; a steady stream of X events cannot block out timers or alternate input sources.

6.9   Dispatching Events

An application dispatches an X event to the appropriate widget by calling XtDispatchEvent.

Boolean XtDispatchEvent(*event*)
    XEvent **event*;

| *event* | Specifies the event to dispatch. |

The event sent to XtDispatchEvent is normally one from XtAppNext-Event but could also be one from an Xlib event-handling routine or even an application-constructed event. The cases where the latter are useful are rather rare.

XtDispatchEvent uses the window field in the event to find a widget to dispatch the event to, and returns TRUE if it found a widget with that window. The only time it should return FALSE is when the application has gone beyond the toolkit event-handling mechanisms and has done something on its own to generate events.

Some applications need more direct control over event processing. They process X events without handling timers or alternate input sources, or process alternate input sources without handling timers or X events. To support these applications the toolkit provides XtAppProcessEvent.

```
void XtAppProcessEvent(app_context, mask)
    XtAppContext app_context;
    XtInputMask mask;
app_context    Specifies the application context.
mask           Specifies which types of events to process.
```

XtAppProcessEvent processes one timer callback, one alternate input callback, or one X event. The mask parameter indicates which types of input to process. It is either a subset of XtIMXEvent, XtIMTimer, and XtIMAlternateInput OR'ed together, or the special value XtIMAll, which tells XtAppProcessEvent to consider all event sources. The values returned from XtAppPending and XtAppPeekEvent are useful for constructing an appropriate input mask. XtAppProcessEvent processes X events by passing them to XtDispatchEvent.

If no events are ready to process for any of the specified sources, XtAppProcessEvent blocks until there is one.

Except for the order in which input gets processed, the following two code fragments do exactly the same thing:

```
while (TRUE) {
    XEvent event;
    XtAppNextEvent(app, &event);
    XtDispatchEvent(&event);
}

while (TRUE) {
    XtAppProcessEvent(app, XtIMAll);
}
```

6.10   Custom Event-Dispatching Loops

Most applications do not need to use any of the procedures described in the last two sections; instead they use XtAppMainLoop. XtAppMainLoop loops forever, calling XtAppNextEvent to get an event and XtDispatchEvent to dispatch the event.

There is nothing special about XtAppMainLoop, however; applications that have particular event-handling needs can create their own event-handling loops. For example, it might be inconvenient to do exit cleanup in the call-back procedure associated with a "quit" widget, so this callback just sets a global flag. The event-handling loop for such a program looks like this:

```
exit_program = FALSE;
while (!exit_program) {
    XEvent event;
    XtAppNextEvent(app, &event);
    XtDispatchEvent(&event);
}
/* Do clean-up here and exit */
```

Another use is in an application that goes into a lengthy computation but still wants to handle Expose events to refresh its windows. At frequent points in the computation the program calls a routine to handle exposures, looking something like this:

```
while (XtAppPending(app) & XtIMXEvent) {
    XEvent event;
    XtAppPeekEvent(app, &event);
    if (event.type == Expose) {
        XtAppProcessEvent(app, XtIMXEvent);
    } else break;
}
```

As long as there are X events pending, this loop peeks at them and, if they are Expose events, processes them. As soon as it encounters a non-Expose event it exits the loop. A more sophisticated loop could use the Xlib event-handling routines to look for Expose events anywhere in the event queue, not just at the front. Using an event loop like this is especially important if the application puts up some sort of "work in progress" widget before starting the calculations; without the loop the widget will not receive the Expose event that tells it to initially display its contents.

A final use is in converting an older, non-event-driven application to the toolkit. The application probably has places where it waits for input events of a particular type, and in these places the converted application fetches and handles events as needed. This code should dispatch any events it does not know how to handle by calling XtDispatchEvent.

Applications with subsidiary event loops can have problems if the application's connection to the X server breaks. XtAppPending does not always perform I/O on the display connection and may not cause the Xlib error handlers to be called if the connection breaks. This is only a concern for applications that go long periods without issuing an X request or blocking for input; other applications will be notified of the broken connection when they issue the request or block. An application that never does output except in response to X events and that does not block for X events should occasionally exercise its display connections by calling XNoOp; see Section 2.3 of *Xlib*.

6.11 Background Work Procedures

The toolkit allows applications to use the time that would otherwise be lost waiting for input by registering *work procedures*. If work procedures are registered, the Intrinsics call them instead of blocking in XtAppPeekEvent, XtAppNextEvent, and XtAppProcessEvent. Application writers should be careful about what their work procedures do, since a work procedure that executes for more than a few milliseconds is likely to make interactive response suffer.

To register a work procedure, use XtAppAddWorkProc.

typedef unsigned long XtWorkProcId;

XtWorkProcId XtAppAddWorkProc(*app_context, proc, client_data*)
    XtAppContext *app_context*;
    XtWorkProc *proc*;
    XtPointer *client_data*;
  app_context   Specifies the application context to add the work procedure to.
  proc   Specifies the work procedure.
  client_data   Specifies a piece of data to pass to the work procedure.

Applications can register multiple work procedures, and the Intrinsics invoke them in the opposite order from which they were added, so the most recently added work procedure is called first. However, if a work procedure adds another work procedure, the newly added procedure has lower priority than the one currently executing.

A work procedure is of type XtWorkProc.

typedef Boolean (*XtWorkProc) (XtPointer)
    XtPointer *client_data*;
  client_data   Specifies the data passed to XtAppAddWorkProc.

The work procedure returns whether it is finished. If it returns TRUE, the Intrinsics remove it from the list of pending work procedures, and if it returns FALSE, the Intrinsics leave it on the list and call it again.

Applications explicitly remove pending work procedures by calling `XtRemoveWorkProc`.

void XtRemoveWorkProc(*id*)
    XtWorkProcId *id*;
id   Specifies the identifier returned from `XtAppAddWorkProc`.

Work procedures do not remove themselves from the list with `XtRemove-WorkProc`; instead they return TRUE to indicate that they are finished.

One common use of work procedures is to create the widgets within pop-up shells. These widgets are not immediately visible when the application starts, so it makes sense to save startup time by creating them in the background. Some coordination must be done to allow the user to invoke pop-ups whose children have not yet been created. The application creates the pop-up shell while creating the user interface, setting the XtNcreatePopupChildProc resource to a procedure that creates the widgets in the shell. The application then registers a work procedure that calls this routine.

Example 6.3 shows a sample version of the work procedure. It casts its *client_data* parameter into the shell to create the children of, then fetches the shell's XtNnumChildren and XtNcreatePopupChildProc resources. If the shell has no children, it means that the children have not yet been created, so the work procedure calls the create procedure.

```
Boolean CreatePopupChild(client_data)
    XtPointer client_data;
{
    Widget shell = (Widget) client_data;
    Cardinal num_children;
    XtCreatePopupChildProc create;
    Arg args[2];
    int n = 0;

    XtSetArg(args[n], XtNnumChildren, &num_children);        n++;
    XtSetArg(args[n], XtNcreatePopupChildProc, &create);     n++;

    XtGetValues(shell, args, n);

    if (num_children == 0) (*create) (shell);

    return TRUE;
}
```

Example 6.3. A work procedure to create pop-up widgets

The application adds this work procedure by calling
```
(void) XtAppAddWorkProc(app, CreatePopupChild,
        (XtPointer) popup_shell);
```
where *popup_shell* is the shell widget. The application can add the work procedure as many times as there are shells to create children for, specifying a different pop-up shell as the client data each time.

Since pop-ups show up more quickly if they are already realized, interactive performance improves by realizing pop-ups in the background. A work procedure to do this casts its *client_data* parameter into a widget and then realizes it; if the widget is already realized, `XtRealizeWidget` returns immediately. If doing this is combined with creating the pop-up children in the background, the application adds the work procedure to realize the pop-up just before the work procedure to create it since the Intrinsics call work procedures in the opposite order from which they were added. An alternative organization is to have the work procedure that created the children add a new work procedure to realize the pop-up's widget tree before it returns.

Work procedures can also update pieces of the user interface that do not need to be kept constantly correct. Consider a mail program that displays information next to each message header indicating whether the message has been read yet. If this information takes long to update on the screen, the mail program uses work procedures whenever a message changes state to update the information in the background. This allows the user to continue interacting with the program without having to wait for the mail program to update the display.

Still another use for work procedures solves the problem of applications that need to do lengthy computations but still respond to user input. The *client_data* for the work procedure is the address of a structure containing the data the computation requires along with some status indicating the current state of the computation. When the Intrinsics call the work procedure, it uses the status information to invoke the next step of the computation. The work procedure computes for a few milliseconds and then updates the status. If the computation is complete, the work procedure returns TRUE; otherwise it returns FALSE. The Intrinsics call the work procedure repeatedly whenever there is no input to process, but input is still handled in a timely fashion. Often, when using this approach, the callback routines for some of the widgets take the same client data value as the work procedure and modify the data to reflect the user's actions; an "Abort computation" callback, for example, can change the status to tell the computation to stop immediately.

A potential problem with work procedures is that if used carelessly they can actually slow down application startup. Typically the last thing the application does before entering its main event loop is to realize its main widget tree. This creates and maps the windows, generating a series of Expose events from the server that makes the widgets draw themselves. It is possible that when the application first requests events in its main loop no Expose events have yet arrived from the server, so the Intrinsics call a work procedure. While the procedure is executing, an Expose event arrives but is not processed immediately because the work procedure is still in process. After the work procedure returns, the Intrinsics process the Expose events and catch up with the server, so they call another work procedure, and the process repeats itself. Another effect occurs when the application and server are running on the same machine; then the work procedure is competing for CPU cycles with the server, possibly causing the server to take longer to generate the Expose events. An application writer who notices her application taking longer to start up than expected can check if this is the cause by temporarily removing the calls that add the work procedures and seeing if the application starts up more quickly. One way to solve these problems is to call XSync after realizing the user interface; this call will not return until all the initial Expose events have arrived. Section 8.6 of *Xlib* describes XSync; the *discard* parameter should be FALSE for this call.

6.12   Using Xlib Event Routines

Xlib presents several input-handling routines with more functionality than those provided by the toolkit, allowing the application to check for, peek at, or wait for events matching various criteria. The application can use these if it needs this extra functionality.

The routines XCheckIfEvent, XCheckWindowEvent, XCheck-MaskEvent, XCheckTypedEvent, and XCheckTypedWindowEvent never block and can be used safely. XIfEvent, XPeekIfEvent, XWindowEvent, and XMaskEvent block if the desired event is not available on the specified display, so they cause problems in an application that uses multiple displays, alternate input, timers, or work procedures. It is best to use one of the check routines to check whether an event already exists before fetching it.

In any case, the event returned from any of these routines besides `XPeekIfEvent` is usually passed to `XtDispatchEvent` for handling.

6.13   Pointer and Keyboard Grabs

An application that needs to grab the keyboard, the pointer, a key, or a pointer button should not use the Xlib routines for this; the Intrinsics provide a parallel set of interfaces to use instead. Since it is primarily widget implementations that use these routines, they are described in the widget writer's part of this chapter. See Section 6.21 for a full description of these routines.

6.14   Sensitivity

The Intrinsics allow an application to temporarily withdraw some of its functionality by making the widget that invokes the functionality *insensitive*. An insensitive widget never receives keyboard or pointer events, so it never invokes its callbacks.

To change the sensitivity of a widget, use `XtSetSensitive`.

void XtSetSensitive(*w, sensitive*)
    Widget *w*;
    Boolean *sensitive*;
w   Specifies the widget whose sensitivity is being changed.
sensitive   Specifies whether to sensitize or desensitize the widget.

If *sensitive* is FALSE, the widget becomes insensitive; if it is TRUE, it becomes sensitive. Changing the sensitivity of a composite widget propagates to its descendants; desensitizing a widget also desensitizes its descendants and sensitizing it also sensitizes its descendants. However, sensitizing a widget does not sensitize any descendants explicitly desensitized with `XtSetSensitive` or any of their descendants; these must be sensitized explicitly.

A newly created widget is insensitive if its parent is. In an Intrinsics misfeature, this also applies to a pop-up child, but changing the parent's sensitivity does not apply to a pop-up child. A pop-up child created with an insensitive parent remains permanently insensitive. To avoid this problem, applications that use pop-ups and insensitive widgets should include the line

    `*OverrideShell.ancestorSensitive : true`

to their application defaults file for each class of shell being used for a pop-up.

To test the sensitivity of a widget, use `XtIsSensitive`.

Boolean XtIsSensitive(*w*)
    Widget *w*;

w   Specifies the widget to check sensitivity for.

`XtIsSensitive` returns FALSE if the widget is insensitive either because the widget was explicitly desensitized or because some ancestor is insensitive.

Writing Widgets

6.15   Event Filters

The Intrinsics provide several ways to reduce the number of events that widgets have to deal with; these are motion compression, enter/leave compression, and exposure compression. The three mechanisms are independent; a particular widget class can use any subset of them. Almost all classes enable all three compression mechanisms.

When motion compression is enabled, the Intrinsics check each pointer motion event for the widget's window to see if additional motion events for the same window are at the head of the event queue. If so, the Intrinsics discard all but the newest motion event. Motion compression only looks at events at the head of the Xlib event queue; it never compresses together motion events with other intervening events or blocks waiting for additional motion events.

Using motion compression reduces the amount of lag time a user sees between when he moves the pointer and when the application responds to the motion. The only widget classes that typically do not use motion compression implement things like bitmap painting tools; in these cases the widget wants to know all the intermediate positions. Widget classes that disable motion compression may also wish to use the X pointer motion history mechanism; see Section 8.11 of *Xlib*. To enable motion compression for a widget class, set the *compress_motion* field in its class record to TRUE.

When enter/leave compression is enabled, any enter event delivered to the window triggers a check to see if a leave event for the same window immediately follows in the event queue. If it does, the Intrinsics discard both the enter and leave events. Enter/leave compression never blocks waiting for a leave event.

If widgets change their display when the pointer enters or leaves their windows, using enter/leave compression reduces the amount of flashing that occurs when the user moves the pointer rapidly across the application without stopping in its windows. The only widget classes that typically do not use enter/leave compression attach semantics beyond appearance changes to enter or leave events or have nonsymmetric display changes that leave the widget looking different after the enter and leave events than it did before. These are rarely good user interface designs; users often move the pointer into a window without intending to. To enable enter/leave compression for a widget class, set the *compress_enterleave* field in its class record to TRUE.

When exposure compression is enabled, the Intrinsics compress series of exposure events for the widget into a single exposure event. The server generates an exposure event for each rectangle of the widget's window that becomes visible, and responding to each exposure can lead to slow redisplays. With exposure compression the rectangle in the event that the Intrinsics finally send to the widget is the smallest rectangle that contains all the rectangles for all the exposure events in the series, and the region passed to the expose procedure is the union of all the exposed rectangles.

The Intrinsics provide options allowing for varying amounts of exposure compression. The *compress_exposure* field in a widget class record takes one of these values:[1]

XtExposeNoCompress

> The Intrinsics perform no exposure compression; they dispatch each event individually to the expose procedure and pass a region argument of NULL.

XtExposeCompressSeries

> The Intrinsics compress exposure events until an event whose *count* field is zero arrives, indicating an end to events from a single exposure. The Intrinsics then deliver the combined event to the expose procedure.

XtExposeCompressMultiple

> The Intrinsics compress adjacent series of exposure events until an event whose *count* field is zero arrives and either the event queue is empty or the next event is not an exposure event. The Intrinsics then deliver the combined event to the expose procedure.

---

[1] *Compress_exposure* is a Boolean field in Intrinsics implementations that conform to specifications earlier than Release 4. The values FALSE and TRUE correspond to the new values XtExposeNoCompress and XtExposeCompressSeries.

XtExposeCompressMaximal

> The Intrinsics compress all exposure events in the event queue, irrespective of any nonexposure events that intervene. If the last exposure event in the event queue does not have a *count* field of zero, the Intrinsics block until such an event arrives. If no further exposure events are in the queue, the Intrinsics deliver the combined event to the expose procedure; otherwise, exposure compression continues.

The most useful value for *compress_exposure* is XtExposeCompressMultiple; using XtExposeCompressMaximal can delay the processing of nonexposure events and can produce confusing displays if the widget changes size between series of exposure events. XtExposeCompressMaximal is the only value that can cause the Intrinsics to block during exposure compression.

Widgets that perform `XCopyArea` or `XCopyPlane` must handle Graphics-Expose and NoExpose events to fill in areas that the server could not copy because they were not available in the source area. Often the code to handle these events is similar to that which handles normal Expose events, so the Intrinsics support dispatching these events to the widget's expose procedure. To enable this dispatching, OR any combination of the following flags into the *compress_exposure* field:

XtExposeGraphicsExpose

> The Intrinsics also dispatch GraphicsExpose events to the widget's expose procedure. The Intrinsics compress GraphicsExpose events in the same way as normal Expose events, according to which of the previous four compression modes are specified.

XtExposeGraphicsExposeMerged

> This flag is only useful if XtExposeCompressMultiple or XtExpose-CompressMaximal is also specified. If XtExposeGraphicsExpose-Merged is set, the Intrinsics compress GraphicsExpose and normal Expose events together, with the type of the event eventually delivered to the expose procedure taken from the final event. If XtExposeGraphicsExposeMerged is not set, the Intrinsics never combine GraphicsExpose and normal Expose events. XtExposeGraphics-ExposeMerged also implies XtExposeGraphicsExpose.

XtExposeNoExpose

> The Intrinsics also deliver NoExpose events to the expose procedure. The Intrinsics never combine NoExpose events with any other events, no matter what other flags are set.

6.16 Handling Exposures

The Intrinsics deliver exposure events for a widget to the widget's expose procedure, which is of type `XtExposeProc`.

```
typedef void (*XtExposeProc) (Widget, XEvent *, Region)
     Widget w;
     XEvent *event;
     Region region;
```

w	Specifies the widget requiring redisplay.
event	Specifies the exposure event.
region	Specifies the union of all the rectangles in the exposure sequence, or NULL.

If exposure compression is not enabled, the Intrinsics send each exposure event to the widget's expose procedure as it arrives and the *region* parameter is always NULL. If exposure compression is enabled, the Intrinsics delay calling the expose procedure until all merged exposure events, as defined by the compression mode, have arrived. The rectangle in the delivered exposure event is the smallest rectangle that contains all the exposed rectangles, and the region is the union of all the rectangles.

The *region* parameter is always NULL when a NoExpose event is delivered to the expose procedure.

The expose procedure is responsible for displaying the contents of the widget. Simple widgets find it easiest to ignore the event and region and just repaint the entire widget for each exposure. More complicated widgets use the region as a clipping region for the redisplay to avoid repainting areas that do not require redisplay.

Widget classes that redisplay the widget contents in their resize procedure can call the expose procedure to do this. This can lead to extra redisplays during set-values processing, though. If the widget has a changed size after all the set_values procedures have been called, and if any of the procedures returned TRUE to indicate that the widget requires a redisplay, the expose procedure can get called twice—once when `XtSetValues` calls the resize procedure after making the geometry request, and once when `XtSetValues` redisplays the widget. There are two ways to avoid this problem, neither particularly clean:

• Rather than calling the expose procedure directly, the resize procedure can do the same thing `XtSetValues` does and call `XClearArea` on the window, specifying *exposures* TRUE (see Section 6.1 of *Xlib*). If exposure compression is set to XtExpose-CompressMultiple, the two series of exposure events will usually be merged into a single call to the expose procedure. If XtExposeCompressMultiple is not appropriate for whatever reason, the resize procedure can set a flag that tells the expose procedure to do its own lookahead for Expose events using the Xlib `XCheckIfEvent` or `XCheckWindowEvent` routine; see Sections 8.8.2 and 8.8.3 of *Xlib*.

• The set_values procedure can set an "expose will be called" flag in the widget if it returns TRUE, and the resize procedure can check the flag, only calling the expose procedure if the flag is unset. The expose procedure resets the flag. This should be done uniformly across the widget set to avoid problems coordinating among superclasses and subclasses, and it applies to constraint set_values procedures that return TRUE as well. In addition, some class near the root of the class hierarchy needs to set the flag if the core *background_pixel* or *background_pixmap* fields change, since Core returns TRUE in this case but does not participate in this protocol.

Unless a widget is particularly expensive to redisplay, it is usually not worth the trouble to work around this problem.

If a widget class does not need to do anything to display its widgets, it specifies NULL as the expose procedure. Most composite widgets fall into this category; all they need is to have the server repaint their backgrounds, which happens automatically upon exposure. Since the Xlib header files contain a macro definition for "Expose", widget implementations must call the expose procedure something else, often "Redisplay".

Example 6.4 shows the Label widget's expose procedure. It concatenates the label string and the accelerator string to obtain the string to draw and then uses the justification value to compute the appropriate x position for the string; the conversions to int are necessary since C's type conversion rules promote signed integers to unsigned instead of the other way around, and the computations might generate a negative value for x. Finally the string is displayed using the label's current graphics context, which contains the appropriate font and foreground color.

Example 6.5 shows the Pushbutton expose procedure. If the widget is currently inverted, it fills the widget with its foreground color, and if it is currently highlighted, it draws a rectangle around the border. It then calls the Label expose procedure to actually display the string. The proper graphics context for displaying the widget in an inverted or insensitive state has already been copied into the *current_gc* field of the widget so Label redisplays using the right context.

```
static void Redisplay(w, event, region)
    Widget w;
    XEvent *event;
    Region region;
{
    LabelWidget lw = (LabelWidget) w;
    char *string;
    Boolean allocated = FALSE;
    int x;

    if (lw->label.accel_string == NULL) {
        string = lw->label.label;
    } else {
        string = XtMalloc(lw->label.label_len + 1);
        (void) strcpy(string, lw->label.label);
        (void) strcat(string, lw->label.accel_string);
        allocated = TRUE;
    }

    switch (lw->label.justify) {
        case Left:
            x = lw->label.space;
            break;
        case Right:
            x = (int) lw->core.width - (int) lw->label.space -
                    (int) lw->label.label_width;
            break;
        case Center:
            x = ((int) lw->core.width -
                    (int) lw->label.label_width) / 2;
            break;
    }

    XDrawString(XtDisplay(w), XtWindow(w), lw->label.current_gc,
            x, lw->label.space + lw->label.font->max_bounds.ascent,
            string, lw->label.label_len);

    if (allocated) XtFree(string);
}
```

Example 6.4. The Label expose procedure

6.17   Visibility

Some widgets require a substantial amount of computation to display themselves, and this computation is pointless if the widget is not currently visible on
the screen. Another application might obscure it, or the widget's application
could be iconified. The *visible* field in the core part of the widget record lets
the implementation know if the widget is currently visible on the screen.

```
static void Redisplay(w, event, region)
    Widget w;
    XEvent *event;
    Region region;
{
    PushbuttonWidget pw = (PushbuttonWidget) w;
    int offset;

    /* If inverted, fill background with the foreground color */

    if (pw->pushbutton.inverted) {
        XFillRectangle(XtDisplay(w), XtWindow(w), pw->label.gc,
                0, 0, pw->core.width, pw->core.height);
    }

    /* If highlighted, draw highlighting border */

    if (pw->pushbutton.highlighted) {
        offset = pw->pushbutton.highlight_border / 2;
        XDrawRectangle(XtDisplay(w), XtWindow(w), pw->label.current_gc,
                offset, offset,
                pw->core.width - pw->pushbutton.highlight_border,
                pw->core.height - pw->pushbutton.highlight_border);
    }

    /* Make Label redisplay the string */

    (*pushbuttonWidgetClass->core_class.superclass->core_class.expose)
            (w, event, region);
}
```

Example 6.5. The Pushbutton expose procedure

If the *visible_interest* flag in the widget class record is FALSE, the widget's *visible* field is always TRUE. If the *visible_interest* flag is TRUE, the Intrinsics request VisibilityNotify events from the X server and keep the *visible* field updated to FALSE if the widget is invisible and TRUE if any part of the widget is visible.

6.18   Implementing Sensitivity

There are two fields in the widget instance that determine sensitivity, *sensitive* and *ancestor_sensitive*. If *sensitive* is FALSE, it means that the widget was explicitly desensitized, and if *ancestor_sensitive* is FALSE, it means that the widget is insensitive because an ancestor was desensitized.

```
/* If sensitivity changing, adjust appearance */

if (NE(core.sensitive) || NE(core.ancestor_sensitive)) {
    if (XtIsSensitive(newpw)) {       /* Just made sensitive */
        newpw->label.current_gc = newpw->label.gc;

    } else {                          /* Just made insensitive */
        newpw->label.current_gc =
                newpw->pushbutton.insensitive_gc;

        /* If currently highlighted, will never receive
           leave event to unhighlight, so unhighlight */
        newpw->pushbutton.highlighted = FALSE;
    }
}
```

Example 6.6. Part of the Pushbutton set_values procedure

The Intrinsics use `XtSetValues` on the XtNsensitive and XtNancestor-Sensitive resources to change a widget's sensitivity in response to a call to `XtSetSensitive`. Widgets that change their appearance when made insensitive check these fields in their set_values procedures.

Example 6.6 shows the part of the Pushbutton set_values procedure that handles sensitivity. It checks to see if either the *sensitive* or *ancestor_sensitive* fields have changed, and if either has, adjusts the pushbutton's appearance accordingly. If both fields are now TRUE, it makes the current graphics context the normal graphics context; otherwise it makes the current graphics context the insensitive graphics context. Additionally, when a pushbutton is made insensitive, it makes sure that highlighting is turned off.

The set_values procedure also, in code not shown here, returns TRUE to indicate that it requires a redisplay if the graphics context has changed.

6.19   Accepting Input Focus

If an application has set the WM_TAKE_FOCUS window manager protocol as described in Sections 6.6 and 6.7, the window manager will sometimes send client messages to the application instructing it to take the input focus. The application does this by calling `XtCallAcceptFocus` for one of its widgets. `XtCallAcceptFocus` in turn calls the accept_focus method for the widget.

Calling the accept_focus method tells the widget to take the input focus if it wants it. The procedure returns a Boolean value that indicates whether it accepted the focus. This return value does not have to be constant; a widget is free to accept the focus at some times but not at others. The accept_focus method can be NULL, indicating that the widget never wants the focus. Accept_focus is non-NULL if the widget *ever* wants the input focus; it returns TRUE if it *currently* wants the input focus.

Widgets that want keyboard events set the focus to their window in their accept_focus procedure by calling XSetInputFocus. There is a snag here: if the widget's window is not currently visible on the screen, the call to XSetInputFocus generates an error from the server. Widget implementations should at the very least make sure that the widget is realized and managed before taking the focus. There is an unfortunate race condition involved here, though—even if the widget is visible when it makes the call, it might be invisible by the time the request gets to the server, for example, if the user iconifies the window. To be absolutely sure the call to XSetInput-Focus does not generate an error, the widget must grab the server, test for visibility, set the focus if the widget is visible, and ungrab the server.

Modifying the Xlib error handling to screen out this error is another approach to get around this; see Section 8.12 of *Xlib*. The accept_focus method synchronizes with the server by calling XSync, then installs an Xlib error handler that ignores BadMatch errors from SetInputFocus protocol requests. It then calls XSetInputFocus, synchronizes again, and restores the previous Xlib error handler. Unfortunately, only Xlib implementations that conform to the Release 4 specification return the old error handler when a new one is installed, so this method does not work with older implementations.

The accept_focus method is of type XtAcceptFocusProc.

```
typedef Boolean (*XtAcceptFocusProc) (Widget, Time *)
     Widget w;
     Time *time;
w               Specifies the widget to take the input focus.
time            Specifies the X time of the event causing the focus to change.
```

If the procedure takes the input focus using XSetInputFocus, it passes the value of the accept_focus procedure's *time* parameter to XSetInputFocus. Note that the *time* parameter is passed by reference.

```
static Boolean AcceptFocus(w, time)
    Widget w;
    Time *time;
{
    BoxWidget box = (BoxWidget) w;
    register int i;

    if (box->box.last_focus != NULL &&
            XtIsManaged(box->box.last_focus)) {
        if (XtCallAcceptFocus(box->box.last_focus, time)) {
            return TRUE;
        }
    }

    for (i = 0; i < box->composite.num_children; i++) {
        if (!XtIsManaged(box->composite.children[i])) continue;
        if (XtCallAcceptFocus(box->composite.children[i], time)) {
            box->box.last_focus = box->composite.children[i];
            return TRUE;
        }
    }

    box->box.last_focus = NULL;
    return FALSE;
}
```

Example 6.7. The Box widget's accept_focus procedure

Composite widgets often have an accept_focus procedure that passes each of its managed children to `XtCallAcceptFocus` to find one that wants the focus. Example 6.7 shows an example of this with the additional enhancement that it keeps track of the last widget that accepted the input focus and tries it first. Composite widgets also often have class methods that their children call to pass the input focus from child to child; for example, the child might have special translations that call "move focus to next child" or "move focus to previous child" methods in the parent when the user hits the Next or Prev keys on his keyboard. This should be done uniformly throughout a widget set so that the children are certain that the parent that happens to contain them has these methods; the easiest way to do this is to have a class supporting these methods that is a superclass of the other composite widgets in the widget set.

6.20   More on the Grab List

When there are widgets on the grab list, special event-handling occurs in the Intrinsics. Some event types are discarded, some are processed normally, and some are *remapped*, or delivered to a different widget than they would be if the grab list were empty.

If an EnterNotify or MotionNotify event occurs for a widget that is not in the active set of the grab list and is not a descendant of a widget in the active set, the Intrinsics discard it.[2]

If a KeyPress, KeyRelease, ButtonPress, or ButtonRelease event arrives for a widget in the active set or a descendant of a widget in the active set, the Intrinsics deliver it normally. If the event arrives for a widget not in the active set, the Intrinsics do not deliver the event to the widget. In either case, the Intrinsics also remap the event: if there is a spring-loaded widget in the active set of the grab list, the Intrinsics deliver the event to the most recently added spring-loaded widget. The Intrinsics thus deliver events that occur within the active set both to their widget and the most recent spring-loaded widget, if any; events occurring outside the active set go only to the spring-loaded widget. The check for remapping occurs at the end of an event dispatch, so if handling an event makes a new spring-loaded widget appear in the active set, the Intrinsics remap the event to that widget. When keyboard events have been redirected using XtSetKeyboardFocus, the redirection takes place first, and then the Intrinsics process the event as if it had occurred in the widget where it was ultimately directed.

All other events are delivered normally.

Note that it is possible for a widget to receive a leave event without a corresponding enter event since grab processing discards enter events but not leave events. Widgets must be prepared to handle extra leave events, usually by ignoring them.

Having events remapped is useful for implementing pop-up menus. When the user presses a pointer button, the server starts a grab for the window that receives the ButtonPress event so that it receives all pointer events no matter where on the screen they occur until the user releases the button. This is inconvenient for pop-up menus since the widgets in the menu need to handle the events. Since the pop-up menu is a spring-loaded pop-up, however, its

---

[2] LeaveNotify events are also discarded in Intrinsics implementations that conform to specifications earlier than Release 4.

shell also gets the pointer events. Section 6.22 shows how to install an event handler on the shell to manipulate the server grab.

6.21   Pointer and Keyboard Grabs

In this section, *grabs* refers to server grabs, not to toolkit grabs.

Some widget implementations use pointer button or key grabs to implement reliable pop-up menus or to trap events that would normally be delivered to their children. The most useful grabs are synchronous grabs, which make the server temporarily suspend event delivery until the application calls XAllowEvents, XUngrabPointer, or XUngrabKeyboard.

Consider a composite widget that allows the user to move the input focus among its children with the Next and Prev keys on the keyboard. The composite widget grabs these two keys so that a keypress event on either gets delivered to the composite widget instead of to the child that currently has the input focus. When the composite widget receives one of these keypress events, it transfers the input focus.

It is possible, however, for the application to lag the server. If the user continues typing after pressing the Next or Prev key, it is likely that the server will already have sent the key events to the application before it receives the request to transfer the input focus. The net result is that the server delivers the first few keystrokes after the Next or Prev key to the old widget instead of to the new one.

The solution lies in synchronous grabs. If the composite issues a synchronous key grab, the server delays delivering further keyboard events until the composite calls XAllowEvents. When it receives the keypress event, the composite widget first transfers the keyboard focus and then calls XAllowEvents to resume event delivery. The server only sends further key events to the application after the focus has changed, so the events go to the correct child.

An analogous process allows "mouse ahead." If pressing a pointer button in a window creates a pop-up menu, a user who knows which menu item will appear underneath the pointer can select that item by releasing the pointer button before the menu appears. By issuing a synchronous pointer button grab, the widget triggering the pop-up delays the delivery of the button release event until the menu has been popped up, making the server deliver the release event to the menu item.

`XtRegisterGrabAction` automatically enables key or button grabs for certain actions; see Section 7.10.

The Intrinsics grab list interferes with key and button grabs. In the first example, the user can type the Next or Prev key while the grab list is non-empty because of a different pop-up widget. The Intrinsics either discard or remap the key event, so the composite widget never receives the event and never calls `XAllowEvents`. The keyboard locks up and becomes useless. In the second example, the user can try to pop up the menu while the grab list is nonempty. Again, the Intrinsics discard or remap the event and the widget triggering the pop-up never receives it, `XAllowEvents` never gets called, and the pointer locks up and becomes useless.

To avoid these problems, the toolkit provides its own version of the Xlib grab routines. This allows the event dispatcher to know when it is discarding or remapping an event that triggers a grab, and it calls `XUngrabPointer` or `XUngrabKeyboard` to prevent pointer or keyboard lock-up.

You should thoroughly understand Sections 7.4 and 7.5 of *Xlib*, on pointer and keyboard grabbing, before attempting to use any of the following routines. All nonwidget parameters in these routines have the same meanings as those in the corresponding Xlib routine.

To passively grab a pointer button, use `XtGrabButton`.

void XtGrabButton (*widget, button, modifiers, owner_events, event_mask, pointer_mode,*
                   keyboard_mode, confine_to, cursor)
    Widget *widget*;
    int *button*;
    Modifiers *modifiers*;
    Boolean *owner_events*;
    unsigned int *event_mask*;
    int *pointer_mode, keyboard_mode*;
    Window *confine_to*;
    Cursor *cursor*;

widget	Specifies the widget in whose window the pointer is to be grabbed.
button	Specifies the button to grab, or AnyButton.
modifiers	Specifies the set of modifiers that limit when the grab activates, or AnyModifiers.
owner_events	Specifies whether pointer events delivered during the grab are delivered to their normal widgets within the application or are all delivered to the grabbing widget.

event_mask   Specifies the pointer event types that will be delivered during the grab.

pointer_mode   Specifies whether to synchronize pointer events; use either GrabModeSync or GrabModeAsync.

keyboard_mode Specifies whether to synchronize keyboard events; use either GrabModeSync or GrabModeAsync.

confine_to   Specifies the window to confine the cursor to during the grab, or None.

cursor   Specifies the cursor to display during the grab, or None.

If the widget is realized, XtGrabButton calls XGrabButton, passing the widget's window as the grab window. If the widget is not realized, the Intrinsics defer the call to XGrabButton until the widget is realized and its window is mapped. If the widget is unrealized and realized again at some future time, the Intrinsics call XGrabButton again.

If at any future time during program execution a pointer button event that triggers the grab arrives and the Intrinsics either discard it or dispatch it to a widget other than the grabbing widget, the Intrinsics also call XUngrab-Pointer to deactivate the grab. However, if a pointer grab is already in progress, the Intrinsics do not call XUngrabPointer.

To release a pointer button grab, use XtUngrabButton.

void XtUngrabButton(*widget, button, modifiers*)
    Widget *widget*;
    int *button*;
    Modifiers *modifiers*;

widget   Specifies the widget whose button grab is to be released.
button   Specifies the button to ungrab, or AnyButton.
modifiers Specifies the set of modifiers that limited when the grab activated, or AnyModifiers.

If the widget is realized, XtUngrabButton calls XUngrabButton, passing the widget's window as the grab window. If the widget is not realized, XtUngrabButton removes the deferred grab caused by XtGrabButton.

To actively grab the pointer, use XtGrabPointer

int XtGrabPointer(*widget, owner_events, event_mask, pointer_mode, keyboard_mode,*
                confine_to, cursor, time)
    Widget *widget*;
    Boolean *owner_events*;
    unsigned int *event_mask*;

```
int pointer_mode, keyboard_mode;
Window confine_to;
Cursor cursor;
Time time;
```

widget   Specifies the widget in whose window the pointer is to be grabbed.

owner_events   Specifies whether pointer events delivered during the grab are
                    delivered to their normal widgets within the application or are all
                    delivered to the grabbing widget.

event_mask   Specifies the pointer event types that will be delivered during the
                    grab.

pointer_mode   Specifies whether to synchronize pointer events; use either
                    GrabModeSync or GrabModeAsync.

keyboard_mode   Specifies whether to synchronize keyboard events; use either
                    GrabModeSync or GrabModeAsync.

confine_to   Specifies the window to confine the cursor to during the grab, or
                    None.

cursor   Specifies the cursor to display during the grab, or None.

time   Specifies the timestamp in the event that initiated the grab, or
                    CurrentTime.

If the widget is realized, `XtGrabPointer` calls `XGrabPointer`, passing the widget's window as the grab window, and returns the result. If the widget is not realized, `XtGrabPointer` immediately returns GrabNotViewable. `XtGrabPointer` allows the Intrinsics grab filtering to know when a pointer grab is active so that it can avoid calling `XUngrabPointer`.

Take care when grabbing the pointer when the grab list is nonempty. Having a widget not in the active set grab the pointer is almost always a mistake since it will not receive the pointer events.

To release a pointer grab, use `XtUngrabPointer`.

```
void XtUngrabPointer(widget, time)
    Widget widget;
    Time time;
```

widget   Specifies the widget that grabbed the pointer.

time   Specifies the timestamp in the event that initiated the grab release,
                    or CurrentTime.

`XtUngrabPointer` calls `XUngrabPointer`, passing the widget's window as the grab window.

To passively grab a key, use `XtGrabKey`.

void XtGrabKey(*widget, keycode, modifiers, owner_events, pointer_mode, keyboard_mode*)
    Widget *widget*;
    KeyCode *keycode*;
    Modifiers *modifiers*;
    Boolean *owner_events*;
    int *pointer_mode, keyboard_mode*;

widget	Specifies the widget in whose window the key is to be grabbed.
keycode	Specifies the keycode of the key to grab, or AnyKey.
modifiers	Specifies the set of modifiers that limit when the grab activates, or AnyModifiers.
owner_events	Specifies whether keyboard events delivered during the grab are delivered to their normal widgets within the application or are all delivered to the grabbing widget.
pointer_mode	Specifies whether to synchronize pointer events; use either GrabModeSync or GrabModeAsync.
keyboard_mode	Specifies whether to synchronize keyboard events; use either GrabModeSync or GrabModeAsync.

If the widget is realized, `XtGrabKey` calls `XGrabKey`, passing the widget's window as the grab window. If the widget is not realized, the Intrinsics defer the call to `XGrabKey` until the widget is realized and its window is mapped. If the widget is unrealized and realized again at some future time, the Intrinsics call `XGrabKey` again.

If at any future time during program execution a keypress event that triggers the grab arrives and the Intrinsics either discard it or dispatch it to a widget other than the grabbing widget, the Intrinsics also call `XUngrab-Keyboard` to deactivate the grab. However, if a keyboard grab is already in progress, the Intrinsics do not call `XUngrabKeyboard`.

The function `XtKeysymToKeycodeList` is particularly useful for finding a keycode for `XtGrabKey`; see Section 7.23.

To release a key grab, use `XtUngrabKey`.

void XtUngrabKey(*widget, keycode, modifiers*)
    Widget *widget*;
    KeyCode *keycode*;
    Modifiers *modifiers*;

widget	Specifies the widget whose key grab is to be released.
keycode	Specifies the keycode of the key to ungrab, or AnyKey.
modifiers	Specifies the set of modifiers that limited when the grab activated, or AnyModifiers.

If the widget is realized, XtUngrabKey calls XUngrabKey, passing the widget's window as the grab window. If the widget is not realized, XtUngrabKey removes the deferred grab caused by XtGrabKey.

To actively grab the keyboard, use XtGrabKeyboard.

int XtGrabKeyboard(*widget, owner_events, pointer_mode, keyboard_mode, time*)
    Widget *widget*;
    Boolean *owner_events*;
    int *pointer_mode, keyboard_mode*;
    Time *time*;

widget	Specifies the widget in whose window the keyboard is to be grabbed.
owner_events	Specifies whether keyboard events delivered during the grab are delivered to their normal widgets within the application or are all delivered to the grabbing widget.
pointer_mode	Specifies whether to synchronize pointer events; use either GrabModeSync or GrabModeAsync.
keyboard_mode	Specifies whether to synchronize keyboard events; use either GrabModeSync or GrabModeAsync.
time	Specifies the timestamp in the event that initiated the grab, or CurrentTime.

If the widget is realized, XtGrabKeyboard calls XGrabKeyboard, passing the widget's window as the grab window, and returns the result. If the widget is not realized, XtGrabKeyboard immediately returns GrabNotViewable. XtGrabKeyboard allows the Intrinsics grab filtering process to know when a keyboard grab is active so that it can avoid calling XUngrabKeyboard.

Take care when grabbing the keyboard when the grab list is nonempty. Having a widget not in the active set grab the keyboard is almost always a mistake since it will not receive the keyboard events.

To release a keyboard grab, use XtUngrabKeyboard.

void XtUngrabKeyboard(*widget, time*)
    Widget *widget*;
    Time *time*;

widget	Specifies the widget that grabbed the keyboard.
time	Specifies the timestamp in the event that initiated the grab release, or CurrentTime.

XtUngrabKeyboard calls XUngrabKeyboard, passing the widget's window as the grab window.

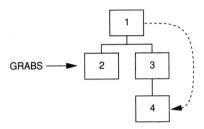

Figure 6.3. Keyboard forwarding and grabs

Key and keyboard grabs affect how `XtSetKeyboardFocus` forwards keyboard events. When event forwarding is in effect, the toolkit simulates part of the processing that the server would do if the final destination of the forwarding actually had the X focus.

Consider the widget tree in Figure 6.3. Keyboard events have been redirected from widget 1 to widget 4, and widgets 2 and 3 have called `XtGrabKey` with *owner_events* FALSE. If a key event that activates the grab occurs in each of the widgets, the following occurs:

Widget 1   The Intrinsics forward the event to widget 4. If widget 4 had actually had the X focus, its parent, widget 3, would have grabbed this event, so the Intrinsics dispatch the event to widget 3.

Widget 2   The Intrinsics forward the event to widget 4. This event triggered a grab on widget 2, but widget 3 would have grabbed the key if widget 4 had had the focus. The Intrinsics dispatch the event to widget 3 after releasing the grab on widget 2.

Widget 3   The Intrinsics forward the event to widget 4, then notice that widget 3 activated a grab and dispatch the event to widget 3.

Widget 4   Cannot happen. Since widget 3 has a grab, no descendant can receive the activating event.

Note that the first two cases leave the keyboard ungrabbed, even though it would have been grabbed if widget 4 had had the focus. There are race conditions in the X protocol that prevent the Intrinsics from precisely duplicating the server behavior.

The exact rules that implement the grab policy are very complicated and you do not really want to know them. In all cases, dispatching an event still goes through the grab list, so the event can be discarded or remapped if its final destination is not in the active set of the grab list. In this case, the Intrinsics automatically cancel any grab the event activated.

6.22   X Event Handlers

Most widget implementations specify their event handling by providing default translations. This provides an application- or user-customizable set of mappings from events into actions; it is discussed in Chapter 7. Some widgets, however, need to deal with events more directly, and for these cases the toolkit provides event handlers.

An event handler is a procedure that the Intrinsics call when a particular type of event arrives for a widget. Event handlers are appropriate when a widget class needs specific processing for some type of event that it does not want to be customizable, or for handling events that are delivered other than through the normal event-handling mechanisms. The toolkit uses them internally to implement selections and translation management. Widgets can have more than one event handler, and XtDispatchEvent always calls all event handlers that match the event type.

An event handler is of type XtEventHandler.

```
typedef void (*XtEventHandler) (Widget, XtPointer, XEvent *, Boolean*);
    Widget w;
    XtPointer client_data;
    XEvent *event;
    Boolean *continue_to_dispatch;
```

w	Specifies the widget that handles the event.
client_data	Specifies a piece of data passed to the toolkit when the event handler was registered.
event	Specifies the X event that triggered the event handler.
continue_to_dispatch	
	Specifies whether the Intrinsics should call the remaining event handlers registered for this event.

The widget implementation specifies the *client_data* parameter when registering the event handler, and the Intrinsics pass it uninterpreted to the event handler.

Before calling any event handlers, the Intrinsics set the Boolean value pointed to by *continue_to_dispatch* to TRUE.[3] If an event handler wishes to abort

---

[3] The *continue_to_dispatch* parameter is not supported by Intrinsics implementations that conform to specifications earlier than Release 4.

further processing of the event, it changes this value to FALSE, and the Intrinsics do not call any remaining event handlers. Aborting further event handling is nonportable and extremely risky; the Intrinsics add private event handlers to widgets to perform internal event processing, and if these do not get called, the Intrinsics' internal state becomes corrupted. The danger of aborting event handlers cannot be overemphasized—before you decide to use it in a widget implementation, study your implementation of the Intrinsics and the implementations of other widgets that might be used with your widget (widgets sometimes add event handlers to their parents, their children, or seemingly unrelated widgets).

The routines that add and remove event handlers all have an *event_mask* parameter that specifies which event types trigger calling the handler. They also have a `Boolean` parameter *nonmaskable* that specifies whether the Intrinsics call the event handler for nonmaskable events. The nonmaskable events are GraphicsExpose, NoExpose, SelectionClear, SelectionRequest, SelectionNotify, ClientMessage, and MappingNotify, none of which have event mask bits defined.

To register a new event handler or to add new events to those that trigger an already registered event handler, use `XtAddEventHandler` or `XtInsertEventHandler`.[4]

In most cases, the ordering of handlers is not important. `XtAddEventHandler` adds an event handler to the list of event handlers in an unspecified place.

typedef unsigned long EventMask;

void XtAddEventHandler(*w, event_mask, nonmaskable, proc, client_data*)
    Widget *w*;
    EventMask *event_mask*;
    Boolean *nonmaskable*;
    XtEventHandler *proc*;
    XtPointer *client_data*;

w	Specifies the widget that the event handler is being registered for.
event_mask	Specifies which event types trigger the event handler.
nonmaskable	Specifies whether the Intrinsics call the handler when a nonmaskable event arrives.

---

[4] `XtInsertEventHandler` is not supported by Intrinsics implementations that conform to specifications earlier than Release 4.

proc   Specifies the event handler.

client_data   Specifies a piece of data passed uninterpreted to the event
                        handler.

If the new event handler specifies mask bits that other event handlers for the
widget have not already selected for, `XtAddEventHandler` calls `XSelect-Input` to update the event mask for the widget's window. If an earlier call to
`XtAddEventHandler` or `XtInsertEventHandler` was made with the
same widget, handler, and client data, the *event_mask* and *nonmaskable*
parameters augment the conditions on which the Intrinsics call the handler.

`XtInsertEventHandler` adds an event handler to either the head or the
tail of the list of event handlers.

typedef enum {XtListHead, XtListTail} XtListPosition;

void XtInsertEventHandler(*w, event_mask, nonmaskable, proc, client_data, position*)
    Widget *w*;
    EventMask *event_mask*;
    Boolean *nonmaskable*;
    XtEventHandler *proc*;
    XtPointer *client_data*;
    XtListPosition *position*;

w   Specifies the widget that the event handler is being registered for.

event_mask   Specifies which event types trigger the event handler.

nonmaskable   Specifies whether the Intrinsics call the handler when a
                        nonmaskable event arrives.

proc   Specifies the event handler.

client_data   Specifies a piece of data passed uninterpreted to the event handler.

position   Specifies whether the new handler should be added before or after
                        already existing handlers.

If *position* is XtListHead, `XtInsertEventHandler` adds the new handler so
that it will be called before any already registered handlers. If *position* is XtList-Tail, `XtInsertEventHandler` adds the new handler so that it will be called
after any already registered handlers. In general, add handlers that should not
be aborted at the head of the list and handlers that can deal with being
aborted at the tail of the list.

To remove a previously registered event handler or to remove events from
those that trigger it, use `XtRemoveEventHandler`.

void XtRemoveEventHandler(*w, event_mask, nonmaskable, proc, client_data*)
     Widget *w*;
     EventMask *event_mask*;
     Boolean *nonmaskable*;
     XtEventHandler *proc*;
     XtPointer *client_data*;

w	Specifies the widget that the handler was registered for.
event_mask	Specifies the events that no longer trigger this handler, or XtAllEvents.
nonmaskable	Specifies whether the Intrinsics should stop calling the handler for nonmaskable events.
proc	Specifies the event handler.
client_data	Specifies the client data.

The widget, event handler, and client data all must match a previously added event handler; otherwise `XtRemoveEventHandler` returns immediately without an error.

`XtRemoveEventHandler` removes events from the set that trigger the specified event handler. If the set of events becomes empty, the Intrinsics remove the event handler from the widget's list of handlers. To remove an event handler completely call `XtRemoveEventHandler` with the special value XtAllEvents as the event mask and with nonmaskable TRUE.

`XtRemoveEventHandler` calls `XSelectInput` to change the event mask for the widget's window if it removes events that no other event handler has registered for.

Some widget implementations need to handle events without making the Intrinsics select for the event. The event may come as a result of a pointer or keyboard grab, may have been delivered to the widget as a result of event remapping, or may be an internally constructed event. In these cases the implementation uses *raw* event handlers to process the event without changing the event mask of the widget's window.

To add a raw event handler or to add new events to those that trigger an already registered raw event handler, use `XtAddRawEventHandler` or `XtInsertRawEventHandler`.[5]

---

[5] `XtInsertRawEventHandler` is not supported by Intrinsics implementations that conform to specifications earlier than Release 4.

void XtAddRawEventHandler(*w, event_mask, nonmaskable, proc, client_data*)
    Widget *w*;
    EventMask *event_mask*;
    Boolean *nonmaskable*;
    XtEventHandler *proc*;
    XtPointer *client_data*;

w	Specifies the widget that the event handler is being registered for.
event_mask	Specifies which event types trigger the event handler.
nonmaskable	Specifies whether the Intrinsics call the handler when a nonmaskable event arrives.
proc	Specifies the event handler.
client_data	Specifies a piece of data passed uninterpreted to the event handler.

void XtInsertRawEventHandler(*w, event_mask, nonmaskable, proc, client_data, position*)
    Widget *w*;
    EventMask *event_mask*;
    Boolean *nonmaskable*;
    XtEventHandler *proc*;
    XtPointer *client_data*;
    XtListPosition *position*;

w	Specifies the widget that the event handler is being registered for.
event_mask	Specifies which event types trigger the event handler.
nonmaskable	Specifies whether the Intrinsics call the handler when a nonmaskable event arrives.
proc	Specifies the event handler.
client_data	Specifies a piece of data passed uninterpreted to the event handler.
position	Specifies whether the new handler should be added before or after already existing handlers.

These routines are identical to their nonraw versions except that they never modify the widget's event mask with `XSelectInput`. However, these events may already be selected for as a result of other, nonraw event handlers.

To remove a previously registered raw event handler or to remove events from those that trigger it, use `XtRemoveRawEventHandler`.

void XtRemoveRawEventHandler(*w, event_mask, nonmaskable, proc, client_data*)
    Widget *w*;
    EventMask *event_mask*;
    Boolean *nonmaskable*;
    XtEventHandler *proc*;
    XtPointer *client_data*;

w	Specifies the widget that the handler was registered for.
event_mask	Specifies the events that no longer trigger this handler, or XtAllEvents.
nonmaskable	Specifies whether the Intrinsics should stop calling the handler for nonmaskable events.
proc	Specifies the event handler.
client_data	Specifies the client data.

XtRemoveRawEventHandler is identical to XtRemoveEventHandler except that it never modifies the widget's input mask with XSelectInput.

Example 6.8 shows the Menu widget's initialize procedure; it adds a raw event handler for button events to the menu's parent. The Menu widget assumes it will be popped up by a ButtonPress event in some widget, and it must transfer the implicit server grab the button event creates to the Menu widget. This allows the widgets in the menu to react to the pointer events. Menus are spring-loaded pop-ups, so a menu's shell always gets a copy of the event that popped up the menu. The Intrinsics dispatch this event to the HandleMenu-Button event handler now on the shell. HandleMenuButton processes the ButtonPress by calling XtGrabPointer to transfer the grab to the shell's window. This makes the server deliver further pointer events to the widgets in the menu tree rather than to the widget that popped the menu up. See Section 6.21 for more information on grabs. The event handler also receives ButtonRelease events and reacts to them by popping down the menu; this makes the menu pop down no matter where the user releases the pointer button. Popping down the menu automatically cancels the grab.

This event handler is raw since the menu's shell does not need to actually select for the pointer events; it only needs to react when the Intrinsics remap them. This also shows an example of the risk involved in aborting event handlers—Menu registers the event handler on its shell widget but the shell widget implementation knows nothing about this event handler. If the shell widget assumed that it knew about all its event handlers and later added a handler to the head of the handler list that aborted further processing, the Intrinsics would never call HandleMenuButton. Not calling this handler makes menus nonfunctional and, if the menu was popped up with a synchronous grab, makes the pointer lock up, rendering it useless.

```
static void HandleMenuButton(w, client_data, event,
        continue_to_dispatch)
    Widget w;
    XtPointer client_data;
    XEvent *event;
    Boolean *continue_to_dispatch;
{
    switch (event->type) {
        case ButtonPress:
            /* The new grab does an implicit AllowEvents */
            (void) XtGrabPointer(w, True,
                    EnterWindowMask | LeaveWindowMask |
                        ButtonReleaseMask,
                    GrabModeAsync, GrabModeAsync, None, None,
                    event->xbutton.time);
            break;

        case ButtonRelease:
            /* Popping down also ungrabs the pointer */
            XtPopdown(w);
            break;
    }
}

static void Initialize(req, new)
    Widget req, new;
{
    ((MenuWidget) new)->menu.save_border = -1;

    if (XtIsShell(XtParent(new))) {
        XtAddRawEventHandler(XtParent(new),
                ButtonPressMask | ButtonReleaseMask,
                FALSE, HandleMenuButton, NULL);
    }
}
```

Example 6.8.   The Menu widget's initialize procedure

6.23   Getting the Current Event Mask

To find out the set of events currently selected for by a widget, call
XtBuildEventMask.

EventMask XtBuildEventMask(*w*)
    Widget *w*;
    w   Specifies the widget.

`XtBuildEventMask` returns the union of the event masks for all the nonraw event handlers for the widget. It is required by widgets that change their cursor during pointer grabs with `XChangeActivePointerGrab` since, in general, the widget does not know which events may have been selected.

Chapter 7

Translation Management

Writing Applications

7.1 Translation Tables

Each widget in a user interface has a *translation table* that defines how that widget reacts to X events. The translation table can be empty, as is normally the case for the Label widget, or it can specify actions to execute when certain sequences of events arrive.

Each widget class defines a set of action names, which are strings that correspond to procedures that implement the functionality of the widget. For example, Pushbutton defines the actions "highlight", "unhighlight", "invert", "uninvert", and "notify". "Highlight" draws a border around the button to tell the user that clicking the pointer button triggers the pushbutton, and "unhighlight" removes the border. "Invert" reverses the colors of the widget to show that it is about to execute, and "uninvert" restores the normal colors. "Notify" makes the pushbutton invoke the callback procedures associated with the widget.

The default translation table for a pushbutton looks like this:

```
"<EnterWindow>  : highlight()          \n\
 <LeaveWindow>  : unhighlight()        \n\
 <Btn1Down>     : invert()             \n\
 <Btn1Up>       : notify() uninvert()"
```

Each line of the table specifies an action to take upon receipt of a particular X event. When the pointer enters the pushbutton's window, the pushbutton highlights itself, and when the pointer leaves, it unhighlights itself. When the user presses pointer button 1 the pushbutton inverts, and when he releases the pointer button the pushbutton invokes the application callback and then restores the pushbutton to its normal colors. The case of alphabetic characters is relevant in all parts of a translation table.

Each widget class has a default set of translations that the widget documentation should describe. Translations can, however, be different for each widget of the class. Application writers only need to worry about translations when they modify the default translations for some widget; many application writers do not need the information in this chapter.

A line in a translation table, called a *translation*, has two parts. The left-hand side consists of a series of specifications of X events separated by commas, and the right-hand side consists of a series of action specifications separated by spaces. If a series of X events that match the left-hand side arrive for the widget, in order from left to right and with no intervening events, the Intrinsics call the actions specified in the right-hand side, in order from left to right. A colon separates the left- and right-hand sides, and a translation table with multiple translations separates them with newline characters.

The major piece of an event specification is the name of an X event surrounded by angle brackets. The Intrinsics define a number of synonyms for the X event types to make writing translation tables easier:

Event	Synonyms
KeyPress	Key, KeyDown
KeyRelease	KeyUp
ButtonPress	BtnDown
ButtonRelease	BtnUp
MotionNotify	Motion, PtrMoved, MouseMoved
EnterNotify	Enter, EnterWindow
LeaveNotify	Leave, LeaveWindow
FocusIn	*none*
FocusOut	*none*
KeymapNotify	Keymap
Expose	*none*
GraphicsExpose	GrExp
NoExpose	NoExp
VisibilityNotify	Visible

Event	Synonyms
CreateNotify	Create
DestroyNotify	Destroy
UnmapNotify	Unmap
MapNotify	Map
MapRequest	MapReq
ReparentNotify	Reparent
ConfigureNotify	Configure
ConfigureRequest	ConfigureReq
GravityNotify	Grav
ResizeRequest	ResReq
CirculateNotify	Circ
CirculateRequest	CirculateReq
PropertyNotify	Prop
SelectionClear	SelClr
SelectionRequest	SelReq
SelectionNotify	Select
ColormapNotify	Clrmap
ClientMessage	Message
MappingNotify	Mapping

Translations for keyboard and pointer events (that is, KeyPress, KeyRelease, ButtonPress, ButtonRelease, MotionNotify, EnterNotify, and LeaveNotify) can specify a set of keys or pointer buttons that must already be in a particular state for the translation to trigger. The X protocol defines a set of eight *modifier* bits that can be associated with keyboard keys. Three of these, the Control, Shift, and Lock modifier bits, are normally associated with the control, shift, and lock keys, although the user can change this. The other five, named Mod1 through Mod5, have no standard bindings; the user can associate them with any key on the keyboard.

For translations, *modifier* refers either to a keyboard modifier bit or to a pointer button bit. If a translation specifies modifiers, it only triggers if the keys or buttons corresponding to the modifiers are in the correct state. Only keyboard and pointer translations can have modifiers; the Intrinsics ignore modifiers specified for other event types. The following table lists the modifiers the Intrinsics accept:

Modifier	Abbreviation	Meaning
None		No modifiers or buttons
Any		Any modifiers or buttons
Ctrl	c	Control modifier bit
Shift	s	Shift modifier bit
Lock	l	Lock modifier bit
Mod1		Mod1 modifier bit
Mod2		Mod2 modifier bit
Mod3		Mod3 modifier bit
Mod4		Mod4 modifier bit
Mod5		Mod5 modifier bit
Meta	m	Meta key modifier
Hyper	h	Hyper key modifier
Super	su	Super key modifier
Alt	a	Alt key modifier
@keysym		Keysym modifier
Button1		Pointer button 1
Button2		Pointer button 2
Button3		Pointer button 3
Button4		Pointer button 4
Button5		Pointer button 5

Modifiers precede the event specification, so, for example, for a pointer button press with shift, write

```
Shift <ButtonPress> : action()
```

Any modifiers that are not mentioned can be in any state, so the above translation also triggers if both the Control and Shift modifiers were set. To specify that certain modifiers must not be set, precede them with a tilde, which may be read as "not." Writing

```
Shift ~Ctrl <ButtonPress> : action()
```

specifies that shift must be set and control must not be. To specify that the given modifiers must be set and no other modifiers can be set, precede the list of modifiers with an exclamation point, which may be read as "none but." Writing

```
!Ctrl Shift <ButtonPress> : action()
```

specifies that Control and Shift must be set and no other modifiers can be. A tilde applies to a single modifier; an exclamation point applies to the entire list of modifiers. In brief,

<Enter> : action()	Any modifiers.
Any <Enter> : action()	Any modifiers.
None <Enter> : action()	No modifiers.
Shift <Enter> : action()	Shift and any others.
!Shift <Enter> : action()	Only Shift.
~Shift <Enter> : action()	Any but Shift.

It is never necessary to use a tilde in an event specification that uses an exclamation point.

The Meta, Hyper, Super, and Alt modifiers are meaningful only if the server's modifier table has one of the modifier bits Mod1 through Mod5 bound to a key with that name. This binding is typically done at session startup using xmodmap or a similar utility.[1] Similarly, if another key has been bound to a modifier bit, translation tables can specify translations using that modifier key by preceding its name with an at-sign (@). Assuming the Help key is bound to a modifier bit, write

```
@Help <ButtonPress> : action()
```

to make the action occur when a button press happens in the widget while the user holds down the Help key.[2]

There are some additional synonyms for event types that include implicit modifiers:

Event	Meaning
Ctrl	KeyPress with Control modifier
Meta	KeyPress with Meta modifier
Shift	KeyPress with Shift modifier
BtnMotion	MotionNotify with any button modifier
Btn1Motion	MotionNotify with Button1 modifier
Btn2Motion	MotionNotify with Button2 modifier
Btn3Motion	MotionNotify with Button3 modifier
Btn4Motion	MotionNotify with Button4 modifier
Btn5Motion	MotionNotify with Button5 modifier

---

[1] The precise interpretation of one of these modifiers is "the modifier bit bound to a key whose list of keysyms contains the corresponding keysym name." In other words, this is a double-indirect lookup, first in the modifier mapping table to find the physical keys bound to the modifier bit and then in the keyboard mapping table to see which of these physical keys is labeled with the appropriate keysym. See Section 7.23 of this guide and Section 7.9 of *Xlib*; alternately, just assume that this all works.

[2] A translation using the Meta modifier is equivalent to a pair of translations that replace Meta with @Meta_L and @Meta_R as modifiers; similarly for Alt, Hyper, and Super.

This means that the following two translations are equivalent:

```
Shift <KeyPress> : action()
<Shift> : action()
```

Event specifications can also have details, often corresponding to values in the detail field of the event. Different event types have details with different meanings; application writers are rarely concerned with details for other than keyboard, pointer button, pointer motion, and client message events. The details for the different event types are

KeyPress, KeyRelease

A keysym for the key that was pressed. This can be a single character if it is not a comma, colon, or space, or can be a keysym name as defined in the header file `<X11/keysymdef.h>` but without the leading "XK_" characters. Keysyms may also be specified as numeric constants; see Appendix B for full details.[3]

ButtonPress, ButtonRelease

The button number (1–5) that was pressed.

MotionNotify   Either NotifyNormal or NotifyHint.

EnterNotify, LeaveNotify

NotifyNormal, NotifyGrab, or NotifyUngrab.

FocusIn, FocusOut

NotifyNormal, NotifyGrab, or NotifyUngrab.

PropertyNotify   The atom for the property that is changing.

SelectionClear   The atom for the selection that was lost.

SelectionRequest   The atom for the requested selection.

SelectionNotify   The atom for the selection that has been sent.

ClientMessage   The atom for the type of the message.

MappingNotify   One of MappingModifier, MappingKeyboard, or MappingPointer.

Just as there are synonyms for events with particular modifiers, there are synonyms for events with particular details.

---

[3] The precise interpretation of the detail is "a keysym that is in the list of keysyms for the key in the event."

Event	Meaning
Btn1Down	ButtonPress for pointer button 1
Btn1Up	ButtonRelease for pointer button 1
Btn2Down	ButtonPress for pointer button 2
Btn2Up	ButtonRelease for pointer button 2
Btn3Down	ButtonPress for pointer button 3
Btn3Up	ButtonRelease for pointer button 3
Btn4Down	ButtonPress for pointer button 4
Btn4Up	ButtonRelease for pointer button 4
Btn5Down	ButtonPress for pointer button 5
Btn5Up	ButtonRelease for pointer button 5

For keyboard translations that specify a key in the detail field, the default interpretation is to trigger the translation for any event that specifies that key, regardless of any modifiers. This means that the two translations

```
<KeyPress> 4 : action()
<KeyPress> $ : action()
```

are the same for many keyboards since the dollar sign is often on the same key as 4. Translations like these can be preceded with a colon to instruct the Intrinsics to apply standard modifiers (usually Shift and Lock) when matching the keysym. This means that the two translation tables

```
~Shift <KeyPress> 4 : four()
 Shift <KeyPress> 4 : dollar()
```

and

```
:<KeyPress> 4 : four()
:<KeyPress> $ : dollar()
```

act the same on keyboards that have 4 and dollar sign on the same key; the second is much preferable since it does not encode knowledge about the particular keyboard layout. The only time you should use a keyboard translation without a colon is to specify a case-insensitive translation; for example,

```
<Key> C : action()
```

triggers on both upper- and lower-case C. The colon should precede any other modifiers and follow the exclamation point, if any, so

```
!:Ctrl <Key> $: action()
```

means to trigger the action when Control is set, whatever standard modifiers are necessary to generate the dollar sign are set, and no other modifier keys or pointer buttons are set.

As a simplification, sequences of key events can be represented as quoted strings. The two translations

```
:<Key>H, :<Key>i : action()
"Hi" : action()
```

are the same. Within a quoted string a caret means the next character must have the Control modifier set and a dollar sign means the next character must have the Meta modifier set. The two translations

```
:Ctrl<Key>x : action()
"^x" : action()
```

are the same. Within a string a backslash quotes any character, particularly a caret, dollar sign, double quote, or backslash. The translation

```
"\^\$\"\\" : action()
```

matches the key sequence caret, dollar sign, double quote, backslash.

Finally, an event can specify a count by including it in parentheses after the event name, but before the detail, if any. The two translations

```
<Enter>, <Enter> : action()
<Enter>(2) : action()
```

are the same. Counts are only really useful for keyboard and pointer events, and for these event types the Intrinsics automatically insert appropriate intermediate events. The two translations

```
<Btn1Up>(2) : action()
<Btn1Down>, <Btn1Up>, <Btn1Down>, <Btn1Up> : action()
```

are the same, and

```
<Btn1Down>(2) : action()
<Btn1Down>, <Btn1Up>, <Btn1Down> : action()
```

are the same. However, with button events, the events must come sufficiently close together in time for the translation to trigger; see Section 7.2. A count can be followed by a plus sign to indicate that the translation triggers after the specified number of repetitions and also after any further repetitions. The two tables

```
<Btn1Up>(2+) : action()
```

and

```
<Btn1Up>(2) : action()
<Btn1Up>(3) : action()
<Btn1Up>(4) : action()
...
```

would be the same if it were possible to specify an infinite translation table.

The preceding described all the possibilities within a single translation. A translation writer must also be aware of how different translations in a translation table interact.

☞ The Intrinsics always take the first translation in the table that matches the input events. This means that specific translations should always precede general ones; for example,

```
Shift <Btn1Down> : action()
<Btn1Down> : anotheraction()
```

is the correct order within the table. If the second translation were first, the Intrinsics would always take it for a button press for button 1, regardless of the state of the Shift modifier, and the action for the shifted press would never occur. This also applies to details:

```
<Key> A : action()
<Key> : anotheraction()
```

If the second translation were first, the Intrinsics would always take it for key events and the action for "A" would never occur.

☞ If one translation specifies an event sequence that is the initial event sequence of another translation, the Intrinsics take both if the longer event sequence occurs. In the table

```
"A" : action()
"AB" : anotheraction()
```

the Intrinsics call the first action if the user types "A" and call both actions if the user types "AB", one action after each keystroke.

This is especially important when using multi-clicks in a translation table. In the table

```
<Btn1Down> : action()
<Btn1Down>(2) : anotheraction()
```

the Intrinsics call the first action for a single press and call both actions for a double press, one after the first press and the other after the second. This implies that the double-click semantics should be a superset of the single-click semantics. For example,

```
<Btn1Down> : moveInsertionPoint()
<Btn1Down>(2) : selectWord()
```

is a good use of double-click. If the user clicks once, the insertion point moves to the pointed-to spot, and if he clicks twice, the insertion point moves and the word being pointed to is selected. A table like

```
<Btn1Down> : capitalizeWord()
<Btn1Down>(2) : italicizeWord()
```

is perfectly legal, but it is not very useful since it does not allow the user to italicize a word without also capitalizing it.

For the purpose of matching translations, the Intrinsics always ignore pointer motion events that occur between other events. This means that the two translations

```
<Btn1Down>, <Btn1Up> : action()
<Btn1Down>, <Motion>, <Btn1Up> : action()
```

are the same. This allows the translation to trigger even if the pointer moves a bit between the two events. Any motion event specification, implicit or explicit, always matches any number of actual motion events. If the final event specification in a translation is for a motion event, the Intrinsics call the translation's action after each motion event.

If a translation specifies an event sequence and the same sequence is specified within another translation but not at the beginning, the Intrinsics do not take the translation with the shorter sequence when the events match the longer sequence. This is independent of the entry order. In the table

```
<Btn1Up> : action()
<Btn1Down>, <Btn1Up> : anotheraction()
```

the Intrinsics only take the first translation if the release event is not immediately preceded by a press event. Again, this can happen when using repeat notation; in the table

```
<Btn1Up> : action()
<Btn1Down>(2) : anotheraction()
```

there is an implicit specification of <Btn1Up> in the second translation, so the first translation rarely triggers. Probably the desired set of translations for this situation is

```
<Btn1Down>, <Btn1Up> : action()
<Btn1Down>(2) : anotheraction()
```

so that the Intrinsics call the first action after the button is pressed and released and call the second after the button is pressed again.

This also occurs with implicit motion events. Assume in a Text widget the programmer wanted to support the following operations:

• If the user clicks a pointer button, move the insertion point to that position in the text.

• If the user presses a button and moves the pointer, highlight the text that the cursor moves past.

• If the user double-clicks the pointer, highlight the word that the cursor points to.

The following translation table does not work:

```
<Btn1Down> : moveInsertionPoint()
<Btn1Down>(2) : highlightWord()
Button1 <Motion> : highlightRegion()
```

because any motion that comes after the first button press matches the implicit motion within the second translation instead of the explicit motion in the third translation.

Another wrong way to write the translations for this is

```
<Btn1Down> : moveInsertionPoint()
<Btn1Down>(2) : highlightWord()
<Btn1Down>, <Motion> : highlightRegion()
```

This does not work for a slightly different reason. When a motion event arrives after a button press, the Intrinsics have no way of knowing if they are in the second translation, where they discard the motion event, or in the third translation, where the motion event triggers the action. Either choice is wrong in some situations. The Intrinsics use the following rule to resolve this dilemma:

    Pointer motion events always match the implicit motion specification between events rather than an explicit motion specification.

This rule makes things quite a bit more difficult for people who need to use motion events, and quite possibly should have been made otherwise, but it is the rule.

So what does the programmer who needs the above functionality do? The only solution is to avoid event sequences, particularly repetitions, in tables that also react to pointer motion. The programmer writes

```
<Btn1Down> : buttonDown()
Button1 <Motion> : buttonMotion()
```

and, within the buttonDown action procedure, keeps track of the timestamp in the button press event. If the Intrinsics call buttonDown with a timestamp that is sufficiently close to the previous one, buttonDown performs the double-click action; otherwise buttonDown performs the single-click action.

7.2   Setting the Multi-Click Timeout

The Intrinsics have a time interval called the multi-click time associated with each display that determines what the maximum time between two consecutive pointer events can be for the Intrinsics to consider them part of a multi-click sequence. This is an application resource with name "multiClickTime" and class "MultiClickTime" that defaults to 200 milliseconds. Applications query or modify this interval by calling `XtGetMultiClickTime` and `XtSetMultiClickTime`.[4]

---

[4] `XtGetMultiClickTime` and `XtSetMultiClickTime` and the corresponding resource are not supported by Intrinsics implementations that conform to specifications earlier than Release 4.

int XtGetMultiClickTime (*display*)
    Display **display;
display   Specifies the display.

`XtGetMultiClickTime` returns the current multi-click time in milliseconds for the specified display.

void XtSetMultiClickTime (*display*, *time*)
    Display **display;
    int *time*;
display   Specifies the display.
time   Specifies the new multi-click time in milliseconds.

The initial value for a display's multi-click time is established from the multi-click resource when the display is initialized.

7.3   Translation Tables in the Program

Most well-written widgets have translation tables that capture everything the widget does. Why does an application need to worry about them at all?

Some applications want a widget to do something slightly different from what the widget designer intended. For example, the Pushbutton widget used in this book invokes the application callback when the pointer button is released, not when it is pressed. This is generally considered a good user interface decision. However, what if an application wants to have pressing the pointer button in a pushbutton pop up a menu? The pushbutton supports all the needed functionality; it just needs a new set of translations. Section 7.11 presents this example of modifying translations, but more toolkit functions must be described before this example will make sense.

Since translations are resources, applications give the user the most flexibility if they specify any translation modifications they make in their application defaults file. However, applications can also manipulate translation tables directly.

The application must first parse any translation table it uses from the table's string representation into a more efficient internal form. `XtParse-TranslationTable` does this conversion.

XtTranslations XtParseTranslationTable (*table*)
    String *table*;
table   Specifies the translation table.

The return type, `XtTranslations`, is opaque; its definition is not available to programmers. `XtParseTranslationTable` is just a simplified interface to an internal type converter.

Once a table is parsed, an application uses it to augment, override, or replace the translations in a widget.

To augment a widget's translations, use `XtAugmentTranslations`.

```
void XtAugmentTranslations(w, translations)
     Widget w;
     XtTranslations translations;
```
w   Specifies the widget whose translations are being modified.
translations   Specifies the new translations.

`XtAugmentTranslations` adds the translations in the new table to those already existing for the widget. If any translation in the new table has a left-hand side that matches a translation in the existing table, `XtAugment-Translations` discards the new translation. Augmenting translations never removes any preexisting translations.

To override a widget's translations, use `XtOverrideTranslations`.

```
void XtOverrideTranslations(w, translations)
     Widget w;
     XtTranslations translations;
```
w   Specifies the widget whose translations are being modified.
translations   Specifies the new translations.

`XtOverrideTranslations` adds the translations in the new table to those already existing for the widget. If any translation in the new table has a left-hand side that matches a translation in the existing table, `XtOverride-Translations` replaces the old translation with the new one.

To completely replace a widget's translation table, give a value for the XtNtranslations resource for the widget either at widget creation or by calling `XtSetValues`:

```
Arg args[1];
int i = 0;

XtSetArg(arg[i], XtNtranslations,
        XtParseTranslationTable(newTranslations)); i++;
XtSetValues(widget, args, i);
```

All three of these methods require the application to parse the translation table with `XtParseTranslationTable` before using it. The value NULL is not a valid value for a parsed translation table; to create a table with no translations, an application can pass an empty string to `XtParse-TranslationTable`.

`XtUninstallTranslations` removes all translations from a widget, which is equivalent to installing the empty table.

void XtUninstallTranslations(*w*)
    Widget *w*;
w   Specifies the widget to remove the translations from.

7.4   Translation Tables in Resource Files

A widget's translation table is one of its resources, and as such is customizable by the user. A user of a Pushbutton widget might want to activate the widget with a different pointer button, and the user of a text-editing widget might want to bind a different set of keys to editing functions like "next line" and "previous line". To allow this, application writers usually put their translation modifications into the application defaults file, letting a predefined resource converter parse the table into its internal form.

To make it more convenient for a user wanting to change just a few translations, a translation table in a resource file can be preceded with a directive telling whether the translation table augments, overrides, or replaces the widget's translations. This is achieved by having the first line of the table be one of the three strings "#augment", "#override", or "#replace". A user binds the next and previous line actions in the text-editing widget to arrow keys by specifying

```
*Text.translations: #augment \n\
    :<Key>downarrow : NextLine() \n\
    :<Key>uparrow : PreviousLine()
```

The "\n" in the first two lines is the newline character that must be present between the lines in a translation table, and the trailing slash allows the resource specification to continue on the next line of the resource file.

If a resource specifies no "#" directive, the Intrinsics assume "#replace".

7.5   Action Tables

Translation tables map event sequences into actions. In the interest of having a representation that can easily be stored in a resource file, translation tables are represented as strings. The Intrinsics must map the name of the action in the translation string into an actual procedure.

The Intrinsics define a data structure, `XtActionsRec`, that contains a string name and a procedure pointer. Each widget class has a table of action records that maps all its defined action names into action procedures, and an application can add its own actions.

An action table is just an array of `XtActionsRec` structures.

```
typedef struct _XtActionsRec {
    String          string;
    XtActionProc    proc;
} XtActionsRec, *XtActionList;
```

The action name is often spelled identically to the procedure.

An action procedure is of type `XtActionProc`.

```
typedef void (*XtActionProc) (Widget, XEvent *, String *, Cardinal *);
    Widget w;
    XEvent *event;
    String *params;
    Cardinal *num_params;
```

w	Specifies the widget causing the action to be called.
event	Specifies the event triggering the action. If the action is called after a sequence of events, this parameter is the last event in the sequence.
params	Specifies a pointer to the list of strings specified as arguments to the action.
num_params	Specifies the number of entries in *params*.

The *params* and *num_params* arguments allow a translation to pass string parameters to an action procedure. A common instance of this is to pass a string to a Text widget; for example, the translation

```
<Key> F1 : insertString("hello")
```

binds function key 1 to the action procedure "insertString", passing the string "hello". The quotation marks around the string are optional unless the parameter contains embedded commas, parentheses, spaces, or tab characters. When the Intrinsics call the action procedure, the *params* parameter points to the string "hello" and *num_params* is 1.

Another common use is to parameterize the operation of an action, for example,

```
<Key> F1 : switchToFont(boldFont)
```

Widget classes should document all their action names and how many parameters they expect, if any.

7.6   Adding Application Actions

Applications add their own action procedures to the translation mechanism by calling `XtAppAddActions`.

void XtAppAddActions(*app_context, actions, num_actions*)
    XtAppContext *app_context*;
    XtActionList *actions*;
    Cardinal *num_actions*;

app_context	Specifies the application context.
actions	Specifies the action table to add.
num_actions	Specifies the number of entries in the action table.

If more than one action is registered with the same name, the Intrinsics use the most recently registered action. If duplicate action names exist in the same action table, the Intrinsics use the first.

7.7   Writing Action Procedures

When writing action procedures, be careful not to make unwarranted assumptions about their parameters.

First, always check the type of the event before accessing any fields in it; the type is available as *event–>type*. User customization might have bound the action to a different event type than the one the program expects, and the action procedure gets unpredictable results if it blindly casts the event to some predetermined type. The most general-purpose action procedures completely ignore their event argument.

Next, do not assume the action procedure has the right number of parameters. If a needed parameter is missing, issue an error or warning message and react appropriately. Action parameter lists are inherently variable-length, which can often be put to good advantage by providing defaults. For example, a "search for string" action in a text editor could search the text for its parameter if given one and could put up a search dialog box if not.

☞   Do not assume that the widget is realized. Under normal circumstances, the widget must be realized before it gets any X events, but if the application or user defines accelerators as described in Section 7.15, the Intrinsics can call the action procedure for an unrealized widget. Also, do not assume that the window in the event refers to the widget's window; with accelerators the action procedure can receive events that occurred in another window.

☞   Finally, do not assume that an action procedure is in a specific place in a list of actions. Your default translation tables may have the action following a special setup action in a single translation, but the user can rebind the actions differently. Actions should ideally be atomic operations.

7.8   XtMenuPopup and XtMenuPopdown

The Intrinsics predefine two actions that are available to translation writers, XtMenuPopup and XtMenuPopdown.[5] Note that these are not the actual procedure names; they are just action names that can be used in translation tables.

XtMenuPopup(*shell_name*)
    String *shell_name*;
shell_name   Specifies the name of the shell to pop up.

XtMenuPopup takes one parameter, the name of the shell to pop up. The Intrinsics search for a pop-up child with this name, starting with the widget that invoked the action and looking upward through its ancestors. When the Intrinsics find the shell, they pop it up. If the triggering action is a ButtonPress event, the Intrinsics pop up the shell as an exclusive, spring-loaded pop-up by calling XtPopupSpringLoaded. If the triggering action is a KeyPress or EnterNotify event, the Intrinsics pop up the shell as a nonexclusive, non-spring-loaded pop-up. No other event types are legal; XtMenuPopup generates an error if specified for other than a button press, key press, or enter window event. The actual action procedure for XtMenuPopup is XtMenuPopupAction; Section 7.10 describes why you might want to know this.

---

[5] These actions are called MenuPopup and MenuPopdown in Intrinsics implementations that conform to specifications earlier than Release 4. The names remain for compatibility.

XtMenuPopdown(*shell_name*)
    String *shell_name*;
shell_name   An optional parameter specifying the shell to pop down.

XtMenuPopdown pops down a pop-up menu. If no name is specified, it pops down the widget for which the translation was specified, which must be a shell widget. If a name is specified, XtMenuPopdown looks for a shell with the specified name using the same rules that XtMenuPopup uses.

7.9   Resolving Action Names

To resolve an action name to the actual action procedure the Intrinsics look in the following places, in order:

• In the actions specified for the class of the widget triggering the action.

• In the actions specified for all superclasses of the widget, starting with the direct superclass and proceeding up the class hierarchy.

• In the actions specified for the class and all superclasses of each ancestor of the widget, starting with the parent and proceeding up the widget tree. The Intrinsics check all superclasses for a particular ancestor before going on to that ancestor's parent.

• In the actions the application added, going from the most recently added table to the oldest.

For actions in a translation table, the action name is bound to an action table using the above rules when the Intrinsics realize the widget or when the application modifies the widget's translation table, not when the translation with the action triggers. Changing application action tables after this binding has no effect on translation actions.

7.10   Registering Grab Actions

In this section, *grabs* refers to server grabs, not to toolkit grabs.

When a widget gets realized, the Intrinsics scan its translation table to find all types of events that the widget wishes to receive and sets the event mask for the widget's window so that the server delivers all appropriate events.

To augment this, the Intrinsics maintain a list of action procedures that, if found in the translation table, enable special processing. In addition to putting the event type into the event mask for the widget's window, the Intrinsics issue a passive grab for the event that triggers the action. A passive grab for an event type modifies the server's event delivery as follows:

- The grab can override event delivery to children; the widget with the grab receives some events that would normally go to its children.

- Grabs can be synchronous, making the server delay delivering certain following events until the application sends notification to resume delivery.

The *owner_events* state of the grab controls overriding event delivery to children after the event that triggered the grab. If the grab has *owner_events* FALSE, the server sends any events that follow the grab and that occur in a child of the grabbing widget to the grabbing widget. If the grab has *owner_event* TRUE, events that would go to the children still go there. Using *owner_events* TRUE grabs is risky for applications, as they can lead to states where the server thinks a grab is in effect but the application does not. This makes the keyboard or pointer lock up and become useless or become "stuck" so that it delivers events only to this application. Unless you understand the server grab model very well, it is best to avoid grabs with *owner_events* TRUE in applications.

Synchronous grabs make the server delay sending certain events that occur after the event that triggers the grab. This is useful for implementing reliable pop-up menus; when the user presses a pointer button to pop up the menu the server can delay sending further pointer events until the application maps the pop-up menu and the menu instructs the server to resume event delivery. Users rapidly come to know where menu entries show up and often release the pointer button before the menu is actually visible on the screen, so delaying event delivery this way guarantees that the server sends the release event to the menu and not to what was on the screen before the menu appeared.

The XtMenuPopup action is by default the only action that receives a passive grab. By default the Intrinsics register it with an asynchronous grab with *owner_events* FALSE so the special synchronous grab processing is not enabled. These defaults provide safety: pop-up widgets must explicitly reenable event delivery if they are to be used with a synchronous grab. If an application only calls XtMenuPopup for pop-ups that understand synchronous grabs (for example, the Menu widget in this book), the application can enable synchronous grabs for XtMenuPopupAction by calling

```
XtRegisterGrabAction(XtMenuPopupAction, FALSE,
        ButtonPressMask | ButtonReleaseMask, GrabModeSync,
        GrabModeAsync);
```

before realizing its widgets. Application writers can treat this call as a magic incantation to modify XtMenuPopup; it is the only call to XtRegister-

`GrabAction` most applications ever use. However, applications and widget implementations can request grab processing for any of their action procedures with `XtRegisterGrabAction`.[6]

> void XtRegisterGrabAction (*action_proc, owner_events, event_mask, pointer_mode,*
> *keyboard_mode*)
> XtActionProc *action_proc*;
> Boolean *owner_events*;
> unsigned int *event_mask*;
> int *pointer_mode, keyboard_mode*;
>
> | | |
> |---|---|
> | *action_proc* | Specifies the action procedure to receive grab processing. |
> | *owner_events* | Specifies the *owner_events* parameter to the grab. |
> | *event_mask* | Specifies the *event_mask* parameter to the grab. |
> | *pointer_mode* | Specifies the *pointer_mode* parameter to the grab. |
> | *keyboard_mode* | Specifies the *keyboard_mode* parameter to the grab. |

Before using `XtRegisterGrabAction` for anything other than the above modification of `XtMenuPopup`, make sure you understand Section 6.21 of this guide and Sections 7.4 and 7.5 of *Xlib*.

`XtRegisterGrabAction` requests grab processing for the specified action procedure. You might wish to do this if you were using some pop-up widgets that understand synchronous grabs and some that do not; you could implement a synonym for `XtMenuPopup` for use with the pop-ups that understand grabs.

`XtRegisterGrabAction` adds the specified action procedure to a list in the Intrinsics. When a widget gets realized the Intrinsics scan its translation table for action names that map to procedures on this list, and if they find any, issue key or button grabs if the last event in the translation is a key or button press event.

If the last event of the translation is a button press, the Intrinsics call `XtGrabButton` for the widget. The button to `XtGrabButton` is the button specified in the detail of the event specification, or AnyButton if there is no detail, and the modifiers are the modifiers specified for the event, or AnyModifiers if the modifiers are explicitly "Any". *Owner_events, event_mask, pointer_mode,* and *keyboard_mode* come from the call to `XtRegisterGrab-Action`. *Confine_to* and *cursor* are always None.

---

[6] `XtRegisterGrabAction` is not supported by Intrinsics implementations that conform to specifications earlier than Release 4.

If the last event of the translation is a key press, the Intrinsics call XtGrabKey for the widget. If there is a detail for the event, the key to XtGrabKey is the keycode corresponding to the keysym in the detail as determined by the keycode translation mechanism (see Section 7.23) and the modifiers are the bitwise OR of the modifiers in the translation table entry and the modifiers as determined by the keycode translation mechanism, or AnyModifiers if the modifiers in the translation are explicitly "Any". If there is more than one keycode/modifier combination that generates the keysym in the detail, the Intrinsics call XtGrabKey for each one. If there is no detail for the event, the key to XtGrabKey is AnyKey and the modifiers are the modifiers for the event, or AnyModifiers. *Owner_events, pointer_mode,* and *keyboard_mode* come from the call to XtRegisterGrabAction; the *event_mask* parameter to XtRegisterGrabAction is ignored.

If the specified action procedure already has grab processing, the parameters to XtRegisterGrabAction replace the previously specified values. Calling XtRegisterGrabAction affects widgets that are realized after the call but not widgets that are already realized.

Note that XtRegisterGrabAction takes an action procedure, not an action name.

7.11   A Translation Example

Example 7.1 shows an action procedure and code that modifies translation tables. The routine RepositionMenu is an action procedure. It centers the global widget *menushell* around the pointer position when a button or key press event occurs. If the event is not a button or key press, Reposition returns immediately. Otherwise it extracts the x and y positions from the event. Calculating the new position requires the menu's width and height, so RepositionMenu realizes the menu shell to ensure that the menu has its real width and height (remember that widgets do not negotiate their geometries until just before being realized). It then extracts the menu's width, height, and border width fields using XtGetValues. RepositionMenu finally calls XtSetValues, setting the menu's position to center it around the pointer.

The action table *actions* binds the string "RepositionMenu" to the RepositionMenu procedure. The string *menuTranslations* contains the new bindings for a press of pointer button 1; it invokes RepositionMenu to reposition the menu and XtMenuPopup to pop up the menu on the screen.

```
Widget menushell;

static void RepositionMenu(w, event, params, num_params)
    Widget w;                       /* unused */
    XEvent *event;
    String *params;                 /* unused */
    Cardinal *num_params;           /* unused */
{
    Dimension width, height, border;
    Position x, y;
    Arg arg[25];
    int n;

    switch (event->type) {
        case ButtonPress:
            x = event->xbutton->x_root;
            y = event->xbutton->y_root;
            continue;
        case KeyPress:
            x = event->xkey->x_root;
            y = event->xkey->y_root;
            continue;
        default:
            return;
    }

    XtRealizeWidget(menushell);

    n = 0;
    XtSetArg(arg[n], XtNwidth, &width);          n++;
    XtSetArg(arg[n], XtNheight, &height);        n++;
    XtSetArg(arg[n], XtNborderWidth, &border);   n++;
    XtGetValues(menushell, arg, n);

    n = 0;
    XtSetArg(arg[n], XtNx, x - width/2 - border);     n++;
    XtSetArg(arg[n], XtNy, y - height/2 - border);    n++;
    XtSetValues(menushell, arg, n);
}
```

(continued)

Example 7.1. A translation example

After initializing the toolkit, the main program calls XtAppAddActions to register the new action and calls XtRegisterGrabAction to enable synchronous processing for XtMenuPopup. It next creates a Pushbutton widget and overrides its translations so that a button press in the pushbutton

```
XtActionsRec actions[] = {
    {"RepositionMenu", RepositionMenu}
};

char *menuTranslations =
    "<Btn1Down> : RepositionMenu() XtMenuPopup(menuShell)";

int main(argc, argv)
    unsigned int argc;
    char **argv;
{
    /* Toolkit initialization code omitted */

    XtAppAddActions(app, actions, XtNumber(actions));

    XtRegisterGrabAction(XtMenuPopupAction, FALSE,
            ButtonPressMask | ButtonReleaseMask, GrabModeSync,
            GrabModeSync);

    /* Creation of box omitted */

    n = 0;
    XtSetArg(arg[n], XtNx, 10); n++;
    XtSetArg(arg[n], XtNy, 10); n++;
    XtSetArg(arg[n], XtNlabel, "Popup menu");    n++;

    pushbutton = XtCreateManagedWidget("pushbutton",
            pushbuttonWidgetClass, box, arg, n);

    XtOverrideTranslations(pushbutton,
            XtParseTranslationTable(menuTranslations));

    menushell = XtCreatePopupShell("menuShell",
            overrideShellWidgetClass, pushbutton, (Arg *) NULL, 0)

    /* Creating menu items and rest of program omitted */
}
```

Example 7.1. A translation example

pops up the menu. There is no need to override the button release action; since the menu is a modal pop-up the pushbutton never receives the button release event. Note that the application parses the translation table before passing it to `XtOverrideTranslations`.

In an actual application, the code to override the translations would most likely be replaced by an entry in the application defaults file:

```
*pushbutton.translations: #override \n\
        <Btn1Down> : RepositionMenu() XtMenuPopup(menuShell)
```

This would allow the user to customize the translations, for example, to use a different button than button 1.

7.12   Calling Action Procedures Directly

Applications can call action procedures directly with `XtCallActionProc`.[7]

void XtCallActionProc(*widget, action, event, params, num_params*)
    Widget *widget*;
    String *action*;
    XEvent **event*;
    String **params*;
    Cardinal *num_params*;

widget	Specifies the widget to invoke the action for.
action	Specifies the action name.
event	Specifies the event to pass to the action procedure.
params	Specifies the list of string parameters to pass to the action procedure, or NULL.
num_params	Specifies the number of entries in the *params* list.

`XtCallActionProc` searches for the action name for the widget using the rules in Section 7.6. If the search finds no action with the specified name, `XtCallActionProc` generates a warning message and returns. Remember that action names are case-sensitive.

Otherwise `XtCallActionProc` calls the action procedure, passing it the specified event, parameters, and parameter count. It is up to the caller to make sure that these arguments are appropriate for the action procedure and, if the action only works when the widget is realized or sensitive, that the widget is in the appropriate state.

Calling action procedures is most useful for implementing new actions in an application that do some additional processing beyond that provided by some widget action procedure. To provide a new action named "UninvertAndDesensitize" for a pushbutton, define this action procedure:

---

[7] `XtCallActionProc` is not supported by Intrinsics implementations that conform to specifications earlier than Release 4.

```
void UninvertAndDesensitize(w, event, params, num_params)
    Widget w;
    XEvent *event;
    String *params;
    Cardinal *num_params;
{
    XtCallActionProc(w, "uninvert", event, params, num_params);
    XtSetSensitive(w, FALSE);
}
```

The desk calculator application in Chapter 10 uses XtCallActionProc in a different way—it calls the "invert" action of the pushbutton used to display the calculator value to indicate that the user selected the value.

7.13   Handling the Keyboard

Programmers of applications that deal with the keyboard directly must understand the X keyboard model as described in Section 7.9 of *Xlib*. Most applications do not need to do this; instead their widgets hide the details and pass character strings to the application through callback procedures. If you have to deal with the keyboard directly, see Sections 7.22 and 7.23 in the widget writer's part of this chapter.

The Xlib keyboard-handling functions create internal Xlib data structures that duplicate structures in the toolkit but provide less functionality. Instead of using the Xlib routines in the following table, use the listed toolkit analog:

Xlib function	Toolkit function
XLookupKeysym	XtGetActionKeysym
XLookupString	XtGetActionKeysym
XKeycodeToKeysym	XtTranslateKey
XKeysymToKeycode	XtKeysymToKeycodeList

The following routines have no toolkit analogs:

XRefreshKeyboardMapping	The Intrinsics perform this automatically.
XRebindKeysym	Specifying strings as parameters to action procedures provides this functionality.
XStringToKeysym	Safe to use.
XKeysymToString	Safe to use.

Using the Xlib routines XLookupKeysym, XLookupString, XKeycodeTo-

`Keysym`, `XKeysymToKeycode`, `XRefreshKeyboardMapping`, or `XRebindKeysym` has the following undesirable effects:

- These routines make Xlib build its redundant data structures, wasting several kilobytes of storage. Xlib does not refresh its data structures automatically upon receipt of a MappingNotify event as the toolkit does.
- They do not use the customizable key-mapping and case conversion facilities of the toolkit. The Intrinsics follow these customizations when doing translation management, so inconsistencies can result.

7.14   Action Hooks

Some kinds of applications need to keep a log of the action procedures that get invoked.

An application could have a "teach" mode in which it replays a stored log of actions to demonstrate the application's functionality to a new user. The easiest way to get the action log is to create a modified version of the application that stores each action into a file as it occurs; running this modified application provides the script for the teach mode.

Another example is a text editor that allows the user to activate a "remember" mode; this mode stores the actions as they occur so that the user can later reinvoke them to perform the same series of editing actions again.

`XtCallActionProc` allows an application to invoke the action procedures in an action log.

To register a procedure that the Intrinsics call before executing each future action, use `XtAppAddActionHook`.[8]

typedef long XtActionHookId;

XtActionHookId XtAppAddActionHook(*app, proc, client_data*)
    XtAppContext *app*;
    XtActionHookProc *proc*;
    XtPointer *client_data*;

app	Specifies the application context.
proc	Specifies the action hook procedure.
client_data	Specifies a piece of data that the Intrinsics pass uninterpreted to the action hook.

---

[8] `XtAppAddActionHook` and `XtRemoveActionHook` are not supported by Intrinsics implementations that conform to specifications earlier than Release 4.

When an application has registered an action hook procedure, the Intrinsics call the hook just before invoking each future action for a widget on a display in the application context. The Intrinsics can either be dispatching an event through a translation table or executing a call to `XtCallActionProc`. If an application has registered more than one action hook, the Intrinsics call each one in reverse order of registration. An action hook procedure is of type `XtActionHookProc`.

```
typedef void (*XtActionHookProc) (Widget, XtPointer, String, XEvent*, String*,
                                  Cardinal*) ;
        Widget w;
        XtPointer client_data;
        String action_name;
        XEvent *event;
        String *params;
        Cardinal *num_params;
```

w	Specifies the widget whose action procedure is about to be called.
client_data	Specifies the client data as passed to `XtAppAddActionHook`.
action_name	Specifies the name of the action that is about to be called.
event	Specifies the event that will be passed to the action procedure.
params	Specifies the action parameters that will be passed to the action procedure.
num_params	Specifies the number of entries in *params*.

The action hook must not modify the data pointed to by any of its arguments other than possibly the *client_data* argument.

To remove an action hook, use `XtRemoveActionHook`.

```
void XtRemoveActionHook(id)
     XtActionHookId id;
```

id	Specifies the action hook to remove.

7.15   Defining Accelerators

Many applications have alternative ways of invoking some functionality. A text editor could have a pushbutton or menu entry to bring up a search dialog box, but it is much more convenient for an experienced user if he can bring up the search dialog through the keyboard so that he does not have to move his hands from the keyboard to the mouse.

The toolkit supports this kind of shortcut by allowing widgets to have *accelerators*. An accelerator is a translation installed on one widget, called the accelerator destination, that invokes the functionality of a different widget, called the accelerator source. Accelerators are specified with accelerator tables, which have exactly the same syntax as translation tables. This section describes how to define accelerators; the next one describes how to install them in a destination widget.

If a widget has multiple functions, it can have multiple entries in its accelerator table, but this is rather rare. Most accelerator tables have only one entry, invoking the widget's main action.

Each widget has an XtNaccelerators resource that contains a table of accelerator translations to access that widget's actions. Each widget is the accelerator source widget for the accelerator translations listed in its own XtNaccelerators resource. Installing these accelerators in another widget adds the translations in the accelerator table to the translations for the destination widget, but an event that triggers an accelerator translation invokes an action for the source widget, not for the destination widget.

Consider the text editor example with the search dialog box; assume the program normally invokes the search dialog box through a menu item. This menu item has a normal translation that looks something like

```
<Btn1Up> : notify()
```

where the notify action invokes a callback procedure in the editor that pops up the search dialog box. The application or user can give the menu item an accelerator that invokes the notify action when the user presses the find key. The accelerator is defined by setting the menu item's accelerator resource to

```
:<Key> Find : notify()
```

Initially this is just a latent accelerator; it is not installed anywhere and cannot trigger. If the application installs the accelerator on its main Text widget, it becomes an active accelerator. The accelerator acts just like any other translation for the Text widget, except that when an event triggers it the Intrinsics invoke the notify action for the menu item with the menu item as the widget parameter. This makes the notify action invoke the callback procedure in the editor just as if the user had triggered it through the menu item's normal translations.

An accelerator only activates if the source widget is sensitive when the event triggering the accelerator occurs. If the source widget is insensitive, the Intrinsics ignore the triggering event.

Action procedures usually do not care whether they were invoked normally or through an accelerator, but if they do, they compare the window field of the event they receive with the window of the widget they receive. If the windows are different, an accelerator invoked the action and the window in the event is the window in which the event occurred. The Intrinsics do not modify the event in any way; they deliver it to the action procedure exactly as it arrived. An action procedure bound to an accelerator can find the widget it was invoked in by calling `XtWindowToWidget` for the window in the event; see Section 9.3.

Each widget has only one accelerator resource, no matter how many places the widget's accelerators are installed. This means that it is impossible to have the widget's actions invoked through different event sequences in different places. Accelerators are almost always defined on keyboard events but need not be; there are cases where having an accelerator trigger on a pointer button is useful.

To define an accelerator for a widget, give a value to the widget's XtNaccelerators resource. This usually comes from the application defaults file, but, as with any resource, it can also be an argument at widget creation or to `XtSetValues`. Applications must parse any accelerator tables they provide internally by calling `XtParseAcceleratorTable`.

XtAccelerators XtParseAcceleratorTable(*source*)
     String *source*;
source   Specifies the accelerator table to parse.

`XtAccelerators` is an opaque data type; its definition is not available to programs.

Just as with normal translations, the Intrinsics convert accelerators in a resource file into their internal form.

Accelerator tables, either in resource files or in a program, can begin with a line containing either "#override" or "#augment"; if neither is present, the Intrinsics assume "#augment". If the table begins with "#override", the accelerators override any preexisting translations for the destination widget— the Intrinsics match incoming events against the accelerators before matching them to the widget's normal translations. If the table begins with "#augment", the accelerators do not override the translations; the Intrinsics only take the accelerator if the event sequence does not match any of the widget's normal translations.

7.16   Installing Accelerators

An application has to decide which widgets in the user interface can trigger accelerators. To make the accelerators available, it calls `XtInstall-Accelerators` or `XtInstallAllAccelerators`.

void XtInstallAccelerators(*destination, source*)
    Widget *destination*;
    Widget *source*;
destination   Specifies the widget that can activate the accelerators.
source   Specifies the widget whose accelerators are being made available.

`XtInstallAccelerators` makes any accelerators defined for the *source* widget available as translations in the *destination* widget.

Usually an application makes the accelerators for all the widgets in its interface available in some widget, and to do this it calls `XtInstallAll-Accelerators`.

void XtInstallAllAccelerators(*destination, source*)
    Widget *destination*;
    Widget *source*;
destination   Specifies the widget that can activate the accelerators.
source   Specifies the root of a widget subtree, all the widgets in which
            have their accelerators made available.

`XtInstallAllAccelerators` recursively descends through the widget tree specified by *source* and installs the accelerators for each widget that it encounters into the *destination* widget. The traversal includes both pop-up and normal children. The most common use is to specify the application's main shell as the source, thereby installing the accelerators for every widget in the application.

The application writer must install the accelerators in each widget that can activate them. The X input model helps with this somewhat, since events propagate outward from the smallest enclosing window through its ancestors until the server finds a window that requested their delivery. If a widget has accelerators installed on it, events that occur in any descendants automatically propagate outward to this widget unless the descendant has requested the events itself. What this means in practice is that applications usually install accelerators in each widget that has translations for the same kind of events as in the accelerators (normally keyboard events) and also install them in the application's main widget to catch events that happen elsewhere.

☞ Some applications do not normally accept keyboard input and so set the XtNinput resource for their shells to FALSE. A common mistake is to install accelerators in such a program but to forget to set XtNinput to TRUE; the symptom that shows up is that the user is unable to set the input focus to the application to type the accelerator keys.

7.17   An Accelerator Example

Example 7.2 shows the main program for a version of "Goodbye, world" that has an accelerator for its button, and Example 7.3 shows the application defaults resource file. The resource file specifies TRUE for the XtNinput resource of its shell (actually the specification applies to all the widgets, but XtNinput only exists for the shell) and specifies an accelerator for control–A that activates the pushbutton. The final resource, the accelerator string, is a string that the pushbutton displays to show the user its accelerator. Note that the accelerator translation does not use a colon; this makes it case-insensitive.

The only thing the program must do to make the accelerator available is to install the accelerators for all descendants of the Box widget on the Box widget by calling `XtInstallAllAccelerators`. Figure 7.1 shows how the program's window looks with the installed accelerator.

7.18   Using a Widget as a Window

If an application needs to provide some sort of user interface functionality that is not available as a widget, the programmer must decide whether to write a widget that supports the new functionality or to work around the problem. Usually writing a new widget is a better way, since it makes the functionality available to other programs (and it really is not all that difficult). However, it is also possible to instantiate some existing widget class and to use its window just as a simple X window.

Some widget sets provide a widget class that is expressly for this purpose, but in the absence of this, a Core widget works just as well. The application creates the widget with appropriate values for its geometry and background resources and, after the widget is realized, uses `XtWindow` to extract the widget's window. The application draws into this window using Xlib calls.

If the application must react to events that occur in the window, it defines action procedures that process the events and creates a translation table to

```
int main(argc, argv)
    unsigned int argc;
    char **argv;
{

    Widget toplevel, box, pushbutton;
    XtAppContext app;

    toplevel = XtAppInitialize(&app, "AcceleratorExample",
            (XrmOptionDescList) NULL, 0, &argc, argv,
            (Xtring *) NULL, (Arg *) NULL, 0);

    box = XtCreateManagedWidget("box", boxWidgetClass, toplevel,
            (Arg *) NULL, 0);

    pushbutton = XtCreateManagedWidget("pushbutton",
            pushbuttonWidgetClass, box, (Arg *) NULL, 0);

    XtAddCallback(pushbutton, XtNcallback, Goodbye, NULL);

    XtInstallAllAccelerators(box, box);

    XtRealizeWidget(toplevel);
    XtAppMainLoop(app);
}
```

Example 7.2. An accelerator example

```
*input: TRUE
*pushbutton.x: 10
*pushbutton.y: 10
*pushbutton.label: Click and die
*pushbutton.accelerators: Ctrl<Key>a: notify()
*pushbutton.acceleratorString: (^A)
```

Example 7.3. The resources for the accelerator example

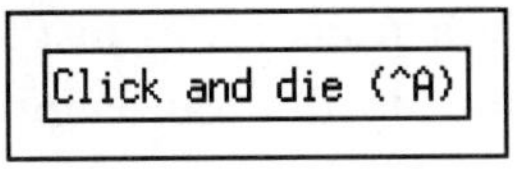

Figure 7.1. "Goodbye, world" with an installed accelerator

invoke these actions when the events occur. The translation table must include a translation for Expose events so that the application redraws the contents of the window when necessary. The application must obey all the usual rules for drawing into windows; in particular, it must wait for the first Expose event before drawing into the window or it runs the risk of having the contents lost because the window is not yet mapped to the screen when the drawing occurs.

Example 7.4 shows a simple program that creates a 100 by 100 widget and draws in it as a result of exposure events.

Writing Widgets

7.19   More on Translation Tables

The first part of this chapter covered all the rules for writing translations; Appendix B contains a formal definition of translation table syntax.

Translation tables also have a canonical form that eliminates many of the options possible in normal translation tables. This canonical form is what the Intrinsics pass to the display_accelerator method, described in Section 7.21, when installing an accelerator. Appendix B also contains the syntax for the canonical form; the differences are that the canonical form replaces synonyms for events with the full event name, replaces quoted strings with key sequences, and always quotes all parameters to action procedures.

7.20   Default Translations and Action Tables

The documentation for a widget class should list the default translations for widgets of that class and should describe all the action procedures with their parameters, if any.

The widget implementation stores the default translations in the *tm_table* field of the widget class record. This is a pointer to the translations in their text representation; the Intrinsics take care of parsing them into the internal form. The special value XtInheritTranslations means to use the same default translations as its superclass. If a widget class has no default translations, *tm_table* is NULL.

The widget implementation stores the widget's action table in the *actions* field of the widget class record and the number of entries in the *num_actions*

```
#include <X11/Intrinsic.h>
#include <X11/StringDefs.h>

void DrawContents(widget, event, params, num_params)
    Widget widget;
    XEvent *event;
    String *params;                 /* Unused */
    Cardinal *num_params;           /* Unused */
{
    Window window = XtWindow(widget);
    Display display = XtDisplay(widget);

    if (event->type != Expose) return;
    /* Draw in the window... */
}

int main(argc, argv)
    unsigned int argc;
    char **argv;
{
    Widget toplevel, panel;
    Arg args[25];
    int n;
    XtAppContext app;
    static XtActionsRec actions[] = {{"refresh", DrawContents}};
    static char translations[] = "<Expose> : refresh()";

    toplevel = XtAppInitialize(&app, "Draw",
            (XrmOptionDescList) NULL, 0, &argc, argv,
            (String *) NULL, (ArgList) NULL, 0);

    XtAppAddActions(app, actions, XtNumber(actions));

    n = 0;
    XtSetArg(args[n], XtNwidth, 100);                   n++;
    XtSetArg(args[n], XtNheight, 100);                  n++;
    XtSetArg(args[n], XtNtranslations,
            XtParseTranslationTable(translations));     n++;
    panel = XtCreateManagedWidget("panel", widgetClass, toplevel,
            args, n);

    XtRealizeWidget(toplevel);
    XtAppMainLoop(app);
}
```

Example 7.4. A program that uses a widget as a window

```
static char defaultTranslations[] =
        "<EnterWindow>   : highlight()                \n\
        <LeaveWindow>   : unhighlight()              \n\
        <Btn1Down>      : invert()                   \n\
        <Btn1Up>        : notify() uninvert()";

static void Highlight(), Unhighlight(), Invert(), Uninvert(), Notify();

static XtActionsRec actions[] = {
  {"highlight",        Highlight},
  {"unhighlight",      Unhighlight},
  {"invert",           Invert},
  {"uninvert",         Uninvert},
  {"notify",           Notify},
};
```

Example 7.5.   The Pushbutton default translations and actions

field. If a widget has no action table, *actions* is NULL and *num_actions* is zero.
Actions is a chained data field; the action tables in all superclasses are always
available to the widget class.

Example 7.5 shows the default translations and the action table for Pushbutton. The implementation stores them in the class record as follows:

```
PushbuttonClassRec pushbuttonClassRec = {
    ...
    /* actions      */    actions,
    /* num_actions */    XtNumber(actions),
    ...
    /* tm_table     */    defaultTranslations,
    ...
};
```

Example 7.6 shows the action procedures for the Pushbutton widget. The
Highlight action checks if the widget is already highlighted and, if not, sets the
highlighted field to TRUE. If the widget is realized, Highlight clears the widget's
window and calls the widget's expose procedure to have the widget redrawn in
its highlighted state. Clearing the window is not absolutely necessary for the
way Pushbutton highlights widgets, but a subclass might highlight them in a
completely different way. Clearing makes the action procedure more generally
useful. Unhighlight does the same thing as Highlight, only setting the
highlighted field to FALSE.

The Invert and Uninvert action procedures are similar to Highlight and
Unhighlight. The difference is that they reset the *current_gc* field before
redrawing the widget so that the expose procedure draws the widget in its new

```
static void Highlight(w, event, params, num_params)
    Widget w;
    XEvent *event;
    String *params;
    Cardinal *num_params;
{
    PushbuttonWidget pw = (PushbuttonWidget) w;

    if (!pw->pushbutton.highlighted) {
        pw->pushbutton.highlighted = TRUE;
        if (XtIsRealized(w)) {
            XClearWindow(XtDisplay(w), XtWindow(w));
            (*(XtClass(w)->core_class.expose))(w, event, NULL);
        }
    }
}

static void Unhighlight(w, event, params, num_params)
    Widget w;
    XEvent *event;
    String *params;
    Cardinal *num_params;
{
    PushbuttonWidget pw = (PushbuttonWidget) w;

    if (pw->pushbutton.highlighted) {
        pw->pushbutton.highlighted = FALSE;
        if (XtIsRealized(w)) {
            XClearWindow(XtDisplay(w), XtWindow(w));
            (*(XtClass(w)->core_class.expose))(w, event, NULL);
        }
    }
}

static void Invert(w, event, params, num_params)
    Widget w;
    XEvent *event;
    String *params;
    Cardinal *num_params;
{
    PushbuttonWidget pw = (PushbuttonWidget) w;

    if (!pw->pushbutton.inverted) {
        pw->pushbutton.inverted = TRUE;
        pw->label.current_gc = pw->pushbutton.inverted_gc;
```

(continued)

Example 7.6. The Pushbutton action procedures

```
        if (XtIsRealized(w)) {
            XClearWindow(XtDisplay(w), XtWindow(w));
            (*(XtClass(w)->core_class.expose))(w, event, NULL);
        }
    }
}

static void Uninvert(w, event, params, num_params)
    Widget w;
    XEvent *event;
    String *params;
    Cardinal *num_params;
{
    PushbuttonWidget pw = (PushbuttonWidget) w;

    if (pw->pushbutton.inverted) {
        pw->pushbutton.inverted = FALSE;
        if (XtIsSensitive(w)) {
            pw->label.current_gc = pw->label.gc;
        } else pw->label.current_gc = pw->pushbutton.insensitive_gc;

        if (XtIsRealized(w)) {
            XClearWindow(XtDisplay(w), XtWindow(w));
            (*(XtClass(w)->core_class.expose))(w, event, NULL);
        }
    }
}

static void Notify(w, event, params, num_params)
    Widget w;
    XEvent *event;
    String *params;
    Cardinal *num_params;
{
    PushbuttonWidget pw = (PushbuttonWidget) w;

    /* If event is a button event, and the event's window is the
       widget's window, we were invoked normally.  Make sure
       the pointer is really in the window */

    if (event != NULL && event->type == ButtonRelease &&
            event->xany.window == XtWindow(w)) {
        XButtonEvent *b = &event->xbutton;
        if (b->x < 0 || b->y < 0 ||
            b->x >= w->core.width || b->y >= w->core.height) return;
    }

    XtCallCallbackList(pw, pw->pushbutton.callback, NULL);
}
```

Example 7.6. The Pushbutton action procedures

state. Uninvert has to check whether to restore *current_gc* to the normal or to the insensitive graphics context.

The Notify action is slightly more complicated than the others to account for the fact that the pushbutton still receives the ButtonRelease event if the user presses the pointer button in the widget, moves the pointer outside, and releases the button elsewhere. In this case Notify does not invoke the widget's callback. Notify checks if it was passed a button event for the widget's window and, if so, whether the coordinates of the release are within the window. Notify returns without doing anything for a button release for the widget's window that is outside the window and invokes the widget's callback in all other cases.

The set of actions for Pushbutton illustrates an important facet of widget design. Since both "notify" and "uninvert" occur on a button release, there is a temptation to bundle them up into a single action. Separating them gives more flexibility to users and application programmers. A user who prefers not to have his pushbuttons invert overrides the translations for the button press and release to eliminate the inverting. Also, if the pushbutton gets an accelerator, the accelerated action is normally just "notify" (although some users might prefer to have the pushbutton invert and uninvert around the notification). By having the different functions be different actions more possibilities for customization present themselves.

7.21   Displaying Accelerators

When an application installs a widget's accelerators, the Intrinsics call the display_accelerator method for the source widget so that the widget can modify its appearance to include a description of the accelerator. The display_accelerator method is of type `XtStringProc`.

typedef void (*XtStringProc) (Widget, String);
        Widget *w*;
        String *accelerators*;
   w   Specifies the widget that has had its accelerators installed.
   accelerators   Specifies the string representation of the accelerators for the widget.

If a widget class does not need to be notified when accelerators are installed, it specifies NULL as its display_accelerator method.

```
static void DisplayAccelerator(w, string)
    Widget w;
    String string;
{
    PushbuttonWidget pw = (PushbuttonWidget) w;
    Arg args[1];

    if (pw->pushbutton.accelerator_string != NULL) {
        XtSetArg(args[0], XtNaccelString,
                pw->pushbutton.accelerator_string);
        XtSetValues(w, args, 1);
    }
}
```

Example 7.7. The display_accelerator method for Pushbutton

The *accelerators* parameter is the string representation of the accelerator table, in canonical form (see Appendix B). Ambitious widget programmers can parse this table into a form more suitable for displaying in the widget; more modest programmers define an additional widget resource that is the string to display and rely upon the person specifying the accelerators to make sure that the string actually matches the widget's accelerators.

Example 7.7 shows the display_accelerator method for Pushbutton. It uses the XtNacceleratorString resource as the string to display and sets the XtNaccelString resource to this value using `XtSetValues`. The set_values and expose methods for Label automatically display this string in the widget.

Two resources, XtNacceleratorString and XtNaccelString, are necessary to make this work right, since the accelerator string should not be displayed unless the accelerator is installed somewhere. XtNaccelString is an internal resource; it is not defined in the public header files. An alternative approach is to just have one accelerator string resource and a Boolean resource that controls whether to display the accelerator string.

7.22   Getting a Keysym from a Keyboard Event

Action procedures that the programmer intends to be invoked on key translations often need to know which key was pressed or released to trigger the action. The keycode of the key is present in the event, but usually the keysym for the key is much more useful. Action procedures find the keysym for the event that triggered them by calling `XtGetActionKeysym`.[9]

KeySym XtGetActionKeysym(*event, modifiers_return*)
    XEvent **event*;
    Modifiers **modifiers_return*;
event   Specifies the event that the Intrinsics passed to the action procedure.
modifiers_return   Returns the modifiers; may be NULL.

If the event is not a KeyPress or KeyRelease event, `XtGetActionKeysym` returns the special value NoSymbol. Otherwise it returns the keysym that corresponds to the keycode and modifiers in the event and updates the *modifiers_return* parameter to be the modifiers used to generate the keysym. Few programs care about the modifiers.

`XtGetActionKeysym` is most useful within action procedures, but it can also find the keysym for a keyboard event obtained in other ways (such as through an event handler).

The modifiers `XtGetActionKeysym` returns are the subset of those in the event that were used to match the keysym, not those in the event. For example, if the translation

    `:Ctrl<Key> $ : action()`

was taken using a keyboard that requires Shift to type a dollar sign, `XtGetActionKeysym` normally returns ShiftMask in *modifiers_return* (or possibly LockMask if the lock key on the terminal is a shift lock key). The action procedure still has to look in the key event to find the actual modifiers. If the translation

    `<Key> : action()`

was taken when the user typed a capital "A", the returned modifiers are normally either ShiftMask or LockMask. If the translation was taken when the user typed a lower-case "a", the returned modifiers are normally zero.

Toolkit programs use `XtGetActionKeysym` instead or `XLookupKeysym` or `XLookupString`. Mapping from the returned keysym to a character is character-set-dependent; Example 7.8 shows a mapping from keysyms to ISO Latin-1 characters (a superset of ASCII). Note that this code does not do any special processing for control characters like backspace or return; widgets usually handle these by having special action procedures for the functions

---

[9] `XtGetActionKeysym` is not supported by Intrinsics implementations that conform to specifications earlier than Release 4.

```
KeySym k;
char ch;

/* Don't care about the modifiers, so pass NULL */
k = XtGetActionKeysym(event, NULL);

if (k == NoSymbol) {
    /* Not a keyboard event or no keysym for the keycode in the
       event.  Do whatever is appropriate. */
} else {
    /* Compensate for servers that call a minus a hyphen */
    if (k == XK_hyphen) k = XK_minus;

    if (k & 0xFF00 != 0) {
        /* Not a keysym for an ISO Latin-1 character.  Do whatever
           is appropriate.  If restricting to ASCII, mask with
           0xFF80 instead. */
    } else {
        /* ISO Latin-1 keysyms are the same as the character */
        ch = (char) k;

        /* If control is set, mask off high bits */
        if (event->xkey.modifiers & ControlMask) ch &= 0x1F;
    }
}

/* Do whatever is appropriate with the character */
```

Example 7.8. Mapping from keysyms to ISO Latin-1 characters

these characters invoke and binding them to translations that specify the control characters.

7.23   Keycodes and Keysyms: Here Be Dragons

This section is quite esoteric and is of interest only to the few programmers who need to modify how the Intrinsics translate keycodes specified in keyboard events into keysyms. Most programs use the default functionality provided by the toolkit; anyone using any of the routines in this section must have a thorough understanding of the X keyboard-handling model as described in Section 7.9 of *Xlib*.

When the server delivers a keyboard event to the application, the event contains a keycode that represents the physical key on the keyboard that the user pressed or released. These keycodes need not bear any relation at all to the characters the key generates; they are just numbers assigned to the keys. Key event translations, however, have keysyms as their details; the keysyms represent actual symbols logically associated with the key.

For example, assume the key with 4 and dollar sign on it generates the keycode 42. If a keyboard event arrives with 42 as the keycode, the Intrinsics must translate the number 42 into the keysyms representing 4 and dollar sign in order to know whether to trigger a translation that specifies 4 or dollar sign as its detail.

The toolkit allows a programmer to write her own keycode-to-keysym conversion routine, which is of type `XtKeyProc`.

```
typedef unsigned long Modifiers;

typedef void (*XtKeyProc) (Display *, KeyCode, Modifiers, Modifiers *, KeySym *);
    Display *display;
    KeyCode keycode;
    Modifiers modifiers;
    Modifiers *modifiers_return;
    KeySym *keysym_return;
```

display	Specifies the display that the keycode is from.
keycode	Specifies the keycode to translate.
modifiers	Specifies the modifiers to apply to the keycode when doing the translation.
modifiers_return	Returns all the modifiers that this translator ever examines.
keysym_return	Returns the resulting keysym.

A keycode translator must examine the keycode and the modifiers and return the keysym that results from applying these modifiers to the keycode; if the keycode/modifier combination is not meaningful, the translator returns the special value NoSymbol. Continuing the above example, if the procedure gets passed 42 as the keycode, it returns XK_4 in *keysym_return* if the Shift bit is not set in the modifiers and XK_dollar if it is.

The translator must also return in *modifiers_return* the subset of the modifier bits that it ever considers when doing translations. A keycode translator must always return the same value in *modifiers_return* no matter what its other parameters are; this value is a constant. In `XtGetActionKeysym`, the *modifiers_return* argument is set to the modifiers in the event ANDed with the *modifiers_return* from the keycode translator.

The Intrinsics maintain a key translator for each display the application has open; they use each display's translator for keyboard events from that display. To register a new translator for a display, use `XtSetKeyTranslator`.

```
void XtSetKeyTranslator(display, proc)
    Display *display;
    XtKeyProc proc;
```

display   Specifies the display to register the translator for.
proc   Specifies the translator procedure.

The default keycode translator is `XtTranslateKey`. It uses standard modifiers (normally Shift and Lock) to look up the keysym in the keycode-to-keysym table described below. Applications pass `XtTranslateKey` to `XtSetKeyTranslator` to reinstall the default translations, and keycode translators can call `XtTranslateKey` to get the default translations.

To call the keycode translator directly, use `XtTranslateKeycode`.

```
void XtTranslateKeycode(display, keycode, modifiers, modifiers_return, keysym_return)
    Display *display;
    KeyCode keycode;
    Modifiers modifiers;
    Modifiers *modifiers_return;
    KeySym *keysym_return;
```

display   Specifies the display the keycode is from.
keycode   Specifies the keycode to translate.
modifiers   Specifies the modifiers to apply to the keycode when doing the translation.
modifiers_return   Returns all the modifiers that the installed translator ever examines.
keysym_return   Returns the resulting keysym.

`XtTranslateKeycode` just calls the currently installed keycode translator for the display, passing it the specified arguments.

The Intrinsics maintain a table mapping keycodes to keysyms. The Intrinsics fetch the table from the server the first time it is needed and update it whenever the application receives a MappingNotify event. Other than being kept up-to-date, this table is identical to the one Xlib would maintain internally to support the Xlib key-handling procedures. See Section 7.9 of *Xlib* for full details on the format of this table. Keycode translators can look in this table to find out what the default server keysyms are for a keycode, but they are under no obligation to return a keysym from the table. To fetch this table, use `XtGetKeysymTable`.[10]

KeySym *XtGetKeysymTable(*display, min_keycode_return, keysyms_per_keycode_return*)
    Display **display;
    KeyCode **min_keycode_return*;
    int **keysyms_per_keycode_return*;
display   Specifies the display whose table is required.
min_keycode_return
                 Returns the minimum keycode valid for that display.
keysyms_per_keycode_return
                 Returns the number of keysyms stored for each keycode.

`XtGetKeysymTable` returns a pointer to the Intrinsics' copy of the keycode-to-keysym table. The caller must not modify this table and should call `XtGetKeysymTable` whenever it needs the table; caching the table or values in it is not allowed since the cached values become invalid if the application receives a MappingNotify event.

The keysym table consists of a single array of keysym values, with *keysyms_per_keycode_return* keysyms contiguously stored for each keycode. The keysyms for a keycode *k* start at the index

    *(k - min_keycode_return) * keysyms_per_keycode_return*

Code must only index this table with a real keycode; using illegal keycode values can result in accessing undefined memory.

Any entries in the list that have no assigned keycodes have the special value NoSymbol. The Intrinsics might or might not have already updated entries for which case conversion is appropriate, using the case conversion mechanism described later in this section. If it matters, the keycode translator should use `XtConvertCase` directly.

Meanings are associated with each position in the keysym table; for example, the first keysym for a keycode represents the keysym with no modifiers applied. For a full discussion of the interpretation, consult Section 7.9 of *Xlib*.

To find out which keycodes in the table have a particular keysym associated with them, call `XtKeysymToKeycodeList`.[11] This procedure is particularly useful for finding keycodes to pass to `XtGrabKey`.

---

[10] `XtGetKeysymTable` is not supported by Intrinsics implementations that conform to specifications earlier than Release 4.

[11] `XtKeysymToKeycodeList` is not supported by Intrinsics implementations that conform to specifications earlier than Release 4.

void XtKeysymToKeycodeList(*display, keysym, keycodes_return, keycount_return*)
　　Display **display*;
　　KeySym *keysym*;
　　KeyCode ***keycodes_return*;
　　Cardinal **keycount_return*;

display	Specifies the display whose table should be searched.
keysym	Specifies a keysym to look for.
keycodes_return	Returns a list of the keycodes that have the keysym associated with them.
keycount_return	Returns the number of keycodes in the keycode list.

The caller frees the keycode list using `XtFree` when it is no longer useful. The keycode list includes all keycodes that have the specified keysym anywhere in their list of keysyms. `XtKeysymToKeycodeList` does not call the key translator, so it does not return keycodes that the translator converts to the specified keysym if the keysym is not also in the keysym table for that keycode. To find the modifiers that produce the keysym, call `XtTranslateKeycode` with each possible modifier combination (as determined by the *modifiers_return* parameter to `XtTranslateKeycode`) to find one that produces the keysym, or less generally, call `XtGetKeysymTable` and look at the appropriate entries. A caller using `XtTranslateKeycode` should be prepared to find that there is no modifier combination that produces the keysym, since key translators are not obliged to use the keysyms in the keysym table. A caller using `XtGetKeysymTable` risks using a keycode that the installed key translator never translates to that keysym.

The default keycode-to-keysym table stored in the server has both lower- and upper-case keysyms for keys like 4/$, where the keysyms are substantially different for the shifted and unshifted cases. For other keys, particularly those with letters, it may have just one keysym, and it is the responsibility of the client program to provide the upper- and lower-case values. When the toolkit gets the keycode-to-keysym table from the server it uses *case converters* to determine what the upper- and lower-case values are for these keys.

A case converter is of type `XtCaseProc`.

typedef void (*XtCaseProc) (Display *, KeySym *, KeySym *, KeySym *);
　　Display **display*;
　　KeySym **keysym*;
　　KeySym **lower_return*;
　　KeySym **upper_return*;

display	Specifies the display.
keysym	Specifies the keysym to convert.
lower_return	Returns the lower-case version of the keysym.
upper_return	Returns the upper-case version of the keysym.

If the keysym is an upper-case keysym, the case converter stores it into *upper_return* and store its lower-case equivalent into *lower_return*. If it is a lower-case keysym, the case converter stores it into *lower_return* and stores its upper-case equivalent into *upper_return*. If it is a keysym for which there is no case distinction, the case converter stores it into both *lower_return* and *upper_return*.

To register a case converter, use `XtRegisterCaseConverter`.

void XtRegisterCaseConverter(*display, proc, start, stop*)
    Display **display*;
    XtCaseProc *proc*;
    KeySym *start*;
    KeySym *stop*;

display	Specifies the display that this converter is for.
proc	Specifies the case converter.
start	Specifies the lowest keysym value that this converter is valid for.
stop	Specifies the highest keysym value that this converter is valid for.

A display can have multiple case converters registered for different ranges of keysyms.[12] The new converter overrides any previous converters for keysyms in that range. No interface exists to remove case converters; instead a program registers an identity converter for keysyms in the range. The default case conversion routine understands case conversions for all keysyms defined by the X protocol; new case converters are only necessary for nonstandard keysyms or nonstandard interpretations of the standard keysyms.

A keycode translator that does case conversion can call `XtConvertCase` to find the upper- and lower-case equivalents for a keysym.

void XtConvertCase(*display, keysym, lower_return, upper_return*)
    Display **display*;
    KeySym *keysym*;
    KeySym **lower_return*;
    KeySym **upper_return*;

display	Specifies the display that the keysym is from.

---

[12] Only one converter could be registered for a display in some Intrinsics implementations that conform to specifications earlier than Release 4.

keysym   Specifies the keysym to convert.
lower_return   Returns the lower-case equivalent of the keysym.
upper_return   Returns the upper-case equivalent of the keysym.

XtConvertCase invokes the currently registered case converter for the range encompassing the specified keysym.

Chapter 8

Nonwidget Objects

Writing Applications

8.1   Background

Before Release 4 of the Intrinsics specification, Core was truly the root of the widget class hierarchy.[1] With Release 4, Core is no longer the root; there are three superclasses:

Object
: The Object class is the root of the class hierarchy. It supports creation, deletion, and resource handling but not geometry, windows, or event handling.

RectObj
: This is a subclass of Object that supports geometry but not windows or event handling.

unnamed
: This is a subclass of RectObj that the Intrinsics reserve for future use.

The Core class is actually a subclass of the unnamed class. Figure 8.1 shows the true hierarchy of all Intrinsics-defined classes.

Like Core, Composite, and Constraint, the Object and RectObj classes are not intended for direct instantiation; applications normally create instances of subclasses of these instead.

The Object class supports manipulating data structures with subclassing and resource handling. Consider a suite of editor applications that share a common set of application resources. Rather than requiring each application

---

[1] Some Release 3 Intrinsics implementations had preliminary implementations for some of the functionality in this chapter, but the functionality is only supported in implementations that conform to specification Release 4.

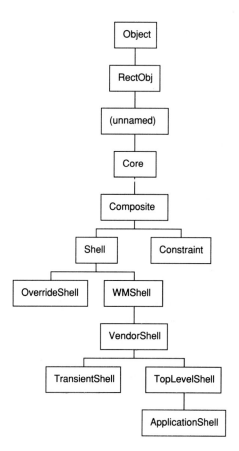

Figure 8.1. The Intrinsics class hierarchy

programmer to duplicate the code to define and fetch the application resources, one programmer could write a subclass of Object that handles them. Each application creates an instance of this class; the Intrinsics initialize the instance's resources to the values specified in the resource database, the command line, and any override values specified in the call to the creation routine. The application fetches values from the instance using XtGet-Values and modifies them during execution using XtSetValues. If an application needs to extend the set of resources, the programmer either creates a new subclass or uses application resources.

The RectObj class adds geometry handling to the Object class. Applications treat subclasses of RectObj the same as widgets, except that instances of RectObj do not have windows or event handling. Instances of RectObj subclasses are frequently called *gadgets*; in return for giving up event handling, using gadgets saves memory both in the application (the Intrinsics event-handling data structures) and in the X server (the storage for the window that is not created). Some widget sets include gadget analogs for simple widgets like Label and Pushbutton. Since gadgets have no windows, the server delivers events that it would deliver to the gadget were it a widget to the gadget's parent instead. This means that gadgets cannot be children of just any composite widget; programmers must consult the documentation for the parent's class to find out which gadget classes the parent accepts as children.

The original motivation for gadgets was to reduce the number of windows an X server needs to store. Many newer servers have greatly reduced the amount of storage for each window, so the impact of using gadgets instead of widgets is much smaller. Since gadgets are not able to maintain the same black-box abstraction that widgets do, their use is not as widespread.

8.2 The Base Object Classes

All resources defined by the Object and RectObj classes have the same meanings as those defined by the Core class.

8.2.1 The Object and Its Resource

Applications never create instances of the Object class, but the type `Object` can be used for instances of any subclasses. The Object class defines one resource.

Name	Class	Type	Default
XtNdestroyCallback	XtCCallback	XtCallbackList	NULL

8.2.2 The Rectangle Object and Its Resources

Applications never create instances of the RectObj class, but the type `RectObj` can be used for gadget instances. The RectObj class defines the following resources:

Name	Class	Type	Default
XtNx	XtCPosition	Position	0
XtNy	XtCPosition	Position	0
XtNwidth	XtCWidth	Dimension	0
XtNheight	XtCHeight	Dimension	0
XtNborderWidth	XtCBorderWidth	Dimension	1
XtNsensitive	XtCSensitive	Boolean	TRUE
XtNancestorSensitive	XtCSensitive	Boolean	special

8.2.3   Resources Not Defined for Objects

Core defines the following resources that are not defined for Object or RectObj:

Name	Class	Type	Default
XtNscreen	XtCScreen	Screen *	special
XtNdepth	XtCDepth	Cardinal	special
XtNcolormap	XtCColormap	Colormap	special
XtNbackground	XtCBackground	Pixel	special
XtNbackgroundPixmap	XtCPixmap	Pixmap	special
XtNborderColor	XtCBorderColor	Pixel	special
XtNborderPixmap	XtCPixmap	Pixmap	special
XtNmappedWhenManaged	XtCMappedWhenManaged	Boolean	TRUE
XtNtranslations	XtCTranslations	XtTranslations	special
XtNaccelerators	XtCAccelerators	XtAccelerators	none

8.3   Types and Intrinsic Routines

The parameter and return types for Intrinsics routines are never `Object` or `RectObj`. Most of the routines predate the nonwidget object classes, and if the types had changed when the new classes were added, all existing code would require modification to avoid type mismatches. For uniformity, all new routines avoid `Object` and `RectObj` parameters as well.

Appendix F lists all Intrinsics routines that have `Widget`, `WidgetList`, or `WidgetClass` parameters or return values along with any class restrictions.

8.4   Object Information Functions

XtDisplay, XtScreen, and XtWindow work only for widgets. The Intrinsics provide three analogous routines that work regardless of their argument's class, returning the value from the argument's closest widget ancestor if the argument is not a widget.

Display *XtDisplayOfObject(*w*)
       Widget *w*;
   w   Specifies the object to get the display for.

Screen *XtScreenOfObject(*w*)
       Widget *w*;
   w   Specifies the object to get the screen for.

Window XtWindowOfObject(*w*)
       Widget *w*;
   w   Specifies the object to get the window for.

There is no harm in always using these routines instead of the widget-specific ones, but if the caller knows that the argument is in fact a widget, using XtDisplay, XtScreen, and XtWindow is often more efficient, especially in widget implementations.

The functions XtIsObject and XtIsRectObj test the class of an object.

Boolean XtIsObject(*w*)
Boolean XtIsRectObj(*w*)
       Widget *w*;
   w   Specifies the object to check.

8.5   Using Objects in Applications

Applications handle objects in much the same way as they handle widgets. They create objects with XtCreateWidget, destroy them with XtDestroy-Widget, modify their resource values with XtSetValues, and fetch their resource values with XtGetValues.

An application that creates objects for its own personal use creates them as children of its main application shell. No Intrinsics classes besides Application-Shell accept object children, although classes in a widget set might.

Objects can also be visible to applications as subparts of widgets. The Graph widget in Chapter 10 has a display handler subpart that takes care of displaying the widget's data. Different implementations of the display handler display the data as a pie chart, as a bar graph, or as a simple table. When an application creates a Graph widget, it specifies what display handler the Graph widget uses.

A display handler contains data like fonts and pixel values. It also contains implementations of procedures to compute the size needed for the graph and to display the graph. Different implementations of the display handler implement the procedures in different ways, and often extend the data and functionality.

In other words, display handlers act just like widget classes except that they have no screen representation. Before the Object class existed, a Graph widget implementation had to use ad hoc mechanisms to create and interact with display handlers. Now, a Graph widget writer defines a new Object class, GraphDisplay, that defines the data and procedures required for all display handlers. Different subclasses of GraphDisplay implement bar graphs, tables, pie charts, and so on.

There is no standard way for applications to interact with widgets that use objects as subparts; programmers must consult the widget documentation. Using the Graph example, application writers might encounter these arrangements:

- Graph might define a resource, XtNdisplayClass, and require the application to set this to a subclass of GraphDisplay when creating a graph. Graph creates an instance of this class to handle display.

- Graph might require the application to create an instance of some subclass of GraphDisplay as a child of the Graph widget, possibly requiring the application to pass the resulting object to the graph by doing an `XtSetValues` on an XtNdisplayHandler resource.

- Graph might expose the display handler to the application through calling `XtGetValues` on an XtNdisplayHandler resource. To fetch or set the resources for the handler, the application uses `XtGetValues` or `XtSetValues` on the value it fetched through `XtGetValues`.

- Graph might hide the handler completely; to fetch or set resources for the handler, the application uses `XtGetValues` or `XtSetValues` on the Graph widget and relies on the Graph implementation to relay the request to the display handler.

Chapter 10 provides an implementation of Graph that requires that the application create the display handler as a child of the graph before realizing it.

Applications use `XtSetValues` or `XtGetValues` on the display handler as needed.

8.6   Using Gadgets

For the most part, applications treat gadgets the same way they treat widgets. Since gadgets have no windows or event handling, there are some restrictions:

- Gadgets have no background or border colors or pixmaps.
- Gadgets cannot have event handlers.
- Gadgets have no translations, accelerators, or actions.
- Gadgets cannot have pop-up children.
- Gadgets cannot do grabs.
- Gadgets cannot redirect the Intrinsics keyboard focus or take the X focus.
- Gadgets cannot own or request selections.
- Gadgets do not need to be and cannot be realized.
- Gadgets cannot have their window, display, or screen queried; use the procedures in Section 8.4 instead.
- Gadgets have no stacking order.

Widget sets that provide gadgets provide various ways to work around some of these restrictions. For example, Pushbutton gadgets have no translations, but they can have resources that their parent uses to decide what to do when a pointer button press occurs while the pointer is in a Pushbutton gadget's area. The Intrinsics define no background color resource for gadgets, but a particular gadget class might define a background color resource that the parent uses to paint the gadget. Resources like these can be defined by the parent's class instead of by the gadget's class, indicating a value that applies to all gadget children.

In general, the coupling between parent and child is much stronger when the child is a gadget than it is when the child is a widget. Composite widgets can typically contain widgets of any class at all, but they can only contain gadget children that are of classes the composite widget's implementation knows how to handle. The documentation for a composite class should list all the gadget classes that the composite can handle.

Writing Widgets

8.7   The Base Object Classes

When Object and RectObj were added to the Intrinsics, the data structures had to be defined in a way that avoided breaking all preexisting widget implementations. If the class records had used the normal conventions, programmers would have had to change the static class initializations for widget subclasses.

Instead of having separate parts, the class records for Object and RectObj have just a single part with padding for fields that do not exist for Object or RectObj. The padding fields have names beginning with "obj" or "rect" and must be NULL or zero in the static initialization for nonwidget subclasses of Object.

The instance records do follow the normal conventions and have separate parts, so memory is saved for each object or rectangle object instance. The Core instance record, however, does not use these parts; doing so would change the names of fields in Core subclass instances, requiring changes to all existing code.

The Intrinsics specification does not require the fields within the class instance parts for Intrinsics-defined classes to be in any particular order. However, any implementation must guarantee that fields in the Object and RectObj instance records have the same offset as the corresponding fields in the Core instance part. In other words, fields within the Core instance record must have the same offsets as they would if the Core instance were defined as

```
typedef struct {
    ObjectPart      object;
    RectObjPart     rectangle;
    UnnamedPart     unnamed;
} CoreWidgetRec;
```

instead of its actual definition,

```
typedef struct {
    CorePart        core;
} CoreWidgetRec;
```

This permits the Intrinsics to operate upon widgets and nonwidget objects with the same code. Assuring this alignment may involve inserting some padding fields into the Core instance part on some architectures.

All this guide's descriptions of chained methods that start or end with Core have been white lies. These methods actually start or end with Object.

8.7.1 The Object Class Structure

The Object class part record is identical to the Core class part record except that some fields have been renamed to start with the characters "obj".

```
typedef struct {
    WidgetClass         superclass;
    String              class_name;
    Cardinal            widget_size;
    XtProc              class_initialize;
    XtWidgetClassProc   class_part_initialize;
    XtEnum              class_inited;
    XtInitProc          initialize;
    XtArgsProc          initialize_hook;
    XtProc              obj1;                   /* realize */
    XtPointer           obj2;                   /* actions */
    Cardinal            obj3;                   /* num_actions */
    XtResourceList      resources;
    Cardinal            num_resources;
    XrmClass            xrm_class;
    Boolean             obj4;                   /* compress_motion */
    XtEnum              obj5;                   /* compress_exposure */
    Boolean             obj6;                   /* compress_enterleave */
    Boolean             obj7;                   /* visible_interest */
    XtWidgetProc        destroy;
    XtProc              obj8;                   /* resize */
    XtProc              obj9;                   /* expose */
    XtSetValuesFunc     set_values;
    XtArgsFunc          set_values_hook;
    XtProc              obj10;                  /* set_values_almost */
    XtArgsProc          get_values_hook;
    XtProc              obj11;                  /* accept_focus */
    XtVersionType       version;
    XtPointer           callback_private;
    String              obj12;                  /* tm_table */
    XtProc              obj13;                  /* query_geometry */
```

```
XtProc              obj14;                /* display_accelerator */
XtPointer           extension;
} ObjectClassPart;
```

All fields not beginning with "obj" have the same meanings as the corresponding fields in CoreClassPart. Fields beginning with "obj" are padding fields that must be initialized to NULL or zero in static class record declarations, depending upon the field type. There is no standard extension for Object.

The full class record for Object is `ObjectClassRec`.

```
typedef struct _ObjectClassRec {
    ObjectClassPart     object_class;
} ObjectClassRec, *ObjectClass;
```

8.7.2   The Object Instance Structure

The Object instance part consists of the following fields from the beginning of the Core instance part:

```
typedef struct _ObjectPart {
    Widget              self;
    WidgetClass         widget_class;
    Widget              parent;
    XrmName             xrm_name;
    Boolean             being_destroyed;
    XtCallbackList      destroy_callbacks;
    XtPointer           constraints;
} ObjectPart;
```

All fields have the same meanings as the corresponding fields in CorePart.

The full class record for Object is `ObjectRec`.

```
typedef struct _ObjectRec {
    ObjectPart      object;
} ObjectRec, *Object;
```

8.7.3   The Rectangle Object Class Structure

The RectObj class part record is identical to the Core class part record except that some fields have been renamed to start with the characters "rect".

```
typedef struct {
    WidgetClass            superclass;
    String                 class_name;
    Cardinal               widget_size;
    XtProc                 class_initialize;
    XtWidgetClassProc      class_part_initialize;
    XtEnum                 class_inited;
    XtInitProc             initialize;
    XtArgsProc             initialize_hook;
    XtProc                 rect1;                  /* realize */
    XtPointer              rect2;                  /* actions */
    Cardinal               rect3;                  /* num_actions */
    XtResourceList         resources;
    Cardinal               num_resources;
    XrmClass               xrm_class;
    Boolean                rect4;                  /* compress_motion */
    XtEnum                 rect5;                  /* compress_exposure */
    Boolean                rect6;                  /* compress_enterleave */
    Boolean                rect7;                  /* visible_interest */
    XtWidgetProc           destroy;
    XtWidgetProc           resize;
    XtExposeProc           expose;
    XtSetValuesFunc        set_values;
    XtArgsFunc             set_values_hook;
    XtAlmostProc           set_values_almost;
    XtArgsProc             get_values_hook;
    XtProc                 rect9;                  /* accept_focus */
    XtVersionType          version;
    XtPointer              callback_private;
    String                 rect10;                 /* tm_table */
    XtGeometryHandler      query_geometry;
    XtProc                 rect11;                 /* display_accelerator */
    XtPointer              extension;
} RectObjClassPart;
```

All fields not beginning with "rect" have the same meanings as the corresponding fields in CoreClassPart. Fields beginning with "rect" are padding fields that must be initialized to NULL or zero in static class record declarations, depending upon the field type; note that there is no *rect8* field. There is no standard extension for RectObj.

The full class record for RectObj is `RectObjClassRec`.

```
typedef struct _RectObjClassRec {
    RectObjClassPart     rect_class;
} RectObjClassRec, *RectObjClass;
```

8.7.4   The Rectangle Object Instance Structure

The RectObj instance part consists of the following subset of fields from the Core instance part:

```
typedef struct _RectObjPart {
    Position      x, y;
    Dimension     width, height;
    Dimension     border_width;
    Boolean       managed;
    Boolean       sensitive;
    Boolean       ancestor_sensitive;
} RectObjPart;
```

All fields have the same meanings as the corresponding fields in CorePart.

The reasons for including the sensitivity resources and fields within RectObj are obscure. Having them there allows a gadget to visibly adjust its appearance in a manner similar to widgets and allows its parent to decide whether it should respond to events in the gadget's area. However, the Intrinsics never dispatch events to gadgets regardless of their sensitivity.

The full class record for RectObj is `RectObjRec`.

```
typedef struct _RectObjRec {
    ObjectPart      object;
    RectObjPart     rectangle;
} RectObjRec, *RectObj;
```

Note that the member name for RectObjPart does not conform to the standard naming conventions. There is, unfortunately, no good reason for this.

8.7.5   The Unnamed Class

The name and contents of the unnamed class between RectObj and Core are undefined. The results of attempting to subclass this class or to reference any fields in it are undefined as well. This class is reserved for possible future definition by the X Consortium.

8.7.6 Object and Rectangle Object Declarations

The Intrinsics header file `<X11/Intrinsic.h>` contains external definitions for the class records for Object and RectObj.

/* Declarations for the Object class */
extern ObjectClassRec objectClassRec;
extern WidgetClass objectWidgetClass;

/* Declarations for the RectObj class */
extern RectObjClassRec rectObjClassRec;
extern WidgetClass rectObjWidgetClass;

8.8 Using Objects in Widgets

One of the main motivations for adding the Object class to the Intrinsics was to simplify using subresources in widgets like the Graph widget described in Section 8.5. The display handler data structures have resources and methods just like widgets, but the Intrinsics provided no direct support. Worse, since there was no subclassing, writing a new display handler, even one that differed only slightly from an existing one, meant providing a completely new implementation.

With Object, the Graph widget programmer defines a new object class, GraphDisplay, that defines the resources and protocols needed for any display handler. Programmers subclass GraphDisplay or an existing GraphDisplay subclass to provide a new display handler.

Another example occurs with the Text widget. The mechanisms to store the text being displayed are independent of the mechanisms to display it. The Text widget implementor defines an object class, TextSource, that defines resources and methods for storing text. Different TextSource subclasses provide text storage in a character string, in a file, or even in a complex data structure suitable for a sophisticated text editor. As long as the text source is able to provide the Text widget with the characters needed, the Text widget does not care how the text is stored.

There are several ways a widget with an accompanying object can handle the object.

The widget can define a resource for the object's class, create an accompanying object of this class in its initialize procedure, and store the object's identifier in the widget instance. To give the application access to the object, the widget can define a resource for the field holding the object, and the application can query this field with `XtGetValues`. This scheme is the simplest for applications that do not need to worry about the object very much.

Alternatively, the widget can require the application to create the object as a child of the widget. The widget can be a composite widget and look for the object in its child list, or it can be a simple widget and require the application to supply the object identifier by calling `XtSetValues` on some resource. If it chooses the composite solution, the *accepts_objects* field in the Composite standard extension record must be TRUE and the insert_child procedure should check that the child being added is of the correct class. This scheme is the simplest if the object has many resources that the application might wish to specify at creation, and is the one used by the Graph widget in Chapter 10.

In either case, the widget can use Intrinsics subresource handling to make the object nearly invisible to the application by allowing the application to specify resources for the object as if they were resources for the widget; see Section 3.25. When the Intrinsics call initialize, set_values, or get_values_hook procedures in the widget, the procedure passes the argument list to a subresource procedure, thereby applying resource specifications in the argument list to the object. To make this work well, the widget must make sure that the object's resource list and the widget's resource list do not have too many collisions. There will always be a collision for the XtNdestroyCallback resource; if the application specifies it in an argument list, the callbacks end up on the destroy callback lists for both the widget and the object unless the widget implementation checks for XtNdestroyCallback in the argument list.

There is not yet enough experience with objects to recommend any of these approaches over the others.

8.9   Writing Composite Widgets to Support Gadgets

Composite parents of gadgets are responsible for much more than composite parents of widgets. Since the events that would go to the child if it were a widget go to the parent instead, the parent must perform appropriate actions on the child's behalf when it receives the event. Widget set designers should set some policies for handling the events so that the composite widgets in the set all act consistently.

There are many different options for how a composite parent interacts with its gadget children, and the documentation for the composite should document what conventions it expects gadget children to follow. If a composite is only prepared to handle gadgets of certain classes, it should perform a class check in its insert_child procedure to help eliminate programming errors. This check should be sure to allow widget children; for example,

```
if (!XtIsWidget(child) && !XtIsSubclass(child, allowedClass)) {
    /* Issue error message */
}
```

Any composite widget that accepts object or gadget children must declare a standard composite extension record and set its *accepts_objects* field to TRUE. If *accepts_objects* is FALSE, the Intrinsics will disallow any attempts to create nonwidget children.

No matter what else it does, the parent is responsible for redisplaying gadget children in its expose procedure. The easiest way to do this is to call the expose procedures for any gadget children whose areas intersect the exposed region, passing it an Expose event and a region. The Intrinsics do not define the contents of the Expose event or the region that are passed to the child's expose procedure; there are several possibilities:

- The x, y, width, and height in the Expose event can either be left in parent coordinates or be translated to be in the coordinate system of the child, and can either be left unmodified or be clipped by the child's rectangle.

- The region parameter can be left as is or be intersected with the child's rectangle.

- If the parent modifies the expose rectangle or region, it choses whether to include the child's border in the modifications.

- The parent can either draw the background and border for the child or leave it up to the child.

In Figure 8.2 assume the shaded area has just been exposed and that the solid rectangle represents a gadget child. The Intrinsics have just called the expose procedure of the widget with the shaded area as the region and the dashed rectangle as the rectangle in the Expose event.

- If the parent leaves the event and region alone, it passes the Expose event and the region to the child's expose procedure. The child is responsible for figuring out what part of itself it must redisplay.

- If the parent transforms the event into child coordinates, it subtracts (150, 150) from the coordinates in the event. The child is still responsible for figuring out what part of itself it must redisplay.

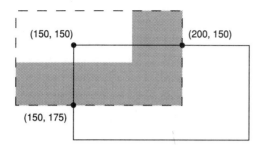

Figure 8.2. Exposures and gadget children

- If the parent clips the event with the child's rectangle, it changes the x and y in the event to (0, 0) and changes the width and height to (50, 25). This tells the child what part it must redisplay.

Intersection of the exposed region with the child's area is only marginally useful. Most expose procedures use the region as a clipping mask if they use it at all, and since the gadget should not be drawing outside its area anyway, the effect of using either the intersected or unintersected region is the same. The same thing applies to children that use the region to figure out which parts of their contents they must redisplay by checking if certain points are in the region; the child should not be checking coordinates outside its area.

If the parent relies upon the child to draw its border, the parent should include the child's border in any modifications it makes to the exposed rectangle or the region. If it draws the border for the child, it must choose whether to include the border in the expose procedure call.

If the parent draws the background or border for the gadget child, it has to find out the pixel values to use. There are three ways it can do this.

- The parent can know a great deal about its gadget children, including their instance declarations. The parent uses resource values from the child to draw the background or border.

- The parent can only accept gadgets that are subclasses of some standard gadget class. The standard class defines the resources for drawing, so the parent knows where to find them. This works well if any of a number of classes of composite widgets can contain the gadgets.

- The parent can have resources of its own that it uses for drawing all gadget children. This reduces flexibility since the same values must apply to all children, but eliminates fields in the instance records of the children. In most applications the same resources apply to all the children anyway, so the lost flexibility is not a problem; if an application writer needs some children with different background or border colors, she makes those children widgets instead of gadgets.

The most general solution of all is to leave it up to each child to draw its own border and background; this complicates the gadget implementations but requires the parent to know almost nothing about the children.

Parents of gadgets also have the option of ignoring their children's expose procedures completely and drawing all their contents for them. This requires the composite to know all about the gadget classes it supports, including how to display each one of them. The advantage to this scheme is that the parent can draw things in a different order than would occur if it called each child's expose procedure: the parent can draw all the backgrounds first, then all the borders, and then all the contents. This reduces the number of graphics context switches required of the server; these switches are expensive operations in some server implementations, and avoiding them can speed up redisplay. Having the parent do all the redisplay is most appropriate when the parent uses its own resources to do drawing since this reduces the number of potential graphics context switches even further.

Having the parent draw the backgrounds and borders is midway between having it draw nothing and having it draw everything. The parent can draw all backgrounds, then all borders, and then call the expose procedures. In many cases the expose procedures all use the same graphics context for drawing, so the effect is almost the same as when the parent does all the drawing.

The Intrinsics clear areas of a gadget's parent, generating Expose events, whenever they manage or unmanage a gadget child, whenever any set_values procedure returned TRUE in response to XtSetValues on a gadget child, and whenever a gadget child's geometry changes. The Expose events replace the ones the server would generate if the gadget child were a widget. If a gadget child's geometry changes, the Intrinsics clear areas both for any area previously occupied by the child, representing areas of the parent that are now exposed, and for the new area of the child, representing the exposure event for the child. The areas cleared always include the gadget's border width.

Parents of gadgets are free to define whatever semantics they desire if their gadget children overlap, including making this an error. If they allow gadgets to overlap, they should make the region parameter to the child's expose procedure actually represent a visible region of the child, and they must require that the child only draw within this region. If the child ignored the region and redisplayed all of itself, it might write over the area of another gadget that overlaps it.

In addition to exposure processing, the composite is also responsible for handling other events for its gadget children, like pointer button presses in Pushbutton gadgets. The guidelines for handling these events are even more vague than those for handling exposures.

The composite parent must somehow decide what logical translations it uses for its gadget children. The easiest way to do this is to have the parent define the translations, not allowing individual event customization. The parent could define a translation for button press, for example, and in the associated action procedure figure out which gadget child the event applied to by comparing the coordinates in the event with the area of each gadget child. If the button press did not occur within a gadget child or occurred within a gadget like a label that does nothing for the button press, the action procedure does nothing. If the button press occurred in a Pushbutton gadget, the action procedure calls some callback in the Pushbutton gadget by using XtCallCallbacks for the gadget. The action procedure must know the callback somehow, usually hard-coding in the appropriate callback resource name for the particular gadget class.

If the parent must support enter or leave events for its gadget children, it specifies a translation for pointer motion events and performs the enter or leave processing whenever the pointer moves into or out of a gadget child.

If the composite parent wants to allow individual event-handling customization for different gadget children, it has to adapt its own event handling based upon resources specified for the child. It can find these resources in the same ways it finds resources for drawing:

• The composite widget can know all about its children's classes, including which event customization resources each supported child class defines.

• The composite widget can look for event customization resources in the instance part of some class that is the superclass for all supported gadget classes.

Whichever solution is chosen, the task of modifying the parent's event handling to reflect the desired child semantics is not trivial. It is generally much easier to do this by installing event handlers on the parent than by trying to modify the parent's translations. Widget writers should consider the option of not allowing individual event-handling customizations; if an application requires them, it uses widgets instead of gadgets for the children requiring customization.

Yet another approach is to rely upon the gadget child to install event handlers on its parent for events in which the child is interested. This even works for Expose events, leading to parents that need to do almost nothing to support their gadget children.

This section presented many alternatives but few recommendations. There is not enough experience yet with gadgets to say which solutions work out the best. In particular, the area of allowing individual event handling for gadget children has been explored only superficially; any guidelines for what the resources should look like and how parents should handle them would be premature. Indeed, the more input semantics required of a gadget, the closer it becomes to being a full widget. If the semantics do not match the window semantics defined by the X protocol, programmer confusion is likely to result. The closer the semantics are to the window semantics, the more the composite widget's code will look like the insides of an X server. The widget set designer should analyze very carefully whether the code versus data trade-offs make complex gadgets desirable in her particular environment.

The implementations of the Box, MinMax, and Menu widgets presented in Chapter 10 support Label gadgets. Since labels define no event handling, the only procedures that need to know about gadgets are the insert_child procedure, which checks the subclass of new children, and the expose procedure, which draws the Label gadgets.

Example 8.1 shows the insert_child procedure for the Box widget. It checks the subclass of the new child to make sure it is either a widget or a Label gadget and issues an error message if it is neither.

Example 8.2 shows the expose procedure for the Box widget. For each managed child that is a Label gadget, the expose procedure checks if the rectangle for the child intersects the exposed region and calls the child's expose procedure if it does.

```
static void InsertChild(w)
    Widget w;
{
    String params[2];
    Cardinal num_params;
    Widget parent = XtParent(w);

    if (!XtIsWidget(w) && !XtIsSubclass(w, labelGadgetClass)) {
        params[0] = XtClass(w)->core_class.class_name;
        params[1] = XtClass(parent)->core_class.class_name;
        num_params = 2;
        XtAppErrorMsg(XtWidgetToApplicationContext(w),
                "childError", "class", "WidgetError",
                "Children of class %s cannot be added to %n widgets",
                params, &num_params);
    }

    (*((CompositeWidgetClass)(boxWidgetClass->core_class.superclass))->
            composite_class.insert_child) (w);
}
```

Example 8.1.   The Box insert_child procedure

```
static void Redisplay(w, event, region)
    Widget w;
    XEvent *event;
    Region region;
{
    CompositeWidget comp = (CompositeWidget) w;
    int i;
    Widget c;                /* child */

    for (i = 0; i < comp->composite.num_children; i++) {
        c = comp->composite.children[i];
        if (XtIsManaged(c) && XtIsSubclass(c, labelGadgetClass) &&
                XRectInRegion(region, c->core.x, c->core.y,
                        c->core.width + 2*c->core.border_width,
                        c->core.height + 2*c->core.border_width)
                    != RectangleOut) {
            (*(XtClass(c)->core_class.expose))(c, event, region);
        }
    }
}
```

Example 8.2.   The Box expose procedure

8.10   Writing Gadgets

Writing a gadget is pretty much the same as writing a widget. The gadget implementation must follow whatever conventions for event handling and redisplay are set forth by the composite widgets that can hold the gadgets.

☞   A gadget implementation must pay close attention to its width and height fields. Unlike a widget, which can often ignore those fields and rely upon the X server to clip its output, a gadget has no boundaries automatically enforced for it. Gadgets that ignore their width and height can overwrite their parent's contents and the contents of other gadget children.

Chapter 10 contains an implementation of a Label gadget. This implementation is almost the same as that of the Label widget, with a few changes:

- The Label gadget does not support the *accel_string* field.
- The Label gadget defines two additional resources, XtNbackground and XtNborder, so that it can draw its own background and border.
- The implementation has two additional graphics context fields for the background and border graphics contexts. The initialize and set_values procedures maintain these contexts.
- The resize procedure updates the border graphics context if the border width changes. It uses a new internal field, *old_border*, to know when this happens.
- The resize and expose procedures draw in the gadget's parent's window.
- The expose procedure draws the background and border and uses a region to clip its output.

Example 8.3 shows the expose procedure for the Label gadget. It plays a bit fast and loose with the rules concerning shared graphics contexts, but since it restores the graphics context before it exits and calls no toolkit routines, no problems result. See Section 10.6 of *Xlib* for more information on regions.

```
static void Redisplay(w, event, region)
    Widget w;
    XEvent *event;
    Region region;
{
    LabelGadget lw = (LabelGadget) w;
    int offset, x;
    XRectangle rect;
    Region r1, r2;

    /* Draw the background */
    XFillRectangle(XtDisplayOfObject(w), XtWindowOfObject(w),
            lw->label.current_bg_gc,
            lw->rectObj.x + lw->rectObj.border_width,
            lw->rectObj.y + lw->rectObj.border_width,
            lw->rectObj.width, lw->rectObj.height);

    /* Draw the border */
    if (lw->rectObj.border_width != 0) {
        offset = lw->rectObj.border_width / 2;
        XDrawRectangle(XtDisplayOfObject(w), XtWindowOfObject(w),
                lw->label.border_gc,
                lw->rectObj.x + offset, lw->rectObj.y + offset,
                lw->rectObj.width + lw->rectObj.border_width,
                lw->rectObj.height + lw->rectObj.border_width);
    }

    switch (lw->label.justify) {
        case Left:
            x = lw->label.space;
            break;
        case Right:
            x = (int) lw->rectObj.width - (int) lw->label.space -
                    (int) lw->label.label_width;
            break;
        case Center:
            x = ((int) lw->rectObj.width -
                    (int) lw->label.label_width) / 2;
            break;
    }

    /* Temporarily change the clip mask in the gc */
    rect.x = lw->rectObj.x + lw->rectObj.border_width;
    rect.y = lw->rectObj.y + lw->rectObj.border_width;
    rect.width = lw->rectObj.width;
    rect.height = lw->rectObj.height;
```

(continued)

Example 8.3. The LabelGadget expose procedure

```
        r1 = XCreateRegion();
        r2 = XCreateRegion();
        if (region != NULL) {
            XUnionRectWithRegion(&rect, r1, r2);     /* r2 = rectangle */
            XIntersectRegion(region, r2, r1);        /* r1 = intersection */
        } else XUnionRectWithRegion(&rect, r2, r1); /* r1 = rectangle */

        XSetRegion(XtDisplayOfObject(w), lw->label.current_gc, r1);
        XDestroyRegion(r1);
        XDestroyRegion(r2);

        XDrawString(XtDisplayOfObject(w), XtWindowOfObject(w),
                lw->label.current_gc,
                lw->rectObj.x + lw->rectObj.border_width + x,
                lw->rectObj.y + lw->rectObj.border_width +
                    lw->label.space + lw->label.font->max_bounds.ascent,
                lw->label.label, lw->label.label_len);

        /* Restore the GC */
        XSetClipMask(XtDisplayOfObject(w), lw->label.current_gc, None);
}
```

Example 8.3. The LabelGadget expose procedure

Chapter 9

Odds and Ends

Writing Applications

This chapter presents an assortment of utility routines and miscellaneous information functions. They provide consistent and convenient interfaces to many commonly performed operations.

9.1   Toolkit Version

To write code that works with Intrinsics implementations that conform to different specification releases but that takes advantage of newer features when possible, use the preprocessor symbol XtSpecificationRelease.

#define XtSpecificationRelease 4

The value of XtSpecificationRelease will change with each new specification version. XtSpecificationRelease is new to the Intrinsics with Release 4, so assume a Release 3 toolkit if XtSpecificationRelease is not defined:

```
#ifndef XtSpecificationRelease
/* Toolkit is Release 3 */
#else
#if XtSpecificationRelease == 4
/* Toolkit is Release 4 */
#else
/* Toolkit is beyond Release 4 */
#endif
#endif
```

9.2   The Size of Arrays

There are many cases where toolkit programs must deal with counted arrays: argument lists, options lists, action tables, resource lists, and so on. XtNumber is a macro that returns the number of elements in a fixed-size array.

Cardinal XtNumber(*array*)
    ArrayVariable *array*;

array   Specifies a fixed-size array.

XtNumber divides the size of the array passed to it by the size of its first element to find the number of elements in the array. For example,

```
int a[] = {6, 26, 57};
Cardinal b = XtNumber(a);
```

stores 3 into *b*.

9.3   Finding Widgets

Some applications need to find a widget identifier given only a window or a widget name. The Intrinsics provide two routines to support this, XtWindowToWidget and XtNameToWidget.

Widget XtWindowToWidget(*display, window*)
    Display *display;
    Window *window*;

display   Specifies the display the widget is defined on.
window   Specifies the window to get the widget for.

XtWindowToWidget returns the widget on the specified display that has the specified window. If no such widget exists, XtWindowToWidget returns NULL.

Widget XtNameToWidget(*reference, name_list*) ;
    Widget *reference*;
    String *name_list*;

reference   Specifies the widget that the search is to start from.
name_list   Specifies the qualified name of the widget to find.

The *name_list* parameter is a list of widget names separated by periods or asterisks. XtNameToWidget looks for a descendant of the *reference* widget such that the ordered list of widget names between the *reference* widget and the descendant, including the descendant but not the *reference* widget, matches the widget names in the *name_list* parameter using these rules:

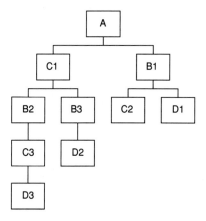

Figure 9.1. A sample widget tree

- Each widget named in the *name_list* parameter must match a name in the list, and the order of the names in *name_list* must match the order of the names in the list.

- If a period separates two widget names in the *name_list* parameter, the matching widgets must be adjacent in the list.

- If an asterisk separates two widget names in the *name_list* parameter, any number, including zero, of intervening widgets can come between the matching widgets in the list.[1]

If such a descendant exists, XtNameToWidget returns it; otherwise it returns NULL. If more than one descendant qualifies, the XtNameToWidget returns the one closest to the *reference* widget in the widget tree. If the closest descendant is not unique, XtNameToWidget returns any equally close descendant.

Consider the widget tree in Figure 9.1. The name of each widget is the letter in the box; the numbers just serve to uniquely identify the widgets. If you called XtNameToWidget with A as the *reference* widget and the string in the first column as the *name_list* parameter, XtNameToWidget returns the widget in the second column:

---

[1] Asterisks in the name list are not supported by Intrinsics implementations that conform to specifications earlier than Release 4.

Name_list	Resulting widget
B	B1
C*B	B2 or B3
*D	D1
*B*C	C2
*C*D	D2

9.4 Memory Management

The toolkit provides memory management routines that give some extra conveniences to programmers. They are completely compatible and can be used interchangeably with the standard C library routines malloc, calloc, realloc, and free. The toolkit routines provide the following added functionality:

- XtMalloc, XtCalloc, and XtRealloc generate a fatal error message if unable to allocate the requested memory.
- XtFree just returns if passed a NULL pointer.
- XtRealloc allocates new storage if passed a NULL pointer.

Their arguments and return types are the same as the C library routines, with Cardinal replacing unsigned and XtPointer replacing char*.

```
char *XtMalloc(size);
    Cardinal size;
    size            Specifies the number of bytes desired.
```

XtMalloc returns a pointer to a block of storage that is at least as large as the specified size. The storage is aligned using the most stringent alignment requirements of the machine architecture so that any data type can be safely copied into the allocated storage. If insufficient storage is available, XtMalloc calls XtErrorMsg.

```
char *XtCalloc(num, size);
    Cardinal num;
    Cardinal size;
    num             Specifies the number of array elements to allocate.
    size            Specifies the size of an array element in bytes.
```

XtCalloc allocates an array with the specified number of elements, each of the specified size, and sets every byte in the returned storage to zero. If insufficient storage is available, XtCalloc calls XtErrorMsg.

char *XtRealloc(*ptr, size*);
    char *ptr*;
    Cardinal *size*;

ptr	Specifies a pointer to a block of storage allocated with XtMalloc.
size	Specifies the new size for the storage.

XtRealloc returns a pointer to a block of storage that is at least as large as the specified size. The storage contains the same contents as the old storage specified in *ptr* up to the minimum of the sizes of the old and new storage blocks. The returned pointer might be the same as the old pointer; if it is not, XtRealloc frees the storage pointed to by *ptr* before returning. *Ptr* must point to a block of storage allocated by one of the memory allocation routines or be NULL; if it is NULL, XtRealloc just calls XtMalloc for a block of the specified size. If insufficient storage is available, XtRealloc calls XtErrorMsg.

void XtFree(*ptr*);
    char *ptr*;

ptr	Specifies a pointer to a block of storage to free.

XtFree frees the specified storage, which must have been returned by one of the memory allocation procedures. If *ptr* is NULL, XtFree returns immediately.

type *XtNew(*type*);
    type;

type	Specifies a data type.

XtNew is a convenience macro that allocates storage sufficient to hold an instance of the passed type. It is defined to be

```
((type *) XtMalloc((unsigned) sizeof(type)))
```

Here are some examples of XtNew in variable declarations:

```
int *i = XtNew(int);
XFontStruct *fontStruct = XtNew(XFontStruct);
```

XtNew is most useful within widget implementations, but applications may find it useful on occasion as well.

String XtNewString(*string*) ;
    String *string*;

string   Specifies a string to copy.

`XtNewString` is a convenience macro that allocates a copy of the specified string. It is defined to be

```
(strcpy(XtMalloc((unsigned) strlen(str) + 1), (str)))
```

Here is an example of `XtNewString`:

```
char *greeting = XtNewString("Hello, world");
```

`XtNewString` is also most useful within widget implementations; its major use is to copy string reference resources.

9.5   Translating Coordinates

To translate x/y coordinates from a widget's coordinate system to screen coordinates, use `XtTranslateCoords`.

void XtTranslateCoords(*w, x, y, rootx_return, rooty_return*)
    Widget *w*;
    Position *x, y*;
    Position **rootx_return, *rooty_return*;

w   Specifies the widget.
x, y   Specify the widget-relative coordinates.
rootx_return   Returns the screen-relative coordinates.
rooty_return   Returns the screen-relative coordinates.

`XtTranslateCoords` is similar to the Xlib `XTranslateCoordinates` function but does not require a round trip to the server. It relies upon the user's window manager to keep the application informed whenever the application's window gets moved, and so can return incorrect coordinates if the window manager misbehaves.

You can use two calls to `XtTranslateCoords` to find the location of one widget relative to another:

```
Position src_x, src_y, dst_x, dst_y;
Position offset_x, offset_y;

XtTranslateCoords(src_widget, 0, 0, &src_x, &src_y);
XtTranslateCoords(dst_widget, 0, 0, &dst_x, &dst_y);

offset_x = src_x - dst_x;
offset_y = src_y - dst_y;
```

This leaves *offset_x* and *offset_y* holding the location of *src_widget* in the coor-

dinate system of *dst_widget*. Doing this directly with XTranslate-
Coordinates would require two server round trips.

9.6   Error Handling

Whenever the Intrinsics detect an error condition, the condition is reported
through a central error-reporting mechanism. Applications and widgets are
encouraged to use the same mechanism for their own error reporting. In
addition, applications can modify the output location or the style of error
messages.

The Intrinsics provide two sets of error routines:

• A high-level interface that takes an error name and class and looks the error message
string up in an error database.

• A low-level interface that takes a simple error message string.

The default operation of the high-level routines is to construct a string and
pass it to the corresponding low-level routine. The default operation of the
low-level routines is to print out the message in some standard place, usually
stderr on Unix-based systems, and to terminate if the error is fatal and to
return if it is not. Applications can install their own error handlers to override
the default operation; they might format the error messages differently, filter
out some warning messages, or report the errors in a different way.

Error handlers must be very careful about using toolkit facilities to report
errors, for example, creating a pop-up dialog box with the error message. It is
generally safe to report errors from the application or nonfatal warning messages this way, but reporting fatal Intrinsics errors often leads to generating
still more errors. If, for example, the handler receives an error indicating that
memory could not be allocated, the Intrinsics are unlikely to be able to allocate the storage they need to pop up widgets. One way to get around this is
to have the handler first install a new error handler that reports the error
without using the Intrinsics and then proceed; if another error results, the
new handler catches it. The two handlers must cooperate to allow the second
handler to report the first handler's error and not its own error, since its error
is just an artifact of the error-handling mechanism.

The toolkit error facilities are not invoked when Xlib reports errors. An
application that wants to unify its error handling must install new Xlib error
handlers to invoke the toolkit facilities; see Section 8.12.2 of *Xlib*.

All these routines take an application context parameter; the routines that install handlers install them for a particular application context, and the routines that report errors use the application context to determine which handler to invoke. There are, however, places in the Intrinsics that generate error messages but that in many implementations do not have enough local context to find an application context. An example is when `XtMalloc` is unable to allocate the desired storage; `XtMalloc` has no parameters that indicate an application context. These implementations typically ignore application contexts completely in their error handling, providing one global set of error handlers for each address space. If different handlers are installed for different application contexts, the most recently installed handler reports errors for all application contexts. Appendix C describes error-reporting interfaces that do not require an application context; these interfaces may be useful to library layers that find themselves in the same predicament as `XtMalloc`.

High-level error routines take an error name, an error type, and an error class. The name is a general category for the error, the type is additional qualification (often the name of the routine generating the error), and the class defines which component is generating the error. All errors generated by the Intrinsics have "XtToolkitError" as their class. It is recommended that widget sets choose an alternative but uniform class for their own error and warning messages. High-level error handlers normally call `XtAppGet-ErrorDatabaseText` to construct an error message; `XtAppGetErrorDatabaseText` uses the name, type, and class to look up the error message in an error database. When `XtMalloc` fails to allocate requested storage, it calls `XtErrorMsg` with error name "allocError", error type "malloc", and error class "XtToolkitError".

The error database is in the format of a resource database. The error name and type make up the left-hand side of the resource specification and the error message is the value of the resource.

The error class is useful in error handlers that handle errors from different sources differently. An error handler can report errors arising from the Intrinsics, from the widgets, and from the application in different ways.

High-level handlers also take a default string to use as the error in case no matching entry is in the error database. This makes error reporting work sensibly if no error database is installed on the system. Error databases are useful when the error text needs to be changed for some reason, particularly for reporting errors in a language other than English.

High-level handlers also take a set of parameters that they substitute into the error message, which contains standard `printf` substitutions to indicate where the parameters go. For example, the default warning message issued by the Intrinsics when it cannot find action procedures to bind to action names is "Actions not found: %s" and the parameter is a string containing the unbound action names.

If you are concerned about writing error messages that can easily be translated into other languages, it is best to avoid messages with more than one parameter substitution. The parameters are always substituted in the string in the order that they occur in the parameter list, and trying to write error messages in another language that preserve this order can lead to extremely contorted syntax.

To generate a fatal error message, use `XtAppErrorMsg`.

void XtAppErrorMsg(*app_context, name, type, class, default, params, num_params*)
    XtAppContext *app_context*;
    String *name*;
    String *type*;
    String *class*;
    String *default*;
    String **params*;
    Cardinal **num_params*;

app_context	Specifies the application context to look for the error handler in. Some implementations ignore this parameter.
name	Specifies the name of the error.
type	Specifies additional detail for the error.
class	Specifies the class of the error.
default	Specifies the default error message.
params	Specifies values to substitute into the error message.
num_params	Specifies the number of values in the *params* parameter.

`XtAppErrorMsg` calls the error handler for the specified application context, or the global error handler in implementations that do not support per-application-context error handlers. It passes the rest of the parameters to the error handler. Use `XtAppErrorMsg` to report fatal errors, that is, errors from which the program cannot recover. The programmer can assume that `XtAppErrorMsg` never returns; it would be an error (of a different kind) if it did.

To generate a warning message, use `XtAppWarningMsg`.

void XtAppWarningMsg(*app_context, name, type, class, default, params, num_params*)
    XtAppContext *app_context*;
    String *name*;
    String *type*;
    String *class*;
    String *default*;
    String *params;
    Cardinal *num_params;

app_context	Specifies the application context to look for the warning handler in. Some implementations ignore this parameter.
name	Specifies the name of the error.
type	Specifies additional detail for the error.
class	Specifies the class of the error.
default	Specifies the default error message.
params	Specifies values to substitute into the error message.
num_params	Specifies the number of values in the *params* parameter.

`XtAppWarningMsg` calls the warning handler for the specified application context, or the global warning handler in implementations that do not support per-application context warning handlers. It passes the rest of the parameters to the warning handler. Use `XtAppWarningMsg` to report non-fatal errors, that is, errors that do not prevent the program from continuing.

If you do not need to modify the Intrinsics' default error handling, skip the rest of this section.

Applications alter the built-in handling of error and warning messages by supplying new error or warning handlers. There are both high-level and low-lever error handlers.

High-level error and warning handlers are of type `XtErrorMsgHandler`.

typedef void (*XtErrorMsgHandler) (String, String, String, String, String *,
                                    Cardinal *)
    String *name*;
    String *type*;
    String *class*;
    String *default*;
    String *params;
    Cardinal *num_params;

name	Specifies the name of the error.

type   Specifies additional detail for the error.

class   Specifies the class of the error.

default   Specifies the default error message.

params   Specifies values to substitute into the error message.

num_params   Specifies the number of values in the *params* parameter.

To install a new high-level error handler, use `XtAppSetErrorMsgHandler`.

XtErrorMsgHandler XtAppSetErrorMsgHandler(*app_context, msg_handler*)
     XtAppContext *app_context*;
     XtErrorMsgHandler *msg_handler*;

app_context   Specifies the application context to install the error handler on.
                      Some implementations ignore this parameter.

msg_handler   Specifies the new error handler.

`XtAppSetErrorMsgHandler` returns the previously installed error handler; this allows error handlers to filter errors and call the previous handler for some of them.

The error handler should not return. The default high-level error handler is `_XtDefaultErrorMsg`; it calls `XtGetErrorDatabaseText` to construct an error message and passes the message to `XtAppError`. Custom handlers can call `_XtDefaultErrorMsg` if appropriate. To restore the default behavior after installing some other error handler, set the error handler to `_XtDefaultErrorMsg`.

To install a new high-level warning handler, use `XtAppSetWarningMsg-Handler`.

XtErrorMsgHandler XtAppSetWarningMsgHandler(*app_context, msg_handler*)
     XtAppContext *app_context*;
     XtErrorMsgHandler *msg_handler*;

app_context   Specifies the application context to install the warning handler on.
                      Some implementations ignore this parameter.

msg_handler   Specifies the new warning handler.

`XtAppSetWarningMsgHandler` returns the previously installed warning handler; this allows warning handlers to filter warnings and call the previous handler for some of them.

The warning handler should return after reporting the warning. The default high-level warning handler is `_XtDefaultWarningMsg`; it calls `XtGetErrorDatabaseText` to construct a warning message and passes the message to `XtAppWarning`. Custom handlers can call `_XtDefault-`

`WarningMsg` if appropriate. To restore the default behavior after installing some other warning handler, set the error handler to `_XtDefault-WarningMsg`.

Error and warning handlers retrieve the error text from the error database by calling `XtAppGetErrorDatabaseText`.

void XtAppGetErrorDatabaseText(*app_context, name, type, class, default, buffer_return,*
nbytes, database)

    XtAppContext *app_context*;
    char **name, *type, *class*;
    char **default*;
    char **buffer_return*;
    int *nbytes*;
    XrmDatabase *database*;

app_context	Specifies the application context to use for the error database. Some implementations ignore this parameter.
name	Specifies the name of the error.
type	Specifies the type of the error.
class	Specifies the class of the error.
default	Specifies the default value for the error string.
buffer_return	Specifies the buffer the error string should be copied into.
nbytes	Specifies the size of the error buffer.
database	Specifies an alternative database to use for the database lookup, or NULL to use the database in the application context.

`XtAppGetErrorDatabaseText` looks up the error message in the error database for the application context, or in the override database if one is specified. The name and type form the resource name for the lookup, so calling `XtAppGetErrorDatabaseText` with name "allocError", type "malloc", and class "XtToolkitError" causes a database query with name "allocError.malloc" and class "XtToolkitError". If it finds a database entry, `XtAppGetErrorDatabaseText` copies the message text into *buffer_return* and, if not, copies the default message into *buffer_return*. In either case at most *nbytes* are copied.

Error handlers substitute any parameters in their *params* argument into this string. Unfortunately there is no good general way to do this in the C language; probably the cleanest way is to have some maximum number of parameters that the handler can report and use `sprintf` calls within a switch statement:

```
char message[2000], buffer_return[1000];

XtAppGetErrorDatabaseText(app, name, type, class, default,
        buffer_return, 1000, NULL);

switch(num_params) {
    case 0:
        strcpy(message, buffer_return);
        break;
    case 1:
        (void) sprintf(message, buffer_return, params[0]);
        break;
    case 2:
        (void) sprintf(message, buffer_return, params[0],
                params[1]);
        break;
    ...
}
```

Programmers who like to live dangerously can do something like

```
(void) sprintf(message, buffer_return, params[0], params[1],
        params[2], params[3], params[4], params[5]);
```

They must still handle the case for zero parameters separately since *params* is NULL in this case. Currently no Intrinsics error messages have more than three parameters.

An error or warning handler finds the application name and class for inclusion in an error message by calling `XtGetApplicationNameAndClass`.

void XtGetApplicationNameAndClass(*display, name_return, class_return*);
    Display **display*;
    String **name_return*;
    String **class_return*;

display	Specifies an open display connection that has been initialized with `XtDisplayInitialize`.
name_return	Returns the application name.
class_return	Returns the application class.

`XtGetApplicationNameAndClass` returns the application name and class passed to `XtDisplayInitialize` for that display. The caller must not modify the returned strings.

Error and warning handlers obtain the error database for an application context by calling `XtAppGetErrorDatabase`.

XrmDatabase *XtAppGetErrorDatabase(*app_context*)
    XtAppContext *app_context*;
app_context   Specifies the application context to fetch the database for.
                  Some implementations ignore this parameter.

`XtAppGetErrorDatabase` returns the address of the error database. Some error handlers modify this database, for example, to merge in a database of application-specific error messages. Most error handlers do not need `XtAppGetErrorDatabase`.

The Intrinsics do not load the error database until the first call to `XtAppGetErrorDatabaseText`, so `XtAppGetErrorDatabase` can return NULL. To force loading the database, call `XtAppGetErrorDatabaseText` before calling `XtAppGetErrorDatabase`.

The low-level error routines exist mainly as a holdover from earlier versions of the toolkit that did not support the high-level routines. `XtAppErrorMsg` and `XtAppWarningMsg` are the preferred interface. Setting the low-level error handlers is still a reasonable thing to do, however, since the default high-level handlers call them to report the error strings they construct. New high-level handlers can do this also; this is the only real remaining use for `XtAppError` and `XtAppWarning`.

To report a fatal error with the low-level interface, use `XtAppError`.

void XtAppError(*app_context, message*)
    XtAppContext *app_context*;
    String *message*;
app_context   Specifies the application context to look for the error handler in.
                  Some implementations ignore this parameter.
message   Specifies the error message.

`XtAppError` calls the low-level error handler for the specified application context, or the global low-level error handler in implementations that do not support per-application-context error handlers. It passes the message to the handler.

To report a warning with the low-level interface, use `XtAppWarning`.

void XtAppWarning(*app_context, message*)
    XtAppContext *app_context*;
    String *message*;

app_context	Specifies the application context to look for the warning handler in. Some implementations ignore this parameter.
message	Specifies the warning message.

XtAppWarning calls the low-level warning handler for the specified application context, or the global low-level warning handler in implementations that do not support per-application-context error handlers. It passes the message to the handler.

Low-level error and warning handlers are of type XtErrorHandler.

typedef void (*XtErrorHandler) (String)
     String *message*;

message	Specifies the error message.

To install a new low-level error handler, use XtAppSetErrorHandler.

XtErrorHandler XtAppSetErrorHandler(*app_context, handler*)
     XtAppContext *app_context*;
     XtErrorHandler *handler*;

app_context	Specifies the application context to install the error handler on. Some implementations ignore this parameter.
handler	Specifies the new error handler.

XtAppSetErrorHandler returns the previously installed error handler; this allows error handlers to filter errors and call the previous handler for some of them.

The error handler should not return. The default low-level error handler is _XtDefaultError; on Unix systems it prints the message on stderr and terminates the application. Custom handlers can call _XtDefaultError if appropriate. To restore the default behavior after installing some other error handler, set the error handler to _XtDefaultError.

To install a new low-level warning handler, use XtAppSetWarning-Handler.

XtErrorHandler XtAppSetWarningHandler(*app_context, handler*)
     XtAppContext *app_context*;
     XtErrorHandler *handler*;

app_context	Specifies the application context to install the warning handler on. Some implementations ignore this parameter.
handler	Specifies the new warning handler.

`XtAppSetWarningHandler` returns the previously installed warning handler; this allows warning handlers to filter warnings and call the previous handler for some of them.

The warning handler should return after reporting the warning. The default low-level warning handler is `_XtDefaultWarning`; on Unix systems, it prints the message on `stderr` and returns to the caller. Custom handlers can call `_XtDefaultWarning` if appropriate. To restore the default behavior after installing some other warning handler, set the error handler to `_XtDefaultWarning`.

9.7 Setting Colormap Windows

Applications that use more than one colormap must inform the window manager which widgets have colormaps different from the one their application shell uses. This allows the window manager to install the application's colormaps when the application is *colormap-active*, where the window manager defines just how it decides which applications are colormap-active. Most window managers make whichever application has the X input focus colormap-active. Applications that are colormap-active are more likely to display in their correct colors than applications that are not colormap-active.

An application that uses only one colormap for all its widgets, whether or not that colormap is the default colormap for the application's screen, only needs to ensure that the application shell widget specifies the desired colormap resource.

To inform the window manager that an application uses multiple colormaps, use `XtSetWMColormapWindows`.[2]

void XtSetWMColormapWindows(*widget, list, count*)
    Widget *widget*;
    Widget **list*;
    Cardinal *count*;

widget	Specifies a shell widget.
list	Specifies a list of widgets with colormaps that may be different from the shell's.
count	Specifies the number of widgets in the widget list.

The shell widget is any nonoverride shell. Generally the application calls

---

[2] `XtSetWMColormapWindows` is not supported by Intrinsics implementations that conform to specifications earlier than Release 4.

XtSetWMColormapWindows for each nonoverride shell tree containing widgets that do not use the same colormap as their parent and lists all such widgets in the shell's tree. Most applications also call XtSetWMColormap-Windows for their main shell, listing all widgets in the application that do not use the same colormap as their parent.

The order of the widgets in the list is important; when an X server supports fewer simultaneous installed colormaps than the application requests, widgets nearer the head of the list will have their colormaps installed in preference to those at the end of the list.

XtSetWMColormapWindows examines each widget in the widget list in order and constructs another list of widgets as follows:

- If the widget is not realized, XtSetWMColormapWindows ignores it.
- If the widget is realized and its colormap is different from the colormap of any widget already on the list, XtSetWMColormapWindows adds it to the list.

XtSetWMColormapWindows then notifies the window manager of the colormaps. It sets the WM_COLORMAPS property on the specified shell's window to a list of all windows for widgets on the internal list. Since the default value for a widget's colormap is its parent's colormap, an application only puts widgets on the list whose colormaps it set explicitly—their children, if included, would not end up on the internal list since their colormaps duplicate their parents'.

When the window manager makes the shell's window colormap-active, it installs as many of the colormaps for windows on the list as the X server supports. Widgets that use these colormaps display in their correct colors. Most servers only support one colormap, so applications that use more than one are unlikely to have all their widgets display with the correct colors simultaneously.

To accommodate servers with just one colormap, applications should use the same colormap for all widgets within each nonoverride shell tree. Widgets within an override shell tree should use the same colormap as used by the shell's parent. If the application calls XtSetWMColormapWindows for the shell of each nonoverride tree, specifying the shell as the widget list, the window manager can make the widgets within that shell display correctly. Applications written this way allow for servers with more than one colormap by calling XtSetWMColormapWindows for its main shell, specifying all its nonoverride shells, starting with the main shell, in the widget list.

Since `XtSetWMColormapWindows` ignores unrealized widgets, calling it before realizing the widget tree is useless. The application must prerealize any pop-up trees that contain widgets on the widget list.

An application writer who uses multiple colormaps must also be aware of visual types; see Section 2.7.

9.8 Finding Files

To search for a file that may exist in any of a number of places, call `XtFindFile`.[3]

String XtFindFile(*path, substitutions, num_substitutions, predicate*)
    String *path*;
    Substitution *substitutions*;
    Cardinal *num_substitutions*;
    XtFilePredicate *predicate*;

path	Specifies a path of file names that can include substitution characters.
substitutions	Specifies a list of substitutions to make into the path.
num_substitutions	Specifies the number of substitutions in the list.
predicate	Specifies a procedure called to judge each potential file name, or NULL.

The *path* parameter specifies a list of file names, separated by colons. `XtFindFile` takes each file name in the path and passes it to the predicate procedure, which is of type `XtFilePredicate`.

typedef Boolean (*XtFilePredicate) (String);
    String *filename*;

filename	Specifies a potential file name.

If the file name is suitable, the predicate returns TRUE; if not, it returns FALSE. `XtFindFile` returns the first name that the predicate returns TRUE for, or NULL if the predicate never returns TRUE. If the predicate passed to `XtFindFile` is NULL, `XtFindFile` uses an internal predicate that returns TRUE if the file specified by the name exists, is readable, and is not a directory.

Before passing the file name to the file predicate, `XtFindFile` scans the file name for substitutions as specified in the *substitutions* parameter. The *substitutions* parameter points to an array of `SubstitutionRec` structures.

---

[3] `XtFindFile` is not supported by Intrinsics implementations that conform to specifications earlier than Release 4.

```
typedef struct {
    char      match;
    String    substitution;
} SubstitutionRec, *Substitution;
```

`XtFindFile` replaces any occurrences of a percent sign followed by one of the match characters with the contents of the corresponding substitution string. In the code

```
static SubstitutionRec sub[] = {
    {'N', "datafile"}
};

file = XtFindFile("/lib/%N:/usr/lib/%N:/usr/local/lib/%N",
        sub, XtNumber(sub), NULL);
```

`XtFindFile` calls the internal file predicate for the strings

```
/lib/datafile
/usr/lib/datafile
/usr/local/lib/datafile
```

in that order. If the *substitution* field of a substitution record is NULL, `XtFindFile` treats it as the empty string.

Within the path specification the characters "%:" represent a single colon that does not separate file names and the characters "%%" represent a single percent character. `XtFindFile` leaves unmodified any percent sign followed by any other character that is not a match character.

After resolving substitutions, `XtFindFile` collapses any adjacent name separators in the file name into a single separator if the operating system does not treat multiple separators the same as a single separator and if the adjacent separators do not appear at the beginning of the name. For example, if the result after substitution is "`/usr/local/lib//datafile`" `XtFindFile` transforms it into "`/usr/local/lib/datafile`" before calling the file predicate. This happens most often when the path contains a substitution between separators and the string to be substituted is the empty string.

The caller of `XtFindFile` must free the returned file name using `XtFree` when it is no longer needed.

The Intrinsics also provide `XtResolvePathname`, a higher-level interface that uses a predefined set of substitutions.[4]

---

[4] `XtResolvePathname` is not supported by Intrinsics implementations that conform to specifications earlier than Release 4.

String XtResolvePathname (*dpy, type, filename, suffix, substitutions, num_substitutions,*
path, predicate)

Display *dpy;
String *type, filename, suffix*;
String *path*;
Substitution *substitutions*;
Cardinal *num_substitutions*;
XtFilePredicate *predicate*;

dpy	Specifies the display to use to find the language substitution string.
type	Specifies a value to substitute into the path.
filename	Specifies a value to substitute into the path.
suffix	Specifies a value to substitute into the path.
path	Specifies a path for XtFindFile, or NULL.
substitutions	Specifies a list of substitutions to make into the path.
num_substitutions	Specifies the number of substitutions in the list.
predicate	Specifies a predicate for XtFindFile, or NULL.

XtResolvePathname uses the value of the xnlLanguage resource fetched from the database for the specified display. The language resource is a string that consists of three parts, a language, a territory, and a codeset, encoded as

```
language[_territory] [.codeset]
```

(the square brackets indicate optional parts). These three parts contain any characters suitable for inclusion in file names other than the separating characters. XtResolvePathname places no interpretation upon them other than to use them in path substitutions. The xnlLanguage resource specifying French as spoken in Belgium could be "French_Belgian", "Fr_Be", or even "abc_zqx3".

XtResolvePathname calls XtFindFile, augmenting the substitutions with the following:

%N	The value of the *filename* parameter, or the application's class if *filename* is NULL.
%T	The value of the *type* parameter.
%S	The value of the *suffix* parameter.
%L	The value of the xnlLanguage resource for the specified display.
%l	The language part of the xnlLanguage resource. (This is a lower-case L, not a one.)

%t   The territory part of the xnlLanguage resource, if any.

%c   The codeset part of the xnlLanguage resource, if any.

If its *path* parameter is not NULL, XtResolvePathname passes it to XtFindFile. If *path* is NULL, XtResolvePathname checks if the XFILESEARCHPATH variable is set in the user's environment, and uses its value as the path if so. If XFILESEARCHPATH is not set, XtResolvePathname passes an implementation-dependent path name that on Unix systems contains at least the string "/usr/lib/X11/%T/%N%S".

If the path (wherever it came from) begins with a colon, XtResolve-Pathname passes a modified path to XtFindFile, consisting of "%N%S" followed by the path. If the path contains two sequential colons not preceded by a percent sign, XtResolvePathname passes a modified path consisting of the original path with "%N%S" inserted between the colons. Starting a path with a colon or using two sequential colons makes XtResolvePathname look for the file in the current directory.

The *type* parameter is a general category of file, usually corresponding to a directory in the search path. Possible values include "app-defaults", "help", and "bitmaps".

The *suffix* parameter is an extension appended to the file name; possible values include ".txt" and ".dat". You can also use the suffix to look for a file in a directory named by the *filename* parameter. For example, if the bitmaps directory of /usr/include/X11 includes a directory named with the *filename* parameter, and this directory includes a file named "icon.bm", a program calls XtResolvePathname with type "bitmaps" and with suffix "/icon.bm".

The caller of XtResolvePathname must free the returned file name using XtFree when it is no longer needed.

The language resource allows a system to have installed data files so that application text can be in different languages. Applications usually store all their displayable text as strings in their application defaults file, so translating the application can be as simple as providing an application defaults file with translated strings. A suggested default value for the default XtResolve-Pathname path on Unix systems is

/usr/lib/X11/%L/%T/%N%S:/usr/lib/X11/%l/%T/%N%S:/usr/lib/X11/%T/%N%S

This supports a system that has language directories in /usr/include/X11 for each installed language; the language directories in turn contain `app-defaults` directories, `help` directories, and so forth. If xnlLanguage has the value "Fr_Be" for Belgian French, `XtResolvePathname` looks for the following application defaults files for an application with class "Myprog".

```
/usr/lib/X11/Fr_Be/app-defaults/Myprog
/usr/lib/X11/Fr/app-defaults/Myprog
/usr/lib/X11/app-defaults/Myprog
```

`XtResolvePathname` first looks for the Belgian French application defaults file; if no such file exists, it looks for the plain French application defaults file and finally for the system default application defaults file.

The meaningful values for the xnlLanguage resource thus depend upon the names of the language directories the system supports.

The Intrinsics use `XtResolvePathname` to find the names of the application defaults file and the per-user application defaults file; see Section 3.5. To find the application defaults file, the Intrinsics call

```
XtResolvePathname(dpy,
        "app-defaults",            /* type */
        (String) NULL,             /* filename */
        (String) NULL,             /* suffix */
        (String) NULL,             /* path */
        (Substitution) NULL,       /* substitutions */
        0,                         /* num_substitutions */
        (XtFilePredicate) NULL);   /* predicate */
```

Finding the per-user application defaults file is more complicated since the Intrinsics must compatibly support an earlier lookup scheme from before `XtResolvePathname`. The Intrinsics call

```
XtResolvePathname(dpy,
        (String) NULL,             /* type */
        (String) NULL,             /* filename */
        (String) NULL,             /* suffix */
        path,                      /* path */
        (Substitution) NULL,       /* substitutions */
        0,                         /* num_substitutions */
        (XtFilePredicate) NULL);   /* predicate */
```

where *path* is defined in an operating-system-specific way. On Unix systems

- If the variable XUSERFILESEARCHPATH is defined in the user's environment, its value is the path.

- Else, if the variable XAPPLRESDIR is defined in the user's environment, the path is
  $XAPPLRESDIR/%L/%N:$XAPPLRESDIR/%l/%N:$XAPPLRESDIR/%N:$HOME/%N
  where $XAPPLRESDIR is replaced by the value of the XAPPLRESDIR variable and $HOME is replaced by the user's home directory.

• Else, the path is

    $HOME/%L/%N:$HOME/%1/%N:$HOME/%N

where $HOME is replaced by the user's home directory.

9.9   Selections

The X selection mechanism allows cooperating applications to pass data among themselves, using the X server as an intermediary. It is the mechanism applications and widgets use to implement "cut and paste." Most toolkit applications do not handle selections themselves; their widgets do this for them. If you need to handle selections in an application, read Section 9.13.

9.10   Getting the Most Recent Timestamp

Sometimes an application or widget needs a timestamp but does not have access to the event that triggered the action. This is especially true when working with selections. The calculator application in Chapter 10 provides an example; it needs a timestamp to request the selection value in the callback procedure for a menu item, but the callback does not pass an event or a timestamp. Similarly, an application must pass a timestamp to XtCallAcceptFocus but may not have one. XtLastTimestamp-Processed solves these problems.[5]

Time XtLastTimestampProcessed(*display*)
    Display **display*;
display   Specifies a display connection.

XtLastTimestampProcessed returns the timestamp from the most recent KeyPress, KeyRelease, ButtonPress, ButtonRelease, MotionNotify, EnterNotify, LeaveNotify, PropertyNotify, or SelectionClear event from the specified display that has gone through XtDispatchEvent. If no such event exists, XtLastTimestampProcessed returns zero.

In most circumstances where a programmer would be tempted to pass the symbolic constant CurrentTime to a procedure, it is more correct and therefore preferable to use XtLastTimestampProcessed. This will make the user less likely to encounter difficulties when running the application across a network with delays.

---

[5] XtLastTimestampProcessed is not supported by Intrinsics implementations that conform to specifications earlier than Release 4.

Writing Widgets

9.11   Graphics Contexts

Every widget that draws anything needs at least one graphics context. In many cases widget instances share these graphics contexts, considerably reducing the total number of contexts needed.

The Intrinsics provide routines to manage shared contexts. These contexts are treated as read-only; widget implementations are not allowed to modify the values in them since changing them would affect all widgets that use the same context. If an implementation needs a modifiable graphics context, it must use the Xlib XCreateGC and XFreeGC routines directly.

To obtain a read-only, shareable graphics context, use XtGetGC.

typedef unsigned long XtGCMask;

GC XtGetGC(*w, value_mask, values*)
    Widget *w*;
    XtGCMask *value_mask*;
    XGCValues **values*;

w	Specifies a widget used to find the screen and depth for the graphics context.
value_mask	Specifies the fields in the graphics context that are of interest.
values	Specifies the values for the fields specified in the value mask.

The widget parameter determines the screen and depth for which the graphics context is valid; the Intrinsics share graphics contexts only among widgets with the same screen and depth.

The value mask is the same as that passed to XCreateGC; see Section 5.3 of *Xlib* for a list of valid values and their meanings. The XGCValues structure is also the same as used by Xlib.

If XtGetGC cannot find a graphics context with the needed values, it creates one; otherwise, it increments a reference count for the shared context.

To release a graphics context obtained with XtGetGC, use XtReleaseGC.

void XtReleaseGC(*w, gc*)
    Widget *w*;
    GC *gc*;

w	Specifies a widget on the same display as the widget used to allocate the graphics context.
gc	Specifies the graphics context to release.

`XtReleaseGC` decrements the reference count for the graphics context and frees it if no more uses exist. Using `XtReleaseGC` on a graphics context created with `XCreateGC` is an error.

Programmers maintaining old code may encounter references to `XtDestroyGC`. This is an obsolete function and should be replaced with `XtReleaseGC` wherever it occurs.

9.12   Merging Exposures

Applications that choose not to use Intrinsics exposure compression (see, for example, Section 7.18) can still use the toolkit to merge rectangular areas specified by exposure events into a region. See Sections 10.5 and 10.6 of *Xlib* for more information on regions.

To add the rectangle in an Expose or GraphicsExpose event to a region, use XtAddExposureToRegion.

void XtAddExposureToRegion(*event, region*)
    XEvent *event*;
    Region *region*;
event   Specifies the exposure event.
region   Specifies the region.

If the event is not an Expose or GraphicsExpose event, `XtAddExposure-ToRegion` returns without modifying the region. Otherwise it sets the region to be the union of the rectangle specified in the event and the current value of the region.

To reset a region to the empty set of points, intersect it with an empty region.

9.13   Selections

X allows client applications to exchange data through a mechanism called *selections*. Selections are conceptually simple, but the mechanics of dealing with them directly through Xlib in a manner compliant with the ICCCM are quite complex. The Intrinsics offer a set of routines that simplify selection handling.

A selection refers to a piece of data that can be sent from one application to another. Selections are global to the X server; at any one time there is only one selection with a given name among all applications connected to a server.

Possible uses for selections include

- Selecting text in one application and inserting it in another.

- Selecting two pieces of text, possibly in different applications, and asking for them to be exchanged.

- Selecting text containing a file name and having an editor open the selected file.

- Selecting a line of text in an editor and having a debugger insert a breakpoint at that line.

- Selecting two pieces of text in a multifont text editor and requesting that the text in the first selection be displayed using the font of the second.

The selection model is very simple:

- An application tells the server that it wants to take ownership of the selection. The server notifies whichever application previously owned the selection, if any, that it is no longer the owner.

- Later, another application requests the selection value.

- The server asks the owning application for the selection value and notifies the requesting application, which retrieves it from the server.

The selection value is not actually transferred until an application requests it; the provider does not prestore the selection in the server.

One source of complexity arises from the way applications deliver selections. A selection request returns immediately. At a later time the server sends events to the requesting application indicating that the selection is available, and the requestor then must get the selection value from the server. The selection owner can transmit the value in several pieces if the value is large, and the requestor must get each piece and put them together into the selection.

The Intrinsics hide this by having the requestor supply a callback procedure. The toolkit handles all the communication with the server, only involving the application after fetching the selection and assembling the pieces.

Applications own and request selections by name, and there can be many different selections simultaneously active as long as they have different names. Names are represented by X atoms; PRIMARY and SECONDARY are predefined atoms that refer to selections, but cooperating applications are free to choose other selection names if this is useful.

As an example, consider three active applications, P, R, and S. Assume application P has taken ownership of the primary selection and application S has taken ownership of the secondary selection. Application R requests the value of either selection by name; it does not have to know which application happens to own the desired selection when it makes the request.

Although the X protocol does not assign any meanings to selection names, the ICCCM defines conventions for the meanings of selections:

PRIMARY   The main selection; most operations that use just one selection use the primary selection. Examples include text transfer between applications, opening a selected file name in an editor, and setting a debugger breakpoint at a selected line in a file.

SECONDARY   An alternative selection used for operations that need two selections or for operations that do not want to disturb the primary selection. Examples include swapping two selected text strings and applying the looks of one string to another string in a multifont editor.

CLIPBOARD   A selection sometimes used for cutting and pasting pieces of data between applications; its use overlaps with the primary selection. Application suites that use the clipboard selection often include a special clipboard application that maintains the value of the clipboard selection; this allows a user to make a clipboard selection in one application, exit that application, and then start up another application that fetches the value from the clipboard.

Only documentation can resolve which selection names to use, since applications must agree on the names. An application that stores selected text in the primary selection cannot interact with another application that requests it from the clipboard selection.

Selections have target types associated with them, but these types are not quite the same thing as types in a programming language. They reflect different kinds of information about the selection that the provider is willing to supply. For example, an editor could provide the selection as a text string, meaning the actual characters selected; as a file name, meaning the name of the file being edited; and as a line number, meaning the line in the file that the selection occurs on. The selection requestor specifies the target type of the selection when requesting it. A terminal emulator requests the selection as text and inserts it as characters typed by the user. A text editor requests it as text and uses it as the name of a file to edit. A debugger requests the selection twice, as a file name and as a line number, to set a breakpoint within the file.

The selection target type is just another atom. The ICCCM defines a list of types that applications use, including STRING, FILE_NAME, LINE_NUMBER, and many others. This list is not exclusive; any two applications can agree on additional target types that they use to communicate. All applications using a particular target type must agree on the format of the data in the selection value. The ICCCM defines formats for ICCCM target types. The STRING target type, for example, uses a string of bytes from the ISO Latin-1 encoding with null bytes separating any subparts. The LINE_NUMBER target type uses two 32-bit integers to indicate the lines on which the selection begins and ends. Selection values always come with their lengths so that the requestor knows the size of the data.

Some of the atoms used in selections have predefined atom values; instead of converting a string to an atom you can use the predefined atom values. The predefined atoms most useful for selections are XA_PRIMARY, XA_SECONDARY, XA_ATOM, and XA_STRING, but any of the predefined atoms described in Section 4.2 of *Xlib* can be used. Use the Intrinsics string-to-atom conversion rather than XInternAtom since the Intrinsics cache the atom values.

You now have enough background to understand the actual toolkit selection routines. Examples of their use are given in the calculator application and Label implementation in Chapter 10. Programmers need not go to any special effort to shortcut the selection mechanism when communicating selections within a single application; the Intrinsics do this automatically.

9.13.1 Getting the Selection Value

A program requests the current value of a selection by using XtGet-SelectionValue.

```
void XtGetSelectionValue(w, selection, target, callback, client_data, time)
    Widget w;
    Atom selection;
    Atom target;
    XtSelectionCallbackProc callback;
    XtPointer client_data;
    Time time;
```

w	Specifies the widget that is making the request. This widget must be realized.
selection	Specifies the selection desired (e.g., XA_PRIMARY).

target	Specifies the type of information that is requested about the selection.
callback	Specifies the procedure to call when the selection becomes available.
client_data	Specifies a piece of data to pass to the callback procedure.
time	Specifies the timestamp of the event that triggered the selection request.

The Intrinsics call the callback procedure at some time in the future to deliver the selection data; they may call it before or after `XtGetSelectionValue` returns, but they always call it exactly once for each call to `XtGet-SelectionValue`.

The *time* parameter avoids race conditions in the selection mechanism that could result in delivering the value of a selection made after the selection request. This must be a valid timestamp from some X event; the value Current-Time is not acceptable. Programs normally request the selection as a result of receiving some event from the user and pass the timestamp in this event. `XtLastTimestampProcessed` is also useful for finding a timestamp; see Section 9.10.

When the selection value is ready, the Intrinsics call the selection callback procedure. This procedure is of type `XtSelectionCallbackProc`.

```
typedef void (*XtSelectionCallbackProc) (Widget, XtPointer, Atom *, Atom *,
                                  XtPointer, unsigned long *, int *);
    Widget w;
    XtPointer client_data;
    Atom *selection;
    Atom *type;
    XtPointer value;
    unsigned long *length;
    int *format;
```

w	Specifies the widget that requested the selection value.
client_data	Specifies the client data passed to `XtGetSelectionValue`.
selection	Specifies the atom name of the selection being supplied.
type	Specifies the type of the selection.
value	Specifies the selection value. This storage must be freed using `XtFree` when it is no longer useful.
length	Specifies the length of the selection in the units specified by format.
format	Specifies the unit size.

The Intrinsics only call the selection callback procedure after assembling the selection from any subparts in which it may have arrived.

If the Intrinsics could not fetch the selection value, *type* points to the value None and value is NULL. This happens if there was no selection currently available with the specified name or if the owner of the selection could not provide it in the target type requested.

The *type* parameter points to an atom describing the format of the returned data; it can be a predefined atom like XA_STRING or XA_INTEGER or it can be a special value defined by the target type. Each target type must define which atom goes with that target type. *Type* has the special value XT_CONVERT_FAIL when the Intrinsics cannot fetch the selection because the owner failed to respond within the selection timeout interval; this usually means that the selection owner died in the midst of transferring the selection.

Format points to 8, 16, or 32, depending upon whether the selection value is 8-bit bytes, 16-bit words, or 32-bit words. The format allows the X server to perform any necessary byte swapping when exchanging data between different machine architectures. *Length* specifies the size of the data in value in the units of *format*; in other words it contains the length in bytes if *format* is 8 and the length in words if *format* is 16 or 32. *Length* is the only way to know for sure how large the selection is; byte stream selections do not normally include a terminating null byte.

A program requests the current selection in more than one target type simultaneously by using `XtGetSelectionValues`. This helps, for example, a debugger that fetches the current selection both as a file name and as a line number. `XtGetSelectionValues` is atomic; the selection cannot change in the midst of getting the selection values so all returned values always apply to the same instance of the selection.

```
void XtGetSelectionValues(w, selection, targets, count, callback, client_data, time)
    Widget w;
    Atom selection;
    Atom *targets;
    int count;
    XtSelectionCallbackProc callback;
    XtPointer *client_data;
    Time time;
```
w   Specifies the widget that is making the request. This widget must be realized.

selection   Specifies the selection desired (e.g., XA_PRIMARY).

targets	Specifies a list of the types of information that are requested about the selection.
count	Specifies the number of target types in targets.
callback	Specifies the procedure to call when the selection becomes available.
client_data	Specifies a list of pieces of data to pass to the callback procedure.
time	Specifies the timestamp of the event that triggered the selection request.

A call to `XtGetSelectionValues` is similar to *count* calls to `XtGet-SelectionValue`, one for each target type. The Intrinsics call the selection callback once for each target type and pass the corresponding value in the client data list to the selection callback. All other parameters, both to `XtGet-SelectionValues` and to the selection callback, are identical to those with `XtGetSelectionValue`. The order in which the Intrinsics return the selection values is not defined.

9.13.2   Providing the Selection

A widget asserts ownership of a selection by calling `XtOwnSelection`.

Boolean XtOwnSelection(*w, selection, time, convert_proc, lose_selection, done_proc*)
    Widget *w*;
    Atom *selection*;
    Time *time*;
    XtConvertSelectionProc *convert_proc*;
    XtLoseSelectionProc *lose_selection*;
    XtSelectionDoneProc *done_proc*;

w	Specifies the widget wishing to become the selection owner. This widget must be realized.
selection	Specifies the selection desired (e.g., XA_PRIMARY.
time	Specifies the timestamp of the event that triggered selection ownership.
convert_proc	Specifies a procedure to call whenever the selection value is requested.
lose_selection	Specifies a procedure to call if the widget loses ownership of the selection, or NULL if the widget is not interested in being notified of this.
done_proc	Specifies a procedure to call after successfully transferring a supplied selection, or NULL if the widget is not interested in being notified of this.

`XtOwnSelection` informs the Intrinsics that the widget wants to own the selection. It returns TRUE if the widget successfully becomes the owner and FALSE if the attempt failed, usually because another client has requested ownership with a timestamp that is later than the one supplied in the *time* parameter. Widgets often highlight the selection in some way to inform the user what the current selection is, but they should not do so if the attempt to take ownership fails.

The *time* parameter must be a valid timestamp from an X event; the value CurrentTime is not acceptable. Widgets usually assert ownership of the selection as a result of some user event, and the timestamp is the one from the event that triggered ownership.

If, at a future time, an application requests the value of the selection, the Intrinsics call the convert procedure. This is of type `XtConvert-SelectionProc`.

```
typedef Boolean (*XtConvertSelectionProc) (Widget, Atom *, Atom *, Atom *,
                                           XtPointer *, unsigned long *, int *);
        Widget w;
        Atom *selection;
        Atom *target;
        Atom *type_return;
        XtPointer *value_return;
        unsigned long *length_return;
        int *format_return;
```

w	Specifies the widget that asserted ownership of the selection.
selection	Specifies the selection.
target	Specifies the type of information about the selection that is desired.
type_return	Specifies a pointer to an atom that the type of the returned data should be stored into.
value_return	Specifies a pointer to a pointer that the selection value should be stored into.
length_return	Specifies a pointer to a size field that the length of the selection should be stored into, in units of *format_return*.
format_return	Specifies a pointer to a size field that the size in bits of the data elements of the selection should be stored into.

This is called a selection conversion procedure since it is responsible for converting the selection into the specified target type. If this procedure is unable to provide the current selection in the desired target type, it returns FALSE and does not update any of the return parameters. If it can provide the selection in the desired target type, it returns TRUE and updates the return parameters.

The convert procedure sets *type_return* to an atom that represents the type of the data. This is constant for each target type.

Value_return returns the actual selection value. If the widget specified no corresponding done procedure in the call to XtOwnSelection, *value_return* must point to a block of storage allocated by XtMalloc. The Intrinsics automatically free this storage after transferring the selection to the requestor. If there is a corresponding done procedure, the selection owner manages the storage any way it wishes; the Intrinsics will call the done procedure later to notify the widget that the selection has been transferred and that the storage can be reclaimed.

The convert procedure sets *length_return* and *format_return* to indicate the size of the selection data. *Format_return* should be 8 if the selection value consists of bytes and 16 or 32 if it consists of a series of words; mixing data of different sizes within the same selection is disallowed since it prevents the byte swapping that may be necessary when communicating between different machine architectures. *Length_return* should specify the length of the selection in units of *format_return*: in bytes if *format_return* is 8 and in words if *format_return* is 16 or 32.

If the selection is requested more than once, the Intrinsics call the convert procedure for each selection request; no caching of the selection value occurs.

The ICCCM specifies three target types that any selection owner must support, MULTIPLE, TIMESTAMP, and TARGETS. MULTIPLE requests the selection in multiple target types, and TIMESTAMP requests the timestamp used to assert selection ownership. The Intrinsics handle both of these target types internally, translating a MULTIPLE request into a series of calls to the convert procedure.

Convert procedures must respond to the TARGETS type themselves. They return as the selection a list of the target types that they are willing to convert to. The returned selection is a list of atoms, and the type is XA_ATOM.

The code to reply to TARGETS generally looks something like this, where NUM is the number of supported target types:

```
Atom targets;
XrmValue source, dest;

source.size = strlen("TARGETS")+1;
source.addr = "TARGETS";
dest.size = sizeof(Atom);
dest.addr = &targets;
```

```
(void) XtConvertAndStore(w, XtRString, &source, XtRAtom, &dest);

if (*target == targets) {
    Atom *targets = (Atom *) XtMalloc(NUM * sizeof(Atom));
    *type = XA_ATOM;
    targets[0] = <first supported target type>;
    targets[1] = <second supported target type>;
    ...
    *value = (XtPointer) targets;
    *length = NUM;
    *format = 32;
    return TRUE;
}
```

The Intrinsics notify the selection owner that they successfully transferred the selection by calling the selection done procedure passed to `XtOwn-Selection`. This is of type `XtSelectionDoneProc`.

typedef void (*XtSelectionDoneProc) (Widget, Atom *, Atom *);
> Widget *w*;
> Atom **selection*;
> Atom **target*;

w	Specifies the widget that asserted ownership of the selection.
selection	Specifies the selection.
target	Specifies the type of information about the selection that was requested.

After the Intrinsics transfer the selection to the requestor they call the selection done procedure. They call it once for each selection request; it is responsible for freeing the selection value if appropriate. There is no guarantee that calls to the selection convert and selection done procedures will alternate; the Intrinsics can call the convert procedure several times before calling the done procedure.

Selection done procedures are optional; if a request to take ownership specifies NULL as the *done_proc* parameter to `XtOwnSelection`, the Intrinsics assume that the selection value is in allocated storage and free it after transferring the selection.

Applications lose ownership of a selection in two ways. If some application (it can be the same application or another one) requests selection ownership at a later time, the current owner loses ownership. Alternatively, the application that requested ownership can voluntarily give it up by calling `XtDisownSelection`. In either case the Intrinsics notify the current selection owner that it lost the selection by calling the lose selection procedure specified in the call to `XtOwnSelection`. A lose selection procedure is of type `XtLoseSelectionProc`.

```
typedef void (*XtLoseSelectionProc) (Widget, Atom *);
    Widget w;
    Atom *selection;
w               Specifies the widget that asserted ownership of the selection.
selection       Specifies the selection.
```

Lose selection procedures are optional; if a widget does not need to know when it loses the selection, it specifies NULL as the *lose_selection* parameter to `XtOwnSelection`. The Intrinsics do not call the lose selection procedure if the attempt to own the selection failed in the first place. The Intrinsics call the lose selection procedure to notify the widget that it has already lost the selection, not to ask it to relinquish the selection; this procedure should not call `XtDisownSelection`.

Example 9.1 shows the selection convert and lose selection procedures for Label. DeliverSelection lets the Intrinsics take care of freeing the selection value by returning it in allocated storage and providing no done procedure. LoseSelection notifies the application that the selection has been lost by executing the XtNloseSelection callbacks.

Widgets that have previously taken selection ownership relinquish it by calling `XtDisownSelection`.

```
void XtDisownSelection(w, selection, time)
    Widget w;
    Atom selection;
    Time time;
w               Specifies the widget that wishes to relinquish ownership.
selection       Specifies the selection the widget no longer wishes to own.
time            Specifies the timestamp from the event that triggered relinquishing
                the selection.
```

If the widget does not currently own the selection, either because it never had the selection to begin with or because the selection has already been lost, `XtDisownSelection` returns without doing anything. Otherwise it relinquishes the selection and calls the lose selection procedure specified when ownership was asserted, if any.

```
static Boolean DeliverSelection(w, selection, target,
        type, value, length, format)
    Widget w;
    Atom *selection, *target, *type;
    XtPointer *value;
    unsigned long *length;
    int *format;
{
    LabelWidget lw = (LabelWidget) w;
    static Atom targets = 0;

    if (targets == 0) {
        targets = FetchAtom(w, "TARGETS");
    }

    if (*target == targets) {
        *type = XA_ATOM;
        *value = (XtPointer) XtNew(Atom);
        *(Atom *) *value = XA_STRING;
        *length = 1;
        *format = 32;
        return TRUE;
    }

    if (*target == XA_STRING) {
        *type = XA_STRING;
        *value = (XtPointer) XtNewString(lw->label.label);
        *length = lw->label.label_len;
        *format = 8;
        return TRUE;
    }

    return FALSE;
}

static void LoseSelection(w, selection)
    Widget w;
    Atom *selection;
{
    LabelWidget lw = (LabelWidget) w;

    XtCallCallbackList(lw, lw->label.lose_selection,
            (XtPointer) selection);
}
```

Example 9.1. The Label selection handling procedures

```
Boolean LabelSelectText(w, selection, own)
    Widget w;
    Atom selection;
    Boolean own;
{
    /* Check that we're in Label or a subclass */

    XtCheckSubclass(w, labelWidgetClass, NULL);

    /* Call the class method */

    return (*((LabelWidgetClass) XtClass(w))->label_class.select)
            (w, selection, own);
}

/* Label's select implementation */

static Boolean SelectText(w, selection, own)
    Widget w;
    Atom selection;
    Boolean own;
{
    LabelWidget lw = (LabelWidget) w;

    if (own) {
        return XtOwnSelection(w, selection,
                XtLastTimestampProcessed(XtDisplay(w)),
                DeliverSelection, LoseSelection,
                (XtSelectionDoneProc) NULL);
    } else {
        XtDisownSelection(w, selection,
                XtLastTimestampProcessed(XtDisplay(w)));
        return TRUE;
    }
}
```

Example 9.2. The Label select text method

After a widget calls XtDisownSelection the Intrinsics no longer call the
selection convert procedure, even to handle selection requests with timestamps within the period when the widget owned the selection. The Intrinsics
still call the selection done procedure, however, if a selection provided before
the call to XtDisownSelection is not fully transferred until after the call to
XtDisownSelection.

Example 9.2 shows the Label widget's implementation of its select method.
LabelSelectText is the external entry point applications call; it extracts the

select procedure from the class method and calls it. SelectText is Label's select procedure.

If the *own* parameter is TRUE, SelectText attempts to take selection ownership by calling XtOwnSelection, passing DeliverSelection as the selection conversion procedure, LoseSelection as the lose selection procedure, and no selection done procedure. If the *own* parameter is FALSE, SelectText disowns the selection by calling XtDisownSelection. Both calls use XtLast-TimestampProcessed (see Section 9.10) since the application calling the method usually has no idea what timestamp to pass.

9.14   Incremental Selections

The X protocol allows selections to be passed between applications incrementally: rather than supplying the selection as one single piece, a selection owner can send it in multiple, smaller pieces. This is useful for transmitting very large selections, since the protocol has a maximum selection size, and is also useful for applications like text editors that do not store the data the selection comes from contiguously. Rather than concatenating all the individual pieces of data into a single selection, the owner provides them using incremental selection transfers.

The Intrinsics selection mechanism handles incremental selections transparently. If a supplied selection value is larger than the protocol maximum, the Intrinsics break it up into smaller pieces. If a selection arrives in pieces, the Intrinsics gather all the pieces and concatenate them before delivering them to the requestor.

The Intrinsics also provide a parallel set of selection routines that allows the selection owner to send the selection incrementally or the selection requestor to receive each selection piece as it arrives.[6] There is no need for the selection owner and requestor to agree on whether they are using incremental selections—if a selection delivered incrementally is requested as one piece, the Intrinsics concatenate the pieces, and if a selection delivered as one piece is requested incrementally, the Intrinsics only deliver one piece to the requestor.

The following descriptions of the incremental selection interface only explain how the incremental routines differ from the atomic interface that handles the selection as one piece.

---

[6] The incremental selection interface is not supported by Intrinsics implementations that conform to specifications earlier than Release 4.

9.14.1   Getting the Selection Value Incrementally

A program requests the current value of a selection incrementally by using
`XtGetSelectionValueIncremental`.

void XtGetSelectionValueIncremental(*w, selection, target, selection_callback, client_data,*
time)

> Widget *w*;
> Atom *selection*;
> Atom *target*;
> XtSelectionCallbackProc *selection_callback*;
> XtPointer *client_data*;
> Time *time*;

w	Specifies the widget that is making the request. This widget must be realized.
selection	Specifies the selection desired (e.g., XA_PRIMARY).
target	Specifies the type of information that is requested about the selection.
selection_callback	Specifies the procedure to call whenever a piece of the selection becomes available.
client_data	Specifies a piece of data to pass to the callback procedures.
time	Specifies the timestamp of the event that triggered the selection request.

The Intrinsics call the selection callback procedure whenever a piece of the selection arrives; after all pieces arrive, the Intrinsics call it once more with a *length* of zero and a non-NULL *value*. If the selection arrives in one piece, the Intrinsics call the selection callback twice; once with the data and once with *length* zero. The selection callback must always free the value when the value is not NULL, even if the length is zero.

As with atomic transfers, the Intrinsics pass XT_CONVERT_FAIL as the type if they cannot fully fetch the selection, usually because the selection owner terminated before supplying all the pieces of the selection. The Intrinsics may have already delivered some pieces; it is up to the callback to decide if the partially delivered selection is meaningful.

To request the selection for multiple target types with incremental delivery, use `XtGetSelectionValuesIncremental`.

void XtGetSelectionValuesIncremental(*w, selection, targets, count, selection_callback,*
client_data, time)

> Widget *w*;

> Atom *selection*;
> Atom **targets*;
> int *count*;
> XtSelectionCallbackProc *selection_callback*;
> XtPointer *client_data*;
> Time *time*;

w	Specifies the widget that is making the request. This widget must be realized.
selection	Specifies the selection desired (e.g., XA_PRIMARY).
targets	Specifies a list of the types of information that are requested about the selection.
count	Specifies the number of target types in targets.
selection_callback	Specifies the procedure to call whenever a piece of the selection becomes available.
client_data	Specifies a piece of data to pass to the callback procedures.
time	Specifies the timestamp of the event that triggered the selection request.

There is no interface to request the selection in multiple target types with some targets being atomic and some incremental.

9.14.2 Providing the Selection Incrementally

A widget asserts ownership of a selection and provides it incrementally by calling XtOwnSelectionIncremental.

> Boolean XtOwnSelectionIncremental(*w, selection, time, convert_callback, lose_callback,*
> *done_callback, cancel_callback, client_data*)
> Widget *w*;
> Atom *selection*;
> Time *time*;
> XtConvertSelectionIncrProc *convert_callback*;
> XtLoseSelectionIncrProc *lose_callback*;
> XtSelectionDoneIncrProc *done_callback*;
> XtCancelConvertSelectionProc *cancel_callback*;
> XtPointer *client_data*;

w	Specifies the widget wishing to become the selection owner. This widget must be realized.
selection	Specifies the selection desired (e.g., XA_PRIMARY).
time	Specifies the timestamp of the event that triggered selection ownership.
convert_proc	Specifies a procedure to call whenever a piece of the selection value is requested.

lose_selection   Specifies a procedure to call if the widget loses ownership of the selection, or NULL if the widget is not interested in being notified of this.

done_proc   Specifies a procedure to call after successfully transferring a supplied selection, or NULL if the widget is not interested in being notified of this.

cancel_callback   Specifies a callback procedure to call if the owner aborts sending the rest of the selection, or NULL if the widget is not interested in being notified of this.

client_data   Specifies a piece of data to be passed to each of the callback procedures.

XtOwnSelectionIncremental differs from XtOwnSelection in that it has a cancel callback that the Intrinsics call if the requesting application fails to respond within the selection timeout interval. This usually means that the requesting application terminated. XtOwnSelectionIncremental also passes client data to each callback, which should have also been done with XtOwnSelection but somehow was not.

The procedures involved all take an additional parameter, the *request_id*. This enables the selection owner to distinguish multiple requests that are going on in parallel. If the owner has already provided the first chunk of the selection to one requestor when another request comes in, the *request_id* allows the selection owner to distinguish the first request, for which it should return the second chunk, from the second request, for which it should return the first chunk.

The incremental selection conversion procedure is of type XtConvert-SelectionIncrProc.

```
typedef XtPointer XtRequestId;

typedef Boolean (*XtConvertSelectionIncrProc) (Widget, Atom *, Atom *, Atom *,
                                               XtPointer *, unsigned long *, int *,
                                               unsigned long *, XRequestId *);
        Widget w;
        Atom *selection;
        Atom *target;
        Atom *type_return;
        XtPointer *value_return;
        unsigned long *length_return;
        int *format_return;
```

```
        unsigned long *max_length;
        XtPointer client_data;
        XtRequestId *request_id;
```

w	Specifies the widget that asserted ownership of the selection.
selection	Specifies the selection.
target	Specifies the type of information about the selection that is desired.
type_return	Specifies a pointer to an atom that the type of the returned data should be stored into.
value_return	Specifies a pointer to a pointer that the selection value should be stored into.
length_return	Specifies a pointer to a size field that the length of the selection should be stored into, in units of *format_return*.
format_return	Specifies a pointer to a size field that the size in bits of the data elements of the selection should be stored into.
max_length	Specifies the maximum amount of data, in bytes, that the convert procedure can return.
client_data	Specifies the client data passed to `XtOwnSelection-Incremental`.
request_id	Specifies the request id.

The Intrinsics call this procedure to request each piece of the selection. When there is no more data to transfer, it stores zero into *length_return*.

When a program takes ownership of the selection atomically, the Intrinsics automatically break up the selection value and send it incrementally if the length is greater than the maximum allowable transfer size. If a program takes ownership incrementally, the Intrinsics do not break up the individual pieces. It is up to the convert procedure to make sure that it does not provide more data than the value in *max_length* in any one piece.

If the incremental selection owner wants to be notified when the selection is transferred, it provides a selection done procedure of type `XtSelectionDoneIncrProc`.

```
typedef void (*XtSelectionDoneIncrProc) (Widget, Atom *, Atom *, XtRequestId *,
                                         XtPointer);
    Widget w;
    Atom *selection;
    Atom *target;
    XtRequestId *request_id;
    XtPointer client_data;
```

w	Specifies the widget that asserted ownership of the selection.
selection	Specifies the selection.
target	Specifies the type of information about the selection that was requested.
client_data	Specifies the client data passed to `XtOwnSelection-Incremental`.
request_id	Specifies the request id.

If the selection owner does not provide a selection done procedure, the Intrinsics assume each piece of the selection was stored in allocated storage and free the pieces after the selection has been transferred. As with the atomic procedures, the Intrinsics guarantee no ordering among calls to the convert selection procedure and the selection done procedure, but they always call the done procedure once for each series of calls to the convert procedure with one *request_id*.

If the incremental selection owner wants to be notified when it loses the selection, it provides a lose selection procedure of type `XtLoseSelection-IncrProc`.

```
typedef void (*XtLoseSelectionselectionIncrProc) (Widget, Atom *, XtPointer);
    Widget w;
    Atom *selection;
    XtPointer client_data;
```

w	Specifies the widget that asserted ownership of the selection.
selection	Specifies the selection.
client_data	Specifies the client data passed to `XtOwnSelection-Incremental`.

The Intrinsics notify the selection owner that the application requesting the selection failed to respond within the selection timeout by calling the cancel convert procedure, which is of type `XtCancelConvertSelectionProc`.

```
typedef void (*XtCancelConvertSelectionProc) (Widget, Atom *, Atom *,
                                              XtRequestId *, XtPointer);
    Widget w;
    Atom *selection;
    Atom *target;
    XtRequestId *request_id;
    XtPointer client_data;
```

w	Specifies the widget that asserted ownership of the selection.
selection	Specifies the selection.

target	Specifies the type of information about the selection that was requested.
client_data	Specifies the client data passed to `XtOwnSelection-Incremental`.
request_id	Specifies the request id.

After calling this procedure, the Intrinsics will not call the convert procedure to supply any further pieces of the selection with this *request_id*. The widget frees any memory or other resources involved in the selection.

If the cancel convert procedure is NULL, the Intrinsics assume, as with the done procedure, that each piece already delivered is in allocated storage and free the pieces. Usually both of these procedures are NULL if either one is.

Selection owners using the incremental interface voluntarily relinquish ownership with `XtDisownSelection` just as do atomic selection owners.

9.15 Getting the Selection Request Event

The Intrinsics automatically handle calling the selection convert procedure when they receive a SelectionRequest event. All the information most convert procedures need is passed into the procedure as parameters; however, a convert procedure can retrieve the selection request event if it needs to use other fields by calling `XtGetSelectionRequest`.[7]

```
XSelectionRequestEvent *XtGetSelectionRequest(w, selection, request_id);
    Widget w;
    Atom selection;
    XtRequestId request_id;
```

w	Specifies the widget that currently owns the selection.
selection	Specifies the current selection being processed.
request_id	Specifies the request id.

If called from within a convert selection procedure, `XtGetSelection-Request` returns the event that triggered the selection conversion. If called elsewhere, it returns NULL. *Request_id* is only meaningful for incremental selection conversions; atomic conversions specify NULL.

Consult the ICCCM for information on selection targets that require additional fields from the selection event.

---

[7] `XtGetSelectionRequest` is not supported by Intrinsics implementations that conform to specifications earlier than Release 4.

9.16   Selection Timeouts

Transferring a selection between applications involves many transactions between the selection provider and the selection requestor. The Intrinsics have a maximum time that they wait for a response from another application involved in a selection transfer. This timeout can be set by specifying the XtNselectionTimeout application resource in the application default file, by specifying the –selectionTimeout command line option, or by calling `XtAppSetSelectionTimeout`.

```
void XtAppSetSelectionTimeout(app_context, timeout)
    XtAppContext app_context;
    unsigned long timeout;
```
app_context   Specifies the application context.
timeout   Specifies the selection timeout in milliseconds.

To get the current timeout value, use `XtAppGetSelectionTimeout`.

```
unsigned long XtAppGetSelectionTimeout(app_context)
    XtAppContext app_context;
```
app_context   Specifies the application context.

The return value is the selection timeout value in milliseconds.

The default value for the selection timeout is five seconds. You rarely, if ever, have to concern yourself with this value unless you are running an application across a network with long delays.

Chapter 10

Pulling It All Together

Writing Applications

This chapter describes the widget set used in this guide and gives some complete sample applications. The applications include suggested modifications as programming exercises.

10.1 The Sample Widgets

The sample programs presented here use the widgets implemented in the second part of this chapter.

10.1.1 The Label Widget

The Label widget class has *labelWidgetClass* as its class pointer. It is a subclass of Widget and so supports all widget resources and the following additional ones:

Name	Class	Type	Default
XtNlabel	XtCLabel	String	special
XtNfont	XtCFont	XFontStruct *	XtDefaultFont
XtNforeground	XtCForeground	Pixel	XtDefaultForeground
XtNjustify	XtCJustify	Justify	Left
XtNspace	XtCSpace	Dimension	2
XtNloseSelection	XtCLoseSelection	XtCallbackList	NULL

XtNlabel is the text to display in the label. Its default value is the name of the widget instance.

XtNfont is the font to use to display the label text. The Label widget does not make its own copy of the font since its value usually comes from the resource cache, so applications must be sure to allocate permanent storage for this resource if they specify it directly.

XtNforeground is the pixel value to use to display the label text.

XtNjustify is an enumeration that defines whether the label text is left-justified, centered, or right-justified in the label's window. Its definition is

```
typedef enum { Center, Left, Right } Justify;
```

Label provides a type converter to convert the strings "center", "left", and "right" to justification values.

XtNspace is the amount of space to leave between the label text and the edges of the label's window.

XtNloseSelection is a callback list to notify the application that selection ownership requested through LabelSelectText has been lost. It passes the address of the lost selection in *call_data.*

Label modifies the default value of the XtNborderWidth resource to be zero. Labels by default have no translations.

If no width is specified for a label or if the width is set to zero through XtSetValues, the label computes a width equal to the width of its text string in its font plus twice the value of its XtNspace resource. If no height is specified or if the height is set to zero, the label computes a height equal to the height of characters in its font plus twice the value of its XtNspace resource. Label automatically recomputes calculated dimensions whenever the text string or the font changes.

Label provides one new class method, LabelSelectText:

Boolean LabelSelectText(*w, selection, own*);
    Widget *w;*
    Atom *selection;*
    Boolean *own;*

If *own* is TRUE, Label takes ownership of the specified selection; the selection value is the label's text string. If *own* is FALSE, Label relinquishes ownership of the selection. If a Label widget loses ownership of a selection, either through LabelSelectText with *own* FALSE or because another client takes ownership of the selection, Label calls the XtNloseSelection callbacks.

10.1.2　The Pushbutton Widget

The Pushbutton widget class has *pushbuttonWidgetClass* as its class pointer. It is a subclass of Label and so supports all of Label's resources and the following additional ones:

Name	Class	Type	Default
XtNcallback	XtCCallback	XtCallbackList	NULL
XtNinsensitiveForeground	XtCForeground	Pixel	special
XtNinsensitivePixmap	XtCPixmap	Pixmap	special
XtNhighlightBorder	XtCBorderWidth	Dimension	1
XtNacceleratorString	XtCAcceleratorString	String	NULL

XtNcallback is the list of callback procedures to execute when the user activates the button.

XtNinsensitiveForeground is the foreground color to use to display the pushbutton text when the button is insensitive. It has no default value; if unspecified, the pushbutton uses the insensitive pixmap instead.

XtNinsensitivePixmap is the pixmap to use as the foreground when displaying the pushbutton text when the button is insensitive. Pushbutton only uses it when XtNinsensitiveForeground is not specified. Its default value is a pixmap with the foreground color stippled to be at half intensity.

XtNhighlightBorder is the width of the extra border drawn to indicate that the widget is highlighted.

XtNacceleratorString is the string to display in the pushbutton to describe the widget's accelerator.

The Pushbutton widget modifies the default value of the XtNborderWidth resource to 1, overriding the Label widget's modification to zero.

The default translations for a pushbutton are

```
"<EnterWindow>  : highlight()           \n\
 <LeaveWindow>  : unhighlight()         \n\
 <Btn1Down>     : invert()              \n\
 <Btn1Up>       : notify() uninvert()"
```

Pushbutton defines the following actions:

highlight()　　　Draws an extra border within the pushbutton, normally to indicate that the button is armed and will activate if the user clicks a pointer button in the widget.

unhighlight()   Removes the extra border added by the highlight action.

invert()   Inverts the foreground and background colors of the widget, nor-
                   mally to indicate that the button will activate if the user releases the
                   pointer button in the widget.

uninvert()   Undoes the inversion performed by the invert action.

notify()   Calls the callback procedures specified by the XtNcallback resource.

Figure 10.1 shows pushbuttons in their normal, insensitive, highlighted, and
inverted states.

Figure 10.1. Pushbuttons in various states

10.1.3   The MenuItem Widget

The MenuItem widget class has *menuItemWidgetClass* as its class pointer. It is a
subclass of Pushbutton and so supports all of its resources. The only difference
is that it has a different set of default translations:

```
"<EnterWindow>  : invert()                \n\
 <LeaveWindow>  : uninvert()              \n\
 <BtnUp>        : notify() uninvert()"
```

This reflects the behavior of menus; when the menu pops up, the pointer
button is already depressed, and the menu item under the cursor inverts to
indicate that it will activate if the user releases the pointer button in that menu
item.

Figure 10.2 shows a menu with an inverted menu item.

Figure 10.2. A menu with an inverted item

10.1.4   **The Box Widget**

The Box widget class has *boxWidgetClass* as its class pointer. It is a subclass of Composite and so supports all resources defined for composite widgets and the following additional one:

Name	Class	Type	Default
XtNmargin	XtCMargin	Dimension	10

XtNmargin is the amount of extra space to leave on the right and bottom of the box when computing the ideal size to hold all the box's children.

The Box widget's layout algorithm is to accept the sizes and positions of its children as specified in their geometry resources. It allows its children to overlap each other if their geometries intersect. Box widgets always attempt to be sufficiently large to hold all their children, clipping the children if they cannot be large enough.

Box widgets can contain Label gadgets. The implementation tests if children are subclasses of labelGadgetClass, so any program that links in `Box.o` must also link in `LabelGadge.o`.

10.1.5   **The MinMax Widget**

The MinMax widget class has *minMaxWidgetClass* as its class pointer. It is a subclass of Constraint, and has the same resources as Box. MinMax defines the following constraint resources that applications can specify for children of a MinMax widget:

Name	Class	Type	Default
XtNminWidth	XtCMinWidth	int	special
XtNmaxWidth	XtCMaxWidth	int	special
XtNminHeight	XtCMinHeight	int	special
XtNmaxHeight	XtCMaxHeight	int	special

XtNminWidth is the minimum width for the child. Its default value is 1 if XtNmaxWidth is specified for the child or the child's initial width otherwise.

XtNmaxWidth is the maximum width for the child. Its default value is infinitely large if XtNminWidth is specified for the child or the child's initial width otherwise.

XtNminHeight is the minimum height for the child. Its default value is 1 if XtNmaxHeight is specified for the child or the child's initial height otherwise.

XtNmaxHeight is the maximum height for the child. Its default value is infinitely large if XtNminHeight is specified for the child or the child's initial height otherwise.

MinMax's layout algorithm is to accept the sizes and positions of its children as specified in their geometry resources. It always attempts to be sufficiently large to hold all the children. If it cannot be large enough to hold its children, it shrinks the children that would otherwise be clipped until either the children fit or they reach their minimum size. If any children are smaller than their maximum size and can grow without extending past the MinMax widget's boundaries, MinMax expands the children up to its boundaries or to their maximum size, whichever is smaller.

MinMax never moves its children; it only resizes them. It is usually not appropriate to specify width ranges for children that have other widgets to their right or height ranges for children that have other widgets below them. If a MinMax widget resizes such a child, it does not move the other children to keep the widgets from bumping into each other.

MinMax widgets can contain Label gadgets. The implementation tests if children are subclasses of labelGadgetClass, so any program that links in `MinMax.o` must also link in `LabelGadge.o`.

Figure 10.3 depicts the same MinMax widget in various sizes, showing how it resizes a child. In the first picture the MinMax widget is short enough that its child would have to be smaller than its minimum height to still fit, so the MinMax widget clips the child. In the last picture the MinMax widget is so tall that its child would have to be larger than its maximum height to fill it up, so there is unused space.

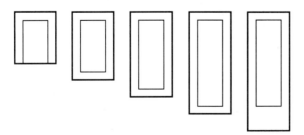

Figure 10.3. The same MinMax widget at different sizes

10.1.6   The Confirm Widget

The Confirm widget class has *confirmWidgetClass* as its class pointer. It is a compound widget that contains a label to display a text message and a push-button to dismiss the Confirm widget. Two implementations exist, one as a subclass of Box and one as a simple widget. Both define the same resources beyond those defined by Box:

Name	Class	Type	Default
XtNlabel	XtCLabel	String	"Click to confirm"
XtNbuttonLabel	XtCButtonLabel	String	"OK"
XtNcallback	XtCCallback	XtCallbackList	NULL
XtNlabelWidget	XtCReadOnly	Widget	special
XtNbuttonWidget	XtCReadOnly	Widget	special

XtNlabel is the text string to display in the Confirm widget.

XtNbuttonLabel is the text string to display in the Confirm widget's push-button.

XtNcallback is a list of callback procedures to execute when the user dismisses the Confirm widget.

XtNlabelWidget and XtNbuttonWidget are the two children of the Confirm widget. These are read-only resources and cannot be changed.

The two children of a Confirm widget are named "label" and "button". Applications specify resources for these two widgets in the normal manner in a resource file. If an application needs to change their resources dynamically, it finds the widget identifiers by calling `XtGetValues` for the XtNlabelWidget and XtNbuttonWidget resources of a Confirm widget.

The default callback procedure for the Confirm widget's pushbutton executes the callback procedures in the Confirm widget's XtNcallback resource and, if the Confirm widget is a child of a shell widget, pops down the shell. If the application creates a Confirm widget that is not a child of a shell, it is responsible for dismissing the Confirm widget itself in the application callback procedure.

The default size for a Confirm widget is large enough to hold its two children, stacked vertically.

Figure 10.4 shows a Confirm widget with its default strings.

Figure 10.4. A Confirm widget

10.1.7   The Menu Widget

The Menu widget class has *menuWidgetClass* as its class pointer. It is a subclass of Constraint and defines no additional resources. Menu modifies the default value of the XtNinsertPosition resource so that rather than always adding a new widget to the end of the menu, the menu inserts the child just before the widget specified by the XtNinsertBefore constraint resource of the new widget.

Menu defines the following constraint resource that applications specify for children of a menu:

Name	Class	Type	Default
XtNinsertBefore	XtCInsertBefore	Widget	NULL

XtNinsertBefore specifies which already existing child of the menu the new child precedes. If XtNinsertBefore is NULL, the new child goes at the end of the menu. Changing XtNinsertBefore using `XtSetValues` changes the order of the children. Querying XtNinsertBefore using `XtGetValues` returns the child that follows the queried child, or NULL if the child is the last one.

Menu provides a type converter from strings to widgets, allowing an application to specify a value for XtNinsertBefore in a resource file. The converter converts the string to the child of the menu that has the string as its name.

Menu's layout algorithm ignores the position information in its children's geometry resources and aligns the children vertically, packing them together so that their borders overlap. All children have the width of the widest child. Menu honors its children's height and border width values. Menus always attempt to be just large enough to hold their children.

Applications can safely pop up menus with a synchronous grab, and menus can contain Label gadgets. The implementation tests if children are subclasses of labelGadgetClass, so any program that links in `Menu.o` must also link in `LabelGadge.o`.

Figure 10.2 shows a menu.

10.1.8 The Label Gadget

The Label gadget class supports most of the functionality of the Label widget except selection handling and translations.[1] Its class pointer is *labelGadgetClass*, and it is a subclass of RectObj and so supports all resources defined for rectangle objects and the following additional ones:

Name	Class	Type	Default
XtNlabel	XtCLabel	String	special
XtNfont	XtCFont	XFontStruct *	XtDefaultFont
XtNforeground	XtCForeground	Pixel	XtDefaultForeground
XtNjustify	XtCJustify	Justify	Left
XtNspace	XtCSpace	Dimension	2
XtNbackground	XtCBackground	Pixel	XtDefaultBackground
XtNborder	XtCBorder	Pixel	XtDefaultForeground

All resources have the same semantics as the corresponding ones for the Label widget. Since the Label gadget does not support selections, there is no XtNloseSelection resource.

XtNbackground is the pixel value to use for displaying the background.

XtNborder is the pixel value to use for displaying the border.

Like the Label widget, the Label gadget modifies the default value of the XtNborderWidth resource to be zero. It uses the same procedure as the Label widget to calculate the width and height.

The Label gadget provides no new class methods.

The implementation of the Label gadget uses procedures in the Label widget implementation. Any program that links in `LabelGadge.o` must also link in `Label.o`.

10.1.9 The Graph Widget

The Graph widget class has *graphWidgetClass* as its class pointer. It is a subclass of Composite and so supports all resources defined for composite widgets and the following additional ones:

---

[1] Since a Label gadget is not a widget, it cannot support functionality that is limited to widgets. This includes installing event handlers on the gadget, changing the stacking order of overlapping gadgets, unmapping the gadget, and creating pop-up children of the gadget.

Name	Class	Type	Default
XtNnumEntries	XtCNumEntries	int	0
XtNlabels	XtCLabels	String *	NULL
XtNvalues	XtCValues	int *	NULL
XtNmaxValue	XtCMaxValue	int	100
XtNscale	XtCScale	int	1

XtNnumEntries is the number of entries in the XtNlabels and XtNvalues resources.

XtNlabels is a list of strings used to label the values being graphed. The Graph widget does not copy this resource; both the list and the strings in the list must be in permanent storage.

XtNvalues is a list of the values to display in the graph. The Graph widget copies this resource.

XtNmaxValue is the maximum value that can be displayed. It is usually used to scale the size of the graphics displaying the values.

XtNscale is a scale factor for the values being displayed. It does not usually affect the size of the graphics, but display methods that print the value as a number are expected to divide the values by the scale factor to obtain the number to display.

The application must give every Graph widget exactly one child, and this child must be a subclass of *graphDisplayObjectClass*. The class of the child determines the Graph widget's default size and how the Graph widget displays its values. See the system monitor application in Section 10.4 for an example of using a Graph widget.

Graph provides a type converter from XtRString to XtRStringTable. The source string should be NULL-terminated and contain embedded newline characters to separate the component strings.

10.1.10 The GraphDisplay Object

The GraphDisplay object class has *graphDisplayObjectClass* as its class pointer. It is a subclass of Object and so supports the resource defined for objects and the following additional ones:

Name	Class	Type	Default
XtNfont	XtCFont	XFontStruct *	XtDefaultFont
XtNforeground	XtCForeground	Pixel	XtDefaultForeground

XtNfont is a font used to display the graph contents.

XtNforeground is a color used to display the graph contents.

GraphDisplay is an abstract class; applications do not create instances of GraphDisplay. It exists to define the protocols that the Graph widget uses to communicate with its child and to provide resources commonly used by GraphDisplay subclasses.

10.1.11 The BarDisplay Object

The BarDisplay object class has *barDisplayObjectClass* as its class pointer. It is a subclass of GraphDisplay and so supports all the resources defined for Graph-Display and the following additional ones:

Name	Class	Type	Default
XtNspace	XtCSpace	Dimension	5
XtNdefaultGraphWidth	XtCDefaultGraphWidth	Dimension	200
XtNformat	XtCFormat	String	"%g"

XtNspace controls how much space the BarDisplay leaves between its bars and between the label, the bar, and the value for each entry.

XtNdefaultGraphWidth is the width that the bars in the bar graph take when at their maximum value, in the absence of other size constraints.

XtNformat is a `printf` format string that BarDisplay uses to display the value for each entry. It should contain a single conversion specification suitable for displaying a floating- point number (normally "%f", "%e", or "%g"), or it can be the empty string to disable displaying the value. It may not be NULL.

BarDisplay displays the values of its parent Graph widget as a horizontal bar graph with the labels at the left and the formatted value following the bar. The thickness of the bars equals the height of the BarDisplay's font as determined by the XtNfont resource of its superclass, GraphDisplay.

A BarDisplay child calculates its parent Graph widget's default size. The default width is the value of the XtNdefaultGraphWidth resource plus the amount of space needed to display the Graph widget's initial labels and values displayed in the BarDisplay's font, plus some space between the components as defined by the XtNspace resource. The default height is the number of items times the font height with XtNspace left between the bars and above and below the entire graph.

A BarDisplay child adjusts its display to use the actual width of its parent Graph widget, modifying the space it uses to display the bars. If a BarDisplay finds that its parent Graph widget is not wide enough to display the entire bar graph, it eliminates the bars and displays as a two-column table. It does not adjust to different heights of its parent; if the parent is not tall enough to display all the bars, the bottom bars are clipped.

BarDisplay objects should only be created as children of Graph widgets. See Figure 10.8 in the description of the system monitor program for a sample graph with a BarDisplay child.

10.2   A Desktop Calculator

The first sample application is a simple four-function calculator. It uses a Box widget to hold the calculator and Pushbutton widgets for all the buttons. It also uses a Pushbutton widget to display the current value; having this be a Pushbutton widget allows the application to invert the displayed number when the user selects it.

Figure 10.5 shows the calculator on the screen, and Figure 10.6 shows its widget tree.

Three functions are available through a pop-up menu. The user can select the value currently displayed to copy into another window, can request a selected number or equation from another window and evaluate it in the calculator, and can exit the application. These are in a pop-up menu only to illustrate how the Menu widget works; they could equally well be made into additional buttons on the calculator.

All buttons and menu items have text accelerators so the user can operate the calculator from the keyboard.

The calculator operates by maintaining two numeric values, the current input number and the running total. When the user invokes an operation, the calculator updates the running total with the current input number, using the

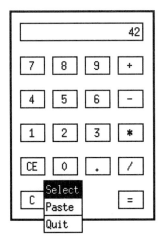

Figure 10.5. The calculator

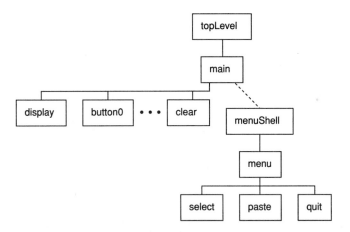

Figure 10.6. The calculator's widget tree

previous operation. For example, if the user enters 2 * 3 − 1 =, the following actions are performed:

2   Set the current input to 2.

*   Set the total to 2 since there is no pending operation, reset the current input to 0, and set the pending operation to "multiply".

3   Set the current input to 3.

−   Use the pending operation, multiply, to operate on the total and the current input, giving a new total, 6. Reset the current input to 0 and set the pending operation to "subtract".

1   Set the current input to 1.

=   Use the pending operation, subtract, to operate on the total and the current input, giving a new total, 5. Reset the current input to 0 and set the pending operation to nothing.

The first operation after an equals can do two different things. If no number was input between the equals and the next operation, the calculator keeps the current total; if a number was input, the total gets set to the current input. So in the two sequences

1 + 2 = * 3 =   The result is 9.

1 + 2 = 2 * 3 =   The result is 6.

This behavior duplicates that of most calculators.

10.2.1   The Implementation

The following pages give a running commentary on the calculator implementation. You can ignore the selection procedures if you are not interested in knowing how to implement selections.

The calculator must include `<X11/Xatom.h>` to fetch the current selection.

```
#include <X11/Intrinsic.h>
#include <X11/StringDefs.h>
#include <X11/Shell.h>
#include <X11/Xatom.h>
```

The four widget classes used are Box, Pushbutton, MenuItem, and Menu.

```
#include "Box.h"
#include "Pushbutton.h"
#include "MenuItem.h"
#include "Menu.h"
```

The *currentInput* and *total* variables hold the two values upon which the calculator operates. *InputDecimal* indicates whether the user has entered a decimal point in the current number, and *inputNumber* indicates whether he has entered any number at all since the last operation. *Scale* tells how much to scale new digits after the user enters a decimal point. *NumberToDisplay* points either to *total* or to *currentInput*, indicating which one should be displayed.

The *lastOp* variable holds the pending operation. *Start* is a special state indicating that there is no pending operation.

```
/* Calculator variables */
double currentInput = 0, total = 0;
Boolean inputDecimal = FALSE, inputNumber = FALSE;
double scale;
double *numberToDisplay = &total;

/* Pending operation */
typedef enum {Start, Equal, Add, Sub, Mul, Div} operation;
operation lastOp = Start;
```

The calculator needs to know when it owns the selection so that it can release it when the displayed value changes.

```
/* Interface variables */
XtAppContext app;
Widget display;              /* Calculator's display */
Widget menuShell;
Boolean hasSelection = FALSE;

void CreateInterface(), InputDigit(), InputDecimal(), Function(),
        Clear(), RefreshDisplay(), RepositionMenu(), Quit(), Select(),
        Paste(), PasteData(), LoseSelection();
```

The *actions* table associates the new action name "RepositionMenu" with the RepositionMenu action procedure.

```
XtActionsRec actions[] = {
    {"RepositionMenu", RepositionMenu}
};
```

The main program initializes the toolkit, getting an application shell to hold the calculator, and then registers the action names in the *actions* table with the Intrinsics. CreateInterface creates the widgets in the calculator, and Refresh-Display makes the *display* widget start up showing zero. The main program finally realizes the widgets and enters the application main loop.

```
int main(argc, argv)
    int argc;
    char *argv[];
{
    Widget toplevel;

    toplevel = XtAppInitialize(&app, "DemoCalc",
```

```
            (XrmOptionDescList) NULL, 0, &argc, argv,
            (String *) NULL, (ArgList) NULL, 0);

    XtAppAddActions(app, actions, XtNumber(actions));

    /* Make XtMenuPopup synchronous */
    XtRegisterGrabAction(XtMenuPopupAction, FALSE,
            ButtonPressMask | ButtonReleaseMask, GrabModeSync,
            GrabModeAsync);

    CreateInterface(toplevel);
    RefreshDisplay();
    XtRealizeWidget(toplevel);
    XtAppMainLoop(app);
}
```

CreateInterface creates the widgets in the calculator's user interface, using its
parameter as its shell. None of the widgets created here have any override
arguments; all resource values come from the application default file. Create-
Interface first creates a Box widget named "main" within the shell and then
creates a Pushbutton widget within the box for the calculator's display. It adds
the callback procedure LoseSelection to the XtNloseSelection callback list of
the *display* widget so the calculator knows when it has lost the selection.
CreateInterface then creates buttons for the digits and operations, associating
the appropriate callback procedure with each pushbutton. It creates a pop-up
shell to hold the menu, a menu within this pop-up shell, and the three items
in the menu. Finally it installs all the accelerators for descendants of the main
widget on the main widget, allowing the calculator to be operated from the
keyboard.

```
void CreateInterface(toplevel)
    Widget toplevel;
{
    Widget main, widget, menu;

    main = XtCreateManagedWidget("main", boxWidgetClass,
            toplevel, (Arg *) NULL, 0);
    display = XtCreateManagedWidget("display", pushbuttonWidgetClass,
            main, (Arg *) NULL, 0);
    XtAddCallback(display, XtNloseSelection,
            LoseSelection, (XtPointer) NULL);

#define CreatePushbutton(name, callback, data) \
        widget = XtCreateManagedWidget(name, pushbuttonWidgetClass, \
                main, (Arg *) NULL, 0); \
        XtAddCallback(widget, XtNcallback, callback, (XtPointer) data);
```

```
        CreatePushbutton("button0", InputDigit, 0);
        CreatePushbutton("button1", InputDigit, 1);
        CreatePushbutton("button2", InputDigit, 2);
        CreatePushbutton("button3", InputDigit, 3);
        CreatePushbutton("button4", InputDigit, 4);
        CreatePushbutton("button5", InputDigit, 5);
        CreatePushbutton("button6", InputDigit, 6);
        CreatePushbutton("button7", InputDigit, 7);
        CreatePushbutton("button8", InputDigit, 8);
        CreatePushbutton("button9", InputDigit, 9);

        CreatePushbutton("decimal", InputDecimal, NULL);

        CreatePushbutton("plus", Function, Add);
        CreatePushbutton("minus", Function, Sub);
        CreatePushbutton("times", Function, Mul);
        CreatePushbutton("divide", Function, Div);
        CreatePushbutton("equals", Function, Equal);

        CreatePushbutton("clearEntry", Clear, FALSE);
        CreatePushbutton("clear", Clear, TRUE);
#undef CreatePushbutton

        menuShell = XtCreatePopupShell("menuShell",
                overrideShellWidgetClass, main, (Arg *) NULL, 0);
        menu = XtCreateManagedWidget("menu", menuWidgetClass, menuShell,
                (Arg *) NULL, 0);

#define CreateMenuItem(name, callback) \
        widget = XtCreateManagedWidget(name, menuItemWidgetClass, \
                menu, (Arg *) NULL, 0); \
        XtAddCallback(widget, XtNcallback, callback, (XtPointer) NULL);

        CreateMenuItem("select", Select);
        CreateMenuItem("paste", Paste);
        CreateMenuItem("quit", Quit);
#undef CreateMenuItem
        XtInstallAllAccelerators(main, main);
}
```

InputDigit is the callback procedure associated with the number buttons. The *client_data* parameter is the digit displayed on the button. If the user has entered a decimal point, InputDigit multiplies the digit by the current scale factor, adds the result to the current input, and divides the scale factor by 10. Otherwise InputDigit multiplies the current input by 10 and adds in the new digit. In either case, InputDigit makes the display show the current input by setting *numberToDisplay* to *currentInput* and calling RefreshDisplay. InputDigit sets *inputNumber* to TRUE to inform the operation code that a number exists.

```
void InputDigit(w, client_data, call_data)
    Widget w;
    XtPointer client_data;        /* Digit to input */
    XtPointer call_data;
{
    int num = (int) client_data;

    if (inputDecimal) {
        currentInput += num * scale;
        scale /= 10;
    } else currentInput = currentInput * 10 + num;

    numberToDisplay = &currentInput;
    RefreshDisplay();
    inputNumber = TRUE;
}
```

InputDecimal is the callback procedure associated with the decimal point button. It does not change the current input; instead it sets the *inputDecimal* and *scale* variables so that InputDigit interprets future digits differently.

```
void InputDecimal(w, client_data, call_data)
    Widget w;
    XtPointer client_data, call_data;
{
    inputDecimal = inputNumber = TRUE;
    scale = 0.1;
    numberToDisplay = &currentInput;
    RefreshDisplay();
}
```

Function is the callback procedure associated with the four function keys and with the equals key. The *client_data* parameter is the operation displayed on the button. Function first uses the previous operation to operate on the total and the current input and then resets the previous operation to the one on the current key. If the previous operation was an equals, Function uses the *inputNumber* flag to decide whether it replaces the total with the current input as described earlier. Function displays the total in the display widget by setting *numberToDisplay* to point to the total and calling RefreshDisplay.

```
void Function(w, client_data, call_data)
    Widget w;
    XtPointer client_data;        /* Operation code */
    XtPointer call_data;
{
    switch (lastOp) {
```

```
            case Add:
                total += currentInput;
                break;
            case Sub:
                total -= currentInput;
                break;
            case Mul:
                total *= currentInput;
                break;
            case Div:
                if (currentInput == 0.0) XBell(XtDisplay(display), 100);
                else total /= currentInput;
                break;
            case Equal:
                if (inputNumber) total = currentInput;
                break;
            case Start:
                total = currentInput;
                break;
        }
        lastOp = (operation) client_data;
        currentInput = 0;
        inputDecimal = inputNumber = FALSE;

        numberToDisplay = &total;
        RefreshDisplay();
    }
```

Clear is the callback procedure associated with the "clear" and "clear entry" buttons; its *client_data* is TRUE if being called for "clear" and FALSE if being called for "clear entry." Clear just resets the appropriate variables to their starting states.

```
void Clear(w, client_data, call_data)
    Widget w;
    XtPointer client_data;        /* FALSE for Clear Entry */
    XtPointer call_data;
{
    currentInput = 0;
    if ((Boolean) client_data) {
        total = 0;
        lastOp = Start;
    }
    inputDecimal = inputNumber = FALSE;

    numberToDisplay = &currentInput;
    RefreshDisplay();
}
```

RefreshDisplay updates the string displayed in the display widget to reflect the current number. When the user is entering a number, *numberToDisplay* points to the current input, and after performing an operation *numberToDisplay* points to the running total. The calculator calls RefreshDisplay whenever the displayed value changes, so RefreshDisplay relinquishes the selection if the calculator currently owns it. This prevents race conditions in the selection mechanism; if the calculator did not relinquish the selection, the selection value could change between the time another application requests the selection and the time the calculator was notified of the selection request, leading to the wrong value being provided as the selection.

```
void RefreshDisplay()
{
    char buffer[100];
    Arg args[10];
    int i = 0;

    if (hasSelection) {            /* Get rid of it */
        LabelSelectText(display, XA_PRIMARY, FALSE);
        /* LoseSelection resets hasSelection and uninverts display */
    }

    sprintf(buffer, "%g", *numberToDisplay);
    XtSetArg(args[i], XtNlabel, buffer);            i++;
    XtSetValues(display, args, i);
}
```

RepositionMenu is an action procedure that moves the menu shell to center it around the coordinates in a ButtonPress event. RepositionMenu fetches the menu's size and uses this size and the root coordinates of the button press to calculate new x and y positions for the menu. RepositionMenu realizes the menu shell to make sure that the menu's dimensions are correct.

```
void RepositionMenu(w, event, params, num_params)
    Widget w;
    XEvent *event;
    String *params;
    Cardinal *num_params;
{
    XButtonEvent *b = &event->xbutton;
    Dimension width, height, border;
    Arg arg[25];
    int n;

    if (event->type != ButtonPress) return;
```

```
/* Size isn't valid before realizing */
XtRealizeWidget(menuShell);

/* Fetch size */
n = 0;
XtSetArg(arg[n], XtNwidth, &width);        n++;
XtSetArg(arg[n], XtNheight, &height);      n++;
XtSetArg(arg[n], XtNborderWidth, &border); n++;
XtGetValues(menuShell, arg, n);

/* Reposition menu */
n = 0;
XtSetArg(arg[n], XtNx, b->x_root - width/2 - border);    n++;
XtSetArg(arg[n], XtNy, b->y_root - height/2 - border);   n++;
XtSetValues(menuShell, arg, n);
}
```

Quit is the callback for the "quit" menu item. It exits the program.

```
void Quit(w, client_data, call_data)
    Widget w;
    XtPointer client_data, call_data;
{
    exit(0);
}
```

Select is the callback procedure for the "select" menu item. It calls Label-SelectText for the display widget to select the displayed text. If Label-SelectText is successful, Select sets the *hasSelection* flag and inverts the display.

```
void Select(w, client_data, call_data)
    Widget w;
    XtPointer client_data, call_data;
{
    if (hasSelection) return;

    /* Ask for selection */
    if (LabelSelectText(display, XA_PRIMARY, TRUE)) {
        hasSelection = TRUE;

        /* Invert display widget */
        XtCallActionProc(display, "invert", (XEvent *) NULL,
            (String *) NULL, 0);
    }
}
```

The Label widget calls LoseSelection to notify the calculator that it has lost the selection. LoseSelection resets the *hasSelection* flag and uninverts the display.

```
void LoseSelection(w, client_data, call_data)
    Widget w;
    XtPointer client_data, call_data;
{

    hasSelection = FALSE;

    /* Uninvert the display */
    XtCallActionProc(display, "uninvert", (XEvent *) NULL,
            (String *) NULL, 0);
}
```

Paste is the callback procedure for the "paste" menu item. It requests the value
of the current selection as a string, telling the Intrinsics to call PasteData when
the selection value is available.

```
void Paste(w, client_data, call_data)
    Widget w;
    XtPointer client_data, call_data;
{
    XtGetSelectionValue(display, XA_PRIMARY, XA_STRING, PasteData,
            (XtPointer) NULL, XtLastTimestampProcessed(XtDisplay(w)));
}
```

The Intrinsics call PasteData upon successfully fetching the selection value as a
character string. PasteData makes sure that the selection value is of the expected type and then processes the characters one by one, calling the same
callback procedure as would be executed if the corresponding button were
activated.

```
void PasteData(w, client_data, selection, type, value, length, format)
    Widget w;
    XtPointer client_data;
    Atom *selection, *type;
    XtPointer value;
    unsigned long *length;
    int *format;
{
    register int i;
    char *ch = (char *) value;

    /* Make sure we got what we expected */
    if (*selection != XA_PRIMARY || *type != XA_STRING ||
            *format != 8 || value == NULL) return;

    for (i = 0; i < *length; i++) {
        if (ch[i] >= '0' && ch[i] <= '9') {
            InputDigit(display, (XtPointer) (ch[i] - '0'),
                    (XtPointer) NULL);
```

```
        } else switch (ch[i]) {
            case '+':
                Function(display, (XtPointer) Add, (XtPointer) NULL);
                break;
            case '-':
                Function(display, (XtPointer) Sub, (XtPointer) NULL);
                break;
            case '*':
                Function(display, (XtPointer) Mul, (XtPointer) NULL);
                break;
            case '/':
                Function(display, (XtPointer) Div, (XtPointer) NULL);
                break;
            case '=':
                Function(display, (XtPointer) Equal, (XtPointer) NULL);
                break;
            case '.':
                InputDecimal(display, (XtPointer) NULL,
                        (XtPointer) NULL);
                break;
            default:
                return;
        }
    }
    Function(display, (XtPointer) Equal, (XtPointer) NULL);

    XtFree((XtPointer) value);
}
```

The appropriate Makefile lines for compiling the calculator are, assuming the widget binaries have been made into the library libwidgets.a,

```
WIDGETS = libwidgets.a
XT = -lXt
XLIB = -lX11
DEPENDS = ${WIDGETS}

democalc:  democalc.c ${DEPENDS}
        cc -o democalc democalc.o ${WIDGETS} ${XT} ${XLIB}
```

10.2.2   The Application Defaults File

The application defaults file should be given the name DemoCalc to match the application class passed to XtAppInitialize. If it cannot be installed in the normal application defaults file location (normally /usr/lib/X11/ app-defaults), the XFILESEARCHPATH environment variable should be set to point to its location; see Sections 3.5 and 9.8.

The input resource is TRUE to allow the user to use keyboard input. The main widget gets a new translation table that repositions the pop-up menu and pops it up upon a press of pointer button 2. Button 1 will not work; it would override the events in the individual pushbuttons, and it is too much trouble to work around this.

```
*input : TRUE
*main.translations : <Btn2Down>:RepositionMenu() XtMenuPopup(menuShell)
```

The *display* widget is right-justified and its translation table is replaced with the empty table.

```
*display.x : 10
*display.y : 10
*display.width : 130
*display.justify : Right
*display.translations : #replace
```

All other pushbuttons are 25 pixels wide and centered; this does not apply to the display pushbutton since its resources, specified by name, override these set by class.

```
*Pushbutton.width : 25
*Pushbutton.justify : Center
```

Each button has a position, a label, and an accelerator. These accelerators allow the user to operate the calculator from the keyboard; other than installing the accelerators the main program does nothing to support keyboard entry.

```
*button0.x : 45
*button0.y : 150
*button0.label :0
*button0.accelerators : :<Key>0 : notify()

*button1.x : 10
*button1.y : 115
*button1.label :1
*button1.accelerators : :<Key>1 : notify()

*button2.x : 45
*button2.y : 115
*button2.label :2
*button2.accelerators : :<Key>2 : notify()

*button3.x : 80
*button3.y : 115
*button3.label :3
*button3.accelerators : :<Key>3 : notify()
```

```
*button4.x : 10
*button4.y : 80
*button4.label :4
*button4.accelerators : :<Key>4 : notify()

*button5.x : 45
*button5.y : 80
*button5.label :5
*button5.accelerators : :<Key>5 : notify()

*button6.x : 80
*button6.y : 80
*button6.label :6
*button6.accelerators : :<Key>6 : notify()

*button7.x : 10
*button7.y : 45
*button7.label :7
*button7.accelerators : :<Key>7 : notify()

*button8.x : 45
*button8.y : 45
*button8.label :8
*button8.accelerators : :<Key>8 : notify()

*button9.x : 80
*button9.y : 45
*button9.label :9
*button9.accelerators : :<Key>9 : notify()

*decimal.x : 80
*decimal.y : 150
*decimal.label :.
*decimal.accelerators : :<Key>. : notify()

*plus.x : 115
*plus.y : 45
*plus.label :+
*plus.accelerators : :<Key>+ : notify()

*minus.x : 115
*minus.y : 80
*minus.label :-
*minus.accelerators : :<Key>- : notify()

*times.x : 115
*times.y : 115
*times.label :*
*times.accelerators : :<Key>* : notify()
```

```
*divide.x : 115
*divide.y : 150
*divide.label :/
*divide.accelerators : :<Key>/ : notify()

*equals.x : 115
*equals.y : 185
*equals.label :=
*equals.accelerators : :<Key>= : notify()

*clearEntry.x : 10
*clearEntry.y : 150
*clearEntry.label :CE
*clearEntry.accelerators : :<Key>c : notify()

*clear.x : 10
*clear.y : 185
*clear.label :C
*clear.accelerators : :<Key>C : notify()
```

The accelerators for the three menu items do not specify a colon. This allows the accelerators to activate regardless of the case of the letter; e.g., *select* activates on either an upper- or a lower-case S.

```
*select.label :Select
*select.accelerators : <Key>S : notify()

*paste.label :Paste
*paste.accelerators : <Key>P : notify()

*quit.label :Quit
*quit.accelerators : <Key>Q : notify()
```

10.2.3   Suggested Programming Exercises

- Make the three functions in the pop-up menu be direct buttons on the calculator instead.

- Make the pop-up selection menu be active only in the *display* widget and have it be activated with button 1.

- Make clicking button 1 in the *display* widget take ownership of the selection without changing the behavior of button 2. Can you do this without modifying the program?

- Modify RepositionMenu to make sure the entire menu is on the screen.

- Add some additional functions to the calculator. If your system supplies a font that contains the square root character, make the button for square root use that font. (Harder) Make the button still display sensibly if the font cannot be found.

- Delay creating the contents of the pop-up menu until just before it is popped up by using the XtNcreatePopupChildProc resource. Then add work procedures to create and realize these children in the background.

- The calculator rings the bell on an error. Instead, make it show the string "Error" in its display when an error occurs.

- Rather than showing "Error" in the display, create a separate Label widget with the string "Error". Rearrange the layout to make room for this widget. Make the label be initially unmapped and use XtSetMappedWhenManaged to make the label appear and disappear.

- Add an application resource that controls which selection name the calculator uses. This resource should be of type XtRAtom; set up the resource so that the Intrinsics automatically convert from a string to an atom. To test this, start up two instances of the calculator that use the same selection name and copy values between them.

- Add an application resource that controls whether a selection pasted into the calculator automatically ends with the equals key.

- Improve the selection handling of the calculator so that the display remains selected even if it changes. One way to do this is to not simply relinquish the selection when the display changes but to reassert ownership with the new value.

- Use fallback resources and a Label widget to display an informative error message in the calculator window if the application defaults file has not been loaded into the resource database. (Hint: Add an extra application resource explicitly for this purpose.)

- (Ambitious) If you are also a widget writer, change the calculator program into a calculator widget. Write a new version of the calculator program that just creates an instance of this widget.

- (Ambitious) Add an application resource that controls whether the calculator acts as an infix calculator as it does now or a reverse Polish notation calculator. Create different buttons depending upon the mode.

- (Very ambitious) Add a button or a menu item that switches between infix and reverse Polish operation. Use managing and unmanaging to control which buttons appear in the two modes.

10.3   A Mail Notifier

The second application is a mail notifier; it pops up a window on the user's screen whenever he has new mail. It uses a Confirm widget to display the notification.

Figure 10.7. The mail notifier and its widget tree

Figure 10.7 shows the mail notifier's window and its widget tree. This diagram only shows the widgets the application creates; the internal implementation of the Confirm widget might or might not be public information.

The notifier illustrates using application resources for customization. It has five application resources:

Name	Class	Type	Default
"quiet"	"Quiet"	Boolean	FALSE
"mailFile"	"MailFile"	String	special
"interval"	"Interval"	int	60
"defaultMessage"	"DefaultMessage"	String	"New mail from someone"
"fromMessage"	"FromMessage"	String	"New mail from %s"

These resources have no symbolic names since the strings only occur in one place in the program; symbolic names would serve no useful purpose.

The "quiet" resource controls whether the notifier rings the workstation bell when it pops up the notification window.

The "mailFile" resource specifies a file to use to check for mail. If no file is specified, the notifier constructs one based upon the identity of the user running the program.

The "interval" resource specifies how often the notifier checks for new mail, in seconds.

The "defaultMessage" resource specifies the message the notifier uses if it is unable to figure out whom a mail message is from.

The "fromMessage" resource specifies the message the notifier uses to display whom a mail message is from. It should have one "%s" `printf` substitution that the notifier fills in with the user who sent the mail message.

The notifier supplies command line options for some of these resources:

Option	Resource Name	Resource Value
–quiet	*quiet	"on"
–file	*mailFile	next argument
–interval	*interval	next argument

10.3.1   The Implementation

The following pages give a running commentary on the notifier implementation. This particular implementation is for Unix operating systems that store a user's incoming mail locally; the code for dealing with the mail file will be different under different mail and operating systems.

```
#include <X11/Intrinsic.h>
#include <X11/StringDefs.h>
#include <X11/Shell.h>
#include "Confirm.h"
```

The notifier needs these header files to read the mail file, to construct its name, and to check whether it can be read.

```
#include <stdio.h>
#include <strings.h>
#include <unistd.h>
#include <pwd.h>
#include <sys/stat.h>

XtAppContext app;
Widget toplevel, confirm = NULL;
unsigned long fileSize;

void GetMailFile(), Timer(), Popup(), CreatePopup(), Callback();
Boolean CheckNewMail();
String FindWhoFrom();
```

OptionsRec is the structure into which the application resources will be stored.

```
typedef struct {
    Boolean quiet;
    String mail_file;
    int timeout;
    String default_message;
    String from_message;
} OptionsRec;
```

```
OptionsRec options;
#define BUFSIZE 1000
```

The *resources* table defines the application resources the notifier supports.

```
#define Offset(field) XtOffsetOf(OptionsRec, field)

XtResource resources[] = {
    {"quiet", "Quiet", XtRBoolean, sizeof(Boolean),
        Offset(quiet), XtRImmediate, (XtPointer) FALSE},
    {"mailFile", "MailFile", XtRString, sizeof(String),
        Offset(mail_file), XtRString, (XtPointer) NULL},
    {"interval", "Interval", XtRInt, sizeof(int),
        Offset(timeout), XtRImmediate, (XtPointer) 60},
    {"defaultMessage", "DefaultMessage", XtRString, sizeof(String),
        Offset(default_message), XtRString, "New mail from someone"},
    {"fromMessage", "FromMessage", XtRString, sizeof(String),
        Offset(from_message), XtRString, "New mail from %s"}
};

#undef Offset
```

The *optionDesc* table defines the command line options the notifier supports.

```
XrmOptionDescRec optionDesc[] = {
    {"-quiet", "*quiet", XrmoptionNoArg, (XtPointer) "on"},
    {"-file", "*mailFile", XrmoptionSepArg, (XtPointer) NULL},
    {"-interval", "*interval", XrmoptionSepArg, (XtPointer) NULL}
};
```

The main program initializes the toolkit and fetches the application resources. As a result of calling `XtGetApplicationResources` the fields in the structure *options* contain values as specified on the command line, in resource files, or in the *resources* table if specified nowhere else. Next the main program calls GetMailFile to check that the mail file is readable, and adds a timer, set to go off after the interval specified by the "interval" resource, that checks if new mail exists. Finally the main program enters the application main loop.

```
main(argc, argv)
    int argc;
    char *argv[];
{
    toplevel = XtAppInitialize(&app, "DemoBiff",
            optionDesc, XtNumber(optionDesc), &argc, argv,
            (String *) NULL, (ArgList) NULL, 0);

    XtGetApplicationResources(toplevel, (XtPointer) &options,
            resources, XtNumber(resources), (Arg *) NULL, 0);
```

```
        GetMailFile();
        (void) XtAppAddTimeOut(app, options.timeout * 1000,
                Timer, (XtPointer) NULL);
        XtAppMainLoop(app);
}
```

If no file name was specified with the "mailFile" resource, GetMailFile constructs one from the user's name. `Access` checks that the file exists and can be read and `stat` gets the file status. The initial file length comes from the file status buffer.

```
void GetMailFile()
{
        extern int getuid();
        struct passwd *pw;
        extern struct passwd *getpwuid();
        struct stat status;
        char buffer[BUFSIZE];

        if (options.mail_file == NULL) {
            pw = getpwuid(getuid());
            if (pw == NULL) {
                XtAppErrorMsg(app, "noUser", "getMailFile",
                        "DemoBiffError", "Could not get user name",
                        (String *) NULL, (Cardinal *) NULL);
            }

            (void) sprintf(buffer, "/usr/spool/mail/%s", pw->pw_name);
            options.mail_file = XtNewString(buffer);
        }

        if (access(options.mail_file, R_OK) != 0 ||
                stat(options.mail_file, &status) != 0) {
            XtAppErrorMsg(app, "noAccess", "getMailFile", "DemoBiffError",
                    "Could not read mail spool file",
                    (String *) NULL, (Cardinal *) NULL);
        }

        fileSize = status.st_size;
}
```

Timer is the timer callback procedure; the Intrinsics call it after the user-specified interval has passed. Timer calls CheckNewMail, which pops up the notification box and returns TRUE if new mail exists or FALSE if there is no new mail. If no new mail exists, Timer reregisters itself so that the Intrinsics will call it again after the appropriate interval.

```
void Timer(client_data, id)
    XtPointer client_data;
    XtIntervalId *id;
{
    if (!CheckNewMail()) {
        (void) XtAppAddTimeOut(app, options.timeout * 1000,
                Timer, (XtPointer) NULL);
    }
}
```

CheckNewMail checks to see if the mail file has grown since the last time it was called. Access determines whether the file exists and is readable, and stat returns a status block containing, among other things, the file size. If the current size of the file is less than or equal to the previous size, there is no new mail, so CheckNewMail returns FALSE. Otherwise CheckNewMail calls Find-WhoFrom to find whom the mail is from and calls Popup to pop the confirmation box up with FindWhoFrom's message as the confirmation text. If the quiet resource is FALSE, CheckNewMail rings the bell.

```
Boolean CheckNewMail()
{
    struct stat status;

    if (access(options.mail_file, R_OK) != 0 ||
            stat(options.mail_file, &status) != 0) {
        XtAppErrorMsg(app, "noAccess", "checkNewMail", "DemoBiffError",
            "Could not read mail spool file",
            (String *) NULL, (Cardinal *) NULL);
    }

    if (status.st_size <= fileSize) {
        fileSize = status.st_size;
        return FALSE;
    }

    Popup(FindWhoFrom());
    if (!options.quiet) XBell(XtDisplay(toplevel), 100);
    fileSize = status.st_size;
    return TRUE;
}
```

FindWhoFrom attempts to figure out whom the new mail is from and returns a string containing the appropriate message. It opens the mail file and then calls fseek to reset the position to the last known file length; the new mail message begins after this position. FindWhoFrom reads lines from the mail file until it finds one that begins with the string "From: " and uses the rest of the line as the name of the sender of the message. If FindWhoFrom is unable to open the file, unable to f seek to the appropriate place, or unable to find a "From" line before encountering the end of the file or a blank line in the file, it returns the default message. If it figures out who sent the mail, it uses *options.from_message* to format its message.

```
String FindWhoFrom()
{
    char buffer[BUFSIZE];
    static char message[BUFSIZE];
    FILE *mail = fopen(options.mail_file, "r");
    int fromLen = strlen("From: ");

    if (mail == NULL) {
        return options.default_message;
    }

    if (fseek(mail, fileSize, 0) == -1) {
        fclose(mail);
        return options.default_message;
    }

    while (1) {
        if (fgets(buffer, BUFSIZE, mail) == NULL ||
                buffer[0] == '\n') {
            fclose(mail);
            return options.default_message;
        }
        if (strncmp(buffer, "From: ", fromLen) == 0) {
            buffer[strlen(buffer)-1] = '\0';     /* Replace \n */
            (void) sprintf(message, options.from_message,
                    &buffer[fromLen]);
            fclose(mail);
            return message;
        }
    }
}
```

Popup checks to see if the notifier has created the Confirm widget yet and creates it if not. Popup then sets the label in the confirmation box to be whatever string was passed in and pops up the *toplevel* shell on the screen.

```
void Popup(string)
    String string;
{
    Arg args[10];
    int i = 0;

    if (confirm == NULL) CreatePopup();
```

```
XtSetArg(args[i], XtNlabel, string);       i++;
XtSetValues(confirm, args, i);
XtPopup(toplevel, XtGrabNone);
}
```

CreatePopup creates the Confirm widget, specifying that it calls the procedure Callback when the confirmation box is dismissed.

```
void CreatePopup()
{
    confirm = XtCreateManagedWidget("confirm", confirmWidgetClass,
            toplevel, (Arg *) NULL, 0);
    XtAddCallback(confirm, XtNcallback, Callback, (XtPointer) NULL);
}
```

Callback is the callback procedure for the confirmation box. It registers the procedure Timer as a timer callback that the Intrinsics will call after zero seconds. Timer checks for new mail, so the net effect is that immediately after dismissing the confirmation box the notifier checks to see if any new mail arrived while the confirmation box was up.

```
void Callback(w, client_data, call_data)
    Widget w;
    XtPointer client_data, call_data;
{
    (void) XtAppAddTimeOut(app, 0, Timer, (XtPointer) NULL);
}
```

The appropriate `Makefile` lines for compiling the notifier are, assuming the widget binaries have been made into the library `libwidgets.a`,

```
WIDGETS = libwidgets.a
XT = -lXt
XLIB = -lX11
DEPENDS = ${WIDGETS}

demobiff:  demobiff.c ${DEPENDS}
        cc -o demobiff demobiff.o ${WIDGETS} ${XT} ${XLIB}
```

10.3.2   The Application Defaults File

The application defaults file should be given the name DemoBiff to match the application class passed to `XtAppInitialize`. If it cannot be installed in the normal application defaults file location (normally `/usr/lib/X11/app-defaults`), the XFILESEARCHPATH environment variable should be set to point to its location; see Sections 3.5 and 9.8.

The application defaults file sets the XtNallowShellResize resource to TRUE for shells in the interface, allowing the confirmation box to grow to accommodate long messages, and sets the title of the window to "Mail Notifier".

```
*AllowShellResize : TRUE
*Title : Mail Notifier
```

10.3.3   Suggested Programming Exercises

• The mail notifier stops checking for new mail when it finds some. Make it continue to check and alter the label in the confirmation box to reflect whom the newest mail is from.

• Instead of altering the label, pop up additional confirmation boxes for each new message. Offset the positions of any additional pop-ups from the position of the first pop-up.

• Reorganize the program so that it does not pop up; instead always have a window and change the message in the window depending upon whether there is new mail.

• Make the program from the previous exercise capable of displaying several new mail messages. If it exceeds some maximum, eliminate the oldest messages. Use an application resource to control how many messages to display.

• Figure out how to know when the user has incorporated (processed) his new mail. Modify the program from the previous exercise so that it automatically gets rid of all its messages when the user incorporates his mail.

• Use the selection mechanism to provide a way for other applications to find out if the user has mail by asking the DemoBiff application.

10.4   A System Monitor

The third application is a system monitor. It uses a Graph widget to display the data.

Figure 10.8 shows the system monitor's window and its widget tree.

The system monitor has three application resources:

Name	Class	Type	Default
"interval"	"Interval"	int	5
"numFields"	"NumFields"	int	3
"command"	"Command"	String	See description

These resources have no symbolic names since the strings only occur in one place in the program; symbolic names would serve no useful purpose.

Figure 10.8. The system monitor and its widget tree

The "interval" resource controls how often the system monitor updates its displayed values.

The "numFields" resource indicates how many fields the "command" resource provides.

The "command" resource gives a command to execute that generates the field values. It should print out the number of fields indicated by the "numFields" resource, separated by spaces or newlines, and these should all be integers. The default value is

```
vmstat 1 2 | awk '{if (NR == 4) print $(NF-2), $(NF-1), $(NF)}'
```

which prints out the percentages of time the CPU is spending in user mode, system mode, and idle time. This command works on Unix systems derived from Berkeley Unix; a different command is required on other operating systems. The suggested programming exercises at the end of this section give some other commands that produce other useful graphs.

The system monitor provides one command line option:

Option	Resource Name	Resource Value
–interval	*interval	next argument

10.4.1   The Implementation

The following pages give a running commentary on the system monitor implementation. The application contains no operating system dependencies other than its use of the standard I/O package to run the command as a subprocess; all other dependencies are encapsulated in the "command" resource.

```
#include <stdio.h>
#include <X11/Intrinsic.h>
#include <X11/StringDefs.h>
#include "Graph.h"
#include "BarDisplay.h"

XtAppContext app;
Widget graph;
int *fields;

void Timer(), CreateGraphWidget(), GetGraphData();
```

OptionsRec is the structure into which the application resources will be stored.

```
typedef struct {
    int timeout;
    int num_fields;
    String command;
} OptionsRec;

OptionsRec options;
```

The *resources* table defines the application resources the monitor supports.

```
#define Offset(field) XtOffsetOf(OptionsRec, field)

XtResource resources[] = {
    {"interval", "Interval", XtRInt, sizeof(int),
        Offset(timeout), XtRImmediate, (XtPointer) 5},
    {"numFields", "NumFields", XtRInt, sizeof(int),
        Offset(num_fields), XtRImmediate, (XtPointer) 3},
    {"command", "Command", XtRString, sizeof(String),
        Offset(command), XtRString,
    "vmstat 1 2 | awk '{if (NR == 4) print $(NF-2), $(NF-1), $(NF)}'"}
};

#undef Offset
```

The *optionDesc* table defines the command line options the monitor supports.

```
XrmOptionDescRec optionDesc[] = {
    {"-interval", "*interval", XrmoptionSepArg, (XtPointer) NULL}
};
```

The main program initializes the toolkit and fetches the application resources. As a result of calling XtGetApplicationResources the fields in the structure *options* contain values as specified on the command line, in resource files, or in the resources if specified nowhere else. Next the main program allocates an array to hold the field values as specified by the "numFields" resource. It

creates and realizes the Graph widget and adds a timer, set to go off after the
interval specified by the "interval" resource, that will update the graph. Finally
the main program enters the application main loop.

```
main(argc, argv)
    int argc;
    char *argv[];
{
    Widget toplevel;

    toplevel = XtAppInitialize(&app, "DemoMonitor",
            optionDesc, XtNumber(optionDesc), &argc, argv,
            (String *) NULL, (ArgList) NULL, 0);

    XtGetApplicationResources(toplevel, (XtPointer) &options,
            resources, XtNumber(resources), (Arg *) NULL, 0);

    fields = (int *) XtCalloc(options.num_fields, sizeof(int));

    CreateGraphWidget(toplevel);
    XtRealizeWidget(toplevel);

    (void) XtAppAddTimeOut(app, options.timeout * 1000,
            Timer, (XtPointer) NULL);

    XtAppMainLoop(app);
}
```

CreateGraphWidget calls GetGraphData to fetch the initial values for the
monitor data, then creates a Graph widget to display these values. It creates a
BarDisplay child of the Graph widget to indicate that it wants the data displayed as a horizontal bar graph.

```
void CreateGraphWidget(parent)
    Widget parent;
{
    Arg args[10];
    int n;

    GetGraphData();

    n = 0;
    XtSetArg(args[n], XtNnumEntries, options.num_fields);   n++;
    XtSetArg(args[n], XtNvalues, fields);                   n++;
    graph = XtCreateManagedWidget("graph", graphWidgetClass, parent,
            args, n);

    (void) XtCreateWidget("bar", barDisplayObjectClass, graph,
            (Arg *) NULL, 0);
}
```

Timer is the timer callback procedure; the Intrinsics call it after the user-specified interval has passed. It gets new values for the monitor data and updates the values displayed in the graph. Finally it calls `XtAppAddTimeOut` to reregister itself to be called again after the appropriate interval.

```
void Timer(client_data, id)
    XtPointer client_data;
    XtIntervalId *id;
{
    Arg args[10];
    int n;

    GetGraphData();

    n = 0;
    XtSetArg(args[n], XtNvalues, fields);    n++;
    XtSetValues(graph, args, n);

    (void) XtAppAddTimeOut(app, options.timeout * 1000,
            Timer, (XtPointer) NULL);
}
```

GetGraphData is responsible for filling in the *fields* array with the values from the command. It uses `popen` to run the command as a subprocess and make its output available in a pipe. GetGraphData reads the values from the pipe into the *fields* array, issuing a warning message and filling the missing fields with zero if it finds insufficient data.

```
void GetGraphData()
{
    int status;
    FILE *f;
    int i;

    f = popen(options.command, "r");

    for (i = 0; i < options.num_fields; i++) {
        status = fscanf(f, "%d", &fields[i]);
        if (status != 1) {
            XtAppWarningMsg(app, "noData", "getGraphData",
                    "DemoLoadError", "Not enough fields in data",
                    (String *) NULL, (Cardinal *) NULL);
            for (; i < options.num_fields; i++) fields[i] = 0;
            break;
        }
    }

    pclose(f);
}
```

The appropriate Makefile lines for compiling the system monitor are, assuming the widget binaries have been made into the library libwidgets.a,

```
WIDGETS = libwidgets.a
XT = -lXt
XLIB = -lX11
DEPENDS = ${WIDGETS}

demomonitor:  demomonitor.c ${DEPENDS}
        cc -o demomonitor demomonitor.o ${WIDGETS} ${XT} ${XLIB}
```

10.4.2   The Application Defaults File

The application defaults file should be given the name DemoMonitor to match the application class passed to XtAppInitialize. If it cannot be installed in the normal application defaults file location (normally /usr/lib/X11/app-defaults), the XFILESEARCHPATH environment variable should be set to point to its location; see Sections 3.5 and 9.8.

The application defaults file sets the XtNlabels and XtNmaxValue resources of the Graph widget.

```
*graph.labels: User\nSystem\nIdle
*graph.maxValue : 100
```

10.4.3   Suggested Programming Exercises

• Experiment with putting different commands in your .Xdefaults file. Look for different system monitor commands on your computer and figure out how to extract the relevant information. For example,

```
lpq | awk 'END {if (NR < 3) print 0; else print NR-2}'
```

displays the number of entries in the line printer queue. If your system supports the uptime utility,

```
uptime | awk '{print substr($10,0,4)*100,
        substr($11,0,4)*100, $12*100}'
```

(all one line) displays the one-, five-, and fifteen-minute load averages.

• Set up your .Xdefaults file so that you can run simultaneous monitors displaying different data. (Hint: use the −name command line option.)

• Add a title to the monitor's output. This will involve adding a composite widget between the shell and the graph. Make this a MinMax and set up the constraints so that resizing the application resizes the graph.

• Add additional application resources so that you can use a command that outputs floating-point numbers. You will need to scale them to integers before passing them to the graph.

- (For widget writers) Create a widget class that encapsulates the monitor, updating itself automatically. The application resources of the monitor application will become resources of this widget. The easiest way is to subclass Graph and to have the widget do `XtSetValues` on itself in the timer callback to change the values displayed. Write a version of the monitor program that uses this class (it will be very short).

- Modify the monitor program to display multiple graphs simultaneously. This will be much easier if you did the previous exercise.

- Try some of the suggested exercises for BarDisplay; writing a new GraphDisplay subclass is less work than writing a new widget. Add an option to make the monitor program display as a pie chart.

Writing Widgets

10.5   The Label Widget

The Label implementation is fairly straightforward, complicated only by some functionality that is not used by Label but that makes the implementation of Pushbutton much simpler. It illustrates the basic structure of a display-only widget and the use of widget-specific resource type converters. The converter allows resource files to use descriptive strings rather than predefined integer constants.

There is a field in the widget instance record, *accel_string*, that Label concatenates with the label text to form the string to display. *Accel_string* is always NULL for labels, but pushbuttons with installed accelerators set this to a string describing the accelerator, for example "(^C)". The resource corresponding to *accel_string*, XtNaccelString, is defined by Pushbutton since only pushbuttons use it.

The Label instance also contains an additional graphics context field, *current_gc*. For Label widgets this is always the same as the normal graphics context, but in pushbuttons this is sometimes a different context in order to display the button in an insensitive or an inverted state. Label's expose procedure always draws the text using *current_gc*, so the Pushbutton implementation uses Label's expose procedure to display the contents of a pushbutton.

Label contains one new class method, LabelSelectText, which applications use to select the text string displayed in the label.

10.5.1   The Public Header File

```
/* Make it safe to include this file more than once. */
#ifndef LABEL_H
#define LABEL_H

/* Label is derived from Core, so no need to include the superclass
   public header file.  */

/* New resource */

#define XtNloseSelection "loseSelection"
#define XtCLoseSelection "LoseSelection"

/* New type for justification */
typedef enum { Center, Left, Right } Justify;

/* External reference to the class record pointer */
extern WidgetClass labelWidgetClass;

/* Type definition for label widgets */
typedef struct _LabelRec *LabelWidget;

/* Method declaration */
extern Boolean LabelSelectText();
    /* Widget    w;        */
    /* Atom      selection;  */
    /* Boolean   select;     */

/* End of preprocessor directives */
#endif /* LABEL_H */
```

10.5.2   The Private Header File

```
/* Make it safe to include this file more than once. */
#ifndef LABELP_H
#define LABELP_H

/* Include the public header file for Label */
#include "Label.h"

/* Label is derived from Core, so no need to include the superclass
   private header file.  No internal types need to be defined. */

/* Define the Label instance part */
typedef struct {
  /* New resource fields */
    String       label;          /* Text to display */
    Pixel        foreground;     /* Foreground pixel value */
    XFontStruct  *font;          /* Font to display in */
```

```
    Justify         justify;        /* The justification value */
    Dimension       space;          /* Inner padding value */
    XtCallbackList  lose_selection; /* Notify app. of lost selection */

  /* New internal fields */
    GC              gc;             /* Graphics context for displaying */
    Dimension       label_width;    /* The calculated width */
    Dimension       label_height;   /* The calculated height */
    Cardinal        label_len;      /* The length of the text string */
    Boolean         size_computed;  /* Whether the size was computed */
    Dimension       desired_width;  /* The width the widget wants to be */
    Dimension       desired_height; /* The height the widget wants to be */
    String          accel_string;   /* Accelerator string */
    GC              current_gc;     /* GC we are currently using */
} LabelPart;

/* Define the full instance record */
typedef struct _LabelRec {
    CorePart    core;
    LabelPart   label;
} LabelRec;

/* Define new type for the class method */
typedef Boolean (*LabelSelectionProc)();
    /* Widget   w;              */
    /* Atom     selection;      */
    /* Boolean  own;            */
/* Define class part structure */
typedef struct {
    LabelSelectionProc  select;
    XtPointer           extension;
} LabelClassPart;

/* Define the full class record */
typedef struct _LabelClassRec {
    CoreClassPart       core_class;
    LabelClassPart      label_class;
} LabelClassRec, *LabelWidgetClass;

/* External definition for class record */
extern LabelClassRec labelClassRec;

/* Inheritance constant for select_text method */
#define InheritSelectText ((LabelSelectionProc) _XtInherit)

/* End of preprocessor directives */
#endif /* LABELP_H */
```

10.5.3 The Implementation

```
#include <X11/Xos.h>          /* Needed for string manipulation */
#include <X11/IntrinsicP.h>   /* Intrinsics header file */
#include <X11/StringDefs.h>   /* Resource string definitions */
#include <X11/Xatom.h>        /* For selection atoms */
#include "LabelP.h"           /* Label private header file */
```

The resource specification for XtNborderWidth duplicates the core border width specification but gives a new default value, zero. Doing this overrides the superclass's default.

```
#define Offset(field) XtOffsetOf(LabelRec, label.field)

static XtResource resources[] = {
    {XtNlabel, XtCLabel, XtRString, sizeof(String),
        Offset(label), XtRString, (XtPointer) NULL},
    {XtNfont,  XtCFont, XtRFontStruct, sizeof(XFontStruct *),
        Offset(font), XtRString, (XtPointer) XtDefaultFont},
    {XtNforeground, XtCForeground, XtRPixel, sizeof(Pixel),
        Offset(foreground), XtRString,
        (XtPointer) XtDefaultForeground},
    {XtNjustify, XtCJustify, XtRJustify, sizeof(Justify),
        Offset(justify), XtRImmediate, (XtPointer) Left},
    {XtNspace, XtCSpace, XtRDimension, sizeof(Dimension),
        Offset(space), XtRImmediate, (XtPointer) 2},
    {XtNloseSelection, XtCLoseSelection, XtRCallback,
        sizeof(XtCallbackList), Offset(lose_selection),
        XtRCallback, (XtPointer) NULL},
    {XtNborderWidth, XtCBorderWidth, XtRDimension, sizeof(Dimension),
        XtOffsetOf(LabelRec, core.border_width),
        XtRImmediate, (XtPointer) 0},
};
#undef Offset
```

An alternative to giving forward declarations for all the procedures in the class record is to put the declaration of the class record at the end of the file.

```
/* Forward declarations */

static void ClassInitialize(), ClassPartInitialize(), Initialize(),
        Redisplay(), Destroy(), Resize(), LoseSelection();
static Boolean SetValues(), SelectText();
static XtGeometryResult QueryGeometry();

/* Class record declaration */

LabelClassRec labelClassRec = {
    /* Core class part */
```

```
{
    /* superclass              */ (WidgetClass) &widgetClassRec,
    /* class_name              */ "Label",
    /* widget_size             */ sizeof(LabelRec),
    /* class_initialize        */ ClassInitialize,
    /* class_part_initialize   */ ClassPartInitialize,
    /* class_inited            */ FALSE,
    /* initialize              */ Initialize,
    /* initialize_hook         */ NULL,
    /* realize                 */ XtInheritRealize,
    /* actions                 */ NULL,
    /* num_actions             */ 0,
    /* resources               */ resources,
    /* num_resources           */ XtNumber(resources),
    /* xrm_class               */ NULLQUARK,
    /* compress_motion         */ TRUE,
    /* compress_exposure       */ XtExposeCompressMultiple,
    /* compress_enterleave     */ TRUE,
    /* visible_interest        */ FALSE,
    /* destroy                 */ Destroy,
    /* resize                  */ Resize,
    /* expose                  */ Redisplay,
    /* set_values              */ SetValues,
    /* set_values_hook         */ NULL,
    /* set_values_almost       */ XtInheritSetValuesAlmost,
    /* get_values_hook         */ NULL,
    /* accept_focus            */ NULL,
    /* version                 */ XtVersion,
    /* callback offsets        */ NULL,
    /* tm_table                */ NULL,
    /* query_geometry          */ QueryGeometry,
    /* display_accelerator     */ NULL,
    /* extension               */ NULL
},
    /* Label class part */
{
    /* select                  */ SelectText,
    /* extension               */ NULL
}
};

/* Class record pointer */

WidgetClass labelWidgetClass = (WidgetClass) &labelClassRec;
```

The string-to-justification converter uses LowerCase to convert any potential justification values to lower-case. If the string passed in is too long to fit into the destination buffer, LowerCase returns TRUE.

```
static Boolean LowerCase(from, to, size)
    register String from, to;
    int size;
{
    register char ch;
    register int i;

    for (i = 0; i < size; i++) {
        ch = from[i];
        if (ch >= 'A' && ch <= 'Z') to[i] = ch - 'A' + 'a';
        else to[i] = ch;
        if (ch == '\0') return FALSE;
    }
    return TRUE;
}
```

CvtStringToJustify is the string-to-justification converter. LOWER_SIZE is the size of the buffer to hold the lower-case version of the source string; it is larger than any valid value for the converter. The procedure first checks that it was passed the correct number of additional conversion arguments, zero, and issues an error message if it was not. After converting the source string to lower-case, it sets the variable j to the appropriate value from the Justify enumeration. The variable j is static so that when its address is returned through *to–>addr* its value lasts long enough to be copied into the resource cache. If the source string is too long or if it does not match any of the valid justification strings, CvtStringToJustify fails by returning FALSE.

```
Boolean CvtStringToJustify(dpy, args, num_args, from, to, data)
    Display *dpy;
    XrmValuePtr args;
    Cardinal *num_args;
    XrmValuePtr from, to;
    XtPointer *data;
{
#define LOWER_SIZE 10
    char lower[LOWER_SIZE];       /* Lower-cased string value */
    register int i;
    Boolean badConvert;
    static Justify j;

    if (*num_args != 0) {         /* Check for correct number */
        XtAppErrorMsg(XtDisplayToApplicationContext(dpy),
                "cvtStringToJustify", "wrongParameters",
                "XtToolkitError",
                "String to justify conversion needs no extra arguments",
                (String *) NULL, (Cardinal *) NULL);
    }
```

```
        /* Lower case the value */
        badConvert = LowerCase(from->addr, lower, LOWER_SIZE);

        /* Try to convert if a short enough string specified */
        if (!badConvert) {
            if (strcmp(lower, "left") == 0) j = Left;
            else if (strcmp(lower, "center") == 0) j = Center;
            else if (strcmp(lower, "right") == 0) j = Right;
            else badConvert = TRUE;
        }

        /* String too long or unknown value -- issue warning */
        if (badConvert) {
            XtDisplayStringConversionWarning(dpy, from->addr, "Justify");
        } else {
            if (to->addr == NULL) to->addr = (caddr_t) &j;
            else if (to->size < sizeof(Justify)) badConvert = TRUE;
            else *(Justify *) to->addr = j;

            to->size = sizeof(Justify);
        }
        return !badConvert;
#undef LOWER_SIZE
}
```

An alternative implementation of this converter uses quarks to avoid string comparisons. It has three static quarks, *Qleft, Qcenter,* and *Qright,* that it initializes to the quark values for the three valid justification strings the first time it gets called. CvtStringToJustify converts the source string to a quark and compares the resulting value to the three possible quarks. Since there are only three possible correct values, the quark version is less efficient than the string version, but it illustrates the use of quarks.

```
#if 0
Boolean CvtStringToJustify(dpy, args, num_args, from, to, data)
    Display *dpy;
    XrmValuePtr args;
    Cardinal *num_args;
    XrmValuePtr from, to;
    XtPointer *data;
{
#define LOWER_SIZE 10
    char lower[LOWER_SIZE];        /* Lower-cased string value */
    register int i;
    Boolean badConvert;
    XrmQuark q;
    static Justify j;
    static XrmQuark Qleft, Qcenter, Qright;
```

```
        static Boolean haveQuarks = FALSE;

    if (*num_args != 0) {          /* Check for correct number */
        XtAppErrorMsg(XtDisplayToApplicationContext(dpy),
                "cvtStringToJustify", "wrongParameters",
                "XtToolkitError",
                "String to justify conversion needs no extra arguments",
                (String *) NULL, (Cardinal *) NULL);
    }

    if (!haveQuarks) {
        Qleft   = XrmStringToQuark("left");
        Qcenter = XrmStringToQuark("center");
        Qright  = XrmStringToQuark("right");
        haveQuarks = TRUE;
    }

    badConvert = LowerCase(from->addr, lower, LOWER_SIZE);

    /* Try to convert if a short enough string specified */

    if (!badConvert) {
        q = XrmStringToQuark(lower);
        if (q == Qleft) j = Left;
        else if (q == Qcenter) j = Center;
        else if (q == Qright) j = Right;
        else badConvert = TRUE;
    }

    /* String too long or unknown value -- issue warning */

    if (badConvert) {
        XtDisplayStringConversionWarning(dpy, from->addr, "Justify");
    } else {
        if (to->addr == NULL) to->addr = (caddr_t) &j;
        else if (to->size < sizeof(Justify)) badConvert = TRUE;
        else *(Justify *) to->addr = j;

        to->size = sizeof(Justify);
    }
    return !badConvert;
#undef LOWER_SIZE
}
#endif
```

The Intrinsics call DeliverSelection if the label owns the selection and some
application requests its value. If the selection target type is TARGETS, Deliver-
Selection must reply with a list of targets that it supports, in this case only
XA_STRING. If the selection target type is XA_STRING, DeliverSelection stores the

label's text as the selection value. DeliverSelection always stores the selection value in allocated storage; since the call to `XtOwnSelection` in SelectText specifies no selection done procedure, the Intrinsics free this storage after delivering the selection.

```
static Atom FetchAtom(w, name)
    Widget w;
    String name;
{
    Atom a;
    XrmValue source, dest;

    source.size = strlen(name)+1;
    source.addr = name;
    dest.size = sizeof(Atom);
    dest.addr = (caddr_t) &a;

    (void) XtConvertAndStore(w, XtRString, &source, XtRAtom, &dest);
    return a;
}


static Boolean DeliverSelection(w, selection, target,
        type, value, length, format)
    Widget w;
    Atom *selection, *target, *type;
    XtPointer *value;
    unsigned long *length;
    int *format;
{
    LabelWidget lw = (LabelWidget) w;
    static Atom targets = 0;

    if (targets == 0) {
        targets = FetchAtom(w, "TARGETS");
    }

    if (*target == targets) {
        *type = XA_ATOM;
        *value = (XtPointer) XtNew(Atom);
        *(Atom *) *value = XA_STRING;
        *length = 1;
        *format = 32;
        return TRUE;
    }

    if (*target == XA_STRING) {
        *type = XA_STRING;
        *value = (XtPointer) XtNewString(lw->label.label);
```

```
        *length = lw->label.label_len;
        *format = 8;
        return TRUE;
    }

    return FALSE;
}
```

The Intrinsics call LoseSelection when the label loses a selection that it previously owned. LoseSelection calls the XtNloseSelection callback to inform the application that the selection has been lost.

```
static void LoseSelection(w, selection)
    Widget w;
    Atom *selection;
{
    LabelWidget lw = (LabelWidget) w;

    XtCallCallbackList(lw, lw->label.lose_selection,
            (XtPointer) selection);
}
```

LabelSelectText is the entry point to access Label's new class method. It checks to be sure that the widget being passed in is a Label widget; XtCheckSubclass issues an error message if not. LabelSelectText extracts the *select* field from the widget's class record and calls it, passing the widget, the selection, and whether to own or disown the selection. This allows subclasses of Label to reimplement the select method with a different procedure if appropriate.

```
Boolean LabelSelectText(w, selection, own)
    Widget w;
    Atom selection;
    Boolean own;
{
    /* Check that we're in Label or a subclass */

    XtCheckSubclass(w, labelWidgetClass, NULL);

    /* Call the class method */

    return (*((LabelWidgetClass) XtClass(w))->label_class.select)
            (w, selection, own);
}
```

SelectText is the procedure that implements LabelSelectText for Label widgets. The *own* parameter tells whether to attempt to own or to relinquish the selection. Having this method take a timestamp parameter would place an undue burden on applications; both the attempt to own and to relinquish the selection use `XtLastTimestampProcessed`.

```
/* Label's select implementation */

static Boolean SelectText(w, selection, own)
    Widget w;
    Atom selection;
    Boolean own;
{
    LabelWidget lw = (LabelWidget) w;

    if (own) {
        return XtOwnSelection(w, selection,
                XtLastTimestampProcessed(XtDisplay(w)),
                DeliverSelection, LoseSelection,
                (XtSelectionDoneProc) NULL);
    } else {
        XtDisownSelection(w, selection,
                XtLastTimestampProcessed(XtDisplay(w)));
        return TRUE;
    }
}
```

The Intrinsics call ClassInitialize before creating any Label widgets. Class-Initialize registers the string-to-justification converter with the resource conversion mechanism. To avoid multiple string comparisons, this is registered as a cached converter. (If it were registered as an uncached converter, the quark version of the CvtStringToJustify would be the preferred implementation. The conversion cache avoids the multiple string comparisons for each conversion that would otherwise be necessary.) Since the converter allocates no extra storage, there is no destructor procedure.

```
static void ClassInitialize()
{
    /* Register a converter for string to justification */

    XtSetTypeConverter(XtRString, XtRJustify, CvtStringToJustify,
            (XtConvertArgList) NULL, 0,
            XtCacheAll, (XtDestructor) NULL);
}
```

The Intrinsics call ClassPartInitialize for each subclass of Label used by an application, passing the class record for the subclass. ClassPartInitialize is responsible for resolving the inheritance of the select method, which it does by comparing the value of the *select* field with the special value Inherit-SelectText and copying the superclass's value for the field into the class record if a match occurs.

```
static void ClassPartInitialize(widget_class)
    WidgetClass widget_class;
{
    register LabelWidgetClass wc = (LabelWidgetClass) widget_class;
    LabelWidgetClass super =
            (LabelWidgetClass) wc->core_class.superclass;

    if (wc->label_class.select == InheritSelectText) {
        wc->label_class.select = super->label_class.select;
    }
}
```

Label's initialize and set_values procedures call SetTextWidthAndHeight to compute the dimensions of the widget's text and accelerator strings when rendered in the widget's font. If the accelerator string is NULL, as it always is for label instances, only the text field is used. Being able to do this calculation without involving the server is the reason for using an XFontStruct rather than just a Font in the widget instance.

```
static void SetTextWidthAndHeight(lw)
    register LabelWidget lw;
{
    register XFontStruct *fs = lw->label.font;
    int accel_len;

    lw->label.label_len = strlen(lw->label.label);
    lw->label.label_width =
            XTextWidth(fs, lw->label.label, lw->label.label_len);
    lw->label.label_height =
            fs->max_bounds.ascent + fs->max_bounds.descent;

    if (lw->label.accel_string != NULL) {
        accel_len = strlen(lw->label.accel_string);
        lw->label.label_len += accel_len;
        lw->label.label_width +=
                XTextWidth(fs, lw->label.accel_string, accel_len);
    }
}
```

GetNormalGC allocates a graphics context to use to display the label text. Only the foreground and font values in the graphics context are relevant.

```
static GC GetNormalGC(lw)
    LabelWidget lw;
{

    XGCValues    values;

    /* Allocate a graphics context with the foreground and font */

    values.foreground = lw->label.foreground;
    values.font = lw->label.font->fid;
    return XtGetGC((Widget) lw, GCForeground | GCFont, &values);
}
```

The Intrinsics call Initialize to initialize any new Label widgets. If *label* is NULL, Initialize uses the widget's name; in any case it creates a new copy of the text to be sure that the text remains valid, even if the application used a local variable as the text when creating the widget. Initialize clears the *accel_string* field to NULL, calls SetTextWidthAndHeight to compute the label dimensions, and calls GetNormalGC to allocate the graphics context. If both the width and height are zero, the *size_computed* field is TRUE, so the label knows that it must recompute its size if the text string or the font changes later through XtSetValues. Initialize calculates the width and height if they are zero, and the *desired_width* and *desired_height* fields are copies of the width and height. Label's query_geometry procedure uses *desired_width* and *desired_height* to report back the size that the label prefers to be.

```
static void Initialize(request, new, args, num_args)
    Widget request, new;
    ArgList args;
    Cardinal *num_args;
{
    LabelWidget lw = (LabelWidget) new;

    /* If no label is specified, use the name */
    if (lw->label.label == NULL) lw->label.label = lw->core.name;

    /* Copy the label */
    lw->label.label = XtNewString(lw->label.label);

    /* Clear accelerator string */
    lw->label.accel_string = NULL;

    /* Compute the text dimensions and get a graphics context. */
    SetTextWidthAndHeight(lw);
    lw->label.gc = lw->label.current_gc = GetNormalGC(lw);

    /* If no size specified, compute one */
```

```
    lw->label.size_computed =
            (lw->core.width == 0) && (lw->core.height == 0);

    if (lw->core.width == 0) {
        lw->core.width = lw->label.label_width + 2 * lw->label.space;
    }
    if (lw->core.height == 0) {
        lw->core.height = lw->label.label_height + 2 * lw->label.space;
    }

    lw->label.desired_width = lw->core.width;
    lw->label.desired_height = lw->core.height;
}
```

The Intrinsics call SetValues whenever `XtSetValues` gets called for a Label widget. If the new label text is NULL, SetValues resets it to the widget's name. If the application sets both the width and the height to zero, the *size_computed* flag becomes TRUE to indicate that the size should be recomputed. If either one changed from its previous value to a nonzero value, *size_computed* becomes FALSE to indicate that the size should not be recomputed if the text or the font changes. SetValues then copies a new width or height into *desired_width* or *desired_height*. If the width and height are not zero, and neither changed, *size_computed* retains its previous value.

If the label, the font, or the accelerator string changed, SetValues must recompute the size of the displayed text. In addition, if the label or accelerator string changed, SetValues must free the old value and copy the new value. The *redisplay* flag becomes TRUE to indicate that these changes require a redisplay of the label to reflect its new state. If the size needs to be recomputed or if the width or height is zero, SetValues computes new values. Testing both *size_computed* and the actual field is necessary since the application might specify one dimension as zero, meaning to compute it, but specify the other as a real value. *Size_computed* is FALSE in this case since automatic recalculation upon a text or font change only occurs when the application sets both width and height to zero.

If the foreground or font changed, a new graphics context is necessary. If *current_gc* equals the old value of *gc*, the widget is currently displayed using the old graphics context and should now be displayed with the new one, so SetValues updates *current_gc*. This is always true for Label widgets but is false if the font or foreground is changed for a pushbutton currently displayed in its inverted or insensitive state. SetValues sets *redisplay* if *current_gc* changes to make the Intrinsics redraw the widget with the new graphics context.

Finally SetValues returns whether the label requires a redisplay. This is true if earlier code set redisplay, if the internal spacing changed, or if the justification value changed.

```
static Boolean SetValues(old, request, new, args, num_args)
    Widget  old, request, new;
    ArgList args;
    Cardinal *num_args;
{
    LabelWidget oldlw = (LabelWidget) old;
    LabelWidget newlw = (LabelWidget) new;
    Boolean redisplay = FALSE;

#define NE(field) (oldlw->field != newlw->field)

    /* If the label has been reset to NULL, change to the name */

    if (newlw->label.label == NULL) {
        newlw->label.label = newlw->core.name;
    }

    /* Decide whether to compute the size */

    if (newlw->core.width == 0 && newlw->core.height == 0) {
        newlw->label.size_computed = TRUE;
    } else if (NE(core.width) || NE(core.height)) {
        newlw->label.size_computed = FALSE;
        if (NE(core.width)) {
            newlw->label.desired_width = newlw->core.width;
        }
        if (NE(core.height)) {
            newlw->label.desired_height = newlw->core.height;
        }
    } /* else leave the same */

    /* If label, font, or accelerator string has changed,
       compute size and recopy */

    if (NE(label.label) || NE(label.font) || NE(label.accel_string)) {
        SetTextWidthAndHeight(newlw);
        redisplay = TRUE;

        if (NE(label.label)) {
            XtFree((char *) oldlw->label.label);
            newlw->label.label = XtNewString(newlw->label.label);
        }
        if (NE(label.accel_string)) {
            XtFree((char *) oldlw->label.accel_string);
            newlw->label.accel_string =
```

```
                              XtNewString(newlw->label.accel_string);
            }
        }


        /* Compute the size if necessary */

        if ((newlw->label.size_computed && redisplay) ||
                newlw->core.width == 0) {
            newlw->label.desired_width = newlw->core.width =
                    newlw->label.label_width + 2 * newlw->label.space;
        }
        if ((newlw->label.size_computed && redisplay) ||
                newlw->core.height == 0) {
            newlw->label.desired_height = newlw->core.height =
                    newlw->label.label_height + 2 * newlw->label.space;
        }


        /* If foreground or font has changed, update GC */

        if (NE(label.foreground) || NE(label.font->fid)) {
            XtReleaseGC(newlw, oldlw->label.gc);
            newlw->label.gc = GetNormalGC(newlw);

            if (newlw->label.current_gc == oldlw->label.gc) {
                newlw->label.current_gc = newlw->label.gc;
                redisplay = TRUE;
            }
        }

    return redisplay || NE(label.space) || NE(label.justify);
#undef NE
}
```

Destroy notifies the implementation that a Label widget is being destroyed. It
frees the label text and releases the label's graphics context.

```
static void Destroy(w)
    Widget w;
{
    LabelWidget lw = (LabelWidget) w;

    XtFree((char *) lw->label.label);
    XtReleaseGC(w, lw->label.gc);
}
```

Redisplay is Label's expose procedure; it is responsible for actually displaying
the label's contents. Since labels are simple to display, Redisplay ignores the
event and region parameters and draws the entire label each time. Redisplay
creates the string to display by concatenating the label text and the accelerator

string, if any. It then calculates the appropriate x coordinate for the text based upon the justification value. Since the width and space are stored as unsigned values, Redisplay casts them to integers to allow the calculation to yield a negative value if appropriate.

```
static void Redisplay(w, event, region)
    Widget w;
    XEvent *event;
    Region region;
{
    LabelWidget lw = (LabelWidget) w;
    char *string;
    Boolean allocated = FALSE;
    int x;

    if (lw->label.accel_string == NULL) {
        string = lw->label.label;
    } else {
        string = XtMalloc(lw->label.label_len + 1);
        (void) strcpy(string, lw->label.label);
        (void) strcat(string, lw->label.accel_string);
        allocated = TRUE;
    }

    switch (lw->label.justify) {
        case Left:
            x = lw->label.space;
            break;
        case Right:
            x = (int) lw->core.width - (int) lw->label.space -
                    (int) lw->label.label_width;
            break;
        case Center:
            x = ((int) lw->core.width -
                    (int) lw->label.label_width) / 2;
            break;
    }

    XDrawString(XtDisplay(w), XtWindow(w), lw->label.current_gc,
            x, lw->label.space + lw->label.font->max_bounds.ascent,
            string, lw->label.label_len);

    if (allocated) XtFree(string);
}
```

The Intrinsics call Resize whenever the size of a Label widget changes. If the widget is realized, Resize redisplays it by clearing it to its background and calling the expose procedure. Note that it calls the expose procedure in the

widget class record rather than calling Redisplay. This allows a subclass of
Label to inherit its resize procedure but override its expose procedure. Any
subclasses of Label must have expose procedures that can accept *region* and
event parameters of NULL. (This sort of information would normally go into
the widget set documentation.)

```
static void Resize(w)
    Widget w;
{
    /* If widget is realized, clear and redisplay */

    if (XtIsRealized(w)) {
        XClearWindow(XtDisplay(w), XtWindow(w));
        (*(XtClass(w)->core_class.expose))(w,
                (XEvent *) NULL, (Region) NULL);
    }
}
```

QueryGeometry is responsible for returning the desired size of the widget.
Label cares about the width and height fields and is willing to accept any x, y,
border width, and stacking position. If the proposed geometry has a width and
a height that match the desired dimensions, and the parent intends to use
these values (i.e., CWWidth and CWHeight are set in *proposed–>request_mode*),
QueryGeometry returns XtGeometryYes. If the parent intends to use values for
width and height that differ from the desired size, QueryGeometry returns
either XtGeometryNo if the desired size is equal to the current size or
XtGeometryAlmost if the desired size is different from the current size.

```
static XtGeometryResult QueryGeometry(w, proposed, desired)
    Widget w;
    XtWidgetGeometry *proposed, *desired;
{
    LabelWidget lw = (LabelWidget) w;
#define Set(bit) (proposed->request_mode & bit)

    desired->width = lw->label.desired_width;
    desired->height = lw->label.desired_height;
    desired->request_mode = CWWidth | CWHeight;

    if (Set(CWWidth) && proposed->width == desired->width &&
            Set(CWHeight) && proposed->height == desired->height) {
        return XtGeometryYes;
    }

    if (desired->width == lw->core.width &&
            desired->height == lw->core.height) {
```

```
            return XtGeometryNo;
    }
    return XtGeometryAlmost;
#undef Set
}
```

10.5.4   Suggested Programming Exercises

- Give Label a new resource XtNbitmap. If the application sets this resource, display a bitmap instead of the text string.

- Write a string-to-bitmap converter to go along with the resource. The string should be the name of a file containing the bitmap; see XReadBitmapFile in Section 10.10 of *Xlib*. Think about how this conversion should be cached. Does it need a destructor procedure?

10.6   The Pushbutton Widget

Pushbutton is a subclass of Label and uses the Label implementation to handle the text string displayed in the pushbutton. The procedures in the Pushbutton implementation concern themselves only with adding the additional functionality for pushbuttons. Pushbutton illustrates how widgets handle X events, particularly keyboard and pointer events.

The most complicated thing about Pushbutton is its use of resource default procedures to handle the resources for displaying an insensitive pushbutton. Pushbuttons have two foreground resources, XtNinsensitiveForeground and XtNinsensitivePixmap, that applications can use to specify the foreground for insensitive pushbuttons. If only one is specified, Pushbutton uses it. If both are specified, Pushbutton uses XtNinsensitiveForeground.[2] If neither is specified, Pushbutton constructs a pixmap consisting of the normal foreground pixel stippled to half intensity and uses it.

10.6.1   The Public Header File

```
/* Make it safe to include this file more than once. */

#ifndef PUSHBUTTON_H
#define PUSHBUTTON_H
```

---

[2] These semantics are intentionally different from the ones Core uses for its background and border colors. Since there is no special value that can be reserved for "unspecified pixel," this widget illustrates a technique that widget programmers may find useful in similar situations.

```
/* Include the public header file for Label, our superclass */

#include "Label.h"

/* New resource definitions */

#define XtNinsensitiveForeground "insensitiveForeground"
#define XtNinsensitivePixmap "insensitivePixmap"
#define XtNhighlightBorder "highlightBorder"
#define XtNacceleratorString "acceleratorString"
#define XtCAcceleratorString "AcceleratorString"

/* External reference to the class record pointer */

extern WidgetClass pushbuttonWidgetClass;

/* Type definition for pushbutton widgets */

typedef struct _PushbuttonRec *PushbuttonWidget;

/* End of preprocessor directives */

#endif /* PUSHBUTTON_H */
```

10.6.2   The Private Header File

```
/* Make it safe to include this file more than once. */

#ifndef PUSHBUTTONP_H
#define PUSHBUTTONP_H

/* Include the public header file for Pushbutton */

#include "Pushbutton.h"

/* Include the private header file for Label, our superclass */

#include "LabelP.h"

/* Define a new, private resource */

#define XtNaccelString "accelString"
#define XtCAccelString "AccelString"

/* Define the Pushbutton instance part */

typedef struct {
  /* New resource fields */
    XtCallbackList callback;              /* Application callback */
    Pixel          insensitive_foreground; /* Insensitive colors */
```

```
    Pixmap       insensitive_pixmap;
    Dimension    highlight_border;        /* Highlight border width */
    String       accelerator_string;      /* String for accelerator */

  /* New internal fields */
    GC           insensitive_gc;     /* GC for displaying insensitive */
    GC           inverted_gc;        /* GC for displaying inverted */
    Boolean      highlighted;        /* Whether highlighted */
    Boolean      inverted;           /* Whether inverted */
    Boolean      use_insens_pixel;   /* Whether using insensitive pixel */
} PushbuttonPart;

/* Define the full instance record */

typedef struct _PushbuttonRec {
    CorePart            core;
    LabelPart           label;
    PushbuttonPart      pushbutton;
} PushbuttonRec;
/* Define class part structure */

typedef struct {
    XtPointer           extension;
} PushbuttonClassPart;

/* Define the full class record */

typedef struct _PushbuttonClassRec {
    CoreClassPart       core_class;
    LabelClassPart      label_class;
    PushbuttonClassPart pushbutton_class;
} PushbuttonClassRec, *PushbuttonWidgetClass;

/* External definition for class record */

extern PushbuttonClassRec pushbuttonClassRec;

/* End of preprocessor directives */
#endif /* PUSHBUTTONP_H */
```

10.6.3   The Implementation

```
#include <string.h>              /* Needed for string manipulation */
#include <X11/IntrinsicP.h>      /* Intrinsics header file */
#include <X11/StringDefs.h>      /* Resource string definitions */
#include "PushbuttoP.h"          /* Pushbutton private header file */
```

Use_insens_pixel is a flag field that defines whether to use the insensitive foreground pixel specified by XtNinsensitiveForeground or to use the insensitive foreground pixmap specified by XtNinsensitivePixmap. The resource default procedures for these resources set *use_insens_pixel*; if the default procedure gets called for one of the resources, it means that that resource was not specified, so the default procedure sets this flag to make the pushbutton use the other resource. This value is not really a resource; its entry in the resource list is to force it to have a known value before either default procedure is called since the initial contents of any widget field without a resource entry are undefined. The name and class contain a period to make it impossible to specify a value for this resource in a resource file.

The ordering of the three resource specifications dealing with the insensitive foreground is significant; recall that the Intrinsics always initialize resource fields in the order that the resources occur in resource lists. First *use_insens_pixel* becomes TRUE. Next the Intrinsics fetch XtNinsensitive-Foreground; if they find no value, they call the default procedure, which sets *use_insens_pixel* to FALSE to make the pushbutton use the insensitive pixmap. Finally the Intrinsics fetch XtNinsensitivePixmap; its default procedure checks *use_insens_pixel* to determine whether to set *insensitive_pixmap* to None or to the new stippled pixmap.

The reason for all this complexity is that every possible pixel value, from 0 to $2^{32} - 1$, is valid. Without the default procedure setting *use_insens_pixel*, there is no way for the rest of the implementation to know whether XtNinsensitive-Foreground took its default value. It must know this to know whether to use the insensitive pixel or the insensitive pixmap. Consult Section 3.17 for more details on how these resources work.

```
static void InsPixel(), InsPixmap();

#define Offset(field) XtOffsetOf(PushbuttonRec, pushbutton.field)

static XtResource resources[] = {
    {XtNcallback, XtCCallback, XtRCallback, sizeof(XtCallbackList),
        Offset(callback), XtRCallback, (XtPointer) NULL},
    {"pri.vate", "Pri.vate", XtRBoolean, sizeof(Boolean),
        Offset(use_insens_pixel), XtRImmediate, (XtPointer) TRUE},
    {XtNinsensitiveForeground, XtCForeground, XtRPixel, sizeof(Pixel),
        Offset(insensitive_foreground),
        XtRCallProc, (XtPointer) InsPixel},
    {XtNinsensitivePixmap, XtCPixmap, XtRPixmap, sizeof(Pixmap),
        Offset(insensitive_pixmap),
        XtRCallProc, (XtPointer) InsPixmap},
```

```
    {XtNhighlightBorder, XtCBorderWidth,
        XtRDimension, sizeof(Dimension),
        Offset(highlight_border), XtRImmediate, (XtPointer) 1},
    {XtNaccelString, XtCAccelString, XtRString, sizeof(String),
        XtOffsetOf(PushbuttonRec, label.accel_string),
        XtRString, NULL},
    {XtNacceleratorString, XtCAcceleratorString,
        XtRString, sizeof(String),
        Offset(accelerator_string), XtRString, NULL},
    {XtNborderWidth, XtCBorderWidth,
        XtRDimension, sizeof(Dimension),
        XtOffsetOf(PushbuttonRec, core.border_width),
        XtRImmediate, (XtPointer) 1},
};

#undef Offset

static void InsPixel(w, offset, value)
    Widget w;
    int offset;          /* Not used */
    XrmValue *value;
{
    PushbuttonWidget p = (PushbuttonWidget) w;

    /* Any value will work; it won't be used */
    value->addr = (caddr_t) &p->label.foreground;
    p->pushbutton.use_insens_pixel = FALSE;
}

/* Return a 2x2 pixmap with the foreground at 50% */

static Pixmap GetPixmap(pw)
    PushbuttonWidget pw;
{
    static char bits[] = {0x01, 0x02};

    return XCreatePixmapFromBitmapData(XtDisplay(pw),
            RootWindowOfScreen(XtScreen(pw)), bits, 2, 2,
            pw->label.foreground, pw->core.background_pixel,
            pw->core.depth);
}

static void InsPixmap(w, offset, value)
    Widget w;
    int offset;          /* Not used */
    XrmValue *value;
{
    PushbuttonWidget pw = (PushbuttonWidget) w;
    static Pixmap pixmap;

    if (pw->pushbutton.use_insens_pixel) pixmap = None;
```

```
        else pixmap = GetPixmap(pw);

        value->addr = (caddr_t) &pixmap;
}
```

The first part of this chapter describes Pushbutton's default translations and actions.

```
static char defaultTranslations[] =
        "<EnterWindow>  : highlight()           \n\
        <LeaveWindow>   : unhighlight()         \n\
        <Btn1Down>      : invert()              \n\
        <Btn1Up>        : notify() uninvert()";

static void Highlight(), Unhighlight(), Invert(), Uninvert(), Notify();

static XtActionsRec actions[] = {
  {"highlight",         Highlight},
  {"unhighlight",       Unhighlight},
  {"invert",            Invert},
  {"uninvert",          Uninvert},
  {"notify",            Notify},
};

/* Forward declarations */

static void Initialize(), DisplayAccelerator(), Destroy(), Redisplay();
static Boolean SetValues();

/* Class record declaration */

PushbuttonClassRec pushbuttonClassRec = {
    /* Core class part */
  {
    /* superclass              */ (WidgetClass) &labelClassRec,
    /* class_name              */ "Pushbutton",
    /* widget_size             */ sizeof(PushbuttonRec),
    /* class_initialize        */ NULL,
    /* class_part_initialize   */ NULL,
    /* class_inited            */ FALSE,
    /* initialize              */ Initialize,
    /* initialize_hook         */ NULL,
    /* realize                 */ XtInheritRealize,
    /* actions                 */ actions,
    /* num_actions             */ XtNumber(actions),
    /* resources               */ resources,
    /* num_resources           */ XtNumber(resources),
    /* xrm_class               */ NULLQUARK,
    /* compress_motion         */ TRUE,
    /* compress_exposure       */ XtExposeCompressMultiple,
    /* compress_enterleave     */ TRUE,
```

```
        /* visible_interest       */ FALSE,
        /* destroy                 */ NULL,
        /* resize                  */ XtInheritResize,
        /* expose                  */ Redisplay,
        /* set_values              */ SetValues,
        /* set_values_hook         */ NULL,
        /* set_values_almost       */ XtInheritSetValuesAlmost,
        /* get_values_hook         */ NULL,
        /* accept_focus            */ NULL,
        /* version                 */ XtVersion,
        /* callback offsets        */ NULL,
        /* tm_table                */ defaultTranslations,
        /* query_geometry          */ XtInheritQueryGeometry,
        /* display_accelerator     */ DisplayAccelerator,
        /* extension               */ NULL
    },
    /* Label class part */
    {
        /* select_text             */ InheritSelectText,
        /* extension               */ NULL
    },
    /* Pushbutton class part */
    {
        /* extension               */ NULL
    }
};

/* Class record pointer */

WidgetClass pushbuttonWidgetClass = (WidgetClass) &pushbuttonClassRec;
```

The Highlight action procedure just sets the *highlighted* field to TRUE and, if
the widget is realized, clears it and calls the expose procedure to redraw the
widget in its highlighted state.

```
static void Highlight(w, event, params, num_params)
    Widget w;
    XEvent *event;
    String *params;
    Cardinal *num_params;
{
    PushbuttonWidget pw = (PushbuttonWidget) w;

    if (!pw->pushbutton.highlighted) {
        pw->pushbutton.highlighted = TRUE;
        if (XtIsRealized(w)) {
            XClearWindow(XtDisplay(w), XtWindow(w));
            (*(XtClass(w)->core_class.expose))(w, event, NULL);
        }
    }
}
```

```
static void Unhighlight(w, event, params, num_params)
    Widget w;
    XEvent *event;
    String *params;
    Cardinal *num_params;
{
    PushbuttonWidget pw = (PushbuttonWidget) w;

    if (pw->pushbutton.highlighted) {
        pw->pushbutton.highlighted = FALSE;
        if (XtIsRealized(w)) {
            XClearWindow(XtDisplay(w), XtWindow(w));
            (*(XtClass(w)->core_class.expose))(w, event, NULL);
        }
    }
}
```

The Invert action procedure is similar to the Highlight action procedure except that it also changes the *current_gc* field so that redisplaying the pushbutton draws it in its inverted state. The Uninvert action procedure also has to check whether the widget is sensitive to know whether to restore *current_gc* to the normal or to the insensitive graphics context.

```
static void Invert(w, event, params, num_params)
    Widget w;
    XEvent *event;
    String *params;
    Cardinal *num_params;
{
    PushbuttonWidget pw = (PushbuttonWidget) w;

    if (!pw->pushbutton.inverted) {
        pw->pushbutton.inverted = TRUE;
        pw->label.current_gc = pw->pushbutton.inverted_gc;
        if (XtIsRealized(w)) {
            XClearWindow(XtDisplay(w), XtWindow(w));
            (*(XtClass(w)->core_class.expose))(w, event, NULL);
        }
    }
}

static void Uninvert(w, event, params, num_params)
    Widget w;
    XEvent *event;
    String *params;
    Cardinal *num_params;
{
    PushbuttonWidget pw = (PushbuttonWidget) w;
```

```
        if (pw->pushbutton.inverted) {
            pw->pushbutton.inverted = FALSE;
            if (XtIsSensitive(w)) {
                pw->label.current_gc = pw->label.gc;
            } else pw->label.current_gc = pw->pushbutton.insensitive_gc;

            if (XtIsRealized(w)) {
                XClearWindow(XtDisplay(w), XtWindow(w));
                (*(XtClass(w)->core_class.expose))(w, event, NULL);
            }
        }
    }
```

The Notify action is a little more complicated. The X server normally
guarantees that the window that received a pointer button press also receives
the button release no matter where the pointer is when the release occurs. To
handle the case where the user presses the pointer button inside the pushbutton, changes his mind, and aborts the pushbutton by moving the pointer
out before releasing, the Notify action checks whether the pointer coordinates
in the release event are actually inside the pushbutton's window. It only does
this check if the event is a button release event for the widget's window; if not,
an accelerator invoked the action or the user bound the action to a different
event type, so the check is inappropriate.

```
static void Notify(w, event, params, num_params)
    Widget w;
    XEvent *event;
    String *params;
    Cardinal *num_params;
{
    PushbuttonWidget pw = (PushbuttonWidget) w;

    /* If event is a button event, and the event's window is the
       widget's window, we were invoked normally.  Make sure
       the pointer is really in the window */

    if (event != NULL && event->type == ButtonRelease &&
            event->xany.window == XtWindow(w)) {
        XButtonEvent *b = &event->xbutton;
        if (b->x < 0 || b->y < 0 ||
            b->x >= w->core.width || b->y >= w->core.height) return;
    }

    XtCallCallbackList(pw, pw->pushbutton.callback, NULL);
}
```

Pushbutton has two graphics context fields in addition to those in Label. GetInvertedGC creates an inverted graphics context, using the widget's background as the graphics context foreground. GetInsensitiveGC creates a graphics context for use when the widget is insensitive. It uses *use_insens_pixel* to decide whether to use the insensitive foreground or the insensitive pixmap in the graphics context.

The Intrinsics call Initialize for every new Pushbutton widget, but only after first calling Label's initialize procedure. Pushbutton's initialize procedure only needs to worry about fields in its instance part. It fetches the insensitive and inverted graphics contexts and creates a new copy of the accelerator string, then initializes the *highlighted* and *inverted* flags to FALSE. If the pushbutton is insensitive, the current graphics context becomes the insensitive graphics context.

```
static GC GetInvertedGC(pw)
    PushbuttonWidget pw;
{
    XGCValues    values;

    values.foreground = pw->core.background_pixel;
    values.font = pw->label.font->fid;
    return XtGetGC((Widget) pw, GCForeground | GCFont, &values);
}

static GC GetInsensitiveGC(pw)
    PushbuttonWidget pw;
{
    XGCValues    values;

    values.font = pw->label.font->fid;

    if (pw->pushbutton.use_insens_pixel) {
        values.foreground = pw->pushbutton.insensitive_foreground;
        return XtGetGC((Widget) pw, GCForeground | GCFont, &values);
    } else {
        values.tile = pw->pushbutton.insensitive_pixmap;
        values.fill_style = FillTiled;
        return XtGetGC((Widget) pw,
                GCTile | GCFont | GCFillStyle, &values);
    }
}

static void Initialize(req, new)
    Widget req, new;
{
```

```
    PushbuttonWidget pw = (PushbuttonWidget) new;

    pw->pushbutton.insensitive_gc = GetInsensitiveGC(pw);
    pw->pushbutton.inverted_gc = GetInvertedGC(pw);
    pw->pushbutton.accelerator_string =
            XtNewString(pw->pushbutton.accelerator_string);

    pw->pushbutton.highlighted = pw->pushbutton.inverted = FALSE;

    if (!XtIsSensitive(pw)) {
        pw->label.current_gc = pw->pushbutton.insensitive_gc;
    }
}
```

The Intrinsics call SetValues when the application changes some widget resources through XtSetValues. If either the insensitive foreground pixel or the insensitive pixmap has changed, SetValues updates *use_insens_pixel* to reflect which to use. Changing the insensitive pixmap to None makes SetValues call GetPixmap to fetch a new stippled pixmap. If either insensitive foreground field or the font has changed, SetValues releases the old insensitive graphics context, fetches a new one, and sets the current graphics context to this new context if it is equal to the old insensitive context. SetValues updates the inverted graphics context analogously.

If either sensitivity field changed, SetValues updates the current graphics context. If the widget is now sensitive, *current_gc* becomes the normal graphics context; otherwise it becomes the insensitive graphics context. Desensitizing the widget also turns highlighting off since the widget will never receive the leave event that would normally do so.

Finally, SetValues returns whether to redisplay the widget. It needs redisplaying if the current graphics context changed, the foreground changed when the widget is inverted, or the highlighting border changed when the widget is highlighted.

```
static Boolean SetValues(old, req, new, args, num_args)
    Widget  old, req, new;
    ArgList args;
    Cardinal *num_args;
{
    PushbuttonWidget oldpw = (PushbuttonWidget) old;
    PushbuttonWidget newpw = (PushbuttonWidget) new;

#define NE(field) (oldpw->field != newpw->field)

    /* If insensitive fields or button's font has changed,
```

```
         update insensitive GC */

    if (NE(pushbutton.insensitive_foreground)) {
        newpw->pushbutton.use_insens_pixel = TRUE;
    }

    if (NE(pushbutton.insensitive_pixmap)) {
        if (newpw->pushbutton.insensitive_pixmap == None) {
            newpw->pushbutton.insensitive_pixmap = GetPixmap(newpw);
        }
        newpw->pushbutton.use_insens_pixel = FALSE;
    }

    if (NE(pushbutton.insensitive_foreground) ||
            NE(pushbutton.insensitive_pixmap) || NE(label.font->fid)) {
        XtReleaseGC(newpw, oldpw->pushbutton.insensitive_gc);
        newpw->pushbutton.insensitive_gc = GetInsensitiveGC(newpw);

        if (newpw->label.current_gc ==
                oldpw->pushbutton.insensitive_gc) {
            newpw->label.current_gc = newpw->pushbutton.insensitive_gc;
        }
    }

    /* If background or font has changed, update inverted GC */

    if (NE(core.background_pixel) || NE(label.font->fid)) {
        XtReleaseGC(newpw, oldpw->pushbutton.inverted_gc);
        newpw->pushbutton.inverted_gc = GetInvertedGC(newpw);

        if (newpw->pushbutton.inverted) {
            newpw->label.current_gc = newpw->pushbutton.inverted_gc;
        }
    }

    /* If sensitivity changing, adjust appearance */

    if (NE(core.sensitive) || NE(core.ancestor_sensitive)) {
        if (XtIsSensitive(newpw)) {      /* Just made sensitive */
            newpw->label.current_gc = newpw->label.gc;

        } else {                          /* Just made insensitive */
            newpw->label.current_gc =
                    newpw->pushbutton.insensitive_gc;

            /* If currently highlighted, will never receive
               leave event to unhighlight, so unhighlight */
            newpw->pushbutton.highlighted = FALSE;
        }
    }
```

```
        /* If current graphics context has changed, inverted
           and foreground has changed, or highlighted and highlight
           width has changed, redisplay */

        return NE(label.current_gc) ||
               (NE(label.foreground) && newpw->pushbutton.inverted) ||
               (NE(pushbutton.highlight_border) &&
                       newpw->pushbutton.highlighted);
#undef NE
}
```

The Intrinsics call Destroy to destroy a pushbutton. It releases the pushbutton's graphics contexts and frees the accelerator strings.

```
static void Destroy(w)
    Widget w;
{
    PushbuttonWidget pw = (PushbuttonWidget) w;

    /* Release the GCs */

    XtReleaseGC(w, pw->pushbutton.insensitive_gc);
    XtReleaseGC(w, pw->pushbutton.inverted_gc);

    XtFree(pw->pushbutton.accelerator_string);
    XtFree(pw->label.accel_string);
}
```

Redisplay is the expose procedure for pushbuttons; it envelopes its superclass expose procedure. If the button is inverted, Redisplay fills it with the widget's foreground color, and if it is highlighted, Redisplay draws a hollow rectangle around the inside of the pushbutton. Redisplay then calls the expose procedure for its superclass, Label, to finish redisplaying by drawing the text.

```
static void Redisplay(w, event, region)
    Widget w;
    XEvent *event;
    Region region;
{
    PushbuttonWidget pw = (PushbuttonWidget) w;
    int offset;

    /* If inverted, fill background with the foreground color */

    if (pw->pushbutton.inverted) {
        XFillRectangle(XtDisplay(w), XtWindow(w), pw->label.gc,
                0, 0, pw->core.width, pw->core.height);
    }

    /* If highlighted, draw highlighting border */
```

```
      if (pw->pushbutton.highlighted) {
          offset = pw->pushbutton.highlight_border / 2;
          XDrawRectangle(XtDisplay(w), XtWindow(w), pw->label.current_gc,
                  offset, offset,
                  pw->core.width - pw->pushbutton.highlight_border,
                  pw->core.height - pw->pushbutton.highlight_border);
      }

      /* Make Label redisplay the string */

      (*pushbuttonWidgetClass->core_class.superclass->core_class.expose)
              (w, event, region);
  }
```

The Intrinsics call DisplayAccelerator when a pushbutton's accelerators get
installed somewhere. If the pushbutton's *accelerator_string* field is not NULL,
DisplayAccelerator copies it into the *accel_string* field by calling
XtSetValues. The SetValues procedure for Label takes care of displaying
the value.

```
static void DisplayAccelerator(w, string)
    Widget w;
    String string;
{
    PushbuttonWidget pw = (PushbuttonWidget) w;
    Arg args[1];

    if (pw->pushbutton.accelerator_string != NULL) {
        XtSetArg(args[0], XtNaccelString,
                pw->pushbutton.accelerator_string);
        XtSetValues(w, args, 1);
    }
}
```

10.6.4   Suggested Programming Exercises

• Make Pushbutton draw in its window to give the pushbutton a three-dimensional
appearance. Along with this, have the initialize and set_values procedures make the
default size larger to make room for this drawing, as described in Section 2.23. If you
make the suggested change to Label to support bitmaps, be sure your new code still
supports this.

10.7   The MenuItem Widget

MenuItem is a subclass of Pushbutton. Its only difference is that it has a different set of default translations, more appropriate for an entry in a menu.

MenuItem illustrates the bare essentials of specializing an existing widget class by subclassing. Although it may appear to be a lot of code to write for such a minimal change, the writer of the MenuItem widget is guaranteed to be able to track any improvements to Pushbutton with no additional effort.

10.7.1   The Public Header File

```
/* Make it safe to include this file more than once. */

#ifndef MENUITEM_H
#define MENUITEM_H

/* Include the public header file for Pushbutton, our superclass */

#include "Pushbutton.h"

/* External reference to the class record pointer */

extern WidgetClass menuItemWidgetClass;

/* Type definition for menuItem widgets */

typedef struct _MenuItemRec *MenuItemWidget;

/* End of preprocessor directives */

#endif /* MENUITEM_H */
```

10.7.2   The Private Header File

```
/* Make it safe to include this file more than once. */

#ifndef MENUITEMP_H
#define MENUITEMP_H

/* Include the public header file for MenuItem */

#include "MenuItem.h"

/* Include the private header file for Pushbutton, our superclass */

#include "PushbuttoP.h"

/* Define the MenuItem instance part */

typedef struct {
    int         empty;          /* no empty structures allowed */
} MenuItemPart;
```

```
/* Define the full instance record */

typedef struct _MenuItemRec {
    CorePart            core;
    LabelPart           label;
    PushbuttonPart      pushbutton;
    MenuItemPart        menuItem;
} MenuItemRec;

/* Define class part structure */

typedef struct {
    XtPointer           extension;
} MenuItemClassPart;

/* Define the full class record */

typedef struct _MenuItemClassRec {
    CoreClassPart       core_class;
    LabelClassPart      label_class;
    PushbuttonClassPart pushbutton_class;
    MenuItemClassPart   menuItem_class;
} MenuItemClassRec, *MenuItemWidgetClass;

/* External definition for class record */

extern MenuItemClassRec menuItemClassRec;

/* End of preprocessor directives */

#endif /* MENUITEMP_H */
```

10.7.3 The Implementation

```
#include <X11/IntrinsicP.h>     /* Intrinsics header file */
#include "MenuItemP.h"          /* MenuItem private header file */

static char defaultTranslations[] =
        "<EnterWindow>  : invert()              \n\
         <LeaveWindow>  : uninvert()            \n\
         <BtnUp>        : notify() uninvert()";

/* Class record declaration */

MenuItemClassRec menuItemClassRec = {
    /* Core class part */
  {
    /* superclass              */ (WidgetClass) &pushbuttonClassRec,
    /* class_name              */ "MenuItem",
    /* widget_size             */ sizeof(MenuItemRec),
```

```
        /* class_initialize       */ NULL,
        /* class_part_initialize */ NULL,
        /* class_inited           */ FALSE,
        /* initialize             */ NULL,
        /* initialize_hook        */ NULL,
        /* realize                */ XtInheritRealize,
        /* actions                */ NULL,
        /* num_actions            */ 0,
        /* resources              */ NULL,
        /* num_resources          */ 0,
        /* xrm_class              */ NULLQUARK,
        /* compress_motion        */ TRUE,
        /* compress_exposure      */ XtExposeCompressMultiple,
        /* compress_enterleave    */ TRUE,
        /* visible_interest       */ FALSE,
        /* destroy                */ NULL,
        /* resize                 */ XtInheritResize,
        /* expose                 */ XtInheritExpose,
        /* set_values             */ NULL,
        /* set_values_hook        */ NULL,
        /* set_values_almost      */ XtInheritSetValuesAlmost,
        /* get_values_hook        */ NULL,
        /* accept_focus           */ NULL,
        /* version                */ XtVersion,
        /* callback offsets       */ NULL,
        /* tm_table               */ defaultTranslations,
        /* query_geometry         */ XtInheritQueryGeometry,
        /* display_accelerator    */ XtInheritDisplayAccelerator,
        /* extension              */ NULL
    },
        /* Label class part */
    {
        /* select_text            */ InheritSelectText,
        /* extension              */ NULL
    },
        /* Pushbutton class part */
    {
        /* extension              */ NULL
    },
        /* MenuItem class part */
    {
        /* extension              */ NULL
    }
};

/* Class record pointer */

WidgetClass menuItemWidgetClass = (WidgetClass) &menuItemClassRec;
```

10.7.4   Suggested Programming Exercises

- Make MenuItem support cascading menus by defining a new XtNpopupSubmenu-Callback callback resource. If the user moves the pointer into the far right of the menu item, call the XtNpopupSubmenuCallback; this gives the application the opportunity to pop up a submenu after popping down any previous submenu. The application can use the XtNpopdownCallback of the menus to make sure things get popped down correctly. If XtNpopupSubmenuCallback is not empty, make the menu item display some appropriate graphic to indicate that it has a submenu.

10.8   The Box Widget

The Box widget is a simple container for other widgets. It illustrates most of the functionality of composite widgets in a simple, straightforward way.

10.8.1   The Public Header File

```
/* Make it safe to include this file more than once. */

#ifndef BOX_H
#define BOX_H

/* Box is derived from Composite, so no need to include the superclass
   public header file.  */

/* Define the new resource that Box uses */

#define XtNmargin "margin"

/* External reference to the class record pointer */

extern WidgetClass boxWidgetClass;

/* Type definition for box widgets */

typedef struct _BoxRec *BoxWidget;

/* End of preprocessor directives */

#endif /* BOX_H */
```

10.8.2   The Private Header File

```
/* Make it safe to include this file more than once. */

#ifndef BOXP_H
#define BOXP_H
```

```
/* Include the public header file for Box */

#include "Box.h"

/* Box is derived from Composite, so no need to include the superclass
   private header file.  */

/* Define the Box instance part */

typedef struct {
  /* New resource fields */
    Dimension    margin;          /* Extra space to leave on edges */

  /* New internal fields */
    Widget       last_focus;      /* Child that last had the focus */
} BoxPart;

/* Define the full instance record */

typedef struct _BoxRec {
    CorePart            core;
    CompositePart       composite;
    BoxPart             box;
} BoxRec;

/* Define class part structure */

typedef struct {
    XtPointer           extension;
} BoxClassPart;

/* Define the full class record */

typedef struct _BoxClassRec {
    CoreClassPart       core_class;
    CompositeClassPart  composite_class;
    BoxClassPart        box_class;
} BoxClassRec, *BoxClass;

/* External definition for class record */

extern BoxClassRec boxClassRec;

/* End of preprocessor directives */

#endif /* BOXP_H */
```

10.8.3   The Implementation

```
#include <X11/IntrinsicP.h>      /* Intrinsics header file */
#include <X11/StringDefs.h>      /* Resource string definitions */
#include "BoxP.h"                /* Box private header file */
#include "LabelGadge.h"          /* To check LabelGadgets */


#define Offset(field) XtOffsetOf(BoxRec, box.field)

static XtResource resources[] = {
    {XtNmargin, XtCMargin, XtRDimension, sizeof(Dimension),
        Offset(margin), XtRImmediate, (XtPointer) 10},
};

#undef Offset

/* Forward declarations */

static void ChangeManaged(), Initialize(), InsertChild(),
        DeleteChild(), Redisplay();
static XtGeometryResult GeometryManager();
static Boolean SetValues(), AcceptFocus();

static CompositeClassExtensionRec compositeExtension = {
    /* next_extension           */ NULL,
    /* record_type              */ NULLQUARK,
    /* version                  */ XtCompositeExtensionVersion,
    /* record_size              */ sizeof(CompositeClassExtensionRec),
    /* accepts_objects          */ TRUE
};

BoxClassRec boxClassRec = {
    /* Core class part */
  {
    /* superclass               */ (WidgetClass) &compositeClassRec,
    /* class_name               */ "Box",
    /* widget_size              */ sizeof(BoxRec),
    /* class_initialize         */ NULL,
    /* class_part_initialize    */ NULL,
    /* class_inited             */ FALSE,
    /* initialize               */ Initialize,
    /* initialize_hook          */ NULL,
    /* realize                  */ XtInheritRealize,
    /* actions                  */ NULL,
    /* num_actions              */ 0,
    /* resources                */ resources,
    /* num_resources            */ XtNumber(resources),
    /* xrm_class                */ NULLQUARK,
    /* compress_motion          */ TRUE,
    /* compress_exposure        */ XtExposeCompressMultiple,
```

```
                /* compress_enterleave    */ TRUE,
                /* visible_interest       */ FALSE,
                /* destroy                 */ NULL,
                /* resize                  */ NULL,
                /* expose                  */ Redisplay,
                /* set_values              */ SetValues,
                /* set_values_hook         */ NULL,
                /* set_values_almost       */ XtInheritSetValuesAlmost,
                /* get_values_hook         */ NULL,
                /* accept_focus            */ AcceptFocus,
                /* version                 */ XtVersion,
                /* callback offsets        */ NULL,
                /* tm_table                */ NULL,
                /* query_geometry          */ XtInheritQueryGeometry,
                /* display_accelerator     */ NULL,
                /* extension               */ NULL,
        },
        /* Composite class part */
        {
                /* geometry_manager        */ GeometryManager,
                /* change_managed          */ ChangeManaged,
                /* insert_child            */ InsertChild,
                /* delete_child            */ DeleteChild,
                /* extension               */ (XtPointer) &compositeExtension,
        },
        /* Box class part */
        {
                /* extension               */ NULL,
        }
};

WidgetClass boxWidgetClass = (WidgetClass) &boxClassRec;
```

Box supplies an insert_child procedure to check that new children are either widgets or Label gadgets. Any other class of child generates an error message. The error message contains the actual class name of the parent widget rather than just using "Box"; this displays the correct class if a subclass of Box inherits this procedure. InsertChild calls the superclass's insert_child procedure to actually insert the child.

```
static void InsertChild(w)
    Widget w;
{
    String params[2];
    Cardinal num_params;
    Widget parent = XtParent(w);

    if (!XtIsWidget(w) && !XtIsSubclass(w, labelGadgetClass)) {
        params[0] = XtClass(w)->core_class.class_name;
```

```
        params[1] = XtClass(parent)->core_class.class_name;
        num_params = 2;
        XtAppErrorMsg(XtWidgetToApplicationContext(w),
                "childError", "class", "WidgetError",
                "Children of class %s cannot be added to %n widgets",
                params, &num_params);
    }

    (*((CompositeWidgetClass)(boxWidgetClass->core_class.superclass))->
            composite_class.insert_child) (w);
}
```

Box supplies a delete_child procedure to reset the *last_focus* field if the child that last had the focus gets deleted. DeleteChild calls the superclass's delete_child procedure to actually delete the child.

```
static void DeleteChild(w)
    Widget w;
{

    BoxWidget box = (BoxWidget) XtParent(w);

    if (box->box.last_focus == w) box->box.last_focus = NULL;

    (*((CompositeWidgetClass)(boxWidgetClass->core_class.superclass))->
            composite_class.delete_child) (w);
}
```

The Initialize procedure sets the *last_focus* field for new Box widgets to NULL.

```
static void Initialize(req, new, args, num_args)
    Widget req, new;
    ArgList args;
    Cardinal *num_args;
{
    ((BoxWidget) new)->box.last_focus = NULL;
}
```

CalculateNewSize is a utility procedure for Box's change_managed, geometry_manager, and set_values procedures. It computes a new size for *box*, sufficiently large to hold all the box's children. CalculateNewSize computes the right and bottom coordinates for each managed child, and the width and height are maximum values of *right* and *bottom* for any child. *Right* or *bottom* would be negative if a child were completely above or to the left of the parent, and *width* and *height* are unsigned quantities. CalculateNewSize casts *width* and *height* to integers for the comparisons to prevent the compiler from casting *right* and *bottom* to unsigned values. CalculateNewSize adds in the box's margin and checks the width and height to make sure they are not zero.

```
static void CalculateNewSize(box, width, height)
    BoxWidget box;
    register Dimension *width, *height;
{
    register Widget child;
    register int i;
    int right, bottom;

    *width = *height = 0;

    for (i = 0; i < box->composite.num_children; i++) {
        child = box->composite.children[i];
        if (!XtIsManaged(child)) continue;
        right = child->core.x + child->core.width +
                2 * child->core.border_width;
        bottom = child->core.y + child->core.height +
                2 * child->core.border_width;
        if (right > (int) *width) *width = right;
        if (bottom > (int) *height) *height = bottom;
    }

    *width += box->box.margin;
    *height += box->box.margin;

    if (*width == 0) *width = 1;
    if (*height == 0) *height = 1;
}
```

The Intrinsics call ChangeManaged to inform a box that its set of managed children has changed. ChangeManaged calculates a new size based upon the new managed set by calling CalculateNewSize. If this new size is different from the box's current size, ChangeManaged calls XtMakeGeometryRequest to try to become this size. If XtMakeGeometryRequest returns XtGeometry-Almost, ChangeManaged calls it again to accept the compromise.

```
static void ChangeManaged(w)
    Widget w;
{
    BoxWidget box = (BoxWidget) w;
    XtWidgetGeometry request;
    XtGeometryResult result;

    CalculateNewSize(box, &request.width, &request.height);

    if (request.width != box->core.width ||
            request.height != box->core.height) {
        request.request_mode = CWWidth | CWHeight;
```

```
        do {
            result = XtMakeGeometryRequest(w, &request, &request);
        } while (result == XtGeometryAlmost);
    }
}
```

GeometryManager is responsible for deciding whether to allow a child's size to change. The Box widget has a simple decision algorithm: it always grants any change. If the request is a query-only request, GeometryManager just returns XtGeometryYes since this is what it always returns. Otherwise it copies any desired changes into the requesting child and computes a new size based on the changes. If the new size is not the same as the current size, Geometry-Manager issues a geometry request to try to become this size, but regardless of whether this request succeeds it returns XtGeometryYes. GeometryManager implicitly handles stacking requests by returning XtGeometryYes; XtMakeGeometryRequest will restack the widget as requested.

```
static XtGeometryResult GeometryManager(w, desired, allowed)
    Widget w;
    XtWidgetGeometry *desired, *allowed;
{
    BoxWidget box = (BoxWidget) XtParent(w);
    XtWidgetGeometry request;
    XtGeometryResult result;

#define Wants(flag) (desired->request_mode & flag)

    if (Wants(XtCWQueryOnly)) return XtGeometryYes;

    if (Wants(CWWidth)) w->core.width = desired->width;
    if (Wants(CWHeight)) w->core.height = desired->height;
    if (Wants(CWX)) w->core.x = desired->x;
    if (Wants(CWY)) w->core.y = desired->y;
    if (Wants(CWBorderWidth)) {
        w->core.border_width = desired->border_width;
    }

    CalculateNewSize(box, &request.width, &request.height);

    if (request.width != box->core.width ||
            request.height != box->core.height) {
        request.request_mode = CWWidth | CWHeight;
        do {
            result = XtMakeGeometryRequest((Widget) box,
                    &request, &request);
        } while (result == XtGeometryAlmost);
    }
```

```
        return XtGeometryYes;

#undef Wants
}
```

The SetValues procedure reacts to any requested changes to a box's resources. If the box's margin has changed or either the box's width or height is now zero, SetValues calls CalculateNewSize to determine a new size and stores the desired height and width in the widget record. It returns FALSE to indicate that it does not require redisplaying.

```
static Boolean SetValues(old, req, new, args, num_args)
    Widget old, req, new;
    ArgList args;
    Cardinal *num_args;
{
    register BoxWidget oldbox = (BoxWidget) old;
    register BoxWidget newbox = (BoxWidget) new;

    if (newbox->box.margin != oldbox->box.margin ||
            newbox->core.width == 0 || newbox->core.height == 0) {
        CalculateNewSize(newbox, &newbox->core.width,
                &newbox->core.height);
    }

    return FALSE;
}
```

AcceptFocus is responsible for taking the keyboard focus on demand. It calls XtCallAcceptFocus for each managed child, first trying the child that last had the focus, trying to find one that accepts the focus. If no child accepts the focus, AcceptFocus does not either, returning FALSE.

```
static Boolean AcceptFocus(w, time)
    Widget w;
    Time *time;
{
    BoxWidget box = (BoxWidget) w;
    register int i;

    if (box->box.last_focus != NULL &&
            XtIsManaged(box->box.last_focus)) {
        if (XtCallAcceptFocus(box->box.last_focus, time)) {
            return TRUE;
        }
    }

    for (i = 0; i < box->composite.num_children; i++) {
```

```
        if (!XtIsManaged(box->composite.children[i])) continue;
        if (XtCallAcceptFocus(box->composite.children[i], time)) {
            box->box.last_focus = box->composite.children[i];
            return TRUE;
        }
    }

    box->box.last_focus = NULL;
    return FALSE;
}
```

Redisplay takes care of calling the expose procedure for any managed Label gadget children whose areas intersect the exposed region. It relies upon the child to redisplay its background and border and does not modify the exposure event or the region. This could be made more efficient by having ChangeManaged set a flag in the widget record indicating whether there are any gadget children.

```
static void Redisplay(w, event, region)
    Widget w;
    XEvent *event;
    Region region;
{
    CompositeWidget comp = (CompositeWidget) w;
    int i;
    Widget c;                /* child */

    for (i = 0; i < comp->composite.num_children; i++) {
        c = comp->composite.children[i];
        if (XtIsManaged(c) && XtIsSubclass(c, labelGadgetClass) &&
                XRectInRegion(region, c->core.x, c->core.y,
                        c->core.width + 2*c->core.border_width,
                        c->core.height + 2*c->core.border_width)
                    != RectangleOut) {
            (*(XtClass(c)->core_class.expose))(c, event, region);
        }
    }
}
```

10.8.4   Suggested Programming Exercises

• Implement the improvement described in the discussion of the Redisplay procedure.

• Modify the Box geometry manager so that it denies a request to grow larger or move if the child would be clipped by the edge of the box.

• Modify the Box geometry manager so that it denies a request to grow larger or move if the child would overlap another child.

- Add the necessary code to let the parent of a Box widget find the minimum Box dimensions needed to display all children without clipping.

- Make Box a subclass of Constraint and rewrite MinMax as a subclass of Box. This will allow MinMax to inherit resources and methods from Box.

10.9   The MinMax Widget

The MinMax widget is similar to the Box widget except that it allows each child to specify minimum and maximum useful dimensions. It illustrates the use of constraint resources. If a user or application shrinks a MinMax widget, any child that would be clipped by the new geometry shrinks until it reaches its minimum size; similarly, if a MinMax widget expands, each child that is less than its maximum size grows. MinMax is not a subclass of Box because MinMax needs to be a subclass of Constraint and Box is not, so MinMax duplicates much of Box's code. One way to avoid doing this would be to make Box a subclass of Constraint even though it defines no constraints.

10.9.1   The Public Header File

```
/* Make it safe to include this file more than once. */
#ifndef MINMAX_H
#define MINMAX_H

/* MinMax is derived from Constraint, so no need to include the
   superclass public header file.  */

/* Define the new resources that MinMax uses */

#define XtNmargin "margin"
#define XtNminWidth "minWidth"
#define XtNmaxWidth "maxWidth"
#define XtNminHeight "minHeight"
#define XtNmaxHeight "maxHeight"
#define XtCMinWidth "MinWidth"
#define XtCMaxWidth "MaxWidth"
#define XtCMinHeight "MinHeight"
#define XtCMaxHeight "MaxHeight"

/* External reference to the class record pointer */
extern WidgetClass minMaxWidgetClass;

/* Type definition for minMax widgets */
typedef struct _MinMaxRec *MinMaxWidget;
```

```
/* End of preprocessor directives */
#endif /* MINMAX_H */
```

10.9.2   The Private Header File

```
/* Make it safe to include this file more than once. */

#ifndef MINMAXP_H
#define MINMAXP_H

/* Include the public header file for MinMax */

#include "MinMax.h"

/* MinMax is derived from Constraint, so no need to include the
   superclass private header file.  */

/* Define the MinMax instance part */

typedef struct {
  /* New resource fields */
    Dimension    margin;          /* Extra space to leave on edges */

  /* New internal fields */
    Widget       last_focus;      /* Child that last had the focus */
} MinMaxPart;

/* Define the full instance record */

typedef struct _MinMaxRec {
    CorePart             core;
    CompositePart        composite;
    ConstraintPart       constraint;
    MinMaxPart           minMax;
} MinMaxRec;

/* Define class part structure */

typedef struct {
    XtPointer            extension;
} MinMaxClassPart;

/* Define the full class record */

typedef struct _MinMaxClassRec {
    CoreClassPart        core_class;
    CompositeClassPart   composite_class;
    ConstraintClassPart  constraint_class;
    MinMaxClassPart      minMax_class;
} MinMaxClassRec, *MinMaxClass;
```

```
/* Define constraint part structure */

typedef struct {
  /* New resource fields */
    short               min_width;
    short               max_width;
    short               min_height;
    short               max_height;
} MinMaxConstraintPart;

/* Define the full constraint record */

typedef struct _MinMaxConstraintRec {
    MinMaxConstraintPart minMax;
} MinMaxConstraintRec, *MinMaxConstraint;

/* External definition for class record */

extern MinMaxClassRec minMaxClassRec;

/* End of preprocessor directives */

#endif /* MINMAXP_H */
```

10.9.3   The Implementation

```
#include <X11/IntrinsicP.h>     /* Intrinsics header file */
#include <X11/StringDefs.h>     /* Resource string definitions */
#include "MinMaxP.h"            /* MinMax private header file */
#include "LabelGadge.h"         /* To check LabelGadgets */
```

MinMax has the same resource list as Box.

```
#define Offset(field) XtOffsetOf(MinMaxRec, minMax.field)

static XtResource resources[] = {
    {XtNmargin, XtCMargin, XtRDimension, sizeof(Dimension),
        Offset(margin), XtRImmediate, (XtPointer) 10},
};

#undef Offset
```

MinMax's constraint resource list defines the four constraint resources
XtNminWidth, XtNmaxWidth, XtNminHeight, and XtNmaxHeight. They are
of type short rather than Dimension so that they can take default values
that are not legal for Dimension; this allows the implementation to detect
which constraints have been specified for a particular child.

```
#define Offset(field) XtOffsetOf(MinMaxConstraintRec, field)

static XtResource constraintResources[] = {
    {XtNminWidth, XtCMinWidth, XtRShort, sizeof(short),
        Offset(minMax.min_width), XtRImmediate, (XtPointer) -1},
    {XtNmaxWidth, XtCMaxWidth, XtRShort, sizeof(short),
        Offset(minMax.max_width), XtRImmediate, (XtPointer) -1},
    {XtNminHeight, XtCMinHeight, XtRShort, sizeof(short),
        Offset(minMax.min_height), XtRImmediate, (XtPointer) -1},
    {XtNmaxHeight, XtCMaxHeight, XtRShort, sizeof(short),
        Offset(minMax.max_height), XtRImmediate, (XtPointer) -1},
};
#undef Offset

/* Forward declarations */

static void ChangeManaged(), Initialize(), ConstraintInitialize(),
        Resize(), InsertChild(), DeleteChild(), Redisplay();
static XtGeometryResult GeometryManager();
static Boolean SetValues(), AcceptFocus(), ConstraintSetValues();

static CompositeClassExtensionRec compositeExtension = {
    /* next_extension       */ NULL,
    /* record_type          */ NULLQUARK,
    /* version              */ XtCompositeExtensionVersion,
    /* record_size          */ sizeof(CompositeClassExtensionRec),
    /* accepts_objects      */ TRUE
};

MinMaxClassRec minMaxClassRec = {
    /* Core class part */
  {
    /* superclass           */ (WidgetClass) &constraintClassRec,
    /* class_name           */ "MinMax",
    /* widget_size          */ sizeof(MinMaxRec),
    /* class_initialize     */ NULL,
    /* class_part_initialize */ NULL,
    /* class_inited         */ FALSE,
    /* initialize           */ Initialize,
    /* initialize_hook      */ NULL,
    /* realize              */ XtInheritRealize,
    /* actions              */ NULL,
    /* num_actions          */ 0,
    /* resources            */ resources,
    /* num_resources        */ XtNumber(resources),
    /* xrm_class            */ NULLQUARK,
    /* compress_motion      */ TRUE,
    /* compress_exposure    */ XtExposeCompressMultiple,
    /* compress_enterleave  */ TRUE,
    /* visible_interest     */ FALSE,
```

```
        /* destroy            */ NULL,
        /* resize             */ Resize,
        /* expose             */ Redisplay,
        /* set_values         */ SetValues,
        /* set_values_hook    */ NULL,
        /* set_values_almost  */ XtInheritSetValuesAlmost,
        /* get_values_hook    */ NULL,
        /* accept_focus       */ AcceptFocus,
        /* version            */ XtVersion,
        /* callback offsets   */ NULL,
        /* tm_table           */ NULL,
        /* query_geometry     */ XtInheritQueryGeometry,
        /* display_accelerator */ NULL,
        /* extension          */ NULL,
    },
    /* Composite class part */
    {
        /* geometry_manager   */ GeometryManager,
        /* change_managed     */ ChangeManaged,
        /* insert_child       */ InsertChild,
        /* delete_child       */ DeleteChild,
        /* extension          */ (XtPointer) &compositeExtension,
    },
    /* Constraint class part */
    {
        /* resources          */ constraintResources,
        /* num_resources      */ XtNumber(constraintResources),
        /* constraint_size    */ sizeof(MinMaxConstraintRec),
        /* initialize         */ ConstraintInitialize,
        /* destroy            */ NULL,
        /* set_values         */ ConstraintSetValues,
        /* extension          */ NULL
    },
    /* MinMax class part */
    {
        /* extension          */ NULL,
    }
};

WidgetClass minMaxWidgetClass = (WidgetClass) &minMaxClassRec;
```

MinMax has the same InsertChild procedure as Box except for the superclass used to find the insert_child procedure.

```
static void InsertChild(w)
    Widget w;
{
    String params[2];
    Cardinal num_params;
    Widget parent = XtParent(w);
```

```
    if (!XtIsWidget(w) && !XtIsSubclass(w, labelGadgetClass)) {
        params[0] = XtClass(w)->core_class.class_name;
        params[1] = XtClass(parent)->core_class.class_name;
        num_params = 2;
        XtAppErrorMsg(XtWidgetToApplicationContext(w),
                "childError", "class", "WidgetError",
                "Children of class %s cannot be added to %n widgets",
                params, &num_params);
    }

    (*((CompositeWidgetClass)(minMaxWidgetClass->
            core_class.superclass))->composite_class.insert_child) (w);
}
```

MinMax has the same DeleteChild procedure as Box.

```
static void DeleteChild(w)
    Widget w;
{
    MinMaxWidget minMax = (MinMaxWidget) XtParent(w);

    if (minMax->minMax.last_focus == w) {
        minMax->minMax.last_focus = NULL;
    }

    (*((CompositeWidgetClass)(minMaxWidgetClass->
            core_class.superclass))->composite_class.delete_child) (w);
}
```

MinMax has the same Initialize procedure as Box.

```
static void Initialize(req, new, args, num_args)
    Widget req, new;
    ArgList args;
    Cardinal *num_args;
{
    ((MinMaxWidget) new)->minMax.last_focus = NULL;
}
```

CheckConstraint is a utility procedure for MinMax's initialize and set_values procedures. It checks if a minimum constraint value is larger than the corresponding maximum and issues a warning and resets the minimum to the maximum if so.

```
static void CheckConstraint(w, smaller, larger, which)
    Widget w;
    short *smaller, *larger;
    String which;
{
    String params[3];
```

```
        Cardinal num_params;

    if (*smaller > *larger) {
        params[0] = params[1] = which;
        params[2] = XtName(w);
        num_params = 3;
        XtAppWarningMsg(XtWidgetToApplicationContext(w),
                "constraintError",
                "width", "WidgetError",
                "Min %s greater than max %s for widget %s",
                params, &num_params);
        *smaller = *larger;
    }
}
```

ResizeWithinConstraints is another utility procedure for MinMax's constraint initialize and set_values procedures. It checks if a widget size is within its constraints, modifying the size if necessary.

```
static void ResizeWithinConstraints(w, width, height)
    Widget w;
    Dimension *width, *height;
{
    register MinMaxConstraint mmc =
            (MinMaxConstraint) w->core.constraints;

    if (*width < mmc->minMax.min_width) {
        *width = mmc->minMax.min_width;
    } else if (*width > mmc->minMax.max_width) {
        *width = mmc->minMax.max_width;
    }

    if (*height < mmc->minMax.min_height) {
        *height = mmc->minMax.min_height;
    } else if (*height > mmc->minMax.max_height) {
        *height = mmc->minMax.max_height;
    }
}
```

The Intrinsics call ConstraintInitialize to initialize the constraint fields of any child of a MinMax widget. The semantics of the MinMax constraints are that if no constraints are specified for a child in a dimension, the child is never resized; if only one constraint is specified in a dimension, the size is not constrained in the other extreme. If the minimum and maximum width fields are both –1, it means that neither was specified, so ConstraintInitialize sets both to the current width; the same is done for the height. ConstraintInitialize then checks each minimum and maximum constraint for –1 and replaces it either with 1, the minimum legal widget size, or MAXDIM, the maximum legal widget size. Calls to CheckConstraint check the width and the height constraints. Finally, ConstraintInitialize calls ResizeWithinConstraints to see if the child satisfies the constraints; if not, ConstraintInitialize calls `XtResizeWidget` to make it do so.

Note that the Intrinsics call the ConstraintInitialize procedure only after calling all the normal initialize procedures for the child's class and its superclasses. From the point of view of the child, its creation is already complete, so `XtResizeWidget` is the correct procedure to call to modify the child's dimensions.

```
static void ConstraintInitialize(req, new, args, num_args)
    Widget req, new;
    ArgList args;
    Cardinal *num_args;
{
    MinMaxConstraint mmc = (MinMaxConstraint) new->core.constraints;
    Dimension width = new->core.width, height = new->core.height;
#define MAXDIM 32768

    if (mmc->minMax.min_width == -1 && mmc->minMax.max_width == -1) {
        mmc->minMax.min_width = mmc->minMax.max_width = width;
    }
    if (mmc->minMax.min_height == -1 && mmc->minMax.max_height == -1) {
        mmc->minMax.min_height = mmc->minMax.max_height = height;
    }

    if (mmc->minMax.min_width == -1) mmc->minMax.min_width = 1;
    if (mmc->minMax.max_width == -1) mmc->minMax.max_width = MAXDIM;
    if (mmc->minMax.min_height == -1) mmc->minMax.min_height = 1;
    if (mmc->minMax.max_height == -1) mmc->minMax.max_height = MAXDIM;

    CheckConstraint(new, &mmc->minMax.min_width,
            &mmc->minMax.max_width, "width");
    CheckConstraint(new, &mmc->minMax.min_height,
            &mmc->minMax.max_height, "height");
    ResizeWithinConstraints(new, &width, &height);

    if (width != new->core.width || height != new->core.height) {
        XtResizeWidget(new, width, height);
    }
#undef MAXDIM
}
```

MinMax has the same CalculateNewSize procedure as Box.

```
static void CalculateNewSize(minMax, width, height)
    MinMaxWidget minMax;
    register Dimension *width, *height;
{
    register Widget child;
    register int i;
    int right, bottom;

    *width = *height = 0;

    for (i = 0; i < minMax->composite.num_children; i++) {
        child = minMax->composite.children[i];
        if (!XtIsManaged(child)) continue;
        right = child->core.x + child->core.width +
                2 * child->core.border_width;
        bottom = child->core.y + child->core.height +
                2 * child->core.border_width;
        if (right > (int) *width) *width = right;
        if (bottom > (int) *height) *height = bottom;
    }

    *width += minMax->minMax.margin;
    *height += minMax->minMax.margin;

    if (*width == 0) *width = 1;
    if (*height == 0) *height = 1;
}
```

ResizeChildren is a utility procedure for MinMax's change_managed, geometry_manager, and resize procedures; it resizes a MinMax widget's children to reflect a new size for the MinMax widget. If MinMax's geometry manager is calling ResizeChildren, the *initiator* parameter is the child making the geometry request. Since MinMax relies upon the Intrinsics to actually resize the requesting child, ResizeChildren skips resizing the initiator. The *minMax_right* and *minMax_bottom* variables are the maximum right and bottom boundaries to use when computing new sizes for children. ResizeChildren inspects each managed child besides the initiator in turn. If the child's right edge extends beyond *minMax_right* and the child is wider than its minimum width, ResizeChildren shrinks the child so that it no longer extends, but never narrower than the child's minimum width. Similarly, if the child's right edge does not reach *minMax_right* and the child is narrower than its maximum width, ResizeChildren expands the child so that it reaches the right edge, but never wider than the child's maximum width. ResizeChildren adjusts the child's height analogously.

```
static void ResizeChildren(minMax, initiator)
    MinMaxWidget minMax;
    Widget initiator;
{
    register Widget child;
    register MinMaxConstraint mmc;
    register int i;
    int right, bottom;
    int new_width, new_height;
    int minMax_right = minMax->core.width - minMax->minMax.margin,
        minMax_bottom = minMax->core.height - minMax->minMax.margin;

    for (i = 0; i < minMax->composite.num_children; i++) {
        child = minMax->composite.children[i];
        if (!XtIsManaged(child) || child == initiator) continue;

        mmc = (MinMaxConstraint) child->core.constraints;
        new_width = child->core.width;
        new_height = child->core.height;

        right = child->core.x + child->core.width +
                2 * child->core.border_width;
        bottom = child->core.y + child->core.height +
                2 * child->core.border_width;

        if (right > minMax_right &&
                child->core.width > mmc->minMax.min_width) {
            new_width -= right - minMax_right;
            if (new_width < mmc->minMax.min_width) {
                new_width = mmc->minMax.min_width;
            }
        } else if (right < minMax_right &&
                child->core.width < mmc->minMax.max_width) {
            new_width += minMax_right - right;
            if (new_width > mmc->minMax.max_width) {
                new_width = mmc->minMax.max_width;
            }
        }

        if (bottom > minMax_bottom &&
                child->core.height > mmc->minMax.min_height) {
            new_height -= bottom - minMax_bottom;
            if (new_height < mmc->minMax.min_height) {
                new_height = mmc->minMax.min_height;
            }
        } else if (bottom < minMax_bottom &&
                child->core.height < mmc->minMax.max_height) {
            new_height += minMax_bottom - bottom;
            if (new_height > mmc->minMax.max_height) {
                new_height = mmc->minMax.max_height;
```

```
                }
            }

            XtResizeWidget(child, new_width, new_height,
                    child->core.border_width);
        }
}
```

The Intrinsics call Resize to notify a MinMax widget that its size has changed. Resize just calls ResizeChildren with a NULL *initiator* widget to make all the children adapt to the new size.

```
static void Resize(w)
    Widget w;
{
    ResizeChildren((MinMaxWidget) w, (Widget) NULL);
}
```

MinMax's ChangeManaged procedure is identical to Box's except that if having a different managed set makes the MinMax widget's size change, ChangeManaged calls ResizeChildren with a NULL *initiator* widget to make all the children adapt to the new size.

```
static void ChangeManaged(w)
    Widget w;
{
    MinMaxWidget minMax = (MinMaxWidget) w;
    XtWidgetGeometry request;
    XtGeometryResult result;

    CalculateNewSize(minMax, &request.width, &request.height);

    if (request.width != minMax->core.width ||
            request.height != minMax->core.height) {
        request.request_mode = CWWidth | CWHeight;
        do {
            result = XtMakeGeometryRequest(w,
                    &request, (XtWidgetGeometry *) NULL);
        } while (result == XtGeometryAlmost);

        if (result == XtGeometryYes) {
            ResizeChildren(minMax, (Widget) NULL);
        }
    }
}
```

MinMax has a more complicated geometry manager than Box. Geometry-Manager first checks if the child is requesting a size change that exceeds its minimum or maximum dimension and returns XtGeometryNo if so. GeometryManager saves the child's geometry fields and stores the requested new ones into the widget. This allows CalculateNewSize to take the child's requested changes into account when figuring out how large the MinMax widget should be. If changing the child's size does not affect the size of the MinMax widget, GeometryManager grants the geometry request. Otherwise, GeometryManager calls `XtMakeGeometryRequest` to see if the MinMax widget's parent allows the change.

If the parent allows the change and this is not a query-only request, the Intrinsics have resized the MinMax widget, so GeometryManager calls Resize-Children with *initiator* being the widget that made the geometry request, making all other children adapt to the new size, and returns XtGeometryYes. Returning XtGeometryYes makes the Intrinsics inspect the geometry changes stored into the widget and to make them; this is why ResizeChildren does not resize the requesting child.

At this point either the request was query-only or the GeometryManager will not grant the request, so GeometryManager backs out the changes to the widget it made earlier. It then returns the appropriate result.

```
static XtGeometryResult GeometryManager(w, desired, allowed)
    Widget w;
    XtWidgetGeometry *desired, *allowed;
{
    MinMaxWidget minMax = (MinMaxWidget) XtParent(w);
    MinMaxConstraint mmc = (MinMaxConstraint) w->core.constraints;
    XtWidgetGeometry request;
    XtGeometryResult result;
    Dimension save_width, save_height, save_border_width;
    Position save_x, save_y;

#define Wants(flag) (desired->request_mode & flag)
#define RestoreGeometry(w) { \
    w->core.x = save_x;        w->core.y = save_y; \
    w->core.width = save_width; w->core.height = save_height; \
    w->core.border_width = save_border_width; }

    /* If the desired change goes outside the constraints, say no */

    if ((Wants(CWWidth) && (desired->width < mmc->minMax.min_width ||
                desired->width > mmc->minMax.max_width)) ||
            (Wants(CWHeight) &&
                (desired->height < mmc->minMax.min_height ||
                desired->height > mmc->minMax.max_height))) {
```

```
                return XtGeometryNo;
        }

        /* Figure out how big we would be with this change */

        save_x = w->core.x;
        save_y = w->core.y;
        save_width = w->core.width;
        save_height = w->core.height;
        save_border_width = w->core.border_width;
        if (Wants(CWX)) w->core.x = desired->x;
        if (Wants(CWY)) w->core.y = desired->y;
        if (Wants(CWWidth)) w->core.width = desired->width;
        if (Wants(CWHeight)) w->core.height = desired->height;
        if (Wants(CWBorderWidth)) {
            w->core.border_width = desired->border_width;
        }

        CalculateNewSize(minMax, &request.width, &request.height);

        if (request.width == minMax->core.width &&
                request.height == minMax->core.height) {
            if (Wants(XtCWQueryOnly)) RestoreGeometry(w);
            return XtGeometryYes;
        }

        /* We need to change size in order to accommodate; see if we can */

        request.request_mode = CWWidth | CWHeight;
        if (Wants(XtCWQueryOnly)) request.request_mode |= XtCWQueryOnly;

        result = XtMakeGeometryRequest((Widget) minMax, &request, NULL);
        if (result == XtGeometryAlmost) result = XtGeometryNo;

        if (result == XtGeometryYes && !Wants(XtCWQueryOnly)) {
            ResizeChildren(minMax, w);
            return XtGeometryYes;
        }

        /* Undo the saved changes */

        RestoreGeometry(w);
        return result;
#undef Wants
#undef RestoreGeometry
    }
```

MinMax has the same SetValues procedure as Box.

```
static Boolean SetValues(old, req, new, args, num_args)
    Widget old, req, new;
    ArgList args;
    Cardinal *num_args;
{
    register MinMaxWidget oldminMax = (MinMaxWidget) old;
    register MinMaxWidget newminMax = (MinMaxWidget) new;

    if (newminMax->minMax.margin != oldminMax->minMax.margin ||
            newminMax->core.width == 0 ||
            newminMax->core.height == 0) {
        CalculateNewSize(newminMax,
                &newminMax->core.width, &newminMax->core.height);
    }

    return FALSE;
}
```

The Intrinsics call ConstraintSetValues whenever the application attempts to change the resources of a child of a MinMax widget through XtSetValues. It does almost the same thing as the ConstraintInitialize procedure, calling CheckConstraint to verify that the minimums are still less than the maximums and calling ResizeWithinConstraints to make the child adjust to any changes. It does not resize the child if it changes the child's geometry fields; XtSetValues takes care of this.

```
static Boolean ConstraintSetValues(old, req, new, args, num_args)
    Widget old, req;
    ArgList args;
    Cardinal *num_args;
    register Widget new;
{
    register MinMaxConstraint mmc =
            (MinMaxConstraint) new->core.constraints;

    CheckConstraint(new, &mmc->minMax.min_width,
            &mmc->minMax.max_width, "width");
    CheckConstraint(new, &mmc->minMax.min_height,
            &mmc->minMax.max_height, "height");
    ResizeWithinConstraints(new, &new->core.width, &new->core.height);

    return FALSE;
}
```

MinMax has the same AcceptFocus procedure as Box.

```
static Boolean AcceptFocus(w, time)
    Widget w;
    Time *time;
```

```
{
    MinMaxWidget minMax = (MinMaxWidget) w;
    register int i;

    if (minMax->minMax.last_focus != NULL &&
            XtIsManaged(minMax->minMax.last_focus)) {
        if (XtCallAcceptFocus(minMax->minMax.last_focus, time)) {
            return TRUE;
        }
    }

    for (i = 0; i < minMax->composite.num_children; i++) {
        if (!XtIsManaged(minMax->composite.children[i])) continue;
        if (XtCallAcceptFocus(minMax->composite.children[i], time)) {
            minMax->minMax.last_focus = minMax->composite.children[i];
            return TRUE;
        }
    }

    minMax->minMax.last_focus = NULL;
    return FALSE;
}
```

MinMax has the same Redisplay procedure as Box.

```
static void Redisplay(w, event, region)
    Widget w;
    XEvent *event;
    Region region;
{
    CompositeWidget comp = (CompositeWidget) w;
    int i;
    Widget c;            /* child */

    for (i = 0; i < comp->composite.num_children; i++) {
        c = comp->composite.children[i];
        if (XtIsManaged(c) && XtIsSubclass(c, labelGadgetClass) &&
                XRectInRegion(region, c->core.x, c->core.y,
                        c->core.width + 2*c->core.border_width,
                        c->core.height + 2*c->core.border_width)
                    != RectangleOut) {
            (*(XtClass(c)->core_class.expose))(c, event, region);
        }
    }
}
```

10.9.4   Suggested Programming Exercises

• Make a subclass of MinMax that also moves its children around when it resizes them. Add new constraint resources that control which other widget each child should be kept next to horizontally and vertically, and new resources that specify how far away from that widget the child should be. If these resources are specified for a widget, compute its location instead of using its XtNx and XtNy resources. A constraint widget with this behavior is sometimes called a Form widget.

10.10   The Confirm Widget

The Confirm widget is an example of a widget that appears to an application to be a single widget but which actually contains several other widgets. There are two implementations of Confirm, one as a subclass of Box and one as a subclass of Core. Confirm also illustrates the use of the get_values_hook procedure to provide resources that can be queried but not set; indeed, in the Box instance the values provided do not even have a fixed location in the Confirm instance structure.

Both implementations create two widgets, a label and a pushbutton, for a new Confirm widget. In the implementation that is a subclass of Box, these widgets are normal children that reside in the child list, and in the implementation that is a subclass of Core these widgets are subwidgets stored in private fields in the Confirm widget instance record.

The Box subclass is discussed first.

10.10.1   The Public Header File

```
/* Make it safe to include this file more than once. */

#ifndef CONFIRM_H
#define CONFIRM_H

/* Include the public header file for Box, our superclass */

#include "Box.h"

/* Define the new resources that Confirm uses.  There are no resource
   classes corresponding to XtNlabelChild and XtNbuttonChild since
   these cannot be set. */

#define XtNbuttonLabel "buttonLabel"
#define XtCButtonLabel "ButtonLabel"
#define XtNlabelWidget "labelWidget"
```

```
#define XtNbuttonWidget "buttonWidget"

/* External reference to the class record pointer */

extern WidgetClass confirmWidgetClass;

/* Type definition for confirm widgets */

typedef struct _ConfirmRec *ConfirmWidget;

/* End of preprocessor directives */

#endif /* CONFIRM_H */
```

10.10.2 The Private Header File

```
/* Make it safe to include this file more than once. */

#ifndef CONFIRMP_H
#define CONFIRMP_H

/* Include the public header file for Confirm */

#include "Confirm.h"

/* Include the private header file for Box, our superclass */

#include "BoxP.h"

/* Define the Confirm instance part */

typedef struct {
  /* New resource fields */
    String              label;          /* Label string */
    String              button_label;   /* Button string */
    XtCallbackList      callback;       /* Callback to execute */
} ConfirmPart;

/* Define the full instance record */

typedef struct _ConfirmRec {
    CorePart            core;
    CompositePart       composite;
    BoxPart             box;
    ConfirmPart         confirm;
} ConfirmRec;

/* Define class part structure */

typedef struct {
```

```
        XtPointer           extension;
} ConfirmClassPart;

/* Define the full class record */

typedef struct _ConfirmClassRec {
    CoreClassPart       core_class;
    CompositeClassPart  composite_class;
    BoxClassPart        box_class;
    ConfirmClassPart    confirm_class;
} ConfirmClassRec, *ConfirmClass;

/* External definition for class record */

extern ConfirmClassRec confirmClassRec;

/* End of preprocessor directives */

#endif /* CONFIRMP_H */
```

10.10.3 The Implementation

```
#include <X11/IntrinsicP.h>     /* Intrinsics header file */
#include <X11/StringDefs.h>     /* Resource string definitions */
#include "ConfirmP.h"           /* Confirm private header file */
#include "Label.h"              /* Label public header file */
#include "Pushbutton.h"         /* Pushbutton public header file */
```

XtNlabelWidget and XtNbuttonWidget do not appear in the resource list, so applications cannot set their values. Querying these resources is supported through Confirm's get_values_hook procedure.

```
#define Offset(field) XtOffsetOf(ConfirmRec, confirm.field)

static XtResource resources[] = {
    {XtNlabel, XtCLabel, XtRString, sizeof(String),
        Offset(label), XtRString, "Click to confirm"},
    {XtNbuttonLabel, XtCButtonLabel, XtRString, sizeof(String),
        Offset(button_label), XtRString, "OK"},
    {XtNcallback, XtCCallback, XtRCallback, sizeof(XtCallbackList),
        Offset(callback), XtRCallback, (XtPointer) NULL},
};

#undef Offset
```

The Label child is always the first entry in the child list, and the Pushbutton child is always the second. These macros make the rest of the code easier to read.

```
#define LabelChild(w) (((CompositeWidget) w)->composite.children[0])
#define ButtonChild(w) (((CompositeWidget) w)->composite.children[1])

/* Forward declarations */

static void InsertChild(), Initialize(), PositionChildren(),
        GetValuesHook();
static Boolean SetValues();
static XtGeometryResult GeometryManager();

ConfirmClassRec confirmClassRec = {
    /* Core class part */
  {
    /* superclass            */ (WidgetClass) &boxClassRec,
    /* class_name            */ "Confirm",
    /* widget_size           */ sizeof(ConfirmRec),
    /* class_initialize      */ NULL,
    /* class_part_initialize */ NULL,
    /* class_inited          */ FALSE,
    /* initialize            */ Initialize,
    /* initialize_hook       */ NULL,
    /* realize               */ XtInheritRealize,
    /* actions               */ NULL,
    /* num_actions           */ 0,
    /* resources             */ resources,
    /* num_resources         */ XtNumber(resources),
    /* xrm_class             */ NULLQUARK,
    /* compress_motion       */ TRUE,
    /* compress_exposure     */ XtExposeCompressMultiple,
    /* compress_enterleave   */ TRUE,
    /* visible_interest      */ FALSE,
    /* destroy               */ NULL,
    /* resize                */ PositionChildren,
    /* expose                */ NULL,
    /* set_values            */ SetValues,
    /* set_values_hook       */ NULL,
    /* set_values_almost     */ XtInheritSetValuesAlmost,
    /* get_values_hook       */ GetValuesHook,
    /* accept_focus          */ NULL,
    /* version               */ XtVersion,
    /* callback offsets      */ NULL,
    /* tm_table              */ NULL,
    /* query_geometry        */ XtInheritQueryGeometry,
    /* display_accelerator   */ NULL,
    /* extension             */ NULL,
  },
   /* Composite class part */
  {
    /* geometry_manager      */ GeometryManager,
    /* change_managed        */ XtInheritChangeManaged,
```

```
        /* insert_child           */ InsertChild,
        /* delete_child           */ XtInheritDeleteChild,
        /* extension              */ NULL,
    },
    /* Box class part */
    {
        /* extension              */ NULL,
    },
    /* Confirm class part */
    {
        /* extension              */ NULL,
    }
};

WidgetClass confirmWidgetClass = (WidgetClass) &confirmClassRec;
```

Confirm's initialize procedure always adds two children to the Confirm
widget. If the Confirm widget already has two children, it means that the
application is trying to add another child to the Confirm widget, which is an
error. The simplest place to detect this situation is in the insert_child procedure since it is called each time a child is added.

```
static void InsertChild(w)
    Widget w;
{
    String params[1];
    Cardinal num_params;
    CompositeWidget parent = (CompositeWidget) XtParent(w);

    if (parent->composite.num_children >= 2) {
        params[0] = XtClass(parent)->core_class.class_name;
        num_params = 1;
        XtAppErrorMsg(XtWidgetToApplicationContext(w),
                "childError", "number", "WidgetError",
                "Applications cannot add children to %s widgets",
                params, &num_params);
    }

    (*((CompositeWidgetClass)(confirmWidgetClass->
            core_class.superclass))->composite_class.insert_child) (w);
}
```

Confirm adds its own callback procedure to the Pushbutton child's callback
list. Its widget parameter is the pushbutton, so the Confirm widget is the
parent of the widget argument. If the parent of the Confirm widget is a shell,
which is the case when the Confirm widget is used as a pop-up, Callback pops
down the Confirm widget's parent. It then calls the Confirm widget's callback
list to notify the application that the user dismissed the Confirm widget.

```
static void Callback(w, call_data, client_data)
    Widget w;
    XtPointer call_data, client_data;
{
    ConfirmWidget confirm = (ConfirmWidget) XtParent(w);

    if (XtIsShell(XtParent(confirm))) XtPopdown(XtParent(confirm));
    XtCallCallbackList(confirm, confirm->confirm.callback,
            (XtPointer) NULL);
}
```

Confirm's initialize and set_values procedures call CalculateSize to compute the size of a Confirm widget. It sets the width to the width of whichever child is wider plus twice the margin, and sets the height to the sum of the children's heights plus three times the margin.

```
static void CalculateSize(cw, width, height)
    ConfirmWidget cw;
    Dimension *width, *height;
{
    int label_width = LabelChild(cw)->core.width +
            2 * LabelChild(cw)->core.border_width,
        button_width = ButtonChild(cw)->core.width +
            2 * ButtonChild(cw)->core.border_width,
        max;

    max = label_width > button_width ? label_width : button_width;

    *width = max + 2 * cw->box.margin;
    *height = LabelChild(cw)->core.height +
            ButtonChild(cw)->core.height +
            2 * (LabelChild(cw)->core.border_width +
                    ButtonChild(cw)->core.border_width) +
            3 * cw->box.margin;
}
```

PositionChildren is Confirm's resize procedure, and the initialize procedure also calls it to give the children their initial positions. It positions the Label and Pushbutton children so that they are centered in the Confirm widget with the label above the pushbutton, separated by the margin.

```
static void PositionChildren(cw)
    ConfirmWidget cw;
{
    int label_width = LabelChild(cw)->core.width +
            2 * LabelChild(cw)->core.border_width,
        button_width = ButtonChild(cw)->core.width +
            2 * ButtonChild(cw)->core.border_width;
```

```
        XtMoveWidget(LabelChild(cw), (cw->core.width - label_width) / 2,
                cw->box.margin);
        XtMoveWidget(ButtonChild(cw), (cw->core.width - button_width) / 2,
                2 * cw->box.margin +
                2 * LabelChild(cw)->core.border_width +
                LabelChild(cw)->core.height);
    }
```

The Intrinsics call Initialize for each new Confirm widget. Initialize creates a Label widget displaying the Confirm widget's label resource and a Pushbutton widget displaying the button label. Initialize also adds its callback procedure, Callback, to the pushbutton, computes a size for the Confirm widget, and positions the two children.

```
static void Initialize(req, new, args, num_args)
    Widget req, new;
    ArgList args;
    Cardinal *num_args;
{
    ConfirmWidget cw = (ConfirmWidget) new;
    Arg arg[1];

    cw->confirm.label = XtNewString(cw->confirm.label);
    XtSetArg(arg[0], XtNlabel, cw->confirm.label);
    (void) XtCreateManagedWidget("label", labelWidgetClass,
            new, arg, 1);

    cw->confirm.button_label = XtNewString(cw->confirm.button_label);
    XtSetArg(arg[0], XtNlabel, cw->confirm.button_label);
    (void) XtCreateManagedWidget("button", pushbuttonWidgetClass,
            new, arg, 1);
    XtAddCallback(ButtonChild(cw), XtNcallback, Callback, NULL);

    CalculateSize(cw, &cw->core.width, &cw->core.height);
    PositionChildren(cw);
}
```

The Intrinsics call Destroy to destroy a Confirm widget; it must free its text strings.

```
static void Destroy(w)
    Widget w;
{
    ConfirmWidget cw = (ConfirmWidget) w;

    XtFree((char *) cw->confirm.label);
    XtFree((char *) cw->confirm.button_label);
}
```

The Intrinsics call SetValues when an application changes any of a Confirm widget's resources through `XtSetValues`. It propagates changes to the Confirm widget's *label* and *button_label* values to the Label and Pushbutton children and, if the margin or either label changed, computes a new size for the Confirm widget. If the Confirm widget's parent grants this change, the Intrinsics will call Confirm's resize procedure, PositionChildren, to center the children in the new size. Note that when SetValues calls `XtSetValues` on either child, the child is likely to request a size change. This means that Confirm's geometry manager will be involved in this process. Writers of composite widgets with more complex layout semantics should not forget this nested series of method calls.

```
static Boolean SetValues(old, req, new, args, num_args)
    Widget old, req, new;
    ArgList args;
    Cardinal *num_args;
{
    register ConfirmWidget oldcw = (ConfirmWidget) old;
    register ConfirmWidget newcw = (ConfirmWidget) new;
    Arg arg[1];
    Boolean resize = FALSE;

#define NE(field) (oldcw->field != newcw->field)

    if (NE(confirm.label)) {
        XtFree((char *) oldcw->confirm.label);
        newcw->confirm.label = XtNewString(newcw->confirm.label);
        XtSetArg(arg[0], XtNlabel, newcw->confirm.label);
        XtSetValues(LabelChild(newcw), arg, 1);
        resize = TRUE;
    }

    if (NE(confirm.button_label)) {
        XtFree((char *) oldcw->confirm.button_label);
        newcw->confirm.button_label =
                XtNewString(newcw->confirm.button_label);
        XtSetArg(arg[0], XtNlabel, newcw->confirm.button_label);
        XtSetValues(ButtonChild(newcw), arg, 1);
        resize = TRUE;
    }

    if (NE(box.margin) || resize) {
        CalculateSize(newcw, &newcw->core.width, &newcw->core.height);
    }
    return FALSE;
#undef NE
}
```

The Intrinsics call GetValuesHook when an application queries a Confirm widget's resources through XtGetValues. The procedure checks each argument to see if it matches XtNlabelWidget or XtNbuttonWidget and, if so, copies the appropriate widget value into the storage pointed to by the argument list value field. This is the standard way to export computed or derived resource values. If a widget class wants to make such data settable as well, it performs equivalent processing of the argument list passed to the initialize and set_values procedures.

```
static void GetValuesHook(w, args, num_args)
    Widget w;
    ArgList args;
    Cardinal *num_args;
{
    register int i;

    for (i = 0; i < *num_args; i++) {
        if (strcmp(args[i].name, XtNlabelWidget) == 0) {
            *(Widget *) (args[i].value) = LabelChild(w);
        } else if (strcmp(args[i].name, XtNbuttonWidget) == 0) {
            *(Widget *) (args[i].value) = ButtonChild(w);
        }
    }
}
```

All composite widgets need geometry manager procedures. Since Confirm controls its children directly it always grants any geometry requests by returning XtGeometryYes.

```
static XtGeometryResult GeometryManager(w, desired, allowed)
    Widget w;
    XtWidgetGeometry *desired, *allowed;
{
#define Wants(flag) (desired->request_mode & flag)

    if (Wants(CWWidth)) w->core.width = desired->width;
    if (Wants(CWHeight)) w->core.height = desired->height;
    if (Wants(CWX)) w->core.x = desired->x;
    if (Wants(CWY)) w->core.y = desired->y;
    if (Wants(CWBorderWidth)) {
        w->core.border_width = desired->border_width;
    }

    return XtGeometryYes;

#undef Wants
}
```

10.10.4   Suggested Programming Exercises

• Make Confirm create a Label gadget instead of a Label widget.

• Make Confirm optionally display two pushbuttons, with the default label for the second one "Abort". This will require a configuration resource and another callback resource. InsertChild will have to be more clever in order to detect when the application is trying to add children.

• Allow the application to add additional children. This will involve additional positioning and geometry manager logic.

10.11   The Confirm Widget, Alternative Implementation

An alternative implementation of the Confirm widget shows how to use sub-widgets. The primary complication here is the need to provide realize and destroy procedures that handle the subwidgets, functions that the Intrinsics perform automatically in the composite implementation. In exchange for this, the subwidget implementation does not need to test for the application adding more children and does not need to provide insert_child or geometry_manager procedures. Since the Label and Button children are stored directly in the Confirm instance record, there is no need for a get_values_hook procedure. The files are named `Confirm1` to distinguish the implementation.

10.11.1   The Public Header File

```
/* Make it safe to include this file more than once. */

#ifndef CONFIRM_H
#define CONFIRM_H

/* Confirm is derived from Core, so no need to include the superclass
   public header file.  */

/* Define the new resources that Confirm uses */

#define XtNmargin "margin"
#define XtNbuttonLabel "buttonLabel"
#define XtCButtonLabel "ButtonLabel"
#define XtNlabelWidget "labelWidget"
#define XtNbuttonWidget "buttonWidget"

/* External reference to the class record pointer */

extern WidgetClass confirmWidgetClass;
```

```
/* Type definition for confirm widgets */

typedef struct _ConfirmRec *ConfirmWidget;

/* End of preprocessor directives */

#endif /* CONFIRM_H */
```

10.11.2   The Private Header File

```
/* Make it safe to include this file more than once. */

#ifndef CONFIRMP_H
#define CONFIRMP_H

/* Include the public header file for Confirm */

#include "Confirm1.h"

/* Confirm is derived from Core, so no need to include the superclass
   private header file.  */

/* Define the Confirm instance part */

typedef struct {
  /* New resource fields */
    Dimension           margin;         /* Extra space to leave */
    String              label;          /* Label string */
    String              button_label;   /* Button string */
    XtCallbackList      callback;       /* Callback to execute */
    Widget              label_widget;   /* Label subwidget */
    Widget              button_widget;  /* Pushbutton subwidget */
} ConfirmPart;

/* Define the full instance record */

typedef struct _ConfirmRec {
    CorePart            core;
    ConfirmPart         confirm;
} ConfirmRec;

/* Define class part structure */

typedef struct {
    XtPointer           extension;
} ConfirmClassPart;

/* Define the full class record */
```

```
typedef struct _ConfirmClassRec {
    CoreClassPart       core_class;
    ConfirmClassPart    confirm_class;
} ConfirmClassRec, *ConfirmClass;

/* External definition for class record */

extern ConfirmClassRec confirmClassRec;

/* End of preprocessor directives */

#endif /* CONFIRMP_H */
```

10.11.3   The Implementation

```
#include <X11/IntrinsicP.h>     /* Intrinsics header file */
#include <X11/StringDefs.h>     /* Resource string definitions */
#include "Confirm1P.h"          /* Confirm private header file */
#include "Label.h"              /* Label public header file */
#include "Pushbutton.h"         /* Pushbutton public header file */
```

The composite implementation inherited the XtNmargin resource from its superclass Box; this implementation must define it directly.

```
#define Offset(field) XtOffsetOf(ConfirmRec, confirm.field)

static XtResource resources[] = {
    {XtNmargin, XtCMargin, XtRDimension, sizeof(Dimension),
        Offset(margin), XtRImmediate, (XtPointer) 10},
    {XtNlabel, XtCLabel, XtRString, sizeof(String),
        Offset(label), XtRString, "Click to confirm"},
    {XtNbuttonLabel, XtCButtonLabel, XtRString, sizeof(String),
        Offset(button_label), XtRString, "OK"},
    {XtNcallback, XtCCallback, XtRCallback, sizeof(XtPointer),
        Offset(callback), XtRCallback, (XtPointer) NULL},
    {XtNlabelWidget, XtCReadOnly, XtRWidget, sizeof(Widget),
        Offset(label_widget), XtRImmediate, (XtPointer) NULL},
    {XtNbuttonWidget, XtCReadOnly, XtRWidget, sizeof(Widget),
        Offset(button_widget), XtRImmediate, (XtPointer) NULL}
};

#undef Offset
```

Defining the same access macros in this implementation as in the composite implementation makes the code similarities more evident.

```
#define LabelChild(w) (((ConfirmWidget) w)->confirm.label_widget)
#define ButtonChild(w) (((ConfirmWidget) w)->confirm.button_widget)
```

```
/* Forward declarations */

static void Initialize(), PositionChildren(), Realize(), Destroy();
static Boolean SetValues();

ConfirmClassRec confirmClassRec = {
    /* Core class part */
  {
    /* superclass              */ (WidgetClass) &widgetClassRec,
    /* class_name              */ "Confirm",
    /* widget_size             */ sizeof(ConfirmRec),
    /* class_initialize        */ NULL,
    /* class_part_initialize   */ NULL,
    /* class_inited            */ FALSE,
    /* initialize              */ Initialize,
    /* initialize_hook         */ NULL,
    /* realize                 */ Realize,
    /* actions                 */ NULL,
    /* num_actions             */ 0,
    /* resources               */ resources,
    /* num_resources           */ XtNumber(resources),
    /* xrm_class               */ NULLQUARK,
    /* compress_motion         */ TRUE,
    /* compress_exposure       */ XtExposeCompressMultiple,
    /* compress_enterleave     */ TRUE,
    /* visible_interest        */ FALSE,
    /* destroy                 */ Destroy,
    /* resize                  */ PositionChildren,
    /* expose                  */ NULL,
    /* set_values              */ SetValues,
    /* set_values_hook         */ NULL,
    /* set_values_almost       */ XtInheritSetValuesAlmost,
    /* get_values_hook         */ NULL,
    /* accept_focus            */ NULL,
    /* version                 */ XtVersion,
    /* callback offsets        */ NULL,
    /* tm_table                */ NULL,
    /* query_geometry          */ XtInheritQueryGeometry,
    /* display_accelerator     */ NULL,
    /* extension               */ NULL,
  },
   /* Confirm class part */
  {
    /* extension               */ NULL,
  }
};

WidgetClass confirmWidgetClass = (WidgetClass) &confirmClassRec;
```

This implementation uses the same callback procedure as the composite implementation.

```
static void Callback(w, call_data, client_data)
    Widget w;
    XtPointer call_data, client_data;
{
    ConfirmWidget confirm = (ConfirmWidget) XtParent(w);

    if (XtIsShell(XtParent(confirm))) XtPopdown(XtParent(confirm));
    XtCallCallbackList(confirm, confirm->confirm.callback,
            (XtPointer) NULL);
}
```

This implementation uses the same procedure to calculate the Confirm widget's size as the composite implementation.

```
static void CalculateSize(cw, width, height)
    ConfirmWidget cw;
    Dimension *width, *height;
{
    int label_width = LabelChild(cw)->core.width +
            2 * LabelChild(cw)->core.border_width,
        button_width = ButtonChild(cw)->core.width +
            2 * ButtonChild(cw)->core.border_width,
        max;

    max = label_width > button_width ? label_width : button_width;

    *width = max + 2 * cw->confirm.margin;
    *height = LabelChild(cw)->core.height +
            ButtonChild(cw)->core.height +
            2 * (LabelChild(cw)->core.border_width +
                    ButtonChild(cw)->core.border_width) +
            3 * cw->confirm.margin;
}
```

This implementation uses the same procedure to position the children as the composite implementation.

```
static void PositionChildren(cw)
    ConfirmWidget cw;
{
    int label_width = LabelChild(cw)->core.width +
            2 * LabelChild(cw)->core.border_width,
        button_width = ButtonChild(cw)->core.width +
            2 * ButtonChild(cw)->core.border_width;

    XtMoveWidget(LabelChild(cw), (cw->core.width - label_width) / 2,
            cw->confirm.margin);
    XtMoveWidget(ButtonChild(cw), (cw->core.width - button_width) / 2,
            2 * cw->confirm.margin +
            2 * LabelChild(cw)->core.border_width +
```

```
                    LabelChild(cw)->core.height);
    }
```

This Initialize procedure differs from that in the composite implementation only by creating unmanaged widgets and storing the widget identifiers for the two subwidgets in the Confirm widget instance record.

```
static void Initialize(req, new, args, num_args)
    Widget req, new;
    ArgList args;
    Cardinal *num_args;
{
    ConfirmWidget cw = (ConfirmWidget) new;
    Arg arg[1];

    cw->confirm.label = XtNewString(cw->confirm.label);
    XtSetArg(arg[0], XtNlabel, cw->confirm.label);
    LabelChild(cw) = XtCreateWidget("label", labelWidgetClass,
            new, arg, 1);

    cw->confirm.button_label = XtNewString(cw->confirm.button_label);
    XtSetArg(arg[0], XtNlabel, cw->confirm.button_label);
    ButtonChild(cw) = XtCreateWidget("button", pushbuttonWidgetClass,
            new, arg, 1);
    XtAddCallback(ButtonChild(cw), XtNcallback, Callback, NULL);

    CalculateSize(cw, &cw->core.width, &cw->core.height);
    PositionChildren(cw);
}
```

This implementation of Confirm has to realize its subwidgets directly; in the composite implementation the Intrinsics handle this task. Realize calls the superclass realize procedure to realize the Confirm widget, calls XtRealizeWidget for each subwidget, and then maps the two children by calling XMapSubwindows.

```
static void Realize(w, valueMask, attributes)
    Widget w;
    XtValueMask *valueMask;
    XSetWindowAttributes *attributes;
{
    (*confirmWidgetClass->core_class.superclass->core_class.realize)
            (w, valueMask, attributes);
    XtRealizeWidget(LabelChild(w));
    XtRealizeWidget(ButtonChild(w));
    XMapSubwindows(XtDisplay(w), XtWindow(w));
}
```

This implementation of Confirm has to destroy its subwidgets directly; in the composite implementation the Intrinsics handle this task.

```
static void Destroy(w)
    Widget w;
{

    ConfirmWidget cw = (ConfirmWidget) w;

    XtFree((char *) cw->confirm.label);
    XtFree((char *) cw->confirm.button_label);

    XtDestroyWidget(LabelChild(w));
    XtDestroyWidget(ButtonChild(w));
}
```

This SetValues procedure differs from that in the composite implementation only in that it disallows changes to the Label and Button child resources. Since the children are not managed (see the Initialize procedure) any geometry request they make will always be granted. The effect is the same as the composite implementation.

```
static Boolean SetValues(old, req, new, args, num_args)
    Widget old, req, new;
    ArgList args;
    Cardinal *num_args;
{

    register ConfirmWidget oldcw = (ConfirmWidget) old;
    register ConfirmWidget newcw = (ConfirmWidget) new;
    Arg arg[1];
    Boolean resize = FALSE;

#define NE(field) (oldcw->field != newcw->field)

    /* We don't let these change */
    LabelChild(newcw) = LabelChild(oldcw);
    ButtonChild(newcw) = ButtonChild(oldcw);

    if (NE(confirm.label)) {
        XtFree((char *) oldcw->confirm.label);
        newcw->confirm.label = XtNewString(newcw->confirm.label);
        XtSetArg(arg[0], XtNlabel, newcw->confirm.label);
        XtSetValues(LabelChild(newcw), arg, 1);
        resize = TRUE;
    }

    if (NE(confirm.button_label)) {
        XtFree((char *) oldcw->confirm.button_label);
        newcw->confirm.button_label =
                XtNewString(newcw->confirm.button_label);
```

```
        XtSetArg(arg[0], XtNlabel, newcw->confirm.button_label);
        XtSetValues(ButtonChild(newcw), arg, 1);
        resize = TRUE;
    }

    if (NE(confirm.margin) || resize) {
        CalculateSize(newcw, &newcw->core.width, &newcw->core.height);
    }

    return FALSE;
#undef NE
}
```

10.12   The Menu Widget

Menu is the most complicated widget in this set, forcing its children to obey a very strict layout policy. It aligns all children into a vertical column and gives them all the same width. Menu contains extra code that makes it more effective when used within a shell as a pop-up menu

10.12.1   The Public Header File

```
/* Make it safe to include this file more than once. */

#ifndef MENU_H
#define MENU_H

/* Menu is derived from Constraint, so no need to include the
   superclass public header file.  */

/* Define the new resource that Menu uses */

#define XtNinsertBefore "insertBefore"
#define XtCInsertBefore "InsertBefore"

/* External reference to the class record pointer */

extern WidgetClass menuWidgetClass;

/* Type definition for menu widgets */

typedef struct _MenuRec *MenuWidget;

/* End of preprocessor directives */

#endif /* MENU_H */
```

10.12.2 The Private Header File

```
/* Make it safe to include this file more than once. */

#ifndef MENUP_H
#define MENUP_H

/* Include the public header file for Menu */

#include "Menu.h"

/* Menu is derived from Constraint, so no need to include the
   superclass private header file.  */

/* Define the Menu instance part */

typedef struct {
    long        save_border;    /* For geometry request foolishness */
} MenuPart;

/* Define the full instance record */

typedef struct _MenuRec {
    CorePart            core;
    CompositePart       composite;
    ConstraintPart      constraint;
    MenuPart            menu;
} MenuRec;

/* Define class part structure */

typedef struct {
    XtPointer           extension;
} MenuClassPart;

/* Define the full class record */

typedef struct _MenuClassRec {
    CoreClassPart       core_class;
    CompositeClassPart  composite_class;
    ConstraintClassPart constraint_class;
    MenuClassPart       menu_class;
} MenuClassRec, *MenuClass;

/* Define constraint part structure */

typedef struct {
  /* New resource field */
    Widget              insert_before;  /* Widget to insert before */

  /* New bookkeeping fields */
```

```
    Dimension              desired_height;
    Dimension              desired_border_width;
} MenuConstraintPart;

/* Define the full constraint record */

typedef struct _MenuConstraintRec {
    MenuConstraintPart  menu;
} MenuConstraintRec, *MenuConstraint;

/* External definition for class record */

extern MenuClassRec menuClassRec;

/* End of preprocessor directives */

#endif /* MENUP_H */
```

10.12.3 The Implementation

```
#include <X11/IntrinsicP.h>      /* Intrinsics header file */
#include <X11/StringDefs.h>      /* Resource string definitions */
#include "MenuP.h"               /* Menu private header file */
#include "LabelGadge.h"          /* To check LabelGadgets */
```

Menu overrides the default value of the XtNinsertPosition resource with a new
procedure, InsertBefore. This is just a procedure pointer that gets stored in
the widget instance like any other resource and not a resource default procedure; the Intrinsics know this because the resource default type is
XtRImmediate and not XtRCallProc. The insert_child procedure calls Insert-
Before to find out where in the child list the new child goes.

```
static Cardinal InsertBefore();

static XtResource resources[] = {
    {XtNinsertPosition, XtCInsertPosition,
        XtRFunction, sizeof(XtOrderProc),
        XtOffsetOf(MenuRec, composite.insert_position),
        XtRImmediate, (XtPointer) InsertBefore}
};

static Cardinal InsertBefore(w)
    Widget w;
{
    MenuWidget menu = (MenuWidget) XtParent(w);
    MenuConstraint mc = (MenuConstraint) w->core.constraints;
    int i;
```

```
        if (mc->menu.insert_before == NULL) {
            return menu->composite.num_children;
        }

        for (i = 0; i < menu->composite.num_children; i++) {
            if (mc->menu.insert_before == menu->composite.children[i]) {
                return i;
            }
        }

        return menu->composite.num_children;
}
```

InsertBefore looks for the widget specified by the child's XtNinsertBefore constraint resource and returns the number of children that precede this widget.
If XtNinsertBefore is NULL or if the widget does not exist, InsertBefore returns
the number of children in the menu, making the insert_child procedure add
the new child at the end.

The default value of XtNinsertBefore is NULL; this makes InsertBefore add
the new child at the end of the list.

```
static XtResource constraintResources[] = {
    {XtNinsertBefore, XtCInsertBefore, XtRWidget, sizeof(Widget),
        XtOffsetOf(MenuConstraintRec, menu.insert_before),
        XtRImmediate, NULL},
};

/* Forward declarations */

static void ClassInitialize(), ChangeManaged(), Initialize(),
        ConstraintInitialize(), Resize(), InsertChild(),
        Redisplay(), Destroy(), ConstraintGetValuesHook();
static XtGeometryResult GeometryManager();
static Boolean ConstraintSetValues();

static CompositeClassExtensionRec compositeExtension = {
    /* next_extension     */ NULL,
    /* record_type        */ NULLQUARK,
    /* version            */ XtCompositeExtensionVersion,
    /* record_size        */ sizeof(CompositeClassExtensionRec),
    /* accepts_objects    */ TRUE
};

static ConstraintClassExtensionRec constraintExtension = {
    /* next_extension     */ NULL,
    /* record_type        */ NULLQUARK,
    /* version            */ XtConstraintExtensionVersion,
    /* record_size        */ sizeof(ConstraintClassExtensionRec),
```

```
        /* get_values_hook        */ ConstraintGetValuesHook
};

MenuClassRec menuClassRec = {
    /* Core class part */
    {
        /* superclass             */ (WidgetClass) &constraintClassRec,
        /* class_name             */ "Menu",
        /* widget_size            */ sizeof(MenuRec),
        /* class_initialize       */ ClassInitialize,
        /* class_part_initialize  */ NULL,
        /* class_inited           */ FALSE,
        /* initialize             */ Initialize,
        /* initialize_hook        */ NULL,
        /* realize                */ XtInheritRealize,
        /* actions                */ NULL,
        /* num_actions            */ 0,
        /* resources              */ resources,
        /* num_resources          */ XtNumber(resources),
        /* xrm_class              */ NULLQUARK,
        /* compress_motion        */ TRUE,
        /* compress_exposure      */ XtExposeCompressMultiple,
        /* compress_enterleave    */ TRUE,
        /* visible_interest       */ FALSE,
        /* destroy                */ Destroy,
        /* resize                 */ Resize,
        /* expose                 */ Redisplay,
        /* set_values             */ NULL,
        /* set_values_hook        */ NULL,
        /* set_values_almost      */ XtInheritSetValuesAlmost,
        /* get_values_hook        */ NULL,
        /* accept_focus           */ NULL,
        /* version                */ XtVersion,
        /* callback offsets       */ NULL,
        /* tm_table               */ NULL,
        /* query_geometry         */ XtInheritQueryGeometry,
        /* display_accelerator    */ NULL,
        /* extension              */ NULL,
    },
    /* Composite class part */
    {
        /* geometry_manager       */ GeometryManager,
        /* change_managed         */ ChangeManaged,
        /* insert_child           */ InsertChild,
        /* delete_child           */ XtInheritDeleteChild,
        /* extension              */ (XtPointer) &compositeExtension,
    },
    /* Constraint class part */
    {
        /* resources              */ constraintResources,
```

```
    /* num_resources          */ XtNumber(constraintResources),
    /* constraint_size        */ sizeof(MenuConstraintRec),
    /* initialize             */ ConstraintInitialize,
    /* destroy                */ NULL,
    /* set_values             */ ConstraintSetValues,
    /* extension              */ (XtPointer) &constraintExtension,
  },
  /* Menu class part */
  {
    /* extension              */ NULL,
  }
};

WidgetClass menuWidgetClass = (WidgetClass) &menuClassRec;
```

Menu has the same InsertChild procedure as Box except for the superclass used to find the insert_child procedure.

```
static void InsertChild(w)
    Widget w;
{
    String params[2];
    Cardinal num_params;
    Widget parent = XtParent(w);

    if (!XtIsWidget(w) && !XtIsSubclass(w, labelGadgetClass)) {
        params[0] = XtClass(w)->core_class.class_name;
        params[1] = XtClass(parent)->core_class.class_name;
        num_params = 2;
        XtAppErrorMsg(XtWidgetToApplicationContext(w),
                "childError", "class", "WidgetError",
                "Children of class %s cannot be added to %n widgets",
                params, &num_params);
    }

    (*((CompositeWidgetClass)(menuWidgetClass->
            core_class.superclass))->composite_class.insert_child) (w);
}
```

CvtStringToWidget converts a string into a widget instance. This converter takes one conversion argument, a widget, and calls `XtNameToWidget` to look for a child of that widget whose name matches the source string.

```
static Boolean CvtStringToWidget(dpy, args, num_args, from, to, data)
    Display *dpy;
    XrmValuePtr args;
    Cardinal *num_args;
    XrmValuePtr from, to;
    XtPointer *data;
{
```

```
    static Widget w;
    Widget parent;
    Boolean badConvert;

    if (*num_args != 1) {
        XtAppErrorMsg(XtDisplayToApplicationContext(dpy),
                "wrongParameters", "cvtStringToWidget",
                "XtToolkitError",
                "StringToWidget conversion needs parent arg",
                (String *) NULL, (Cardinal *) NULL);
    }

    /* Convert first arg into parent */

    parent = *(Widget*) args[0].addr;

    w = XtNameToWidget(parent, (String) from->addr);
    badConvert = (w == NULL);

    if (badConvert) {
        XtDisplayStringConversionWarning(dpy, from->addr, "Widget");
    } else {
        if (to->addr == NULL) to->addr = (caddr_t) &w;
        else if (to->size < sizeof(Widget)) badConvert = TRUE;
        else *(Widget *) to->addr = w;

        to->size = sizeof(Widget);
    }
    return !badConvert;
}
```

ClassInitialize registers the string-to-widget type converter. It sets up the conversion arguments so that the first one contains the parent of the widget requesting the conversion. Since this conversion depends upon volatile, non-display-specific information (the widget's parent) it is registered as an uncached conversion. Since the converter allocates no extra storage, there is no destructor procedure.

```
static void ClassInitialize()
{
    static XtConvertArgRec parentConvertArgs[] = {
        {XtBaseOffset, (XtPointer) XtOffsetOf(WidgetRec, core.parent),
                sizeof(Widget)},
    };

    /* Register a converter for string to widget */
```

```
        XtSetTypeConverter(XtRString, XtRWidget, CvtStringToWidget,
            parentConvertArgs, XtNumber(parentConvertArgs),
            XtCacheNone, (XtDestructor) NULL);
}
```

HandleMenuButton is an event handler that Initialize installs on the shell
widget containing the menu. When the user presses a pointer button in a
window, the server automatically initiates a pointer grab so that only that window receives pointer events until the user releases the button. HandleMenu-
Button transfers this grab to the menu subtree so that the menu items receive
the events instead of the activating window. The Intrinsics grab semantics
guarantee that the event that made the menu pop up also goes to the menu's
shell when the shell is a spring-loaded pop-up. This guarantees that Handle-
MenuButton always receives the ButtonPress event so it can transfer the grab.
HandleMenuButton also pops down the menu upon a ButtonRelease event to
guarantee that the menu goes away no matter where the user releases the
pointer button.

```
static void HandleMenuButton(w, client_data, event,
        continue_to_dispatch)
    Widget w;
    XtPointer client_data;
    XEvent *event;
    Boolean *continue_to_dispatch;
{
    switch (event->type) {
        case ButtonPress:
            /* The new grab does an implicit AllowEvents */
            (void) XtGrabPointer(w, True,
                    EnterWindowMask | LeaveWindowMask |
                        ButtonReleaseMask,
                    GrabModeAsync, GrabModeAsync, None, None,
                    event->xbutton.time);
            break;

        case ButtonRelease:
            /* Popping down also ungrabs the pointer */
            XtPopdown(w);
            break;
    }
}
```

Initialize just initializes an internal bookkeeping field and installs the Handle-
MenuButton event handler on the menu's shell. HandleMenuButton only
needs to react to the events that the Intrinsics remap and not to select for the
events directly, so Initialize adds it as a raw event handler.

```
static void Initialize(req, new)
    Widget req, new;
{
    ((MenuWidget) new)->menu.save_border = -1;

    if (XtIsShell(XtParent(new))) {
        XtAddRawEventHandler(XtParent(new),
                ButtonPressMask | ButtonReleaseMask,
                FALSE, HandleMenuButton, NULL);
    }
}
```

ConstraintInitialize initializes fields in the new widget's constraint structure. PositionChildren uses the *desired_height* and *desired_border_width* fields during the layout process.

```
static void ConstraintInitialize(req, new, args, num_args)
    Widget req, new;
    ArgList args;
    Cardinal *num_args;
{
    MenuConstraint mc = (MenuConstraint) new->core.constraints;

    mc->menu.desired_height = new->core.height;
    mc->menu.desired_border_width = new->core.border_width;
}
```

Destroy removes the HandleMenuButton event handler from the menu's parent.

```
static void Destroy(w)
    Widget w;
{
    XtRemoveRawEventHandler(XtParent(w), XtAllEvents, TRUE,
            HandleMenuButton, NULL);
}
```

Menu's change_managed, resize, and geometry_manager procedures use PositionChildren to move and resize the menu's children. When the geometry manager calls PositionChildren, it passes the child making the geometry request in the *initiator* parameter. PositionChildren configures all children other than the initiator. Most of PositionChildren's complexity stems from positioning each pair of children so that their borders overlap, with the space between the children equal to whichever child's border is larger. If a child's border is larger than the previous child's border, PositionChildren increases the vertical position for the next child by the difference between the borders. The x coor-

dinate for the child is set to clip the child's left border. PositionChildren
positions the initiator widget by setting its geometry fields rather than by
reconfiguring it since returning XtGeometryYes from the geometry manager
makes these changes take place automatically.

```
static void PositionChildren(menu, initiator)
    register MenuWidget menu;
    Widget initiator;
{
    int i, y;
    register int last_border;
    register Widget child;
    MenuConstraint mc;
    Boolean first = TRUE;

    if (menu->composite.num_children == 0) return;

    for (i = 0; i < menu->composite.num_children; i++) {
        child = menu->composite.children[i];
        if (!XtIsManaged(child)) continue;
        mc = (MenuConstraint) child->core.constraints;

        if (first) {
            first = FALSE;
            last_border = mc->menu.desired_border_width;
            y = -last_border;
        }

        if (child == initiator) {
            if (last_border > child->core.border_width) {
                y += last_border - child->core.border_width;
            }
            last_border = child->core.border_width;

            child->core.x = -last_border;
            child->core.y = y;
            child->core.width = menu->core.width;
        } else {
            if (last_border > mc->menu.desired_border_width) {
                y += last_border - mc->menu.desired_border_width;
            }
            last_border = mc->menu.desired_border_width;

            XtConfigureWidget(child, -last_border, y,
                    menu->core.width, mc->menu.desired_height,
                    last_border);
        }
```

```
            y += (int) child->core.height + last_border;
    }
}

static void Resize(w)
    Widget w;
{
    PositionChildren((MenuWidget) w, (Widget) NULL);
}
```

WidestDesiredSize queries each of a menu's managed children to find the one
with the widest desired width. XtQueryGeometry finds this out for children
other than the one initiating a geometry request; for the initiator the desired
width is always in the widget.

```
static int WidestDesiredSize(menu, initiator)
    MenuWidget menu;
    Widget initiator;
{
    register int i, width = 0;
    register Widget child;
    XtWidgetGeometry desired;

    for (i = 0; i < menu->composite.num_children; i++) {
        child = menu->composite.children[i];
        if (!XtIsManaged(child)) continue;

        if (child == initiator) {
            if (child->core.width > width) {
                width = child->core.width;
            }
        } else {
            (void) XtQueryGeometry(child, NULL, &desired);
            if (desired.width > width) width = desired.width;
        }
    }

    if (width <= 0) return 1;
    else return width;
}
```

CalculateDesiredSizes finds out for each managed child what its desired
height and border width are, given a specific width. This accommodates
children that are willing to make height/width size trade-offs. While it is unlikely that any widgets that one would normally put into a menu do this, it is
safer to allow for it as it makes the Menu widget more flexible. Calculate-
DesiredSizes queries each managed child other than the initiator and stores its

desired height and border width in the constraint record. As with Widest-
DesiredSize, the desired size for the widget initiating a geometry request is in
the widget.

```
static void CalculateDesiredSizes(menu, width, initiator)
    MenuWidget menu;
    Dimension width;
    Widget initiator;
{
    XtWidgetGeometry proposed, desired;
    register Widget child;
    MenuConstraint mc;
    register int i;

    for (i = 0; i < menu->composite.num_children; i++) {
        child = menu->composite.children[i];
        if (!XtIsManaged(child)) continue;
        mc = (MenuConstraint) child->core.constraints;

        if (child == initiator) {
            mc->menu.desired_height = child->core.height;
            mc->menu.desired_border_width =
                    child->core.border_width;
        } else {
            proposed.width = width;
            proposed.request_mode = CWWidth;
            (void) XtQueryGeometry(child, &proposed, &desired);

            mc->menu.desired_height = desired.height;
            mc->menu.desired_border_width = desired.border_width;
        }
    }
}
```

CalculateNewSize uses the previous two routines to compute a new size for a
menu widget. It calls WidestDesiredSize to find the new width for the menu
and then calls CalculateDesiredSizes to find the desired heights and border
widths given that size. CalculateNewSize uses an algorithm identical to that
used by PositionChildren to compute the amount to overlap adjacent widgets.
Its main loop does not need to treat the initiator specially; Calculate-
DesiredSizes copies the initiator's height and border width into the
desired_height and *desired_border_width* fields.

```
static void CalculateNewSize(menu, width, height, initiator)
    register MenuWidget menu;
    Dimension *width, *height;
    Widget initiator;
```

```
{
    register int i;
    register int last_border;
    register Widget child;
    int y;
    MenuConstraint mc;
    Boolean first = TRUE;

    if (menu->composite.num_children == 0) {
        *width = *height = 10;  /* Arbitrary */
        return;
    }

    *width = WidestDesiredSize(menu, initiator);

    CalculateDesiredSizes(menu, *width, initiator);

    for (i = 0; i < menu->composite.num_children; i++) {
        child = menu->composite.children[i];
        if (!XtIsManaged(child)) continue;
        mc = (MenuConstraint) child->core.constraints;

        if (first) {
            first = FALSE;
            last_border = mc->menu.desired_border_width;
            y = -last_border;
        }

        if (last_border > mc->menu.desired_border_width) {
            y += last_border - (int) mc->menu.desired_border_width;
        }
        last_border = mc->menu.desired_border_width;
        y += (int) mc->menu.desired_height + last_border;
    }

    if (y <= 0) y = 1;
    *height = y;
}
```

ChangeManaged simply calls CalculateNewSize and makes a geometry request for the result, then repositions the currently managed children.

```
static void ChangeManaged(w)
    Widget w;
{
    MenuWidget menu = (MenuWidget) w;
    XtWidgetGeometry request;
    XtGeometryResult result;
```

```
      CalculateNewSize(menu, &request.width, &request.height,
            (Widget) NULL);

  if (request.width != menu->core.width ||
          request.height != menu->core.height) {
      request.request_mode = CWWidth | CWHeight;
      do {
          result = XtMakeGeometryRequest(w, &request, &request);
      } while (result == XtGeometryAlmost);
  }


      PositionChildren(menu, (Widget) NULL);
}
```

ConstraintSetValues must reorder the menu's children when one of them changes the widget that it precedes. ConstraintSetValues moves all widgets that follow the requesting one down one spot in the child list, finds the new position, moves the children after the new position up one spot, and inserts the child in its new position. Because of the way the menu overlaps the children's borders, changing the child's position makes the menu change its height if the children newly adjacent to the moving widget have different borders from those previously adjacent. ConstraintSetValues is not allowed to act on this directly since a future subclass might override the change to XtNinsertBefore or handle it differently, so ConstraintSetValues makes an artificial change to the child to force a geometry request. It saves the child's actual border width in the menu's *save_border* field and changes the child's border, triggering a geometry request.

```
static Boolean ConstraintSetValues(old, req, new, args, num_args)
    Widget old, req, new;
    ArgList args;
    Cardinal *num_args;
{
    MenuConstraint newmc = (MenuConstraint) new->core.constraints;
    MenuConstraint oldmc = (MenuConstraint) old->core.constraints;
    register MenuWidget menu;
    register int i, j;

    if (newmc->menu.insert_before != oldmc->menu.insert_before) {
        menu = (MenuWidget) XtParent(new);

        /* Remove child from current position */

        for (i = 0; i < menu->composite.num_children &&
                menu->composite.children[i] != new; i++) {}
```

```
        for (; i < menu->composite.num_children - 1; i++) {
            menu->composite.children[i] =
                    menu->composite.children[i+1];
        }

        /* Find new widget to insert before */

        for (i = 0; i < menu->composite.num_children - 1 &&
                menu->composite.children[i] !=
                        newmc->menu.insert_before;
                i++) {}

        /* Move the rest of them up */

        for (j = menu->composite.num_children - 1; j > i; j--) {
            menu->composite.children[j] =
                    menu->composite.children[j-1];
        }

        menu->composite.children[i] = new;

        /* Cause a geometry request */

        menu->menu.save_border = new->core.border_width;
        new->core.border_width += 1000;
    }

    return FALSE;
}
```

GeometryManager is the most complicated procedure here. If the menu's
save_border field is not −1, GeometryManager knows that the change to the
child's border width was an artificial one just to cause the geometry request, so
it restores the border width to what it was before. Menus never allow their
children to change their x or y values, so GeometryManager denies any request to change them by returning XtGeometryNo. GeometryManager then
calculates a new size for the menu based on the child's requested sizes and
decides what to return.

If the requesting child was not the widest child and requests a width that is
still narrower than the widest child, the requested change does not affect the
menu width—the menu width is still that of the widest child. In this case
CalculateNewSize returns the same width for the menu as before; so
GeometryManager denies the child's request.

If the new width for the menu is equal to the child's requested width, it
means either that the requestor is now the widest child or that the requestor

did not ask for a width change. In either case the menu tries to change size to accommodate the child's request. If it succeeds, it repositions the other children.

The final case is when the new menu width is different from the original, but not equal to what the child requested. This happens if the child that was previously the widest child asks to become narrower than the second-widest child; it means that the child can shrink some but not as much as requested. Menu wants to return XtGeometryAlmost in this case, but it must first check that its parent will let it become this size by issuing a query-only geometry request. If the parent allows the change to the menu, GeometryManager returns XtGeometryAlmost.

```
static XtGeometryResult GeometryManager(w, desired, allowed)
    Widget w;
    XtWidgetGeometry *desired, *allowed;
{
    MenuWidget menu = (MenuWidget) XtParent(w);
    XtWidgetGeometry request;
    XtGeometryResult result;
    Dimension save_width, save_height, save_border_width;

#define Wants(flag) (desired->request_mode & flag)
#define RestoreGeometry(w) { \
        w->core.width = save_width; \
        w->core.height = save_height; \
        w->core.border_width = save_border_width; }

    if (menu->menu.save_border != -1) {
        /* This was caused by a child set-values */
        w->core.border_width = menu->menu.save_border;
        menu->menu.save_border = -1;
        desired->border_width -= 1000;
    }

    if (Wants(CWX) || Wants(CWY)) {
        return XtGeometryNo;
    }

    /* If only requesting a stack mode change, allow it */

    if (!Wants(CWWidth) && !Wants(CWHeight) && !Wants(CWBorderWidth)) {
        return XtGeometryYes;
    }

    /* Figure out how big we would be with this change */

    save_width = w->core.width;
```

```
      save_height = w->core.height;
      save_border_width = w->core.border_width;
      if (Wants(CWWidth)) w->core.width = desired->width;
      if (Wants(CWHeight)) w->core.height = desired->height;
      if (Wants(CWBorderWidth)) {
          w->core.border_width = desired->border_width;
      }

      CalculateNewSize(menu, &request.width, &request.height, w);

      /* If the new width is the same as the old and the child requested
         a width change, CalculateNewSize was not able to accommodate
         the width change, so refuse the geometry request. */

      if (request.width == menu->core.width && Wants(CWWidth)) {
          RestoreGeometry(w);
          return XtGeometryNo;
      }

      /* If new width is equal to child's width, we are going to try
         to accommodate the child.  Make a geometry request.  This also
         covers cases where the child requested no width change since
         that wouldn't cause the menu to change width. */

      if (request.width == w->core.width) {
          request.request_mode = CWWidth | CWHeight;
          if (Wants(XtCWQueryOnly)) {
              request.request_mode |= XtCWQueryOnly;
          }
          result = XtMakeGeometryRequest((Widget) menu, &request, NULL);

          /* Almost isn't good enough here; must be allowed */

          if (result == XtGeometryAlmost) result = XtGeometryNo;
          if (result == XtGeometryNo || Wants(XtCWQueryOnly)) {
              RestoreGeometry(w);
          } else PositionChildren(menu, w);
          return result;
      }

      /* New width is different from child's width, so we want to return
         XtGeometryAlmost.  See if this is allowed. */

      RestoreGeometry(w);

      request.request_mode = CWWidth | CWHeight | XtCWQueryOnly;
      result = XtMakeGeometryRequest((Widget) menu, &request, NULL);

      /* Almost isn't good enough here; must be allowed */

      if (result != XtGeometryYes) return XtGeometryNo;
```

```
    /* It would be allowed, so return suggested geometry */

    *allowed = *desired;
    allowed->width = request.width;
    return XtGeometryAlmost;
#undef Wants
#undef RestoreGeometry
}
```

Menu has the same Redisplay procedure as Box.

```
static void Redisplay(w, event, region)
    Widget w;
    XEvent *event;
    Region region;
{
    CompositeWidget comp = (CompositeWidget) w;
    int i;
    Widget c;                /* child */

    for (i = 0; i < comp->composite.num_children; i++) {
        c = comp->composite.children[i];
        if (XtIsManaged(c) && XtIsSubclass(c, labelGadgetClass) &&
                XRectInRegion(region, c->core.x, c->core.y,
                        c->core.width + 2*c->core.border_width,
                        c->core.height + 2*c->core.border_width)
                    != RectangleOut) {
            (*(XtClass(c)->core_class.expose))(c, event, region);
        }
    }
}
```

The ConstraintGetValuesHook allows an application to query the XtNinsert-Before resource. Since we do not expect this to happen very often, it is easier to provide the information in the hook than to keep it updated in the constraint record.

```
static void ConstraintGetValuesHook(w, args, num_args)
    Widget w;
    ArgList args;
    Cardinal *num_args;
{
    register int i, j;

    for (i = 0; i < *num_args; i++) {
        if (strcmp(args[i].name, XtNinsertBefore) == 0) {
            MenuConstraint mc = (MenuConstraint) w->core.constraints;
            MenuWidget menu = (MenuWidget) XtParent(w);
```

```
                    for (j = 0; j < menu->composite.num_children; j++) {
                        if (menu->composite.children[j] == w) {
                            if (j == menu->composite.num_children - 1) {
                                args[i].value = NULL;
                            } else {
                                *(Widget *) (args[i].value) =
                                        menu->composite.children[j+1];
                            }
                            break;
                        }
                    } /* End of for loop checking children */
                }
            }
        }
```

10.12.4   Suggested Programming Exercises

• If you made the modification to MenuItem to support cascading menus, verify that it works with the Menu implementation. You may need to modify the event handler Menu installs on its shell to support cascading menus.

• Applications that use this Menu implementation have to reposition the menu each time. Add a resource that makes the menu reposition itself around the pointer. One way to do this is to add a pop-up callback to the menu's shell; this callback queries the pointer position to find out where it should go.

10.13   The Label Gadget

Label gadgets support all the functionality of Label widgets except selection and event handling and stacking position. Since a Label gadget cannot process events, it has no need for the code to display an accelerator string. This description focuses on how the gadget implementation differs from the widget implementation.

10.13.1   The Public Header File

```
/* Make it safe to include this file more than once. */
#ifndef LABEL_GADGET_H
#define LABEL_GADGET_H

/* LabelGadget is derived from RectObj, so no need to include the
   superclass public header file.  */

/* Include Label header file to get Justify type */
#include "Label.h"

/* External reference to the class record pointer */
```

```
extern WidgetClass labelGadgetClass;

/* Type definition for label widgets */
typedef struct _LabelGadgetRec *LabelGadget;

/* End of preprocessor directives */
#endif /* LABEL_GADGET_H */
```

10.13.2 The Private Header File

```
/* Make it safe to include this file more than once. */
#ifndef LABEL_GADGETP_H
#define LABEL_GADGETP_H

/* Include the public header file for LabelGadget */
#include "LabelGadge.h"

/* LabelGadget is derived from RectObj, so no need to include the
   superclass private header file.  No internal types need to be
   defined. */

/* Define the LabelGadget instance part */
typedef struct {
  /* New resource fields */
    String      label;          /* Text to display */
    Pixel       foreground;     /* Foreground pixel value */
    XFontStruct *font;          /* Font to display in */
    Justify     justify;        /* The justification value */
    Dimension   space;          /* Inner padding value */
    Pixel       background;     /* Background pixel value */
    Pixel       border;         /* Border pixel value */

  /* New internal fields */
    GC          gc;             /* Graphics context for displaying */
    GC          background_gc;  /* Graphics context for background */
    GC          border_gc;      /* Graphics context for border */
    Dimension   old_border;     /* Previous border width */
    Dimension   label_width;    /* The calculated width */
    Dimension   label_height;   /* The calculated height */
    Cardinal    label_len;      /* The length of the text string */
    Boolean     size_computed;  /* Whether the size was computed */
    Dimension   desired_width;  /* The width the widget wants to be */
    Dimension   desired_height; /* The height the widget wants to be */
    GC          current_gc;     /* GC we are currently using */
    GC          current_bg_gc;  /* GC for current background */
} LabelGadgetPart;

/* Define the full instance record */
typedef struct _LabelGadgetRec {
    ObjectPart          object;
```

```
        RectObjPart        rectObj;
        LabelGadgetPart    label;
    } LabelGadgetRec;

    /* Define class part structure */
    typedef struct {
        XtPointer          extension;
    } LabelGadgetClassPart;

    /* Define the full class record */
    typedef struct _LabelGadgetClassRec {
        RectObjClassPart        rect_class;
        LabelGadgetClassPart    label_class;
    } LabelGadgetClassRec, *LabelGadgetClass;

    /* External definition for class record */
    extern LabelGadgetClassRec labelGadgetClassRec;

    /* End of preprocessor directives */
    #endif /* LABEL_GADGETP_H */
```

10.13.3   The Implementation

```
#include <string.h>            /* Needed for string manipulation */
#include <X11/IntrinsicP.h>    /* Intrinsics header file */
#include <X11/StringDefs.h>    /* Resource string definitions */
#include "LabelGadgP.h"        /* LabelGadget private header file */
```

Since RectObj does not define background or border pixel values, Label-Gadget must define them itself.

```
#define Offset(field) XtOffsetOf(LabelGadgetRec, label.field)

static XtResource resources[] = {
    {XtNlabel, XtCLabel, XtRString, sizeof(String),
        Offset(label), XtRString, (XtPointer) NULL},
    {XtNfont,  XtCFont, XtRFontStruct, sizeof(XFontStruct *),
        Offset(font), XtRString, (XtPointer) XtDefaultFont},
    {XtNforeground, XtCForeground, XtRPixel, sizeof(Pixel),
        Offset(foreground), XtRString,
        (XtPointer) XtDefaultForeground},
    {XtNjustify, XtCJustify, XtRJustify, sizeof(Justify),
        Offset(justify), XtRImmediate, (XtPointer) Left},
    {XtNspace, XtCSpace, XtRDimension, sizeof(Dimension),
        Offset(space), XtRImmediate, (XtPointer) 2},
    {XtNborderWidth, XtCBorderWidth, XtRDimension, sizeof(Dimension),
        XtOffsetOf(LabelGadgetRec, rectObj.border_width),
        XtRImmediate, (XtPointer) 0},
    {XtNbackground, XtCBackground, XtRPixel, sizeof(Pixel),
        Offset(background), XtRString,
```

```
                (XtPointer) XtDefaultBackground},
        {XtNborderColor, XtCBorderColor, XtRPixel, sizeof(Pixel),
            Offset(border), XtRString, (XtPointer) XtDefaultForeground},
};
#undef Offset
```

Since LabelGadget defines no new class methods, it needs no class_part_initialize procedure.

```
/* Forward declarations */

static void ClassInitialize(), Initialize(),
        Redisplay(), Destroy(), Resize();
static Boolean SetValues();
static XtGeometryResult QueryGeometry();

/* Class record declaration */

LabelGadgetClassRec labelGadgetClassRec = {
    /* RectObj class part */
  {
    /* superclass            */ (WidgetClass) &rectObjClassRec,
    /* class_name            */ "LabelGadget",
    /* widget_size           */ sizeof(LabelGadgetRec),
    /* class_initialize      */ ClassInitialize,
    /* class_part_initialize */ NULL,
    /* class_inited          */ FALSE,
    /* initialize            */ Initialize,
    /* initialize_hook       */ NULL,
    /* rect1                 */ NULL,
    /* rect2                 */ NULL,
    /* rect3                 */ 0,
    /* resources             */ resources,
    /* num_resources         */ XtNumber(resources),
    /* xrm_class             */ NULLQUARK,
    /* rect4                 */ 0,
    /* rect5                 */ 0,
    /* rect6                 */ 0,
    /* rect7                 */ 0,
    /* destroy               */ Destroy,
    /* resize                */ Resize,
    /* expose                */ Redisplay,
    /* set_values            */ SetValues,
    /* set_values_hook       */ NULL,
    /* set_values_almost     */ XtInheritSetValuesAlmost,
    /* get_values_hook       */ NULL,
    /* rect9                 */ NULL,
    /* version               */ XtVersion,
    /* callback offsets      */ NULL,
    /* rect10                */ NULL,
```

```
      /* query_geometry        */ QueryGeometry,
      /* rect11                */ NULL,
      /* extension             */ NULL
   },
      /* LabelGadget class part  */
   {
      /* extension             */ NULL
   }
};


/* Class record pointer */

WidgetClass labelGadgetClass = (WidgetClass) &labelGadgetClassRec;

static void ClassInitialize()
{
    extern void CvtStringToJustify();    /* Defined in Label.c */

    /* Register a converter for string to justification */

    XtSetTypeConverter(XtRString, XtRJustify, CvtStringToJustify,
          (XtConvertArgList) NULL, 0,
          XtCacheAll, (XtDestructor) NULL);
}
```

SetTextWidthAndHeight is identical to that for Label except that it does not deal with the accelerator string.

```
static void SetTextWidthAndHeight(lw)
    LabelGadget lw;
{
    register XFontStruct *fs = lw->label.font;

    /* Compute the text dimensions based on the string and the font */

    lw->label.label_len = strlen(lw->label.label);
    lw->label.label_width =
          XTextWidth(fs, lw->label.label, lw->label.label_len);
    lw->label.label_height =
          fs->max_bounds.ascent + fs->max_bounds.descent;
}

static GC GetNormalGC(lw)
    LabelGadget lw;
{
    XGCValues    values;

    /* Allocate a graphics context with the foreground and font */

    values.foreground = lw->label.foreground;
```

```
        values.font = lw->label.font->fid;
        return XtGetGC((Widget) lw, GCForeground | GCFont, &values);
}
```

LabelGadget requires graphics contexts for drawing the background and border since the server does not take care of this. The *current_bg_gc* supports future subclasses that may need to change the background.

```
static GC GetBackgroundGC(lw)
    LabelGadget lw;
{
    XGCValues   values;

    /* Allocate a graphics context with the background */

    values.foreground = lw->label.background;
    return XtGetGC((Widget) lw, GCForeground, &values);
}

static GC GetBorderGC(lw)
    LabelGadget lw;
{
    XGCValues   values;

    if (lw->rectObj.border_width == 0) return NULL;

    /* Allocate a graphics context with the border values */

    values.foreground = lw->label.border;
    values.line_width = lw->rectObj.border_width;
    return XtGetGC((Widget) lw, GCForeground | GCLineWidth, &values);
}
```

Initialize must create the background and border graphics contexts just as it creates the normal graphics context.

```
static void Initialize(request, new, args, num_args)
    Widget request, new;
    ArgList args;
    Cardinal *num_args;
{
    LabelGadget lw = (LabelGadget) new;

    /* If no label is specified, use the name */
    if (lw->label.label == NULL) lw->label.label = XtName(lw);

    /* Copy the label */
    lw->label.label = XtNewString(lw->label.label);

    /* Compute the text dimensions and get graphics contexts. */
```

```
SetTextWidthAndHeight(lw);
lw->label.gc = lw->label.current_gc = GetNormalGC(lw);
lw->label.background_gc =
        lw->label.current_bg_gc = GetBackgroundGC(lw);
lw->label.border_gc = GetBorderGC(lw);

/* If no size specified, compute one */
lw->label.size_computed =
        (lw->rectObj.width == 0) && (lw->rectObj.height == 0);

if (lw->rectObj.width == 0) {
    lw->rectObj.width = lw->label.label_width +
            2 * lw->label.space;
}
if (lw->rectObj.height == 0) {
    lw->rectObj.height = lw->label.label_height +
            2 * lw->label.space;
}

lw->label.old_border = lw->rectObj.border_width;

lw->label.desired_width = lw->rectObj.width;
lw->label.desired_height = lw->rectObj.height;
}
```

SetValues must update the background and border graphics contexts just as it updates the normal graphics context.

```
static Boolean SetValues(old, request, new, args, num_args)
    Widget  old, request, new;
    ArgList args;
    Cardinal *num_args;
{
    LabelGadget oldlw = (LabelGadget) old;
    LabelGadget newlw = (LabelGadget) new;
    Boolean redisplay = FALSE;

#define NE(field) (oldlw->field != newlw->field)

    /* If the label has been reset to NULL, change to the name */

    if (newlw->label.label == NULL) {
        newlw->label.label = XtName(newlw);
    }

    /* Decide whether to compute the size */

    if (newlw->rectObj.width == 0 && newlw->rectObj.height == 0) {
        newlw->label.size_computed = TRUE;
    } else if (NE(rectObj.width) || NE(rectObj.height)) {
```

```
        newlw->label.size_computed = FALSE;
        if (NE(rectObj.width)) {
            newlw->label.desired_width = newlw->rectObj.width;
        }
        if (NE(rectObj.height)) {
            newlw->label.desired_height = newlw->rectObj.height;
        }
    } /* else leave the same */

    /* If label, or font has changed, recopy and compute size */

    if (NE(label.label) || NE(label.font)) {
        if (NE(label.label)) {
            XtFree((char *) oldlw->label.label);
            newlw->label.label = XtNewString(newlw->label.label);
        }
        SetTextWidthAndHeight(newlw);
        redisplay = TRUE;
    }

    /* Compute the size if necessary */

    if (newlw->label.size_computed || newlw->rectObj.width == 0) {
        newlw->label.desired_width = newlw->rectObj.width =
                newlw->label.label_width + 2 * newlw->label.space;
    }
    if (newlw->label.size_computed || newlw->rectObj.height == 0) {
        newlw->label.desired_height = newlw->rectObj.height =
                newlw->label.label_height + 2 * newlw->label.space;
    }

    /* If foreground or font has changed, update GC */

    if (NE(label.foreground) || NE(label.font->fid)) {
        XtReleaseGC(newlw, oldlw->label.gc);
        newlw->label.gc = GetNormalGC(newlw);

        if (newlw->label.current_gc == oldlw->label.gc) {
            newlw->label.current_gc = newlw->label.gc;
            redisplay = TRUE;
        }
    }

    /* If background has changed, update background GC */

    if (NE(label.background)) {
        XtReleaseGC(newlw, oldlw->label.background_gc);
        newlw->label.background_gc = GetBackgroundGC(newlw);

        if (newlw->label.current_bg_gc == oldlw->label.background_gc) {
```

```
                newlw->label.current_bg_gc = newlw->label.background_gc;
                redisplay = TRUE;
            }
        }

        /* If border has changed, update border GC */

        if (NE(label.border) || NE(rectObj.border_width)) {
            if (oldlw->label.border_gc != NULL) {
                XtReleaseGC(newlw, oldlw->label.border_gc);
            }
            newlw->label.border_gc = GetBorderGC(newlw);
            redisplay = TRUE;
        }

        return redisplay || NE(label.space) || NE(label.justify);
#undef NE
    }
```

Destroy must free the new graphics contexts.

```
static void Destroy(w)
    Widget w;
{
    LabelGadget lw = (LabelGadget) w;

    XtFree((char *) lw->label.label);

    XtReleaseGC(w, lw->label.gc);
    XtReleaseGC(w, lw->label.background_gc);
    if (lw->label.border_gc != NULL) {
        XtReleaseGC(w, lw->label.border_gc);
    }
}
```

Redisplay must draw the background and border using the background and border graphics contexts. It draws in the parent's window since the gadget has no window of its own. To avoid displaying text outside of the Label gadget's area, Redisplay sets the clip mask in the current graphics context to the area of the gadget and then restores it after drawing the string. This is not strictly allowed since you are supposed to treat the graphics context as read-only, but since the state is restored before returning, no problems should arise.

```
static void Redisplay(w, event, region)
    Widget w;
    XEvent *event;
    Region region;
{
    LabelGadget lw = (LabelGadget) w;
```

```
        int offset, x;
        XRectangle rect;
        Region r1, r2;

        /* Draw the background */
        XFillRectangle(XtDisplayOfObject(w), XtWindowOfObject(w),
                lw->label.current_bg_gc,
                lw->rectObj.x + lw->rectObj.border_width,
                lw->rectObj.y + lw->rectObj.border_width,
                lw->rectObj.width, lw->rectObj.height);

        /* Draw the border */
        if (lw->rectObj.border_width != 0) {
            offset = lw->rectObj.border_width / 2;
            XDrawRectangle(XtDisplayOfObject(w), XtWindowOfObject(w),
                    lw->label.border_gc,
                    lw->rectObj.x + offset, lw->rectObj.y + offset,
                    lw->rectObj.width + lw->rectObj.border_width,
                    lw->rectObj.height + lw->rectObj.border_width);
        }

        switch (lw->label.justify) {
            case Left:
                x = lw->label.space;
                break;
            case Right:
                x = (int) lw->rectObj.width - (int) lw->label.space -
                        (int) lw->label.label_width;
                break;
            case Center:
                x = ((int) lw->rectObj.width -
                        (int) lw->label.label_width) / 2;
                break;
        }

        /* Temporarily change the clip mask in the gc */
        rect.x = lw->rectObj.x + lw->rectObj.border_width;
        rect.y = lw->rectObj.y + lw->rectObj.border_width;
        rect.width = lw->rectObj.width;
        rect.height = lw->rectObj.height;

        r1 = XCreateRegion();
        r2 = XCreateRegion();
        if (region != NULL) {
            XUnionRectWithRegion(&rect, r1, r2);    /* r2 = rectangle */
            XIntersectRegion(region, r2, r1);       /* r1 = intersection */
        } else XUnionRectWithRegion(&rect, r2, r1); /* r1 = rectangle */

        XSetRegion(XtDisplayOfObject(w), lw->label.current_gc, r1);
        XDestroyRegion(r1);
```

```
    XDestroyRegion(r2);

    XDrawString(XtDisplayOfObject(w), XtWindowOfObject(w),
            lw->label.current_gc,
            lw->rectObj.x + lw->rectObj.border_width + x,
            lw->rectObj.y + lw->rectObj.border_width +
                lw->label.space + lw->label.font->max_bounds.ascent,
            lw->label.label, lw->label.label_len);

    /* Restore the GC */
    XSetClipMask(XtDisplayOfObject(w), lw->label.current_gc, None);
}
```

Resize must update the border graphics context if the border width changes; it uses the field *old_border* to tell when this occurs. It relies upon the Intrinsics to clear its parent's area, generating Expose events. Note that the Intrinsics only call the resize procedure when the width and height change, so if a parent wants to change only the border width of a RectObj child, it must use XtSetValues instead of XtConfigureWidget or XtResizeWidget when the child requires notification of the change.

```
static void Resize(w)
    Widget w;
{
    LabelGadget lw = (LabelGadget) w;

    /* If border width changed, update border GC */

    if (lw->label.old_border != lw->rectObj.border_width) {
        if (lw->label.border_gc != NULL) {
            XtReleaseGC(w, lw->label.border_gc);
        }
        lw->label.border_gc = GetBorderGC(lw);
        lw->label.old_border = lw->rectObj.border_width;
    }
}

static XtGeometryResult QueryGeometry(w, proposed, desired)
    Widget w;
    XtWidgetGeometry *proposed, *desired;
{
    LabelGadget lw = (LabelGadget) w;
#define Set(bit) (proposed->request_mode & bit)

    desired->width = lw->label.desired_width;
    desired->height = lw->label.desired_height;
    desired->request_mode = CWWidth | CWHeight;

    if (Set(CWWidth) && proposed->width == desired->width &&
```

```
                    Set(CWHeight) && proposed->height == desired->height) {
            return XtGeometryYes;
        }

        if (desired->width == lw->rectObj.width &&
                desired->height == lw->rectObj.height) {
            return XtGeometryNo;
        }
        return XtGeometryAlmost;
#undef Set
}
```

10.13.4 Suggested Programming Exercises

• Modify LabelGadget so that it correctly updates its display if the parent calls
XtResizeWidget to change only the border width.

• Describe the environments and circumstances in which the temporary modification of
the shared graphics context in the Redisplay procedure could cause trouble. Modify
the code so that the problem does not occur.

• (Very ambitious) Write a PushbuttonGadget subclass of LabelGadget. Make Box,
MinMax, and Menu able to handle these. You might wish to make an abstract Gadget
support class to allow the composites to treat gadget children uniformly. Pick a way to
make the composites handle input events for a Pushbutton gadget. Do you need a
MenuItem gadget?

10.14   The Graph Widget

The Graph widget displays a data set in a way that is controlled by its Graph-
Display child. Graph illustrates writing a widget that has a component object.

10.14.1   The Public Header File

```
/* Make it safe to include this file more than once. */
#ifndef GRAPH_H
#define GRAPH_H

/* Graph is derived from Composite, so no need to include the
   superclass public header file.  */

/* New resources */

#define XtNnumEntries "numEntries"
#define XtCNumEntries "NumEntries"
#define XtNlabels "labels"
#define XtCLabels "Labels"
```

```
#define XtNvalues "values"
#define XtCValues "Values"
#define XtNmaxValue "maxValue"
#define XtCMaxValue "MaxValue"
#define XtNscale "scale"
#define XtCScale "Scale"

/* External reference to the class record pointer */
extern WidgetClass graphWidgetClass;

/* Type definition for graph widgets */
typedef struct _GraphRec *GraphWidget;

/* End of preprocessor directives */
#endif /* GRAPH_H */
```

10.14.2   The Private Header File

```
/* Make it safe to include this file more than once. */
#ifndef GRAPHP_H
#define GRAPHP_H

/* Include the public header file for Graph */
#include "Graph.h"

/* Graph is derived from Composite, so no need to include the
   superclass private header file. */

/* Define the Graph instance part */
typedef struct {
    int         num_entries;    /* Number of entries to graph */
    String      *labels;        /* Labels for values */
    int         *values;        /* Graph values */
    int         max_value;      /* Maximum graph value */
    int         scale;          /* Scale factor for values */
} GraphPart;

/* Define the full instance record */
typedef struct _GraphRec {
    CorePart            core;
    CompositePart       composite;
    GraphPart           graph;
} GraphRec;

/* Define class part structure */
typedef struct {
    XtPointer           extension;
} GraphClassPart;

/* Define the full class record */
```

```
typedef struct _GraphClassRec {
    CoreClassPart          core_class;
    CompositeClassPart     composite_class;
    GraphClassPart         graph_class;
} GraphClassRec, *GraphWidgetClass;

/* External definition for class record */
extern GraphClassRec graphClassRec;

/* End of preprocessor directives */
#endif /* GRAPHP_H */
```

10.14.3   The Implementation

```
#include <X11/IntrinsicP.h>     /* Intrinsics header file */
#include <X11/StringDefs.h>     /* Resource string definitions */
#include "GraphP.h"             /* Graph private header file */
#include "GraphDispP.h"         /* Graph display object */

#define Offset(field) XtOffsetOf(GraphRec, graph.field)

static XtResource resources[] = {
    {XtNnumEntries, XtCNumEntries, XtRInt, sizeof(int),
        Offset(num_entries), XtRImmediate, (XtPointer) 0},
    {XtNlabels, XtCLabels, XtRStringTable, sizeof(String *),
        Offset(labels), XtRImmediate, (XtPointer) NULL},
    {XtNvalues, XtCValues, XtRPointer, sizeof(int *),
        Offset(values), XtRImmediate, (XtPointer) NULL},
    {XtNmaxValue, XtCMaxValue, XtRInt, sizeof(int),
        Offset(max_value), XtRImmediate, (XtPointer) 100},
    {XtNscale, XtCScale, XtRInt, sizeof(int),
        Offset(scale), XtRImmediate, (XtPointer) 1}
};
#undef Offset
```

Graph has NULL geometry_manager and change_managed procedures. Even though it is a subclass of Composite, its insert_child procedure forbids any children that are not subclasses of GraphDisplay. Since GraphDisplay is not a subclass of RectObj, a Graph widget's child can never be managed and cannot issue geometry requests. This makes these procedures unnecessary.

```
/* Forward declarations */

static void ClassInitialize(), Initialize(),
        Redisplay(), Destroy(), Resize(), Realize(),
        InsertChild();
static Boolean SetValues();
```

```
static CompositeClassExtensionRec compositeExtension = {
    /* next_extension        */ NULL,
    /* record_type           */ NULLQUARK,
    /* version               */ XtCompositeExtensionVersion,
    /* record_size           */ sizeof(CompositeClassExtensionRec),
    /* accepts_objects        */ TRUE
};

GraphClassRec graphClassRec = {
    /* Core class part */
  {
    /* superclass            */ (WidgetClass) &compositeClassRec,
    /* class_name            */ "Graph",
    /* widget_size           */ sizeof(GraphRec),
    /* class_initialize      */ ClassInitialize,
    /* class_part_initialize */ NULL,
    /* class_inited          */ FALSE,
    /* initialize            */ Initialize,
    /* initialize_hook       */ NULL,
    /* realize               */ Realize,
    /* actions               */ NULL,
    /* num_actions           */ 0,
    /* resources             */ resources,
    /* num_resources         */ XtNumber(resources),
    /* xrm_class             */ NULLQUARK,
    /* compress_motion       */ TRUE,
    /* compress_exposure     */ XtExposeCompressMultiple,
    /* compress_enterleave   */ TRUE,
    /* visible_interest      */ FALSE,
    /* destroy               */ Destroy,
    /* resize                */ Resize,
    /* expose                */ Redisplay,
    /* set_values            */ SetValues,
    /* set_values_hook       */ NULL,
    /* set_values_almost     */ XtInheritSetValuesAlmost,
    /* get_values_hook       */ NULL,
    /* accept_focus          */ NULL,
    /* version               */ XtVersion,
    /* callback offsets      */ NULL,
    /* tm_table              */ NULL,
    /* query_geometry        */ NULL,
    /* display_accelerator   */ NULL,
    /* extension             */ NULL
  },
    /* Composite class part */
  {
    /* geometry_manager      */ NULL,
    /* change_managed        */ NULL,
    /* insert_child          */ InsertChild,
    /* delete_child          */ XtInheritDeleteChild,
```

```
      /* extension              */ (XtPointer) &compositeExtension,
  },
    /* Graph class part */
  {
    /* extension               */ NULL
  }
};
```

/* Class record pointer */

WidgetClass graphWidgetClass = (WidgetClass) &graphClassRec;

CvtStringToStringList converts a string with embedded newline characters
into a NULL-terminated list of strings. It copies the contents of the source
string in case the string is in temporary storage passed through an ArgList
and to allow the application to change the contents of the resource database
after the conversion has been performed.

```
static Boolean CvtStringToStringList(dpy, args, num_args,
        from, to, data)
    Display *dpy;
    XrmValuePtr args;
    Cardinal *num_args;
    XrmValuePtr from, to;
    XtPointer *data;
{
    register int i, count = 1;
    register char *ch, *start = from->addr;
    static String *list;
    int len;

    if (*num_args != 0) {
        XtAppErrorMsg(XtDisplayToApplicationContext(dpy),
            "cvtStringToStringList", "wrongParameters",
            "XtToolkitError",
            "String to string list conversion needs no extra arguments",
            (String *) NULL, (Cardinal *) NULL);
    }
    if (to->addr != NULL && to->size < sizeof(String *)) {
        to->size = sizeof(String *);
        return FALSE;
    }
    if (start == NULL || *start == '\0') list = NULL;
    else {
        for (ch = start; *ch != '\0'; ch++) {    /* Count strings */
            if (*ch == '\n') count++;
        }
        list = (String *) XtCalloc(count+1, sizeof(String));
```

```
        for (i = 0; i < count; i++) {
            for (ch = start; *ch != '\n' && *ch != '\0'; ch++) {}
            len = ch - start;
            list[i] = XtMalloc(len + 1);
            (void) strncpy(list[i], start, len);
            list[i][len] = '\0';
            start = ch + 1;
        }
    }
    if (to->addr == NULL) to->addr = (caddr_t) &list;
    else *(String **) to->addr = list;
    to->size = sizeof(String *);
    return TRUE;
}
```

Since the string-to-string-list converter allocates storage to hold the string list, it needs a destructor procedure to free the storage.

```
static void StringListDestructor(app, to, converter_data,
        args, num_args)
    XtAppContext app;
    XrmValuePtr to;
    XtPointer converter_data;
    XrmValuePtr args;
    Cardinal *num_args;
{
    String *list = (String *) to->addr;
    register String *entry;

    if (list == NULL) return;

    for (entry = list; entry != NULL; entry++) {
        XtFree((XtPointer) entry);
    }

    XtFree((XtPointer) list);
}
```

ClassInitialize registers the string-to-string-list converter. Since the labels can take up a fair amount of storage, the conversion is reference-counted.

```
static void ClassInitialize()
{
    /* Register a converter for string to string list */

    XtSetTypeConverter(XtRString, XtRStringTable,
        CvtStringToStringList, (XtConvertArgList) NULL, 0,
        XtCacheAll | XtCacheRefCount, StringListDestructor);
}
```

Initialize copies the graph values into allocated storage so that the application does not need to keep them. Unfortunately there is no good way to tell if there are the right number of values or labels specified; Initialize touches each value and label so that an error will occur here rather than someplace harder to diagnose.

```
static void Initialize(request, new, args, num_args)
    Widget request, new;
    ArgList args;
    Cardinal *num_args;
{
    register GraphWidget gw = (GraphWidget) new;
    int *values;
    register int i;
    String label;

    /* Copy the values */
    values = (int *) XtCalloc(gw->graph.num_entries, sizeof(int));
    for (i = 0; i < gw->graph.num_entries; i++) {
        values[i] = gw->graph.values[i];
    }
    gw->graph.values = values;

    /* If labels is not NULL, make sure there are enough of them now
       to avoid an error some random other place. */
    if (gw->graph.labels != NULL) {
        for (i = 0; i < gw->graph.num_entries; i++) {
            label = gw->graph.labels[i];
        }
    }
}
```

SetValues copies the values if they have changed. If the number of entries is different but the value list or label list is unchanged, the application made an error.

```
static Boolean SetValues(old, req, new, args, num_args)
    Widget old, req, new;
    ArgList args;
    Cardinal *num_args;
{
    register GraphWidget oldgraph = (GraphWidget) old;
    register GraphWidget newgraph = (GraphWidget) new;
    int *values;
    String label;
    register int i;

#define NE(field) (newgraph->graph.field != oldgraph->graph.field)
```

```
#define EQ(field) (newgraph->graph.field == oldgraph->graph.field)

    if (NE(values)) {
        values = (int *) XtCalloc(newgraph->graph.num_entries,
                sizeof(int));
        XtFree(oldgraph->graph.values);
        for (i = 0; i < newgraph->graph.num_entries; i++) {
            values[i] = newgraph->graph.values[i];
        }
        newgraph->graph.values = values;
        return TRUE;
    }

    /* If num_entries changed but not the labels or values,
       something's wrong */
    if (NE(num_entries) && (EQ(labels) || EQ(values))) {
        XtAppErrorMsg(XtWidgetToApplicationContext(new),
            "countError", "numEntries", "WidgetError",
            "Number of graph entries changed but not labels or values",
            (String *) NULL, (Cardinal *) NULL);
    }

    if (NE(labels) && newgraph->graph.labels != NULL) {
        for (i = 0; i < newgraph->graph.num_entries; i++) {
            label = newgraph->graph.labels[i];
        }
    }

    return NE(num_entries) || NE(labels) || NE(max_value);
#undef NE
}
```

Destroy does not free the labels since no private copy was made.

```
static void Destroy(w)
    Widget w;
{
    GraphWidget gw = (GraphWidget) w;

    XtFree((char *) gw->graph.values);
}
```

InsertChild checks to make sure that the new child is a subclass of Graph-Display and that there is no child already there. Once the child has been added, InsertChild calls the child's compute_size method to let it set the Graph widget's size.

```
static void InsertChild(w)
    Widget w;
{
```

```
    String params[2];
    Cardinal num_params;
    CompositeWidget parent = (CompositeWidget) XtParent(w);
    GraphDisplayObjectClass childClass;

    if (!XtIsSubclass(w, graphDisplayObjectClass)) {
        params[0] = XtClass(w)->core_class.class_name;
        params[1] = XtClass(parent)->core_class.class_name;
        num_params = 2;
        XtAppErrorMsg(XtWidgetToApplicationContext(w),
                "childError", "class", "WidgetError",
                "Children of class %s cannot be added to %n widgets",
                params, &num_params);
    }

    if (parent->composite.num_children != 0) {
        params[0] = XtClass(parent)->core_class.class_name;
        num_params = 1;
        XtAppErrorMsg(XtWidgetToApplicationContext(w),
                "childError", "number", "WidgetError",
                "%s widgets can only take one child",
                params, &num_params);
    }

    (*((CompositeWidgetClass)(graphWidgetClass->
            core_class.superclass))->composite_class.insert_child) (w);

    /* Give the child a chance to compute our dimensions */

    childClass = (GraphDisplayObjectClass) XtClass(w);
    if (childClass->graphDisplay_class.compute_size != NULL) {
        (*childClass->graphDisplay_class.compute_size) (parent);
    }
}
```

The GraphDisplay child must be in place by the time the Graph widget gets realized. Realize generates an error message if not.

```
static void Realize(w, valueMask, attributes)
    Widget w;
    XtValueMask *valueMask;
    XSetWindowAttributes *attributes;
{
    GraphWidget gw = (GraphWidget) w;
    String params[2];
    Cardinal num_params;

    if (gw->composite.num_children != 1) {
        params[0] = XtClass(w)->core_class.class_name;
        num_params = 1;
```

```
        XtAppErrorMsg(XtWidgetToApplicationContext(w),
            "childError", "number", "WidgetError",
            "%s widgets must have exactly one child",
            params, &num_params);
    }

    (*graphWidgetClass->core_class.superclass->core_class.realize)
        (w, valueMask, attributes);
}
```

Redisplay just calls the display object's expose procedure to let it draw the graph.

```
static void Redisplay(w, event, region)
    Widget w;
    XEvent *event;
    Region region;
{
    GraphWidget gw = (GraphWidget) w;
    GraphDisplayObject d =
            (GraphDisplayObject) gw->composite.children[0];
    GraphDisplayObjectClass childClass;

    childClass = (GraphDisplayObjectClass) XtClass((Widget) d);
    if (childClass->graphDisplay_class.expose != NULL) {
        (*childClass->graphDisplay_class.expose) (w, event, region);
    }
}
static void Resize(w)
    Widget w;
{
    /* If widget is realized, clear and redisplay */

    if (XtIsRealized(w)) {
        XClearWindow(XtDisplay(w), XtWindow(w));
        (*(XtClass(w)->core_class.expose))(w,
                (XEvent *) NULL, (Region) NULL);
    }
}
```

10.14.4 Suggested Programming Exercises

- Implement the query_geometry method for Graph. Can you do this without modifying GraphDisplay or its subclasses?

- Modify Graph to allow the application to change the number of entries to display without changing the values.

10.15   The GraphDisplay Object

GraphDisplay is an abstract class that defines the methods a display object requires. It defines two methods:

compute_size   If the parent Graph widget's width or height is zero, the compute_size method fills the fields in with an appropriate size to hold the graph.

expose   The expose method is responsible for displaying the graph in its parent's window.

GraphDisplay does not provide implementations of either of these methods; it merely defines them so that Graph can deal with its display object child the same way regardless of its class.

10.15.1   The Public Header File

```
/* Make it safe to include this file more than once. */
#ifndef GRAPHDISPLAY_H
#define GRAPHDISPLAY_H

/* GraphDisplay is derived from Object, so no need to include the
   superclass public header file. */

/* External reference to the class record pointer */
extern WidgetClass graphDisplayObjectClass;

/* Type definition for graphDisplay objects */
typedef struct _GraphDisplayRec *GraphDisplayObject;

/* End of preprocessor directives */
#endif /* GRAPHDISPLAY_H */
```

10.15.2   The Private Header File

```
/* Make it safe to include this file more than once. */
#ifndef GRAPHDISPLAYP_H
#define GRAPHDISPLAYP_H

/* Include the public header file for GraphDisplay */
#include "GraphDispl.h"

/* GraphDisplay is derived from Object, so no need to include the
   superclass private header file. */

/* Define the GraphDisplay instance part */
typedef struct {
```

```
    Pixel       foreground;     /* Foreground pixel value */
    XFontStruct *font;          /* Font to display in */
    GC          gc;             /* Graphics context for displaying */
} GraphDisplayPart;

/* Define the full instance record */
typedef struct _GraphDisplayRec {
    ObjectPart          object;
    GraphDisplayPart    graphDisplay;
} GraphDisplayRec;

/* Define new type for the compute_size method */
typedef void (*ComputeSizeProc)();
    /* GraphWidget     w; */

/* Define class part structure */
typedef struct {
    ComputeSizeProc     compute_size;
    XtExposeProc        expose;
    XtPointer           extension;
} GraphDisplayClassPart;

/* Define the full class record */
typedef struct _GraphDisplayClassRec {
    ObjectClassPart             object_class;
    GraphDisplayClassPart       graphDisplay_class;
} GraphDisplayClassRec, *GraphDisplayObjectClass;

/* External definition for class record */
extern GraphDisplayClassRec graphDisplayClassRec;

/* Inheritance constant for compute_size method */

#define InheritComputeSize ((ComputeSizeProc) _XtInherit)

/* End of preprocessor directives */
#endif /* GRAPHDISPLAYP_H */
```

10.15.3   The Implementation

```
#include <X11/IntrinsicP.h>     /* Intrinsics header file */
#include <X11/StringDefs.h>     /* Resource string definitions */
#include "GraphDispP.h"         /* Graph display object */

#define Offset(field) XtOffsetOf(GraphDisplayRec, graphDisplay.field)

static XtResource resources[] = {
    {XtNfont,  XtCFont, XtRFontStruct, sizeof(XFontStruct *),
        Offset(font), XtRString, (XtPointer) XtDefaultFont},
    {XtNforeground, XtCForeground, XtRPixel, sizeof(Pixel),
```

```
                Offset(foreground), XtRString,
                (XtPointer) XtDefaultForeground},
    };
    #undef Offset

    /* Forward declarations */

    static void ClassPartInitialize(), Initialize(), Destroy();
    static Boolean SetValues();

    /* Class record declaration */

    GraphDisplayClassRec graphDisplayClassRec = {
        /* Object class part */
      {
        /* superclass              */ (WidgetClass) &objectClassRec,
        /* class_name               */ "GraphDisplay",
        /* widget_size              */ sizeof(GraphDisplayRec),
        /* class_initialize         */ NULL,
        /* class_part_initialize    */ ClassPartInitialize,
        /* class_inited             */ FALSE,
        /* initialize               */ Initialize,
        /* initialize_hook          */ NULL,
        /* obj1                     */ NULL,
        /* obj2                     */ NULL,
        /* obj3                     */ 0,
        /* resources                */ resources,
        /* num_resources            */ XtNumber(resources),
        /* xrm_class                */ NULLQUARK,
        /* obj4                     */ 0,
        /* obj5                     */ 0,
        /* obj6                     */ 0,
        /* obj7                     */ 0,
        /* destroy                  */ Destroy,
        /* obj8                     */ NULL,
        /* obj9                     */ NULL,
        /* set_values               */ SetValues,
        /* set_values_hook          */ NULL,
        /* obj10                    */ NULL,
        /* get_values_hook          */ NULL,
        /* obj11                    */ NULL,
        /* version                  */ XtVersion,
        /* callback offsets         */ NULL,
        /* obj12                    */ NULL,
        /* obj13                    */ NULL,
        /* obj14                    */ NULL,
        /* extension                */ NULL
      },
        /* GraphDisplay class part  */
      {
```

```
        /* compute_size          */ NULL,
        /* expose                */ NULL,
        /* extension             */ NULL
    }
};


/* Class record pointer */

WidgetClass graphDisplayObjectClass =
        (WidgetClass) &graphDisplayClassRec;
```

ClassPartInitialize is responsible for resolving the inheritance of Graph-Display's two methods.

```
static void ClassPartInitialize(widgetClass)
    WidgetClass widgetClass;
{
    register GraphDisplayObjectClass wc =
            (GraphDisplayObjectClass) widgetClass;
    GraphDisplayObjectClass super =
            (GraphDisplayObjectClass) wc->object_class.superclass;

    if (wc->graphDisplay_class.compute_size == InheritComputeSize) {
        wc->graphDisplay_class.compute_size =
                super->graphDisplay_class.compute_size;
    }

    if (wc->graphDisplay_class.expose == XtInheritExpose) {
        wc->graphDisplay_class.expose =
                super->graphDisplay_class.expose;
    }
}
```

Since most display objects will need at least one color and a font, Graph-Display defines resources for these and stores them in a graphics context.

```
static GC GetGC(gd)
    GraphDisplayObject gd;
{
    XGCValues    values;

    /* Allocate a graphics context with the foreground and font */

    values.foreground = gd->graphDisplay.foreground;
    values.font = gd->graphDisplay.font->fid;

    return XtGetGC(XtParent((Widget) gd),
            GCForeground | GCFont, &values);
}
```

```
static void Initialize(request, new, args, num_args)
    Widget request, new;
    ArgList args;
    Cardinal *num_args;
{

    GraphDisplayObject gd = (GraphDisplayObject) new;


    /* Get a graphics context */
    gd->graphDisplay.gc = GetGC(gd);
}
```

SetValues updates the graphics context if the foreground or font changes. It also uses a massive kludge to work around a deficiency in the Intrinsics—there is no way for an object child to make its parent redisplay from its set_values procedure. To get around this, SetValues clears the parent itself, generating Expose events. The Intrinsics ignore the return value.

```
static Boolean SetValues(old, request, new, args, num_args)
    Widget  old, request, new;
    ArgList args;
    Cardinal *num_args;
{

    GraphDisplayObject oldgd = (GraphDisplayObject) old;
    GraphDisplayObject newgd = (GraphDisplayObject) new;

#define NE(field) (oldgd->field != newgd->field)

    /* If foreground or font has changed, update GC */

    if (NE(graphDisplay.foreground) || NE(graphDisplay.font->fid)) {
        XtReleaseGC(newgd, oldgd->graphDisplay.gc);
        newgd->graphDisplay.gc = GetGC(newgd);

        /* Kludge.  There's no way to tell the Intrinsics to
           automatically redisplay, so clear the parent, causing
           expose events.  Subclasses will do this too, but multiple
           redisplays are avoided since the parent has
           XtExposeCompressMultiple. */

        if (XtIsRealized(XtParent((Widget) newgd))) {
            XClearArea(XtDisplayOfObject(newgd),
                    XtWindowOfObject(newgd), 0, 0, 0, 0, TRUE);
        }
    }

    return FALSE;
#undef NE
}
```

```
static void Destroy(w)
    Widget w;
{
    GraphDisplayObject gd = (GraphDisplayObject) w;

    XtReleaseGC(XtParent(w), gd->graphDisplay.gc);
}
```

10.16   The BarDisplay Object

BarDisplay is a subclass of GraphDisplay that generates horizontal bar graphs.

10.16.1   The Public Header File

```
/* Make it safe to include this file more than once. */
#ifndef BARDISPLAY_H
#define BARDISPLAY_H

/* Superclass public header file */

#include "GraphDispl.h"

/* New resources */

#define XtNspace "space"
#define XtCSpace "Space"
#define XtNdefaultGraphWidth "defaultGraphWidth"
#define XtCDefaultGraphWidth "DefaultGraphWidth"
#define XtNformat "format"
#define XtCFormat "Format"

/* External reference to the class record pointer */
extern WidgetClass barDisplayObjectClass;

/* Type definition for barDisplay objects */
typedef struct _BarDisplayRec *BarDisplayObject;

/* End of preprocessor directives */
#endif /* BARDISPLAY_H */
```

10.16.2   The Private Header File

```
/* Make it safe to include this file more than once. */
#ifndef BARDISPLAYP_H
#define BARDISPLAYP_H

/* Include the public header file for BarDisplay */
#include "BarDisplay.h"
```

```
/* Include the private header file for GraphDisplay */
#include "GraphDispP.h"

/* Define the BarDisplay instance part */
typedef struct {
    Dimension    space;                /* Space between bars */
    Dimension    default_graph_width;  /* Default width */
    String       format;               /* For displaying value */
} BarDisplayPart;

/* Define the full instance record */
typedef struct _BarDisplayRec {
    ObjectPart          object;
    GraphDisplayPart    graphDisplay;
    BarDisplayPart      barDisplay;
} BarDisplayRec;

/* Define class part structure */
typedef struct {
    XtPointer           extension;
} BarDisplayClassPart;

/* Define the full class record */
typedef struct _BarDisplayClassRec {
    ObjectClassPart          object_class;
    GraphDisplayClassPart    graphDisplay_class;
    BarDisplayClassPart      barDisplay_class;
} BarDisplayClassRec, *BarDisplayObjectClass;

/* External definition for class record */
extern BarDisplayClassRec barDisplayClassRec;

/* End of preprocessor directives */
#endif /* BARDISPLAYP_H */
```

10.16.3   The Implementation

```
#include <X11/IntrinsicP.h>    /* Intrinsics header file */
#include <X11/StringDefs.h>    /* Resource string definitions */
#include "BarDisplaP.h"        /* Bar display object */
#include "GraphP.h"            /* Graph widget */

#define Offset(field) XtOffsetOf(BarDisplayRec, barDisplay.field)

static XtResource resources[] = {
    {XtNspace, XtCSpace, XtRDimension, sizeof(Dimension),
        Offset(space), XtRImmediate, (XtPointer) 5},
    {XtNdefaultGraphWidth, XtCDefaultGraphWidth,
        XtRDimension, sizeof(Dimension),
        Offset(default_graph_width), XtRImmediate, (XtPointer) 200},
```

```
        {XtNformat, XtCFormat, XtRString, sizeof(String),
            Offset(format), XtRString, "%g"}
};
#undef Offset

/* Forward declarations */

static void Initialize(), Redisplay(), ComputeSize();
static Boolean SetValues();

/* Class record declaration */

BarDisplayClassRec barDisplayClassRec = {
    /* Object class part */
    {
    /* superclass              */ (WidgetClass) &graphDisplayClassRec,
    /* class_name              */ "BarDisplay",
    /* widget_size             */ sizeof(BarDisplayRec),
    /* class_initialize        */ NULL,
    /* class_part_initialize   */ NULL,
    /* class_inited            */ FALSE,
    /* initialize              */ Initialize,
    /* initialize_hook         */ NULL,
    /* obj1                    */ NULL,
    /* obj2                    */ NULL,
    /* obj3                    */ 0,
    /* resources               */ resources,
    /* num_resources           */ XtNumber(resources),
    /* xrm_class               */ NULLQUARK,
    /* obj4                    */ 0,
    /* obj5                    */ 0,
    /* obj6                    */ 0,
    /* obj7                    */ 0,
    /* destroy                 */ NULL,
    /* obj8                    */ NULL,
    /* obj9                    */ NULL,
    /* set_values              */ SetValues,
    /* set_values_hook         */ NULL,
    /* obj10                   */ NULL,
    /* get_values_hook         */ NULL,
    /* obj11                   */ NULL,
    /* version                 */ XtVersion,
    /* callback offsets        */ NULL,
    /* obj12                   */ NULL,
    /* obj13                   */ NULL,
    /* obj14                   */ NULL,
    /* extension               */ NULL
    },
```

```
        /* GraphDisplay class part  */
      {
        /* compute_size          */ ComputeSize,
        /* expose                */ Redisplay,
        /* extension             */ NULL
      },
        /* BarDisplay class part  */
      {
        /* extension             */ NULL
      }
};

/* Class record pointer */

WidgetClass barDisplayObjectClass = (WidgetClass) &barDisplayClassRec;

static void Initialize(request, new, args, num_args)
    Widget request, new;
    ArgList args;
    Cardinal *num_args;
{
    BarDisplayObject bd = (BarDisplayObject) new;

    /* Copy format */
    bd->barDisplay.format = XtNewString(bd->barDisplay.format);
}
```

BarDisplay's SetValues uses the same kludge that GraphDisplay's SetValues did.

```
static Boolean SetValues(old, request, new, args, num_args)
    Widget  old, request, new;
    ArgList args;
    Cardinal *num_args;
{
    BarDisplayObject oldbd = (BarDisplayObject) old;
    BarDisplayObject newbd = (BarDisplayObject) new;

#define NE(field) (oldbd->barDisplay.field != newbd->barDisplay.field)

    if (NE(format)) {
        newbd->barDisplay.format =
                XtNewString(newbd->barDisplay.format);
    }

    /* If space or format has changed and we're realized, redisplay */

    if (NE(space) || NE(format)) {

        /* Kludge.  There's no way to tell the Intrinsics to
           automatically redisplay, so clear the parent, causing
```

```
        expose events.  Subclasses will do this too, but multiple
        redisplays are avoided since the parent has
        XtExposeCompressMultiple. */

    if (XtIsRealized(XtParent((Widget) newbd))) {
      XClearArea(XtDisplayOfObject(newbd),
            XtWindowOfObject(newbd), 0, 0, 0, 0, TRUE);
    }
  }

  return FALSE;
}
```

ComputeLabelDimensions computes the width of the widest label and the
height of the font. It also formats the values and computes the widest one,
then adds this to the widest label value to return the width needed to display
both the widest label and the widest formatted value. The value returned in
total_w is the width that would be needed to display the labels and the formatted values in a vertical table.

```
static void ComputeLabelDimensions(bd, label_w, total_w, height)
    BarDisplayObject bd;
    Dimension *label_w, *total_w, *height;
{
    register XFontStruct *fs = bd->graphDisplay.font;
    register int i;
    int width;
    GraphWidget parent = (GraphWidget) XtParent((Widget) bd);
    char buf[100];

    *label_w = *total_w = 0;
    if (parent->graph.labels != NULL) {
        for (i = 0; i < parent->graph.num_entries; i++) {
            width = XTextWidth(fs, parent->graph.labels[i],
                    strlen(parent->graph.labels[i]));
            if (width > *label_w) *label_w = width;
        }
    }

    for (i = 0; i < parent->graph.num_entries; i++) {
        (void) sprintf(buf, bd->barDisplay.format,
                (float) parent->graph.values[i] / parent->graph.scale);
        width = XTextWidth(fs, buf, strlen(buf));
        if (width > *total_w) *total_w = width;
    }

    *total_w += *label_w;
    *height = fs->max_bounds.ascent + fs->max_bounds.descent;
}
```

ComputeSize is responsible for computing a size large enough to hold the bar graph and storing this size in the parent Graph widget if the parent does not already have a size. The desired width is the total width returned from ComputeLabelDimensions plus the default width for the bars plus four times the space resource (to the left of the labels, between the labels and the bars, between the bars and the formatted values, and to the right of the formatted values). The desired height is the font height times the number of entries, with the space added in between the bars and at the top and the bottom.

```
static void ComputeSize(w)
    GraphWidget w;
{
    BarDisplayObject bd = (BarDisplayObject) w->composite.children[0];
    Dimension label_width, total_width, label_height;

    ComputeLabelDimensions(bd, &label_width,
            &total_width, &label_height);

    /* If parent has no width, compute one */
    if (w->core.width == 0) {
        w->core.width = 4*bd->barDisplay.space + total_width +
                bd->barDisplay.default_graph_width;
    }

    /* If parent has no height, compute one */
    if (w->core.height == 0) {
        w->core.height = w->graph.num_entries *
                (bd->barDisplay.space + label_height) +
                bd->barDisplay.space;
    }
}
```

Redisplay is responsible for drawing the bar graph in its parent's window. If the parent is too narrow to display the labels, the bars, and the formatted values, Redisplay omits the bars and displays as a two-column table.

```
static void Redisplay(w, event, region)
    GraphWidget w;
    XEvent *event;
    Region region;
{
    BarDisplayObject bd = (BarDisplayObject) w->composite.children[0];
    Dimension label_width, total_width, label_height;
    Boolean displayBars;
    register int i;
    int x, y, bar_width;
    char buf[100];
```

```
register int *values = w->graph.values;
register String *labels = w->graph.labels;

ComputeLabelDimensions(bd, &label_width, &total_width,
        &label_height);

/* See if there's enough room to display bars */

bar_width = w->core.width - total_width - 4*bd->barDisplay.space;
displayBars = (bar_width > (int) bd->barDisplay.space);

y = bd->barDisplay.space;
for (i = 0; i < w->graph.num_entries; i++) {
    if (labels != NULL) {
        XDrawString(XtDisplay(w), XtWindow(w), bd->graphDisplay.gc,
                bd->barDisplay.space,
                y + bd->graphDisplay.font->max_bounds.ascent,
                labels[i], strlen(labels[i]));
        x = label_width + 2*bd->barDisplay.space;
    } else x = 0;

    if (displayBars) {
        XFillRectangle(XtDisplay(w), XtWindow(w),
                bd->graphDisplay.gc, x, y,
                bar_width * values[i] / w->graph.max_value,
                bd->graphDisplay.font->max_bounds.ascent);
        x += bar_width * values[i] / w->graph.max_value +
                bd->barDisplay.space;
    }

    (void) sprintf(buf, bd->barDisplay.format,
            (float) values[i] / w->graph.scale);
    XDrawString(XtDisplay(w), XtWindow(w), bd->graphDisplay.gc,
            x, y + bd->graphDisplay.font->max_bounds.ascent,
            buf, strlen(buf));

    y += label_height + bd->barDisplay.space;
    }
}
```

10.16.4 Suggested Programming Exercises

- Add a resource to BarDisplay that controls whether it displays the formatted values. Be sure to take this into account in ComputeLabelDimensions and ComputeSize.

- BarDisplay does not check if the values are larger than the maximum; it just displays a bar that extends past the right edge of the graph. Modify Redisplay so that it takes this into account; a bar for an entry larger than the maximum value should be truncated at the maximum value and end with an arrowhead to indicate that it is too large.

- BarDisplay does not handle graphs with open-ended values very well (values like you might get graphing a load average). Write a subclass that keeps track of the maximum graph value for some previous number of data sets, and have the full bar width correspond to this maximum. You should be able to inherit the compute_size method. Add another method that tells this subclass to reset itself.

- Write a subclass that only handles one value but graphs it against time (similar to the `xload` application).

- Add resources so that the labels or formatted values can be in a different color from the bars.

- Add a resource so that each bar can be a different color. Write a string-to-pixel-list converter to handle the colors. Consider an additional resource giving the number of colors; if there are not enough colors, cycle through them multiple times.

- Write a GraphDisplay subclass that displays a vertical bar graph. Decide what to do about the labels.

- Write a GraphDisplay subclass that displays as a pie chart.

- Make the pie chart display in multiple colors.

- Use your imagination. How many different ways can you think of to display the data?

PART II. SPECIFICATION

Ralph Swick

with Paul J. Asente and Joel McCormack

Chapter 1

Intrinsics and Widgets

The Intrinsics are a programming library tailored to the special requirements of user interface construction within a network window system, specifically the X Window System. The Intrinsics and a widget set make up an X Toolkit.

1.1   Intrinsics

The Intrinsics provide the base mechanism necessary to build a wide variety of interoperating widget sets and application environments. The Intrinsics are a layer on top of Xlib, the C Library X Interface. They extend the fundamental abstractions provided by the X Window System while still remaining independent of any particular user interface policy or style.

The Intrinsics use object-oriented programming techniques to supply a consistent architecture for constructing and composing user interface components, known as widgets. This allows programmers to extend a widget set in new ways, either by deriving new widgets from existing ones (subclassing), or by writing entirely new widgets following the established conventions.

When the Intrinsics were first conceived, the root of the object hierarchy was a widget class named Core. In Release 4 of the Intrinsics, three nonwidget superclasses were added above Core. These superclasses are described in Chapter 12.[1] The name of the class now at the root of the Intrinsics class hierarchy is Object. The remainder of this specification refers uniformly to

---

[1] All cross-references in the specification are to chapters and sections within the specification unless an explicit reference is made to another source.

widgets and *Core* as if they were the base class for all Intrinsics operations. The argument descriptions for each Intrinsics procedure and Chapter 12 describe which operations are defined for the nonwidget superclasses of Core. The reader may determine by context whether a specific reference to *widget* actually means "widget" or "object."

1.2   Languages

The Intrinsics are intended to be used for two programming purposes. Programmers writing widgets will be using most of the facilities provided by the Intrinsics to construct user interface components from the simple, such as buttons and scrollbars, to the complex, such as control panels and property sheets. Application programmers will use a much smaller subset of the Intrinsics procedures in combination with one or more sets of widgets to construct and present complete user interfaces on an X display. The Intrinsics programming interfaces primarily intended for application use are designed to be callable from most procedural programming languages. Therefore, most arguments are passed by reference rather than by value. The interfaces primarily intended for widget programmers are expected to be used principally from the C language. In these cases, the usual C programming conventions apply. In this specification, the term *client* refers to any module, widget, or application that calls an Intrinsics procedure.

Applications that use the Intrinsics mechanisms must include the header files ⟨X11/Intrinsic.h⟩ and ⟨X11/StringDefs.h⟩, or their equivalent, and they may also include ⟨X11/Xatoms.h⟩ and ⟨X11/Shell.h⟩. In addition, widget implementations should include ⟨X11/IntrinsicP.h⟩ instead of ⟨X11/Intrinsic.h⟩.

The applications must also include the additional header files for each widget class that they are to use (for example, ⟨X11/Xaw/Label.h⟩ or ⟨X11/Xaw/Scrollbar.h⟩). On a POSIX-based system, the Intrinsics object library file is named libXt.a and is usually referenced as –lXt when linking the application.

1.3   Procedures and Macros

All functions defined in this specification except those specified below may be implemented as C macros with arguments. C applications may use "#undef" to remove a macro definition and ensure that the actual function is referenced.

Any such macro will expand to a single expression that has the same precedence as a function call and that evaluates each of its arguments exactly once, fully protected by parentheses, so that arbitrary expressions may be used as arguments.

The following symbols are macros that do not have function equivalents and that may expand their arguments in a manner other than that described above: `XtCheckSubclass`, `XtNew`, `XtNumber`, `XtOffsetOf`, `XtOffset`, and `XtSetArg`.

1.4   Widgets

The fundamental abstraction and data type of the X Toolkit is the widget, which is a combination of an X window and its associated input and display semantics and which is dynamically allocated and contains state information. Some widgets display information (for example, text or graphics), and others are merely containers for other widgets (for example, a menu box). Some widgets are output-only and do not react to pointer or keyboard input, and others change their display in response to input and can invoke functions that an application has attached to them.

Every widget belongs to exactly one widget class, which is statically allocated and initialized and which contains the operations allowable on widgets of that class. Logically, a widget class is the procedures and data associated with all widgets belonging to that class. These procedures and data can be inherited by subclasses. Physically, a widget class is a pointer to a structure. The contents of this structure are constant for all widgets of the widget class but will vary from class to class. (Here, "constant" means the class structure is initialized at compile time and never changed, except for a one-time class initialization and in-place compilation of resource lists, which takes place when the first widget of the class or subclass is created.) For further information, see Section 2.4.

The distribution of the declarations and code for a new widget class among a public .h file for application programmer use, a private .h file for widget programmer use, and the implementation .c file is described in Section 1.6. The predefined widget classes adhere to these conventions.

A widget instance is composed of two parts:

• A data structure which contains instance-specific values.

• A class structure which contains information that is applicable to all widgets of that class.

Much of the input/output of a widget (for example, fonts, colors, sizes, border widths, and so on) is customizable by users.

This chapter discusses the base widget classes, Core, Composite, and Constraint, and ends with a discussion of widget classing.

1.4.1 Core Widgets

The Core widget class contains the definitions of fields common to all widgets. All widget classes are subclasses of the Core class, which is defined by the `Core-ClassPart` and `CorePart` structures.

1.4.1.1 CoreClassPart Structure

All widget classes contain the fields defined in the `CoreClassPart` structure.

```
typedef struct {
    WidgetClass         superclass;             See Section 1.6
    String              class_name;             See Chapter 9
    Cardinal            widget_size;            See Section 1.6
    XtProc              class_initialize;       See Section 1.6
    XtWidgetClassProc   class_part_initialize;  See Section 1.6
    XtEnum              class_inited;           See Section 1.6
    XtInitProc          initialize;             See Section 2.4
    XtArgsProc          initialize_hook;        See Section 2.4
    XtRealizeProc       realize;                See Section 2.5
    XtActionList        actions;                See Chapter 10
    Cardinal            num_actions;            See Chapter 10
    XtResourceList      resources;              See Chapter 9
    Cardinal            num_resources;          See Chapter 9
    XrmClass            xrm_class;              Private to resource manager
    Boolean             compress_motion;        See Section 7.9
    XtEnum              compress_exposure;      See Section 7.9
    Boolean             compress_enterleave;    See Section 7.9
    Boolean             visible_interest;       See Section 7.10
    XtWidgetProc        destroy;                See Section 2.8
    XtWidgetProc        resize;                 See Chapter 6
    XtExposeProc        expose;                 See Section 7.10
    XtSetValuesFunc     set_values;             See Section 9.7
    XtArgsFunc          set_values_hook;        See Section 9.7
    XtAlmostProc        set_values_almost;      See Section 9.7
    XtArgsProc          get_values_hook;        See Section 9.7
    XtAcceptFocusProc   accept_focus;           See Section 7.3
```

XtVersionType	version;	See Section 1.6
XtPointer	callback_private;	Private to callbacks
String	tm_table;	See Chapter 10
XtGeometryHandler	query_geometry;	See Chapter 6
XtStringProc	display_accelerator;	See Chapter 10
XtPointer	extension;	See Section 1.6

} CoreClassPart;

All widget classes have the Core class fields as their first component. The prototypical `WidgetClass` and `CoreWidgetClass` are defined with only this set of fields.

```
typedef struct _WidgetClassRec {
    CoreClassPart          core_class;
} WidgetClassRec, *WidgetClass, CoreClassRec, *CoreWidgetClass;
```

Various routines can cast widget class pointers, as needed, to specific widget class types. The single occurrences of the class record and pointer for creating instances of Core are

In `IntrinsicP.h`:

```
extern WidgetClassRec widgetClassRec;
#define coreClassRec widgetClassRec
```

In `Intrinsic.h`:

```
extern WidgetClass widgetClass, coreWidgetClass;
```

The opaque types `Widget` and `WidgetClass` and the opaque variable `widgetClass` are defined for generic actions on widgets. In order to make these types opaque and ensure that the compiler does not allow applications to access private data, the Intrinsics use incomplete structure definitions in `Intrinsic.h`.

```
typedef struct _WidgetClassRec *WidgetClass, *CoreWidgetClass;
```

1.4.1.2 CorePart Structure

All widget instances contain the fields defined in the `CorePart` structure.

```
typedef struct _CorePart {
    Widget                self;              Described below
    WidgetClass           widget_class;      See Section 1.6
```

Widget	parent;	See Section 2.4
XrmName	xrm_name;	Private to resource manager
Boolean	being_destroyed;	See Section 2.8
XtCallbackList	destroy_callbacks;	See Section 2.8
XtPointer	constraints;	See Section 3.6
Position	x, y;	See Chapter 6
Dimension	width, height;	See Chapter 6
Dimension	border_width;	See Chapter 6
Boolean	managed;	See Chapter 3
Boolean	sensitive;	See Section 7.7
Boolean	ancestor_sensitive;	See Section 7.7
XtEventTable	event_table;	Private to event manager
XtTMRec	tm;	Private to translation manager
XtTranslations	accelerators;	See Chapter 10
Pixel	border_pixel;	See Section 2.5
Pixmap	border_pixmap;	See Section 2.5
WidgetList	popup_list;	See Chapter 5
Cardinal	num_popups;	See Chapter 5
String	name;	See Chapter 9
Screen	*screen;	See Section 2.5
Colormap	colormap;	See Section 2.5
Window	window;	See Section 2.5
Cardinal	depth;	See Section 2.5
Pixel	background_pixel;	See Section 2.5
Pixmap	background_pixmap;	See Section 2.5
Boolean	visible;	See Section 7.10
Boolean	mapped_when_managed;	See Chapter 3

} CorePart;

All widget instances have the Core fields as their first component. The prototypical type `Widget` is defined with only this set of fields.

```
typedef struct {
    CorePart        core;
} WidgetRec, *Widget, CoreRec, *CoreWidget;
```

Various routines can cast widget pointers, as needed, to specific widget types. In order to make these types opaque and ensure that the compiler does not allow applications to access private data, the Intrinsics use incomplete structure definitions in `Intrinsic.h`.

typedef struct _WidgetRec *Widget, *CoreWidget;

1.4.1.3 Core Resources

The resource names, classes, and representation types specified in the `core-ClassRec` resource list are

Name	Class	Representation
XtNaccelerators	XtCAccelerators	XtRAcceleratorTable
XtNbackground	XtCBackground	XtRPixel
XtNbackgroundPixmap	XtCPixmap	XtRPixmap
XtNborderColor	XtCBorderColor	XtRPixel
XtNborderPixmap	XtCPixmap	XtRPixmap
XtNcolormap	XtCColormap	XtRColormap
XtNdepth	XtCDepth	XtRInt
XtNmappedWhenManaged	XtCMappedWhenManaged	XtRBoolean
XtNscreen	XtCScreen	XtRScreen
XtNtranslations	XtCTranslations	XtRTranslationTable

Additional resources are defined for all widgets via the `objectClassRec` and `rectObjClassRec` resource lists; see Sections 12.2 and 12.3.

1.4.1.4 CorePart Default Values

The default values for the Core fields, which are filled in from the resource lists and by the initialize procedures, are

Field	Default Value
self	Address of the widget structure (may not be changed).
widget_class	*widget_class* argument to `XtCreateWidget` (may not be changed).
parent	*parent* argument to `XtCreateWidget` (may not be changed).
xrm_name	Encoded *name* argument to `XtCreateWidget` (may not be changed).
being_destroyed	Parent's *being_destroyed* value.
destroy_callbacks	NULL
constraints	NULL

Field	Default Value
x	0
y	0
width	0
height	0
border_width	1
managed	`False`
sensitive	`True`
ancestor_sensitive	Logical AND of parent's *sensitive* and *ancestor_sensitive* values.
event_table	Initialized by the event manager.
tm	Initialized by the translation manager.
accelerators	NULL
border_pixel	`XtDefaultForeground`
border_pixmap	`XtUnspecifiedPixmap`
popup_list	NULL
num_popups	0
name	*name* argument to `XtCreateWidget` (may not be changed).
screen	Parent's *screen*; top-level widget gets screen from display specifier (may not be changed).
colormap	Parent's *colormap* value.
window	NULL
depth	Parent's *depth*; top-level widget gets root window depth.
background_pixel	`XtDefaultBackground`
background_pixmap	`XtUnspecifiedPixmap`
visible	`True`
mapped_when_managed	`True`

`XtUnspecifiedPixmap` is a symbolic constant guaranteed to be unequal to any valid Pixmap id, `None`, and `ParentRelative`.

1.4.2   Composite Widgets

The Composite widget class is a subclass of the Core widget class (see Chapter 3). Composite widgets are intended to be containers for other widgets. The additional data used by composite widgets are defined by the `Composite-ClassPart` and `CompositePart` structures.

1.4.2.1 CompositeClassPart Structure

In addition to the Core class fields, widgets of the Composite class have the following class fields.

```
typedef struct {
    XtGeometryHandler    geometry_manager;    See Chapter 6
    XtWidgetProc         change_managed;      See Chapter 3
    XtWidgetProc         insert_child;        See Chapter 3
    XtWidgetProc         delete_child;        See Chapter 3
    XtPointer            extension;           See Section 1.6
} CompositeClassPart;
```

The extension record defined for `CompositeClassPart` with *record_type* equal to NULLQUARK is `CompositeClassExtensionRec`.

```
typedef struct {
    XtPointer    next_extension;    See Section 1.6.12
    XrmQuark     record_type;       See Section 1.6.12
    long         version;           See Section 1.6.12
    Cardinal     record_size;       See Section 1.6.12
    Boolean      accepts_objects;   See Chapter 3
} CompositeClassExtensionRec, *CompositeClassExtension;
```

Composite classes have the Composite class fields immediately following the Core class fields.

```
typedef struct _CompositeClassRec {
    CoreClassPart         core_class;
    CompositeClassPart    composite_class;
} CompositeClassRec, *CompositeWidgetClass;
```

The single occurrences of the class record and pointer for creating instances of Composite are

In `IntrinsicP.h`:

extern CompositeClassRec compositeClassRec;

In `Intrinsic.h`:

extern WidgetClass compositeWidgetClass;

The opaque types `CompositeWidget` and `CompositeWidgetClass` and the opaque variable `compositeWidgetClass` are defined for generic operations on widgets whose class is Composite or a subclass of Composite. The symbolic constant for the `CompositeClassExtension` version identifier is `XtCompositeExtensionVersion` (see Section 1.6.12). `Intrinsic.h` uses an incomplete structure definition to ensure that the compiler catches attempts to access private data.

```
typedef struct _CompositeClassRec *CompositeWidgetClass;
```

1.4.2.2 CompositePart Structure

In addition to the Core instance fields, widgets of the Composite class have the following instance fields defined in the `CompositePart` structure.

```
typedef struct {
    WidgetList      children;         See Chapter 3
    Cardinal        num_children;     See Chapter 3
    Cardinal        num_slots;        See Chapter 3
    XtOrderProc     insert_position;  See Section 3.2
} CompositePart;
```

Composite widgets have the Composite instance fields immediately following the Core instance fields.

```
typedef struct _CompositeRec {
    CorePart            core;
    CompositePart       composite;
} CompositeRec, *CompositeWidget;
```

`Intrinsic.h` uses an incomplete structure definition to ensure that the compiler catches attempts to access private data.

```
typedef struct _CompositeRec *CompositeWidget;
```

1.4.2.3 Composite Resources

The resource names, classes, and representation types that are specified in the `compositeClassRec` resource list are

Name	Class	Representation
XtNchildren	XtCReadOnly	XtRWidgetList
XtNinsertPosition	XtCInsertPosition	XtRFunction
XtNnumChildren	XtCReadOnly	XtRCardinal

1.4.2.4   CompositePart Default Values

The default values for the Composite fields, which are filled in from the Composite resource list and by the Composite initialize procedure, are

Field	Default Value
children	NULL
num_children	0
num_slots	0
insert_position	Internal function to insert at end

The *children, num_children,* and *insert_position* fields are declared as resources; XtNinsertPosition is a settable resource, XtNchildren and XtNnumChildren may be read by any client but should only be modified by the composite widget class procedures.

1.4.3   Constraint Widgets

The Constraint widget class is a subclass of the Composite widget class (see Section 3.6). Constraint widgets maintain additional state data for each child; for example, client-defined constraints on the child's geometry. The additional data used by constraint widgets are defined by the `ConstraintClassPart` and `ConstraintPart` structures.

1.4.3.1   ConstraintClassPart Structure

In addition to the Core and Composite class fields, widgets of the Constraint class have the following class fields.

```
typedef struct {
    XtResourceList      resources;          See Chapter 9
    Cardinal            num_resources;      See Chapter 9
    Cardinal            constraint_size;    See Section 3.6
    XtInitProc          initialize;         See Section 3.6
    XtWidgetProc        destroy;            See Section 3.6
    XtSetValuesFunc     set_values;         See Section 9.7.2
    XtPointer           extension;          See Section 1.6
} ConstraintClassPart;
```

The extension record defined for ConstraintClassPart with *record_type* equal to NULLQUARK is ConstraintClassExtensionRec.

```
typedef struct {
    XtPointer      next_extension;    See Section 1.6.12
    XrmQuark       record_type;       See Section 1.6.12
    long           version;           See Section 1.6.12
    Cardinal       record_size;       See Section 1.6.12
    XtArgsProc     get_values_hook;   See Section 9.7.1
} ConstraintClassExtensionRec, *ConstraintClassExtension;
```

Constraint classes have the Constraint class fields immediately following the Composite class fields.

```
typedef struct _ConstraintClassRec {
    CoreClassPart          core_class;
    CompositeClassPart     composite_class;
    ConstraintClassPart    constraint_class;
} ConstraintClassRec, *ConstraintWidgetClass;
```

The single occurrences of the class record and pointer for creating instances of Constraint are

In IntrinsicP.h:

extern ConstraintClassRec constraintClassRec;

In Intrinsic.h:

extern WidgetClass constraintWidgetClass;

The opaque types ConstraintWidget and ConstraintWidgetClass and the opaque variable constraintWidgetClass are defined for generic operations on widgets whose class is Constraint or a subclass of Constraint. The symbolic constant for the ConstraintClassExtension version id is XtConstraintExtensionVersion (see Section 1.6.12). Intrinsic.h uses an incomplete structure definition to ensure that the compiler catches attempts to access private data.

typedef struct _ConstraintClassRec *ConstraintWidgetClass;

1.4.3.2 ConstraintPart Structure

In addition to the Core and Composite instance fields, widgets of the Constraint class have the following unused instance field defined in the `ConstraintPart` structure.

```
typedef struct {
    int     empty;
} ConstraintPart;
```

Constraint widgets have the Constraint instance fields immediately following the Composite instance fields.

```
typedef struct {
    CorePart            core;
    CompositePart       composite;
    ConstraintPart      constraint;
} ConstraintRec, *ConstraintWidget;
```

`Intrinsic.h` uses an incomplete structure definition to ensure that the compiler catches attempts to access private data.

```
typedef struct _ConstraintRec *ConstraintWidget;
```

1.4.3.3 Constraint Resources

The `constraintClassRec` *core_class* and *constraint_class resources* fields are NULL and the *num_resources* fields are zero; no additional resources beyond those declared by the superclasses are defined for Constraint.

1.5 Implementation-Specific Types

To increase the portability of widget and application source code between different system environments, the Intrinsics define several types whose precise representation is explicitly dependent upon, and chosen by, each individual implementation of the Intrinsics.

These implementation-defined types are

`Boolean`   A datum that contains a zero or nonzero value. Unless explicitly stated, clients should not assume that the nonzero value is equal to the symbolic value `True`.

`Cardinal` An unsigned integer datum with a minimum range of $[0..2^{16}-1]$.

Dimension   An unsigned integer datum with a minimum range of $[0..2^{16}\text{-}1]$.

Position   A signed integer datum with a minimum range of $[\text{-}2^{15}..2^{15}\text{-}1]$.

XtPointer   A datum large enough to contain the largest of a char*, int*, function pointer, structure pointer, or long value. A pointer to any type or function, or a long value may be converted to an XtPointer and back again and the result will compare equal to the original value. In ANSI C environments it is expected that XtPointer will be defined as void*.

XtArgVal   A datum large enough to contain an XtPointer, Cardinal, Dimension, or Position value.

XtEnum   An integer datum large enough to encode at least 128 distinct values, two of which are the symbolic values True and False. The symbolic values TRUE and FALSE are also defined to be equal to True and False, respectively.

In addition to these specific types, the precise order of the fields within the structure declarations for any of the instance part records ObjectPart, RectObjPart, CorePart, CompositePart, ShellPart, WMShellPart, TopLevelShellPart, and ApplicationShellPart is implementation-defined. The ObjectPart, RectObjPart, and CorePart structures must be defined so that any member with the same name appears at the same offset in ObjectRec, RectObjRec and CoreRec (WidgetRec). No other relations between the offsets of any two fields may be assumed.

1.6   Widget Classing

The *widget_class* field of a widget points to its widget class structure, which contains information that is constant across all widgets of that class. As a consequence, widgets usually do not implement directly callable procedures; rather, they implement procedures, called methods, that are available through their widget class structure. These methods are invoked by generic procedures that envelop common actions around the methods implemented by the widget class. Such procedures are applicable to all widgets of that class and also to widgets whose classes are subclasses of that class.

All widget classes are a subclass of Core and can be subclassed further. Subclassing reduces the amount of code and declarations necessary to make a new widget class that is similar to an existing class. For example, you do not have to describe every resource your widget uses in an XtResourceList. Instead, you describe only the resources your widget has that its superclass does not. Subclasses usually inherit many of their superclasses' procedures (for example, the expose procedure or geometry handler).

Subclassing, however, can be taken too far. If you create a subclass that inherits none of the procedures of its superclass, you should consider whether you have chosen the most appropriate superclass.

To make good use of subclassing, widget declarations and naming conventions are highly stylized. A widget consists of three files:

• A public .h file, used by client widgets or applications.

• A private .h file, used by widgets whose classes are subclasses of the widget class.

• A .c file, which implements the widget.

1.6.1 Widget Naming Conventions

The Intrinsics provide a vehicle by which programmers can create new widgets and organize a collection of widgets into an application. To ensure that applications need not deal with as many styles of capitalization and spelling as the number of widget classes it uses, the following guidelines should be followed when writing new widgets:

• Use the X library naming conventions that are applicable. For example, a record component name is all lower case and uses underscores (_) for compound words (for example, background_pixmap). Type and procedure names start with upper case and use capitalization for compound words (for example, `ArgList` or `XtSetValues`).

• A resource name is spelled identically to the field name except that compound names use capitalization rather than underscore. To let the compiler catch spelling errors, each resource name should have a symbolic identifier prefixed with "XtN". For example, the *background_pixmap* field has the corresponding identifier XtNbackgroundPixmap, which is defined as the string "backgroundPixmap". Many predefined names are listed in `<X11/StringDefs.h>`. Before you invent a new name, you should make sure there is not already a name that you can use.

• A resource class string starts with a capital letter and uses capitalization for compound names (for example, "BorderWidth"). Each resource class string should have a symbolic identifier prefixed with "XtC" (for example, XtCBorderWidth). Many predefined classes are listed in `<X11/StringDefs.h>`.

• A resource representation string is spelled identically to the type name (for example, "TranslationTable"). Each representation string should have a symbolic identifier prefixed with "XtR" (for example, XtRTranslationTable). Many predefined representation types are listed in <X11/StringDefs.h>.

- New widget classes start with a capital and use upper case for compound words. Given a new class name AbcXyz, you should derive several names:

  — Additional widget instance structure part name AbcXyzPart.

  — Complete widget instance structure names AbcXyzRec and _AbcXyzRec.

  — Widget instance structure pointer type name AbcXyzWidget.

  — Additional class structure part name AbcXyzClassPart.

  — Complete class structure names AbcXyzClassRec and _AbcXyzClassRec.

  — Class structure pointer type name AbcXyzWidgetClass.

  — Class structure variable abcXyzClassRec.

  — Class structure pointer variable abcXyzWidgetClass.

- Action procedures available to translation specifications should follow the same naming conventions as procedures. That is, they start with a capital letter, and compound names use upper case (for example, "Highlight" and "NotifyClient").

The symbolic identifiers XtN . . . , XtC . . . , and XtR . . . may be implemented as macros, as global symbols, or as a mixture of the two. The (implicit) type of the identifier is String. The pointer value itself is not significant; clients must not assume that inequality of two identifiers implies inequality of the resource name, class, or representation string. Clients should also note that although global symbols permit savings in literal storage in some environments, they also introduce the possibility of multiple definition conflicts when applications attempt to use independently developed widgets simultaneously.

1.6.2   Widget Subclassing in Public .h Files

The public .h file for a widget class is imported by clients and contains

- A reference to the public .h file for the superclass.

- Symbolic identifiers for the names and classes of the new resources that this widget adds to its superclass. The definitions should have a single space between the definition name and the value and no trailing space or comment in order to reduce the possibility of compiler warnings from similar declarations in multiple classes.

- Type declarations for any new resource data types defined by the class.

- The class record pointer variable used to create widget instances.

- The C type that corresponds to widget instances of this class.

- Entry points for new class methods.

For example, the following is the public .h file for a possible implementation of a Label widget:

```
#ifndef LABEL_H
#define LABEL_H

/* New resources */
#define XtNjustify "justify"
#define XtNforeground "foreground"
#define XtNlabel "label"
#define XtNfont "font"
#define XtNinternalWidth "internalWidth"
#define XtNinternalHeight "internalHeight"

/* Class record pointer */
extern WidgetClass labelWidgetClass;

/* C Widget type definition */
typedef struct _LabelRec   *LabelWidget;

/* New class method entry points */
extern void LabelSetText();
        /* Widget w */
        /* String text */

extern String LabelGetText();
        /* Widget w */

#endif LABEL_H
```

The conditional inclusion of the text allows the application to include header files for different widgets without being concerned that they already may be included as a superclass of another widget.

To accommodate operating systems with file name length restrictions, the name of the public .h file is the first ten characters of the widget class. For example, the public .h file for the Constraint widget class is `Constraint.h`.

1.6.3   Widget Subclassing in Private .h Files

The private .h file for a widget is imported by widget classes that are subclasses of the widget and contains

- A reference to the public .h file for the class.

- A reference to the private .h file for the superclass.

- Symbolic identifiers for any new resource representation types defined by the class. The definitions should have a single space between the definition name and the value and no trailing space or comment.

- A structure part definition for the new fields that the widget instance adds to its superclass's widget structure.

- The complete widget instance structure definition for this widget.

- A structure part definition for the new fields this widget class adds to its superclass's constraint structure if the widget class is a subclass of Constraint.

- The complete constraint structure definition if the widget class is a subclass of Constraint.

- Type definitions for any new procedure types used by class methods declared in the widget class part.

- A structure part definition for the new fields that this widget class adds to its superclass's widget class structure.

- The complete widget class structure definition for this widget.

- The complete widget class extension structure definition for this widget, if any.

- The symbolic constant identifying the class extension version, if any.

- The name of the global class structure variable containing the generic class structure for this class.

- An inherit constant for each new procedure in the widget class part structure.

For example, the following is the private .h file for a possible Label widget:

```
#ifndef LABELP_H
#define LABELP_H

#include <X11/Label.h>

/* New representation types used by the Label widget */
#define XtRJustify "Justify"

/* New fields for the Label widget record */
typedef struct {
/* Settable resources */
    Pixel foreground;
    XFontStruct *font;
    String label;                       /* text to display */
    XtJustify justify;
    Dimension internal_width;           /* # pixels horizontal border */
    Dimension internal_height;          /* # pixels vertical border */

/* Data derived from resources */
    GC normal_GC;
    GC gray_GC;
    Pixmap gray_pixmap;
    Position label_x;
    Position label_y;
```

```
        Dimension label_width;
        Dimension label_height;
        Cardinal label_len;
        Boolean display_sensitive;
    } LabelPart;

    /* Full instance record declaration */
    typedef struct _LabelRec {
        CorePart core;
        LabelPart label;
    } LabelRec;

    /* Types for Label class methods */
    typedef void (*LabelSetTextProc)();
        /* Widget w */
        /* String text */

    typedef String (*LabelGetTextProc)();
        /* Widget w */

    /* New fields for the Label widget class record */
    typedef struct {
        LabelSetTextProc set_text;
        LabelGetTextProc get_text;
        XtPointer extension;
    } LabelClassPart;

    /* Full class record declaration */
    typedef struct _LabelClassRec {
        CoreClassPart core_class;
        LabelClassPart label_class;
    } LabelClassRec;

    /* Class record variable */
    extern LabelClassRec labelClassRec;

    #define LabelInheritSetText((LabelSetTextProc)_XtInherit)
    #define LabelInheritGetText((LabelGetTextProc)_XtInherit)
    #endif LABELP_H
```

To accommodate operating systems with file name length restrictions, the name of the private .h file is the first nine characters of the widget class followed by a capital P. For example, the private .h file for the Constraint widget class is `ConstrainP.h`.

1.6.4   Widget Subclassing in .c Files

The .c file for a widget contains the structure initializer for the class record variable, which contains the following parts:

- Class information (for example, *superclass, class_name, widget_size, class_initialize,* and *class_inited*).

- Data constants (for example, *resources* and *num_resources, actions* and *num_actions, visible_interest, compress_motion, compress_exposure,* and *version*).

- Widget operations (for example, *initialize, realize, destroy, resize, expose, set_values, accept_focus,* and any new operations specific to the widget).

The *superclass* field points to the superclass, global class record, declared in the superclass private .h file. For direct subclasses of the generic core widget, *superclass* should be initialized to the address of the `widgetClassRec` structure. The superclass is used for class chaining operations and for inheriting or enveloping a superclass's operations (see Sections 1.6.7, 1.6.9, and 1.6.10).

The *class_name* field contains the text name for this class, which is used by the resource manager. For example, the Label widget has the string "Label". More than one widget class can share the same text class name.

The *widget_size* field is the size of the corresponding widget instance structure (not the size of the class structure).

The *version* field indicates the toolkit implementation version number and is used for runtime consistency checking of the X Toolkit and widgets in an application. Widget writers must set it to the implementation-defined symbolic value `XtVersion` in the widget class structure initialization. Those widget writers who believe that their widget binaries are compatible with other implementations of the Intrinsics can put the special value `XtVersionDontCheck` in the *version* field to disable version checking for those widgets. If a widget needs to compile alternative code for different revisions of the Intrinsics interface definition, it may use the symbol `XtSpecificationRelease`, as described in Chapter 13. Use of `XtVersion` allows the Intrinsics implementation to recognize widget binaries that were compiled with older implementations.

The *extension* field is for future upward compatibility. If the widget programmer adds fields to class parts, all subclass structure layouts change, requiring complete recompilation. To allow clients to avoid recompilation, an extension field at the end of each class part can point to a record that contains any additional class information required.

All other fields are described in their respective sections.

The .c file also contains the declaration of the global class structure pointer variable used to create instances of the class. The following is an abbreviated version of the .c file for a Label widget. The resources table is described in Chapter 9.

```
/* Resources specific to Label */
static XtResource resources[] = {
    {XtNforeground, XtCForeground, XtRPixel, sizeof(Pixel),
     XtOffset(LabelWidget, label.foreground), XtRString,
     XtDefaultForeground},
    {XtNfont, XtCFont, XtRFontStruct, sizeof(XFontStruct *),
     XtOffset(LabelWidget, label.font), XtRString,
     XtDefaultFont},
    {XtNlabel, XtCLabel, XtRString, sizeof(String),
     XtOffset(LabelWidget, label.label), XtRString, NULL},
                    .
                    .
                    .
}

/* Forward declarations of procedures */
static void ClassInitialize();
static void Initialize();
static void Realize();
static void SetText();
static void GetText();
            .
            .
            .

/* Class record constant */
LabelClassRec labelClassRec = {
  {
   /* core_class fields */
        /* superclass              */   (WidgetClass)&coreClassRec,
        /* class_name              */   "Label",
        /* widget_size             */   sizeof(LabelRec),
        /* class_initialize        */   ClassInitialize,
        /* class_part_initialize   */   NULL,
        /* class_inited            */   False,
        /* initialize              */   Initialize,
        /* initialize_hook         */   NULL,
        /* realize                 */   Realize,
        /* actions                 */   NULL,
        /* num_actions             */   0,
        /* resources               */   resources,
        /* num_resources           */   XtNumber(resources),
        /* xrm_class               */   NULLQUARK,
        /* compress_motion         */   True,
        /* compress_exposure       */   True,
        /* compress_enterleave     */   True,
        /* visible_interest        */   False,
        /* destroy                 */   NULL,
        /* resize                  */   Resize,
        /* expose                  */   Redisplay,
        /* set_values              */   SetValues,
        /* set_values_hook         */   NULL,
        /* set_values_almost       */   XtInheritSetValuesAlmost,
```

```
                    /* get_values_hook      */    NULL,
                    /* accept_focus         */    NULL,
                    /* version              */    XtVersion,
                    /* callback_offsets     */    NULL,
                    /* tm_table             */    NULL,
                    /* query_geometry       */    XtInheritQueryGeometry,
                    /* display_accelerator  */    NULL,
                    /* extension            */    NULL
        },
        {
          /* Label_class fields */
                    /* get_text             */    GetText,
                    /* set_text             */    SetText,
                    /* extension            */    NULL
        }
    };

    /* Class record pointer */
    WidgetClass labelWidgetClass = (WidgetClass) &labelClassRec;

    /* New method access routines */
    void LabelSetText(w, text)
            Widget w;
            String text;
    {
            Label WidgetClass lwc = (Label WidgetClass)XtClass(w);
            XtCheckSubclass(w, labelWidgetClass, NULL);
            *(lwc ->label_class.set_text)(w, text)
    }
    /* Private procedures */
                .
                .
                .
```

1.6.5   Widget Class and Superclass Lookup

To obtain the class of a widget, use XtClass.

WidgetClass XtClass(*w*)
    Widget *w*;

    w   Specifies the widget. Must be of class Object or any subclass thereof.

The XtClass function returns a pointer to the widget's class structure.

To obtain the superclass of a widget, use XtSuperclass.

WidgetClass XtSuperclass(*w*)
    Widget *w*;

    w   Specifies the widget. Must be of class Object or any subclass thereof.

The XtSuperclass function returns a pointer to the widget's superclass class structure.

1.6.6   Widget Subclass Verification

To check the subclass to which a widget belongs, use XtIsSubclass.

Boolean XtIsSubclass(*w, widget_class*)
 Widget *w*;
 WidgetClass *widget_class*;
 w   Specifies the widget or object instance whose class is to be checked. Must be of class Object or any subclass thereof.
 widget_class Specifies the widget class for which to test. Must be objectClass or any subclass thereof.

The XtIsSubclass function returns True if the class of the specified widget is equal to or is a subclass of the specified class. The widget's class can be any number of subclasses down the chain and need not be an immediate subclass of the specified class. Composite widgets that need to restrict the class of the items they contain can use XtIsSubclass to find out if a widget belongs to the desired class of objects.

To test if a given widget belongs to a subclass of an Intrinsics-defined class, the Intrinsics define macros or functions equivalent to XtIsSubclass for each of the built-in classes. These procedures are XtIsObject, XtIsRect-Obj, XtIsWidget, XtIsComposite, XtIsConstraint, XtIsShell, XtIs-OverrideShell, XtIsWMShell, XtIsVendorShell, XtIsTransient-Shell, XtIsTopLevelShell and XtIsApplicationShell. All these macros and functions have the same argument description.

Boolean XtIs<*class*> (*w*)
 Widget *w*;
 w   Specifies the widget or object instance whose class is to be checked. Must be of class Object or any subclass thereof.

These procedures may be faster than calling XtIsSubclass directly for the built-in classes.

To check a widget's class and to generate a debugging error message, use XtCheckSubclass, defined in <X11/IntrinsicP.h>.

void XtCheckSubclass(*w*, *widget_class*, *message*)
    Widget *w*;
    WidgetClass *widget_class*;
    String *message*;

w	Specifies the widget or object whose class is to be checked. Must be of class Object or any subclass thereof.
widget_class	Specifies the widget class for which to test. Must be `objectClass` or any subclass thereof.
message	Specifies the message to be used.

The `XtCheckSubclass` macro determines if the class of the specified widget is equal to or is a subclass of the specified class. The widget's class can be any number of subclasses down the chain and need not be an immediate subclass of the specified class. If the specified widget's class is not a subclass, `XtCheckSubclass` constructs an error message from the supplied message, the widget's actual class, and the expected class and calls `XtErrorMsg`. `XtCheckSubclass` should be used at the entry point of exported routines to ensure that the client has passed in a valid widget class for the exported operation.

    `XtCheckSubclass` is only executed when the module has been compiled with the compiler symbol DEBUG defined; otherwise, it is defined as the empty string and generates no code.

1.6.7   Superclass Chaining

While most fields in a widget class structure are self-contained, some fields are linked to their corresponding fields in their superclass structures. With a linked field, the Intrinsics access the field's value only after accessing its corresponding superclass value (called downward superclass chaining) or before accessing its corresponding superclass value (called upward superclass chaining). The self-contained fields are

In all widget classes:
        class_name
        class_initialize
        widget_size
        realize
        visible_interest
        resize
        expose
        accept_focus

	compress_motion
	compress_exposure
	compress_enterleave
	set_values_almost
	tm_table
	version
In Composite widget classes:	*geometry_manager*
	change_managed
	insert_child
	delete_child
	accepts_objects
In Constraint widget classes:	*constraint_size*
In Shell widget classes:	*root_geometry_manager*

With downward superclass chaining, the invocation of an operation first accesses the field from the Object, RectObj, and Core class structures, then from the subclass structure, and so on down the class chain to that widget's class structure. These superclass-to-subclass fields are

class_part_initialize
get_values_hook
initialize
initialize_hook
set_values
set_values_hook
resources

In addition, for subclasses of Constraint, the following fields of the `ConstraintClassPart` and `ConstraintClassExtensionRec` structures are chained from the Constraint class down to the subclass:

resources
initialize
set_values
get_values_hook

With upward superclass chaining, the invocation of an operation first accesses the field from the widget class structure, then from the superclass structure, and so on up the class chain to the Core, RectObj, and Object class structures. The subclass-to-superclass fields are

destroy
actions

For subclasses of Constraint, the following field of `ConstraintClassPart` is chained from the subclass up to the Constraint class:

destroy

1.6.8   Class Initialization: class_initialize and class_part_initialize Procedures

Many class records can be initialized completely at compile or link time. In some cases, however, a class may need to register type converters or perform other sorts of once-only runtime initialization.

Because the C language does not have initialization procedures that are invoked automatically when a program starts up, a widget class can declare a class_initialize procedure that will be automatically called exactly once by the X Toolkit. A class initialization procedure pointer is of type `XtProc`:

typedef void (*XtProc) (void);

A widget class indicates that it has no class initialization procedure by specifying NULL in the *class_initialize* field.

In addition to the class initialization that is done exactly once, some classes perform initialization for fields in their parts of the class record. These are performed not just for the particular class but for subclasses as well, and are done in the class's class part initialization procedure, which is stored in the *class_part_initialize* field. The class_part_initialize procedure pointer is of type `XtWidgetClassProc`.

typedef void (*XtWidgetClassProc) (WidgetClass);
    WidgetClass *widget_class*;
widget_class   Points to the class structure for the class being initialized.

During class initialization, the class part initialization procedures for the class and all its superclasses are called in superclass-to-subclass order on the class record. These procedures have the responsibility of doing any dynamic initializations necessary to their class's part of the record. The most common is the resolution of any inherited methods defined in the class. For example, if a widget class C has superclasses Core, Composite, A, and B, the class record for C first is passed to Core's class_part_initialize procedure. This resolves any inherited Core methods and compiles the textual representations of the resource list and action table that are defined in the class record. Next, Composite's class_part_initialize procedure is called to initialize the composite part of C's class record. Finally, the class_part_initialize procedures for A, B, and C, in that order, are called. For further information, see Section 1.6.9. Classes that do not define any new class fields or that need no extra processing for them can specify NULL in the *class_part_initialize* field.

All widget classes, whether they have a class initialization procedure or not, must start with their *class_inited* field False.

The first time a widget of a class is created, XtCreateWidget ensures that the widget class and all superclasses are initialized, in superclass-to-subclass order, by checking each *class_inited* field and, if it is False, by calling the class_initialize and the class_part_initialize procedures for the class and all its superclasses. The Intrinsics then set the *class_inited* field to a nonzero value. After the one-time initialization, a class structure is constant.

The following example provides the class initialization procedure for a Label class.

```
static void ClassInitialize()
{
    XtSetTypeConverter(XtRString, XtRJustify, CvtStringToJustify,
                    NULL, 0, XtCacheNone, NULL);
}
```

1.6.9 Initializing a Widget Class

A class is initialized when the first widget of that class or any subclass is created. To initialize a widget class without creating any widgets, use XtInitialize-WidgetClass.

void XtInitializeWidgetClass(*object_class*)
    WidgetClass *object_class*;

object_class   Specifies the object class to initialize. May be objectClass or any subclass thereof.

If the specified widget class is already initialized, XtInitializeWidget-Class returns immediately.

If the class initialization procedure registers type converters, these type converters are not available until the first object of the class or subclass is created or XtInitializeWidgetClass is called (see Section 9.6).

1.6.10   Inheritance of Superclass Operations

A widget class is free to use any of its superclass's self-contained operations rather than implementing its own code. The most frequently inherited operations are

expose
realize
insert_child
delete_child
geometry_manager
set_values_almost

To inherit an operation *xyz*, specify the constant XtInherit*Xyz* in your class record.

Every class that declares a new procedure in its widget class part must provide for inheriting the procedure in its class_part_initialize procedure. The chained operations declared in Core and Constraint records are never inherited. Widget classes that do nothing beyond what their superclass does specify NULL for chained procedures in their class records.

Inheriting works by comparing the value of the field with a known, special value and by copying in the superclass's value for that field if a match occurs. This special value, called the inheritance constant, is usually the Intrinsics internal value _XtInherit cast to the appropriate type. _XtInherit is a procedure that issues an error message if it is actually called.

For example, CompositeP.h contains these definitions:

```
#define XtInheritGeometryManager ((XtGeometryHandler) _XtInherit)
#define XtInheritChangeManaged ((XtWidgetProc) _XtInherit)
#define XtInheritInsertChild ((XtArgsProc) _XtInherit)
#define XtInheritDeleteChild ((XtWidgetProc) _XtInherit)
```

Composite's class_part_initialize procedure begins as follows:

```
static void CompositeClassPartInitialize(widgetClass)
    WidgetClass widgetClass;
{
    CompositeWidgetClass wc = (CompositeWidgetClass)widgetClass;
    CompositeWidgetClass super = (CompositeWidgetClass)
        wc ->core_class.superclass;
```

```
if (wc ->composite_class.geometry_manager
    == XtInheritGeometryManager) {
  wc->composite_class.geometry_manager =
      super ->composite_class.geometry_manager;
}

if (wc ->composite_class.change_managed
    == XtInheritChangeManaged) {
  wc ->composite_class.change_managed =
      super ->composite_class.change_managed;
}
    .
    .
    .
```

Nonprocedure fields may be inherited in the same manner as procedure fields. The class may declare any reserved value it wishes for the inheritance constant for its new fields. The following inheritance constants are defined:

For Core:	`XtInheritRealize`
	`XtInheritResize`
	`XtInheritExpose`
	`XtInheritSetValuesAlmost`
	`XtInheritAcceptFocus`
	`XtInheritQueryGeometry`
	`XtInheritTranslations`
	`XtInheritDisplayAccelerator`
For Composite:	`XtInheritGeometryManager`
	`XtInheritChangeManaged`
	`XtInheritInsertChild`
	`XtInheritDeleteChild`
For Shell:	`XtInheritRootGeometryManager`

1.6.11 Invocation of Superclass Operations

A widget sometimes needs to call a superclass operation that is not chained. For example, a widget's expose procedure might call its superclass's *expose* and then perform a little more work on its own. For example, a Composite class with predefined managed children can implement insert_child by first calling its superclass's *insert_child* and then calling `XtManageChild` to add the child to the managed set.

Note   A class method should not use XtSuperclass but should instead call the class method of its own specific superclass directly through the superclass record. That is, it should use its own class pointers only, not the widget's class pointers, as the widget's class may be a subclass of the class whose implementation is being referenced.

This technique is referred to as *enveloping* the superclass's operation.

1.6.12   Class Extension Records

It may be necessary at times to add new fields to already existing widget class structures. To permit this to be done without requiring recompilation of all subclasses, the last field in a class part structure should be an extension pointer. If no extension fields for a class have yet been defined, subclasses should initialize the value of the extension pointer to NULL.

If extension fields exist, as is the case with the Composite, Constraint, and Shell classes, subclasses can provide values for these fields by setting the *extension* pointer for the appropriate part in their class structure to point to a statically declared extension record containing the additional fields. Setting the *extension* field is never mandatory; code that uses fields in the extension record must always check the *extension* field and take some appropriate default action if it is NULL.

In order to permit multiple subclasses and libraries to chain extension records from a single *extension* field, extension records should be declared as a linked list and each extension record definition should contain the following four fields at the beginning of the structure declaration:

```
struct {
        XtPointer    next_extension;
        XrmQuark     record_type;
        long         version;
        Cardinal     record_size;
};
```

next_extension   Specifies the next record in the list, or NULL.

record_type   Specifies the particular structure declaration to which each extension record instance conforms.

version   Specifies a version id symbolic constant supplied by the definer of the structure.

record_size   Specifies the total number of bytes allocated for the extension record.

The *record_type* field identifies the contents of the extension record and is used by the definer of the record to locate its particular extension record in the list. The *record_type* field is normally assigned the result of XrmStringToQuark for a registered string constant. The Intrinsics reserve all record type strings beginning with the two characters "XT" for future standard uses. The value NULLQUARK may also be used by the class part owner in extension records attached to its own class part extension field to identify the extension record unique to that particular class.

The version field is an owner-defined constant that may be used to identify binary files that have been compiled with alternative definitions of the remainder of the extension record data structure. The private header file for a widget class should provide a symbolic constant for subclasses to use to initialize this field.

The *record_size* field value includes the four common header fields and should normally be initialized with sizeof().

Any value stored in the class part extension fields of CompositeClass-Part, ConstraintClassPart, or ShellClassPart must point to an extension record conforming to this definition.

Chapter 2

Widget Instantiation

A hierarchy of widget instances constitutes a widget tree. The shell widget returned by `XtAppCreateShell` is the root of the widget tree instance. The widgets with one or more children are the intermediate nodes of that tree, and the widgets with no children of any kind are the leaves of the widget tree. With the exception of pop-up children (see Chapter 5), this widget tree instance defines the associated X Window tree.

Widgets can be either composite or primitive. Both kinds of widgets can contain children, but the Intrinsics provide a set of management mechanisms for constructing and interfacing between composite widgets, their children, and other clients.

Composite widgets, that is, members of the class `compositeWidgetClass`, are containers for an arbitrary but implementation-defined collection of children, which may be instantiated by the composite widget itself, by other clients, or by a combination of the two. Composite widgets also contain methods for managing the geometry (layout) of any child widget. Under unusual circumstances, a composite widget may have zero children, but it usually has at least one. By contrast, primitive widgets that contain children typically instantiate specific children of known classes themselves and do not expect external clients to do so. Primitive widgets also do not have general geometry management methods.

In addition, the Intrinsics recursively perform many operations (for example, realization and destruction) on composite widgets and all their children.

Primitive widgets that have children must be prepared to perform the recursive operations themselves on behalf of their children.

A widget tree is manipulated by several Intrinsics functions. For example, `XtRealizeWidget` traverses the tree downward and recursively realizes all pop-up widgets and children of composite widgets. `XtDestroyWidget` traverses the tree downward and destroys all pop-up widgets and children of composite widgets. The functions that fetch and modify resources traverse the tree upward and determine the inheritance of resources from a widget's ancestors. `XtMakeGeometryRequest` traverses the tree up one level and calls the geometry manager that is responsible for a widget child's geometry.

To facilitate upward traversal of the widget tree, each widget has a pointer to its parent widget. The shell widget that `XtAppCreateShell` returns has a *parent* pointer of NULL.

To facilitate downward traversal of the widget tree, the *children* field of each composite widget is a pointer to an array of child widgets, which includes all normal children created, not just the subset of children that are managed by the composite widget's geometry manager. Primitive widgets that instantiate children are entirely responsible for all operations that require downward traversal below themselves. In addition, every widget has a pointer to an array of pop-up children.

2.1   Initializing the X Toolkit

Before an application can call any Intrinsics function, it must initialize the X Toolkit by using

- `XtToolkitInitialize`, which initializes the X Toolkit internals.
- `XtCreateApplicationContext`, which initializes the per-application state.
- `XtDisplayInitialize` or `XtOpenDisplay`, which initializes the per-display state.
- `XtAppCreateShell`, which creates the root of a widget tree.

Or an application can call the convenience procedure `XtAppInitialize`, which combines the functions of the preceding procedures.

Multiple instances of X Toolkit applications may be implemented in a single address space. Each instance needs to be able to read input and dispatch events independently of any other instance. Further, an application instance may need multiple display connections to have widgets on multiple screens. From the application's point of view, multiple display connections usually are treated together as a single unit. To accommodate both requirements, the Intrinsics define application contexts, each of which provides the information needed to distinguish one application instance from another. The major component of an application context is a list of one or more X `Display` pointers for that application. The Intrinsics handle all display connections within a single application context simultaneously, handling input in a round-robin fashion. The application context type `XtAppContext` is opaque to clients.

To initialize the X Toolkit internals, use `XtToolkitInitialize`.

void XtToolkitInitialize()

The semantics of calling `XtToolkitInitialize` more than once are undefined.

To create an application context, use `XtCreateApplicationContext`.

XtAppContext XtCreateApplicationContext()

The `XtCreateApplicationContext` function returns an application context, which is an opaque type. Every application must have at least one application context.

To destroy an application context and close any remaining display connections in it, use `XtDestroyApplicationContext`.

void XtDestroyApplicationContext(*app_context*)
    XtAppContext *app_context*;
app_context   Specifies the application context.

The `XtDestroyApplicationContext` function destroys the specified application context as soon as it is safe to do so. If called from within an event dispatch (for example, in a callback procedure), `XtDestroyApplication-Context` does not destroy the application context until the dispatch is complete.

To get the application context in which a given widget was created, use `XtWidgetToApplicationContext`.

XtAppContext XtWidgetToApplicationContext(*w*)
  Widget *w*;

w　　　　　　　　Specifies the widget for which you want the application context. Must be of class Object or any subclass thereof.

The `XtWidgetToApplicationContext` function returns the application context for the specified widget.

To initialize a display and add it to an application context, use `XtDisplay-Initialize`.

void XtDisplayInitialize(*app_context, display, application_name, application_class,*
                options, num_options, argc, argv)
  XtAppContext *app_context*;
  Display **display*;
  String *application_name*;
  String *application_class*;
  XrmOptionDescRec **options*;
  Cardinal *num_options*;
  Cardinal **argc*;
  String **argv*;

app_context	Specifies the application context.
display	Specifies a previously opened display connection. Note that a single display connection can be in at most one application context.
application_name	Specifies the name of the application instance.
application_class	Specifies the class name of this application, which is usually the generic name for all instances of this applicaon.
options	Specifies how to parse the command line for any application-specific resources. The *options* argument is passed as a parameter to `Xrm-ParseCommand`. For further information, see Section 10.11.4 in *Xlib*[1] and Section 2.3 of this specification.
num_options	Specifies the number of entries in the options list.
argc	Specifies a pointer to the number of command line parameters.
argv	Specifies the list of command line parameters.

The `XtDisplayInitialize` function retrieves the language string to be used for the specified display (see Section 11.11), builds the resource database,

---

[1] *Xlib* refers to the C Library X Interface specification of the MIT X Consortium, published in *X Window System—C Library and Protocol Reference* by Robert W. Scheifler, James Gettys, and Ron Newman.

calls the Xlib `XrmParseCommand` function to parse the command line, and performs other per-display initialization. After `XrmParseCommand` has been called, *argc* and *argv* contain only those parameters that were not in the standard option table or in the table specified by the *options* argument. If the modified *argc* is not zero, most applications simply print out the modified *argv* along with a message listing the allowable options. On POSIX-based systems, the application name is usually the final component of *argv*[0]. If the synchronous resource is `True`, `XtDisplayInitialize` calls the Xlib `XSynchronize` function to put Xlib into synchronous mode for this display connection and any others currently open in the application context.

To open a display, initialize it, and then add it to an application context, use `XtOpenDisplay`.

Display *XtOpenDisplay(*app_context, display_string, application_name, application_class,*
                       options, num_options, argc, argv)
  XtAppContext *app_context*;
  String *display_string*;
  String *application_name*;
  String *application_class*;
  XrmOptionDescRec **options*;
  Cardinal *num_options*;
  Cardinal **argc*;
  String **argv*;

app_context	Specifies the application context.
display_string	Specifies the display string, or NULL.
application_name	Specifies the name of the application instance, or NULL.
application_class	Specifies the class name of this application, which is usually the generic name for all instances of this application.
options	Specifies how to parse the command line for any application-specific resources. The options argument is passed as a parameter to `XrmParseCommand`.
num_options	Specifies the number of entries in the options list.
argc	Specifies a pointer to the number of command line parameters.
argv	Specifies the list of command line parameters.

The `XtOpenDisplay` function calls `XOpenDisplay` with the specified *display_string*. If *display_string* is NULL, `XtOpenDisplay` uses the current value of the −display option specified in *argv*. If no display is specified in *argv*, the user's default display is retrieved from the environment. On POSIX-based systems, this is the value of the DISPLAY environment variable.

If this succeeds, XtOpenDisplay then calls XtDisplayInitialize and passes it the opened display and the value of the –name option specified in *argv* as the application name. If no –name option is specified and *application_name* is non-NULL, *application_name* is passed to XtDisplayInitialize. If *application_name* is NULL and if the environment variable RESOURCE_NAME is set, the value of RESOURCE_NAME is used. Otherwise, the application name is the name used to invoke the program. On implementations that conform to ANSI C Hosted Environment support, the application name will be *argv*[0] less any directory and file type components, that is, the final component of *argv*[0], if specified. If *argv*[0] does not exist or is the empty string, the application name is "main". XtOpenDisplay returns the newly opened display, or NULL if it failed.

To close a display and remove it from an application context, use XtCloseDisplay.

void XtCloseDisplay(*display*)
    Display **display*;
    display   Specifies the display.

The XtCloseDisplay function calls XCloseDisplay with the specified *display* as soon as it is safe to do so. If called from within an event dispatch (for example, a callback procedure), XtCloseDisplay does not close the display until the dispatch is complete. Note that applications need only call XtCloseDisplay if they are to continue executing after closing the display; otherwise, they should call XtDestroyApplicationContext or just exit.

2.2   Loading the Resource Database

The XtDisplayInitialize function first determines the language string to be used for the specified display and then loads the application's resource database for this language/display/host/application combination from the following sources in order (i.e., the first named source has lowest precedence):

• Application-specific class resource file on the local host.

• Application-specific user resource file on the local host.

• Resource property on the server or user preference resource file on the local host.

• Per-host user environment resource file on the local host.

• Application command line (argv).

XtDisplayInitialize creates a unique resource database for each Display specified. When creating the database, a language string is determined for the display in a manner equivalent to the following sequence of actions: XtDisplayInitialize initially creates two temporary databases. The first database is constructed by parsing the command line according to Section 2.3 and the second database from the string returned by XResourceManagerString or, if XResourceManagerString returns NULL, the contents of a resource file in the user's home directory. On POSIX-based systems, the usual name for this user preference resource file is $HOME/.Xdefaults. The database constructed from the command line is then queried for the resource *name*.xnlLanguage, class *Class*.XnlLanguage where *name* and *Class* are the specified *application_name* and *application_class*. If this database query fails, the server resource database is queried; if this query also fails, the language is determined from the environment; on POSIX-based systems, this is done by retrieving the value of the LANG environment variable. If no language string is found, the empty string is used.

The application-specific class resource file name is constructed from the language string and class name of the application. It points to a site-specific resource file that usually is installed by the site manager when the application is installed. The file is found by calling XtResolvePathname with the parameters (*display*, "app-defaults", NULL, NULL, NULL, NULL, 0, NULL); see Section 11.11. This file is expected to be provided by the developer of the application and may be required for the application to function properly. A simple application that wants to be assured of having a minimal set of resources in the absence of its class resource file can declare fallback resource specifications with XtAppSetFallbackResources.

The application-specific user resource file name is constructed from the language string and class name of the application and points to a user-specific resource file. This file is owned by the application and typically stores user customizations. Its name is found by calling XtResolvePathname with the parameters (*display*, NULL, NULL, NULL, *path*, NULL, 0, NULL) where *path* is defined in an operating-system-specific way. On POSIX-based systems, *path* is defined to be the value of the environment variable XUSERFILESEARCHPATH if this is defined. If XUSERFILESEARCHPATH is not defined but the environment variable XAPPLRESDIR is defined, *path* is

$XAPPLRESDIR/%L/%N:$XAPPLRESDIR/%l/%N:$XAPPLRESDIR/%N:$HOME/%N

where $XAPPLRESDIR is replaced by the value of that environment variable and $HOME is replaced by the user's home directory. If XAPPLRESDIR is not defined, *path* is

$HOME/%L/%N:$HOME/%l/%N:$HOME/%N

If the resulting resource file exists, it is merged into the resource database. This file may be provided with the application or constructed by the user.

The temporary database constructed from the server resource property or user resource file during language determination is then merged into the resource database. The server resource file is constructed entirely by the user and contains both display-independent and display-specific user preferences.

If one exists, the user's environment resource file is then loaded and merged into the resource database. This file name is user- and host-specific. On POSIX-based systems, the user's environment resource file name is specified by the value of the XENVIRONMENT environment variable. If this environment variable does not exist, XtDisplayInitialize searches the user's home directory for a file named .Xdefaults-*host*, where *host* is the host name of the machine on which the application is running. If the resulting resource file exists, it is merged into the resource database. The environment resource file is expected to contain process-specific resource specifications that are to supplement those user-preference specifications in the server resource file.

Finally, the temporary database constructed by parsing the command line is merged into the resource database.

To obtain the resource database for a particular display, use XtDatabase.

XrmDatabase XtDatabase(*display*)
   Display **display*;
display   Specifies the display.

The XtDatabase function returns the fully merged resource database that was built by XtDisplayInitialize, associated with the specified display. If this display has not been initialized by XtDisplayInitialize, the results are not defined.

To specify a default set of resource values that will be used to initialize the resource database if no application-specific class resource file is found (the first of the five sources listed above), use `XtAppSetFallbackResources`.

void XtAppSetFallbackResources(*app_context, specification_list*)
    XtAppContext *app_context*;
    String *specification_list*;
app_context   Specifies the application context in which the fallback specifications will be used.
specification_list   Specifies a NULL-terminated list of resource specifications to preload the database, or NULL.

Each entry in *specification_list* points to a string in the format of `XrmPutLine-Resource`. Following a call to `XtAppSetFallbackResources`, if `XtDisplayInitialize` is not able to find or read an application-specific class resource file according to the rules given above and if *specification_list* is non-NULL, the display-specific resource database will be initialized with the resource specifications in *specification_list*. `XtAppSetFallbackResources` is not required to copy *specification_list*; the caller must ensure that the contents of the list and of the strings addressed by the list remain valid until all displays are initialized or until `XtAppSetFallbackResources` is called again. The value NULL for *specification_list* removes any previous fallback resource specification for the application context. The intended use is to provide a minimal number of resources that will make the application usable (or at least terminate with helpful diagnostic messages) when some problem exists in finding and loading the application defaults file.

2.3   Parsing the Command Line

The `XtOpenDisplay` function first parses the command line for the following options:

−display   Specifies the display name for `XOpenDisplay`.

−name   Sets the resource name prefix, which overrides the application name passed to `XtOpenDisplay`.

`XtDisplayInitialize` has a table of standard command line options that are passed to `XrmParseCommand` for adding resources to the resource database, and it takes as a parameter additional application-specific resource abbreviations. The format of this table is described in Section 10.11.4 in *Xlib*.

```
typedef enum {
    XrmoptionNoArg,          /* Value is specified in OptionDescRec.value */
    XrmoptionIsArg,          /* Value is the option string itself */
    XrmoptionStickyArg,      /* Value is characters immediately following option */
    XrmoptionSepArg,         /* Value is next argument in argv */
    XrmoptionResArg,         /* Use the next argument as input to
                                XrmPutLineResource*/

    XrmoptionSkipArg,        /* Ignore this option and the next argument in argv */
    XrmoptionSkipNArgs,      /* Ignore this option and the next */
                             /* OptionDescRec.value arguments in argv */

    XrmoptionSkipLine        /* Ignore this option and the rest of argv */
} XrmOptionKind;

typedef struct {
    char             *option;      /* Option name in argv */
    char             *specifier;   /* Resource name (without application name) */
    XrmOptionKind    argKind;      /* Location of the resource value */
    caddr_t          value;        /* Value to provide if XrmoptionNoArg */
} XrmOptionDescRec, *XrmOptionDescList;
```

The standard table contains the following entries:

Option String	Resource Name	Argument Kind	Resource Value
−background	*background	SepArg	next argument
−bd	*borderColor	SepArg	next argument
−bg	*background	SepArg	next argument
−borderwidth	.borderWidth	SepArg	next argument
−bordercolor	*borderColor	SepArg	next argument
−bw	.borderWidth	SepArg	next argument
−display	.display	SepArg	next argument
−fg	*foreground	SepArg	next argument
−fn	*font	SepArg	next argument
−font	*font	SepArg	next argument
−foreground	*foreground	SepArg	next argument
−geometry	.geometry	SepArg	next argument
−iconic	.iconic	NoArg	"true"
−name	.name	SepArg	next argument
−reverse	.reverseVideo	NoArg	"on"
−rv	.reverseVideo	NoArg	"on"
+rv	.reverseVideo	NoArg	"off"

Option String	Resource Name	Argument Kind	Resource Value
−selectionTimeout	.selectionTimeout	SepArg	next argument
−synchronous	.synchronous	NoArg	"on"
+synchronous	.synchronous	NoArg	"off"
−title	.title	SepArg	next argument
−xnllanguage	.xnlLanguage	SepArg	next argument
−xrm	next argument	ResArg	next argument

Note that any unique abbreviation for an option name in the standard table or in the application table is accepted.

If reverseVideo is `True`, the values of `XtDefaultForeground` and `XtDefaultBackground` are exchanged for all screens on the Display.

The value of the synchronous resource specifies whether or not Xlib is put into synchronous mode. If a value is found in the resource database during display initialization, `XtDisplayInitialize` makes a call to `XSynchronize` for all display connections currently open in the application context. Therefore, when multiple displays are initialized in the same application context, the most recent value specified for the synchronous resource is used for all displays in the application context.

The value of the selectionTimeout resource applies to all displays opened in the same application context. When multiple displays are initialized in the same application context, the most recent value specified is used for all displays in the application context.

The −xrm option provides a method of setting any resource in an application. The next argument should be a quoted string identical in format to a line in the user resource file. For example, to give a red background to all command buttons in an application named xmh, you can start it up as

```
xmh −xrm 'xmh*Command.background: red'
```

When it parses the command line, `XtDisplayInitialize` merges the application option table with the standard option table before calling the Xlib `XrmParseCommand` function. An entry in the application table with the same name as an entry in the standard table overrides the standard table entry. If an option name is a prefix of another option name, both names are kept in the merged table. The Intrinsics reserve all option names beginning with the characters "-xt" for future standard uses.

2.4   Creating Widgets

The creation of widget instances is a three-phase process:

1. The widgets are allocated and initialized with resources and are optionally added to the managed subset of their parent.
2. All composite widgets are notified of their managed children in a bottom-up traversal of the widget tree.
3. The widgets create X windows, which then are mapped.

To start the first phase, the application calls `XtCreateWidget` for all its widgets and adds some (usually, most or all) of its widgets to their respective parents' managed set by calling `XtManageChild`. To avoid an $O(n^2)$ creation process where each composite widget lays itself out each time a widget is created and managed, parent widgets are not notified of changes in their managed set during this phase.

After all widgets have been created, the application calls `XtRealize-Widget` with the top-level widget to execute the second and third phases. `XtRealizeWidget` first recursively traverses the widget tree in a postorder (bottom-up) traversal and then notifies each composite widget with one or more managed children by means of its change_managed procedure.

Notifying a parent about its managed set involves geometry layout and possibly geometry negotiation. A parent deals with constraints on its size imposed from above (for example, when a user specifies the application window size) and suggestions made from below (for example, when a primitive child computes its preferred size). One difference between the two can cause geometry changes to ripple in both directions through the widget tree. The parent may force some of its children to change size and position and may issue geometry requests to its own parent in order to better accommodate all its children. You cannot predict where anything will go on the screen until this process finishes.

Consequently, in the first and second phases, no X windows are actually created, because it is likely that they will get moved around after creation. This avoids unnecessary requests to the X server.

Finally, `XtRealizeWidget` starts the third phase by making a preorder (top-down) traversal of the widget tree, allocates an X window to each widget by means of its realize procedure, and finally maps the widgets that are managed.

2.4.1   Creating and Merging Argument Lists

Many Intrinsics functions may be passed pairs of resource names and values. These are passed as an arglist, a pointer to an array of `Arg` structures, which contains

```
typedef struct {
    String      name;
    XtArgVal    value;
} Arg, *ArgList;
```

where `XtArgVal` is as defined in Section 1.5.

If the size of the resource is less than or equal to the size of an `XtArgVal`, the resource value is stored directly in *value*; otherwise, a pointer to it is stored into *value*.

To set values in an arglist, use `XtSetArg`.

```
void XtSetArg(arg, name, value)
    Arg arg;
    String name;
    XtArgVal value;
```

arg	Specifies the *name/value* pair to set.
name	Specifies the name of the resource.
value	Specifies the value of the resource if it will fit in an `XtArgVal`, else the address.

The `XtSetArg` function is usually used in a highly stylized manner to minimize the probability of making a mistake; for example:

```
Arg args[20];
int n;

n = 0;
XtSetArg(args[n], XtNheight, 100);    n++;
XtSetArg(args[n], XtNwidth, 200);     n++;
XtSetValues(widget, args, n);
```

Alternatively, an application can statically declare the argument list and use `XtNumber`:

```
static Args args[] = {
    {XtNheight, (XtArgVal) 100},
    {XtNwidth, (XtArgVal) 200},
};
XtSetValues(Widget, args, XtNumber(args));
```

Note that you should not use expressions with side effects such as auto-increment or auto-decrement within the first argument to XtSetArg. XtSetArg can be implemented as a macro that evaluates the first argument twice.

To merge two arglist arrays, use XtMergeArgLists.

ArgList XtMergeArgLists(*args1*, *num_args1*, *args2*, *num_args2*)
    ArgList *args1*;
    Cardinal *num_args1*;
    ArgList *args2*;
    Cardinal *num_args2*;

args1	Specifies the first argument list.
num_args1	Specifies the number of entries in the first argument list.
args2	Specifies the second argument list.
num_args2	Specifies the number of entries in the second argument list.

The XtMergeArgLists function allocates enough storage to hold the combined arglist arrays and copies them into it. Note that it does not check for duplicate entries. The length of the returned list is the sum of the lengths of the specified lists. When it is no longer needed, free the returned storage by using XtFree.

All Intrinsics interfaces that require ArgList arguments have analogs conforming to the ANSI C variable argument list (traditionally called "varargs") calling convention. The name of the analog is formed by prefixing "Va" to the name of the corresponding ArgList procedure; e.g., XtVaCreateWidget. Each procedure named XtVa*something* takes as its last arguments, in place of the corresponding ArgList/Cardinal parameters, a variable parameter list of resource name and value pairs where each name is of type String and each value is of type XtArgVal. The end of the list is identified by a name entry containing NULL. Developers writing in the C language wishing to pass resource name and value pairs to any of these interfaces may use the ArgList and varargs forms interchangeably.

Two special names are defined for use only in varargs lists: XtVaTypedArg and XtVaNestedList.

#define XtVaTypedArg "XtVaTypedArg"

If the name XtVaTypedArg is specified in place of a resource name, then the following four arguments are interpreted as a *name/type/value/size* tuple, where *name* is of type String, *type* is of type String, *value* is of type XtArgVal, and *size* is of type int. When a varargs list containing XtVaTypedArg is processed, a resource type conversion (see Section 9.6) is performed if necessary to convert the value into the format required by the associated resource. If *type* is XtRString, then *value* contains a pointer to the string and *size* contains the number of bytes allocated, including the trailing null byte. If *type* is not XtRString, then if *size* is less than or equal to sizeof(XtArgVal), the value should be the data cast to the type XtArgVal; otherwise *value* is a pointer to the data. If the type conversion fails for any reason, a warning message is issued and the list entry is skipped.

#define XtVaNestedList "XtVaNestedList"

If the name XtVaNestedList is specified in place of a resource name, then the following argument is interpreted as an XtVarArgsList value, which specifies another varargs list that is logically inserted into the original list at the point of declaration. The end of the nested list is identified with a name entry containing NULL. Varargs lists may nest to any depth.

To dynamically allocate a varargs list for use with XtVaNestedList in multiple calls, use XtVaCreateArgsList.

typedef XtPointer XtVarArgsList;

XtVarArgsList XtVaCreateArgsList(*unused*, . . .)
    XtPointer *unused*;

unused	This argument is not currently used and must be specified as NULL.
. . .	Specifies a variable parameter list of resource name and value pairs.

The XtVaCreateArgsList function allocates memory and copies its arguments into a single list pointer, which may be used with XtVaNestedList. The end of both lists is identified by a *name* entry containing NULL. Any entries of type XtVaTypedArg are copied as specified without applying conversions. Data passed by reference (including Strings) are not copied, only the pointers themselves; the caller must ensure that the data remain valid for the lifetime of the created varargs list. The list should be freed using XtFree when no longer needed.

Use of resource files and the resource database is generally encouraged over lengthy arglist or varargs lists whenever possible in order to permit modification without recompilation.

2.4.2 Creating a Widget Instance

To create an instance of a widget, use XtCreateWidget.

Widget XtCreateWidget(*name, object_class, parent, args, num_args*)
    String *name*;
    WidgetClass *object_class*;
    Widget *parent*;
    ArgList *args*;
    Cardinal *num_args*;

name	Specifies the resource instance name for the created widget, which is used for retrieving resources and, for that reason, should not be the same as any other widget that is a child of the same parent.
object_class	Specifies the widget class pointer for the created object. Must be objectClass or any subclass thereof.
parent	Specifies the parent widget. Must be of class Object or any subclass thereof.
args	Specifies the argument list to override any other resource specifications.
num_args	Specifies the number of entries in the argument list.

The XtCreateWidget function performs all the boilerplate operations of widget creation, doing the following in order:

• Checks to see if the class_initialize procedure has been called for this class and for all superclasses and, if not, calls those necessary in a superclass-to-subclass order.

• If the specified class is not coreWidgetClass or a subclass thereof, and the parent's class is a subclass of compositeWidgetClass and either no extension record in the parent's composite class part extension field exists with the *record_type* NULLQUARK or the *accepts_objects* field in the extension record is False, XtCreateWidget issues a fatal error; see Section 3.1 and Chapter 12.

• Allocates memory for the widget instance.

• If the parent is a member of the class constraintWidgetClass, allocates memory for the parent's constraints and stores the address of this memory into the *constraints* field.

• Initializes the Core nonresource data fields (for example, *parent* and *visible*).

• Initializes the resource fields (for example, *background_pixel*) by using the CoreClassPart resource list specified for this class and all superclasses.

- If the parent is a member of the class `constraintWidgetClass`, initializes the resource fields of the constraints record by using the `ConstraintClassPart` resource list specified for the parent's class and all superclasses up to `constraintWidgetClass`.

- Calls the initialize procedures for the widget by starting at the Object initialize procedure on down to the widget's initialize procedure.

- If the parent is a member of the class `compositeWidgetClass`, puts the widget into its parent's children list by calling its parent's insert_child procedure. For further information, see Section 3.1.

- If the parent is a member of the class `constraintWidgetClass`, calls the `ConstraintClassPart` initialize procedures, starting at `constraintWidgetClass` on down to the parent's `ConstraintClassPart` initialize procedure.

To create an instance of a widget using varargs lists, use `XtVaCreateWidget`.

Widget XtVaCreateWidget(*name, object_class, parent,* . . .)
    String *name*;
    WidgetClass *object_class*;
    Widget *parent*;

name	Specifies the resource name for the created widget.
object_class	Specifies the widget class pointer for the created object. Must be `objectClass` or any subclass thereof.
parent	Specifies the parent widget. Must be of class Object or any subclass thereof.
. . .	Specifies the variable argument list to override any other resource specifications.

The `XtVaCreateWidget` procedure is identical in function to `XtCreateWidget` with the *args* and *num_args* parameters replaced by a varargs list, as described in Section 2.4.1.

2.4.3   Creating an Application Shell Instance

An application can have multiple top-level widgets, each of which specifies a unique widget tree, which can potentially be on different screens or displays. An application uses `XtAppCreateShell` to create independent widget trees.

Widget XtAppCreateShell(*application_name, application_class, widget_class, display,*
                                         args, num_args)
    String *application_name*;
    String *application_class*;

WidgetClass *widget_class*;
Display **display*;
ArgList *args*;
Cardinal *num_args*;

application_name   Specifies the name of the application instance. If *application_name* is NULL, the application name passed to XtDisplayInitialize is used.

application_class   Specifies the class name of this application.

widget_class   Specifies the widget class for the top-level widget (normally applicationShellWidgetClass)

display   Specifies the display.

args   Specifies the argument list to override any other resource specifications.

num_args   Specifies the number of entries in the argument list.

The XtAppCreateShell function saves the specified application name and application class for qualifying all widget resource specifiers and to set the WM_CLASS property on the shell's window. The application name and application class are used as the leftmost components in all widget resource names for this application. XtAppCreateShell should be used to create a new logical application within a program or to create a shell on another display. In the first case, it allows the specification of a new root in the resource hierarchy. In the second case, it uses the resource database associated with the other display.

The widget returned by XtAppCreateShell has the WM_COMMAND and WM_CLASS properties set for window and session managers if the specified *widget_class* is a subclass of ApplicationShell (see Chapter 4).

To create multiple top-level shells within a single (logical) application, you can use one of two methods:

- Designate one shell as the real top-level shell and create the others as pop-up children of it by using XtCreatePopupShell.

- Have all shells as pop-up children of an unrealized top-level shell.

The first method, which is best used when there is a clear choice for what is the main window, leads to resource specifications like the following:

     xmail.geometry: . . .   (the main window)
     xmail.read.geometry: . . .   (the read window)
     xmail.compose.geometry: . . .   (the compose window)

The second method, which is best if there is no main window, leads to resource specifications like the following:

xmail.headers.geometry: . . .   (the headers window)
xmail.read.geometry: . . .   (the read window)
xmail.compose.geometry: . . .   (the compose window)

To create a top-level widget that is the root of a widget tree using varargs lists, use XtVaAppCreateShell.

Widget XtVaAppCreateShell(*application_name, application_class, widget_class, display, . . .*)
    String *application_name*;
    String *application_class*;
    WidgetClass *widget_class*;
    Display **display*;

application_name	Specifies the name of the application instance.
application_class	Specifies the class name of this application.
widget_class	Specifies the widget class for the top-level widget.
display	Specifies the display.
. . .	Specifies the variable argument list to override any other resource specifications.

The XtVaAppCreateShell procedure is identical in function to XtAppCreateShell with the *args* and *num_args* parameters replaced by a varargs list, as described in Section 2.4.1.

2.4.4   Convenience Procedure to Initialize an Application

To initialize the X Toolkit internals, create an application context, open and initialize a display, and create the initial application shell instance, an application may use XtAppInitialize or XtVaAppInitialize.

Widget XtAppInitialize(*app_context_return, application_class, options, num_options,*
                           argc_in_out, argv_in_out, fallback_resources, args, num_args)
    XtAppContext **app_context_return*;
    String *application_class*;
    XrmOptionDescList *options*;
    Cardinal *num_options*;
    Cardinal **argc_in_out*;
    String **argv_in_out*;
    String **fallback_resources*;

ArgList *args*;

Cardinal *num_args*;

app_context_return	Returns the application context, if non-NULL.
application_class	Specifies the class name of the application.
options	Specifies the command line options table.
num_options	Specifies the number of entries in *options*.
argc_in_out	Specifies a pointer to the number of command line arguments.
argv_in_out	Specifies a pointer to the command line arguments.
fallback_resources	Specifies resource values to be used if the application class resource file cannot be opened or read, or NULL.
args	Specifies the argument list to override any other resource specifications for the created shell widget.
num_args	Specifies the number of entries in the argument list.

The `XtAppInitialize` function calls `XtToolkitInitialize` followed by `XtCreateApplicationContext`, then calls `XtOpenDisplay` with *display_string* NULL and *application_name* NULL, and finally calls `XtAppCreate-Shell` with *application_name* NULL, *widget_class* `applicationShellWidget-Class`, and the specified *args* and *num_args* and returns the created shell. The modified *argc* and *argv* returned by `XtDisplayInitialize` are returned in *argc_in_out* and *argv_in_out*. If *app_context_return* is not NULL, the created application context is also returned. If the display specified by the command line cannot be opened, an error message is issued and `XtAppInitialize` terminates the application. If *fallback_resources* is non-NULL, `XtAppSetFallback-Resources` is called with the value prior to calling `XtOpenDisplay`.

Widget XtVaAppInitialize (*app_context_return, application_class, options, num_options, argc_in_out, argv_in_out, fallback_resources, . . .*)

XtAppContext **app_context_return*;

String *application_class*;

XrmOptionDescList *options*;

Cardinal *num_options*;

Cardinal **argc_in_out*;

String **argv_in_out*;

String **fallback_resources*;

app_context_return	Returns the application context, if non-NULL.
application_class	Specifies the class name of the application.
options	Specifies the command line options table.
num_options	Specifies the number of entries in *options*.
argc_in_out	Specifies a pointer to the number of command line arguments.
argv_in_out	Specifies the command line arguments array.

> *fallback_resources*   Specifies resource values to be used if the application class resource file cannot be opened, or NULL.
>
> . . .   Specifies the variable argument list to override any other resource specifications for the created shell.

The `XtVaAppInitialize` procedure is identical in function to `XtApp-Initialize` with the *args* and *num_args* parameters replaced by a varargs list, as described in Section 2.4.1.

2.4.5   Widget Instance Initialization: the initialize Procedure

The initialize procedure pointer in a widget class is of type `XtInitProc`.

```
typedef void (*XtInitProc)(Widget, Widget, ArgList, Cardinal*);
    Widget request;
    Widget new;
    ArgList args;
    Cardinal *num_args;
```

> *request*   Specifies a copy of the widget with resource values as requested by the argument list, the resource database, and the widget defaults.
>
> *new*   Specifies the widget with the new values, both resource and nonresource, that are actually allowed.
>
> *args*   Specifies the argument list passed by the client, for computing derived resource values. If the client created the widget using a varargs form, any resources specified via `XtVaTypedArg` are converted to the widget representation and the list is transformed into the `ArgList` format.
>
> *num_args*   Specifies the number of entries in the argument list.

An initialization procedure performs the following:

• Allocates space for and copies any resources referenced by address that the client is allowed to free or modify after the widget has been created. For example, if a widget has a field that is a `String`, it may choose not to depend on the characters at that address remaining constant but dynamically allocate space for the string and copy it to the new space. Widgets that do not copy one or more resources referenced by address should clearly so state in their user documentation.

Note   It is not necessary to allocate space for or to copy callback lists.

• Computes values for unspecified resource fields. For example, if *width* and *height* are zero, the widget should compute an appropriate width and height based on its other resources.

Note   A widget may only directly assign its own *width* and *height* within the initialize, initialize_hook, set_values, and set_values_hook procedures; see Chapter 6.

• Computes values for uninitialized nonresource fields that are derived from resource fields. For example, graphics contexts (GCs) that the widget uses are derived from resources like background, foreground, and font.

An initialization procedure also can check certain fields for internal consistency. For example, it makes no sense to specify a colormap for a depth that does not support that colormap.

Initialization procedures are called in superclass-to-subclass order after all fields specified in the resource lists have been initialized. The initialize procedure does not need to examine *args* and *num_args* if all public resources are declared in the resource list. Most of the initialization code for a specific widget class deals with fields defined in that class and not with fields defined in its superclasses.

If a subclass does not need an initialization procedure because it does not need to perform any of the above operations, it can specify NULL for the *initialize* field in the class record.

Sometimes a subclass may want to overwrite values filled in by its superclass. In particular, size calculations of a superclass are often incorrect for a subclass, and in this case, the subclass must modify or recalculate fields declared and computed by its superclass.

As an example, a subclass can visually surround its superclass display. In this case, the width and height calculated by the superclass initialize procedure are too small and need to be incremented by the size of the surround. The subclass needs to know if its superclass's size was calculated by the superclass or was specified explicitly. All widgets must place themselves into whatever size is explicitly given, but they should compute a reasonable size if no size is requested.

The *request* and *new* arguments provide the necessary information for a subclass to determine the difference between an explicitly specified field and a field computed by a superclass. The *request* widget is a copy of the widget as initialized by the arglist and resource database. The *new* widget starts with the values in the request, but it has been updated by all superclass initialization procedures called so far. A subclass initialize procedure can compare these two to resolve any potential conflicts.

In the above example, the subclass with the visual surround can see if the *width* and *height* in the *request* widget are zero. If so, it adds its surround size to the *width* and *height* fields in the *new* widget. If not, it must make do with the size originally specified.

The *new* widget will become the actual widget instance record. Therefore, the initialization procedure should do all its work on the *new* widget; the *request* widget should never be modified. If the initialize procedure needs to call any routines that operate on a widget, it should specify *new* as the widget instance.

2.4.6   Constraint Instance Initialization: the ConstraintClassPart initialize Procedure

The constraint initialization procedure pointer, found in the `Constraint-ClassPart` *initialize* field of the widget class record, is of type `XtInitProc`. The values passed to the parent constraint initialization procedures are the same as those passed to the child's class widget initialization procedures.

The *constraints* field of the *request* widget points to a copy of the constraints record as initialized by the arglist and resource database.

The constraint initialization procedure should compute any constraint fields derived from constraint resources. It can make further changes to the *new* widget to make the widget and any other constraint fields conform to the specified constraints, for example, changing the widget's size or position.

If a constraint class does not need a constraint initialization procedure, it can specify NULL for the *initialize* field of the `ConstraintClassPart` in the class record.

2.4.7   Nonwidget Data Initialization: the initialize_hook Procedure

Note   The initialize_hook procedure is obsolete, as the same information is now available to the initialize procedure. The procedure has been retained for those widgets that used it in previous releases.

The initialize_hook procedure pointer is of type `XtArgsProc`.

```
typedef void (*XtArgsProc) (Widget, ArgList, Cardinal*);
    Widget w;
    ArgList args;
    Cardinal *num_args;
```

w	Specifies the widget.
args	Specifies the argument list passed by the client. If the client created the widget using a varargs form, any resources specified via `XtVaTypedArg` are converted to the widget representation and the list is transformed into the `ArgList` format.
num_args	Specifies the number of entries in the argument list.

If this procedure is not NULL, it is called immediately after the corresponding initialize procedure or in its place if the *initialize* field is NULL.

The initialize_hook procedure allows a widget instance to initialize non-resource data using information from the specified argument list as if it were a resource.

2.5   Realizing Widgets

To realize a widget instance, use `XtRealizeWidget`.

void XtRealizeWidget(*w*)
    Widget *w*;
w	Specifies the widget. Must be of class Core or any subclass thereof.

If the widget is already realized, `XtRealizeWidget` simply returns. Otherwise it performs the following:

- Binds all action names in the widget's translation table to procedures (see Section 10.1.2).

- Makes a postorder traversal of the widget tree rooted at the specified widget and calls the change_managed procedure of each composite widget that has one or more managed children.

- Constructs an `XSetWindowAttributes` structure filled in with information derived from the Core widget fields and calls the realize procedure for the widget, which adds any widget-specific attributes and creates the X window.

- If the widget is not a subclass of `compositeWidgetClass`, `XtRealizeWidget` returns; otherwise it continues and performs the following:
  — Descends recursively to each of the widget's managed children and calls the realize procedures. Primitive widgets that instantiate children are responsible for realizing those children themselves.

  — Maps all the managed children windows that have *mapped_when_managed* True. If a widget is managed but *mapped_when_managed* is False, the widget is allocated visual space but is not displayed.

If the widget is a top-level shell widget (that is, it has no parent), and *mapped_when_managed* is True, XtRealizeWidget maps the widget window.

Within a widget tree, XtCreateWidget, XtVaCreateWidget, XtRealizeWidget, XtManageChildren, XtUnmanageChildren, XtUnrealizeWidget, XtSetMappedWhenManaged, and XtDestroy-Widget maintain the following invariants:

• If a composite widget is realized, then all its managed children are realized.

• If a composite widget is realized, then all its managed children that have *mapped_when_managed* True are mapped.

All Intrinsics functions and all widget routines should accept either realized or unrealized widgets. When calling the realize procedures for children of a composite widget, XtRealizeWidget calls the procedures in reverse order of appearance in the CompositePart *children* list. By default, this will result in the stacking order of any newly created subwindows being top-to-bottom in the order of appearance on the list, and the most recently created child will be at the bottom.

To check whether or not a widget has been realized, use XtIsRealized.

Boolean XtIsRealized(*w*)
    Widget *w*;
    w   Specifies the widget. Must be of class Object or any subclass thereof.

The XtIsRealized function returns True if the widget has been realized, that is, if the widget has a nonzero window id. If the specified object is not a widget, the state of the nearest widget ancestor is returned.

Some widget procedures (for example, set_values) might wish to operate differently after the widget has been realized.

2.5.1   Widget Instance Window Creation: the realize Procedure

The realize procedure pointer in a widget class is of type XtRealizeProc.

typedef void (*XtRealizeProc)(Widget, XtValueMask*, XSetWindowAttributes*);
    Widget *w*;
    XtValueMask *value_mask*;
    XSetWindowAttributes *attributes*;
    w   Specifies the widget.

value_mask	Specifies which fields in the *attributes* structure are used.
attributes	Specifies the window attributes to use in the XCreateWindow call.

The realize procedure must create the widget's window.

Before calling the class realize procedure, the generic XtRealizeWidget function fills in a mask and a corresponding XSetWindowAttributes structure. It sets the following fields in *attributes* and corresponding bits in *value_mask* based on information in the widget core structure:

- The *background_pixmap* (or *background_pixel* if *background_pixmap* is XtUnspecifiedPixmap) is filled in from the corresponding field.

- The *border_pixmap* (or *border_pixel* if *border_pixmap* is XtUnspecifiedPixmap) is filled in from the corresponding field.

- The *colormap* is filled in from the corresponding field.

- The *event_mask* is filled in based on the event handlers registered, the event translations specified, whether expose is non-NULL, and whether *visible_interest* is True.

- The *bit_gravity* is set to NorthWestGravity if the *expose* field is NULL.

These or any other fields in attributes and the corresponding bits in *value_mask* can be set by the realize procedure.

Note that because realize is not a chained operation, the widget class realize procedure must update the XSetWindowAttributes structure with all the appropriate fields from non-Core superclasses.

A widget class can inherit its realize procedure from its superclass during class initialization. The realize procedure defined for coreWidgetClass calls XtCreateWindow with the passed *value_mask* and *attributes* and with *window_class* and *visual* set to CopyFromParent. Both compositeWidgetClass and constraintWidgetClass inherit this realize procedure, and most new widget subclasses can do the same (see Section 1.6.10).

The most common noninherited realize procedures set *bit_gravity* in the mask and attributes to the appropriate value and then create the window. For example, depending on its justification, Label might set *bit_gravity* to WestGravity, CenterGravity, or EastGravity. Consequently, shrinking it would just move the bits appropriately, and no exposure event is needed for repainting.

If a composite widget's children should be realized in an order other than that specified (to control the stacking order, for example), it should call XtRealizeWidget on its children itself in the appropriate order from within its own realize procedure.

Widgets that have children and whose class is not a subclass of `composite-WidgetClass` are responsible for calling `XtRealizeWidget` on their children, usually from within the realize procedure.

2.5.2   Window Creation Convenience Routine

Rather than call the Xlib `XCreateWindow` function explicitly, a realize procedure should normally call the Intrinsics analog `XtCreateWindow`, which simplifies the creation of windows for widgets.

> void XtCreateWindow(*w, window_class, visual, value_mask, attributes*)
>   Widget *w*;
>   unsigned int *window_class*;
>   Visual **visual*;
>   XtValueMask *value_mask*;
>   XSetWindowAttributes **attributes*;
>
> | | |
> |---|---|
> | *w* | Specifies the widget that defines the additional window attributes. Must be of class Core or any subclass thereof. |
> | *window_class* | Specifies the Xlib window class (for example, `InputOutput`, `InputOnly`, or `CopyFromParent`). |
> | *visual* | Specifies the visual type (usually `CopyFromParent`). |
> | *value_mask* | Specifies which fields in the *attributes* structure are used. |
> | *attributes* | Specifies the window attributes to use in the `XCreateWindow` call. |

The `XtCreateWindow` function calls the Xlib `XCreateWindow` function with values from the widget structure and the passed parameters. Then, it assigns the created window to the widget's *window* field.

`XtCreateWindow` evaluates the following fields of the widget core structure: *depth, screen, parent –>core.window, x, y, width, height,* and *border_width*.

2.6   Obtaining Window Information from a Widget

The Core widget class definition contains the screen and window ids. The *window* field may be NULL for a while (see Sections 2.4 and 2.5).

The display pointer, the parent widget, screen pointer, and window of a widget are available to the widget writer by means of macros and to the application writer by means of functions.

> Display *XtDisplay(*w*)
>   Widget *w*;
>
> | | |
> |---|---|
> | *w* | Specifies the widget. Must be of class Core or any subclass thereof. |

`XtDisplay` returns the display pointer for the specified widget.

Widget XtParent(*w*)
   Widget *w*;
     w   Specifies the widget. Must be of class Object or any subclass thereof.

`XtParent` returns the parent object for the specified widget. The returned object will be of class Object or a subclass.

Screen *XtScreen(*w*)
   Widget *w*;
     w   Specifies the widget. Must be of class Core or any subclass thereof.

`XtScreen` returns the screen pointer for the specified widget.

Window XtWindow(*w*)
   Widget *w*;
     w   Specifies the widget. Must be of class Core or any subclass thereof.

`XtWindow` returns the window of the specified widget.

The display pointer, screen pointer, and window of a widget or of the closest widget ancestor of a nonwidget object are available by means of `XtDisplay-OfObject`, `XtScreenOfObject`, and `XtWindowOfObject`.

Display *XtDisplayOfObject(*object*)
   Widget *object*;
   object   Specifies the object. Must be of class Object or any subclass thereof.

`XtDisplayOfObject` is identical in function to `XtDisplay` if the object is a widget; otherwise `XtDisplayOfObject` returns the display pointer for the nearest ancestor of *object* that is of class Widget or a subclass thereof.

Screen *XtScreenOfObject(*object*)
   Widget *object*;
   object   Specifies the object. Must be of class Object or any subclass thereof.

`XtScreenOfObject` is identical in function to `XtScreen` if the object is a widget; otherwise `XtScreenOfObject` returns the screen pointer for the nearest ancestor of *object* that is of class Widget or a subclass thereof.

Window XtWindowOfObject(*object*)
   Widget *object*;
   object   Specifies the object. Must be of class Object or any subclass thereof.

XtWindowOfObject is identical in function to XtWindow if the object is a widget; otherwise XtWindowOfObject returns the window for the nearest ancestor of *object* that is of class Widget or a subclass thereof.

To retrieve the instance name of an object, use XtName.

String XtName(*object*)
  Widget *object*;
  object   Specifies the object whose name is desired. Must be of class Object or a subclass thereof.

XtName returns a pointer to the instance name of the specified object. The storage is owned by the Intrinsics and must not be modified. The name is not qualified by the names of any of the object's ancestors.

Several window attributes are locally cached in the widget instance. Thus, they can be set by the resource manager and XtSetValues as well as used by routines that derive structures from these values (for example, *depth* for deriving pixmaps, *background_pixel* for deriving GCs, and so on) or in the XtCreateWindow call.

The *x*, *y*, *width*, *height*, and *border_width* window attributes are available to geometry managers. These fields are maintained synchronously inside the X Toolkit. When an XConfigureWindow is issued by the Intrinsics on the widget's window (on request of its parent), these values are updated immediately rather than some time later when the server generates a Configure-Notify event. (In fact, most widgets do not have SubstructureNotify turned on.) This ensures that all geometry calculations are based on the internally consistent toolkit world rather than on either an inconsistent world updated by asynchronous ConfigureNotify events or a consistent but slow world in which geometry managers ask the server for window sizes whenever they need to lay out their managed children (see Chapter 6).

2.7   Unrealizing Widgets

To destroy the windows associated with a widget and its non-pop-up descendants, use XtUnrealizeWidget.

void XtUnrealizeWidget(*w*)
  Widget *w*;
  w   Specifies the widget. Must be of class Core or any subclass thereof.

If the widget is currently unrealized, `XtUnrealizeWidget` simply returns. Otherwise it performs the following:

• Unmanages the widget if the widget is managed.

• Makes a postorder (child-to-parent) traversal of the widget tree rooted at the specified widget and, for each widget that has declared a callback list resource named "unrealizeCallback", executes the procedures on the XtNunrealizeCallback list.

• Destroys the widget's window and any subwindows by calling `XDestroyWindow` with the specified widget's *window* field.

Any events in the queue or which arrive following a call to `XtUnrealize-Widget` will be dispatched as if the window(s) of the unrealized widget(s) had never existed.

2.8 Destroying Widgets

The Intrinsics provide support

• To destroy all the pop-up children of the widget being destroyed and destroy all children of composite widgets.

• To remove (and unmap) the widget from its parent.

• To call the callback procedures that have been registered to trigger when the widget is destroyed.

• To minimize the number of things a widget has to deallocate when destroyed.

• To minimize the number of `XDestroyWindow` calls when destroying a widget tree.

To destroy a widget instance, use `XtDestroyWidget`.

```
void XtDestroyWidget(w)
    Widget w;
    w                   Specifies the widget. Must be of class Object or any subclass thereof.
```

The `XtDestroyWidget` function provides the only method of destroying a widget, including widgets that need to destroy themselves. It can be called at any time, including from an application callback routine of the widget being destroyed. This requires a two-phase destroy process in order to avoid dangling references to destroyed widgets.

In phase 1, `XtDestroyWidget` performs the following:

• If the *being_destroyed* field of the widget is `True`, it returns immediately.

• Recursively descends the widget tree and sets the *being_destroyed* field to `True` for the widget and all normal and pop-up children.

• Adds the widget to a list of widgets (the destroy list) that should be destroyed when it is safe to do so.

Entries on the destroy list satisfy the invariant that if w2 occurs after w1 on the destroy list, then w2 is not a descendent, either normal or pop-up, of w1.

Phase 2 occurs when all procedures that should execute as a result of the current event have been called, including all procedures registered with the event and translation managers, that is, when the current invocation of XtDispatchEvent is about to return, or immediately if not in XtDispatchEvent.

In phase 2, XtDestroyWidget performs the following on each entry in the destroy list in the order specified:

• Calls the destroy callback procedures registered on the widget and all normal and pop-up descendants in postorder (it calls child callbacks before parent callbacks).

• If the widget is not a pop-up child and the widget's parent is a subclass of compositeWidgetClass, and if the parent is not being destroyed, it calls XtUnmanageChild on the widget and then calls the widget's parent's delete_child procedure (see Section 3.3).

• If the widget is not a pop-up child, and the widget's parent is a subclass of constraintWidgetClass, it calls the ConstraintClassPart destroy procedure for the parent, then for the parent's superclass, until finally it calls the ConstraintClassPart destroy procedure for constraintWidgetClass.

• Calls the destroy procedures for the widget and all normal and pop-up descendants in postorder. For each such widget, it calls the CoreClassPart destroy procedure declared in the widget class, then the destroy procedure declared in its superclass, until finally it calls the destroy procedure declared in the Object class record.

• Calls XDestroyWindow if the specified widget is realized (that is, has an X window). The server recursively destroys all normal descendant windows.

• Recursively descends the tree and destroys the windows for all realized pop-up descendants, deallocates all pop-up descendants, constraint records, callback lists, and if the widget's class is a subclass of compositeWidgetClass, children.

2.8.1   Adding and Removing Destroy Callbacks

When an application needs to perform additional processing during the destruction of a widget, it should register a destroy callback procedure for the widget. The destroy callback procedures use the mechanism described in Chapter 8. The destroy callback list is identified by the resource name XtNdestroyCallback.

For example, the following adds an application-supplied destroy callback procedure *ClientDestroy* with client data to a widget by calling XtAddCallback.

XtAddCallback (*w*, XtNdestroyCallback, *ClientDestroy, client_data*)

Similarly, the following removes the application-supplied destroy callback procedure *ClientDestroy* by calling XtRemoveCallback.

XtRemoveCallback (*w*, XtNdestroyCallback, *ClientDestroy, client_data*)

The *ClientDestroy* argument is of type XtCallbackProc; see Section 8.1.

2.8.2 Dynamic Data Deallocation: the destroy Procedure

The destroy procedure pointers in the ObjectClassPart, RectObjClass-Part, and CoreClassPart structures are of type XtWidgetProc.

```
typedef void (*XtWidgetProc) (Widget);
    Widget w;
    w              Specifies the widget being destroyed.
```

The destroy procedures are called in subclass-to-superclass order. Therefore, a widget's destroy procedure only should deallocate storage that is specific to the subclass and should ignore the storage allocated by any of its superclasses. The destroy procedure should only deallocate resources that have been explicitly created by the subclass. Any resource that was obtained from the resource database or passed in an argument list was not created by the widget and therefore should not be destroyed by it. If a widget does not need to deallocate any storage, the destroy procedure entry in its class record can be NULL.

Deallocating storage includes, but is not limited to, the following steps:

• Calling XtFree on dynamic storage allocated with XtMalloc, XtCalloc, and so on.

• Calling XFreePixmap on pixmaps created with direct X calls.

• Calling XtReleaseGC on GCs allocated with XtGetGC.

• Calling XFreeGC on GCs allocated with direct X calls.

• Calling XtRemoveEventHandler on event handlers added to other widgets.

• Calling XtRemoveTimeOut on timers created with XtAppAddTimeOut.

• Calling XtDestroyWidget for each child if the widget has children and is not a subclass of compositeWidgetClass.

2.8.3   Dynamic Constraint Data Deallocation: the ConstraintClassPart destroy Procedure

The constraint destroy procedure identified in the `ConstraintClassPart` structure is called for a widget whose parent is a subclass of `constraintWidgetClass`. This constraint destroy procedure pointer is of type `XtWidgetProc`. The constraint destroy procedures are called in subclass-to-superclass order, starting at the class of the widget's parent and ending at `constraintWidgetClass`. Therefore, a parent's constraint destroy procedure only should deallocate storage that is specific to the constraint subclass and not storage allocated by any of its superclasses.

If a parent does not need to deallocate any constraint storage, the constraint destroy procedure entry in its class record can be NULL.

2.9   Exiting from an Application

All X Toolkit applications should terminate by calling `XtDestroyApplicationContext` and then exiting using the standard method for their operating system (typically, by calling `exit` for POSIX-based systems). The quickest way to make the windows disappear while exiting is to call `XtUnmapWidget` on each top-level shell widget. The X Toolkit has no resources beyond those in the program image, and the X server will free its resources when its connection to the application is broken.

Depending upon the widget set in use, it may be necessary to explicitly destroy individual widgets or widget trees with `XtDestroyWidget` before calling `XtDestroyApplicationConcept` in order to ensure that any required widget cleanup is properly executed. The application developer must refer to the widget documentation to learn if a widget needs to perform additional cleanup beyond that performed automatically by the operating system. None of the widget classes defined by the Intrinsics require additional cleanup.

Chapter 3

Composite Widgets and Their Children

Composite widgets (widgets whose class is a subclass of `composite-WidgetClass`) can have an arbitrary number of children. Consequently, they are responsible for much more than primitive widgets. Their responsibilities (either implemented directly by the widget class or indirectly by Intrinsics functions) include

- Overall management of children from creation to destruction.
- Destruction of descendants when the composite widget is destroyed.
- Physical arrangement (geometry management) of a displayable subset of children (that is, the managed children).
- Mapping and unmapping of a subset of the managed children.

Overall management is handled by the generic procedures `XtCreateWidget` and `XtDestroyWidget`. `XtCreateWidget` adds children to their parent by calling the parent's insert_child procedure. `XtDestroyWidget` removes children from their parent by calling the parent's delete_child procedure and ensures that all children of a destroyed composite widget also get destroyed.

Only a subset of the total number of children is actually managed by the geometry manager and hence possibly visible. For example, a multibuffer composite editor widget might allocate one child widget for each file buffer, but it might only display a small number of the existing buffers. Widgets that are in this displayable subset are called managed widgets and enter into geometry manager calculations. The other children are called unmanaged widgets and, by definition, are not mapped by the Intrinsics.

Children are added to and removed from their parent's managed set by using XtManageChild, XtManageChildren, XtUnmanageChild, and XtUnmanageChildren, which notify the parent to recalculate the physical layout of its children by calling the parent's change_managed procedure. The XtCreateManagedWidget convenience function calls XtCreateWidget and XtManageChild on the result.

Most managed children are mapped, but some widgets can be in a state where they take up physical space but do not show anything. Managed widgets are not mapped automatically if their *map_when_managed* field is False. The default is True and is changed by using XtSetMappedWhenManaged.

Each composite widget class declares a geometry manager, which is responsible for figuring out where the managed children should appear within the composite widget's window. Geometry management techniques fall into four classes:

Fixed boxes   Fixed boxes have a fixed number of children created by the parent. All these children are managed, and none ever makes geometry manager requests.

Homogeneous boxes   Homogeneous boxes treat all children equally and apply the same geometry constraints to each child. Many clients insert and delete widgets freely.

Heterogeneous boxes   Heterogeneous boxes have a specific location where each child is placed. This location usually is not specified in pixels, because the window may be resized, but is expressed rather in terms of the relationship between a child and the parent or between the child and other specific children. The class of heterogeneous boxes is usually a subclass of Constraint.

Shell boxes   Shell boxes have only one child, which is exactly the size of the shell. The geometry manager must communicate with the window manager, if it exists, and the box must also accept ConfigureNotify events when the window size is changed by the window manager.

3.1 Addition of Children to a Composite Widget: the insert_child Procedure

To add a child to the parent's list of children, the XtCreateWidget function calls the parent's class routine insert_child. The insert_child procedure pointer in a composite widget is of type XtWidgetProc.

```
typedef void (*XtWidgetProc) (Widget);
    Widget w;
w               Passes the newly created child.
```

Most composite widgets inherit their superclass's operation. The insert_child routine in CompositeWidgetClass calls the insert_position procedure and inserts the child at the specified position in the *children* list, expanding it if necessary.

Some composite widgets define their own insert_child routine so that they can order their children in some convenient way, create companion controller widgets for a new widget, or limit the number or class of their child widgets. A composite widget class that wishes to allow nonwidget children (see Chapter 12) must specify a CompositeClassExtension extension record as described in Section 1.4.2.1 and set the *accepts_objects* field in this record to True. If the CompositeClassExtension record is not specified or the *accepts_objects* field is False, the composite widget can assume that all its children are of a subclass of Core without an explicit subclass test in the insert_child procedure.

If there is not enough room to insert a new child in the child array (that is, *num_children* is equal to *num_slots*), the insert_child procedure must first reallocate the array and update *num_slots*. The insert_child procedure then places the child at the appropriate position in the array and increments the *num_children* field.

3.2 Insertion Order of Children: the insert_position Procedure

Instances of composite widgets sometimes need to specify more about the order in which their children are kept. For example, an application may want a set of command buttons in some logical order grouped by function, and it may want buttons that represent file names to be kept in alphabetical order without constraining the order in which the buttons are created.

An application controls the presentation order of a set of children by supplying an XtNinsertPosition resource. The insert_position procedure pointer in a composite widget instance is of type `XtOrderProc`.

```
typedef Cardinal (*XtOrderProc) (Widget);
    Widget w;
    w                Passes the newly created widget.
```

Composite widgets that allow clients to order their children (usually homogeneous boxes) can call their widget instance's insert_position procedure from the class's insert_child procedure to determine where a new child should go in its child array. Thus, a client using a composite class can apply different sorting criteria to widget instances of the class, passing in a different insert_position procedure resource when it creates each composite widget instance.

The return value of the insert_position procedure indicates how many children should go before the widget. Returning zero indicates that the widget should go before all other children, and returning *num_children* indicates that it should go after all other children. The default insert_position function returns *num_children* and can be overridden by a specific composite widget's resource list or by the argument list provided when the composite widget is created.

3.3 Deletion of Children: the delete_child Procedure

To remove the child from the parent's *children* list, the `XtDestroyWidget` function eventually causes a call to the Composite parent's class delete_child procedure. The delete_child procedure pointer is of type `XtWidgetProc`.

```
typedef void (*XtWidgetProc) (Widget);
    Widget w;
    w                Passes the child being deleted.
```

Most widgets inherit the delete_child procedure from their superclass. Composite widgets that create companion widgets define their own delete_child procedure to remove these companion widgets.

3.4 Adding and Removing Children from the Managed Set

The Intrinsics provide a set of generic routines to permit the addition of widgets to or the removal of widgets from a composite widget's managed set.

These generic routines eventually call the composite widget's change_ managed procedure. The change_managed procedure pointer is of type XtWidgetProc. The widget argument specifies the composite widget whose managed child set has been modified.

3.4.1 Managing Children

To add a list of widgets to the geometry-managed (and hence displayable) subset of their Composite parent, use XtManageChildren.

typedef Widget *WidgetList;

void XtManageChildren (*children, num_children*)
    WidgetList *children*;
    Cardinal *num_children*;
    children   Specifies a list of child widgets. Each child must be of class RectObj or any subclass thereof.
    num_children   Specifies the number of children in the list.

The XtManageChildren function performs the following:

• Issues an error if the children do not all have the same parent or if the parent's class is not a subclass of compositeWidgetClass.

• Returns immediately if the common parent is being destroyed; otherwise, for each unique child on the list, XtManageChildren ignores the child if it already is managed or is being destroyed, and marks it if not.

• If the parent is realized and after all children have been marked, it makes some of the newly managed children viewable:
— Calls the change_managed routine of the widgets' parent.

— Calls XtRealizeWidget on each previously unmanaged child that is unrealized.

— Maps each previously unmanaged child that has *map_when_managed* True.

Managing children is independent of the ordering of children and independent of creating and deleting children. The layout routine of the parent should consider children whose *managed* field is True and should ignore all other children. Note that some composite widgets, especially fixed boxes, call XtManageChild from their insert_child procedure.

If the parent widget is realized, its change_managed procedure is called to notify it that its set of managed children has changed. The parent can reposition and resize any of its children. It moves each child as needed by calling

XtMoveWidget, which first updates the *x* and *y* fields and which then calls XMoveWindow.

If the composite widget wishes to change the size or border width of any of its children, it calls XtResizeWidget, which first updates the *width, height,* and *border_width* fields and then calls XConfigureWindow. Simultaneous repositioning and resizing may be done with XtConfigureWidget; see Section 6.6.

To add a single child to its parent widget's set of managed children, use XtManageChild.

void XtManageChild(*child*)
    Widget *child*;
child   Specifies the child. Must be of class RectObj or any subclass thereof.

The XtManageChild function constructs a WidgetList of length 1 and calls XtManageChildren.

To create and manage a child widget in a single procedure, use XtCreate-ManagedWidget or XtVaCreateManagedWidget.

Widget XtCreateManagedWidget(*name, widget_class, parent, args, num_args*)
    String *name*;
    WidgetClass *widget_class*;
    Widget *parent*;
    ArgList *args*;
    Cardinal *num_args*;
name   Specifies the resource instance name for the created widget.
widget_class   Specifies the widget class pointer for the created widget. Must be rectObjClass or any subclass thereof.
parent   Specifies the parent widget. Must be of class Composite or any subclass thereof.
args   Specifies the argument list to override any other resource specifications.
num_args   Specifies the number of entries in the argument list.

The XtCreateManagedWidget function is a convenience routine that calls XtCreateWidget and XtManageChild.

Widget XtVaCreateManagedWidget(*name, widget_class, parent, . . .*)
    String *name*;
    WidgetClass *widget_class*;
    Widget *parent*;

name	Specifies the resource instance name for the created widget.
widget_class	Specifies the widget class pointer for the created widget. Must be `rectObjClass` or any subclass thereof.
parent	Specifies the parent widget. Must be of class Composite or any subclass thereof.
. . .	Specifies the variable argument list to override any other resource specifications.

`XtVaCreateManagedWidget` is identical in function to `XtCreateManaged-Widget` with the *args* and *num_args* parameters replaced by a varargs list, as described in Section 2.4.1.

3.4.2 Unmanaging Children

To remove a list of children from their parent widget's managed set, use `XtUnmanageChildren`.

void XtUnmanageChildren (*children*, *num_children*)
    WidgetList *children*;
    Cardinal *num_children*;

children	Specifies a list of child widgets. Each child must be of class RectObj or any subclass thereof.
num_children	Specifies the number of children.

The `XtUnmanageChildren` function performs the following:

• Issues an error if the children do not all have the same parent or if the parent is not a subclass of `compositeWidgetClass`.

• Returns immediately if the common parent is being destroyed; otherwise, for each unique child on the list, `XtUnmanageChildren` performs the following:
— Ignores the child if it already is unmanaged or is being destroyed, and marks it if not.

— If the child is realized, it makes it nonvisible by unmapping it.

• Calls the change_managed routine of the widgets' parent after all children have been marked if the parent is realized.

`XtUnmanageChildren` does not destroy the child widgets. Removing widgets from a parent's managed set is often a temporary banishment, and some time later the client may manage the children again. To destroy widgets entirely, `XtDestroyWidget` should be called instead; see Section 2.8.

To remove a single child from its parent widget's managed set, use `XtUnmanageChild`.

void XtUnmanageChild(*child*)
   Widget *child*;
child   Specifies the child. Must be of class RectObj or any subclass thereof.

The `XtUnmanageChild` function constructs a widget list of length 1 and calls `XtUnmanageChildren`.

These functions are low-level routines that are used by generic composite widget building routines. In addition, composite widgets can provide widget-specific, high-level convenience procedures.

3.4.3   Determining If a Widget Is Managed

To determine the managed state of a given child widget, use `XtIsManaged`.

Boolean XtIsManaged(*w*)
   Widget *w*;
w   Specifies the widget. Must be of class Object or any subclass thereof.

The `XtIsManaged` macro (for widget programmers) or function (for application programmers) returns `True` if the specified widget is of class RectObj or any subclass thereof and is managed, or `False` otherwise.

3.5   Controlling When Widgets Get Mapped

A widget is normally mapped if it is managed. However, this behavior can be overridden by setting the XtNmappedWhenManaged resource for the widget when it is created or by setting the *map_when_managed* field to `False`.

To change the value of a given widget's *map_when_managed* field, use `XtSet-MappedWhenManaged`.

void XtSetMappedWhenManaged(*w*, *map_when_managed*)
   Widget *w*;
   Boolean *map_when_managed*;
w   Specifies the widget. Must be of class Core or any subclass thereof.
map_when_managed   Specifies a Boolean value that indicates the new value that is stored into the widget's *map_when_managed* field.

If the widget is realized and managed and if *map_when_managed* is `True`, `XtSetMappedWhenManaged` maps the window. If the widget is realized and managed and if *map_when_managed* is `False`, it unmaps the window. `XtSet-MappedWhenManaged` is a convenience function that is equivalent to (but slightly faster than) calling `XtSetValues` and setting the new value for the XtNmappedWhenManaged resource, then mapping the widget as appropriate. As an alternative to using `XtSetMappedWhenManaged` to control mapping, a client may set *mapped_when_managed* to `False` and use `XtMapWidget` and `XtUnmapWidget` explicitly.

To map a widget explicitly, use `XtMapWidget`.

XtMapWidget(*w*)
   Widget *w*;
   w   Specifies the widget. Must be of class Core or any subclass thereof.

To unmap a widget explicitly, use `XtUnmapWidget`.

XtUnmapWidget(*w*)
   Widget *w*;
   w   Specifies the widget. Must be of class Core or any subclass thereof.

3.6   Constrained Composite Widgets

The Constraint widget class is a subclass of `compositeWidgetClass`. The name is derived from the fact that constraint widgets may manage the geometry of their children based on constraints associated with each child. These constraints can be as simple as the maximum width and height the parent will allow the child to occupy or can be as complicated as how other children should change if this child is moved or resized. Constraint widgets let a parent define constraints as resources that are supplied for their children. For example, if the Constraint parent defines the maximum sizes for its children, these new size resources are retrieved for each child as if they were resources that were defined by the child widget's class. Accordingly, constraint resources may be included in the argument list or resource file just like any other resource for the child.

Constraint widgets have all the responsibilities of normal composite widgets and, in addition, must process and act upon the constraint information associated with each of their children.

To make it easy for widgets and the Intrinsics to keep track of the constraints associated with a child, every widget has a *constraints* field, which is the address of a parent-specific structure that contains constraint information about the child. If a child's parent does not belong to a subclass of constraint-WidgetClass, then the child's *constraints* field is NULL.

Subclasses of Constraint can add additional constraint data to their super-class. To allow this, widget writers should define the constraint records in their private .h file by using the same conventions as used for widget records. For example, a widget class that needs to maintain a maximum width and height for each child might define its constraint record as follows:

```
typedef struct {
        Dimension max_width, max_height;
} MaxConstraintPart;

typedef struct {
        MaxConstraintPart max;
} MaxConstraintRecord, *MaxConstraint;
```

A subclass of this widget class that also needs to maintain a minimum size would define its constraint record as follows:

```
typedef struct {
        Dimension min_width, min_height;
} MinConstraintPart;

typedef struct {
        MaxConstraintPart max;
        MinConstraintPart min;
} MaxMinConstraintRecord, *MaxMinConstraint;
```

Constraints are allocated, initialized, deallocated, and otherwise maintained insofar as possible by the Intrinsics. The Constraint class record part has several entries that facilitate this. All entries in ConstraintClassPart are fields and procedures that are defined and implemented by the parent, but they are called whenever actions are performed on the parent's children.

The XtCreateWidget function uses the *constraint_size* field in the par-ent's class record to allocate a constraint record when a child is created. XtCreateWidget also uses the constraint resources to fill in resource fields in the constraint record associated with a child. It then calls the constraint initial-ize procedure so that the parent can compute constraint fields that are derived from constraint resources and can possibly move or resize the child to conform to the given constraints.

When the XtGetValues and XtSetValues functions are executed on a child, they use the constraint resources to get the values or set the values of con-straints associated with that child. XtSetValues then calls the constraint set_values procedures so that the parent can recompute derived constraint fields and move or resize the child as appropriate. If a Constraint widget class or any of its superclasses have declared a `ConstraintClassExtension` record in the `ConstraintClassPart` *extension* fields with a record type of NULLQUARK and the *get_values_hook* field in the extension record is non-NULL, `XtGetValues` calls the get_values_hook procedure(s) to allow the parent to return derived constraint fields.

The `XtDestroyWidget` function calls the constraint destroy procedure to deallocate any dynamic storage associated with a constraint record. The constraint record itself must not be deallocated by the constraint destroy procedure; `XtDestroyWidget` does this automatically.

```

Chapter 4



Shell Widgets

```

Shell widgets hold an application's top-level widgets to allow them to communicate with the window manager. Shells have been designed to be as nearly invisible as possible. Clients have to create them, but they should never have to worry about their sizes.

If a shell widget is resized from the outside (typically by a window manager), the shell widget also resizes its managed child widget automatically. Similarly, if the shell's child widget needs to change size, it can make a geometry request to the shell, and the shell negotiates the size change with the outer environment. Clients should never attempt to change the size of their shells directly.

The four types of public shells are

OverrideShell	Used for shell windows that completely bypass the window manager (for example, pop-up menu shells).
TransientShell	Used for shell windows that have the WM_TRANSIENT_FOR property set. The effect of this property is dependent upon the window manager being used.
TopLevelShell	Used for normal top-level windows (for example, any additional top-level widgets an application needs).
ApplicationShell	Used for the single main top-level window that the window manager identifies as an application instance and that interacts with the session manager.

4.1   Shell Widget Definitions

Widgets negotiate their size and position with their parent widget, that is, the widget that directly contains them. Widgets at the top of the hierarchy do not have parent widgets. Instead, they must deal with the outside world. To provide for this, each top-level widget is encapsulated in a special widget, called a shell widget.

Shell widgets, whose class is a subclass of the Composite class, encapsulate other widgets and can allow a widget to avoid the geometry clipping imposed by the parent-child window relationship. They also can provide a layer of communication with the window manager.

The seven different types of shells are

Shell   The base class for shell widgets; provides the fields needed for all types of shells. Shell is a direct subclass of `composite-WidgetClass`.

OverrideShell   A subclass of Shell; used for shell windows that completely bypass the window manager.

WMShell   A subclass of Shell; contains fields needed by the common window manager protocol.

VendorShell   A subclass of WMShell; contains fields used by vendor-specific window managers.

TransientShell   A subclass of VendorShell; used for shell windows that desire the WM_TRANSIENT_FOR property.

TopLevelShell   A subclass of VendorShell; used for normal top-level windows.

ApplicationShell A subclass of TopLevelShell; used for an application's main top-level window.

Note that the classes Shell, WMShell, and VendorShell are internal and should not be instantiated or subclassed. Only OverrrideShell, TransientShell, TopLevelShell, and ApplicationShell are intended for public use.

4.1.1   ShellClassPart Definitions

Only the Shell class has additional class fields, which are all contained in the `ShellClassExtensionRec`. None of the other Shell classes have any additional class fields:

```
typedef struct {
    XtPointer                    extension;
} ShellClassPart, OverrideShellClassPart,
WMShellClassPart, VendorShellClassPart, TransientShellClassPart,
TopLevelShellClassPart, ApplicationShellClassPart;
```

The full Shell class record definitions are

```
typedef struct _ShellClassRec {
    CoreClassPart                core_class;
    CompositeClassPart           composite_class;
    ShellClassPart               shell_class;
} ShellClassRec;
```

```
typedef struct {
    XtPointer            next_extension;      See Section 1.6.12
    XrmQuark             record_type;         See Section 1.6.12
    long                 version;             See Section 1.6.12
    Cardinal             record_size;         See Section 1.6.12
    XtGeometryHandler    root_geometry_manager;   See below
} ShellClassExtensionRec, *ShellClassExtension;
```

```
typedef struct _OverrideShellClassRec {
    CoreClassPart                core_class;
    CompositeClassPart           composite_class;
    ShellClassPart               shell_class;
    OverrideShellClassPart       override_shell_class;
} OverrideShellClassRec;
```

```
typedef struct _WMShellClassRec {
    CoreClassPart                core_class;
    CompositeClassPart           composite_class;
    ShellClassPart               shell_class;
    WMShellClassPart             wm_shell_class;
} WMShellClassRec;
```

```
typedef struct _VendorShellClassRec {
    CoreClassPart                core_class;
    CompositeClassPart           composite_class;
    ShellClassPart               shell_class;
```

```
        WMShellClassPart              wm_shell_class;
        VendorShellClassPart          vendor_shell_class;
} VendorShellClassRec;

typedef struct _TransientShellClassRec {
        CoreClassPart                 core_class;
        CompositeClassPart            composite_class;
        ShellClassPart                shell_class;
        WMShellClassPart              wm_shell_class;
        VendorShellClassPart          vendor_shell_class;
        TransientShellClassPart       transient_shell_class;
} TransientShellClassRec;

typedef struct _TopLevelShellClassRec {
        CoreClassPart                 core_class;
        CompositeClassPart            composite_class;
        ShellClassPart                shell_class;
        WMShellClassPart              wm_shell_class;
        VendorShellClassPart          vendor_shell_class;
        TopLevelShellClassPart        top_level_shell_class;
} TopLevelShellClassRec;

typedef struct _ApplicationShellClassRec {
        CoreClassPart                 core_class;
        CompositeClassPart            composite_class;
        ShellClassPart                shell_class;
        WMShellClassPart              wm_shell_class;
        VendorShellClassPart          vendor_shell_class;
        TopLevelShellClassPart        top_level_shell_class;
        ApplicationShellClassPart     application_shell_class;
} ApplicationShellClassRec;
```

The single occurrences of the class records and pointers for creating instances of shells are

```
extern ShellClassRec shellClassRec;
extern OverrideShellClassRec overrideShellClassRec;
extern WMShellClassRec wmShellClassRec;
extern VendorShellClassRec vendorShellClassRec;
extern TransientShellClassRec transientShellClassRec;
extern TopLevelShellClassRec topLevelShellClassRec;
extern ApplicationShellClassRec applicationShellClassRec;
```

extern WidgetClass shellWidgetClass;
extern WidgetClass overrideShellWidgetClass;
extern WidgetClass wmShellWidgetClass;
extern WidgetClass vendorShellWidgetClass;
extern WidgetClass transientShellWidgetClass;
extern WidgetClass topLevelShellWidgetClass;
extern WidgetClass applicationShellWidgetClass;

The following opaque types and opaque variables are defined for generic operations on widgets whose class is a subclass of Shell.

Types	Variables
ShellWidget	shellWidgetClass
OverrideShellWidget	overrideShellWidgetClass
WMShellWidget	wmShellWidgetClass
VendorShellWidget	vendorShellWidgetClass
TransientShellWidget	transientShellWidgetClass
TopLevelShellWidget	topLevelShellWidgetClass
ApplicationShellWidget	applicationShellWidgetClass
ShellWidgetClass	
OverrideShellWidgetClass	
WMShellWidgetClass	
VendorShellWidgetClass	
TransientShellWidgetClass	
TopLevelShellWidgetClass	
ApplicationShellWidgetClass	

The declarations for all Intrinsics-defined shells except VendorShell appear in Shell.h and ShellP.h. VendorShell has separate public and private .h files which are included by Shell.h and ShellP.h. Shell.h uses incomplete structure definitions to ensure that the compiler catches attempts to access private data in any of the Shell instance or class data structures.

The symbolic constant for the ShellClassExtension version identifier is XtShellExtensionVersion (see Section 1.6.12).

The root_geometry_manager procedure acts as the parent geometry manager for geometry requests made by shell widgets. When a shell widget calls either XtMakeGeometryRequest or XtMakeResizeRequest, the root_geometry_manager procedure is invoked to negotiate the new geometry with the window manager. If the window manager permits the new geometry, the root_geometry_manager procedure should return XtGeometryYes; if the window manager denies the geometry request or it does not change the window geometry within some timeout interval (equal to *wm_timeout* in the case of WMShells), the root_geometry_manager procedure should return XtGeometryNo. If the window manager makes some alternative geometry change, the root_geometry_manager procedure may either return XtGeometryNo and handle the new geometry as a resize, or may return XtGeometryAlmost in anticipation that the shell will accept the compromise. If the compromise is not accepted, the new size must then be handled as a resize. Subclasses of Shell that wish to provide their own root_-geometry_manager procedures are strongly encouraged to use enveloping to invoke their superclass's root_geometry_manager procedure under most situations, as the window manager interaction may be very complex.

If no ShellClassPart extension record is declared with *record_type* equal to NULLQUARK, then XtInheritRootGeometryManager is assumed.

4.1.2   ShellPart Definition

The various shell widgets have the following additional instance fields defined in their widget records:

```
typedef struct {
    String                    geometry;
    XtCreatePopupChildProc    create_popup_child_proc;
    XtGrabKind                grab_kind;
    Boolean                   spring_loaded;
    Boolean                   popped_up;
    Boolean                   allow_shell_resize;
    Boolean                   client_specified;
    Boolean                   save_under;
    Boolean                   override_redirect;
    XtCallbackList            popup_callback;
    XtCallbackList            popdown_callback;
    Visual                    *visual;
} ShellPart;

typedef struct {
    int                       empty;
} OverrideShellPart;
```

```
typedef struct {
    String              title;
    int                 wm_timeout;
    Boolean             wait_for_wm;
    Boolean             transient;
    struct _OldXSizeHints {
        long                flags;
        int                 x, y;
        int                 width, height;
        int                 min_width, min_height;
        int                 max_width, max_height;
        int                 width_inc, height_inc;
        struct {
            int                 x;
            int                 y;
        } min_aspect, max_aspect;
    } size_hints;
    XWMHints            wm_hints;
    int                 base_width, base_height, win_gravity;
    Atom                title_encoding;
} WMShellPart;

typedef struct {
    int                 vendor_specific;
} VendorShellPart;

typedef struct {
    Widget              transient_for;
} TransientShellPart;

typedef struct {
    String              icon_name;
    Boolean             iconic;
    Atom                icon_name_encoding;
} TopLevelShellPart;

typedef struct {
    char                *class;
    XrmClass            xrm_class;
    int                 argc;
    char                **argv;
} ApplicationShellPart;
```

The full shell widget instance record definitions are

```
typedef struct {
    CorePart                    core;
    CompositePart               composite;
    ShellPart                   shell;
} ShellRec, *ShellWidget;

typedef struct {
    CorePart                    core;
    CompositePart               composite;
    ShellPart                   shell;
    OverrideShellPart           override;
} OverrideShellRec, *OverrideShellWidget;

typedef struct {
    CorePart                    core;
    CompositePart               composite;
    ShellPart                   shell;
    WMShellPart                 wm;
} WMShellRec, *WMShellWidget;

typedef struct {
    CorePart                    core;
    CompositePart               composite;
    ShellPart                   shell;
    WMShellPart                 wm;
    VendorShellPart             vendor;
} VendorShellRec, *VendorShellWidget;

typedef struct {
    CorePart                    core;
    CompositePart               composite;
    ShellPart                   shell;
    WMShellPart                 wm;
    VendorShellPart             vendor;
    TransientShellPart          transient;
} TransientShellRec, *TransientShellWidget;

typedef struct {
    CorePart                    core;
    CompositePart               composite;
```

```
        ShellPart                      shell;
        WMShellPart                    wm;
        VendorShellPart                vendor;
        TopLevelShellPart              topLevel;
} TopLevelShellRec, *TopLevelShellWidget;


typedef struct {
        CorePart                       core;
        CompositePart                  composite;
        ShellPart                      shell;
        WMShellPart                    wm;
        VendorShellPart                vendor;
        TopLevelShellPart              topLevel;
        ApplicationShellPart           application;
} ApplicationShellRec, *ApplicationShellWidget;
```

4.1.3   Shell Resources

The resource names, classes, and representation types specified in the shellClassRec resource list are

Name	Class	Representation
XtNallowShellResize	XtCAllowShellResize	XtRBoolean
XtNcreatePopupChildProc	XtCCreatePopupChildProc	XtRFunction
XtNgeometry	XtCGeometry	XtRString
XtNoverrideRedirect	XtCOverrideRedirect	XtRBoolean
XtNpopdownCallback	XtCCallback	XtRCallback
XtNpopupCallback	XtCCallback	XtRCallback
XtNsaveUnder	XtCSaveUnder	XtRBoolean
XtNvisual	XtCVisual	XtRVisual

OverrideShell declares no additional resources beyond those defined by Shell.

The resource names, classes, and representation types specified in the wmShellClassRec resource list are

Name	Class	Representation
XtNbaseHeight	XtCBaseHeight	XtRInt
XtNbaseWidth	XtCBaseWidth	XtRInt
XtNheightInc	XtCHeightInc	XtRInt
XtNiconMask	XtCIconMask	XtRBitmap

Name	Class	Representation
XtNiconPixmap	XtCIconPixmap	XtRBitmap
XtNiconWindow	XtCIconWindow	XtRWindow
XtNiconX	XtCIconX	XtRInt
XtNiconY	XtCIconY	XtRInt
XtNinitialState	XtCInitialState	XtRInitialState
XtNinput	XtCInput	XtRBool
XtNmaxAspectX	XtCMaxAspectX	XtRInt
XtNmaxAspectY	XtCMaxAspectY	XtRInt
XtNmaxHeight	XtCMaxHeight	XtRInt
XtNmaxWidth	XtCMaxWidth	XtRInt
XtNminAspectX	XtCMinAspectX	XtRInt
XtNminAspectY	XtCMinAspectY	XtRInt
XtNminHeight	XtCMinHeight	XtRInt
XtNminWidth	XtCMinWidth	XtRInt
XtNtitle	XtCTitle	XtRString
XtNtitleEncoding	XtCTitleEncoding	XtRAtom
XtNtransient	XtCTransient	XtRBoolean
XtNwaitForWm	XtCWaitForWm	XtRBoolean
XtNwidthInc	XtCWidthInc	XtRInt
XtNwinGravity	XtCWinGravity	XtRInt
XtNwindowGroup	XtCWindowGroup	XtRWindow
XtNwmTimeout	XtCWmTimeout	XtRInt

The class resource list for VendorShell is implementation-defined.

The resource names, classes, and representation types that are specified in the `transientShellClassRec` resource list are

Name	Class	Representation
XtNtransientFor	XtCTransientFor	XtRWidget

The resource names, classes, and representation types that are specified in the `topLevelShellClassRec` resource list are

Name	Class	Representation
XtNiconName	XtCIconName	XtRString
XtNiconNameEncoding	XtCIconNameEncoding	XtRAtom
XtNiconic	XtCIconic	XtRBoolean

The resource names, classes, and representation types that are specified in the `applicationShellClassRec` resource list are

Name	Class	Representation
XtNargc	XtCArgc	XtRInt
XtNargv	XtCArgv	XtRStringArray

4.1.4   ShellPart Default Values

The default values for fields common to all classes of public shells (filled in by the Shell resource lists and the Shell initialize procedures) are

Field	Default Value
geometry	NULL
create_popup_child_proc	NULL
grab_kind	(none)
spring_loaded	(none)
popped_up	False
allow_shell_resize	False
client_specified	(internal)
save_under	True for OverrideShell and TransientShell, False otherwise
override_redirect	True for OverrideShell, False otherwise
popup_callback	NULL
popdown_callback	NULL
visual	CopyFromParent

The *geometry* field specifies the size and position and is usually given only on a command line or in a defaults file. If the *geometry* field is non-NULL when a widget of class WMShell is realized, the geometry specification is parsed using XWMGeometry with a default geometry string constructed from the values of *x*, *y*, *width*, *height*, *width_inc*, and *height_inc*, and the size and position flags in the window manager size hints are set. If the geometry specifies an x or y position, then USPosition is set. If the geometry specifies a width or height, then USSize is set. Any fields in the geometry specification override the corresponding values in the Core *x*, *y*, *width*, and *height* fields. If *geometry* is NULL or contains only a partial specification, then the Core *x*, *y*, *width*, and *height* fields are used and PPosition and PSize are set as appropriate. The geometry string is not copied by any of the Intrinsics Shell classes; a client specifying the string in an arglist or varargs list must ensure that the value remains valid until the shell widget is realized. For further information on the geometry string, see Section 10.3 in *Xlib*.

The *create_popup_child_proc* procedure is called by the XtPopup procedure and may remain NULL. The *grab_kind, spring_loaded,* and *popped_up* fields maintain widget state information as described under XtPopup, XtMenuPopup, XtPopdown, and XtMenuPopdown. The *allow_shell_resize* field controls whether the widget contained by the child is allowed to try to resize itself. If *allow_ shell_resize* is False, any geometry requests made by the child will always return XtGeometryNo without interacting with the window manager. Setting *save_under* True instructs the server to attempt to save the contents of windows obscured by the shell when it is mapped and to restore those contents automatically when the shell is unmapped. It is useful for pop-up menus. Setting *override_redirect* True determines whether the window manager can intercede when the shell window is mapped. The pop-up and pop-down callbacks are called during XtPopup and XtPopdown. For further information on override_redirect, see Section 3.2 in *Xlib* and the *Inter-Client Communication Conventions Manual.*

The default values for Shell fields in WMShell and its subclasses are

Field	*Default Value*
title	Icon name, if specified, otherwise the application's name.
wm_timeout	Five seconds, in units of milliseconds.
wait_for_wm	True
transient	True for TransientShell, False otherwise
min_width	XtUnspecifiedShellInt
min_height	XtUnspecifiedShellInt
max_width	XtUnspecifiedShellInt
max_height	XtUnspecifiedShellInt
width_inc	XtUnspecifiedShellInt
height_inc	XtUnspecifiedShellInt
min_aspect_x	XtUnspecifiedShellInt
min_aspect_y	XtUnspecifiedShellInt
max_aspect_x	XtUnspecifiedShellInt
max_aspect_y	XtUnspecifiedShellInt
input	False

Field	Default Value
initial_state	Normal
icon_pixmap	None
icon_window	None
icon_x	XtUnspecifiedShellInt
icon_y	XtUnspecifiedShellInt
icon_mask	None
window_group	XtUnspecifiedWindow
base_width	XtUnspecifiedShellInt
base_height	XtUnspecifiedShellInt
win_gravity	XtUnspecifiedShellInt
title_encoding	XA_STRING

The *title* and *title_encoding* fields are stored in the WM_NAME property on the shell's window by the WMShell realize procedure. The *wm_timeout* field specifies, in milliseconds, the amount of time a shell is to wait for confirmation of a geometry request to the window manager. If none comes back within that time, the shell assumes the window manager is not functioning properly and sets *wait_for_wm* to False (later events may reset this value). When *wait_for_wm* is False, the shell does not wait for a response but relies on asynchronous notification. If *transient* is True, the WM_TRANSIENT_FOR property will be stored on the shell window with a value as specified below. The interpretation of this property is specific to the window manager under which the application is run; see the *Inter-Client Communication Conventions Manual* for more details. All other resources specify fields in the window manager hints and the window manager size hints. The realize and set_values procedures of WMShell set the corresponding flag bits in the hints if any of the fields contain non-default values. In addition, if a flag bit is set that refers to a field with the value XtUnspecifiedShellInt, the value of the field is modified as follows:

Field	Replacement
base_width, base_height	0
width_inc, height_inc	1
max_width, max_height	32767
min_width, min_height	1
min_aspect_x, min_aspect_y	-1

Field	Replacement
max_aspect_x, max_aspect_y	-1
icon_x, icon_y	-1
win_gravity	Value returned by XWMGeometry if called, else NorthWestGravity

If the shell widget has a non-NULL parent, then the realize and set_values procedures replace the value XtUnspecifiedWindow in the *window_group* field with the window id of the root widget of the widget tree if the root widget is realized. The symbolic constant XtUnspecifiedWindowGroup may be used to indicate that the *window_group* hint flag bit is not to be set. If *transient* is True and the shell's class is not a subclass of TransientShell and *window_group* is not XtUnspecifiedWindowGroup, the WMShell realize and set_values procedures store the WM_TRANSIENT_FOR property with the value of *window_group*.

Transient shells have the following additional resource:

Field	Default Value
transient_for	NULL

The realize and set_values procedures of TransientShell store the WM_TRANSIENT_FOR property on the shell window if *transient* is True. If *transient_for* is non-NULL and the widget specified by *transient_for* is realized, then its window is used as the value of the WM_TRANSIENT_FOR property; otherwise, the value of *window_group* is used.

TopLevel shells have the the following additional resources:

Field	Default Value
icon_name	Shell widget's name
iconic	False
icon_name_encoding	XA_STRING

The *icon_name* and *icon_name_encoding* fields are stored in the WM_ICON_NAME property on the shell's window by the TopLevelShell realize procedure. The *iconic* field may be used by a client to request that the window manager iconify or deiconify the shell; the TopLevelShell set_values procedure will send the appropriate WM_CHANGE_STATE message (as specified by the *Inter-Client Communication Conventions Manual*) if this resource is changed from `False` to `True`, and will call `XtPopup` specifying *grab_kind* as `XtGrabNone` if *iconic* is changed from `True` to `False`. The XtNiconic resource is also an alternative way to set the XtNinitialState resource to indicate that a shell should be initially displayed as an icon; the TopLevelShell initialize procedure will set *initial_state* to `IconicState` if *iconic* is `True`.

Application shells have the following additional resources:

Field	Default Value
argc	0
argv	NULL

The *argc* and *argv* fields are used to initialize the standard property WM_COMMAND. See the *Inter-Client Communication Conventions Manual* for more information.

Chapter 5

Pop-Up Widgets

Pop-up widgets are used to create windows outside of the window hierarchy defined by the widget tree. Each pop-up child has a window that is a descendant of the root window, so that the pop-up window is not clipped by the pop-up widget's parent window. Therefore, pop-ups are created and attached differently to their widget parent than normal widget children.

A parent of a pop-up widget does not actively manage its pop-up children; in fact, it usually does not operate upon them in any way. The *popup_list* field in the `CorePart` structure contains the list of its pop-up children. This pop-up list exists mainly to provide the proper place in the widget hierarchy for the pop-up to get resources and to provide a place for `XtDestroyWidget` to look for all extant children.

A composite widget can have both normal and pop-up children. A pop-up can be popped up from almost anywhere, not just by its parent. The term *child* always refers to a normal, geometry-managed widget on the composite widget's list of children, and the term *pop-up child* always refers to a widget on the pop-up list.

5.1 Pop-Up Widget Types

There are three kinds of pop-up widgets:

Modeless pop-ups   A modeless pop-up (for example, a dialog box that does not prevent continued interaction with the rest of the application) can usually be manipulated by the window

	manager and looks like any other application window from the user's point of view. The application main window itself is a special case of a modeless pop-up.
Modal pop-ups	A modal pop-up (for example, a dialog box that requires user input to continue) can sometimes be manipulated by the window manager, and except for events that occur in the dialog box, it disables user-event distribution to the rest of the application.
Spring-loaded pop-ups	A spring-loaded pop-up (for example, a menu) can seldom be manipulated by the window manager, and except for events that occur in the pop-up or its descendants, it disables user-event distribution to all other applications.

Modal pop-ups and spring-loaded pop-ups are very similar and should be coded as if they were the same. In fact, the same widget (for example, a ButtonBox or Menu widget) can be used both as a modal pop-up and as a spring-loaded pop-up within the same application. The main difference is that spring-loaded pop-ups are brought up with the pointer and, because of the grab that the pointer button causes, require different processing by the Intrinsics. Further, all user input remap events occurring outside the spring-loaded pop-up (e.g., in a descendant) are also delivered to the spring-loaded pop-up after they have been dispatched to the appropriate descendant, so that, for example, button-up can take down a spring-loaded pop-up no matter where the button-up occurs.

Any kind of pop-up, in turn, can pop up other widgets. Modal and spring-loaded pop-ups can constrain user events to the most recent such pop-up or allow user events to be dispatched to any of the modal or spring-loaded pop-ups currently mapped.

Regardless of their type, all pop-up widget classes are responsible for communicating with the X window manager and therefore are subclasses of one of the Shell widget classes.

5.2   Creating a Pop-Up Shell

For a widget to be popped up, it must be the child of a pop-up shell widget. None of the Intrinsics-supplied shells will simultaneously manage more than one child. Both the shell and child taken together are referred to as the pop-up. When you need to use a pop-up, you always refer to the pop-up by the pop-up shell, not the child.

To create a pop-up shell, use `XtCreatePopupShell`.

Widget XtCreatePopupShell(*name, widget_class, parent, args, num_args*)
    String *name*;
    WidgetClass *widget_class*;
    Widget *parent*;
    ArgList *args*;
    Cardinal *num_args*;

name	Specifies the text name for the created shell widget.
widget_class	Specifies the widget class pointer for the created shell widget.
parent	Specifies the parent widget. Must be of class Core or any subclass thereof.
args	Specifies the argument list to override any other resource specifications.
num_args	Specifies the number of entries in the argument list.

The `XtCreatePopupShell` function ensures that the specified class is a sub-class of Shell and, rather than using insert_child to attach the widget to the parent's *children* list, attaches the shell to the parent's *popup_list* directly.

A spring-loaded pop-up invoked from a translation table via `XtMenuPopup` must already exist at the time that the translation is invoked, so the translation manager can find the shell by name. Pop-ups invoked in other ways can be created when the pop-up actually is needed. This delayed creation of the shell is particularly useful when you pop up an unspecified number of pop-ups. You can look to see if an appropriate unused shell (that is, not currently popped up) exists and create a new shell if needed.

To create a pop-up shell using varargs lists, use `XtVaCreatePopupShell`.

Widget XtVaCreatePopupShell(*name, widget_class, parent, . . .*)
    String *name*;
    WidgetClass *widget_class*;
    Widget *parent*;

name	Specifies the text name for the created shell widget.
widget_class	Specifies the widget class pointer for the created shell widget.
parent	Specifies the parent widget. Must be of class Core or any subclass thereof.
. . .	Specifies the variable argument list to override any other resource specifications.

XtVaCreatePopupShell is identical in function to XtCreatePopupShell with the *args* and *num_args* parameters replaced by a varargs list, as described in Section 2.4.1.

5.3   Creating Pop-Up Children

Once a pop-up shell is created, the single child of the pop-up shell can be created either statically or dynamically.

At startup, an application can create the child of the pop-up shell, which is appropriate for pop-up children composed of a fixed set of widgets. The application can change the state of the subparts of the pop-up child as the application state changes. For example, if an application creates a static menu, it can call XtSetSensitive (or, in general, XtSetValues) on any of the buttons that make up the menu. Creating the pop-up child early means that pop-up time is minimized, especially if the application calls XtRealizeWidget on the pop-up shell at startup. When the menu is needed, all the widgets that make up the menu already exist and need only be mapped. The menu should pop up as quickly as the X server can respond.

Alternatively, an application can postpone the creation of the child until it is needed, which minimizes application startup time and allows the pop-up child to reconfigure itself each time it is popped up. In this case, the pop-up child creation routine might poll the application to find out if it should change the sensitivity of any of its subparts.

Pop-up child creation does not map the pop-up, even if you create the child and call XtRealizeWidget on the pop-up shell.

All shells have pop-up and pop-down callbacks, which provide the opportunity either to make last-minute changes to a pop-up child before it is popped up or to change it after it is popped down. Note that excessive use of pop-up callbacks can make popping up occur more slowly.

5.4   Mapping a Pop-Up Widget

Pop-ups can be popped up through several mechanisms:

• A call to XtPopup or XtPopupSpringLoaded.

• One of the supplied callback procedures XtCallbackNone, XtCallbackNonexclusive, or XtCallbackExclusive.

• The standard translation action XtMenuPopup.

Some of these routines take an argument of type `XtGrabKind`, which is defined as

typedef enum {XtGrabNone, XtGrabNonexclusive, XtGrabExclusive} XtGrabKind;

The create_popup_child_proc procedure pointer in the shell widget instance record is of type `XtCreatePopupChildProc`.

typedef void (*XtCreatePopupChildProc) (Widget);
    Widget *w*;
w   Specifies the shell widget being popped up.

To map a pop-up from within an application, use `XtPopup`.

void XtPopup(*popup_shell, grab_kind*)
    Widget *popup_shell*;
    XtGrabKind *grab_kind*;
popup_shell   Specifies the shell widget.
grab_kind   Specifies the way in which user events should be constrained.

The `XtPopup` function performs the following:

- Calls `XtCheckSubclass` to ensure *popup_shell*'s class is a subclass of `shellWidgetClass`.

- Raises the window and returns if the shell's *popped_up* field is already `True`.

- Calls the callback procedures on the shell's *popup_callback* list.

- Sets the shell *popped_up* field to `True`, the shell *spring_loaded* field to `False`, and the shell *grab_kind* field from *grab_kind*.

- If the shell's *create_popup_child_proc* field is non-NULL, `XtPopup` calls it with *popup_shell* as the parameter.

- If *grab_kind* is either `XtGrabNonexclusive` or `XtGrabExclusive`, it calls
    XtAddGrab(*popup_shell*, (*grab_kind* == XtGrabExclusive), False)

- Calls `XtRealizeWidget` with *popup_shell* specified.

- Calls `XMapRaised` with the window of *popup_shell*.

To map a spring-loaded pop-up from within an application, use `XtPopup-SpringLoaded`.

void XtPopupSpringLoaded(*popup_shell*)
    Widget *popup_shell*;
popup_shell   Specifies the shell widget to be popped up.

The XtPopupSpringLoaded function performs exactly as XtPopup except that it sets the shell *spring_loaded* field to True and always calls XtAddGrab with *exclusive* True and *spring-loaded* True.

To map a pop-up from a given widget's callback list, you also can register one of the XtCallbackNone, XtCallbackNonexclusive, or XtCallback-Exclusive convenience routines as callbacks, using the pop-up shell widget as the client data.

void XtCallbackNone(*w, client_data, call_data*)
    Widget *w*;
    XtPointer *client_data*;
    XtPointer *call_data*;
w   Specifies the widget.
client_data   Specifies the pop-up shell.
call_data   Specifies the callback data argument, which is not used by this procedure.

void XtCallbackNonexclusive(*w, client_data, call_data*)
    Widget *w*;
    XtPointer *client_data*;
    XtPointer *call_data*;
w   Specifies the widget.
client_data   Specifies the pop-up shell.
call_data   Specifies the callback data argument, which is not used by this procedure.

void XtCallbackExclusive(*w, client_data, call_data*)
    Widget *w*;
    XtPointer *client_data*;
    XtPointer *call_data*;
w   Specifies the widget.
client_data   Specifies the pop-up shell.
call_data   Specifies the callback data argument, which is not used by this procedure.

The XtCallbackNone, XtCallbackNonexclusive, and XtCallback-Exclusive functions call XtPopup with the shell specified by the *client_data* argument and *grab_kind* set as the name specifies. XtCallbackNone, XtCallbackNonexclusive, and XtCallbackExclusive specify XtGrab-None, XtGrabNonexclusive, and XtGrabExclusive, respectively. Each function then sets the widget that executed the callback list to be insensitive by calling XtSetSensitive. Using these functions in callbacks is not required. In particular, an application must provide customized code for callbacks that create pop-up shells dynamically or that must do more than desensitizing the button.

Within a translation table, to pop up a menu when a key or pointer button is pressed or when the pointer is moved into a widget, use XtMenuPopup, or its synonym, MenuPopup. From a translation writer's point of view, the definition for this translation action is

```
void XtMenuPopup(shell_name)
    String shell_name;
    shell_name        Specifies the name of the widget shell to pop up.
```

XtMenuPopup is known to the translation manager, which registers the corresponding built-in action procedure XtMenuPopupAction using XtRegisterGrabAction specifying *owner_events* True, *event_mask* Button-PressMask | ButtonReleaseMask, and *pointer_mode* and *keyboard_mode* GrabModeAsync.

If XtMenuPopup is invoked on ButtonPress, it calls XtPopupSpring-Loaded on the specified shell widget. If XtMenuPopup is invoked on Key-Press or EnterWindow, it calls XtPopup on the specified shell widget with *grab_kind* set to XtGrabNonexclusive. Otherwise, the translation manager generates a warning message and ignores the action.

XtMenuPopup tries to find the shell by searching the widget tree starting at the widget in which it is invoked. If it finds a shell with the specified name in the pop-up children of that widget, it pops up the shell with the appropriate parameters. Otherwise, it moves up the parent chain to find a pop-up child with the specified name. If XtMenuPopup gets to the application top-level shell widget and has not found a matching shell, it generates a warning and returns immediately.

5.5   Unmapping a Pop-Up Widget

Pop-ups can be popped down through several mechanisms:

- A call to XtPopdown.
- The supplied callback procedure XtCallbackPcpdown.
- The standard translation action XtMenuPopdown.

To unmap a pop-up from within an application, use XtPopdown.

void XtPopdown(*popup_shell*)
    Widget *popup_shell*;
popup_shell   Specifies the shell widget to pop down.

The XtPopdown function performs the following:

- Calls XtCheckSubclass to ensure *popup_shell*'s class is a subclass of shellWidgetClass.
- Checks that the *popped_up* field of *popup_shell* is True; otherwise, it returns immediately.
- Unmaps *popup_shell*'s window and, if *override_redirect* is False, sends a synthetic UnmapNotify event as specified by the *Inter-Client Communication Conventions Manual.*
- If *popup_shell*'s *grab_kind* is either XtGrabNonexclusive or XtGrabExclusive, it calls XtRemoveGrab.
- Sets *popup_shell*'s *popped_up* field to False.
- Calls the callback procedures on the shell's *popdown_callback* list.

To pop down a pop-up from a callback list, you may use the callback XtCallbackPopdown.

void XtCallbackPopdown(*w, client_data, call_data*)
    Widget *w*;
    XtPointer *client_data*;
    XtPointer *call_data*;
w   Specifies the widget.
client_data   Specifies a pointer to the XtPopdownID structure.
call_data   Specifies the callback data argument, which is not used by this
                   procedure.

The XtCallbackPopdown function casts the *client_data* parameter to a pointer of type XtPopdownID.

```
typedef struct {
    Widget      shell_widget;
    Widget      enable_widget;
} XtPopdownIDRec, *XtPopdownID;
```

The *shell_widget* is the pop-up shell to pop down, and the *enable_widget* is usually the widget that was used to pop it up in one of the pop-up callback convenience procedures.

XtCallbackPopdown calls XtPopdown with the specified *shell_widget* and then calls XtSetSensitive to resensitize *enable_widget*.

Within a translation table, to pop down a spring-loaded menu when a key or pointer button is released or when the pointer is moved into a widget, use XtMenuPopdown or its synonym, MenuPopdown. From a translation writer's point of view, the definition for this translation action is

```
void XtMenuPopdown(shell_name)
    String shell_name;
    shell_name      Specifies the name of the widget shell to pop down.
```

If a shell name is not given, XtMenuPopdown calls XtPopdown with the widget for which the translation is specified. If *shell_name* is specified in the translation table, XtMenuPopdown tries to find the shell by looking up the widget tree starting at the widget in which it is invoked. If it finds a shell with the specified name in the pop-up children of that widget, it pops down the shell; otherwise, it moves up the parent chain to find a pop-up child with the specified name. If XtMenuPopdown gets to the application top-level shell widget and cannot find a matching shell, it generates a warning and returns immediately.

Chapter 6

Geometry Management

A widget does not directly control its size and location; rather, its parent is responsible for controlling them. Although the position of children is usually left up to their parent, the widgets themselves often have the best idea of their optimal sizes and, possibly, preferred locations.

To resolve physical layout conflicts between sibling widgets and between a widget and its parent, the Intrinsics provide the geometry management mechanism. Almost all composite widgets have a geometry manager specified in the *geometry_manager* field in the widget class record that is responsible for the size, position, and stacking order of the widget's children. The only exception is fixed boxes, which create their children themselves and can ensure that their children will never make a geometry request.

6.1   Initiating Geometry Changes

Parents, children, and clients each initiate geometry changes differently. Because a parent has absolute control of its children's geometry, it changes the geometry directly by calling XtMoveWidget, XtResizeWidget, or XtConfigureWidget. A child must ask its parent for a geometry change by calling XtMakeGeometryRequest or XtMakeResizeRequest. An application or other client code initiates a geometry change by calling XtSetValues on the appropriate geometry fields, thereby giving the widget the opportunity to modify or reject the client request before it gets propagated to the parent and the opportunity to respond appropriately to the parent's reply.

When a widget that needs to change its size, position, border width, or stacking depth asks its parent's geometry manager to make the desired changes, the geometry manager can allow the request, disallow the request, or suggest a compromise. When the geometry manager is asked to change the geometry of a child, the geometry manager may also rearrange and resize any or all of the other children that it controls. The geometry manager can move children around freely using `XtMoveWidget`. When it resizes a child (that is, changes the width, height, or border width) other than the one making the request, it should do so by calling `XtResizeWidget`. It can simultaneously move and resize a child with a single call to `XtConfigureWidget`.

Often, geometry managers find that they can satisfy a request only if they can reconfigure a widget that they are not in control of; in particular, the composite widget may want to change its own size. In this case, the geometry manager makes a request to its parent's geometry manager. Geometry requests can cascade this way to arbitrary depth.

Because such cascaded arbitration of widget geometry can involve extended negotiation, windows are not actually allocated to widgets at application startup until all widgets are satisfied with their geometry; see Sections 2.4 and 2.5.

Notes
1. The Intrinsics treatment of stacking requests is deficient in several areas. Stacking requests for unrealized widgets are granted but will have no effect. In addition, there is no way to do an `XtSetValues` that will generate a stacking geometry request.
2. After a successful geometry request (one that returned `XtGeometryYes`), a widget does not know whether its resize procedure has been called. Widgets should have resize procedures that can be called more than once without ill effects.

6.2   General Geometry Manager Requests

When making a geometry request, the child specifies an `XtWidgetGeometry` structure.

```
typedef unsigned long XtGeometryMask;

typedef struct {
    XtGeometryMask        request_mode;
```

Position	x, y;
Dimension	width, height;
Dimension	border_width;
Widget	sibling;
int	stack_mode;

} XtWidgetGeometry;

To make a general geometry manager request from a widget, use `XtMake-GeometryRequest`.

XtGeometryResult XtMakeGeometryRequest(*w, request, reply_return*)
    Widget *w*;
    XtWidgetGeometry **request*;
    XtWidgetGeometry **reply_return*;

w	Specifies the widget that is making the request. Must be of class RectObj or any subclass thereof.
request	Specifies the desired widget geometry (size, position, border width, and stacking order).
reply_return	Returns the allowed widget size, or may be NULL if the requesting widget is not interested in handling `XtGeometryAlmost`.

Depending on the condition, `XtMakeGeometryRequest` performs the following:

- If the widget is unmanaged or the widget's parent is not realized, it makes the changes and returns `XtGeometryYes`.

- If the parent's class is not a subclass of `compositeWidgetClass` or the parent's *geometry_manager* is NULL, it issues an error.

- If the widget's *being_destroyed* field is `True`, it returns `XtGeometryNo`.

- If the widget *x*, *y*, *width*, *height*, and *border_width* fields are all equal to the requested values, it returns `XtGeometryYes`; otherwise, it calls the parent's geometry_manager procedure with the given parameters.

- If the parent's geometry manager returns `XtGeometryYes` and if `XtCWQueryOnly` is not set in *request –>request_mode* and if the widget is realized, `XtMakeGeometryRequest` calls the `XConfigureWindow` Xlib function to reconfigure the widget's window (set its size, location, and stacking order as appropriate).

- If the geometry manager returns `XtGeometryDone`, the change has been approved and actually has been done. In this case, `XtMakeGeometryRequest` does no configuring and returns `XtGeometryYes`. `XtMakeGeometryRequest` never returns `XtGeometryDone`.

- Otherwise, `XtMakeGeometryRequest` just returns the resulting value from the parent's geometry manager.

Children of primitive widgets are always unmanaged; therefore, `XtMake-GeometryRequest` always returns `XtGeometryYes` when called by a child of a primitive widget.

The return codes from geometry managers are

```
typedef enum _XtGeometryResult {
    XtGeometryYes,
    XtGeometryNo,
    XtGeometryAlmost,
    XtGeometryDone
} XtGeometryResult;
```

The *request_mode* definitions are from `<X11/X.h>`.

```
#define    CWX             (1<<0)
#define    CWY             (1<<1)
#define    CWWidth         (1<<2)
#define    CWHeight        (1<<3)
#define    CWBorderWidth   (1<<4)
#define    CWSibling       (1<<5)
#define    CWStackMode     (1<<6)
```

The Intrinsics also support the following value.

```
#define    XtCWQueryOnly   (1<<7)
```

`XtCWQueryOnly` indicates that the corresponding geometry request is only a query as to what would happen if this geometry request were made and that no widgets should actually be changed.

`XtMakeGeometryRequest`, like the `XConfigureWindow` Xlib function, uses *request_mode* to determine which fields in the `XtWidgetGeometry` structure the caller wants to specify.

The *stack_mode* definitions are from `<X11/X.h>`.

```
#define    Above       0
#define    Below       1
#define    TopIf       2
#define    BottomIf    3
#define    Opposite    4
```

The Intrinsics also support the following value.

```
#define    XtSMDontChange    5
```

For the definition and behavior of Above, Below, TopIf, BottomIf, and Opposite, see Section 3.7 in *Xlib*. XtSMDontChange indicates that the widget wants its current stacking order preserved.

6.3   Resize Requests

To make a simple resize request from a widget, you can use XtMakeResize-Request as an alternative to XtMakeGeometryRequest.

XtGeometryResult XtMakeResizeRequest(*w, width, height, width_return, height_return*)
    Widget *w*;
    Dimension *width, height*;
    Dimension **width_return, *height_return*;

w	Specifies the widget that is making the request. Must be of class RectObj or any subclass thereof.
width *height*	Specify the desired widget width and height.
width_return *height_return*	Return the allowed widget width and height.

The XtMakeResizeRequest function, a simple interface to XtMake-GeometryRequest, creates an XtWidgetGeometry structure and specifies that width and height should change by setting *request_mode* to CWWidth|CWHeight. The geometry manager is free to modify any of the other window attributes (position or stacking order) to satisfy the resize request. If the return value is XtGeometryAlmost, *width_return* and *height_return* contain a compromise width and height. If these are acceptable, the widget should immediately call XtMakeResizeRequest again and request that the compromise width and height be applied. If the widget is not interested in XtGeometryAlmost replies, it can pass NULL for *width_return* and *height_return*.

6.4   Potential Geometry Changes

Sometimes a geometry manager cannot respond to a geometry request from a child without first making a geometry request to the widget's own parent (the original requestor's grandparent). If the request to the grandparent would allow the parent to satisfy the original request, the geometry manager can make the intermediate geometry request as if it were the originator. On the other hand, if the geometry manager already has determined that the original request cannot be completely satisfied (for example, if it always denies position changes), it needs to tell the grandparent to respond to the intermediate request without actually changing the geometry because it does not know if the child will accept the compromise. To accomplish this, the geometry manager uses `XtCWQueryOnly` in the intermediate request.

When `XtCWQueryOnly` is used, the geometry manager needs to cache enough information to exactly reconstruct the intermediate request. If the grandparent's response to the intermediate query was `XtGeometryAlmost`, the geometry manager needs to cache the entire reply geometry in the event the child accepts the parent's compromise.

If the grandparent's response was `XtGeometryAlmost`, it may also be necessary to cache the entire reply geometry from the grandparent when `XtCWQueryOnly` is not used. If the geometry manager is still able to satisfy the original request, it may immediately accept the grandparent's compromise and then act on the child's request. If the grandparent's compromise geometry is insufficient to allow the child's request and if the geometry manager is willing to offer a different compromise to the child, the grandparent's compromise should not be accepted until the child has accepted the new compromise.

Note that a compromise geometry returned with `XtGeometryAlmost` is guaranteed only for the next call to the same widget; therefore, a cache of size 1 is sufficient.

6.5 Child Geometry Management: the geometry_manager Procedure

The geometry_manager procedure pointer in a composite widget class is of type `XtGeometryHandler`.

```
typedef XtGeometryResult (*XtGeometryHandler) (Widget, XtWidgetGeometry*,
                                               XtWidgetGeometry*);
    Widget w;
    XtWidgetGeometry *request;
    XtWidgetGeometry *geometry_return;
```

w	Passes the widget that is making the request.
request	Passes the new geometry the child desires.
geometry_return	Passes a geometry structure in which the geometry manager may store a compromise.

A class can inherit its superclass's geometry manager during class initialization.

A bit set to zero in the request's *request_mode* field means that the child widget does not care about the value of the corresponding field, so the geometry manager can change this field as it wishes. A bit set to 1 means that the child wants that geometry element changed to the value in the corresponding field.

If the geometry manager can satisfy all changes requested and if XtCWQueryOnly is not specified, it updates the widget's *x, y, width, height,* and *border_width* fields appropriately. Then, it returns XtGeometryYes, and the values pointed to by the *geometry_return* argument are undefined. The widget's window is moved and resized automatically by XtMakeGeometryRequest.

Homogeneous composite widgets often find it convenient to treat the widget making the request the same as any other widget, possibly reconfiguring it as part of its layout process, unless XtCWQueryOnly is specified. If it does this, it should return XtGeometryDone to inform XtMakeGeometryRequest that it does not need to do the configuration itself.

Note   To remain compatible with layout techniques used in older widgets (before XtGeometryDone was added to the Intrinsics), a geometry manager should avoid using XtResizeWidget or XtConfigureWidget on the child making the request because the layout process of the child may be in an intermediate state in which it is not prepared to handle a call to its resize procedure. A self-contained widget set may choose this alternative geometry management scheme, however, provided that it clearly warns widget developers of the compatibility consequences.

Although XtMakeGeometryRequest resizes the widget's window (if the geometry manager returns XtGeometryYes), it does not call the widget class's resize procedure. The requesting widget must perform whatever resizing calculations are needed explicitly.

If the geometry manager disallows the request, the widget cannot change its geometry. The values pointed to by *geometry_return* are undefined, and the geometry manager returns XtGeometryNo.

Sometimes the geometry manager cannot satisfy the request exactly but may be able to satisfy a similar request. That is, it could satisfy only a subset of the requests (for example, size but not position) or a lesser request (for example, it cannot make the child as big as the request but it can make the child bigger than its current size). In such cases, the geometry manager fills in the structure pointed to by *geometry_return* with the actual changes it is willing to make, including an appropriate *request_mode* mask, and returns XtGeometryAlmost. If a bit in *geometry_return –>request_mode* is zero, the geometry manager agrees not to change the corresponding value if *geometry_return* is used immediately in a new request. If a bit is 1, the geometry manager does change that element to the corresponding value in *geometry_return.* More bits may be set in *geometry_return –>request_mode* than in the original request if the geometry manager intends to change other fields should the child accept the compromise.

When XtGeometryAlmost is returned, the widget must decide if the compromise suggested in *geometry_return* is acceptable. If it is, the widget must not change its geometry directly; rather, it must make another call to XtMake-GeometryRequest.

If the next geometry request from this child uses the *geometry_return* values filled in by the geometry manager with an XtGeometryAlmost return and if there have been no intervening geometry requests on either its parent or any of its other children, the geometry manager must grant the request, if possible. That is, if the child asks immediately with the returned geometry, it should get an answer of XtGeometryYes. However, dynamic behavior in the user's window manager may affect the final outcome.

To return XtGeometryYes, the geometry manager frequently rearranges the position of other managed children by calling XtMoveWidget. However, a few geometry managers may sometimes change the size of other managed children by calling XtResizeWidget or XtConfigureWidget. If XtCWQueryOnly is specified, the geometry manager must return data describing how it would react to this geometry request without actually moving or resizing any widgets.

Geometry managers must not assume that the *request* and *geometry_return* arguments point to independent storage. The caller is permitted to use the same field for both, and the geometry manager must allocate its own temporary storage, if necessary.

6.6   Widget Placement and Sizing

To move a sibling widget of the child making the geometry request, the parent uses XtMoveWidget.

void XtMoveWidget(*w, x, y*)
    Widget *w*;
    Position *x*;
    Position *y*;
w   Specifies the widget. Must be of class RectObj or any subclass thereof.
x, y   Specify the new widget x and y coordinates.

The `XtMoveWidget` function returns immediately if the specified geometry fields are the same as the old values. Otherwise, `XtMoveWidget` writes the new *x* and *y* values into the object and, if the object is a widget and is realized, issues an Xlib `XMoveWindow` call on the widget's window.

To resize a sibling widget of the child making the geometry request, the parent uses `XtResizeWidget`.

void XtResizeWidget(*w, width, height, border_width*)
    Widget *w*;
    Dimension *width*;
    Dimension *height*;
    Dimension *border_width*;
w   Specifies the widget. Must be of class RectObj or any subclass thereof.
width   Specify the new widget size.
height
border_width

The `XtResizeWidget` function returns immediately if the specified geometry fields are the same as the old values. Otherwise, `XtResizeWidget` writes the new *width, height,* and *border_width* values into the object and, if the object is a widget and is realized, issues an `XConfigureWindow` call on the widget's window.

If the new width or height is different from the old values, `XtResizeWidget` calls the object's resize procedure to notify it of the size change.

To move and resize the sibling widget of the child making the geometry request, the parent uses `XtConfigureWidget`.

void XtConfigureWidget(*w, x, y, width, height, border_width*)
    Widget *w*;
    Position *x*;
    Position *y*;

Dimension *width*;
Dimension *height*;
Dimension *border_width*;

w	Specifies the widget. Must be of class RectObj or any subclass thereof.
x, y	Specify the new widget x and y coordinates.
width	Specify the new widget size.
height	
border_width	

The `XtConfigureWidget` function returns immediately if the specified new geometry fields are all equal to the current values. Otherwise, `XtConfigureWidget` writes the new *x, y, width, height,* and *border_width* values into the object and, if the object is a widget and is realized, makes an Xlib `XConfigureWindow` call on the widget's window.

If the new width or height is different from its old value, `XtConfigureWidget` calls the object's resize procedure to notify it of the size change; otherwise, it simply returns.

To resize a child widget that already has the new values of its width, height, and border width, the parent uses `XtResizeWindow`.

void XtResizeWindow(*w*)
  Widget *w*;

w	Specifies the widget. Must be of class Core or any subclass thereof.

The `XtResizeWindow` function calls the `XConfigureWindow` Xlib function to make the window of the specified widget match its width, height, and border width. This request is done unconditionally because there is no inexpensive way to tell if these values match the current values. Note that the widget's resize procedure is not called.

There are very few times to use `XtResizeWindow`; instead, the parent should use `XtResizeWidget`.

6.7 Preferred Geometry

Some parents may be willing to adjust their layouts to accommodate the preferred geometries of their children. They can use `XtQueryGeometry` to obtain the preferred geometry and, as they see fit, can use or ignore any portion of the response.

To query a child widget's preferred geometry, use `XtQueryGeometry`.

XtGeometryResult XtQueryGeometry(*w, intended, preferred_return*)
   Widget *w*;
   XtWidgetGeometry **intended, *preferred_return*;

w	Specifies the widget. Must be of class RectObj or any subclass thereof.
intended	Specifies the new geometry the parent plans to give to the child, or NULL.
preferred_return	Returns the child widget's preferred geometry.

To discover a child's preferred geometry, the child's parent stores the new geometry in the corresponding fields of the intended structure, sets the corresponding bits in *intended –>request_mode*, and calls `XtQueryGeometry`. The parent should set only those fields that are important to it so that the child can determine whether it may be able to attempt changes to other fields.

   `XtQueryGeometry` clears all bits in the *preferred_return –>request_mode* field and checks the *query_geometry* field of the specified widget's class record. If *query_geometry* is not NULL, `XtQueryGeometry` calls the query_geometry procedure and passes as arguments the specified widget, *intended*, and *preferred_return* structures. If the *intended* argument is NULL, `XtQuery-Geometry` replaces it with a pointer to an `XtWidgetGeometry` structure with *request_mode* equal to zero before calling the query_geometry procedure.

Note   If `XtQueryGeometry` is called from within a geometry_manager procedure for the widget that issued `XtMakeGeometryRequest` or `XtMakeResize-Request`, the results are not guaranteed to be consistent with the requested changes. The change request passed to the geometry manager takes precedence over the preferred geometry.

   The query_geometry procedure pointer is of type `XtGeometryHandler`.

typedef XtGeometryResult (*XtGeometryHandler) (Widget, XtWidgetGeometry*,
                                                     XtWidgetGeometry*);

   Widget *w*;
   XtWidgetGeometry **request*;
   XtWidgetGeometry **preferred_return*;

w	Passes the child widget whose preferred geometry is required.
request	Passes the geometry changes which the parent plans to make.
preferred_return	Passes a structure in which the child returns its preferred geometry.

The query_geometry procedure is expected to examine the bits set in *request ->* *request_mode*, evaluate the preferred geometry of the widget, and store the result in *preferred_return* (setting the bits in *preferred_return ->request_mode* corresponding to those geometry fields that it cares about). If the proposed geometry change is acceptable without modification, the query_geometry procedure should return XtGeometryYes. If at least one field in *preferred_return* with a bit set in *preferred_return ->request_mode* is different from the corresponding field in *request* or if a bit was set in *preferred_return ->request_mode* that was not set in the request, the query_geometry procedure should return XtGeometryAlmost. If the preferred geometry is identical to the current geometry, the query_geometry procedure should return XtGeometryNo.

Note   The query_geometry procedure may assume that no XtMakeResizeRequest or XtMakeGeometryRequest is in progress for the specified widget; that is, it is not required to construct a reply consistent with the requested geometry if such a request were actually outstanding.

After calling the query_geometry procedure or if the *query_geometry* field is NULL, XtQueryGeometry examines all the unset bits in *preferred_return ->* *request_mode* and sets the corresponding fields in *preferred_return* to the current values from the widget instance. If CWStackMode is not set, the *stack_mode* field is set to XtSMDontChange. XtQueryGeometry returns the value returned by the query_geometry procedure or XtGeometryYes if the *query_geometry* field is NULL.

Therefore, the caller can interpret a return of XtGeometryYes as not needing to evaluate the contents of the reply and, more important, not needing to modify its layout plans. A return of XtGeometryAlmost means either that both the parent and the child expressed interest in at least one common field and the child's preference does not match the parent's intentions or that the child expressed interest in a field that the parent might need to consider. A return value of XtGeometryNo means that both the parent and the child expressed interest in a field and that the child suggests that the field's current value in the widget instance is its preferred value. In addition, whether or not the caller ignores the return value or the reply mask, it is guaranteed that the *preferred_return* structure contains complete geometry information for the child.

Parents are expected to call `XtQueryGeometry` in their layout routine and wherever else the information is significant after change_managed has been called. The changed_managed procedure may assume that the child's current geometry is its preferred geometry. Thus, the child is still responsible for storing values into its own geometry during its initialize procedure.

6.8   Size Change Management: the resize Procedure

A child can be resized by its parent at any time. Widgets usually need to know when they have changed size so that they can lay out their displayed data again to match the new size. When a parent resizes a child, it calls `XtResizeWidget`, which updates the geometry fields in the widget, configures the window if the widget is realized, and calls the child's resize procedure to notify the child. The resize procedure pointer is of type `XtWidget-Proc`.

If a class need not recalculate anything when a widget is resized, it can specify NULL for the *resize* field in its class record. This is an unusual case and should occur only for widgets with very trivial display semantics. The resize procedure takes a widget as its only argument. The *x, y, width, height*, and *border_width* fields of the widget contain the new values. The resize procedure should recalculate the layout of internal data as needed. (For example, a centered Label in a window that changes size should recalculate the starting position of the text.) The widget must obey resize as a command and must not treat it as a request. A widget must not issue an `XtMakeGeometryRequest` or `XtMakeResize-Request` call from its resize procedure.

Chapter 7

Event Management

While Xlib allows the reading and processing of events anywhere in an application, widgets in the X Toolkit neither directly read events nor grab the server or pointer. Widgets register procedures that are to be called when an event or class of events occurs in that widget.

A typical application consists of startup code followed by an event loop that reads events and dispatches them by calling the procedures that widgets have registered. The default event loop provided by the Intrinsics is `XtAppMainLoop`.

The event manager is a collection of functions to perform the following tasks:

- Add or remove event sources other than X server events (in particular, timer interrupts and file input).
- Query the status of event sources.
- Add or remove procedures to be called when an event occurs for a particular widget.
- Enable and disable the dispatching of user-initiated events (keyboard and pointer events) for a particular widget.
- Constrain the dispatching of events to a cascade of pop-up widgets.
- Register procedures to be called when specific events arrive.

Most widgets do not need to call any of the event handler functions explicitly. The normal interface to X events is through the higher-level translation manager, which maps sequences of X events, with modifiers, into procedure calls. Applications rarely use any of the event manager routines besides `XtAppMainLoop`.

7.1   Adding and Deleting Additional Event Sources

While most applications are driven only by X events, some applications need to incorporate other sources of input into the X Toolkit event-handling mechanism. The event manager provides routines to integrate notification of timer events and file data pending into this mechanism.

The next section describes functions that provide input gathering from files. The application registers the files with the Intrinsics read routine. When input is pending on one of the files, the registered callback procedures are invoked.

7.1.1   Adding and Removing Input Sources

To register a new file as an input source for a given application context, use XtAppAddInput.

XtInputId XtAppAddInput(*app_context, source, condition, proc, client_data*)
    XtAppContext *app_context*;
    int *source*;
    XtPointer *condition*;
    XtInputCallbackProc *proc*;
    XtPointer *client_data*;

app_context	Specifies the application context that identifies the application.
source	Specifies the source file descriptor on a POSIX-based system or other operating-system-dependent device specification.
condition	Specifies the mask that indicates a read, write, or exception condition or some other operating-system-dependent condition.
proc	Specifies the procedure to be called when the condition is found.
client_data	Specifies an argument passed to the specified procedure when it is called.

The XtAppAddInput function registers with the Intrinsics read routine a new source of events, which is usually file input but can also be file output. Note that *file* should be loosely interpreted to mean any sink or source of data. XtAppAddInput also specifies the conditions under which the source can generate events. When an event is pending on this source, the callback procedure is called.

The legal values for the *condition* argument are operating-system-dependent. On a POSIX-based system, *source* is a file number and the condition is some union of the following:

XtInputReadMask — Specifies that *proc* is to be called when *source* has data to be read.

XtInputWriteMask — Specifies that *proc* is to be called when *source* is ready for writing.

XtInputExceptMask — Specifies that *proc* is to be called when *source* has exception data.

Callback procedure pointers used to handle file events are of type XtInput-CallbackProc.

```
typedef void (*XtInputCallbackProc)(XtPointer, int*, XtInputId*);
    XtPointer client_data;
    int *source;
    XtInputId *id;
```
client_data — Passes the client data argument that was registered for this procedure in XtAppAddInput.

source — Passes the source file descriptor generating the event.

id — Passes the id returned from the corresponding XtAppAddInput call.

To discontinue a source of input, use XtRemoveInput.

```
void XtRemoveInput(id)
    XtInputId id;
```
id — Specifies the id returned from the corresponding XtAppAddInput call.

The XtRemoveInput function causes the Intrinsics read routine to stop watching for events from the file source specified by *id*.

7.1.2 Adding and Removing Timeouts

The timeout facility notifies the application or the widget through a callback procedure that a specified time interval has elapsed. Timeout values are uniquely identified by an interval id.

To register a timeout callback, use XtAppAddTimeOut.

```
XtIntervalId XtAppAddTimeOut(app_context, interval, proc, client_data)
    XtAppContext app_context;
    unsigned long interval;
    XtTimerCallbackProc proc;
    XtPointer client_data;
```

app_context	Specifies the application context for which the timer is to be set.
interval	Specifies the time interval in milliseconds.
proc	Specifies the procedure to be called after the time expires.
client_data	Specifies an argument passed to the specified procedure when it is called.

The `XtAppAddTimeOut` function creates a timeout and returns an identifier for it. The timeout value is set to *interval.* The callback procedure *proc* is called when `XtAppNextEvent` or `XtAppProcessEvent` is next called after the time interval elapses, and then the timeout is removed.

Callback procedure pointers used with timeouts are of type `XtTimer-CallbackProc`.

typedef void (*XtTimerCallbackProc) (XtPointer, XtIntervalId*);
    XtPointer *client_data*;
    XtIntervalId *timer*;

client_data	Passes the client data argument that was registered for this procedure in `XtAppAddTimeOut`.
timer	Passes the id returned from the corresponding `XtAppAddTimeOut` call.

To clear a timeout value, use `XtRemoveTimeOut`.

void XtRemoveTimeOut(*timer*)
    XtIntervalId *timer*;

timer	Specifies the id for the timeout request to be cleared.

The `XtRemoveTimeOut` function removes the pending timeout. Note that timeouts are automatically removed once they trigger.

7.2   Constraining Events to a Cascade of Widgets

Modal widgets are widgets that, except for the input directed to them, lock out user input to the application.

When a modal menu or modal dialog box is popped up using `XtPopup`, user events (keyboard and pointer events) that occur outside the modal widget should be delivered to the modal widget or ignored. In no case will user events be delivered to a widget outside the modal widget.

Menus can pop up submenus, and dialog boxes can pop up further dialog boxes, to create a pop-up cascade. In this case, user events may be delivered to one of several modal widgets in the cascade.

Display-related events should be delivered outside the modal cascade so that exposure events and the like keep the application's display up-to-date. Any event that occurs within the cascade is delivered as usual. The user events delivered to the most recent spring-loaded shell in the cascade when they occur outside the cascade are called remap events and are `KeyPress`, `KeyRelease`, `ButtonPress`, and `ButtonRelease`. The user events ignored when they occur outside the cascade are `MotionNotify` and `EnterNotify`. All other events are delivered normally. In particular, note that this is one way in which widgets can receive `LeaveNotify` events without first receiving `EnterNotify` events; they should be prepared to deal with this, typically by ignoring any unmatched `LeaveNotify` events.

`XtPopup` uses the `XtAddGrab` and `XtRemoveGrab` functions to constrain user events to a modal cascade and subsequently to remove a grab when the modal widget is popped down. Usually you should have no need to call them explicitly.

To constrain or redirect user input to a modal widget, use `XtAddGrab`.

```
void XtAddGrab(w, exclusive, spring_loaded)
    Widget w;
    Boolean exclusive;
    Boolean spring_loaded;
```

w	Specifies the widget to add to the modal cascade. Must be of class Core or any subclass thereof.
exclusive	Specifies whether user events should be dispatched exclusively to this widget or also to previous widgets in the cascade.
spring_loaded	Specifies whether this widget was popped up because the user pressed a pointer button.

The `XtAddGrab` function appends the widget to the modal cascade and checks that *exclusive* is `True` if *spring_loaded* is `True`. If this condition is not met, `XtAddGrab` generates a warning message.

The modal cascade is used by `XtDispatchEvent` when it tries to dispatch a user event. When at least one modal widget is in the widget cascade, `XtDispatchEvent` first determines if the event should be delivered. It starts at the most recent cascade entry and follows the cascade up to and including the most recent cascade entry added with the *exclusive* parameter `True`.

This subset of the modal cascade along with all descendants of these widgets comprise the active subset. User events that occur outside the widgets in this subset are ignored or remapped. Modal menus with submenus generally add a submenu widget to the cascade with *exclusive* `False`. Modal dialog boxes that need to restrict user input to the most deeply nested dialog box add a subdialog widget to the cascade with *exclusive* `True`. User events that occur within the active subset are delivered to the appropriate widget, which is usually a child or further descendant of the modal widget.

Regardless of where in the application they occur, remap events are always delivered to the most recent widget in the active subset of the cascade registered with *spring_loaded* `True`, if any such widget exists. If the event occurred in the active subset of the cascade but outside the spring-loaded widget, it is delivered normally before being delivered also to the spring-loaded widget.

To remove the redirection of user input to a modal widget, use `XtRemove-Grab`.

void XtRemoveGrab(*w*)
    Widget *w*;
    w   Specifies the widget to remove from the modal cascade.

The `XtRemoveGrab` function removes widgets from the modal cascade starting at the most recent widget up to and including the specified widget. It issues a warning if the specified widget is not on the modal cascade.

7.2.1   Requesting Key and Button Grabs

The Intrinsics provide a set of key and button grab interfaces that are parallel to those provided by Xlib and that allow the Intrinsics to modify event dispatching when necessary. X Toolkit applications and widgets that need to passively grab keys or buttons or actively grab the keyboard or pointer should use the following Intrinsics routines rather than the corresponding Xlib routines.

To passively grab a single key of the keyboard, use `XtGrabKey`.

void XtGrabKey(*widget, keycode, modifiers, owner_events, pointer_mode, keyboard_mode*)
    Widget *widget*;
    KeyCode *keycode*;

Modifiers *modifiers*;
Boolean *owner_events*;
int *pointer_mode, keyboard_mode*;

widget	Specifies the widget in whose window the key is to be grabbed. Must be of class Core or any subclass thereof.
keycode	Specify arguments to XGrabKey; see Section 7.5 in *Xlib*.
modifiers	
owner_events	
pointer_mode	
keyboard_mode	

XtGrabKey calls XGrabKey, specifying the widget's window as the grab window if the widget is realized. The remaining arguments are exactly as for XGrabKey. If the widget is not realized, or is later unrealized, the call to XGrabKey will be performed (again) when the widget is realized and its window becomes mapped. In the future, if a KeyPress event matching the specified keycode and modifiers (which may be AnyKey or AnyModifier, respectively) arrives for the widget's window, and there is a modal cascade and the widget is not in the active subset of the cascade and the keyboard was not previously grabbed, then the Intrinsics will call XtUngrabKeyboard with the timestamp from the KeyPress event.

To cancel a passive key grab, use XtUngrabKey.

void XtUngrabKey(*widget, keycode, modifiers*)
    Widget *widget*;
    KeyCode *keycode*;
    Modifiers *modifiers*;

widget	Specifies the widget in whose window the key was grabbed.
keycode	Specify arguments to XUngrabKey; see Section 7.5 in *Xlib*.
modifiers	

The XtUngrabKey procedure calls XUngrabKey, specifying the widget's window as the ungrab window if the widget is realized. The remaining arguments are exactly as for XUngrabKey. If the widget is not realized, XtUngrabKey removes a deferred XtGrabKey request, if any, for the specified widget, keycode, and modifiers.

To actively grab the keyboard, use `XtGrabKeyboard`.

int XtGrabKeyboard(*widget, owner_events, pointer_mode, keyboard_mode, time*)
    Widget *widget*;
    Boolean *owner_events*;
    int *pointer_mode, keyboard_mode*;
    Time *time*;

widget	Specifies the widget for whose window the keyboard is to be grabbed. Must be of class Core or any subclass thereof.
owner_events *pointer_mode* *keyboard_mode* *time*	Specify arguments to `XGrabKeyboard`; see Section 7.5 in *Xlib*.

If the specified widget is realized, `XtGrabKeyboard` calls `XGrabKeyboard`, specifying the widget's window as the grab window. The remaining arguments and return value are exactly as for `XGrabKeyboard`. If the widget is not realized, `XGrabKeyboard` immediately returns `GrabNotViewable`. No future automatic ungrab is implied by `XtGrabKeyboard`.

To cancel an active keyboard grab, use `XtUngrabKeyboard`.

void XtUngrabKeyboard(*widget, time*)
    Widget *widget*;
    Time *time*;

widget	Specifies the widget that has the active keyboard grab.
time	Specifies the additional argument to `XUngrabKeyboard`; see Section 7.5 in *Xlib*.

`XtUngrabKeyboard` calls `XUngrabKeyboard` with the specified time.

To passively grab a single pointer button, use `XtGrabButton`.

void XtGrabButton(*widget, button, modifiers, owner_events, event_mask, pointer_mode,
                keyboard_mode, confine_to, cursor*)
    Widget *widget*;
    int *button*;
    Modifiers *modifiers*;
    Boolean *owner_events*;
    unsigned int *event_mask*;

int *pointer_mode, keyboard_mode*;
Window *confine_to*;
Cursor *cursor*;

widget	Specifies the widget in whose window the button is to be grabbed. Must be of class Core or any subclass thereof.
button	Specify arguments to XGrabButton; see Section 7.4 in *Xlib*.
modifiers	
owner_events	
event_mask	
pointer_mode	
keyboard_mode	
confine_to	
cursor	

XtGrabButton calls XGrabButton, specifying the widget's window as the grab window if the widget is realized. The remaining arguments are exactly as for XGrabButton. If the widget is not realized, or is later unrealized, the call to XGrabButton will be performed (again) when the widget is realized and its window becomes mapped. In the future, if a ButtonPress event matching the specified button and modifiers (which may be AnyButton or AnyModifier, respectively) arrives for the widget's window, and there is a modal cascade and the widget is not in the active subset of the cascade and the pointer was not previously grabbed, then the Intrinsics will call XtUngrabPointer with the timestamp from the ButtonPress event.

To cancel a passive button grab, use XtUngrabButton.

void XtUngrabButton(*widget, button, modifiers*)
    Widget *widget*;
    unsigned int *button*;
    Modifiers *modifiers*;

widget	Specifies the widget in whose window the button was grabbed.
button	Specify arguments to XUngrabButton; see Section 7.4 in *Xlib*.
modifiers	

The XtUngrabButton procedure calls XUngrabButton, specifying the widget's window as the ungrab window if the widget is realized. The remaining arguments are exactly as for XUngrabButton. If the widget is not realized, XtUngrabButton removes a deferred XtGrabButton request, if any, for the specified widget, button, and modifiers.

To actively grab the pointer, use XtGrabPointer.

int XtGrabPointer(*widget, owner_events, event_mask, pointer_mode, keyboard_mode,*
                    confine_to, cursor, time)
    Widget *widget*;
    Boolean *owner_events*;
    unsigned int *event_mask*;
    int *pointer_mode, keyboard_mode*;
    Window *confine_to*;
    Cursor *cursor*;
    Time *time*;

widget   Specifies the widget for whose window the pointer is to be grabbed.
                      Must be of class Core or any subclass thereof.

owner_events   Specify arguments to XGrabPointer; see Section 7.4 in *Xlib*.
event_mask
pointer_mode
keyboard_mode
confine_to
cursor
time

If the specified widget is realized, XtGrabPointer calls XGrabPointer, specifying the widget's window as the grab window. The remaining arguments and return value are exactly as for XGrabPointer. If the widget is not realized, XGrabPointer immediately returns GrabNotViewable. No future automatic ungrab is implied by XtGrabPointer.

To cancel an active pointer grab, use XtUngrabPointer.

void XtUngrabPointer(*widget, time*)
    Widget *widget*;
    Time *time*;

widget   Specifies the widget that has the active pointer grab.
time   Specifies the time argument to XUngrabPointer; see Section 7.4 in
                      Xlib.

XtUngrabPointer calls XUngrabPointer with the specified time.

7.3   Focusing Events on a Child

To redirect keyboard input to a normal descendant of a widget without calling XSetInputFocus, use XtSetKeyboardFocus.

void XtSetKeyboardFocus(*subtree, descendant*)
  Widget *subtree, descendant;*

subtree	Specifies the subtree of the hierarchy for which the keyboard focus is to be set. Must be of class Core or any subclass thereof.
descendant	Specifies either the normal (non-pop-up) descendant of *subtree* to which keyboard events are logically directed, or None. It is not an error to specify None when no input focus was previously set. Must be of class Object or any subclass thereof.

XtSetKeyboardFocus causes XtDispatchEvent to remap keyboard events occurring within the specified subtree and dispatch them to the specified descendant widget or to an ancestor. If the descendant's class is not a subclass of Core, the descendant is replaced by its closest windowed ancestor.

When there is no modal cascade, keyboard events can be dispatched to a widget in one of four ways. Assume the server delivered the event to the window for widget E (because of X input focus, key or keyboard grabs, or pointer position).

• If neither E nor any of E's ancestors have redirected the keyboard focus, or if the event activated a grab for E as specified by a call to XtGrabKey with any value of *owner_events*, or if the keyboard is actively grabbed by E with *owner_events* False via XtGrab-Keyboard or XtGrabKey on a previous key press, the event is dispatched to E.

• Beginning with the ancestor of E closest to the root that has redirected the keyboard focus or E if no such ancestor exists, if the target of that focus redirection has in turn redirected the keyboard focus, recursively follow this focus chain to find a widget F that has not redirected focus.

— If E is the final focus target widget F or a descendant of F, the event is dispatched to E.

— If E is not F, an ancestor of F, or a descendant of F, and the event activated a grab for E as specified by a call to XtGrabKey for E, XtUngrabKeyboard is called.

— If E is an ancestor of F, and the event is a key press, and either
   • E has grabbed the key with XtGrabKey and *owner_events* False, or
   • E has grabbed the key with XtGrabKey and *owner_events* True, and the coordinates of the event are outside the rectangle specified by E's geometry,
   then the event is dispatched to E.

— Otherwise, define A as the closest common ancestor of E and F:
   • If there is an active keyboard grab for any widget via either XtGrabKeyboard or XtGrabKey on a previous key press, or if no widget between F and A (noninclusive)

has grabbed the key and modifier combination with XtGrabKey and any value of *owner_events*, the event is dispatched to F.
- Else, the event is dispatched to the ancestor of F closest to A that has grabbed the key and modifier combination with XtGrabKey.

When there is a modal cascade, if the final destination widget as identified above is in the active subset of the cascade, the event is dispatched; otherwise the event is remapped to a spring-loaded shell or discarded.

When *subtree* or one of its descendants acquires the X input focus or the pointer moves into the subtree such that keyboard events would now be delivered to the subtree, a FocusIn event is generated for the descendant if FocusChange events have been selected by the descendant. Similarly, when *subtree* loses the X input focus or the keyboard focus for one of its ancestors, a FocusOut event is generated for descendant if FocusChange events have been selected by the descendant.

A widget tree may also actively manage the X server input focus. To do so, a widget class specifies an accept_focus procedure.

The accept_focus procedure pointer is of type XtAcceptFocusProc.

```
typedef Boolean (*XtAcceptFocusProc)(Widget, Time*);
    Widget w;
    Time *time;
w               Specifies the widget.
time            Specifies the X time of the event causing the accept focus.
```

Widgets that need the input focus can call XSetInputFocus explicitly, pursuant to the restrictions of the *Inter-Client Communication Conventions Manual*. To allow outside agents, such as the parent, to cause a widget to take the input focus, every widget exports an accept_focus procedure. The widget returns a value indicating whether it actually took the focus or not, so that the parent can give the focus to another widget. Widgets that need to know when they lose the input focus must use the Xlib focus notification mechanism explicitly (typically by specifying translations for FocusIn and FocusOut events). Widget classes that never want the input focus should set the *accept_focus* field to NULL.

To call a widget's accept_focus procedure, use XtCallAcceptFocus.

```
Boolean XtCallAcceptFocus(w, time)
    Widget w;
    Time *time;
```

w   Specifies the widget. Must be of class Core or any subclass thereof.

time   Specifies the X time of the event that is causing the focus change.

The `XtCallAcceptFocus` function calls the specified widget's accept_focus procedure, passing it the specified widget and time, and returns what the accept_focus procedure returns. If *accept_focus* is NULL, `XtCallAcceptFocus` returns `False`.

7.4   Querying Event Sources

The event manager provides several functions to examine and read events (including file and timer events) that are in the queue. The next three functions are Intrinsics equivalents of the `XPending`, `XPeekEvent`, and `XNext-Event` Xlib calls.

To determine if there are any events on the input queue for a given application, use `XtAppPending`.

XtInputMask XtAppPending(*app_context*)
    XtAppContext *app_context*;

app_context   Specifies the application context that identifies the application queue to check.

The `XtAppPending` function returns a nonzero value if there are events pending from the X server, timer pending, or other input sources pending. The value returned is a bit mask that is the OR of `XtIMXEvent`, `XtIMTimer`, and `XtIMAlternateInput` (see `XtAppProcessEvent`). If there are no events pending, `XtAppPending` flushes the output buffers of each Display in the application context and returns zero.

To return the event from the head of a given application's input queue without removing input from the queue, use `XtAppPeekEvent`.

Boolean XtAppPeekEvent(*app_context, event_return*)
    XtAppContext *app_context*;
    XEvent *event_return*;

app_context   Specifies the application context that identifies the application.

event_return   Returns the event information to the specified event structure.

If there is an X event in the queue, `XtAppPeekEvent` copies it into *event_return* and returns `True`. If no X input is on the queue, `XtAppPeekEvent` flushes the output buffers of each Display in the application context and blocks until some input is available (possibly calling some timeout callbacks in the interim). If the next available input is an X event, `XtAppPeekEvent` fills in *event_return* and returns `True`. Otherwise, the input is for an input source registered with `XtAppAddInput`, and `XtAppPeekEvent` returns `False`.

To remove and return the event from the head of a given application's X event queue, use `XtAppNextEvent`.

void XtAppNextEvent(*app_context, event_return*)
    XtAppContext *app_context*;
    XEvent **event_return*;

app_context	Specifies the application context that identifies the application.
event_return	Returns the event information to the specified event structure.

If the X event queue is empty, `XtAppNextEvent` flushes the X output buffers of each Display in the application context and waits for an X event while looking at the other input sources and timeout values and calling any callback procedures triggered by them. This wait time can be used for background processing; see Section 7.8.

7.5   Dispatching Events

The Intrinsics provide functions that dispatch events to widgets or other application code. Every client interested in X events on a widget uses `XtAddEvent-Handler` to register which events it is interested in and a procedure (event handler) to be called when the event happens in that window. The translation manager automatically registers event handlers for widgets that use translation tables; see Chapter 10.

Applications that need direct control of the processing of different types of input should use `XtAppProcessEvent`.

void XtAppProcessEvent(*app_context, mask*)
    XtAppContext *app_context*;
    XtInputMask *mask*;

app_context	Specifies the application context that identifies the application for which to process input.

mask   Specifies what types of events to process. The mask is the bitwise
                    inclusive OR of any combination of XtIMXEvent, XtIMTimer,
                    and XtIMAlternateInput. As a convenience, Intrinsic.h
                    defines the symbolic name XtIMAll to be the bitwise inclusive OR of
                    all event types.

The XtAppProcessEvent function processes one timer, input source, or X
event. If there is no event or input of the appropriate type to process, then
XtAppProcessEvent blocks until there is. If there is more than one type of
input available to process, it is undefined which will get processed. Usually, this
procedure is not called by client applications; see XtAppMainLoop. XtApp-
ProcessEvent processes timer events by calling any appropriate timer callbacks, input sources by calling any appropriate input callbacks, and X events by
calling XtDispatchEvent.

When an X event is received, it is passed to XtDispatchEvent, which calls
the appropriate event handlers and passes them the widget, the event, and
client-specific data registered with each procedure. If no handlers for that
event are registered, the event is ignored and the dispatcher simply returns.

Boolean XtDispatchEvent(*event*)
    XEvent **event;
event   Specifies a pointer to the event structure that is to be dispatched to
                    the appropriate event handlers.

The XtDispatchEvent function sends the event to the event handler functions that have been previously registered with the dispatch routine.
XtDispatchEvent returns True if it dispatched the event to some handler
and False if it found no handler to which to dispatch the event. The most
common use of XtDispatchEvent is to dispatch events acquired with the
XtAppNextEvent procedure. However, it also can be used to dispatch user-
constructed events. XtDispatchEvent records the last timestamp in any
event that contains a timestamp (see XtLastTimestampProcessed) and
also is responsible for implementing the grab semantics of XtAddGrab.

7.6   The Application Input Loop

To process all input from a given application in a continuous loop, use the convenience procedure XtAppMainLoop.

void XtAppMainLoop(*app_context*)
    XtAppContext *app_context*;
app_context   Specifies the application context that identifies the application.

The XtAppMainLoop function first reads the next incoming X event by calling XtAppNextEvent and then dispatches the event to the appropriate registered procedure by calling XtDispatchEvent. This constitutes the main loop of X Toolkit applications and, as such, it does not return. Applications are expected to exit in response to some user action within a callback procedure. There is nothing special about XtAppMainLoop; it is simply an infinite loop that calls XtAppNextEvent and then XtDispatchEvent.

Applications can provide their own version of this loop, which tests some global termination flag or tests that the number of top-level widgets is larger than zero before circling back to the call to XtAppNextEvent.

7.7   Setting and Checking the Sensitivity State of a Widget

Many widgets have a mode in which they assume a different appearance (for example, are grayed out or stippled), do not respond to user events, and become dormant.

When dormant, a widget is considered to be insensitive. If a widget is insensitive, the event manager does not dispatch any events to the widget with an event type of KeyPress, KeyRelease, ButtonPress, ButtonRelease, MotionNotify, EnterNotify, LeaveNotify, FocusIn, or FocusOut.

A widget can be insensitive because its *sensitive* field is False, or because one of its ancestors is insensitive and thus the widget's *ancestor_sensitive* field also is False. A widget can but does not need to distinguish these two cases visually.

Note   Pop-up shells will have *ancestor_sensitive* False if the parent was insensitive when the shell was created. Since XtSetSensitive on the parent will not modify the resource of the pop-up child, clients are advised to include a resource specification of the form "*TransientShell.ancestorSensitive: True" in the application defaults resource file or to ensure that the parent is sensitive when creating pop-up shells.

To set the sensitivity state of a widget, use `XtSetSensitive`.

void XtSetSensitive(*w, sensitive*)
   Widget *w*;
   Boolean *sensitive*;
   w   Specifies the widget. Must be of class RectObj or any subclass thereof.
   sensitive   Specifies whether the widget should receive keyboard, pointer, and focus events.

The `XtSetSensitive` function first calls `XtSetValues` on the current widget with an argument list specifying the XtNsensitive resource and the new value. If *sensitive* is `False` and the widget's class is a subclass of Composite, `XtSetSensitive` recursively propagates the new value down the child tree by calling `XtSetValues` on each child to set *ancestor_sensitive* to `False`. If *sensitive* is `True` and the widget's class is a subclass of Composite and the widget's *ancestor_sensitive* field is `True`, `XtSetSensitive` sets the *ancestor_sensitive* field of each child to `True` and then recursively calls `XtSetValues` on each normal descendant that is now sensitive to set *ancestor_sensitive* to `True`.

`XtSetSensitive` calls `XtSetValues` to change the *sensitive* and *ancestor_sensitive* fields of each affected widget. Therefore, when one of these changes, the widget's set_values procedure should take whatever display actions are needed (for example, graying out or stippling the widget).

`XtSetSensitive` maintains the invariant that if the parent has either *sensitive* or *ancestor_sensitive* `False`, then all children have *ancestor_sensitive* `False`.

To check the current sensitivity state of a widget, use `XtIsSensitive`.

Boolean XtIsSensitive(*w*)
   Widget *w*;
   w   Specifies the object. Must be of class Object or any subclass thereof.

The `XtIsSensitive` function returns `True` or `False` to indicate whether user input events are being dispatched. If the object's class is a subclass of RectObj and both *sensitive* and *ancestor_sensitive* are `True`, `XtIsSensitive` returns `True`; otherwise, it returns `False`.

7.8   Adding Background Work Procedures

The Intrinsics have some limited support for background processing. Because most applications spend most of their time waiting for input, you can register an idle-time work procedure that will be called when the toolkit would otherwise block in `XtAppNextEvent` or `XtAppProcessEvent`. Work procedure pointers are of type `XtWorkProc`.

typedef Boolean (*XtWorkProc) (XtPointer);
    XtPointer *client_data*;

client_data	Passes the client data specified when the work procedure was registered.

This procedure should return `True` when it is done to indicate that it should be removed. If the procedure returns `False`, it will remain registered and will be called again when the application is next idle. Work procedures should be very judicious about how much they do. If they run for more than a small part of a second, interactive feel is likely to suffer.

To register a work procedure for a given application, use `XtAppAddWorkProc`.

XtWorkProcId XtAppAddWorkProc(*app_context, proc, client_data*)
    XtAppContext *app_context*;
    XtWorkProc *proc*;
    XtPointer *client_data*;

app_context	Specifies the application context that identifies the application.
proc	Specifies the procedure to be called when the application is idle.
client_data	Specifies the argument passed to the specified procedure when it is called.

The `XtAppAddWorkProc` function adds the specified work procedure for the application identified by *app_context* and returns an opaque unique identifier for this work procedure. Multiple work procedures can be registered, and the most recently added one is always the one that is called. However, if a work procedure adds another work procedure, the newly added one has lower priority than the current one.

To remove a work procedure, either return `True` from the procedure when it is called or use `XtRemoveWorkProc`.

void XtRemoveWorkProc(*id*)
    XtWorkProcId *id*;

id	Specifies which work procedure to remove.

The `XtRemoveWorkProc` function explicitly removes the specified background work procedure.

7.9   X Event Filters

The event manager provides filters that can be applied to specific X events. The filters, which screen out events that are redundant or are temporarily unwanted, handle pointer motion compression, enter/leave compression, and exposure compression.

7.9.1   Pointer Motion Compression

Widgets can have a hard time keeping up with a rapid stream of pointer motion events. Further, they usually do not care about every motion event. To throw out redundant motion events, the widget class field *compress_motion* should be `True`. When a request for an event would return a motion event, the Intrinsics check if there are any other motion events for the same widget immediately following the current one and, if so, skip all but the last of them.

7.9.2   Enter/Leave Compression

To throw out pairs of enter and leave events that have no intervening events, as can happen when the user moves the pointer across a widget without stopping in it, the widget class field *compress_enterleave* should be `True`. These enter and leave events are not delivered to the client if they are found together in the input queue.

7.9.3   Exposure Compression

Many widgets prefer to process a series of exposure events as a single expose region rather than as individual rectangles. Widgets with complex displays might use the expose region as a clip list in a graphics context, and widgets with simple displays might ignore the region entirely and redisplay their whole window or might get the bounding box from the region and redisplay only that rectangle.

In either case, these widgets do not care about getting partial exposure events. The *compress_exposure* field in the widget class structure specifies the type and number of exposure events that will be dispatched to the widget's expose procedure. This field must be initialized to one of the following values,

#define XtExposeNoCompress   ((XtEnum)False)
#define XtExposeCompressSeries   ((XtEnum)True)
#define XtExposeCompressMultiple   <implementation-defined>
#define XtExposeCompressMaximal   <implementation-defined>

optionally ORed with any combination of the following flags (all with implementation-defined values): XtExposeGraphicsExpose, XtExpose-GraphicsExposeMerged, and XtExposeNoExpose.

If the *compress_exposure* field in the widget class structure does not specify XtExposeNoCompress, the event manager calls the widget's expose procedure only once for a series of exposure events. In this case, all Expose or GraphicsExpose events are accumulated into a region. When the final event is received, the event manager replaces the rectangle in the event with the bounding box for the region and calls the widget's expose procedure, passing the modified exposure event and the region. For more information on regions, see Section 10.6 in *Xlib*.

The values have the following interpretation:

XtExposeNoCompress
: No exposure compression is performed; every selected event is individually dispatched to the expose procedure with a *region* argument of NULL.

XtExposeCompressSeries
: Each series of exposure events is coalesced into a single event, which is dispatched when an exposure event with count equal to zero is reached.

XtExposeCompressMultiple
: Consecutive series of exposure events are coalesced into a single event, which is dispatched when an exposure event with count equal to zero is reached and either the event queue is empty or the next event is not an exposure event for the same widget.

XtExposeCompressMaximal
: All expose series currently in the queue for the widget are coalesced into a single event without regard to intervening nonexposure events. If a partial series is in the end of the queue, the Intrinsics will block until the end of the series is received.

The additional flags have the following meaning:

`XtExposeGraphicsExpose`	Specifies that `GraphicsExpose` events are also to be dispatched to the expose procedure. `GraphicsExpose` events will be compressed, if specified, in the same manner as `Expose` events.
`XtExposeGraphicsExposeMerged`	Specifies in the case of `XtExpose-CompressMultiple` and `XtExpose-CompressMaximal` that series of `GraphicsExpose` and `Expose` events are to be compressed together, with the final event type determining the type of the event passed to the expose procedure. If this flag is not set, then only series of the same event type as the event at the head of the queue are coalesced. This flag also implies `XtExpose-GraphicsExpose`.
`XtExposeNoExpose`	Specifies that `NoExpose` events are also to be dispatched to the expose procedure. `NoExpose` events are never coalesced with other exposure events or with each other.

7.10   Widget Exposure and Visibility

Every primitive widget and some composite widgets display data on the screen by means of direct Xlib calls. Widgets cannot simply write to the screen and forget what they have done. They must keep enough state to redisplay the window or parts of it if a portion is obscured and then reexposed.

7.10.1   Redisplay of a Widget: the expose Procedure

The expose procedure pointer in a widget class is of type `XtExposeProc`.

```
typedef void (*XtExposeProc) (Widget, XEvent*, Region);
    Widget w;
    XEvent *event;
    Region region;
```

w	Specifies the widget instance requiring redisplay.
event	Specifies the exposure event giving the rectangle requiring redisplay.
region	Specifies the union of all rectangles in this exposure sequence.

The redisplay of a widget upon exposure is the responsibility of the expose procedure in the widget's class record. If a widget has no display semantics, it can specify NULL for the *expose* field. Many composite widgets serve only as containers for their children and have no expose procedure.

Note   If the *expose* field is NULL, XtRealizeWidget fills in a default bit gravity of NorthWestGravity before it calls the widget's realize procedure.

If the widget's *compress_exposure* class field specifies XtExposeNoCompress or the event type is NoExpose (see Section 7.9.3), *region* is NULL; otherwise, the event is the final event in the compressed series but *x, y, width,* and *height* contain the bounding box for *region.*

A small simple widget (for example, Label) can ignore the bounding box information in the event and redisplay the entire window. A more complicated widget (for example, Text) can use the bounding box information to minimize the amount of calculation and redisplay it does. A very complex widget uses the region as a clip list in a GC and ignores the event information. The expose procedure is not chained and is therefore responsible for exposure of all superclass data as well as its own.

However, it often is possible to anticipate the display needs of several levels of subclassing. For example, rather than implement separate display procedures for the widgets Label, Pushbutton, and Toggle, you could write a single display routine in Label that uses display state fields like

```
Boolean invert;
Boolean highlight;
Dimension highlight_width;
```

Label would have *invert* and *highlight* always False and *highlight_width* zero. Pushbutton would dynamically set *highlight* and *highlight_width* but would leave *invert* always False. Finally, Toggle would dynamically set all three. In this case, the expose procedures for Pushbutton and Toggle inherit their superclass's expose procedure; see Section 1.6.10.

7.10.2   Widget Visibility

Some widgets may use substantial computing resources to produce the data they will display. However, this effort is wasted if the widget is not actually visible on the screen, that is, if the widget is obscured by another application or is iconified.

The *visible* field in the core widget structure provides a hint to the widget that it need not compute display data. This field is guaranteed to be `True` by the time an exposure event is processed if any part of the widget is visible but is `False` if the widget is fully obscured.

Widgets can use or ignore the *visible* hint. If they ignore it, they should have *visible_interest* in their widget class record set `False`. In such cases, the *visible* field is initialized `True` and never changes. If *visible_interest* is `True`, the event manager asks for `VisibilityNotify` events for the widget and sets *visible* to `True` on `VisibilityUnobscured` or `VisibilityPartiallyObscured` events and `False` on `VisibilityFullyObscured` events.

7.11   X Event Handlers

Event handlers are procedures called when specified events occur in a widget. Most widgets need not use event handlers explicitly. Instead, they use the Intrinsics translation manager. Event handler procedure pointers are of the type `XtEventHandler`.

```
typedef void (*XtEventHandler) (Widget, XtPointer, XEvent*, Boolean*);
    Widget w;
    XtPointer client_data;
    XEvent *event;
    Boolean *continue_to_dispatch;
```

w	Specifies the widget for which the event arrived.
client_data	Specifies any client-specific information registered with the event handler.
event	Specifies the triggering event.
continue_to_dispatch	Specifies whether the remaining event handlers registered for the current event should be called.

After receiving an event and before calling any event handlers, the Boolean pointed to by *continue_to_dispatch* is initialized to `True`. When an event handler is called, it may decide that further processing of the event is not desirable and may store `False` in this Boolean, in which case any handlers remaining to be called for the event will be ignored.

The circumstances under which the Intrinsics may add event handlers to a widget are currently implementation-dependent. Clients must therefore be aware that storing `False` into the *continue_to_dispatch* argument can lead to portability problems.

7.11.1   Event Handlers That Select Events

To register an event handler procedure with the dispatch mechanism, use `XtAddEventHandler`.

> void XtAddEventHandler(*w, event_mask, nonmaskable, proc, client_data*)
>   Widget *w*;
>   EventMask *event_mask*;
>   Boolean *nonmaskable*;
>   XtEventHandler *proc*;
>   XtPointer *client_data*;
>
> | | |
> |---|---|
> | *w* | Specifies the widget for which this event handler is being registered. Must be of class Core or any subclass thereof. |
> | *event_mask* | Specifies the event mask for which to call this procedure. |
> | *nonmaskable* | Specifies whether this procedure should be called on the nonmaskable events (`GraphicsExpose`, `NoExpose`, `SelectionClear`, `SelectionRequest`, `SelectionNotify`, `ClientMessage`, and `MappingNotify`). |
> | *proc* | Specifies the procedure to be called. |
> | *client_data* | Specifies additional data to be passed to the event handler. |

The `XtAddEventHandler` function registers a procedure with the dispatch mechanism that is to be called when an event that matches the mask occurs on the specified widget. Each widget has a single registered event handler list, which will contain any procedure–client_data pair exactly once regardless of the manner in which it is registered. If the procedure is already registered with the same *client_data* value, the specified mask augments the existing mask. If the widget is realized, `XtAddEventHandler` calls `XSelectInput`, if necessary. The order in which this procedure is called relative to other handlers registered for the same event is not defined.

To remove a previously registered event handler, use `XtRemoveEvent-Handler`.

> void XtRemoveEventHandler(*w, event_mask, nonmaskable, proc, client_data*)
>   Widget *w*;
>   EventMask *event_mask*;
>   Boolean *nonmaskable*;
>   XtEventHandler *proc*;
>   XtPointer *client_data*;

w	Specifies the widget for which this procedure is registered. Must be of class Core or any subclass thereof.
event_mask	Specifies the event mask for which to unregister this procedure.
nonmaskable	Specifies whether this procedure should be removed on the nonmaskable events (`GraphicsExpose`, `NoExpose`, `SelectionClear`, `SelectionRequest`, `SelectionNotify`, `ClientMessage`, and `MappingNotify`).
proc	Specifies the procedure to be removed.
client_data	Specifies the registered client data.

The `XtRemoveEventHandler` function unregisters an event handler registered with `XtAddEventHandler` or `XtInsertEventHandler` for the specified events. The request is ignored if *client_data* does not match the value given when the handler was registered. If the widget is realized and no other event handler requires the event, `XtRemoveEventHandler` calls `XSelect-Input`. If the specified procedure has not been registered or if it has been registered with a different value of *client_data*, `XtRemoveEventHandler` returns without reporting an error.

To stop a procedure registered with `XtAddEventHandler` or `XtInsert-EventHandler` from receiving all selected events, call `XtRemoveEvent-Handler` with *event_mask* `XtAllEvents` and *nonmaskable* `True`. The procedure will continue to receive any events that have been specified in calls to `XtAddRawEventHandler` or `XtInsertRawEventHandler`.

To register an event handler procedure that receives events before or after all previously registered event handlers, use `XtInsertEventHandler`.

```
typedef enum {XtListHead, XtListTail} XtListPosition;
```

void XtInsertEventHandler(*w*, *event_mask*, *nonmaskable*, *proc*, *client_data*, *position*)
  Widget *w*;
  EventMask *event_mask*;
  Boolean *nonmaskable*;
  XtEventHandler *proc*;
  XtPointer *client_data*;
  XtListPosition *position*;

w	Specifies the widget for which this event handler is being registered. Must be of class Core or any subclass thereof.
event_mask	Specifies the event mask for which to call this procedure.

nonmaskable	Specifies whether this procedure should be called on the nonmaskable events (GraphicsExpose, NoExpose, SelectionClear, SelectionRequest, SelectionNotify, ClientMessage, and MappingNotify).
proc	Specifies the procedure to be called.
client_data	Specifies additional data to be passed to the client's event handler.
position	Specifies when the event handler is to be called relative to other previously registered handlers.

XtInsertEventHandler is identical to XtAddEventHandler with the additional *position* argument. If *position* is XtListHead, the event handler is registered so that it will be called before any event handlers that were previously registered for the same widget. If *position* is XtListTail, the event handler is registered to be called after any previously registered event handlers. If the procedure is already registered with the same *client_data* value, the specified mask augments the existing mask and the procedure is repositioned in the list.

7.11.2   Event Handlers That Do Not Select Events

On occasion, clients need to register an event handler procedure with the dispatch mechanism without explicitly causing the X server to select for that event. To do this, use XtAddRawEventHandler.

void XtAddRawEventHandler(*w, event_mask, nonmaskable, proc, client_data*)
    Widget *w*;
    EventMask *event_mask*;
    Boolean *nonmaskable*;
    XtEventHandler *proc*;
    XtPointer *client_data*;

w	Specifies the widget for which this event handler is being registered. Must be of class Core or any subclass thereof.
event_mask	Specifies the event mask for which to call this procedure.
nonmaskable	Specifies whether this procedure should be called on the nonmaskable events (GraphicsExpose, NoExpose, SelectionClear, SelectionRequest, SelectionNotify, ClientMessage, and MappingNotify).
proc	Specifies the procedure to be called.
client_data	Specifies additional data to be passed to the client's event handler.

The XtAddRawEventHandler function is similar to XtAddEventHandler except that it does not affect the widget's event mask and never causes an XSelectInput for its events. Note that the widget might already have those

mask bits set because of other nonraw event handlers registered on it. If the
procedure is already registered with the same *client_data* value, the specified
mask augments the existing mask. The order in which this procedure is called
relative to other handlers registered for the same event is not defined.

To remove a previously registered raw event handler, use `XtRemoveRaw-`
`EventHandler`.

void XtRemoveRawEventHandler(*w, event_mask, nonmaskable, proc, client_data*)
    Widget *w*;
    EventMask *event_mask*;
    Boolean *nonmaskable*;
    XtEventHandler *proc*;
    XtPointer *client_data*;

w	Specifies the widget for which this procedure is registered. Must be of class Core or any subclass thereof.
event_mask	Specifies the event mask for which to unregister this procedure.
nonmaskable	Specifies whether this procedure should be removed on the nonmaskable events (`GraphicsExpose`, `NoExpose`, `SelectionClear`, `SelectionRequest`, `SelectionNotify`, `ClientMessage`, and `MappingNotify`).
proc	Specifies the procedure to be registered.
client_data	Specifies the registered client data.

The `XtRemoveRawEventHandler` function unregisters an event handler
registered with `XtAddRawEventHandler` or `XtInsertRawEventHandler`
for the specified events without changing the window event mask. The request
is ignored if *client_data* does not match the value given when the handler was
registered. If the specified procedure has not been registered or if it has been
registered with a different value of *client_data*, `XtRemoveRawEventHandler`
returns without reporting an error.

To stop a procedure registered with `XtAddRawEventHandler` or
`XtInsertRawEventHandler` from receiving all nonselected events, call
`XtRemoveRawEventHandler` with *event_mask* `XtAllEvents` and *nonmaskable* `True`. The procedure will continue to receive any events that have been
specified in calls to `XtAddEventHandler` or `XtInsertEventHandler`.

To register an event handler procedure that receives events before or after
all previously registered event handlers without selecting for the events, use
`XtInsertRawEventHandler`.

void XtInsertRawEventHandler(*w, event_mask, nonmaskable, proc, client_data, position*)
  Widget *w*;
  EventMask *event_mask*;
  Boolean *nonmaskable*;
  XtEventHandler *proc*;
  XtPointer *client_data*;
  XtListPosition *position*;

w	Specifies the widget for which this event handler is being registered. Must be of class Core or any subclass thereof.
event_mask	Specifies the event mask for which to call this procedure.
nonmaskable	Specifies whether this procedure should be called on the nonmaskable events (`GraphicsExpose`, `NoExpose`, `SelectionClear`, `SelectionRequest`, `SelectionNotify`, `ClientMessage`, and `MappingNotify`).
proc	Specifies the procedure to be registered.
client_data	Specifies additional data to be passed to the client's event handler.
position	Specifies when the event handler is to be called relative to other previously registered handlers.

The `XtInsertRawEventHandler` function is similar to `XtInsertEvent-Handler` except that it does not modify the widget's event mask and never causes an `XSelectInput` for the specified events. If the procedure is already registered with the same *client_data* value, the specified mask augments the existing mask and the procedure is repositioned in the list.

7.11.3 Current Event Mask

To retrieve the event mask for a given widget, use `XtBuildEventMask`.

EventMask XtBuildEventMask(*w*)
  Widget *w*;

w	Specifies the widget. Must be of class Core or any subclass thereof.

The `XtBuildEventMask` function returns the event mask representing the logical OR of all event masks for event handlers registered on the widget with `XtAddEventHandler` and `XtInsertEventHandler` and all event translations, including accelerators, installed on the widget. This is the same event mask stored into the `XSetWindowAttributes` structure by `XtRealize-Widget` and sent to the server when event handlers and translations are installed or removed on the realized widget.

```
┌─────────────────────────────────────┐
│  Chapter 8                           │
│                                      │
│                                      │
│                                      │
│  Callbacks                           │
│                                      │
└─────────────────────────────────────┘
```

Applications and other widgets often need to register a procedure with a widget that gets called under certain prespecified conditions. For example, when a widget is destroyed, every procedure on the widget's *destroy_callbacks* list is called to notify clients of the widget's impending doom.

Every widget has a *destroy_callbacks* list. Widgets can define additional callback lists as they see fit. For example, the Pushbutton widget has a callback list to notify clients when the button has been activated.

Except where otherwise noted, it is the intent that all Intrinsics functions may be called at any time, including from within callback procedures, action routines, and event handlers.

8.1   Using Callback Procedures and Callback List Definitions

Callback procedure pointers for use in callback lists are of type XtCallback-Proc.

typedef void (*XtCallbackProc) (Widget, XtPointer, XtPointer);
    Widget *w*;
    XtPointer *client_data*;
    XtPointer *call_data*;
    w   Specifies the widget owning the list in which the callback is registered.
    client_data   Specifies additional data supplied by the client when the procedure was registered.

call_data   Specifies any callback-specific data the widget wants to pass to the
                     client. For example, when Scrollbar executes its XtNthumbChanged
                     callback list, it passes the new position of the thumb.

The *client_data* argument provides a way for the client registering the callback procedure also to register client-specific data, for example, a pointer to additional information about the widget, a reason for invoking the callback, and so on. The *client_data* value may be NULL if all necessary information is in the widget. The *call_data* argument is a convenience to avoid having simple cases where the client would otherwise always call XtGetValues or a widget-specific function to retrieve data from the widget. Widgets should generally avoid putting complex state information in *call_data*. The client can use the more general data retrieval methods, if necessary.

Whenever a client wants to pass a callback list as an argument in an XtCreateWidget, XtSetValues, or XtGetValues call, it should specify the address of a NULL-terminated array of type XtCallbackList.

```
typedef struct {
    XtCallbackProc      callback;
    XtPointer           closure;
} XtCallbackRec, *XtCallbackList;
```

For example, the callback list for procedures A and B with client data client-DataA and clientDataB, respectively, is

```
static XtCallbackRec callbacks[] = {
    {A, (XtPointer) clientDataA},
    {B, (XtPointer) clientDataB},
    {(XtCallbackProc) NULL, (XtPointer) NULL}
};
```

Although callback lists are passed by address in arglists and varargs lists, the Intrinsics recognize callback lists through the widget resource list and will copy the contents when necessary. Widget initialize and set_values procedures should not allocate memory for the callback list contents. The Intrinsics automatically do this, potentially using a different structure for their internal representation.

8.2   Identifying Callback Lists

Whenever a widget contains a callback list for use by clients, it also exports in its public .h file the resource name of the callback list. Applications and client widgets never access callback list fields directly. Instead, they always identify the desired callback list by using the exported resource name. All the callback manipulation functions described in this chapter except XtCallCallback-List check to see that the requested callback list is indeed implemented by the widget.

For the Intrinsics to find and correctly handle callback lists, they must be declared with a resource type of XtRCallback. The internal representation of a callback list is implementation-dependent; widgets may make no assumptions about the value stored in this resource if it is non-NULL. Except to compare the value to NULL (which is equivalent to XtCallbackStatus XtCallback-HasNone), access to callback list resources must be made through other Intrinsics procedures.

8.3   Adding Callback Procedures

To add a callback procedure to a widget's callback list, use XtAddCallback.

void XtAddCallback(*w, callback_name, callback, client_data*)
    Widget *w*;
    String *callback_name*;
    XtCallbackProc *callback*;
    XtPointer *client_data*;

w	Specifies the widget. Must be of class Object or any subclass thereof.
callback_name	Specifies the callback list to which the procedure is to be appended.
callback	Specifies the callback procedure.
client_data	Specifies additional data to be passed to the specified procedure when it is invoked, or NULL.

A callback will be invoked as many times as it occurs in the callback list.

To add a list of callback procedures to a given widget's callback list, use XtAddCallbacks.

void XtAddCallbacks(*w, callback_name, callbacks*)
    Widget *w*;
    String *callback_name*;
    XtCallbackList *callbacks*;

w	Specifies the widget. Must be of class Object or any subclass thereof.
callback_name	Specifies the callback list to which the procedures are to be appended.
callbacks	Specifies the NULL-terminated list of callback procedures and corresponding client data.

8.4   Removing Callback Procedures

To delete a callback procedure from a widget's callback list, use XtRemove-Callback.

void XtRemoveCallback(*w, callback_name, callback, client_data*)
    Widget *w*;
    String *callback_name*;
    XtCallbackProc *callback*;
    XtPointer *client_data*;

w	Specifies the widget. Must be of class Object or any subclass thereof.
callback_name	Specifies the callback list from which the procedure is to be deleted.
callback	Specifies the callback procedure.
client_data	Specifies the client data to match with the registered callback entry.

The XtRemoveCallback function removes a callback only if both the procedure and the client data match.

To delete a list of callback procedures from a given widget's callback list, use XtRemoveCallbacks.

void XtRemoveCallbacks(*w, callback_name, callbacks*)
    Widget *w*;
    String *callback_name*;
    XtCallbackList *callbacks*;

w	Specifies the widget. Must be of class Object or any subclass thereof.
callback_name	Specifies the callback list from which the procedures are to be deleted.
callbacks	Specifies the NULL-terminated list of callback procedures and corresponding client data.

To delete all callback procedures from a given widget's callback list and free all storage associated with the callback list, use XtRemoveAllCallbacks.

void XtRemoveAllCallbacks(*w, callback_name*)
    Widget *w*;
    String *callback_name*;

w	Specifies the widget. Must be of class Object or any subclass thereof.
callback_name	Specifies the callback list to be cleared.

8.5 Executing Callback Procedures

To execute the procedures in a given widget's callback list, specifying the callback list by resource name, use `XtCallCallbacks`.

void XtCallCallbacks(*w, callback_name, call_data*)
    Widget *w*;
    String *callback_name*;
    XtPointer *call_data*;

w	Specifies the widget. Must be of class Object or any subclass thereof.
callback_name	Specifies the callback list to be executed.
call_data	Specifies a callback-list-specific data value to pass to each of the callback procedures in the list, or NULL.

`XtCallCallbacks` calls each of the callback procedures in the list named by *callback_name* in the specified widget, passing the client data registered with the procedure and *call_data*.

To execute the procedures in a callback list, specifying the callback list by address, use `XtCallCallbackList`.

void XtCallCallbackList(*widget, callbacks, call_data*)
    Widget *widget*;
    XtCallbackList *callbacks*;
    XtPointer *call_data*;

widget	Specifies the widget instance that contains the callback list. Must be of class Object or any subclass thereof.
callbacks	Specifies the callback list to be executed.
call_data	Specifies a callback-list-specific data value to pass to each of the callback procedures in the list, or NULL.

The *callbacks* parameter must specify the contents of a widget or object resource declared with representation type XtRCallback. If *callbacks* is NULL, `XtCallCallbackList` returns immediately; otherwise it calls each of the callback procedures in the list, passing the client data and *call_data*.

8.6 Checking the Status of a Callback List

To find out the status of a given widget's callback list, use `XtHasCallbacks`.

typedef enum {XtCallbackNoList, XtCallbackHasNone, XtCallbackHasSome}
    XtCallbackStatus;

XtCallbackStatus XtHasCallbacks(*w*, *callback_name*)
    Widget *w*;
    String *callback_name*;
  w   Specifies the widget. Must be of class Object or any subclass thereof.
  callback_name   Specifies the callback list to be checked.

The XtHasCallbacks function first checks to see if the widget has a callback list identified by *callback_name*. If the callback list does not exist, XtHas-Callbacks returns XtCallbackNoList. If the callback list exists but is empty, it returns XtCallbackHasNone. If the callback list exists and has at least one callback registered, it returns XtCallbackHasSome.

Chapter 9

Resource Management

A resource is a field in the widget record with a corresponding resource entry in the *resources* list of the widget or any of its superclasses. This means that the field is settable by XtCreateWidget (by naming the field in the argument list), by an entry in a resource file (by using either the name or class), and by XtSet-Values. In addition, it is readable by XtGetValues. Not all fields in a widget record are resources. Some are for bookkeeping use by the generic routines (like *managed* and *being_destroyed*). Others can be for local bookkeeping, and still others are derived from resources (many graphics contexts and pixmaps).

Widgets typically need to obtain a large set of resources at widget creation time. Some of the resources come from the argument list supplied in the call to XtCreateWidget, some from the resource database, and some from the internal defaults specified by the widget. Resources are obtained first from the argument list, then from the resource database for all resources not specified in the argument list, and last, from the internal default, if needed.

9.1   Resource Lists

A resource entry specifies a field in the widget, the textual name and class of the field that argument lists and external resource files use to refer to the field, and a default value that the field should get if no value is specified. The declaration for the XtResource structure is

```
typedef struct {
    String      resource_name;
    String      resource_class;
```

```
        String        resource_type;
        Cardinal      resource_size;
        Cardinal      resource_offset;
        String        default_type;
        XtPointer     default_addr;
} XtResource, *XtResourceList;
```

The *resource_name* field contains the name used by clients to access the field in the widget. By convention, it starts with a lower-case letter and is spelled exactly like the field name, except all underscores (_) are deleted and the next letter is replaced by its upper-case counterpart. For example, the resource name for background_pixel becomes backgroundPixel. Resource names beginning with the two-character sequence "xt" and resource classes beginning with the two-character sequence "Xt" are reserved to the Intrinsics for future standard and implementation-dependent uses. Widget header files typically contain a symbolic name for each resource name. All resource names, classes, and types used by the Intrinsics are named in `<X11/StringDefs.h>`. The Intrinsics's symbolic resource names begin with "XtN" and are followed by the string name (for example, XtNbackgroundPixel for backgroundPixel).

The *resource_class* field contains the class used by clients to access the field. A resource class provides two functions:

• It isolates an application from different representations that widgets can use for a similar resource.

• It lets you specify values for several actual resources with a single name. A resource class should be chosen to span a group of closely related fields.

For example, a widget can have several pixel resources: background, foreground, border, block cursor, pointer cursor, and so on. Typically, the background defaults to white and everything else to black. The resource class for each of these resources in the resource list should be chosen so that it takes the minimal number of entries in the resource database to make the background offwhite and everything else darkblue.

In this case, the background pixel should have a resource class of "Background" and all the other pixel entries a resource class of "Foreground". Then, the resource file needs only two lines to change all pixels to offwhite or darkblue:

```
*Background:    offwhite
*Foreground:    darkblue
```

Similarly, a widget may have several font resources (such as normal and bold), but all fonts should have the class Font. Thus, changing all fonts simply requires only a single line in the default resource file:

```
*Font:6x13
```

By convention, resource classes are always spelled starting with a capital letter to distinguish them from resource names. Their symbolic names are preceded with "XtC" (for example, XtCBackground).

The *resource_type* field gives the physical representation type of the resource and also encodes information about the specific usage of the field. By convention, it starts with an upper-case letter and is spelled identically to the type name of the field. The resource type is used when resources are fetched to convert from the resource database format (usually `String`) or the default resource format (almost anything, but often `String`) to the desired physical representation (see Section 9.6). The Intrinsics define the following resource types:

Resource Type	Structure or Field Type
XtRAcceleratorTable	XtAccelerators
XtRAtom	Atom
XtRBitmap	Pixmap, depth=1
XtRBoolean	Boolean
XtRBool	Bool
XtRCallback	XtCallbackList
XtRCardinal	Cardinal
XtRColor	XColor
XtRColormap	Colormap
XtRCursor	Cursor
XtRDimension	Dimension
XtRDisplay	Display*
XtREnum	XtEnum
XtRFile	FILE*
XtRFloat	float
XtRFont	Font
XtRFontStruct	XFontStruct*
XtRFunction	(*)()
XtRGeometry	char*, format as defined by `XParseGeometry`
XtRInitialState	int
XtRInt	int
XtRLongBoolean	long

Resource Type	Structure or Field Type
XtRObject	Object
XtRPixel	Pixel
XtRPixmap	Pixmap
XtRPointer	XtPointer
XtRPosition	Position
XtRScreen	Screen*
XtRShort	short
XtRString	String
XtRStringArray	String*
XtRStringTable	String*
XtRTranslationTable	XtTranslations
XtRUnsignedChar	unsigned char
XtRVisual	Visual*
XtRWidget	Widget
XtRWidgetClass	WidgetClass
XtRWidgetList	WidgetList
XtRWindow	Window

`<X11/StringDefs.h>` also defines the following resource types as a convenience for widgets, although they do not have any corresponding data type assigned: XtREditMode, XtRJustify, and XtROrientation.

The *resource_size* field is the size of the physical representation in bytes; you should specify it as `sizeof`(*type*) so that the compiler fills in the value. The *resource_offset* field is the offset in bytes of the field within the widget. You should use the `XtOffsetOf` macro to retrieve this value. The *default_type* field is the representation type of the default resource value. If *default_type* is different from *resource_type* and the default value is needed, the resource manager invokes a conversion procedure from *default_type* to *resource_type*. Whenever possible, the default type should be identical to the resource type in order to minimize widget creation time. However, there are sometimes no values of the type that the program can easily specify. In this case, it should be a value for which the converter is guaranteed to work (for example, `XtDefaultForeground` for a pixel resource). The *default_addr* field specifies the address of the default resource value. As a special case, if *default_type* is XtRString, then the value in the *default_addr* field is the pointer to the string rather than a pointer to the pointer. The default is used if a resource is not specified in the argument list or in the resource database, or if the conversion from the representation type stored in the resource database fails, which can happen for various reasons (for example, a misspelled entry in a resource file).

Two special representation types (XtRImmediate and XtRCallProc) are usable only as default resource types. XtRImmediate indicates that the value in the *default_addr* field is the actual value of the resource rather than the address of the value. The value must be in the correct representation type for the resource, coerced to an `XtPointer`. No conversion is possible, since there is no source representation type. XtRCallProc indicates that the value in the *default_addr* field is a procedure pointer. This procedure is automatically invoked with the widget, *resource_offset*, and a pointer to an `XrmValue` in which to store the result. XtRCallProc procedure pointers are of type `XtResource-DefaultProc`.

typedef void (*XtResourceDefaultProc) (Widget, int, XrmValue*);
    Widget *w*;
    int *offset*;
    XrmValue *value*;

w	Specifies the widget whose resource value is to be obtained.
offset	Specifies the offset of the field in the widget record.
value	Specifies the resource value descriptor to return.

The `XtResourceDefaultProc` procedure should fill in the *value –>addr* field with a pointer to the resource value in its correct representation type.

To get the resource list structure for a particular class, use `XtGetResource-List`.

void XtGetResourceList(*class, resources_return, num_resources_return*)
    WidgetClass *class*;
    XtResourceList *resources_return*;
    Cardinal *num_resources_return*;

class	Specifies the object class to be queried. It must be `objectClass` or any subclass thereof.
resources_return	Returns the resource list.
num_resources_return	Returns the number of entries in the resource list.

If `XtGetResourceList` is called before the class is initialized, it returns the resource list as specified in the class record. If it is called after the class has been initialized, `XtGetResourceList` returns a merged resource list that includes the resources for all superclasses. The list returned by `XtGetResourceList` should be freed using `XtFree` when it is no longer needed.

To get the constraint resource list structure for a particular widget class, use
XtGetConstraintResourceList.

void XtGetConstraintResourceList(*class, resources_return, num_resources_return*)
    WidgetClass *class*;
    XtResourceList **resources_return*;
    Cardinal **num_resources_return*;

class	Specifies the object class to be queried. It must be objectClass or any subclass thereof.
resources_return	Returns the constraint resource list.
num_resources_return	Returns the number of entries in the constraint resource list.

If XtGetConstraintResourceList is called before the widget class is initialized, the resource list as specified in the widget class Constraint part is
returned. If XtGetConstraintResourceList is called after the widget class
has been initialized, the merged resource list for the class and all Constraint
superclasses is returned. If the specified class is not a subclass of constraint-
WidgetClass, **resources_return* is set to NULL and **num_resources_return* is set
to zero. The list returned by XtGetConstraintResourceList should be
freed using XtFree when it is no longer needed.

The routines XtSetValues and XtGetValues also use the resource list to
set and get widget state; see Sections 9.7.1 and 9.7.2.

Here is an abbreviated version of a possible resource list for a Label widget:

```
/* Resources specific to Label */
static XtResource resources[] = {
{XtNforeground, XtCForeground, XtRPixel, sizeof(Pixel),
   XtOffsetOf(LabelRec, label.foreground), XtRString,
   XtDefaultForeground},
{XtNfont, XtCFont, XtRFontStruct, sizeof(XFontStruct*),
   XtOffsetOf(LabelRec, label.font), XtRString, XtDefaultFont},
{XtNlabel, XtCLabel, XtRString, sizeof(String),
   XtOffsetOf(LabelRec, label.label), XtRString, NULL},
                    .
                    .
                    .
};
```

The complete resource name for a field of a widget instance is the concatenation of the application shell name (from XtAppCreateShell), the instance
names of all the widget's parents up to the top of the widget tree, the instance
name of the widget itself, and the resource name of the specified field of the
widget. Similarly, the full resource class of a field of a widget instance is the

concatenation of the application class (from XtAppCreateShell), the widget class names of all the widget's parents up to the top of the widget tree, the widget class name of the widget itself, and the resource class of the specified field of the widget.

9.2   Byte Offset Calculations

To determine the byte offset of a field within a structure type, use XtOffsetOf.

Cardinal XtOffsetOf(*structure_type, field_name*)
  Type structure_type;
  Field field_name;
  structure_type   Specifies a type that is declared as a structure.
  field_name   Specifies the name of a member within the structure.

The XtOffsetOf macro expands to a constant expression that gives the offset in bytes to the specified structure member from the beginning of the structure. It is normally used to statically initialize resource lists and is more portable than XtOffset, which serves the same function.

To determine the byte offset of a field within a structure pointer type, use XtOffset.

Cardinal XtOffset(*pointer_type, field_name*)
  Type pointer_type;
  Field field_name;
  pointer_type   Specifies a type that is declared as a pointer to a structure.
  field_name   Specifies the name of a member within the structure.

The XtOffset macro expands to a constant expression that gives the offset in bytes to the specified structure member from the beginning of the structure. It may be used to statically initialize resource lists. XtOffset is less portable than XtOffsetOf.

9.3   Superclass-to-Subclass Chaining of Resource Lists

The XtCreateWidget function gets resources as a superclass-to-subclass chained operation. That is, the resources specified in the objectClass resource list are fetched, then those in rectObjClass, and so on down to the resources specified for this widget's class. Within a class, resources are fetched in the order they are declared.

In general, if a widget resource field is declared in a superclass, that field is included in the superclass's resource list and need not be included in the subclass's resource list. For example, the Core class contains a resource entry for *background_pixel.* Consequently, the implementation of Label need not also have a resource entry for *background_pixel.* However, a subclass, by specifying a resource entry for that field in its own resource list, can override the resource entry for any field declared in a superclass. This is most often done to override the defaults provided in the superclass with new ones. At class initialization time, resource lists for that class are scanned from the superclass down to the class to look for resources with the same offset. A matching resource in a subclass will be reordered to override the superclass entry. If reordering is necessary, a copy of the superclass resource list is made to avoid affecting other subclasses of the superclass.

Also at class initialization time, the Intrinsics produce an internal representation of the resource list to optimize access time when creating widgets. In order to save memory, the Intrinsics may overwrite the storage allocated for the resource list in the class record; therefore, widgets must allocate resource lists in writable storage and must not access the list contents directly after the class_initialize procedure has returned.

9.4   Subresources

A widget does not do anything to retrieve its own resources; instead, XtCreateWidget does this automatically before calling the class initialize procedure.

Some widgets have subparts that are not widgets but for which the widget would like to fetch resources. Such widgets call XtGetSubresources to accomplish this.

```
void XtGetSubresources(w, base, name, class, resources, num_resources, args, num_args)
    Widget w;
    XtPointer base;
    String name;
    String class;
    XtResourceList resources;
    Cardinal num_resources;
```

    ArgList *args*;
    Cardinal *num_args*;

w	Specifies the object used to qualify the subpart resource name and class. Must be of class Object or any subclass thereof.
base	Specifies the base address of the subpart data structure into which the resources will be written.
name	Specifies the name of the subpart.
class	Specifies the class of the subpart.
resources	Specifies the resource list for the subpart.
num_resources	Specifies the number of entries in the resource list.
args	Specifies the argument list to override any other resource specifications.
num_args	Specifies the number of entries in the argument list.

The `XtGetSubresources` function constructs a name and class list from the application name and class, the name and classes of all the object's ancestors, and the object itself. Then it appends to this list the *name* and *class* pair passed in. The resources are fetched from the argument list, the resource database, or the default values in the resource list. Then they are copied into the subpart record. If *args* is NULL, *num_args* must be zero. However, if *num_args* is zero, the argument list is not referenced.

    `XtGetSubresources` may overwrite the specified resource list with an equivalent representation in an internal format, which optimizes access time if the list is used repeatedly. The resource list must be allocated in writable storage, and the caller must not modify the list contents after the call if the same list is to be used again. Resources fetched by `XtGetSubresources` are reference-counted as if they were referenced by the specified object. Subresources might therefore be freed from the conversion cache and destroyed when the object is destroyed, but not before then.

    To fetch resources for widget subparts using varargs lists, use `XtVaGetSubresources`.

void XtVaGetSubresources(*w, base, name, class, resources, num_resources, . . .*)
    Widget *w*;
    XtPointer *base*;
    String *name*;
    String *class*;
    XtResourceList *resources*;
    Cardinal *num_resources*;

w	Specifies the object used to qualify the subpart resource name and class. Must be of class Object or any subclass thereof.
base	Specifies the base address of the subpart data structure into which the resources will be written.
name	Specifies the name of the subpart.
class	Specifies the class of the subpart.
resources	Specifies the resource list for the subpart.
num_resources	Specifies the number of entries in the resource list.
. . .	Specifies the variable argument list to override any other resource specifications.

XtVaGetSubresources is identical in function to XtGetSubresources with the *args* and *num_args* parameters replaced by a varargs list, as described in Section 2.4.1.

9.5   Obtaining Application Resources

To retrieve resources that are not specific to a widget but apply to the overall application, use XtGetApplicationResources.

void XtGetApplicationResources(*w, base, resources, num_resources, args, num_args*)
    Widget *w*;
    XtPointer *base*;
    XtResourceList *resources*;
    Cardinal *num_resources*;
    ArgList *args*;
    Cardinal *num_args*;

w	Specifies the object that identifies the resource database to search (the database is that associated with the display for this object). Must be of class Object or any subclass thereof.
base	Specifies the base address into which the resource values will be written.
resources	Specifies the resource list.
num_resources	Specifies the number of entries in the resource list.
args	Specifies the argument list to override any other resource specifications.
num_args	Specifies the number of entries in the argument list.

The XtGetApplicationResources function first uses the passed object, which is usually an application shell widget, to construct a resource name and class list. The full name and class of the specified object (that is, including its ancestors, if any) is logically added to the front of each resource name and class. Then it retrieves the resources from the argument list, the resource database, or the resource list default values. XtGetApplicationResources copies the resources into the addresses obtained by adding *base* to each *offset* in the resource list. If *args* is NULL, *num_args* must be zero. However, if *num_args* is zero, the argument list is not referenced. The portable way to specify application resources is to declare them as members of a structure and pass the address of the structure as the *base* argument.

XtGetApplicationResources may overwrite the specified resource list with an equivalent representation in an internal format, which optimizes access time if the list is used repeatedly. The resource list must be allocated in writable storage, and the caller must not modify the list contents after the call if the same list is to be used again. Any per-display resources fetched by XtGet-ApplicationResources will not be freed from the resource cache until the display is closed.

To retrieve resources for the overall application using varargs lists, use XtVaGetApplicationResources.

void XtVaGetApplicationResources(*w, base, resources, num_resources, . . .*)
    Widget *w*;
    XtPointer *base*;
    XtResourceList *resources*;
    Cardinal *num_resources*;

w	Specifies the object that identifies the resource database to search (the database is that associated with the display for this object). Must be of class Object or any subclass thereof.
base	Specifies the base address into which the resource values will be written.
resources	Specifies the resource list.
num_resources	Specifies the number of entries in the resource list.
. . .	Specifies the variable argument list to override any other resource specifications.

XtVaGetApplicationResources is identical in function to XtGet-ApplicationResources with the *args* and *num_args* parameters replaced by a varargs list, as described in Section 2.4.1.

9.6   Resource Conversions

The Intrinsics provide a mechanism for registering representation converters that are automatically invoked by the resource-fetching routines. The Intrinsics additionally provide and register several commonly used converters. This resource conversion mechanism serves several purposes:

• It permits user and application resource files to contain textual representations of nontextual values.

• It allows textual or other representations of default resource values that are dependent on the display, screen, or colormap, and thus must be computed at runtime.

• It caches conversion source and result data. Conversions that require much computation or space (for example, string-to-translation-table) or that require round-trips to the server (for example, string-to-font or string-to-color) are performed only once.

9.6.1   Predefined Resource Converters

The Intrinsics define all the representations used in the Object, RectObj, Core, Composite, Constraint, and Shell widget classes. It registers the following resource converters:

From XtRString to	XtRAcceleratorTable, XtRAtom, XtRBoolean, XtRBool, XtRCursor, XtRDimension, XtRDisplay, XtRFile, XtRFloat, XtRFont, XtRFontStruct, XtRInt, XtRInitialState, XtRPixel, XtRPosition, XtRShort, XtRTranslationTable, XtRUnsignedChar, and XtRVisual.
From XtRColor to	XtRPixel
From XRInt to	XtRBoolean, XtRBool, XtRColor, XtRDimension, XtRFloat, XtRFont, XtRPixel, XtRPixmap, XtRPosition, XtRShort, and XtRUnsignedChar.
From XtRPixel to	XtRColor.

The String-to-Pixel conversion has two predefined constants that are guaranteed to work and contrast with each other: XtDefaultForeground and XtDefaultBackground. They evaluate to the black and white pixel values of the widget's screen, respectively. If the application resource reverse-Video is True, they evaluate to the white and black pixel values of the widget's screen, respectively. Similarly, the String-to-Font and String-to-FontStruct converters recognize the constant XtDefaultFont and evaluate this in the following manner:

• Query the resource database for the resource whose full name is "xtDefaultFont", class "XtDefaultFont" (that is, no widget name/class prefixes) and use a type XtRString value returned as the font name, or a type XtRFont or XtRFontStruct value directly as the resource value.

- If the resource database does not contain a value for xtDefaultFont, class XtDefaultFont, or if the returned font name cannot be successfully opened, an implementation-defined font in ISO8859-1 character set encoding is opened. (One possible algorithm is to perform an XListFonts using a wildcard font name and use the first font in the list. This wildcard font name should be as broad as possible to maximize the probability of locating a useable font; for example, "–*–*–*–R–*–*–*–120–*–*–*–ISO8859–1".)

- If no suitable ISO8859-1 font can be found, issue an error message.

The String-to-InitialState conversion accepts the values `NormalState` or `IconicState` as defined by the *Inter-Client Communication Conventions Manual.*

The String-to-Visual conversion calls `XMatchVisualInfo` using the *screen* and *depth* fields from the core part and returns the first matching Visual on the list. The widget resource list must be certain to specify any resource of type XtRVisual after the depth resource. The allowed string values are the visual class names defined in *Xlib*, Protocol, Section 8; `StaticGray`, `StaticColor`, `TrueColor`, `GrayScale`, `PseudoColor`, and `DirectColor`.

9.6.2   New Resource Converters

Type converters use pointers to `XrmValue` structures (defined in `<X11/Xresource.h>`; see Section 10.11 in *Xlib*) for input and output values.

```
typedef struct {
    unsigned int    size;
    caddr_t         addr;
} XrmValue, *XrmValuePtr;
```

The *addr* field specifies the address of the data, and the *size* field gives the total number of significant bytes in the data. For values of type `String`, *addr* is the address of the first character and *size* includes the NULL terminating byte.

A resource converter procedure pointer is of type `XtTypeConverter`.

```
typedef Boolean (*XtTypeConverter) (Display*, XrmValue*, Cardinal*,
                                    XrmValue*, XrmValue*, XtPointer*);
    Display *display;
    XrmValue *args;
    Cardinal *num_args;
    XrmValue *from;
    XrmValue *to;
    XtPointer *converter_data;
```

display	Specifies the display connection with which this conversion is associated.
args	Specifies a list of additional XrmValue arguments to the converter if additional context is needed to perform the conversion, or NULL. For example, the String-to-Font converter needs the widget's *screen*, and the String-to-Pixel converter needs the widget's *screen* and *colormap*.
num_args	Specifies the number of entries in *args*.
from	Specifies the value to convert.
to	Specifies a descriptor for a location into which to store the converted value.
converter_data	Specifies a location into which the converter may store converter-specific data associated with this conversion.

The *display* argument is normally used only when generating error messages, to identify the application context (with the function XtDisplayTo-ApplicationContext).

The *to* argument specifies the size and location into which the converter should store the converted value. If the *addr* field is NULL, the converter should allocate appropriate storage and store the size and location into the *to* descriptor. If the type converter allocates the storage, it remains under the ownership of the converter and must not be modified by the caller. The type converter is permitted to use static storage for this purpose, and therefore the caller must immediately copy the data upon return from the converter. If the *addr* field is not NULL, the converter must check the *size* field to ensure that sufficient space has been allocated before storing the converted value. If insufficient space is specified, the converter should update the *size* field with the number of bytes required and return False without modifying the data at the specified location. If sufficient space was allocated by the caller, the converter should update the *size* field with the number of bytes actually occupied by the converted value. For converted values of type XtRString, the size should include the NULL terminating byte, if any. The converter may store any value in the location specified in *converter_data*; this value will be passed to the destructor, if any, when the resource is freed by the Intrinsics.

The converter must return True if the conversion was successful and False otherwise. If the conversion cannot be performed because of an improper source value, a warning message should also be issued with XtAppWarning-Msg.

Most type converters just take the data described by the specified *from* argument and return data by writing into the location specified in the *to* argument. A few need other information, which is available in *args*. A type converter can invoke another type converter, which allows differing sources that may convert into a common intermediate result to make maximum use of the type converter cache.

Note that if an address is written into *to→addr*, it cannot be that of a local variable of the converter because the data will not be valid after the converter returns. Static variables may be used, as in the following example.

The following is an example of a converter that takes a `String` and converts it to a `Pixel`. Note that the *display* parameter is only used to generate error messages; the `Screen` conversion argument is still required to inform the Intrinsics that the converted value is a function of the particular display (and colormap).

```
#define done(type, value) \
    {                                                        \
        if (toVal ->addr != NULL) {                          \
            if (toVal ->size < sizeof(type)) {               \
                toVal ->size = sizeof(type);                 \
                return False;                                \
            }                                                \
            *(type*)(toVal ->addr) = (value);                \
        }                                                    \
        else {                                               \
            static type static_val;                          \
            static_val = (value);                            \
            toVal ->addr = (XtPointer)&static_val;           \
        }                                                    \
        toVal ->size = sizeof(type);                         \
        return True;                                         \
    }


static Boolean CvtStringToPixel(dpy, args, num_args, fromVal,
                                toVal, converter_data)
    Display     *dpy;
    XrmValue    *args;
    Cardinal    *num_args;
    XrmValue    *fromVal;
    XrmValue    *toVal;
    XtPointer   *converter_data;
{
    static XColor   screenColor;
    XColor          exactColor;
    Screen          *screen;
```

```
        Colormap        colormap;
        Status          status;
        char            message[1000];

    if (*num_args != 2)
        XtAppErrorMsg(XtDisplayToApplicationContext(dpy),
            "cvtStringToPixel", "wrongParameters",
            "XtToolkitError",
            "String to pixel conversion needs screen and \
colormap arguments",
            (String *)NULL, (Cardinal *)NULL);

    screen = *((Screen **) args[0].addr);
    colormap = *((Colormap *) args[1].addr);

    LowerCase((char *) fromVal->addr, message);

    if (strcmp(message, "xtdefaultbackground") == 0)
        done(&WhitePixelOfScreen(screen), Pixel);
    if (strcmp(message, "xtdefaultforeground") == 0)
        done(&BlackPixelOfScreen(screen), Pixel);

    if ((char) fromVal->addr[0] == '#') {  /* some rgb spec */
        status = XParseColor(DisplayOfScreen(screen), colormap,
                            (char*)fromVal->addr, &screenColor);
        if (status != 0)
            status = XAllocColor(DisplayOfScreen(screen),
                                colormap, &screenColor);
    } else  /* some color name */
        status = XAllocNamedColor(DisplayOfScreen(screen),
                                colormap, (char*)fromVal->addr,
                                &screenColor, &exactColor);

    if (status == 0) {
        String params[1];
        Cardinal num_params = 1;
        params[0] = (String)fromVal->addr;
        XtAppWarningMsg(XtDisplayToApplicationContext(dpy),
            "cvtStringToPixel", "noColormap", "XtToolkitError",
            "Cannot allocate colormap entry for \"%s\"",
            params, &num_params);
    } else {
        done( &screenColor.pixel, Pixel );
    }

    /* converter_data not used here */
};
```

All type converters should define some set of conversion values for which they are guaranteed to succeed so these can be used in the resource defaults. This issue arises only with conversions, such as fonts and colors, where there is no string representation that all server implementations will necessarily recognize. For resources like these, the converter should define a symbolic constant in the same manner as `XtDefaultForeground`, `XtDefaultBackground`, and `XtDefaultFont`.

To allow the Intrinsics to deallocate resources produced by type converters, a resource destructor procedure may also be provided.

A resource destructor procedure pointer is of type `XtDestructor`.

typedef void (*XtDestructor) (XtAppContext, XrmValue*, XtPointer, XrmValue*,
                                    Cardinal*);
    XtAppContext *app*;
    XrmValue **to;
    XtPointer *converter_data*;
    XrmValue **args;
    Cardinal **num_args;

app	Specifies an application context in which the resource is being freed.
to	Specifies a descriptor for the resource produced by the type converter.
converter_data	Specifies the converter-specific data returned by the type converter.
args	Specifies the additional converter arguments as passed to the type converter when the conversion was performed.
num_args	Specifies the number of entries in *args*.

The destructor procedure is responsible for freeing the resource specified by the *to* argument, including any auxiliary storage associated with that resource, but not the memory directly addressed by the size and location in the *to* argument nor the memory specified by *args*.

9.6.3 Issuing Conversion Warnings

The `XtDisplayStringConversionWarning` procedure is a convenience routine for resource type converters that convert from string values.

void XtDisplayStringConversionWarning (*display, from_value, to_type*)
    Display **display;
    String *from_value, to_type*;

display	Specifies the display connection with which the conversion is associated.

from_value	Specifies the string that could not be converted.
to_type	Specifies the target representation type requested.

The `XtDisplayStringConversionWarning` procedure issues a warning message using `XtAppWarningMsg` with *name* "conversionError", *type* "string", *class* "XtToolkitError", and the default message string "Cannot convert "*from_value*" to type *to_type*".

To issue other types of warning or error messages, the type converter should use `XtAppWarningMsg` or `XtAppErrorMsg`.

To retrieve the application context associated with a given display connection, use `XtDisplayToApplicationContext`.

XtAppContext XtDisplayToApplicationContext(*display*)
    Display **display*;

display	Specifies an open and initialized display connection.

The `XtDisplayToApplicationContext` function returns the application context in which the specified display was initialized. If the display is not known to the Intrinsics, an error message is issued.

9.6.4   Registering a New Resource Converter

When registering a resource converter, the client must specify the manner in which the conversion cache is to be used when there are multiple calls to the converter. Conversion cache control is specified via an `XtCacheType` argument.

typedef int XtCacheType;

An `XtCacheType` field may contain one of the following values:

`XtCacheNone`	Specifies that the results of a previous conversion may not be reused to satisfy any other resource requests; the specified converter will be called each time the converted value is required.
`XtCacheAll`	Specifies that the results of a previous conversion should be reused for any resource request that depends upon the same source value and conversion arguments.

XtCacheByDisplay — Specifies that the results of a previous conversion should be used as for XtCacheAll but the destructor will be called, if specified, if XtCloseDisplay is called for the display connection associated with the converted value, and the value will be removed from the conversion cache.

The qualifier XtCacheRefCount may be ORed with any of the above values. If XtCacheRefCount is specified, calls to XtCreateWidget, XtCreate-ManagedWidget, XtGetApplicationResources, and XtGetSub-resources that use the converted value will be counted. When a widget using the converted value is destroyed, the count is decremented, and if the count reaches zero, the destructor procedure will be called and the converted value will be removed from the conversion cache.

To register a type converter for all application contexts in a process, use XtSetTypeConverter, and to register a type converter in a single application context, use XtAppSetTypeConverter.

void XtSetTypeConverter(*from_type, to_type, converter, convert_args, num_args, cache_type, destructor*)
    String *from_type*;
    String *to_type*;
    XtTypeConverter *converter*;
    XtConvertArgList *convert_args*;
    Cardinal *num_args*;
    XtCacheType *cache_type*;
    XtDestructor *destructor*;

from_type — Specifies the source type.
to_type — Specifies the destination type.
converter — Specifies the resource type converter procedure.
convert_args — Specifies additional conversion arguments, or NULL.
num_args — Specifies the number of entries in *convert_args*.
cache_type — Specifies whether or not resources produced by this converter are shareable or display-specific and when they should be freed.
destructor — Specifies a destroy procedure for resources produced by this conversion, or NULL if no additional action is required to deallocate resources produced by the converter.

void XtAppSetTypeConverter(*app_context, from_type, to_type, converter, convert_args, num_args, cache_type, destructor*)
    XtAppContext *app_context*;
    String *from_type*;
    String *to_type*;

XtTypeConverter *converter*;
XtConvertArgList *convert_args*;
Cardinal *num_args*;
XtCacheType *cache_type*;
XtDestructor *destructor*;

app_context	Specifies the application context.
from_type	Specifies the source type.
to_type	Specifies the destination type.
converter	Specifies the resource type converter procedure.
convert_args	Specifies additional conversion arguments, or NULL.
num_args	Specifies the number of entries in *convert_args*.
cache_type	Specifies whether or not resources produced by this converter are shareable or display-specific and when they should be freed.
destructor	Specifies a destroy procedure for resources produced by this conversion, or NULL if no additional action is required to deallocate resources produced by the converter.

`XtSetTypeConverter` registers the specified type converter and destructor in all application contexts created by the calling process, including any future application contexts that may be created. `XtAppSetTypeConverter` registers the specified type converter in the single application context specified. If the same *from_type* and *to_type* are specified in multiple calls to either function, the most recent overrides the previous ones.

For the few type converters that need additional arguments, the Intrinsics conversion mechanism provides a method of specifying how these arguments should be computed. The enumerated type `XtAddressMode` and the structure `XtConvertArgRec` specify how each argument is derived. These are defined in `<X11/Intrinsic.h>`.

```
typedef enum {
    /*address mode          parameter representation */
    XtAddress                /* address */
    XtBaseOffset,            /* offset */
    XtImmediate,             /* constant */
    XtResourceString,        /* resource name string */
    XtResourceQuark,         /* resource name quark */
    XtWidgetBaseOffset,      /* offset */
    XtProcedureArg           /* procedure to call */
} XtAddressMode;
```

```
typedef struct {
    XtAddressMode     address_mode;
    XtPointer         address_id;
    Cardinal          size;
} XtConvertArgRec, *XtConvertArgList;
```

The *size* field specifies the length of the data in bytes. The *address_mode* field specifies how the *address_id* field should be interpreted. XtAddress causes *address_id* to be interpreted as the address of the data. XtBaseOffset causes *address_id* to be interpreted as the offset from the widget base. XtImmediate causes *address_id* to be interpreted as a constant. XtResourceString causes *address_id* to be interpreted as the name of a resource that is to be converted into an offset from the widget base. XtResourceQuark causes *address_id* to be interpreted as the result of an XrmStringToQuark conversion on the name of a resource, which is to be converted into an offset from the widget base. XtWidgetBaseOffset is similar to XtBaseOffset except that it searches for the closest windowed ancestor if the object is not of a subclass of Core (see Chapter 12). XtProcedureArg specifies that *address_id* is a pointer to a procedure to be invoked to return the conversion argument. If XtProcedureArg is specified, *address_id* must contain the address of a function of type XtConvertArgProc.

```
typedef void (*XtConvertArgProc) (Widget, Cardinal*, XrmValue*);
    Widget object;
    Cardinal *size;
    XrmValue *value;
```

object	Passes the object for which the resource is being converted, or NULL if the converter was invoked by XtCallConverter or XtDirectConvert.
size	Passes a pointer to the *size* field from the XtConvertArgRec.
value	Passes a pointer to a descriptor into which the procedure must store the conversion argument.

When invoked, the XtConvertArgProc procedure must derive a conversion argument and store the address and size of the argument in the location pointed to by *value*.

In order to permit reentrancy, the XtConvertArgProc should return the address of storage whose lifetime is no shorter than the lifetime of *object*. If *object* is NULL, the lifetime of the conversion argument must be no shorter than the lifetime of the resource with which the conversion argument is associated. The Intrinsics do not guarantee to copy this storage but do guarantee not to reference it if the resource is removed from the conversion cache.

The following example illustrates how to register the CvtStringToPixel routine given earlier:

```
static XtConvertArgRec colorConvertArgs[] = {
    {XtWidgetBaseOffset,
     (XtPointer)XtOffset(Widget, core.screen), sizeof(Screen*)},
    {XtWidgetBaseOffset,
     (XtPointer)XtOffset(Widget, core.colormap),sizeof(Colormap)}
};

XtSetTypeConverter(XtRString, XtRPixel, CvtStringToPixel,
    colorConvertArgs, XtNumber(colorConvertArgs),
    XtCacheByDisplay, NULL);
```

The conversion argument descriptors colorConvertArgs and screen-ConvertArg are predefined by the Intrinsics. Both take the values from the closest windowed ancestor if the object is not of a subclass of Core. The screenConvertArg descriptor puts the widget's *screen* field into *args*[0]. The colorConvertArgs descriptor puts the widget's *screen* field into *args*[0] and the widget's *colormap* field into *args*[1].

Conversion routines should not just put a descriptor for the address of the base of the widget into *args*[0] and use that in the routine. They should pass in the actual values on which the conversion depends. By keeping the dependencies of the conversion procedure specific, it is more likely that subsequent conversions will find what they need in the conversion cache. This way the cache is smaller and has fewer and more widely applicable entries.

If any conversion arguments of type XtBaseOffset, XtResourceString, XtResourceQuark, and XtWidgetBaseOffset are specified for conversions performed by XtGetApplicationResources, XtGet-Subresources, XtVaGetApplicationResources, or XtVaGet-Subresources, the arguments are computed with respect to the specified widget, not the base address or resource list specified in the call.

9.6.5   Resource Converter Invocation

All resource-fetching routines (for example, XtGetSubresources, XtGet-ApplicationResources, and so on) call resource converters if the resource database or varargs list specifies a value that has a different representation from the desired representation or if the widget's default resource value representation is different from the desired representation.

To invoke explicit resource conversions, use `XtConvertAndStore` or `XtCallConverter`.

typedef Opaque XtCacheRef;

Boolean XtCallConverter(*display, converter, args, num_args, from, to_in_out,*
                               cache_ref_return)
    Display* *display*;
    XtTypeConverter *converter*;
    XrmValuePtr *args*;
    Cardinal *num_args*;
    XrmValuePtr *from*;
    XrmValuePtr *to_in_out*;
    XtCacheRef * *cache_ref_return*;

display	Specifies the display with which the conversion is to be associated.
converter	Specifies the conversion procedure that is to be called.
args	Specifies the additional conversion arguments needed to perform the conversion, or NULL.
num_args	Specifies the number of entries in *args*.
from	Specifies a descriptor for the source value.
to_in_out	Returns the converted value.
cache_ref_return	Returns a conversion cache id.

The `XtCallConverter` function looks up the specified type converter in the application context associated with the display and, if the converter was not registered or was registered with cache type `XtCacheAll` or `XtCacheBy-Display`, looks in the conversion cache to see if this conversion procedure has been called with the specified arguments. If so, it checks the success status of the prior call, and if the conversion failed, `XtCallConverter` returns `False` immediately; otherwise it checks the size specified in the *to* argument and, if it is greater than or equal to the size stored in the cache, copies the information stored in the cache into the location specified by *to—>addr*, stores the cache size into *to—>size*, and returns `True`. If the size specified in the *to* argument is smaller than the size stored in the cache, `XtCallConverter` copies the cache size into *to—>size* and returns `False`. If the converter was registered with cache type `XtCacheNone` or no value was found in the conversion cache,

XtCallConverter calls the converter and, if it was not registered with cache type XtCacheNone, enters the result in the cache. XtCallConverter then returns what the converter returned.

The *cache_ref_return* field specifies storage allocated by the caller in which an opaque value will be stored. If the type converter has been registered with the XtCacheRefCount modifier and if the value returned in *cache_ref_return* is non-NULL, then the caller should store the *cache_ref_return* value in order to decrement the reference count when the converted value is no longer required. The *cache_ref_return* argument should be NULL if the caller is unwilling or unable to store the value.

To explicitly decrement the reference counts for resources obtained from XtCallConverter, use XtAppReleaseCacheRefs.

void XtAppReleaseCacheRefs(*app_context, refs*)
    XtAppContext *app_context*;
    XtCacheRef **refs*;
app_context   Specifies the application context.
refs   Specifies the list of cache references to be released.

XtAppReleaseCacheRefs decrements the reference count for the conversion entries identified by the *refs* argument. This argument is a pointer to a NULL-terminated list of XtCacheRef values. If any reference count reaches zero, the destructor, if any, will be called and the resource removed from the conversion cache.

As a convenience to clients needing to explicitly decrement reference counts via a callback function, the Intrinsics define two callback procedures, XtCallbackReleaseCacheRef and XtCallbackReleaseCacheRef-List.

void XtCallbackReleaseCacheRef(*object, client_data, call_data*)
    Widget *object*;
    XtPointer *client_data*;
    XtPointer *call_data*;
object   Specifies the object with which the resource is associated.
client_data   Specifies the conversion cache entry to be released.
call_data   Is ignored.

This callback procedure may be added to a callback list to release a previously returned `XtCacheRef` value. When adding the callback, the callback *client_data* argument must be specified as the value of the `XtCacheRef` data cast to type `XtPointer`.

void XtCallbackReleaseCacheRefList(*object, client_data, call_data*)
    Widget *object*;
    XtPointer *client_data*;
    XtPointer *call_data*;
object   Specifies the object with which the resources are associated.
client_data   Specifies the conversion cache entries to be released.
call_data   Is ignored.

This callback procedure may be added to a callback list to release a list of previously returned `XtCacheRef` values. When adding the callback, the callback *client_data* argument must be specified as a pointer to a NULL-terminated list of `XtCacheRef` values.

To look up and call a resource converter, copy the resulting value, and free a cached resource when a widget is destroyed, use `XtConvertAndStore`.

Boolean XtConvertAndStore(*object, from_type, from, to_type, to_in_out*)
    Widget *object*;
    String *from_type*;
    XrmValuePtr *from*;
    String *to_type*;
    XrmValuePtr *to_in_out*;
object   Specifies the object to use for additional arguments, if any are needed, and the destroy callback list. Must be of class Object or any subclass thereof.
from_type   Specifies the source type.
from   Specifies the value to be converted.
to_type   Specifies the destination type.
to_in_out   Specifies a descriptor for storage into which the converted value will be returned.

The `XtConvertAndStore` function looks up the type converter registered to convert *from_type* to *to_type*, computes any additional arguments needed, and then calls `XtCallConverter` (or `XtDirectConvert` if an old-style converter was registered with `XtAddConverter` or `XtAppAddConverter`; see

Appendix C) with the *from* and *to_in_out* arguments. The *to_in_out* argument specifies the size and location into which the converted value will be stored and is passed directly to the converter. If the location is specified as NULL, it will be replaced with a pointer to private storage and the size will be returned in the descriptor. The caller is expected to copy this private storage immediately and must not modify it in any way. If a non-NULL location is specified, the caller must allocate sufficient storage to hold the converted value and must also specify the size of that storage in the descriptor. If the conversion succeeds, `XtConvertAndStore` returns `True`; otherwise, it returns `False`.

`XtConvertAndStore` adds `XtCallbackReleaseCacheRef` to the destroyCallback list of the specified object if the conversion returns an `XtCacheRef` value. The resulting resource should not be referenced after the object has been destroyed.

`XtCreateWidget` performs processing equivalent to `XtConvertAndStore` when initializing the object instance. Because there is extra memory overhead required to implement reference counting, clients may distinguish those objects that are never destroyed before the application exits from those that may be destroyed and whose resources should be deallocated.

To specify whether reference counting is to be enabled for the resources of a particular object when the object is created, the client can specify a value for the `Boolean` resource XtNinitialResourcesPersistent, class XtCInitialResourcesPersistent.

When `XtCreateWidget` is called, if this resource is not specified as `False` in either the arglist or the resource database, then the resources referenced by this object are not reference-counted, regardless of how the type converter may have been registered. The effective default value is `True`; thus clients that expect to destroy one or more objects and want resources deallocated must explicitly specify `False` for XtNinitialResourcesPersistent.

The resources are still freed and destructors called when `XtCloseDisplay` is called if the conversion was registered as `XtCacheByDisplay`.

9.7   Reading and Writing Widget State

Any resource field in a widget can be read or written by a client. On a write operation, the widget decides what changes it will actually allow and updates all derived fields appropriately.

9.7.1   Obtaining Widget State

To retrieve the current values of resources associated with a widget instance, use XtGetValues.

void XtGetValues(*object, args, num_args*)
    Widget *object*;
    ArgList *args*;
    Cardinal *num_args*;

object	Specifies the object whose resource values are to be returned. Must be of class Object or any subclass thereof.
args	Specifies the argument list of name/address pairs that contain the resource names and the addresses into which the resource values are to be stored. The resource names are widget-dependent.
num_args	Specifies the number of entries in the argument list.

The XtGetValues function starts with the resources specified for the Object class and proceeds down the subclass chain to the class of the object. The *value* field of a passed argument list must contain the address into which to store the corresponding resource value. It is the caller's responsibility to allocate and deallocate this storage according to the size of the resource representation type used within the object.

If the class of the object's parent is a subclass of constraint-WidgetClass, XtGetValues then fetches the values for any constraint resources requested. It starts with the constraint resources specified for constraintWidgetClass and proceeds down the subclass chain to the parent's constraint resources. If the argument list contains a resource name that is not found in any of the resource lists searched, the value at the corresponding address is not modified. If any get_values_hook procedures in the object's class or superclass records are non-NULL, they are called in superclass-to-subclass order after all the resource values have been fetched by XtGetValues. Finally, if the object's parent is a subclass of constraintWidgetClass, and if any of the parent's class or superclass records have declared ConstraintClassExtension records in the Constraint class part *extension* field with a record type of NULLQUARK, and if the *get_values_hook* field in the extension record is non-NULL, XtGetValues calls the get_values_hook procedures in superclass-to-subclass order. This permits a Constraint parent to provide nonresource constraint data via XtGetValues.

To retrieve the current values of resources associated with a widget instance using varargs lists, use XtVaGetValues.

void XtVaGetValues(*object*, . . .)
    Widget *object*;

object	Specifies the object whose resource values are to be returned. Must be of class Object or any subclass thereof.
. . .	Specifies the variable argument list for the resources to be returned.

XtVaGetValues is identical in function to XtGetValues with the *args* and *num_args* parameters replaced by a varargs list, as described in Section 2.4.1. All value entries in the list must specify pointers to storage allocated by the caller to which the resource value will be copied. It is the caller's responsibility to ensure that sufficient storage is allocated. If XtVaTypedArg is specified, the *type* argument specifies the representation desired by the caller and the *size* argument specifies the number of bytes allocated to store the result of the conversion. If the size is insufficient, a warning message is issued and the list entry is skipped.

9.7.1.1 Widget Subpart Resource Data: the get_values_hook Procedure

Widgets that have subparts can return resource values from them through XtGetValues by supplying a get_values_hook procedure. The get_values_ hook procedure pointer is of type XtArgsProc.

typedef void (*XtArgsProc)(Widget, ArgList, Cardinal*);
    Widget *w*;
    ArgList *args*;
    Cardinal **num_args*;

w	Specifies the widget whose subpart resource values are to be retrieved.
args	Specifies the argument list that was passed to XtGetValues or the transformed varargs list passed to XtVaGetValues.
num_args	Specifies the number of entries in the argument list.

The widget with subpart resources should call XtGetSubvalues in the get_values_hook procedure and pass in its subresource list and the *args* and *num_args* parameters.

9.7.1.2 Widget Subpart State

To retrieve the current values of subpart resource data associated with a widget instance, use XtGetSubvalues. For a discussion of subpart resources, see Section 9.4.

void XtGetSubvalues(*base, resources, num_resources, args, num_args*)
    XtPointer *base*;
    XtResourceList *resources*;
    Cardinal *num_resources*;
    ArgList *args*;
    Cardinal *num_args*;

base	Specifies the base address of the subpart data structure for which the resources should be retrieved.
resources	Specifies the subpart resource list.
num_resources	Specifies the number of entries in the resource list.
args	Specifies the argument list of name/address pairs that contain the resource names and the addresses into which the resource values are to be stored.
num_args	Specifies the number of entries in the argument list.

The `XtGetSubvalues` function obtains resource values from the structure identified by *base*. The *value* field in each argument entry must contain the address into which to store the corresponding resource value. It is the caller's responsibility to allocate and deallocate this storage according to the size of the resource representation type used within the subpart. If the argument list contains a resource name that is not found in the resource list, the value at the corresponding address is not modified.

To retrieve the current values of subpart resources associated with a widget instance using varargs lists, use `XtVaGetSubvalues`.

void XtVaGetSubvalues(*base, resources, num_resources, . . .*)
    XtPointer *base*;
    XtResourceList *resources*;
    Cardinal *num_resources*;

base	Specifies the base address of the subpart data structure for which the resources should be retrieved.
resources	Specifies the subpart resource list.
num_resources	Specifies the number of entries in the resource list.
. . .	Specifies a variable argument list of name/address pairs that contain the resource names and the addresses into which the resource values are to be stored.

XtVaGetSubvalues is identical in function to XtGetSubvalues with the *args* and *num_args* parameters replaced by a varargs list, as described in Section 2.4.1. XtVaTypedArg is not supported for XtVaGetSubvalues. If XtVa- TypedArg is specified in the list, a warning message is issued and the entry is ignored.

9.7.2   Setting Widget State

To modify the current values of resources associated with a widget instance, use XtSetValues.

void XtSetValues(*object, args, num_args*)
    Widget *object*;
    ArgList *args*;
    Cardinal *num_args*;

object	Specifies the object whose resources are to be modified. Must be of class Object or any subclass thereof.
args	Specifies the argument list of name/value pairs that contain the resources to be modified and their new values.
num_args	Specifies the number of entries in the argument list.

The XtSetValues function starts with the resources specified for the Object class fields and proceeds down the subclass chain to the object. At each stage, it replaces the *object* resource fields with any values specified in the argument list. XtSetValues then calls the set_values procedures for the object in superclass-to-subclass order. If the object has any non-NULL *set_values_hook* fields, these are called immediately after the corresponding set_values procedure. This procedure permits subclasses to set subpart data via XtSet- Values.

If the class of the object's parent is a subclass of constraintWidget- Class, XtSetValues also updates the object's constraints. It starts with the constraint resources specified for constraintWidgetClass and proceeds down the subclass chain to the parent's class. At each stage, it replaces the con- straint resource fields with any values specified in the argument list. It then calls the constraint set_values procedures from constraintWidgetClass down to the parent's class. The constraint set_values procedures are called with widget arguments, as for all set_values procedures, not just the constraint records, so that they can make adjustments to the desired values based on full information about the widget. Any arguments specified that do not match a resource list entry are silently ignored.

If the object is of a subclass of RectObj, XtSetValues determines if a geometry request is needed by comparing the old object to the new object. If any geometry changes are required, it restores the original geometry, then makes the request, and the geometry manager returns XtGeometryYes, XtGeometryAlmost, or XtGeometryNo. If XtGeometryYes, XtSet-Values calls the object's resize procedure. If XtGeometryNo, XtSetValues ignores the geometry request and continues. If XtGeometryAlmost, XtSet-Values calls the set_values_almost procedure, which determines what should be done. XtSetValues then repeats this process, deciding once more whether the geometry manager should be called.

Finally, if any of the set_values procedures returned True, and the widget is realized, XtSetValues causes the widget's expose procedure to be invoked by calling XClearArea on the widget's window.

To modify the current values of resources associated with a widget instance using varargs lists, use XtVaSetValues.

```
void XtVaSetValues(object, . . .)
    Widget object;
```
object   Specifies the object whose resources are to be modified.
     Must be of class Object or any subclass thereof.
. . .   Specifies the variable argument list of name/value pairs that contain
     the resources to be modified and their new values.

XtVaSetValues is identical in function to XtSetValues with the *args* and *num_args* parameters replaced by a varargs list, as described in Section 2.4.1.

9.7.2.1 Widget State: the set_values Procedure

The set_values procedure pointer in a widget class is of type XtSetValues-Func.

```
typedef Boolean (*XtSetValuesFunc) (Widget, Widget, Widget, ArgList, Cardinal*);
    Widget current;
    Widget request;
    Widget new;
    ArgList args;
    Cardinal *num_args;
```

current   Specifies a copy of the widget as it was before the `XtSetValues` call.

request   Specifies a copy of the widget with all values changed as asked for by the `XtSetValues` call before any class set_values procedures have been called.

new   Specifies the widget with the new values that are actually allowed.

args   Specifies the argument list passed to `XtSetValues` or the transformed argument list passed to `XtVaSetValues`.

num_args   Specifies the number of entries in the argument list.

The set_values procedure should recompute any field derived from resources that are changed (for example, many GCs depend on foreground and background pixels). If no recomputation is necessary and if none of the resources specific to a subclass require the window to be redisplayed when their values are changed, you can specify NULL for the *set_values* field in the class record.

Like the initialize procedure, set_values mostly deals only with the fields defined in the subclass, but it has to resolve conflicts with its superclass, especially conflicts over width and height.

Sometimes a subclass may want to overwrite values filled in by its superclass. In particular, size calculations of a superclass are often incorrect for a subclass and, in this case, the subclass must modify or recalculate fields declared and computed by its superclass.

As an example, a subclass can visually surround its superclass display. In this case, the width and height calculated by the superclass set_values procedure are too small and need to be incremented by the size of the surround. The subclass needs to know if its superclass's size was calculated by the superclass or was specified explicitly. All widgets must place themselves into whatever size is explicitly given, but they should compute a reasonable size if no size is requested. How does a subclass know the difference between a specified size and a size computed by a superclass?

The *request* and *new* parameters provide the necessary information. The *request* widget is a copy of the widget, updated as originally requested. The *new* widget starts with the values in the request, but it has additionally been updated by all superclass set_values procedures called so far. A subclass set_values procedure can compare these two to resolve any potential conflicts. The set_values procedure need not refer to the *request* widget unless it must resolve conflicts between the *current* and *new* widgets. Any changes the widget needs to make, including geometry changes, should be made in the *new* widget.

In the above example, the subclass with the visual surround can see if the *width* and *height* in the *request* widget are zero. If so, it adds its surround size to the *width* and *height* fields in the *new* widget. If not, it must make do with the size originally specified. In this case, zero is a special value defined by the class to permit the application to invoke this behavior.

The *new* widget is the actual widget instance record. Therefore, the set_values procedure should do all its work on the *new* widget; the *request* widget should never be modified. If the set_values procedure needs to call any routines that operate on a widget, it should specify *new* as the widget instance.

Before calling the set_values procedures, the Intrinsics modify the resources of the *request* widget according to the contents of the arglist; if the widget names all its resources in the class resource list, it is never necessary to examine the contents of *args*.

Finally, the set_values procedure must return a Boolean that indicates whether the widget needs to be redisplayed. Note that a change in the geometry fields alone does not require the set_values procedure to return `True`; the X server will eventually generate an `Expose` event, if necessary. After calling all the set_values procedures, `XtSetValues` forces a redisplay by calling `XClearArea` if any of the set_values procedures returned `True`. Therefore, a set_values procedure should not try to do its own redisplaying.

Set_values procedures should not do any work in response to changes in geometry because `XtSetValues` eventually will perform a geometry request, and that request might be denied. If the widget actually changes size in response to a call to `XtSetValues`, its resize procedure is called. Widgets should do any geometry-related work in their resize procedure.

Note that it is permissible to call `XtSetValues` before a widget is realized. Therefore, the set_values procedure must not assume that the widget is realized.

9.7.2.2 Widget State: the set_values_almost Procedure

The set_values_almost procedure pointer in the widget class record is of type `XtAlmostProc`.

```
typedef void (*XtAlmostProc) (Widget, Widget, XtWidgetGeometry*,
                              XtWidgetGeometry*);
    Widget old;
    Widget new;
```

XtWidgetGeometry *_request_;
XtWidgetGeometry *_reply_;

old	Specifies a copy of the object as it was before the XtSetValues call.
new	Specifies the object instance record.
request	Specifies the original geometry request that was sent to the geometry manager that caused XtGeometryAlmost to be returned.
reply	Specifies the compromise geometry that was returned by the geometry manager with XtGeometryAlmost.

Most classes inherit the set_values_almost procedure from their superclass by specifying XtInheritSetValuesAlmost in the class initialization. The set_values_almost procedure in rectObjClass accepts the compromise suggested.

The set_values_almost procedure is called when a client tries to set a widget's geometry by means of a call to XtSetValues, and the geometry manager cannot satisfy the request but instead returns XtGeometryNo or XtGeometry-Almost and a compromise geometry. The _new_ object is the actual instance record. The _x_, _y_, _width_, _height_, and _border_width_ fields contain the original values as they were before the XtSetValues call and all other fields contain the new values. The _request_ parameter contains the new geometry request that was made to the parent. The _reply_ parameter contains _reply_-> _request_mode_ equal to zero if the parent returned XtGeometryNo and contains the parent's compromise geometry otherwise. The set_values_almost procedure takes the original geometry and the compromise geometry and determines if the compromise is acceptable or whether to try a different compromise. It returns its results in the _request_ parameter, which is then sent back to the geometry manager for another try. To accept the compromise, the procedure must copy the contents of the _reply_ geometry into the _request_ geometry; to attempt an alternative geometry, the procedure may modify any part of the _request_ argument; to terminate the geometry negotiation and retain the original geometry, the procedure must set _request_-> _request_mode_ to zero. The geometry fields of the _old_ and _new_ instances must not be modified directly.

9.7.2.3   Widget State: the ConstraintClassPart set_values Procedure

The constraint set_values procedure pointer is of type XtSetValuesFunc. The values passed to the parent's constraint set_values procedure are the same as those passed to the child's class set_values procedure. A class can specify

NULL for the *set_values* field of the `ConstraintPart` if it need not compute anything.

The constraint set_values procedure should recompute any constraint fields derived from constraint resources that are changed. Further, it may modify other widget fields as appropriate. For example, if a constraint for the maximum height of a widget is changed to a value smaller than the widget's current height, the constraint set_values procedure may reset the *height* field in the widget.

9.7.2.4   Widget Subpart State

To set the current values of subpart resources associated with a widget instance, use `XtSetSubvalues`. For a discussion of subpart resources, see Section 9.4.

void XtSetSubvalues(*base, resources, num_resources, args, num_args*)	
XtPointer *base*;	
XtResourceList *resources*;	
Cardinal *num_resources*;	
ArgList *args*;	
Cardinal *num_args*;	
base	Specifies the base address of the subpart data structure into which the resources should be written.
resources	Specifies the subpart resource list.
num_resources	Specifies the number of entries in the resource list.
args	Specifies the argument list of name/value pairs that contain the resources to be modified and their new values.
num_args	Specifies the number of entries in the argument list.

The `XtSetSubvalues` function updates the resource fields of the structure identified by *base*. Any specified arguments that do not match an entry in the resource list are silently ignored.

To set the current values of subpart resources associated with a widget instance using varargs lists, use `XtVaSetSubvalues`.

void XtVaSetSubvalues(*base, resources, num_resources, . . .*)
    XtPointer *base*;
    XtResourceList *resources*;
    Cardinal *num_resources*;

base	Specifies the base address of the subpart data structure into which the resources should be written.
resources	Specifies the subpart resource list.
num_resources	Specifies the number of entries in the resource list.
. . .	Specifies the variable argument list of name/value pairs that contain the resources to be modified and their new values.

XtVaSetSubvalues is identical in function to XtSetSubvalues with the *args* and *num_args* parameters replaced by a varargs list, as described in Section 2.4.1. XtVaTypedArg is not supported for XtVaSetSubvalues. If an entry containing XtVaTypedArg is specified in the list, a warning message is issued and the entry is ignored.

9.7.2.5 Widget Subpart Resource Data: the set_values_hook Procedure

Note   The set_values_hook procedure is obsolete, as the same information is now available to the set_values procedure. The procedure has been retained for those widgets that used it in versions prior to Release 4.

Widgets that have a subpart can set the subpart resource values through XtSetValues by supplying a set_values_hook procedure. The set_values_ hook procedure pointer in a widget class is of type XtArgsFunc.

```
typedef Boolean (*XtArgsFunc)(Widget, Arglist, Cardinal*);
    Widget w;
    Arglist args;
    Cardinal *num_args;
```

w	Specifies the widget whose subpart resource values are to be changed.
args	Specifies the argument list that was passed to XtSetValues or the transformed varargs list passed to XtVaSetValues.
num_args	Specifies the number of entries in the argument list.

The widget with subpart resources may call XtSetSubvalues from the set_values_hook procedure and pass in its subresource list and the *args* and *num_args* parameters.

Chapter 10

Translation Management

Except under unusual circumstances, widgets do not hardwire the mapping of user events into widget behavior by using the event manager. Instead, they provide a default mapping of events into behavior that you can override.

The translation manager provides an interface to specify and manage the mapping of X event sequences into widget-supplied functionality, for example, calling procedure *Abc* when the *y* key is pressed.

The translation manager uses two kinds of tables to perform translations:

• The action tables, which are in the widget class structure, specify the mapping of externally available procedure name strings to the corresponding procedure implemented by the widget class.

• A translation table, which is in the widget class structure, specifies the mapping of event sequences to procedure name strings.

You can override the translation table in the class structure for a specific widget instance by supplying a different translation table for the widget instance. The resource name is XtNtranslations.

10.1 Action Tables

All widget class records contain an action table, an array of `XtActionsRec` entries. In addition, an application can register its own action tables with the translation manager so that the translation tables it provides to widget instances can access application functionality directly. The translation action procedure pointer is of type `XtActionProc`.

```
typedef void (*XtActionProc) (Widget, XEvent*, String*, Cardinal*);
    Widget w;
    XEvent *event;
    String *params;
    Cardinal *num_params;
```

w	Specifies the widget that caused the action to be called.
event	Specifies the event that caused the action to be called. If the action is called after a sequence of events, then the last event in the sequence is used.
params	Specifies a pointer to the list of strings that were specified in the translation table as arguments to the action, or NULL.
num_params	Specifies the number of entries in *params*.

```
typedef struct _XtActionsRec {
    String          string;
    XtActionProc    proc;
} XtActionsRec, *XtActionList;
```

The *string* field is the name that is used in translation tables to access the procedure. The *proc* field is a pointer to a procedure that implements the functionality.

Action procedures should not assume that the widget in which they are invoked is realized; an accelerator specification can cause an action procedure to be called for a widget that does not yet have a window. Widget writers should also note which of a widget's callback lists are invoked from action procedures and warn clients not to assume the widget is realized in those callbacks.

For example, a Pushbutton widget has procedures to take the following actions:

• Set the button to indicate it is activated.

• Unset the button back to its normal mode.

• Highlight the button borders.

• Unhighlight the button borders.

• Notify any callbacks that the button has been activated.

The action table for the Pushbutton widget class makes these functions available to translation tables written for Pushbutton or any subclass. The string entry is the name used in translation tables. The procedure entry (usually spelled identically to the string) is the name of the C procedure that implements that function:

```
XtActionsRec actionTable[] = {
    {"Set",         Set},
    {"Unset",       Unset},
    {"Highlight",   Highlight},
    {"Unhighlight", Unhighlight}
    {"Notify",      Notify},
};
```

The Intrinsics reserve all action names and parameters starting with the characters "Xt" for future standard enhancements. Users, applications, and widgets should not declare action names or pass parameters starting with these characters except to invoke specified built-in Intrinsics functions.

10.1.1 Action Table Registration

The *actions* and *num_actions* fields of `CoreClassPart` specify the actions implemented by a widget class. These are automatically registered with the Intrinsics when the class is initialized.

To declare an action table within an application and register it with the translation manager, use `XtAppAddActions`.

> void XtAppAddActions(*app_context, actions, num_actions*)
>   XtAppContext *app_context*;
>   XtActionList *actions*;
>   Cardinal *num_actions*;
> *app_context*   Specifies the application context.
> *actions*   Specifies the action table to register.
> *num_actions*   Specifies the number of entries in this action table.

If more than one action is registered with the same name, the most recently registered action is used. If duplicate actions exist in an action table, the first is used. The Intrinsics register an action table containing XtMenuPopup and XtMenuPopdown as part of XtCreateApplicationContext.

10.1.2 Action Names to Procedure Translations

The translation manager uses a simple algorithm to resolve the name of a procedure specified in a translation table into the actual procedure specified in an action table. When the widget is realized, the translation manager performs a search for the name in the following tables, in order:

• The widget's class and all superclass action tables, in subclass-to-superclass order.

• The parent's class and all superclass action tables, in subclass-to-superclass order, then on up the ancestor tree.

• The action tables registered with `XtAppAddActions` and `XtAddActions` from the most recently added table to the oldest table.

As soon as it finds a name, the translation manager stops the search. If it cannot find a name, the translation manager generates a warning message.

10.1.3   Action Hook Registration

An application can specify a procedure that will be called just before every action routine is dispatched by the translation manager. To do so, the application supplies a procedure pointer of type `XtActionHookProc`.

typedef void (*XtActionHookProc) (Widget, XtPointer, String, XEvent*, String*,
Cardinal*);
    Widget *w*;
    XtPointer *client_data*;
    String *action_name*;
    XEvent* *event*;
    String* *params*;
    Cardinal* *num_params*;

w	Specifies the widget whose action is about to be dispatched.
client_data	Specifies the application-specific closure that was passed to `XtAppAddActionHook`.
action_name	Specifies the name of the action to be dispatched.
event	Specifies the event argument that will be passed to the action routine.
params	Specifies the action parameters that will be passed to the action routine.
num_params	Specifies the number of entries in *params*.

Action hooks should not modify any of the data pointed to by the arguments other than the *client_data* argument.

To add an action hook, use `XtAppAddActionHook`.

XtActionHookId XtAppAddActionHook(*app, proc, client_data*)
    XtAppContext *app*;
    XtActionHookProc *proc*;
    XtPointer *client_data*;

app   Specifies the application context.
proc   Specifies the action hook procedure.
client_data   Specifies application-specific data to be passed to the action hook.

`XtAppAddActionHook` adds the specified procedure to the front of a list maintained in the application context. In the future, when an action routine is about to be invoked for any widget in this application context, either through the translation manager or via `XtCallActionProc`, the action hook procedures will be called in reverse order of registration just prior to invoking the action routine.

Action hook procedures are removed automatically and the `XtAction-HookIds` destroyed when the application context in which they were added is destroyed.

To remove an action hook procedure without destroying the application context, use `XtRemoveActionHook`.

void XtRemoveActionHook(*id*)
    XtActionHookId *id*;
    id   Specifies the action hook id returned by `XtAppAddActionHook`.

`XtRemoveActionHook` removes the specified action hook procedure from the list in which it was registered.

10.2   Translation Tables

All widget instance records contain a translation table, which is a resource with a default value specified elsewhere in the class record. A translation table specifies what action procedures are invoked for an event or a sequence of events. A translation table is a string containing a list of translations from an event sequence into one or more action procedure calls. The translations are separated from one another by newline characters (ASCII LF). The complete syntax of translation tables is specified in Appendix B.

As an example, the default behavior of Pushbutton is

• Highlight on enter window.

• Unhighlight on exit window.

• Invert on left button down.

• Call callbacks and reinvert on left button up.

The following illustrates Pushbutton's default translation table:

```
static String defaultTranslations =
    "<EnterWindow>:    Highlight()\n \
    <LeaveWindow>:    Unhighlight()\n \
    <Btn1Down>:       Set()\n \
    <Btn1Up>:         Notify() Unset()";
```

The *tm_table* field of the `CoreClassPart` should be filled in at static initialization time with the string containing the class's default translations. If a class wants to inherit its superclass's translations, it can store the special value `XtInheritTranslations` into *tm_table*. In Core's class part initialization procedure, the Intrinsics compile this translation table into an efficient internal form. Then, at widget creation time, this default translation table is combined with the XtNtranslations resource.

The resource conversion mechanism automatically compiles string translation tables that are specified in the resource database. If a client uses translation tables that are not retrieved via a resource conversion, it must compile them itself using `XtParseTranslationTable`.

The Intrinsics use the compiled form of the translation table to register the necessary events with the event manager. Widgets need do nothing other than specify the action and translation tables for events to be processed by the translation manager.

10.2.1   Event Sequences

An event sequence is a comma-separated list of X event descriptions that describes a specific sequence of X events to map to a set of program actions. Each X event description consists of three parts: the X event type, a prefix consisting of the X modifier bits, and an event-specific suffix.

Various abbreviations are supported to make translation tables easier to read. The events must match incoming events in left-to-right order to trigger the action sequence.

10.2.2   Action Sequences

Action sequences specify what program or widget actions to take in response to incoming X events. An action sequence consists of space-separated action procedure call specifications. Each action procedure call consists of the name of an action procedure and a parenthesized list of zero or more comma-separated string parameters to pass to that procedure. The actions are invoked in left-to-right order as specified in the action sequence.

10.2.3 Multi-Click Time

Translation table entries may specify actions that are taken when two or more identical events occur consecutively within a short time interval, called the multi-click time. The multi-click time value may be specified as an application resource with name "multiClickTime" and class "MultiClickTime" and may also be modified dynamically by the application. The multi-click time is unique for each Display value and is retrieved from the resource database by `XtDisplayInitialize`. If no value is specified, the initial value is 200 milliseconds.

To set the multi-click time dynamically, use `XtSetMultiClickTime`.

```
void XtSetMultiClickTime(display, time)
    Display *display;
    int time;
```

display	Specifies the display connection.
time	Specifies the multi-click time in milliseconds.

`XtSetMultiClickTime` sets the time interval used by the translation manager to determine when multiple events are interpreted as a repeated event. When a repeat count is specified in a translation entry, the interval between the timestamps in each pair of repeated events (e.g., between two `ButtonPress` events) must be less than the multi-click time in order for the translation actions to be taken.

To read the multi-click time, use `XtGetMultiClickTime`.

```
int XtGetMultiClickTime(display)
    Display *display;
```

display	Specifies the display connection.

`XtGetMultiClickTime` returns the time in milliseconds that the translation manager uses to determine if multiple events are to be interpreted as a repeated event for purposes of matching a translation entry containing a repeat count.

10.3   Translation Table Management

Sometimes an application needs to merge its own translations with a widget's translations. For example, a window manager provides functions to move a window. It usually may move the window when any pointer button is pressed down in a title bar, but it allows the user to specify other translations for the middle or right button down in the title bar, and it ignores any user translations for left button down.

To accomplish this, the window manager should first create the title bar and then should merge the two translation tables into the title bar's translations. One translation table contains the translations that the window manager wants only if the user has not specified a translation for a particular event or event sequence. The other translation table contains the translations that the window manager wants regardless of what the user has specified.

Three Intrinsics functions support this merging:

`XtParseTranslationTable`	Compiles a translation table.
`XtAugmentTranslations`	Merges a compiled translation table into a widget's compiled translation table, ignoring any new translations that conflict with existing translations.
`XtOverrideTranslations`	Merges a compiled translation table into a widget's compiled translation table, replacing any existing translations that conflict with new translations.

To compile a translation table, use `XtParseTranslationTable`.

XtTranslations XtParseTranslationTable(*table*)
   String *table*;
   table   Specifies the translation table to compile.

The `XtParseTranslationTable` function compiles the translation table, provided in the format given in Appendix B, into an opaque internal representation of type `XtTranslations`. Note that if an empty translation table is required for any purpose, one can be obtained by calling `XtParse-TranslationTable` and passing an empty string.

To merge additional translations into an existing translation table, use `XtAugmentTranslations`.

void XtAugmentTranslations(*w*, *translations*)
   Widget *w*;
   XtTranslations *translations*;
   w   Specifies the widget into which the new translations are to be merged.
                           Must be of class Core or any subclass thereof.
   translations   Specifies the compiled translation table to merge in.

The `XtAugmentTranslations` function merges the new translations into
the existing widget translations, ignoring any `#replace`, `#augment`, or
`#override` directive that may have been specified in the translation string.
The translation table specified by *translations* is not altered by this process. If
the new translations contain an event or event sequence that already exists in
the widget's translations, the new translation is ignored.

To overwrite existing translations with new translations, use `XtOverride-`
`Translations`.

void XtOverrideTranslations(*w*, *translations*)
   Widget *w*;
   XtTranslations *translations*;
   w   Specifies the widget into which the new translations are to be merged.
                           Must be of class Core or any subclass thereof.
   translations   Specifies the compiled translation table to merge in.

The `XtOverrideTranslations` function merges the new translations into
the existing widget translations, ignoring any `#replace`, `#augment`, or
`#override` directive that may have been specified in the translation string.
The translation table specified by *translations* is not altered by this process. If
the new translations contain an event or event sequence that already exists in
the widget's translations, the new translation is merged in and overrides the
widget's translation.

To replace a widget's translations completely, use `XtSetValues` on the
XtNtranslations resource and specifiy a compiled translation table as the value.

To make it possible for users to easily modify translation tables in their
resource files, the string-to-translation-table resource type converter allows the
string to specify whether the table should replace, augment, or override any
existing translation table in the widget. To specify this, a sharp sign (#) is given

as the first character of the table followed by one of the keywords "replace", "augment", or "override" to indicate whether to replace, augment, or override the existing table. The replace or merge operation is performed during the Core instance initialization and during the Core set_values invocation. At instance initialization the widget class translation table (if any) is copied into the widget prior to a merge operation. The merge operation produces a new translation resource value; if the original table was shared by other widgets, they are unaffected. If no directive is specified, "#replace" is assumed.

To completely remove existing translations, use `XtUninstall-Translations`.

void XtUninstallTranslations(*w*)
    Widget *w*;

w   Specifies the widget from which the translations are to be removed.
                       Must be of class Core or any subclass thereof.

The `XtUninstallTranslations` function causes the entire translation table for the widget to be removed.

10.4   Using Accelerators

It is often desirable to be able to bind events in one widget to actions in another. In particular, it is often useful to be able to invoke menu actions from the keyboard. The Intrinsics provide a facility, called accelerators, that lets you accomplish this. An accelerator table is a translation table that is bound with its actions in the context of a particular widget, the *source* widget. The accelerator table can then be installed on one or more *destination* widgets. When an event sequence in the destination widget would cause an accelerator action to be taken, and if the source widget is sensitive, the actions are executed as though triggered by the same event sequence in the accelerator source widget. The event is passed to the action procedure without modification. The action procedures used within accelerators must not assume that the source widget is realized nor that any fields of the event are in reference to the source widget's window if the widget is realized.

Each widget instance contains that widget's exported accelerator table as a resource. Each class of widget exports a method that takes a displayable string representation of the accelerators so that widgets can display their current

accelerators. The representation is the accelerator table in canonical translation table form (see Appendix B). The display_accelerator procedure pointer
is of type `XtStringProc`.

typedef void (*XtStringProc) (Widget, String);
    Widget *w*;
    String *string*;

w   Specifies the source widget that supplied the accelerators.
string   Specifies the string representation of the accelerators for this widget.

Accelerators can be specified in resource files, and the string representation is
the same as for a translation table. However, the interpretation of the
#augment and #override directives applies to what will happen when the
accelerator is installed; that is, whether or not the accelerator translations will
override the translations in the destination widget. The default is #augment,
which means that the accelerator translations have lower priority than the destination translations. The #replace directive is ignored for accelerator tables.

To parse an accelerator table, use `XtParseAcceleratorTable`.

XtAccelerators XtParseAcceleratorTable (*source*)
    String *source*;
source   Specifies the accelerator table to compile.

The `XtParseAcceleratorTable` function compiles the accelerator table
into an opaque internal representation. The client should set the XtNaccelerators resource of each widget that is to be activated by these translations to the
returned value.

To install accelerators from a widget on another widget, use `XtInstall-`
`Accelerators`.

void XtInstallAccelerators(*destination, source*)
    Widget *destination*;
    Widget *source*;
destination   Specifies the widget on which the accelerators are to be installed.
                            Must be of class Core or any subclass thereof.
source   Specifies the widget from which the accelerators are to come.
                            Must be of class Core or any subclass thereof.

The XtInstallAccelerators function installs the *accelerators* resource value from *source* onto *destination* by merging the source accelerators into the destination translations. If the source *display_accelerator* field is non-NULL, XtInstallAccelerators calls it with the source widget and a string representation of the accelerator table, which indicates that its accelerators have been installed and that it should display them appropriately. The string representation of the accelerator table is its canonical translation table representation.

As a convenience for installing all accelerators from a widget and all its descendants onto one destination, use XtInstallAllAccelerators.

void XtInstallAllAccelerators(*destination, source*)
    Widget *destination*;
    Widget *source*;

destination	Specifies the widget on which the accelerators are to be installed. Must be of class Core or any subclass thereof.
source	Specifies the root widget of the widget tree from which the accelerators are to come. Must be of class Core or any subclass thereof.

The XtInstallAllAccelerators function recursively descends the widget tree rooted at *source* and installs the accelerators resource value of each widget encountered onto *destination*. A common use is to call XtInstallAll-Accelerators and pass the application main window as the source.

10.5   KeyCode-to-KeySym Conversions

The translation manager provides support for automatically translating Key-Codes in incoming key events into KeySyms. KeyCode-to-KeySym translator procedure pointers are of type XtKeyProc.

typedef void (*XtKeyProc)(Display*, KeyCode, Modifiers, Modifiers*, KeySym*);
    Display *display*;
    KeyCode *keycode*;
    Modifiers *modifiers*;
    Modifiers *modifiers_return*;
    KeySym *keysym_return*;

display	Specifies the display that the KeyCode is from.
keycode	Specifies the KeyCode to translate.
modifiers	Specifies the modifiers to the KeyCode.

    modifiers_return   Specifies a location in which to store a mask that indicates the subset of all modifiers that are examined by the key translator.

    keysym_return   Specifies a location in which to store the resulting KeySym.

This procedure takes a KeyCode and modifiers and produces a KeySym. For any given key translator function, *modifiers_return* will be a constant that indicates the subset of all modifiers that are examined by the key translator.

    The Intrinsics maintain tables internally to map KeyCodes to KeySyms for each open display. Translator procedures and other clients may share a single copy of this table to perform the same mapping.

    To return a pointer to the KeySym-to-KeyCode mapping table for a particular display, use XtGetKeysymTable.

```
KeySym *XtGetKeysymTable (display, min_keycode_return, keysyms_per_keycode_return)
    Display *display;
    KeyCode *min_keycode_return;
    int *keysyms_per_keycode_return;
```

    display   Specifies the display whose table is required.

    min_keycode_return   Returns the minimum KeyCode valid for the display.

    keysyms_per_keycode_return   Returns the number of KeySyms stored for each KeyCode.

XtGetKeysymTable returns a pointer to the Intrinsics' copy of the server's KeyCode-to-KeySym table. This table must not be modified. There are *keysyms_per_keycode_return* KeySyms associated with each KeyCode, located in the table with indices starting at index

$$(\text{test\_keycode} - \text{min\_keycode\_return}) * \text{keysyms\_per\_keycode\_return}$$

for KeyCode *test_keycode*. Any entries that have no KeySyms associated with them contain the value NoSymbol. Clients should not cache the KeySym table but should call XtGetKeysymTable each time the value is needed, as the table may change prior to dispatching each event.

    For more information on this table, see Section 7.9 in *Xlib*.

    To register a key translator, use XtSetKeyTranslator.

```
void XtSetKeyTranslator (display, proc)
    Display *display;
    XtKeyProc proc;
```

display   Specifies the display from which to translate the events.

proc   Specifies the procedure that is to perform key translations.

The `XtSetKeyTranslator` function sets the specified procedure as the current key translator. The default translator is `XtTranslateKey`, an `XtKeyProc` that uses the Shift, Lock, and group modifiers with the interpretations defined in *Xlib*, Protocol, Section 5. It is provided so that new translators can call it to get default KeyCode-to-KeySym translations and so that the default translator can be reinstalled.

To invoke the currently registered KeyCode-to-KeySym translator, use `XtTranslateKeycode`.

void XtTranslateKeycode(*display, keycode, modifiers, modifiers_return, keysym_return*)
    Display **display*;
    KeyCode *keycode*;
    Modifiers *modifiers*;
    Modifiers **modifiers_return*;
    KeySym **keysym_return*;

display   Specifies the display that the KeyCode is from.

keycode   Specifies the KeyCode to translate.

modifiers   Specifies the modifiers to the KeyCode.

modifiers_return   Returns a mask that indicates the modifiers actually used to generate the KeySym.

keysym_return   Returns the resulting KeySym.

The `XtTranslateKeycode` function passes the specified arguments directly to the currently registered KeyCode-to-KeySym translator.

To handle capitalization of nonstandard KeySyms, the Intrinsics allow clients to register case conversion routines. Case converter procedure pointers are of type `XtCaseProc`.

typedef void (*XtCaseProc)(Display*, KeySym, KeySym*, KeySym*);
    Display **display*;
    KeySym *keysym*;
    KeySym **lower_return*;
    KeySym **upper_return*;

display   Specifies the display connection for which the conversion is required.

keysym   Specifies the KeySym to convert.

lower_return   Specifies a location into which to store the lower-case equivalent for the KeySym.

upper_return   Specifies a location into which to store the upper-case equivalent for the KeySym.

If there is no case distinction, this procedure should store the KeySym into both return values.

To register a case converter, use `XtRegisterCaseConverter`.

void XtRegisterCaseConverter(*display, proc, start, stop*)
   Display *display;
   XtCaseProc *proc*;
   KeySym *start*;
   KeySym *stop*;
display   Specifies the display from which the key events are to come.
proc   Specifies the `XtCaseProc` that is to do the conversions.
start   Specifies the first KeySym for which this converter is valid.
stop   Specifies the last KeySym for which this converter is valid.

The `XtRegisterCaseConverter` registers the specified case converter. The *start* and *stop* arguments provide the inclusive range of KeySyms for which this converter is to be called. The new converter overrides any previous converters for KeySyms in that range. No interface exists to remove converters; you need to register an identity converter. When a new converter is registered, the Intrinsics refresh the keyboard state if necessary. The default converter understands case conversion for all Latin KeySyms defined in *Xlib*, Protocol, Appendix E.

To determine upper- and lower-case equivalents for a given KeySym, use `XtConvertCase`.

void XtConvertCase(*display, keysym, lower_return, upper_return*)
   Display *display;
   KeySym *keysym*;
   KeySym *lower_return;
   KeySym *upper_return;
display   Specifies the display that the KeySym came from.
keysym   Specifies the KeySym to convert.
lower_return   Returns the lower-case equivalent of the KeySym.
upper_return   Returns the upper-case equivalent of the KeySym.

The XtConvertCase function calls the appropriate converter and returns the results. A user-supplied XtKeyProc may need to use this function.

10.6   Obtaining a KeySym in an Action Procedure

When an action procedure is invoked on a KeyPress or KeyRelease event, it often has a need to retrieve the KeySym and modifiers corresponding to the event that caused it to be invoked. In order to avoid repeating the processing that was just performed by the Intrinsics to match the translation entry, the KeySym and modifiers are stored for the duration of the action procedure and are made available to the client.

To retrieve the KeySym and modifiers that matched the final event specification in the translation table entry, use XtGetActionKeysym.

KeySym XtGetActionKeysym (*event, modifiers_return*)
    XEvent **event*;
    Modifiers **modifiers_return*;
event   Specifies the event pointer passed to the action procedure by the Intrinsics.
modifiers_return   Returns the modifiers that caused the match, if non-NULL.

If XtGetActionKeysym is called after an action procedure has been invoked by the Intrinsics and before that action procedure returns, and if the event pointer has the same value as the event pointer passed to that action routine, and if the event is a KeyPress or KeyRelease event, then XtGetAction-Keysym returns the KeySym that matched the final event specification in the translation table and, if *modifiers_return* is non-NULL, the modifier state actually used to generate this KeySym; otherwise, if the event is a KeyPress or Key-Release event, then XtGetActionKeysym calls XtTranslateKeycode and returns the results; else it returns NoSymbol and does not examine *modifiers_return*.

Note that if an action procedure invoked by the Intrinsics invokes a subsequent action procedure (and so on) via XtCallActionProc, the nested action procedure may also call XtGetActionKeysym to retrieve the Intrinsics' KeySym and modifiers.

10.7   KeySym-to-KeyCode Conversions

To return the list of KeyCodes that map to a particular KeySym in the keyboard mapping table maintained by the Intrinsics, use XtKeysymToKeycodeList.

void XtKeysymToKeycodeList(*display, keysym, keycodes_return, keycount_return*)
    Display **display*;
    KeySym *keysym*;
    KeyCode ***keycodes_return*;
    Cardinal **keycount_return*;

display	Specifies the display whose table is required.
keysym	Specifies the KeySym for which to search.
keycodes_return	Returns a list of KeyCodes that have *keysym* associated with them, or NULL if *keycount_return* is zero.
keycount_return	Returns the number of KeyCodes in the keycode list.

The `XtKeysymToKeycodeList` procedure returns all the KeyCodes that have *keysym* in their entry for the keyboard mapping table associated with *display*. For each entry in the table, the first four KeySyms (groups 1 and 2) are interpreted as specified by *Xlib*, Protocol, Section 5. If no KeyCodes map to the specified KeySym, *keycount_return* is zero and **keycodes_return* is NULL.

The caller should free the storage pointed to by *keycodes_return* using `XtFree` when it is no longer useful. If the caller needs to examine the KeyCode-to-KeySym table for a particular KeyCode, it should call `XtGetKeysymTable`.

10.8   Registering Button and Key Grabs for Actions

To register button and key grabs for a widget's window according to the event bindings in the widget's translation table, use `XtRegisterGrabAction`.

void XtRegisterGrabAction(*action_proc, owner_events, event_mask, pointer_mode,*
                                keyboard_mode)
    XtActionProc *action_proc*;
    Boolean *owner_events*;
    unsigned int *event_mask*;
    int *pointer_mode, keyboard_mode*;

action_proc	Specifies the action procedure to search for in translation tables.
owner_events	Specify arguments to `XtGrabButton` or `XtGrabKey`.
event_mask	
pointer_mode	
keyboard_mode	

`XtRegisterGrabAction` adds the specified *action_proc* to a list known to the translation manager. When a widget is realized, or when the translations of a realized widget or the accelerators installed on a realized widget are modified, its translation table and any installed accelerators are scanned for action procedures on this list. If any are invoked on `ButtonPress` or `KeyPress` events as the only or final event in a sequence, the Intrinsics will call `XtGrabButton` or `XtGrabKey` for the widget with every button or KeyCode which maps to the event detail field, passing the specified *owner_events, event_mask, pointer_mode,* and *keyboard_mode*. For `ButtonPress` events, the modifiers specified in the grab are determined directly from the translation specification and *confine_to* and *cursor* are specified as `None`. For `KeyPress` events, if the translation table entry specifies colon (:) in the modifier list, the modifiers are determined by calling the key translator procedure registered for the display and calling `XtGrabKey` for every combination of standard modifiers which map the Key-Code to the specified event detail KeySym, and ORing any modifiers specified in the translation table entry, and *event_mask* is ignored. If the translation table entry does not specify colon in the modifier list, the modifiers specified in the grab are those specified in the translation table entry only. For both `Button-Press` and `KeyPress` events, don't-care modifiers are ignored unless the translation entry explicitly specifies "Any" in the *modifiers* field.

If the specified *action_proc* is already registered for the calling process, the new values will replace the previously specified values for any widgets that become realized following the call, but existing grabs are not altered on currently-realized widgets.

When translations or installed accelerators are modified for a realized widget, any previous key or button grabs registered as a result of the old bindings are released if they do not appear in the new bindings and are not explicitly grabbed by the client with `XtGrabKey` or `XtGrabButton`.

10.9   Invoking Actions Directly

Normally action procedures are invoked by the Intrinsics when an event or event sequence arrives for a widget. To invoke an action procedure directly, without generating (or synthesizing) events, use `XtCallActionProc`.

```
void XtCallActionProc(widget, action, event, params, num_params)
    Widget widget;
    String action;
    XEvent *event;
    String *params;
    Cardinal num_params;
```

widget	Specifies the widget in which the action is to be invoked. Must be of class Core or any subclass thereof.
action	Specifies the name of the action routine.
event	Specifies the contents of the *event* passed to the action routine.
params	Specifies the contents of the *params* passed to the action routine.
num_params	Specifies the number of entries in *params*.

XtCallActionProc searches for the named action routine in the same manner and order as translation tables are bound, as described in Section 10.1.2, except that application action tables are searched, if necessary, as of the time of the call to XtCallActionProc. If found, the action routine is invoked with the specified widget, event pointer, and parameters. It is the responsibility of the caller to ensure that the contents of the *event, params,* and *num_params* arguments are appropriate for the specified action routine and, if necessary, that the specified widget is realized or sensitive. If the named action routine cannot be found, XtCallActionProc generates a warning message and returns.

Chapter 11

Utility Functions

The Intrinsics provide a number of utility functions that you can use to

• Determine the number of elements in an array.

• Translate strings to widget instances.

• Manage memory usage.

• Share graphics contexts.

• Manipulate selections.

• Merge exposure events into a region.

• Translate widget coordinates.

• Locate a widget given a window id.

• Handle errors.

11.1   Determining the Number of Elements in an Array

To determine the number of elements in a fixed-size array, use `XtNumber`.

Cardinal XtNumber(*array*)
    ArrayType array;
    array   Specifies a fixed-size array.

The `XtNumber` macro returns the number of elements allocated to the array.

11.2   Translating Strings to Widget Instances

To translate a widget name to a widget instance, use `XtNameToWidget`.

Widget XtNameToWidget(*reference, names*)
    Widget *reference*;
    String *names*;
 reference   Specifies the widget from which the search is to start.
                            Must be of class Core or any subclass thereof.
 names   Specifies the partially qualified name of the desired widget.

The `XtNameToWidget` function searches for a descendant of the *reference* widget whose name matches the specified name. The *names* parameter specifies a simple object name or a series of simple object name components separated by periods or asterisks. `XtNameToWidget` returns the descendant with the shortest name matching the specification according to the following rules, where child is either a pop-up child or a normal child if the widget's class is a subclass of Composite:

• Enumerate the object subtree rooted at the reference widget in breadth-first order, qualifying the name of each object with the names of all its ancestors up to but not including the reference widget. The ordering between children of a common parent is not defined.

• Return the first object in the enumeration that matches the specified name, where each component of *names* matches exactly the corresponding component of the qualified object name, and asterisk matches any series of components, including none.

• If no match is found, return NULL.

Since breadth-first traversal is specified, the descendant with the shortest matching name (i.e., the fewest number of components), if any, will always be returned. However, since the order of enumeration of children is undefined and since the Intrinsics do not require that all children of a widget have unique names, `XtNameToWidget` may return any child that matches if there are multiple objects in the subtree with the same name. Consecutive separators (periods or asterisks) including at least one asterisk are treated as a single asterisk. Consecutive periods are treated as a single period.

11.3   Managing Memory Usage

The Intrinsics' memory management functions provide uniform checking for null pointers and error reporting on memory allocation errors. These functions are completely compatible with their standard C language runtime counterparts `malloc`, `calloc`, `realloc`, and `free` with the following added functionality:

- `XtMalloc`, `XtCalloc`, and `XtRealloc` give an error if there is not enough memory.
- `XtFree` simply returns if passed a NULL pointer.
- `XtRealloc` simply allocates new storage if passed a NULL pointer.

See the standard C library documentation on `malloc`, `calloc`, `realloc`, and `free` for more information.

To allocate storage, use `XtMalloc`.

```
char *XtMalloc(size)
    Cardinal size;
```
size   Specifies the number of bytes desired.

The `XtMalloc` function returns a pointer to a block of storage of at least the specified *size* bytes. If there is insufficient memory to allocate the new block, `XtMalloc` calls `XtErrorMsg`.

To allocate and initialize an array, use `XtCalloc`.

```
char *XtCalloc(num, size)
    Cardinal num;
    Cardinal size;
```
num   Specifies the number of array elements to allocate.
size   Specifies the size of each array element in bytes.

The `XtCalloc` function allocates space for the specified number of array elements of the specified size and initializes the space to zero. If there is insufficient memory to allocate the new block, `XtCalloc` calls `XtErrorMsg`. `XtCalloc` returns the address of the allocated storage.

To change the size of an allocated block of storage, use `XtRealloc`.

```
char *XtRealloc(ptr, num)
    char *ptr;
    Cardinal num;
```
ptr   Specifies a pointer to the old storage allocated with `XtMalloc`, `XtCalloc`, or `XtRealloc`, or NULL.
num   Specifies the number of bytes desired in new storage.

The XtRealloc function changes the size of a block of storage, possibly moving it. Then it copies the old contents (or as much as will fit) into the new block and frees the old block. If there is insufficient memory to allocate the new block, XtRealloc calls XtErrorMsg. If *ptr* is NULL, XtRealloc simply calls XtMalloc. XtRealloc then returns the address of the new block.

To free an allocated block of storage, use XtFree.

void XtFree(*ptr*)
   char **ptr*;
ptr   Specifies a pointer to a block of storage allocated with XtMalloc, XtCalloc, or XtRealloc, or NULL.

The XtFree function returns storage, allowing it to be reused. If *ptr* is NULL, XtFree returns immediately.

To allocate storage for a new instance of a type, use XtNew.

type*XtNew(*type*)
   type t;
type   Specifies a previously declared type.

XtNew returns a pointer to the allocated storage. If there is insufficient memory to allocate the new block, XtNew calls XtErrorMsg. XtNew is a convenience macro that calls XtMalloc with the following arguments specified:

```
((type *) XtMalloc((unsigned) sizeof(type)))
```

The storage allocated by XtNew should be freed using XtFree.

To copy an instance of a string, use XtNewString.

String XtNewString(*string*)
   String *string*;
string   Specifies a previously declared string.

XtNewString returns a pointer to the allocated storage. If there is insufficient memory to allocate the new block, XtNewString calls XtErrorMsg. XtNewString is a convenience macro that calls XtMalloc with the following arguments specified:

```
(strcpy(XtMalloc((unsigned)strlen(str) + 1), str))
```

The storage allocated by XtNewString should be freed using XtFree.

11.4   Sharing Graphics Contexts

The Intrinsics provide a mechanism whereby cooperating clients can share a graphics context (GC), thereby reducing both the number of GCs created and the total number of server calls in any given application. The mechanism is a simple caching scheme, and all GCs obtained by means of this mechanism must be treated as read-only. If a changeable GC is needed, the Xlib XCreateGC function should be used instead.

To obtain a read-only, shareable GC, use XtGetGC.

GC XtGetGC(*object, value_mask, values*)
    Widget *object*;
    XtGCMask *value_mask*;
    XGCValues *values;

object	Specifies an object, giving the screen and depth for which the returned GC is valid. Must be of class Object or any subclass thereof.
value_mask	Specifies which fields of the *values* structure are specified.
values	Specifies the actual values for this GC.

The XtGetGC function returns a shareable, read-only GC. The parameters to this function are the same as those for XCreateGC except that an object is passed instead of a display. The *depth* field of the specified widget or of the nearest widget ancestor of the specified object specifies the drawable depths for which this GC is valid. XtGetGC shares only GCs in which all values in the GC returned by XCreateGC are the same. In particular, it does not use the *value_mask* provided to determine which fields of the GC a widget considers relevant. The *value_mask* is used only to tell the server which fields should be filled in from *values* and which it should fill in with default values. For further information about *value_mask* and *values,* see XCreateGC in Section 5.3 in *Xlib.*

To deallocate a shared GC when it is no longer needed, use XtReleaseGC.

void XtReleaseGC(*object, gc*)
    Widget *object*;
    GC *gc*;

object	Specifies any object on the Display for which the GC was created. Must be of class Object or any subclass thereof.
gc	Specifies the shared GC to be deallocated.

References to shareable GCs are counted and a free request is generated to the server when the last user of a given GC releases it.

11.5   Managing Selections

Arbitrary widgets in multiple applications can communicate with each other by means of the X Toolkit global selection mechanism, which conforms to the specifications in the *Inter-Client Communication Conventions Manual.* The Intrinsics supply functions for providing and receiving selection data in one logical piece (atomic transfers) or in smaller logical segments (incremental transfers).

The incremental interface is provided for a selection owner or selection requestor that cannot or prefers not to pass the selection value to and from the Intrinsics in a single call. For instance, either an application that is running on a machine with limited memory may not be able to store the entire selection value in memory, or a selection owner may already have the selection value available in discrete chunks, and it would be more efficient not to have to allocate additional storage to copy the pieces contiguously. Any owner or requestor that prefers to deal with the selection value in segments can use the incremental interfaces to do so. The transfer between the selection owner or requestor and the Intrinsics is not required to match the underlying transport protocol between the application and the X server; the Intrinsics will break a too large selection into smaller pieces for transport if necessary and will coalesce a selection transmitted incrementally if the value was requested atomically.

11.5.1   Setting and Getting the Selection Timeout Value

To set the Intrinsics selection timeout, use `XtAppSetSelectionTimeout`.

```
void XtAppSetSelectionTimeout(app_context, timeout)
    XtAppContext app_context;
    unsigned long timeout;
```
app_context   Specifies the application context.
timeout   Specifies the selection timeout in milliseconds.

To get the current selection timeout value, use `XtAppGetSelection-Timeout`.

```
unsigned long XtAppGetSelectionTimeout(app_context)
    XtAppContext app_context;
```
app_context   Specifies the application context.

The `XtAppGetSelectionTimeout` function returns the current selection timeout value, in milliseconds. The selection timeout is the time within which the two communicating applications must respond to one another. The initial timeout value is set by the selectionTimeout application resource as retrieved by `XtDisplayInitialize`. If XtNselectionTimeout is not specified, the default is 5 seconds.

11.5.2   Using Atomic Transfers

When using atomic transfers, the owner will completely process one selection request at a time. The owner may consider each request individually, since there is no possibility for overlap between evaluation of two requests.

11.5.2.1   Atomic Transfer Procedures

The following procedures are used by the selection owner when providing selection data in a single unit.

The procedure pointer specified by the owner to supply the selection data to the Intrinsics is of type `XtConvertSelectionProc`.

```
typedef Boolean (*XtConvertSelectionProc) (Widget, Atom*, Atom*, Atom*,
                                  XtPointer*, unsigned long*, int*);
    Widget w;
    Atom *selection;
    Atom *target;
    Atom *type_return;
    XtPointer *value_return;
    unsigned long *length_return;
    int *format_return;
```

w	Specifies the widget that currently owns this selection.
selection	Specifies the atom naming the selection requested (for example, XA_PRIMARY or XA_SECONDARY).
target	Specifies the target type of the selection that has been requested, which indicates the desired information about the selection (for example, File Name, Text, Window).
type_return	Specifies a pointer to an atom into which the property type of the converted value of the selection is to be stored. For instance, either File Name or Text might have property type XA_STRING.
value_return	Specifies a pointer into which a pointer to the converted value of the selection is to be stored. The selection owner is responsible for allocating this storage. If the selection owner has provided an

XtSelectionDoneProc for the selection, this storage is owned by the selection owner; otherwise, it is owned by the Intrinsics selection mechanism, which frees it by calling XtFree when it is done with it.

length_return Specifies a pointer into which the number of elements in *value_return*, each of size indicated by *format_return*, is to be stored.

format_return Specifies a pointer into which the size in bits of the data elements of the selection value is to be stored.

This procedure is called by the Intrinsics selection mechanism to get the value of a selection as a given type from the current selection owner. It returns True if the owner successfully converted the selection to the target type or False otherwise. If the procedure returns False, the values of the return arguments are undefined. Each XtConvertSelectionProc should respond to target value TARGETS by returning a value containing the list of the targets into which it is prepared to convert the selection. The value returned in *format_return* must be one of 8, 16, or 32 to allow the server to byte-swap the data if necessary.

This procedure does not need to worry about responding to the MULTIPLE or the TIMESTAMP target values (see the *Inter-Client Communication Conventions Manual*). A selection request with the MULTIPLE target type will be transparently transformed into a series of calls to this procedure, one for each target type, and a selection request with the TIMESTAMP target value will be answered automatically by the Intrinsics using the time specified in the call to XtOwnSelection or XtOwnSelectionIncremental.

To retrieve the SelectionRequest event that triggered the XtConvertSelectionProc procedure, use XtGetSelectionRequest.

XSelectionRequestEvent *XtGetSelectionRequest(*w, selection, request_id*)
 Widget *w*;
 Atom *selection*;
 XtRequestId *request_id*;

w Specifies the widget that currently owns this selection. Must be of class Core or any subclass thereof.

selection Specifies the selection being processed.

request_id Specifies the requestor id in the case of incremental sele NULL in the case of atomic transfers.

XtGetSelectionRequest may only be called from wi SelectionProc procedure and returns a pointe Request event that caused the conversion proced

specifies a unique id for the individual request in the case that multiple incremental transfers are outstanding. For atomic transfers, *request_id* must be specified as NULL. If no `SelectionRequest` event is being processed for the specified *widget, selection,* and *request_id,* `XtGetSelectionRequest` returns NULL.

The procedure pointer specified by the owner when it desires notification upon losing ownership is of type `XtLoseSelectionProc`.

```
typedef void (*XtLoseSelectionProc)(Widget, Atom*);
   Widget w;
   Atom *selection;
```

w	Specifies the widget that has lost selection ownership.
selection	Specifies the atom naming the selection.

This procedure is called by the Intrinsics selection mechanism to inform the specified widget that it has lost the given selection. Note that this procedure does not ask the widget to relinquish the selection ownership; it is merely informative.

The procedure pointer specified by the owner when it desires notification of receipt of the data or when it manages the storage containing the data is of type `XtSelectionDoneProc`.

```
typedef void (*XtSelectionDoneProc)(Widget, Atom*, Atom*);
   Widget w;
   Atom *selection;
   Atom *target;
```

w	Specifies the widget that owns the converted selection.
selection	Specifies the atom naming the selection that was converted.
target	Specifies the target type to which the conversion was done.

This procedure is called by the Intrinsics selection mechanism to inform the selection owner that a selection requestor has successfully retrieved a selection value. If the selection owner has registered an `XtSelectionDoneProc`, it should expect it to be called once for each conversion that it performs, after the converted value has been successfully transferred to the requestor. If the selection owner has registered an `XtSelectionDoneProc`, it also owns the storage containing the converted selection value.

11.5.2.2   Getting the Selection Value

The procedure pointer specified by the requestor to receive the selection data from the Intrinsics is of type `XtSelectionCallbackProc`.

typedef void (*XtSelectionCallbackProc) (Widget, XtPointer, Atom*, Atom*, XtPointer,
                                         unsigned long*, int*);
    Widget *w*;
    XtPointer *client_data*;
    Atom *selection*;
    Atom *type*;
    XtPointer *value*;
    unsigned long *length*;
    int *format*;

w	Specifies the widget that requested the selection value.
client_data	Specifies a value passed in by the widget when it requested the selection.
selection	Specifies the name of the selection that was requested.
type	Specifies the representation type of the selection value (for example, XA_STRING). Note that it is not the target that was requested (which the client must remember for itself) but the type that is used to represent the target. The special X Toolkit atom XT_CONVERT_FAIL is used to indicate that the selection conversion failed because the selection owner did not respond within the Intrinsics selection timeout interval.
value	Specifies a pointer to the selection value. The requesting client owns this storage and is responsible for freeing it by calling XtFree when it is done with it.
length	Specifies the number of elements in value.
format	Specifies the size in bits of the data elements of value.

This procedure is called by the Intrinsics selection mechanism to deliver the requested selection to the requestor.

If the `SelectionNotify` event returns a property of None, meaning the conversion has been refused because there is no owner for the specified selection or the owner cannot convert the selection to the requested target for any reason, the procedure is called with a value of NULL and a length of zero.

To obtain the selection value in a single logical unit, use `XtGetSelection-Value` or `XtGetSelectionValues`.

void XtGetSelectionValue(*w, selection, target, callback, client_data, time*)
    Widget *w*;
    Atom *selection*;

```
Atom target;
XtSelectionCallbackProc callback;
XtPointer client_data;
Time time;
```

w	Specifies the widget that is making the request. Must be of class Core or any subclass thereof.
selection	Specifies the particular selection desired; for example, XA_PRIMARY.
target	Specifies the type of the information needed about the selection.
callback	Specifies the procedure to be called when the selection value has been obtained. Note that this is how the selection value is communicated back to the client.
client_data	Specifies additional data to be passed to the specified procedure when it is called.
time	Specifies the timestamp that indicates when the selection request was initiated. This should be the timestamp of the event that triggered this request; the value CurrentTime is not acceptable.

The XtGetSelectionValue function requests the value of the selection converted to the target type. The specified callback will be called at some time after XtGetSelectionValue is called, when the selection value is received from the X server. It may be called before or after XtGetSelectionValue returns. For more information about *selection*, *target*, and *time*, see the *Inter-Client Communication Conventions Manual*.

```
void XtGetSelectionValues(w, selection, targets, count, callback, client_data, time)
Widget w;
Atom selection;
Atom *targets;
int count;
XtSelectionCallbackProc callback;
XtPointer *client_data;
Time time;
```

w	Specifies the widget that is making the request. Must be of class Core or any subclass thereof.
selection	Specifies the particular selection desired (that is, primary or secondary).
targets	Specifies the types of information needed about the selection.
count	Specifies the length of the *targets* and *client_data* lists.
callback	Specifies the callback procedure to be called with each selection value obtained. Note that this is how the selection values are communicated back to the client.

client_data	Specifies a list of additional data values, one for each target type, that are passed to the callback procedure when it is called for that target.
time	Specifies the timestamp that indicates when the selection request was initiated. This should be the timestamp of the event that triggered this request; the value CurrentTime is not acceptable.

The XtGetSelectionValues function is similar to multiple calls to XtGet-SelectionValue except that it guarantees that no other client can assert ownership between requests and therefore that all the conversions will refer to the same selection value. The callback is invoked once for each target value with the corresponding client data. For more information about *selection, target,* and *time,* see the *Inter-Client Communication Conventions Manual.*

11.5.2.3 Setting the Selection Owner

To set the selection owner and indicate that the selection value will be provided in one piece, use XtOwnSelection.

Boolean XtOwnSelection(*w, selection, time, convert_proc, lose_selection, done_proc*)
    Widget *w*;
    Atom *selection*;
    Time *time*;
    XtConvertSelectionProc *convert_proc*;
    XtLoseSelectionProc *lose_selection*;
    XtSelectionDoneProc *done_proc*;

w	Specifies the widget that wishes to become the owner. Must be of class Core or any subclass thereof.
selection	Specifies the name of the selection (for example, XA_PRIMARY).
time	Specifies the timestamp that indicates when the ownership request was initiated. This should be the timestamp of the event that triggered ownership; the value CurrentTime is not acceptable.
convert_proc	Specifies the procedure to be called whenever a client requests the current value of the selection.
lose_selection	Specifies the procedure to be called whenever the widget has lost selection ownership, or NULL if the owner is not interested in being called back.
done_proc	Specifies the procedure called after the requestor has received the selection value, or NULL if the owner is not interested in being called back.

The XtOwnSelection function informs the Intrinsics selection mechanism that a widget wishes to own a selection. It returns True if the widget successfully becomes the owner and `False` otherwise. The widget may fail to become the owner if some other widget has asserted ownership at a time later than this widget. The widget can lose selection ownership either because some other client asserted later ownership of the selection or because the widget voluntarily gave up ownership of the selection. The lose_selection procedure is not called if the widget fails to obtain selection ownership in the first place.

If a done_proc is specified, the client owns the storage allocated for passing the value to the Intrinsics. If *done_proc* is NULL, the convert_proc must allocate storage using `XtMalloc`, `XtRealloc`, or `XtCalloc`, and the value specified will be freed by the Intrinsics when the transfer is complete.

Usually, a selection owner maintains ownership indefinitely until some other client requests ownership, at which time the Intrinsics selection mechanism informs the previous owner that it has lost ownership of the selection. However, in response to some user actions (for example, when a user deletes the information selected), the application may wish to explicitly inform the Intrinsics that it no longer is to be the selection owner by using `XtDisown-Selection`.

void XtDisownSelection (*w, selection, time*)
    Widget *w*;
    Atom *selection*;
    Time *time*;

w	Specifies the widget that wishes to relinquish ownership.
selection	Specifies the atom naming the selection it is giving up.
time	Specifies the timestamp that indicates when the request to relinquish selection ownership was initiated.

The `XtDisownSelection` function informs the Intrinsics selection mechanism that the specified widget is to lose ownership of the selection. If the widget does not currently own the selection, either because it lost the selection or because it never had the selection to begin with, `XtDisownSelection` does nothing.

After a widget has called `XtDisownSelection`, its convert procedure is not called even if a request arrives later with a timestamp during the period that this widget owned the selection. However, its done procedure will be called if a conversion that started before the call to `XtDisownSelection` finishes after the call to `XtDisownSelection`.

11.5.3   Using Incremental Transfers

When using the incremental interface, an owner may have to process more than one selection request for the same selection, converted to the same target, at the same time. The incremental functions take a *request_id* argument, which is an identifier that is guaranteed to be unique among all incremental requests that are active concurrently.

For example, consider the following:

- Upon receiving a request for the selection value, the owner sends the first segment.

- While waiting to be called to provide the next segment value but before sending it, the owner receives another request from a different requestor for the same selection value.

- To distinguish between the requests, the owner uses the request_id value. This allows the owner to distinguish between the first requestor, which is asking for the second segment, and the second requestor, which is asking for the first segment.

11.5.3.1   Incremental Transfer Procedures

The following procedures are used by selection owners who wish to provide the selection data in multiple segments.

The procedure pointer specified by the incremental owner to supply the selection data to the Intrinsics is of type `XtConvertSelectionIncrProc`.

typedef XtPointer XtRequestId;

typedef Boolean (*XtConvertSelectionIncrProc) (Widget, Atom*, Atom*, Atom*,
            XtPointer*, unsigned long*, int*, unsigned long*, XtPointer,
            XtRequestId*);
    Widget *w*;
    Atom *selection*;
    Atom *target*;
    Atom *type_return*;
    XtPointer *value_return*;
    unsigned long *length_return*;
    int *format_return*;
    unsigned long *max_length*;
    XtPointer *client_data*;
    XtRequestId *request_id*;

w	Specifies the widget that currently owns this selection.
selection	Specifies the atom that names the selection requested.
target	Specifies the type of information required about selection.
type_return	Specifies a pointer to an atom into which the property type of the converted value of the selection is to be stored.

value_return	Specifies a pointer into which a pointer to the converted value of the selection is to be stored. The selection owner is responsible for allocating this storage.
length_return	Specifies a pointer into which the number of elements in *value_return*, each of size indicated by *format_return*, is to be stored.
format_return	Specifies a pointer into which the size in bits of the data elements of the selection value is to be stored so that the server may byte-swap the data if necessary.
max_length	Specifies the maximum number of bytes that may be transferred at any one time.
client_data	Specifies the value passed in by the widget when it took ownership of the selection.
request_id	Specifies an opaque identification for a specific request.

This procedure is called repeatedly by the Intrinsics selection mechanism to get the next incremental chunk of data from a selection owner who has called `XtOwnSelectionIncremental`. It must return `True` if the procedure has succeeded in converting the selection data or `False` otherwise. On the first call with a particular request id, the owner must begin a new incremental transfer for the requested selection and target. On subsequent calls with the same request id, the owner may assume that the previously supplied value is no longer needed by the Intrinsics; that is, a fixed transfer area may be allocated and returned in *value_return* for each segment to be transferred. This procedure should store a non-NULL value in *value_return* and zero in *length_return* to indicate that the entire selection has been delivered. After returning this final segment, the request id may be reused by the Intrinsics to begin a new transfer.

To retrieve the `SelectionRequest` event that triggered the selection conversion procedure, use `XtGetSelectionRequest`, described in Section 11.5.2.1.

The procedure pointer specified by the incremental selection owner when it desires notification upon no longer having ownership is of type `XtLose-SelectionIncrProc`.

```
typedef void (*XtLoseSelectionIncrProc)(Widget, Atom*, XtPointer);
    Widget w;
    Atom *selection;
    XtPointer client_data;
```

w	Specifies the widget that has lost the selection ownership.
selection	Specifies the atom that names the selection.
client_data	Specifies the value passed in by the widget when it took ownership of the selection.

This procedure, which is optional, is called by the Intrinsics to inform the selection owner that it no longer owns the selection.

The procedure pointer specified by the incremental selection owner when it desires notification of receipt of the data or when it manages the storage containing the data is of type `XtSelectionDoneIncrProc`.

```
typedef void (*XtSelectionDoneIncrProc) (Widget, Atom*, Atom*, XtRequestId*,
                                         XtPointer);
```

Widget *w*;
Atom **selection*;
Atom **target*;
XtRequestId **request_id*;
XtPointer *client_data*;

w	Specifies the widget that owns the selection.
selection	Specifies the atom that names the selection being transferred.
target	Specifies the target type to which the conversion was done.
request_id	Specifies an opaque identification for a specific request.
client_data	Specifies the value passed in by the widget when it took ownership of the selection.

This procedure, which is optional, is called by the Intrinsics after the requestor has retrieved the final (zero-length) segment of the incremental transfer to indicate that the entire transfer is complete. If this procedure is not specified, the Intrinsics will free only the final value returned by the selection owner using `XtFree`.

The procedure pointer specified by the incremental selection owner to notify it if a transfer should be terminated prematurely is of type `XtCancel-ConvertSelectionProc`.

```
typedef void (*XtCancelConvertSelectionProc) (Widget, Atom*, Atom*, XtRequestId*,
                                              XtPointer);
```

Widget *w*;
Atom **selection*;
Atom **target*;

XtRequestId *request_id;
XtPointer client_data;

w	Specifies the widget that owns the selection.
selection	Specifies the atom that names the selection being transferred.
target	Specifies the target type to which the conversion was done.
request_id	Specifies an opaque identification for a specific request.
client_data	Specifies the value passed in by the widget when it took ownership of the selection.

This procedure is called by the Intrinsics when it has been determined by means of a timeout or other mechanism that any remaining segments of the selection no longer need to be transferred. Upon receiving this callback, the selection request is considered complete and the owner can free the memory and any other resources that have been allocated for the transfer.

11.5.3.2 Getting the Selection Value Incrementally

To obtain the value of the selection using incremental transfers, use `XtGetSelectionValueIncremental` or `XtGetSelectionValues-Incremental`.

void XtGetSelectionValueIncremental(w, selection, target, selection_callback, client_data, time)

Widget w;
Atom selection;
Atom target;
XtSelectionCallbackProc selection_callback;
XtPointer client_data;
Time time;

w	Specifies the widget that is making the request. Must be of class Core or any subclass thereof.
selection	Specifies the particular selection desired.
target	Specifies the type of the information needed about the selection.
selection_callback	Specifies the callback procedure to be called to receive each data segment.
client_data	Specifies client-specific data to be passed to the specified callback procedure when it is invoked.
time	Specifies the timestamp that indicates when the selection request was initiated. This should be the timestamp of the event that triggered this request; the value CurrentTime is not acceptable.

The `XtGetSelectionValueIncremental` function is similar to `XtGet-SelectionValue` except that the selection_callback procedure will be called repeatedly upon delivery of multiple segments of the selection value. The end of the selection value is indicated when selection_callback is called with a non-NULL value of length zero, which must still be freed by the client. If the transfer of the selection is aborted in the middle of a transfer (for example, because of timeout), the selection_callback procedure is called with a type of XT_CONVERT_FAIL so that the requestor can dispose of the partial selection value it has collected up until that point. Upon receiving XT_CONVERT_FAIL, the requesting client must determine for itself whether or not a partially completed data transfer is meaningful. For more information about *selection, target,* and *time,* see the *Inter-Client Communication Conventions Manual.*

void XtGetSelectionValuesIncremental(*w, selection, targets, count, selection_callback,*
client_data, time)

    Widget *w*;
    Atom *selection*;
    Atom **targets*;
    int *count*;
    XtSelectionCallbackProc *selection_callback*;
    XtPointer **client_data*;
    Time *time*;

w	Specifies the widget that is making the request. Must be of class Core or any subclass thereof.
selection	Specifies the particular selection desired.
targets	Specifies the types of information needed about the selection.
count	Specifies the length of the *targets* and *client_data* lists.
selection_callback	Specifies the callback procedure to be called to receive each selection value.
client_data	Specifies a list of client data (one for each target type) values that are passed to the callback procedure when it is invoked for the corresponding target.
time	Specifies the timestamp that indicates when the selection request was initiated. This should be the timestamp of the event that triggered this request; the value `CurrentTime` is not acceptable.

The `XtGetSelectionValuesIncremental` function is similar to `XtGet-SelectionValueIncremental` except that it takes a list of targets and client data. `XtGetSelectionValuesIncremental` is equivalent to calling

XtGetSelectionValueIncremental successively for each *target/client_data* pair except that XtGetSelectionValuesIncremental does guarantee that all the conversions will use the same selection value because the ownership of the selection cannot change in the middle of the list, as would be possible when calling XtGetSelectionValueIncremental repeatedly. For more information about *selection, target,* and *time,* see the *Inter-Client Communication Conventions Manual.*

11.5.3.3 Setting the Selection Owner for Incremental Transfers

To set the selection owner when using incremental transfers, use XtOwn-SelectionIncremental.

Boolean XtOwnSelectionIncremental(*w, selection, time, convert_callback, lose_callback,*
                                              done_callback, cancel_callback, client_data)
    Widget *w*;
    Atom *selection*;
    Time *time*;
    XtConvertSelectionIncrProc *convert_callback*;
    XtLoseSelectionIncrProc *lose_callback*;
    XtSelectionDoneIncrProc *done_callback*;
    XtCancelConvertSelectionProc *cancel_callback*;
    XtPointer *client_data*;

w	Specifies the widget that wishes to become the owner. Must be of class Core or any subclass thereof.
selection	Specifies the atom that names the selection.
time	Specifies the timestamp that indicates when the selection ownership request was initiated. This should be the timestamp of the event that triggered ownership; the value CurrentTime is not acceptable.
convert_callback	Specifies the procedure to be called whenever the current value of the selection is requested.
lose_callback	Specifies the procedure to be called whenever the widget has lost selection ownership, or NULL if the owner is not interested in being notified.
done_callback	Specifies the procedure called after the requestor has received the entire selection, or NULL if the owner is not interested in being notified.
cancel_callback	Specifies the callback procedure to be called when a selection request aborts because a timeout expires, or NULL if the owner is not interested in being notified.
client_data	Specifies the argument to be passed to each of the callback procedures when they are called.

The XtOwnSelectionIncremental procedure informs the Intrinsics incremental selection mechanism that the specified widget wishes to own the selection. It returns True if the specified widget successfully becomes the selection owner or False otherwise. For more information about *selection, target,* and *time,* see the *Inter-Client Communication Conventions Manual.*

If a done_callback procedure is specified, the client owns the storage allocated for passing the value to the Intrinsics. If *done_callback* is NULL, the convert_callback procedure must allocate storage using XtMalloc, XtRealloc, or XtCalloc, and the final value specified will be freed by the Intrinsics when the transfer is complete. After a selection transfer has started, only one of the done_callback or cancel_callback procedures will be invoked to indicate completion of the transfer.

The lose_callback procedure does not indicate completion of any in-progress transfers; it will be invoked at the time a SelectionClear event is dispatched regardless of any active transfers, which are still expected to continue.

A widget that becomes the selection owner using XtOwnSelection-Incremental may use XtDisownSelection to relinquish selection ownership.

11.5.4 Retrieving the Most Recent Timestamp

To retrieve the timestamp from the most recent call to XtDispatchEvent that contained a timestamp, use XtLastTimestampProcessed.

Time XtLastTimestampProcessed(*display*)
   Display **display*;
display   Specifies an open display connection.

If no KeyPress, KeyRelease, ButtonPress, ButtonRelease, Motion-Notify, EnterNotify, LeaveNotify, PropertyNotify, or Selection-Clear event has yet been passed to XtDispatchEvent for the specified display, XtLastTimestampProcessed returns zero.

11.6 Merging Exposure Events into a Region

The Intrinsics provide an XtAddExposureToRegion utility function that merges Expose and GraphicsExpose events into a region for clients to process at once rather than processing individual rectangles. For further information about regions, see Section 10.6 in *Xlib.*

To merge `Expose` and `GraphicsExpose` events into a region, use `XtAdd-ExposureToRegion`.

void XtAddExposureToRegion(*event, region*)
    XEvent **event*;
    Region *region*;
    event   Specifies a pointer to the `Expose` or `GraphicsExpose` event.
    region   Specifies the region object (as defined in `<X11/Xutil.h>`).

The `XtAddExposureToRegion` function computes the union of the rectangle defined by the exposure event and the specified region. Then it stores the results back in *region*. If the event argument is not an `Expose` or `Graphics-Expose` event, `XtAddExposureToRegion` returns without an error and without modifying *region*.

This function is used by the exposure compression mechanism; see Section 7.9.3.

11.7   Translating Widget Coordinates

To translate an x-y coordinate pair from widget coordinates to root window absolute coordinates, use `XtTranslateCoords`.

void XtTranslateCoords(*w, x, y, rootx_return, rooty_return*)
    Widget *w*;
    Position *x, y*;
    Position **rootx_return, *rooty_return*;
    w   Specifies the widget. Must be of class RectObj or any subclass thereof.
    x, y   Specify the widget-relative x and y coordinates.
    rootx_return   Return the root-relative x and y coordinates.
    rooty_return

While `XtTranslateCoords` is similar to the Xlib `XTranslate-Coordinates` function, it does not generate a server request because all the required information already is in the widget's data structures.

11.8   Translating a Window to a Widget

To translate a given window and display pointer into a widget instance, use `XtWindowToWidget`.

Widget XtWindowToWidget(*display, window*)
    Display **display*;
    Window *window*;

display	Specifies the display on which the window is defined.
window	Specifies the window for which you want the widget.

If there is a realized widget whose window is the specified *window* on the specified *display*, XtWindowToWidget returns that widget; otherwise, it returns NULL.

11.9 Handling Errors

The Intrinsics allow a client to register procedures that will be called whenever a fatal or nonfatal error occurs. These facilities are intended for both error reporting and logging and for error correction or recovery.

Two levels of interface are provided:

- A high-level interface that takes an error name and class and retrieves the error message text from an error resource database.

- A low-level interface that takes a simple string to display.

The high-level functions construct a string to pass to the lower-level interface. On POSIX-based systems, the error database usually is loaded from /usr/lib/X11/XtErrorDB.

Note The application-context-specific error handling is not implemented on many systems, although the interfaces are always present. Most implementations will have just one set of error handlers for all application contexts within a process. If they are set for different application contexts, the ones registered last will prevail.

To obtain the error database (for example, to merge with an application- or widget-specific database), use XtAppGetErrorDatabase.

XrmDatabase *XtAppGetErrorDatabase(*app_context*)
   XtAppContext *app_context*;
app_context   Specifies the application context.

The XtAppGetErrorDatabase function returns the address of the error database. The Intrinsics do a lazy binding of the error database and do not merge in the database file until the first call to XtAppGetErrorDatabase-Text.

For a complete listing of all errors and warnings that can be generated by the Intrinsics, see Appendix D.

The high-level error and warning handler procedure pointers are of type `XtErrorMsgHandler`.

```
typedef void (*XtErrorMsgHandler) (String, String, String, String, String*, Cardinal*);
    String name;
    String type;
    String class;
    String defaultp;
    String *params;
    Cardinal *num_params;
```

name	Specifies the name to be concatenated with the specified type to form the resource name of the error message.
type	Specifies the type to be concatenated with the name to form the resource name of the error message.
class	Specifies the resource class of the error message.
defaultp	Specifies the default message to use if no error database entry is found.
params	Specifies a pointer to a list of parameters to be substituted in the message.
num_params	Specifies the number of entries in *params*.

The specified name can be a general kind of error, like "invalidParameters" or "invalidWindow", and the specified type gives extra information such as the name of the routine in which the error was detected. Standard `printf` notation is used to substitute the parameters into the message.

An error message handler can obtain the error database text for an error or a warning by calling `XtAppGetErrorDatabaseText`.

```
void XtAppGetErrorDatabaseText( app_context, name, type, class, default, buffer_return,
                                nbytes, database)
    XtAppContext app_context;
    String name, type, class;
    String default;
    String buffer_return;
    int nbytes;
    XrmDatabase database;
```

app_context	Specifies the application context.
name, type	Specify the name and type concatenated to form the resource name of the error message.
class	Specifies the resource class of the error message.

default	Specifies the default message to use if an error database entry is not found.
buffer_return	Specifies the buffer into which the error message is to be returned.
nbytes	Specifies the size of the buffer in bytes.
database	Specifies the name of the alternative database to be used, or NULL if the application context's error database is to be used.

The `XtAppGetErrorDatabaseText` returns the appropriate message from the error database or returns the specified default message if one is not found in the error database.

To return the application name and class as passed to `XtDisplay-Initialize` for a particular Display, use `XtGetApplicationNameAnd-Class`.

void XtGetApplicationNameAndClass(*display, name_return, class_return*)
    Display* *display*;
    String* *name_return*;
    String* *class_return*;

display	Specifies an open display connection that has been initialized with `XtDisplayInitialize`.
name_return	Returns the application name.
class_return	Returns the application class.

`XtGetApplicationNameAndClass` returns the application name and class passed to `XtDisplayInitialize` for the specified display. If the display was never initialized or has been closed, the result is undefined. The returned strings are owned by the Intrinsics and must not be modified or freed by the caller.

To register a procedure to be called on fatal error conditions, use `XtAppSetErrorMsgHandler`.

XtErrorMsgHandler XtAppSetErrorMsgHandler(*app_context, msg_handler*)
    XtAppContext *app_context*;
    XtErrorMsgHandler *msg_handler*;

app_context	Specifies the application context.
msg_handler	Specifies the new fatal error procedure, which should not return.

`XtAppSetErrorMsgHandler` returns a pointer to the previously installed high-level fatal error handler. The default high-level fatal error handler provided by the Intrinsics is named _XtDefaultErrorMsg and constructs a string from the error resource database and calls XtError. Fatal error message handlers should not return. If one does, subsequent Intrinsics behavior is undefined.

To call the high-level error handler, use XtAppErrorMsg.

void XtAppErrorMsg(*app_context, name, type, class, default, params, num_params*)
    XtAppContext *app_context*;
    String *name*;
    String *type*;
    String *class*;
    String *default*;
    String **params*;
    Cardinal **num_params*;

app_context	Specifies the application context.
name	Specifies the general kind of error.
type	Specifies the detailed name of the error.
class	Specifies the resource class.
default	Specifies the default message to use if an error database entry is not found.
params	Specifies a pointer to a list of values to be stored in the message.
num_params	Specifies the number of entries in params.

The Intrinsics internal errors all have class "XtToolkitError".

To register a procedure to be called on nonfatal error conditions, use XtAppSetWarningMsgHandler.

XtErrorMsgHandler XtAppSetWarningMsgHandler(*app_context, msg_handler*)
    XtAppContext *app_context*;
    XtErrorMsgHandler *msg_handler*;

app_context	Specifies the application context.
msg_handler	Specifies the new nonfatal error procedure, which usually returns.

XtAppSetWarningMsgHandler returns a pointer to the previously installed high-level warning handler. The default high-level warning handler provided by the Intrinsics is named _XtDefaultWarningMsg and constructs a string from the error resource database and calls XtWarning.

To call the installed high-level warning handler, use `XtAppWarningMsg`.

void XtAppWarningMsg(*app_context, name, type, class, default, params, num_params*)
    XtAppContext *app_context*;
    String *name*;
    String *type*;
    String *class*;
    String *default*;
    String **params*;
    Cardinal **num_params*;

app_context	Specifies the application context.
name	Specifies the general kind of error.
type	Specifies the detailed name of the error.
class	Specifies the resource class.
default	Specifies the default message to use if an error database entry is not found.
params	Specifies a pointer to a list of values to be stored in the message.
num_params	Specifies the number of entries in *params*.

The Intrinsics internal warnings all have class "XtToolkitError".

The low-level error and warning handler procedure pointers are of type `XtErrorHandler`.

typedef void (*XtErrorHandler)(String);
    String *message*;

message	Specifies the error message.

The error handler should display the message string in some appropriate fashion.

To register a procedure to be called on fatal error conditions, use `XtAppSetErrorHandler`.

XtErrorHandler XtAppSetErrorHandler(*app_context, handler*)
    XtAppContext *app_context*;
    XtErrorHandler *handler*;

app_context	Specifies the application context.
handler	Specifies the new fatal error procedure, which should not return.

`XtAppSetErrorHandler` returns a pointer to the previously installed low-level fatal error handler. The default low-level error handler provided by the Intrinsics is `_XtDefaultError`. On POSIX-based systems, it prints the message to standard error and terminates the application. Fatal error message handlers should not return. If one does, subsequent Intrinsics behavior is undefined.

To call the installed fatal error procedure, use `XtAppError`.

void XtAppError(*app_context*, *message*)
    XtAppContext *app_context*;
    String *message*;
app_context   Specifies the application context.
message   Specifies the message that is to be reported.

Most programs should use `XtAppErrorMsg`, not `XtAppError`, to provide for customization and internationalization of error messages.

To register a procedure to be called on nonfatal error conditions, use `XtAppSetWarningHandler`.

XtErrorHandler XtAppSetWarningHandler(*app_context*, *handler*)
    XtAppContext *app_context*;
    XtErrorHandler *handler*;
app_context   Specifies the application context.
handler   Specifies the new nonfatal error procedure, which usually returns.

`XtAppSetWarningHandler` returns a pointer to the previously installed low-level warning handler. The default low-level warning handler provided by the Intrinsics is `_XtDefaultWarning`. On POSIX-based systems, it prints the message to standard error and returns to the caller.

To call the installed nonfatal error procedure, use `XtAppWarning`.

void XtAppWarning(*app_context*, *message*)
    XtAppContext *app_context*;
    String *message*;
app_context   Specifies the application context.
message   Specifies the nonfatal error message that is to be reported.

Most programs should use `XtAppWarningMsg`, not `XtAppWarning`, to provide for customization and internationalization of warning messages.

11.10   Setting WM_COLORMAP_WINDOWS

A client may set the value of the WM_COLORMAP_WINDOWS property on a widget's window by calling `XtSetWMColormapWindows`.

> void XtSetWMColormapWindows(*widget, list, count*)
>   Widget *widget*;
>   Widget* *list*;
>   Cardinal *count*;

widget	Specifies the widget on whose window the WM_COLORMAP_WINDOWS property will be stored. Must be of class Core or any subclass thereof.
list	Specifies a list of widgets whose windows are potentially to be listed in the WM_COLORMAP_WINDOWS property.
count	Specifies the number of widgets in *list*.

`XtSetWMColormapWindows` returns immediately if *widget* is not realized or if *count* is zero. Otherwise, `XtSetWMColormapWindows` constructs an ordered list of windows by examining each widget in *list* in turn and ignoring the widget if it is not realized, or adding the widget's window to the window list if the widget is realized and if its colormap resource is different from the colormap resources of all widgets whose windows are already on the window list. Finally, `XtSetWMColormapWindows` stores the resulting window list in the WM_COLORMAP_WINDOWS property on the specified widget's window. Refer to the *Inter-Client Communication Conventions Manual* for details of the semantics of the WM_COLORMAP_WINDOWS property.

11.11   Finding File Names

The Intrinsics provide procedures to look for a file by name, allowing string substitutions in a list of file specifications. Two routines are provided for this: `XtFindFile` and `XtResolvePathname`. `XtFindFile` uses an arbitrary set of client-specified substitutions, and `XtResolvePathname` uses a set of standard substitutions corresponding to the *X/Open Portability Guide* language localization conventions. Most applications should use `XtResolvePathname`.

    A string substitution is defined by a list of `Substitution` entries.

> typedef struct {
>   char   match;
>   String   substitution;
> } SubstitutionRec, *Substitution;

File name evaluation is handled in an operating-system-dependent fashion by an XtFilePredicate procedure.

typedef Boolean (*XtFilePredicate) (String);
    String *filename*;
filename   Specifies a potential file name.

A file predicate procedure will be called with a string that is potentially a file name. It should return True if this string specifies a file that is appropriate for the intended use and False otherwise.

To search for a file using substitutions in a path list, use XtFindFile.

String XtFindFile (*path, substitutions, num_substitutions, predicate*)
    String *path*;
    Substitution *substitutions*;
    Cardinal *num_substitutions*;
    XtFilePredicate *predicate*;
path   Specifies a path of file names, including substitution characters.
substitutions   Specifies a list of substitutions to make into the path.
num_substitutions   Specifies the number of substitutions passed in.
predicate   Specifies a procedure called to judge each potential file name,
                      or NULL.

The *path* parameter specifies a string that consists of a series of potential file names delimited by colons. Within each name, the percent character specifies a string substitution selected by the following character. The character sequence "%:" specifies an embedded colon that is not a delimiter; the sequence is replaced by a single colon. The character sequence "%%" specifies a percent character that does not introduce a substitution; the sequence is replaced by a single percent character. If a percent character is followed by any other character, XtFindFile looks through the specified *substitutions* for that character in the *match* field and if found replaces the percent and match characters with the string in the corresponding *substitution* field. A *substitution* field entry of NULL is equivalent to a pointer to an empty string. If the operating system does not interpret multiple embedded name separators in the path (i.e., "/" in POSIX) the same way as a single separator, XtFindFile will collapse multiple separators into a single one after performing all string substitutions. Except for collapsing embedded separators, the contents of the string substitutions are not interpreted by XtFindFile and may therefore contain any operating-system-dependent characters, including additional name separators. Each resulting string is passed to the predicate procedure until a string is found for which the procedure returns `True`; this string is the return value for `XtFindFile`. If no string yields a `True` return from the predicate, `XtFindFile` returns NULL.

If the *predicate* parameter is NULL, an internal procedure that checks if the file exists, is readable, and is not a directory will be used.

It is the responsibility of the caller to free the returned string using `XtFree` when it is no longer needed.

To search for a file using standard substitutions in a path list, use `XtResolvePathname`.

String XtResolvePathname (*dpy, type, filename, suffix, path, substitutions, num_substitutions,*
                                                predicate)
    Display **dpy*;
    String *type, filename, suffix, path*;
    Substitution *substitutions*;
    Cardinal *num_substitutions*;
    XtFilePredicate *predicate*;

dpy	Specifies the display to use to find the language for language substitutions.
type *filename* *suffix*	Specify values to substitute into the path.
path	Specifies the list of file specifications, or NULL.
substitutions	Specifies a list of additional substitutions to make into the path, or NULL.
num_substitutions	Specifies the number of entries in *substitutions*.
predicate	Specifies a procedure called to judge each potential file name, or NULL.

The substitutions specified by `XtResolvePathname` are determined from the value of the language string retrieved by `XtDisplayInitialize` for the specified display. A language string is specified from three parts, two of which are optional: the language, the territory, and the codeset. These parts are combined into a single string as language_territory.codeset; the parts consist of arbitrary strings of letters and numbers. The underscore is omitted if territory is omitted, and the period is omitted if codeset is omitted. No interpretation of the parts of the language is done other than to use them in substitutions. To set the language for all applications specify "*xnlLanguage: *lang*" in the resource database.

`XtResolvePathname` calls `XtFindFile` with the following substitutions in addition to any passed by the caller and returns the value returned by `XtFindFile`:

%N   The value of the *filename* parameter, or the application's class name if *filename* is NULL.
%T   The value of the *type* parameter.
%S   The value of the *suffix* parameter.
%L   The language string associated with the specified display.
%l   The language part of the display's language string.
%t   The territory part of the display's language string.
%c   The codeset part of the display's language string.

If a path is passed to `XtResolvePathname`, it will be passed along to `XtFind-File`. If the *path* argument is NULL, the value of the XFILESEARCHPATH environment variable will be passed to `XtFindFile`. If XFILESEARCHPATH is not defined, an implementation-specific default path will be used which contains at least `/usr/lib/X11/%T/%N%S`. If the path begins with a colon, it will be preceded by `%N%S`. If the path includes two adjacent colons, `%N%S` will be inserted between them.

The *type* parameter is intended to be a category of files, usually being translated into a directory in the path name. Possible values might include "app-defaults", "help", and "bitmap".

The *suffix* parameter is intended to be appended to the file name. Possible values might include ".txt", ".dat", and ".bm".

A suggested value for the default path on POSIX-based systems is

```
/usr/lib/X11/%L/%T/%N%S:/usr/lib/X11/%l/%T/%N%S:/
    /usr/lib/X11/%T/%N%S
```

Using this example, if the user has specified a language, it will be used as a sub-directory of `/usr/lib/X11` that will be searched for other files. If the desired file is not found there, the lookup will be tried again using just the language part of the specification. If the file is not there, it will be looked for in `/usr/lib/X11`. The *type* parameter is used as a subdirectory of the language directory or of `/usr/lib/X11`, and *suffix* is appended to the file name.

It is the responsibility of the caller to free the returned string using `XtFree` when it is no longer needed.

Chapter 12

Nonwidget Objects

Although widget writers are free to treat Core as the base class of the widget hierarchy, there are actually three classes above it. These classes are Object, RectObj (Rectangle Object) and (*unnamed*) and members of these classes are referred to generically as *objects*. By convention, the term *widget* refers only to objects that are a subclass of Core, and the term *nonwidget* refers to objects that are not a subclass of Core. In the preceding portion of this specification, the interface descriptions indicate explicitly whether the generic *widget* argument is restricted to particular subclasses of Object. Sections 12.2.5, 12.3.5, and 12.5 summarize the permissible classes of the arguments to, and return values from, each of the Intrinsics routines.

12.1   Data Structures

In order not to conflict with previous widget code, the data structures used by nonwidget objects do not follow all the same conventions as those for widgets. In particular, the class records are not composed of parts but instead are complete data structures with filler for the widget fields they do not use. This allows the static class initializers for existing widgets to remain unchanged.

12.2   Object Objects

The Object object contains the definitions of fields common to all objects. It encapsulates the mechanisms for resource management. All objects and widgets are members of subclasses of Object, which is defined by the `Object-ClassPart` and `ObjectPart` structures.

12.2.1   ObjectClassPart Structure

The common fields for all object classes are defined in the `ObjectClassPart`
structure. All fields have the same purpose and function as the corresponding
fields in `CoreClassPart`; fields whose names are obj$n$ for some integer n are
not used for Object but exist to pad the data structure so that it matches Core's
class record. The class record initialization must fill all obj$n$ fields with NULL or
zero as appropriate to the type.

```
typedef struct _ObjectClassPart {
    WidgetClass         superclass;
    String              class_name;
    Cardinal            widget_size;
    XtProc              class_initialize;
    XtWidgetClassProc   class_part_initialize;
    XtEnum              class_inited;
    XtInitProc          initialize;
    XtArgsProc          initialize_hook;
    XtProc              obj1;
    XtPointer           obj2;
    Cardinal            obj3;
    XtResourceList      resources;
    Cardinal            num_resources;
    XrmClass            xrm_class;
    Boolean             obj4;
    XtEnum              obj5;
    Boolean             obj6;
    Boolean             obj7;
    XtWidgetProc        destroy;
    XtProc              obj8;
    XtProc              obj9;
    XtSetValuesFunc     set_values;
    XtArgsFunc          set_values_hook;
    XtProc              obj10;
    XtArgsProc          get_values_hook;
    XtProc              obj11;
    XtVersionType       version;
    XtPointer           callback_private;
    String              obj12;
    XtProc              obj13;
    XtProc              obj14;
    XtPointer           extension;
} ObjectClassPart;
```

The prototypical `ObjectClass` consists of just the `ObjectClassPart`.

```
typedef struct _ObjectClassRec {
    ObjectClassPart    object_class;
} ObjectClassRec, *ObjectClass;
```

The predefined class record and pointer for `ObjectClassRec` are
In `IntrinsicP.h`:

```
extern ObjectClassRec objectClassRec;
```

In `Intrinsic.h`:

```
extern WidgetClass objectClass;
```

The opaque types Object and `ObjectClass` and the opaque variable `objectClass` are defined for generic actions on objects. `Intrinsic.h` uses an incomplete structure definition to ensure that the compiler catches attempts to access private data:

```
typedef struct _ObjectClassRec* ObjectClass;
```

12.2.2 ObjectPart Structure

The common fields for all object instances are defined in the `ObjectPart` structure. All fields have the same meaning as the corresponding fields in `CorePart`.

```
typedef struct _ObjectPart {
    Widget          self;
    WidgetClass     widget_class;
    Widget          parent;
    XrmName         xrm_name;
    Boolean         being_destroyed;
    XtCallbackList  destroy_callbacks;
    XtPointer       constraints;
} ObjectPart;
```

All object instances have the Object fields as their first component. The prototypical type Object is defined with only this set of fields. Various routines can
cast object pointers, as needed, to specific object types.

In `IntrinsicP.h`:

```
typedef struct _ObjectRec {
    ObjectPart    object;
} ObjectRec, *Object;
```

In `Intrinsic.h`:

```
typedef struct _ObjectRec*Object;
```

12.2.3   Object Resources

The resource names, classes, and representation types specified in the `objectClassRec` resource list are

Name	Class	Representation
XtNdestroyCallback	XtCCallback	XtRCallback

12.2.4   ObjectPart Default Values

All fields in `ObjectPart` have the same default values as the corresponding fields in `CorePart`.

12.2.5   Object Arguments to Intrinsics Routines

The WidgetClass arguments to the following procedures may be `objectClass` or any subclass:

`XtInitializeWidgetClass, XtCreateWidget, XtVaCreateWidget`

`XtIsSubclass, XtCheckSubclass`

`XtGetResourceList, XtGetConstraintResourceList`

The Widget arguments to the following procedures may be of class Object or any subclass:

`XtCreateWidget, XtVaCreateWidget`

`XtAddCallback, XtAddCallbacks, XtRemoveCallback,`
`XtRemoveCallbacks, XtRemoveAllCallbacks, XtCallCallbacks,`
`XtHasCallbacks, XtCallCallbackList`

`XtClass, XtSuperclass, XtIsSubclass, XtCheckSubclass, XtIsObject,`
`XtIsRectObj, XtIsWidget, XtIsComposite, XtIsConstraint, XtIsShell,`

XtIsOverrideShell, XtIsWMShell, XtIsVendorShell, XtIsTransient-Shell, XtIsToplevelShell, XtIsApplicationShell

XtIsManaged, XtIsSensitive (both will return False if argument is not a subclass of RectObj)

XtIsRealized (returns the state of the nearest windowed ancestor if class of argument is not a subclass of Core)

XtWidgetToApplicationContext

XtDestroyWidget

XtParent, XtDisplayOfObject, XtScreenOfObject, XtWindowOfObject

XtSetKeyboardFocus (descendant)

XtGetGC, XtReleaseGC

XtName

XtSetValues, XtGetValues, XtVaSetValues, XtVaGetValues

XtGetSubresources, XtGetApplicationResources, XtVaGetSubresources, XtVaGetApplicationResources

XtConvert, XtConvertAndStore

The return value of the following procedures will be of class Object or a subclass:

XtCreateWidget, XtVaCreateWidget

XtParent

XtNameToWidget

The return value of the following procedures will be objectClass or a subclass:

XtClass, XtSuperclass

12.2.6 Use of Objects

The Object class exists to enable programmers to use the Intrinsics' classing and resource-handling mechanisms for things smaller and simpler than widgets. Objects make obsolete many common uses of subresources as described in Sections 9.4, 9.7.2.4, and 9.7.2.5.

Composite widget classes that wish to accept nonwidget children must set the *accepts_objects* field in the CompositeClassExtension structure to True.

`XtCreateWidget` will otherwise generate an error message on an attempt to create a nonwidget child.

Of the classes defined by the Intrinsics, only ApplicationShell accepts nonwidget children, and the class of any nonwidget child must not be `rectObjClass` or any subclass. The intent of allowing Object children of ApplicationShell is to provide clients a simple mechanism for establishing the resource-naming root of an object hierarchy.

12.3   Rectangle Objects

The class of rectangle objects is a subclass of Object and represents rectangular areas. It encapsulates the mechanisms for geometry management and is called RectObj to avoid conflict with the Xlib `Rectangle` data type.

12.3.1   RectObjClassPart Structure

As with the `ObjectClassPart` structure, all fields in the `RectObjClassPart` structure have the same purpose and function as the corresponding fields in `CoreClassPart`; fields whose names are rect*n* for some integer *n* are not used for RectObj but exist to pad the data structure so that it matches Core's class record. The class record initialization must fill all rect*n* fields with NULL or zero as appropriate to the type.

```
typedef struct _RectObjClassPart {
    WidgetClass             superclass;
    String                  class_name;
    Cardinal                widget_size;
    XtProc                  class_initialize;
    XtWidgetClassProc       class_part_initialize;
    XtEnum                  class_inited;
    XtInitProc              initialize;
    XtArgsProc              initialize_hook;
    XtProc                  rect1;
    XtPointer               rect2;
    Cardinal                rect3;
    XtResourceList          resources;
    Cardinal                num_resources;
    XrmClass                xrm_class;
    Boolean                 rect4;
```

XtEnum	rect5;
Boolean	rect6;
Boolean	rect7;
XtWidgetProc	destroy;
XtWidgetProc	resize;
XtExposeProc	expose;
XtSetValuesFunc	set_values;
XtArgsFunc	set_values_hook;
XtAlmostProc	set_values_almost;
XtArgsProc	get_values_hook;
XtProc	rect9;
XtVersionType	version;
XtPointer	callback_private;
String	rect10;
XtGeometryHandler	query_geometry;
XtProc	rect11;
XtPointer	extension;

} RectObjClassPart;

The RectObj class record consists of just the `RectObjClassPart`.

```
typedef struct _RectObjClassRec {
    RectObjClassPart    rect_class;
} RectObjClassRec, *RectObjClass;
```

The predefined class record and pointer for `RectObjClassRec` are
In `IntrinsicP.h`:

```
extern RectObjClassRec rectObjClassRec;
```

In `Intrinsic.h`:

```
extern WidgetClass rectObjClass;
```

The opaque types `RectObj` and `RectObjClass` and the opaque variable
`rectObjClass` are defined for generic actions on objects whose class is
RectObj or a subclass of RectObj. `Intrinsic.h` uses an incomplete structure
definition to ensure that the compiler catches attempts to access private data:

```
typedef struct _RectObjClassRec* RectObjClass;
```

12.3.2   RectObjPart Structure

In addition to the `ObjectPart` fields, RectObj objects have the following fields defined in the `RectObjPart` structure. All fields have the same meaning as the corresponding field in `CorePart`.

```
typedef struct _RectObjPart {
    Position      x, y;
    Dimension     width, height;
    Dimension     border_width;
    Boolean       managed;
    Boolean       sensitive;
    Boolean       ancestor_sensitive;
} RectObjPart;
```

RectObj objects have the RectObj fields immediately following the Object fields.

```
typedef struct _RectObjRec {
    ObjectPart     object;
    RectObjPart    rectangle;
} RectObjRec, *RectObj;
```

In `Intrinsic.h`:

```
typedef struct _RectObjRec* RectObj;
```

12.3.3   RectObj Resources

The resource names, classes, and representation types that are specified in the `rectObjClassRec` resource list are

Name	Class	Representation
XtNancestorSensitive	XtCSensitive	XtRBoolean
XtNborderWidth	XtCBorderWidth	XtRDimension
XtNheight	XtCHeight	XtRDimension
XtNsensitive	XtCSensitive	XtRBoolean
XtNwidth	XtCWidth	XtRDimension
XtNx	XtCPosition	XtRPosition
XtNy	XtCPosition	XtRPosition

12.3.4 RectObjPart Default Values

All fields in `RectObjPart` have the same default values as the corresponding fields in `CorePart`.

12.3.5 RectObj Arguments to Intrinsics Routines

The WidgetClass arguments to the following procedures may be `rectObjClass` or any subclass:

`XtCreateManagedWidget, XtVaCreateManagedWidget`

The Widget arguments to the following procedures may be of class RectObj or any subclass:

`XtConfigureWidget, XtMoveWidget, XtResizeWidget`

`XtMakeGeometryRequest, XtMakeResizeRequest`

`XtManageChildren, XtManageChild, XtUnmanageChildren, XtUnmanageChild`

`XtQueryGeometry`

`XtSetSensitive`

`XtTranslateCoords`

The return value of the following procedures will be of class RectObj or a subclass:

`XtCreateManagedWidget, XtVaCreateManagedWidget`

12.3.6 Use of Rectangle Objects

RectObj can be subclassed to provide widgetlike objects (sometimes called gadgets) that do not use windows and do not have features often unused in simple widgets. This can save memory resources both in the server and in applications but requires additional support code in the parent. In the following discussion, *rectobj* refers only to objects whose class is RectObj or a subclass of RectObj but not Core or a subclass of Core.

Composite widget classes that wish to accept rectobj children must set the *accepts_objects* field in the `CompositeClassExtension` extension structure to `True`. `XtCreateWidget` or `XtCreateManagedWidget` will otherwise generate an error if called to create a nonwidget child. If the composite widget supports only children of class RectObj or a subclass (i.e., not of the general Object class), it must declare an insert_child procedure and check the subclass of each new child in that procedure. None of the classes defined by the Intrinsics accept rectobj children.

If gadgets are defined in an object set, the parent is responsible for much more than the parent of a widget. The parent must request and handle input events that occur for the gadget and is responsible for making sure that when it receives an exposure event the gadget children get drawn correctly. Rectobj children may have expose procedures specified in their class records, but the parent is free to ignore them, instead drawing the contents of the child itself. This can potentially save graphics context switching. The precise contents of the exposure event and region arguments to the RectObj expose procedure are not specified by the Intrinsics; a particular rectangle object is free to define the coordinate system origin (self-relative or parent-relative) and whether or not the rectangle or region is assumed to have been intersected with the visible region of the object.

In general, it is expected that a composite widget that accepts nonwidget children will document those children it is able to handle, since a gadget cannot be viewed as a completely self-contained entity, as can a widget. Since a particular composite widget class is usually designed to handle nonwidget children of only a limited set of classes, it should check the classes of newly added children in its insert_child procedure to make sure that it can deal with them.

The Intrinsics will clear areas of a parent window obscured by rectobj children, causing exposure events, under the following circumstances:

• A rectobj child is managed or unmanaged.

• In a call to XtSetValues on a rectobj child, one or more of the set_values procedures returns True.

• In a call to XtConfigureWidget on a rectobj child, areas will be cleared corresponding to both the old and the new child geometries, including the border, if the geometry changes.

• In a call to XtMoveWidget on a rectobj child, areas will be cleared corresponding to both the old and the new child geometries, including the border, if the geometry changes.

• In a call to XtResizeWidget on a rectobj child, a single rectangle will be cleared corresponding to the larger of the old and the new child geometries if they are different.

• In a call to `XtMakeGeometryRequest` (or `XtMakeResizeRequest`) on a rectobj child with `XtQueryOnly` not set, if the manager returns `XtGeometryYes`, two rectangles will be cleared corresponding to both the old and the new child geometries.

Stacking order is not supported for rectobj children. Composite widgets with rectobj children are free to define any semantics desired if the child geometries overlap, including making this an error.

When a rectobj is playing the role of a widget, developers must be reminded to avoid making assumptions about the object passed in the Widget argument to a callback procedure.

12.4 Undeclared Class

The Intrinsics define an unnamed class between RectObj and Core for possible future use by the X Consortium. The only assumptions that may be made about the unnamed class are

• The *core_class.superclass* field of `coreWidgetClassRec` contains a pointer to the unnamed class record.

• A pointer to the unnamed class record when dereferenced as an `ObjectClass` will contain a pointer to `rectObjClassRec` in its *object_class.superclass* field.

Except for the above, the contents of the class record for this class and the result of an attempt to subclass or to create a widget of this unnamed class are undefined.

12.5 Widget Arguments to Intrinsics Routines

The WidgetClass arguments to the following procedures must be of class Shell or a subclass:

```
XtCreatePopupShell, XtVaCreatePopupShell, XtAppCreateShell,
XtVaAppCreateShell
```

The Widget arguments to the following procedures must be of class Core or any subclass:

```
XtCreatePopupShell, XtVaCreatePopupShell

XtAddEventHandler, XtAddRawEventHandler,
XtRemoveEventHandler, XtRemoveRawEventHandler,
XtInsertEventHandler, XtInsertRawEventHandler
```

```
XtAddGrab, XtRemoveGrab, XtGrabKey, XtGrabKeyboard, XtUngrabKey,
XtUngrabKeyboard, XtGrabButton, XtGrabPointer, XtUngrabButton,
XtUngrabPointer
```

```
XtBuildEventMask
```

```
XtCreateWindow, XtDisplay, XtScreen, XtWindow
```

```
XtNameToWidget
```

```
XtGetSelectionValue, XtGetSelectionValues, XtOwnSelection,
XtDisownSelection, XtOwnSelectionIncremental,
XtGetSelectionValueIncremental, XtGetSelectionValuesIncremental,
XtGetSelectionRequest
```

```
XtInstallAccelerators, XtInstallAllAccelerators (both destination and
source)
```

```
XtAugmentTranslations, XtOverrideTranslations,
XtUninstallTranslations, XtCallActionProc
```

```
XtMapWidget, XtUnmapWidget
```

```
XtRealizeWidget, XtUnrealizeWidget
```

```
XtSetMappedWhenManaged
```

```
XtCallAcceptFocus, XtSetKeyboardFocus (subtree)
```

```
XtResizeWindow
```

```
XtSetWMColormapWindows
```

The Widget arguments to the following procedures must be of class Composite or any subclass:

```
XtCreateManagedWidget, XtVaCreateManagedWidget
```

The Widget arguments to the following procedures must be of a subclass of Shell:

```
XtPopdown, XtCallbackPopdown, XtPopup, XtCallbackNone,
XtCallbackNonexclusive, XtCallbackExclusive, XtPopupSpringLoaded
```

The return value of the following procedure will be of class Core or a subclass:

```
XtWindowToWidget
```

The return value of the following procedures will be of a subclass of Shell:

```
XtAppCreateShell, XtVaAppCreateShell, XtAppInitialize,
XtVaAppInitialize, XtCreatePopupShell, XtVaCreatePopupShell
```

Chapter 13

Evolution of
the Intrinsics

The interfaces described by this specification have undergone several sets of revisions in the course of adoption as an X Consortium standard specification. Having now been adopted by the Consortium as a standard part of the X Window System, it is expected that this and future revisions will retain backward compatibility in the sense that fully conforming implementations of these specifications may be produced that provide source compatibility with widgets and applications written to previous Consortium standard revisions.

The Intrinsics do not place any special requirement on widget programmers to retain source or binary compatibility for their widgets as they evolve, but several conventions have been established to assist those developers who want to provide such compatibility.

In particular, widget programmers may wish to conform to the convention described in Section 1.6.12 when defining class extension records.

13.1 Determining Specification Revision Level

Widget and application developers who wish to maintain a common source pool that will build properly with implementations of the Intrinsics at different revision levels of these specifications but that take advantage of newer features added in later revisions may use the symbolic macro `XtSpecification-Release`.

#define XtSpecificationRelease 4

As the symbol `XtSpecificationRelease` is new to Release 4, widgets and applications desiring to build against earlier implementations should test for the presence of this symbol and assume only Release 3 interfaces if the definition is not present.

13.2   Release 3 to Release 4 Compatibility

At the data structure level, Release 4 retains binary compatibility with Release 3 (the first X Consortium standard release) for all data structures except `WMShellPart`, `TopLevelShellPart`, and `TransientShellPart`. Release 4 changed the argument type to most procedures that now take arguments of type `XtPointer` and structure members that are now of type `XtPointer` in order to avoid potential ANSI C conformance problems. It is expected that most implementations will be binary compatible with the previous definition.

Two fields in `CoreClassPart` were changed from `Boolean` to `XtEnum` to allow implementations additional freedom in specifying the representations of each. This change should require no source modification.

13.2.1   Additional Arguments

Arguments were added to the procedure definitions for `XtInitProc`, `XtSetValuesFunc`, and `XtEventHandler` to provide more information and to allow event handlers to abort further dispatching of the current event (caution is advised!). The added arguments to `XtInitProc` and `XtSetValuesFunc` make the initialize_hook and set_values_hook methods obsolete, but the hooks have been retained for those widgets that used them in Release 3.

13.2.2   set_values_almost Procedures

The use of the arguments by a set_values_almost procedure was poorly described in Release 3 and was inconsistent with other conventions.

The current specification for the manner in which a set_values_almost procedure returns information to the Intrinsics is not compatible with the Release 3 specification, and all widget implementations should verify that any set_values_almost procedures conform to the current interface.

No known implementation of the Intrinsics correctly implemented the Release 3 interface, so it is expected that the impact of this specification change is small.

13.2.3 Query Geometry

A composite widget layout routine that calls `XtQueryGeometry` is now expected to store the complete new geometry in the intended structure; previously the specification said "store the changes it intends to make." Only by storing the complete geometry does the child have any way to know what other parts of the geometry may still be flexible. Existing widgets should not be affected by this, except to take advantage of the new information.

13.2.4 unrealizeCallback Callback List

In order to provide a mechanism for widgets to be notified when they become unrealized through a call to `XtUnrealizeWidget`, the callback list name "unrealizeCallback" has been defined by the Intrinsics. A widget class that requires notification on unrealize may declare a callback list resource by this name. No class is required to declare this resource, but any class that did so in a prior revision may find it necessary to modify the resource name if it does not wish to use the new semantics.

13.2.5 Subclasses of WMShell

The formal adoption of the *Inter-Client Communication Conventions Manual* as an X Consortium standard has meant the addition of four fields to `WMShellPart` and one field to `TopLevelShellPart`. In deference to some widget libraries that had developed their own additional conventions to provide binary compatibility, these five new fields were added at the end of the respective data structures.

To provide more convenience for TransientShells, a field was added to the previously empty `TransientShellPart`. On some architectures the size of the part structure will not have changed as a result of this.

Any widget implementation whose class is a subclass of TopLevelShell or TransientShell must at minimum be recompiled with the new data structure declarations. Because `WMShellPart` no longer contains a contiguous `XSizeHints` data structure, a subclass that expected to do a single structure assignment of an XSizeHints structure to the *size_hints* field of WMShell-Part must be revised, though the old fields remain at the same positions within WMShellPart.

13.2.6   Resource Type Converters

A new interface declaration for resource type converters was defined to provide more information to converters, to support conversion cache cleanup with resource reference counting, and to allow additional procedures to be declared to free resources. The old interfaces remain (in the compatibility section) and a new set of procedures was defined that work only with the new type converter interface.

In the now obsolete old type converter interface, converters are reminded that they must return the size of the converted value as well as its address. The example indicated this, but the description of XtConverter was incomplete.

13.2.7   KeySym Case Conversion Procedure

The specification for the XtCaseProc function type has been changed to match the Release 3 implementation, which included necessary additional information required by the function (a pointer to the display connection), and corrects the argument type of the source KeySym parameter. No known implementation of the Intrinsics implemented the previously documented interface.

13.2.8   Nonwidget Objects

Formal support for nonwidget objects is new to Release 4. A prototype implementation was latent in at least one Release 3 implementation of the Intrinsics, but the specification has changed somewhat. The most significant change is the requirement for a composite widget to declare the CompositeClass-Extension record with the *accepts_objects* field set to True in order to permit a client to create a nonwidget child.

The addition of this extension field ensures that composite widgets written under Release 3 will not encounter unexpected errors if an application attempts to create a nonwidget child. In Release 4 there is no requirement that all composite widgets implement the extra functionality required to manage windowless children, so the *accept_objects* field allows a composite widget to declare that it is not prepared to do so.

PART III. APPENDIXES

Appendix A

Resource File Format

The format of resource files is defined by *Xlib* and is reproduced here for convenience only.

The format of a resource specification is

ResourceLine	= Comment | ResourceSpec
Comment	= "!" string | <empty line>
ResourceSpec	= WhiteSpace ResourceName WhiteSpace ":" WhiteSpace value
ResourceName	= [Binding] ComponentName {Binding ComponentName}
Binding	= "." | "*"
WhiteSpace	= {" " | "\t"}
ComponentName	= {"A"-"Z" | "a"-"z" | "0"-"9" | "_" | "-"}
value	= string
string	= {<any character not including "\n">}

where {. . .} means zero or more occurrences of the enclosed elements.

If the last character on a line is a backslash (\), that line is assumed to continue on the next line.

To include a newline character in a string, use "\n". To include arbitrary octets in a string, use the four-character sequence "\nnn" where nnn is the numeric value of the octet specified as an octal constant. For example, a value containing a NULL byte may be stored by including "\000" in the string.

---

* This appendix is part of the formal Intrinsics Specification.

```
┌─────────────────────────────────────────┐
│                                         │
│  Appendix B                             │
│                                         │
│                                         │
│                                         │
│                                         │
│  Translation                            │
│  Table Syntax                           │
│                                         │
└─────────────────────────────────────────┘
```

B.1   Notation

Syntax is specified in EBNF notation with the following conventions:

[a]   Means either nothing or "a"
{ a }   Means zero or more occurrences of "a"
(a | b)   Means either "a" or "b"
\n   Is the newline character

All terminals are enclosed in double quotation marks (" "). Informal descriptions are enclosed in angle brackets (< >).

B.2   Syntax

The syntax of a translation table is

```
translationTable   = [ directive ] { production }
directive          = ( "#replace" | "#override" | "#augment" ) "\n"
production         = lhs ":" rhs "\n"
lhs                = ( event | keyseq ) { "," (event | keyseq) }
keyseq             = " " " keychar {keychar} " " "
keychar            = [ "^" | "$" | "\" ] <ISO Latin 1 character>
event              = [modifier_list] "<"event_type">" [ "(" count["+"] ")" ] {detail}
modifier_list      = ( ["!"] [":"] {modifier} ) | "None"
modifier           = ["~"] modifier_name
count              = ("1" | "2" | "3" | "4" | ...)
```

    * This appendix is part of the formal Intrinsics Specification.

modifier_name	= "@" <keysym>	<see ModifierNames table below>
event_type	= <see Event Types table below>
detail	= <event specific details>
rhs	= { name "(" [params] ")" }
name	= namechar { namechar }
namechar	= { "a"-"z"	"A"-"Z"	"0"-"9"	"_"	"-" }
params	= string {"," string}
string	= quoted_string	unquoted_string
quoted_string	= " " " {<Latin 1 character>} " " "
unquoted_string	= {<Latin 1 character except space, tab, ",", "\n", ")">}

B.3   Modifier Names

The modifier field is used to specify standard X keyboard and button modifier mask bits. Modifiers are legal on event types `KeyPress`, `KeyRelease`, `ButtonPress`, `ButtonRelease`, `MotionNotify`, `EnterNotify`, `Leave-Notify`, and their abbreviations. An error is generated when a translation table that contains modifiers for any other events is parsed.

• If the modifier list has no entries and is not "None", it means "don't care" on all modifiers.

• If an exclamation point (!) is specified at the beginning of the modifier list, it means that the listed modifiers must be in the correct state and no other modifiers can be asserted.

• If any modifiers are specified and an exclamation point (!) is not specified, it means that the listed modifiers must be in the correct state and "don't care" about any other modifiers.

• If a modifier is preceded by a tilde (˜), it means that the modifier must not be asserted.

• If "None" is specified, it means no modifiers can be asserted.

• If a colon (:) is specified at the beginning of the modifier list, it directs the Intrinsics to apply any standard modifiers in the event to map the event keycode into a KeySym. The default standard modifiers are Shift and Lock, with the interpretation as defined in *Xlib*, Protocol, Section 5. The resulting KeySym must exactly match the specified KeySym, and the nonstandard modifiers in the event must match the modifier list. For example, ":<Key>a" is distinct from ":<Key>A", and ":Shift<Key>A" is distinct from ":<Key>A".

• If both an exclamation point (!) and a colon (:) are specified at the beginning of the modifier list, it means that the listed modifiers must be in the correct state and that no other modifiers except the standard modifiers can be asserted. Any standard modifiers in the event are applied as for colon (:) above.

• If a colon (:) is not specified, no standard modifiers are applied. Then, for example, "<Key>A" and "<Key>a" are equivalent.

In key sequences, a circumflex (^) is an abbreviation for the Control modifier, a dollar sign ($) is an abbreviation for Meta, and a backslash (\) can be used to quote any character, in particular a double quote ("), a circumflex (^), a dollar sign ($), and another backslash (\). Briefly:

No modifiers:	None <event> detail
Any modifiers:	<event> detail
Only these modifiers:	! mod1 mod2 <event> detail
These modifiers and any others:	mod1 mod2 <event> detail

The use of "None" for a modifier list is identical to the use of an exclamation point with no modifiers.

Modifier	Abbreviation	Meaning
Ctrl	c	Control modifier bit
Shift	s	Shift modifier bit
Lock	l	Lock modifier bit
Meta	m	Meta key modifier
Hyper	h	Hyper key modifier
Super	su	Super key modifier
Alt	a	Alt key modifier
Mod1		Mod1 modifier bit
Mod2		Mod2 modifier bit
Mod3		Mod3 modifier bit
Mod4		Mod4 modifier bit
Mod5		Mod5 modifier bit
Button1		Button1 modifier bit
Button2		Button2 modifier bit
Button3		Button3 modifier bit
Button4		Button4 modifier bit
Button5		Button5 modifier bit
None		No modifiers
Any		Any modifier combination

A key modifier is any modifier bit one of whose corresponding KeyCodes contains the corresponding left or right KeySym. For example, "m" or "Meta" means any modifier bit mapping to a KeyCode whose KeySym list contains XK_Meta_L or XK_Meta_R. Note that this interpretation is for each display, not global or even for each application context. The Control, Shift, and Lock modifier names refer explicitly to the corresponding modifier bits; there is no additional interpretation of KeySyms for these modifiers.

Because it is possible to associate arbitrary KeySyms with modifiers, the set of key modifiers is extensible. The "@" <keysym> syntax means any modifier bit whose corresponding KeyCode contains the specified KeySym name.

A modifier_list/KeySym combination in a translation matches a modifiers/KeyCode combination in an event in the following ways:

1. If a colon (:) is used, the Intrinsics call the display's XtKeyProc with the KeyCode and modifiers. To match, (*modifiers* & ~*modifiers_return*) must equal *modifier_list*, and *keysym_return* must equal the given KeySym.
2. If (:) is not used, the Intrinsics mask off all don't-care bits from the modifiers. This value must be equal to *modifier_list*. Then, for each possible combination of don't-care modifiers in the modifier list, the Intrinsics call the display's XtKeyProc with the KeyCode and that combination ORed with the cared-about modifier bits from the event. *Keysym_return* must match the KeySym in the translation.

B.4 Event Types

The event-type field describes XEvent types. In addition to the standard Xlib symbolic event type names, the following event type synonyms are defined:

Type	*Meaning*
Key	KeyPress
KeyDown	KeyPress
KeyUp	KeyRelease
BtnDown	ButtonPress
BtnUp	ButtonRelease
Motion	MotionNotify
PtrMoved	MotionNotify
MouseMoved	MotionNotify
Enter	EnterNotify
EnterWindow	EnterNotify
Leave	LeaveNotify
LeaveWindow	LeaveNotify
FocusIn	FocusIn
FocusOut	FocusOut
Keymap	KeymapNotify
Expose	Expose

Type	*Meaning*
GrExp	`GraphicsExpose`
NoExp	`NoExpose`
Visible	`VisibilityNotify`
Create	`CreateNotify`
Destroy	`DestroyNotify`
Unmap	`UnmapNotify`
Map	`MapNotify`
MapReq	`MapRequest`
Reparent	`ReparentNotify`
Configure	`ConfigureNotify`
ConfigureReq	`ConfigureRequest`
Grav	`GravityNotify`
ResReq	`ResizeRequest`
Circ	`CirculateNotify`
CircReq	`CirculateRequest`
Prop	`PropertyNotify`
SelClr	`SelectionClear`
SelReq	`SelectionRequest`
Select	`SelectionNotify`
Clrmap	`ColormapNotify`
Message	`ClientMessage`
Mapping	`MappingNotify`

The supported abbreviations are

Abbreviation	*Event Type*	*Including*
Ctrl	`KeyPress`	with Control modifier
Meta	`KeyPress`	with Meta modifier
Shift	`KeyPress`	with Shift modifier
Btn1Down	`ButtonPress`	with Button1 detail
Btn1Up	`ButtonRelease`	with Button1 detail
Btn2Down	`ButtonPress`	with Button2 detail
Btn2Up	`ButtonRelease`	with Button2 detail
Btn3Down	`ButtonPress`	with Button3 detail
Btn3Up	`ButtonRelease`	with Button3 detail
Btn4Down	`ButtonPress`	with Button4 detail
Btn4Up	`ButtonRelease`	with Button4 detail
Btn5Down	`ButtonPress`	with Button5 detail

Abbreviation	*Event Type*	*Including*
Btn5Up	`ButtonRelease`	with Button5 detail
BtnMotion	`MotionNotify`	with any button modifier
Btn1Motion	`MotionNotify`	with Button1 modifier
Btn2Motion	`MotionNotify`	with Button2 modifier
Btn3Motion	`MotionNotify`	with Button3 modifier
Btn4Motion	`MotionNotify`	with Button4 modifier
Btn5Motion	`MotionNotify`	with Button5 modifier

The detail field is event-specific and normally corresponds to the detail field of the corresponding event as described by *Xlib*, Protocol, Section 11. The detail field is supported for the following event types:

Event	*Event Field*
KeyPress	KeySym from event *detail* (keycode)
KeyRelease	KeySym from event *detail* (keycode)
ButtonPress	Button from event *detail*
ButtonRelease	Button from event *detail*
MotionNotify	Event *detail*
EnterNotify	Event *mode*
LeaveNotify	Event *mode*
FocusIn	Event *mode*
FocusOut	Event *mode*
PropertyNotify	*atom*
SelectionClear	*selection*
SelectionRequest	*selection*
SelectionNotify	*selection*
ClientMessage	*type*
MappingNotify	*request*

If the event type is `KeyPress` or `KeyRelease`, the detail field specifies a KeySym name in standard format which is matched against the event as described above, for example, <Key>A.

For the `PropertyNotify`, `SelectionClear`, `SelectionRequest`, `SelectionNotify` and `ClientMessage` events the detail field is specified as an atom name; for example, <Message>WM_PROTOCOLS. For the `MotionNotify`, `EnterNotify`, `LeaveNotify`, `FocusIn`, `FocusOut` and `MappingNotify` events, either the symbolic constants as defined by *Xlib*, Protocol, Section 11, or the numeric values may be specified.

If no detail field is specified, then any value in the event detail is accepted as a match.

A KeySym can be specified as any of the standard KeySym names, a hexadecimal number prefixed with "0x" or "0X", an octal number prefixed with "0" or a decimal number. A KeySym expressed as a single digit is interpreted as the corresponding Latin 1 KeySym, for example, "0" is the KeySym XK_0. Other single character KeySyms are treated as literal constants from Latin 1, for example, "!" is treated as 0x21. Standard keysym names are as defined in `<X11/keysymdef.h>` with the "XK_" prefix removed.

B.5   Canonical Representation

Every translation table has a unique, canonical text representation. This representation is passed to a widget's `display_accelerator` procedure to describe the accelerators installed on that widget. The canonical representation of a translation table is (see also "Syntax")

translationTable	= { production }
production	= lhs ":" rhs "\n"
lhs	= event { "," event }
event	= [modifier_list] "<"event_type">" ["(" count["+"] ")"] {detail}
modifier_list	= ["!"] [":"] {modifier}
modifier	= ["~"] modifier_name
count	= ("1" | "2" | "3" | "4" | ...)
modifier_name	= "@" <keysym>	<see canonical modifier names below>
event_type	= <see canonical event types below>
detail	= <event specific details>
rhs	= { name "(" [params] ")" }
name	= namechar { namechar }
namechar	= { "a"-"z"	"A"-"Z"	"0"-"9"	"_"	"-" }
params	= string {"," string}
string	= quoted_string
quoted_string	= " " " {<Latin 1 character>} " " "

The canonical modifier names are

Ctrl	Mod1	Button1
Shift	Mod2	Button2
Lock	Mod3	Button3
	Mod4	Button4
	Mod5	Button5

The canonical event types are

KeyPress	KeyRelease
ButtonPress	ButtonRelease
MotionNotify	EnterNotify
LeaveNotify	FocusIn
FocusOut	KeymapNotify
Expose	GraphicsExpose,
NoExpose	VisibilityNotify
CreateNotify	DestroyNotify
UnmapNotify	MapNotify
MapRequest	ReparentNotify
ConfigureNotify	ConfigureRequest
GravityNotify	ResizeRequest
CirculateNotify	CirculateRequest
PropertyNotify	SelectionClear
SelectionRequest	SelectionNotify
ColormapNotify	ClientMessage

B.6   Examples

• Always put more specific events in the table before more general ones:

```
Shift <Btn1Down> : twas()\n\
<Btn1Down> : brillig()
```

• For double-click on Button1 Up with Shift, use this specification:

```
Shift<Btn1Up>(2) : and()
```

This is equivalent to the following line with appropriate timers set between events:

```
Shift<Btn1Down>, Shift<Btn1Up>, Shift<Btn1Down>, Shift<Btn1Up>:and()
```

• For double-click on Button1 Down with Shift, use this specification:

```
Shift<Btn1Down>(2):the()
```

This is equivalent to the following line with appropriate timers set between events:

```
Shift<Btn1Down>, Shift<Btn1Up>, Shift<Btn1Down>:the()
```

• Mouse motion is always discarded when it occurs between events in a table where no motion event is specified:

```
<Btn1Down>,<Btn1Up> : slithy()
```

This action is taken, even if the pointer moves a bit between the down and up events. Similarly, any motion event specified in a translation matches any number of motion events. If the motion event causes an action procedure to be invoked, the procedure is invoked after each motion event.

- If an event sequence consists of a sequence of events that is also a non-initial subsequence of another translation, it is not taken if it occurs in the context of the longer sequence. This occurs mostly in sequences like the following:

```
<Btn1Down>,<Btn1Up> : toves()\n\
<Btn1Up> :  did()
```

The second translation is taken only if the button release is not preceded by a button press or if there are intervening events between the press and the release. Be particularly aware of this when using the repeat notation, above, with buttons and keys, because their expansion includes additional events; and when specifying motion events, because they are implicitly included between any two other events. In particular, pointer motion and double-click translations cannot coexist in the same translation table.

- For single click on Button1 Up with Shift and Meta, use this specification:

```
Shift Meta <Btn1Down>, Shift Meta<Btn1Up>: gyre()
```

- For multiple clicks greater or equal to a minimum number, a plus sign (+) may be appended to the final (rightmost) count in an event sequence. The actions will be invoked on the *count*-th click and each subsequent one arriving within the multi-click time interval. For example:

```
Shift <Btn1Up>(2+) : and()
```

- To indicate EnterNotify with any modifiers, use this specification:

```
<Enter> : gimble()
```

- To indicate EnterNotify with no modifiers, use this specification:

```
None<Enter> : in()
```

- To indicate EnterNotify with Button1 down and Button2 up and "don't care" about the other modifiers, use this specification:

```
Button1 ~Button2 <Enter> : the()
```

- To indicate EnterNotify with Button1 down and Button2 down exclusively, use this specification:

```
! Button1 Button2<Enter> : wabe()
```

You do not need to use a tilde (˜) with an exclamation point (!).

Appendix C

Compatibility Functions

In prototype versions of the X Toolkit each widget class implemented an Xt<*Widget*>Create (for example, `XtLabelCreate`) function, in which most of the code was identical from widget to widget. In the Intrinsics, a single generic `XtCreateWidget` performs most of the common work and then calls the initialize procedure implemented for the particular widget class.

Each Composite class also implemented the procedures Xt<*Widget*>Add and an Xt<*Widget*>Delete (for example, `XtButtonBoxAddButton` and `XtButtonBoxDeleteButton`). In the Intrinsics, the Composite generic procedures `XtManageChildren` and `XtUnmanageChildren` perform error checking and screening out of certain children. Then they call the change_managed procedure implemented for the widget's Composite class. If the widget's parent has not yet been realized, the call to the change_managed procedure is delayed until realization time.

Old style calls can be implemented in the X Toolkit by defining one-line procedures or macros that invoke a generic routine. For example, you could define the macro `XtLabelCreate` as

```
#define XtLabelCreate (name, parent, args, num_args) \
    ((LabelWidget) XtCreateWidget(name, labelWidgetClass, parent, args, num_args))
```

Pop-up shells in some of the prototypes automatically performed an `XtManageChild` on their child within their insert_child procedure. Creators of pop-up children need to call `XtManageChild` themselves.

---

* This appendix is part of the formal Intrinsics Specification.

As a convenience to people converting from earlier versions of the toolkit, the following routines exist: XtInitialize, XtMainLoop, XtNextEvent, XtProcessEvent, XtPeekEvent, XtPending, XtAddInput, XtAddTime-Out, XtAddWorkProc, and XtCreateApplicationShell.

Widget XtInitialize(*shell_name, application_class, options, num_options, argc, argv*)
    String *shell_name*;
    String *application_class*;
    XrmOptionDescRec *options*[];
    Cardinal *num_options*;
    Cardinal *argc*;
    String *argv*[];

shell_name	This parameter is ignored; therefore, you can specify NULL.
application_class	Specifies the class name of this application.
options	Specifies how to parse the command line for any application-specific resources. The *options* argument is passed as a parameter to XrmParseCommand.
num_options	Specifies the number of entries in the options list.
argc	Specifies a pointer to the number of command line parameters.
argv	Specifies the command line parameters.

XtInitialize calls XtToolkitInitialize to initialize the toolkit internals, creates a default application context for use by the other convenience routines, calls XtOpenDisplay with *display_string* NULL and *application_name* NULL, and finally calls XtAppCreateShell with *application_name* NULL and returns the created shell. The semantics of calling XtInitialize more than once are undefined. This routine has been replaced by XtAppInitialize.

void XtMainLoop()

XtMainLoop first reads the next alternate input, timer, or X event by calling XtNextEvent. Then it dispatches this to the appropriate registered procedure by calling XtDispatchEvent. This routine has been replaced by XtAppMainLoop.

void XtNextEvent(*event_return*)
    XEvent *event_return*;

event_return	Returns the event information to the specified event structure.

If no input is on the X input queue for the default application context, XtNext-Event flushes the X output buffer and waits for an event while looking at the alternate input sources and timeout values and calling any callback procedures triggered by them. This routine has been replaced by XtAppNextEvent. XtInitialize must be called before using this routine.

void XtProcessEvent(*mask*)
    XtInputMask *mask*;
mask   Specifies the type of input to process.

XtProcessEvent processes one X event, timeout, or alternate input source (depending on the value of *mask*), blocking if necessary. It has been replaced by XtAppProcessEvent. XtInitialize must be called before using this function.

Boolean XtPeekEvent(*event_return*)
    XEvent *event_return*;
event_return   Returns the event information to the specified event structure.

If there is an event in the queue for the default application context, XtPeekEvent fills in the event and returns a nonzero value. If no X input is on the queue, XtPeekEvent flushes the output buffer and blocks until input is available, possibly calling some timeout callbacks in the process. If the input is an event, XtPeekEvent fills in the event and returns a nonzero value. Otherwise, the input is for an alternate input source, and XtPeekEvent returns zero. This routine has been replaced by XtAppPeekEvent. XtInitialize must be called before using this routine.

Boolean XtPending()

XtPending returns a nonzero value if there are events pending from the X server or alternate input sources in the default application context. If there are no events pending, it flushes the output buffer and returns a zero value. It has been replaced by XtAppPending. XtInitialize must be called before using this routine.

XtInputId XtAddInput(*source, condition, proc, client_data*)
    int *source*;
    XtPointer *condition*;
    XtInputCallbackProc *proc*;
    XtPointer *client_data*;

source	Specifies the source file descriptor on a POSIX-based system or other operating-system-dependent device specification.
condition	Specifies the mask that indicates either a read, write, or exception condition, or some operating-system-dependent condition.
proc	Specifies the procedure called when input is available.
client_data	Specifies the parameter to be passed to *proc* when input is available.

The `XtAddInput` function registers in the default application context a new source of events, which is usually file input but can also be file output. (The word *file* should be loosely interpreted to mean any sink or source of data.) `XtAddInput` also specifies the conditions under which the source can generate events. When input is pending on this source in the default application context, the callback procedure is called. This routine has been replaced by `XtAppAddInput`. `XtInitialize` must be called before using this routine.

XtIntervalId XtAddTimeOut(*interval, proc, client_data*)
    unsigned long *interval*;
    XtTimerCallbackProc *proc*;
    XtPointer *client_data*;

interval	Specifies the time interval in milliseconds.
proc	Specifies the procedure to be called when time expires.
client_data	Specifies the parameter to be passed to *proc* when it is called.

The `XtAddTimeOut` function creates a timeout in the default application context and returns an identifier for it. The timeout value is set to *interval*. The callback procedure will be called after the time interval elapses, after which the timeout is removed. This routine has been replaced by `XtAppAddTimeOut`. `XtInitialize` must be called before using this routine.

XtWorkProcId XtAddWorkProc(*proc, client_data*)
    XtWorkProc *proc*;
    XtPointer *client_data*;

proc	Procedure to call to do the work.
client_data	Client data to pass to *proc* when it is called.

This routine registers a work procedure in the default application context. It has been replaced by `XtAppAddWorkProc`. `XtInitialize` must be called before using this routine.

Widget XtCreateApplicationShell(*name, widget_class, args, num_args*)
    String *name*;
    WidgetClass *widget_class*;
    ArgList *args*;
    Cardinal *num_args*;

name	This parameter is ignored; therefore, you can specify NULL.
widget_class	Specifies the widget class pointer for the created application shell widget. This will usually be `topLevelShellWidgetClass` or a subclass thereof.
args	Specifies the argument list to override any other resource specifications.
num_args	Specifies the number of entries in *args*.

The procedure `XtCreateApplicationShell` calls `XtAppCreateShell` with *application_name* NULL, the application class passed to `XtInitialize`, and the default application context created by `XtInitialize`. This routine has been replaced by `XtAppCreateShell`.

An old-format resource type converter procedure pointer is of type `XtConverter`.

typedef void (*XtConverter) (XrmValue*, Cardinal*, XrmValue*, XrmValue*);
    XrmValue *args*;
    Cardinal *num_args*;
    XrmValue *from*;
    XrmValue *to*;

args	Specifies a list of additional `XrmValue` arguments to the converter if additional context is needed to perform the conversion, or NULL.
num_args	Specifies the number of entries in *args*.
from	Specifies the value to convert.
to	Specifies the descriptor to use to return the converted value.

Type converters should perform the following actions:

• Check to see that the number of arguments passed is correct.

• Attempt the type conversion.

• If successful, return the size and pointer to the data in the *to* argument; otherwise, call XtWarningMsg and return without modifying the *to* argument.

Most type converters just take the data described by the specified *from* argument and return data by writing into the specified *to* argument. A few need other information, which is available in the specified argument list. A type converter can invoke another type converter, which allows differing sources that may convert into a common intermediate result to make maximum use of the type converter cache.

Note that the address returned in *to –>addr* cannot be that of a local variable of the converter because this is not valid after the converter returns. It should be a pointer to a static variable.

The procedure type XtConverter has been replaced by XtType-Converter.

The XtStringConversionWarning function is a convenience routine for old-format resource converters that convert from strings.

void XtStringConversionWarning (*src, dst_type*)
  String *src, dst_type*;
src   Specifies the string that could not be converted.
dst_type   Specifies the name of the type to which the string could not be converted.

The XtStringConversionWarning function issues a warning message with name "conversionError", type "string", class "XtToolkitError", and the default message string "Cannot convert "*src*" to type *dst_type*". This routine has been superseded by XtDisplayStringConversionWarning.

To register an old-format converter, use XtAddConverter or XtAppAdd-Converter.

void XtAddConverter (*from_type, to_type, converter, convert_args, num_args*)
  String *from_type*;
  String *to_type*;
  XtConverter *converter*;
  XtConvertArgList *convert_args*;
  Cardinal *num_args*;
from_type   Specifies the source type.
to_type   Specifies the destination type.

converter	Specifies the type converter procedure.
convert_args	Specifies how to compute the additional arguments to the converter, or NULL.
num_args	Specifies the number of entries in *convert_args*.

`XtAddConverter` is equivalent in function to `XtSetTypeConverter` with *cache_type* equal to `XtCacheAll` for old-format type converters. It has been superseded by `XtSetTypeConverter`.

void XtAppAddConverter(*app_context, from_type, to_type, converter, convert_args, num_args*)
    XtAppContext *app_context*;
    String *from_type*;
    String *to_type*;
    XtConverter *converter*;
    XtConvertArgList *convert_args*;
    Cardinal *num_args*;

app_context	Specifies the application context.
from_type	Specifies the source type.
to_type	Specifies the destination type.
converter	Specifies the type converter procedure.
convert_args	Specifies how to compute the additional arguments to the converter, or NULL.
num_args	Specifies the number of entries in *convert_args*.

`XtAppAddConverter` is equivalent in function to `XtAppSetType-Converter` with *cache_type* equal to `XtCacheAll` for old-format type converters. It has been superseded by `XtAppSetTypeConverter`.

To invoke resource conversions, a client may use `XtConvert` or, for old-format converters only, `XtDirectConvert`.

void XtConvert(*w, from_type, from, to_type, to_return*)
    Widget *w*;
    String *from_type*;
    XrmValuePtr *from*;
    String *to_type*;
    XrmValuePtr *to_return*;

w	Specifies the widget to use for additional arguments, if any are needed. Must be of class Object or any subclass thereof.
from_type	Specifies the source type.
from	Specifies the value to be converted.

to_type   Specifies the destination type.

to_return   Returns the converted value.

void XtDirectConvert(*converter, args, num_args, from, to_return*)

    XtConverter *converter*;

    XrmValuePtr *args*;

    Cardinal *num_args*;

    XrmValuePtr *from*;

    XrmValuePtr *to_return*;

converter   Specifies the conversion procedure to be called.

args   Specifies the argument list that contains the additional arguments
                    needed to perform the conversion (often NULL).

num_args   Specifies the number of entries in *args*.

from   Specifies the value to be converted.

to_return   Returns the converted value.

The `XtConvert` function looks up the type converter registered to convert *from_type* to *to_type*, computes any additional arguments needed, and then calls `XtDirectConvert` or `XtCallConverter`. The `XtDirectConvert` function looks in the converter cache to see if this conversion procedure has been called with the specified arguments. If so, it returns a descriptor for information stored in the cache; otherwise, it calls the converter and enters the result in the cache.

Before calling the specified converter, `XtDirectConvert` sets the return value size to zero and the return value address to NULL. To determine if the conversion was successful, the client should check *to_return.address* for non-NULL. The data returned by `XtConvert` must be copied immediately by the caller, as it may point to static data in the type converter.

`XtConvert` has been replaced by `XtConvertAndStore`, and `XtDirect-Convert` has been superseded by `XtCallConverter`.

To deallocate a shared GC when it is no longer needed, use `XtDestroyGC`.

void XtDestroyGC(*w, gc*)

    Widget *w*;

    GC *gc*;

w   Specifies any object on the display for which the shared GC was
                    created. Must be of class Object or any subclass thereof.

gc   Specifies the shared GC to be deallocated.

References to sharable GCs are counted and a free request is generated to the server when the last user of a given GC destroys it. Note that some earlier versions of XtDestroyGC had only a *gc* argument. Therefore, this function is not very portable, and you are encouraged to use XtReleaseGC instead.

To declare an action table in the default application context and register it with the translation manager, use XtAddActions.

void XtAddActions(*actions, num_actions*)
    XtActionList *actions*;
    Cardinal *num_actions*;
actions   Specifies the action table to register.
num_actions   Specifies the number of entries in actions.

If more than one action is registered with the same name, the most recently registered action is used. If duplicate actions exist in an action table, the first is used. The Intrinsics register an action table for XtMenuPopup and XtMenu-Popdown as part of X Toolkit initialization. This routine has been replaced by XtAppAddActions. XtInitialize must be called before using this routine.

To set the Intrinsics selection timeout in the default application context, use XtSetSelectionTimeout.

void XtSetSelectionTimeout(*timeout*)
    unsigned long *timeout*;
timeout   Specifies the selection timeout in milliseconds.

This routine has been replaced by XtAppSetSelectionTimeout. XtInitialize must be called before using this routine.

To get the current selection timeout value in the default application context, use XtGetSelectionTimeout.

unsigned long XtGetSelectionTimeout()

The selection timeout is the time within which the two communicating applications must respond to one another. If one of them does not respond within this interval, the Intrinsics abort the selection request. This routine has been replaced by XtAppGetSelectionTimeout. XtInitialize must be called before using this routine.

To obtain the global error database (for example, to merge with an application- or widget-specific database), use `XtGetErrorDatabase`.

XrmDatabase *XtGetErrorDatabase()

The `XtGetErrorDatabase` function returns the address of the error database. The Intrinsics do a lazy binding of the error database and do not merge in the database file until the first call to `XtGetErrorDatabaseText`. This routine has been replaced by `XtAppGetErrorDatabase`.

An error message handler can obtain the error database text for an error or a warning by calling `XtGetErrorDatabaseText`.

void XtGetErrorDatabaseText(*name, type, class, default, buffer_return, nbytes*)
    String *name, type, class*;
    String *default*;
    String *buffer_return*;
    int *nbytes*;

name, type	Specify the name and type that are concatenated to form the resource name of the error message.
class	Specifies the resource class of the error message.
default	Specifies the default message to use if an error database entry is not found.
buffer_return	Specifies the buffer into which the error message is to be returned.
nbytes	Specifies the size of the buffer in bytes.

`XtGetErrorDatabaseText` returns the appropriate message from the error database associated with the default application context or returns the specified default message if one is not found in the error database. This routine has been superseded by `XtAppGetErrorDatabaseText`.

To register a procedure to be called on fatal error conditions, use `XtSet-ErrorMsgHandler`.

void XtSetErrorMsgHandler(*msg_handler*)
    XtErrorMsgHandler *msg_handler*;

msg_handler	Specifies the new fatal error procedure, which should not return.

The default error handler provided by the Intrinsics constructs a string from the error resource database and calls `XtError`. Fatal error message handlers should not return. If one does, subsequent X Toolkit behavior is undefined. This routine has been superseded by `XtAppSetErrorMsgHandler`.

To call the high-level error handler, use `XtErrorMsg`.

void XtErrorMsg(*name, type, class, default, params, num_params*)
    String *name*;
    String *type*;
    String *class*;
    String *default*;
    String **params*;
    Cardinal **num_params*;

name	Specifies the general kind of error.
type	Specifies the detailed name of the error.
class	Specifies the resource class.
default	Specifies the default message to use if an error database entry is not found.
params	Specifies a pointer to a list of values to be stored in the message.
num_params	Specifies the number of entries in *params*.

This routine has been superseded by `XtAppErrorMsg`.

To register a procedure to be called on nonfatal error conditions, use `XtSetWarningMsgHandler`.

void XtSetWarningMsgHandler(*msg_handler*)
    XtErrorMsgHandler *msg_handler*;

msg_handler	Specifies the new nonfatal error procedure, which usually returns.

The default warning handler provided by the Intrinsics constructs a string from the error resource database and calls `XtWarning`. This routine has been superseded by `XtAppSetWarningMsgHandler`.

To call the installed high-level warning handler, use `XtWarningMsg`.

void XtWarningMsg(*name, type, class, default, params, num_params*)
    String *name*;
    String *type*;
    String *class*;
    String *default*;
    String **params*;
    Cardinal **num_params*;

name	Specifies the general kind of error.
type	Specifies the detailed name of the error.
class	Specifies the resource class.

default	Specifies the default message to use if an error database entry is not found.
params	Specifies a pointer to a list of values to be stored in the message.
num_params	Specifies the number of entries in *params*.

This routine has been superseded by `XtAppWarningMsg`.

To register a procedure to be called on fatal error conditions, use `XtSet-ErrorHandler`.

void XtSetErrorHandler(*handler*)
   XtErrorHandler *handler*;

handler	Specifies the new fatal error procedure, which should not return.

The default error handler provided by the Intrinsics is `_XtError`. On POSIX-based systems, it prints the message to standard error and terminates the application. Fatal error message handlers should not return. If one does, subsequent X Toolkit behavior is undefined. This routine has been superseded by `XtAppSetErrorHandler`.

To call the installed fatal error procedure, use `XtError`.

void XtError(*message*)
   String *message*;

message	Specifies the message to be reported.

Most programs should use `XtAppErrorMsg`, not `XtError`, to provide for customization and internationalization of error messages. This routine has been superseded by `XtAppError`.

To register a procedure to be called on nonfatal error conditions, use `XtSetWarningHandler`.

void XtSetWarningHandler(*handler*)
   XtErrorHandler *handler*;

handler	Specifies the new nonfatal error procedure, which usually returns.

The default warning handler provided by the Intrinsics is `_XtWarning`. On POSIX-based systems, it prints the message to standard error and returns to the caller. This routine has been superseded by `XtAppSetWarningHandler`.

To call the installed nonfatal error procedure, use `XtWarning`.

void XtWarning(*message*)
    String *message*;
message   Specifies the nonfatal error message to be reported.

Most programs should use `XtAppWarningMsg`, not `XtWarning`, to provide for customization and internationalization of warning messages. This routine has been superseded by `XtAppWarning`.

Appendix D

Intrinsics Error Messages

All Intrinsics errors and warnings have class "XtToolkitError". The following two sections summarize all the errors and warnings that can be generated by the Intrinsics.

D.1   Error Messages

Name	Type	Default Message
allocError	calloc	Cannot perform calloc
allocError	malloc	Cannot perform malloc
allocError	realloc	Cannot perform realloc
communicationError	select	Select failed
internalError	shell	Shell's window manager interaction is broken
invalidArgCount	xtGetValues	Argument count > 0 on NULL argument list in XtGetValues
invalidArgCount	xtSetValues	Argument count > 0 on NULL argument list in XtSetValues
invalidClass	constraintSetValue	Subclass of Constraint required in CallConstraintSetValues

* This appendix is part of the formal Intrinsics Specification.

Name	Type	Default Message
invalidClass	xtAppCreateShell	XtAppCreateShell requires non-NULL widget class
invalidClass	xtCreatePopupShell	XtCreatePopupShell requires non-NULL widget class
invalidClass	xtCreateWidget	XtCreateWidget requires non-NULL widget class
invalidClass	xtPopdown	XtPopdown requires a subclass of shellWidgetClass
invalidClass	xtPopup	XtPopup requires a subclass of shellWidgetClass
invalidDimension	xtCreateWindow	Widget %s has zero width and /or height
invalidDimension	shellRealize	Shell widget %s has zero width and /or height
invalidDisplay	xtInitialize	Can't Open display
invalidGeometryManager	xtMakeGeometryRequest	XtMakeGeometryRequest —parent has no geometry manager
invalidParameter	removePopupFromParent	RemovePopupFromParent requires non-NULL popuplist
invalidParameter	xtAddInput	invalid condition passed to XtAddInput
invalidParameters	xtMenuPopupAction	MenuPopup wants exactly one argument
invalidParameters	xtmenuPopdown	XtMenuPopdown called with num_params != 0 or 1
invalidParent	realize	Application shell is not a windowed widget?
invalidParent	xtCreatePopupShell	XtCreatePopupShell requires non-NULL parent

Name	*Type*	*Default Message*
invalidParent	xtCreateWidget	XtCreateWidget requires non-NULL parent
invalidParent	xtMakeGeometryRequest	XtMakeGeometryRequest —NULL parent. Use SetValues instead
invalidParent	xtMakeGeometryRequest	XtMakeGeometryRequest —parent not composite
invalidParent	xtManageChildren	Attempt to manage a child when parent is not Composite
invalidParent	xtUnmanageChildren	Attempt to unmanage a child when parent is not Composite
invalidPopup	xtMenuPopup	Can't find popup in _XtMenuPopup
invalidPopup	xtMenuPopup	Can't find popup in _XtMenuPopup
invalidProcedure	inheritanceProc	Unresolved inheritance operation
invalidProcedure	realizeProc	No realize class procedure defined
invalidWindow	eventHandler	Event with wrong window
missingEvent	shell	Events are disappearing from under Shell
noAppContext	widgetToApplicationContext	Couldn't find ancestor with display information
noPerDisplay	closeDisplay	Couldn't find per display information
noPerDisplay	getPerDisplay	Couldn't find per display information
noSelectionProperties	freeSelectionProperty	internal error: no selection property context for display
nullProc	insertChild	NULL insert_child procedure

Name	Type	Default Message
subclassMismatch	xtCheckSubclass	Widget class %s found when subclass of %s expected: %s
translationError	mergingTablesWithCycles	Trying to merge translation tables with cycles, and can't resolve this cycle.
wrongParameters	cvtIntOrPixelToXColor	Pixel to color conversion needs screen and colormap arguments
wrongParameters	cvtStringToCursor	String to cursor conversion needs screen argument
wrongParameters	cvtStringToFont	String to font conversion needs screen argument
wrongParameters	cvtStringToFontStruct	String to cursor conversion needs screen argument
wrongParameters	cvtStringToPixel	String to pixel conversion needs screen and colormap arguments

D.2   Warning Messages

Name	Type	Default Message
ambigiousParent	xtManageChildren	Not all children have same parent in XtManageChildren
ambigiousParent	xtUnmanageChildren	Not all children have same parent in XtUnmanageChildren
communicationError	windowManager	Window Manager is confused
conversionError	string	Cannot convert string "%s" to type %s

Name	Type	Default Message
displayError	invalidDisplay	Can't find display structure
grabError	grabDestroyCallback	XtAddGrab requires exclusive grab if spring_loaded is TRUE
grabError	grabDestroyCallback	XtAddGrab requires exclusive grab if spring_loaded is TRUE
grabError	xtRemoveGrab	XtRemoveGrab asked to remove a widget not on the grab list
initializationError	xtInitialize	Initializing Resource Lists twice
invalidArgCount	getResources	argument count > 0 on NULL argument list
invalidCallbackList	xtAddCallbacks	Cannot find callback list in XtAddCallbacks
invalidCallbackList	xtCallCallback	Cannot find callback list in XtCallCallbacks
invalidCallbackList	xtOverrideCallback	Cannot find callback list in XtOverrideCall-backs
invalidCallbackList	xtRemoveAllCallback	Cannot find callback list in XtRemoveAll-Callbacks
invalidCallbackList	xtRemoveCallbacks	Cannot find callback list in XtRemoveCall-backs
invalidChild	xtManageChildren	null child passed to XtManageChildren
invalidChild	xtUnmanageChildren	Null child passed to XtUnmanageChildren
invalidDepth	setValues	Can't change widget depth
invalidGeometry	xtMakeGeometryRequest	Shell subclass did not take care of geometry in XtSetValues

Name	Type	Default Message
invalidParameters	compileAccelerators	String to Accelerator-Table needs no extra arguments
invalidParameters	compileTranslations	String to Translation-Table needs no extra arguments
invalidParameters	mergeTranslations	MergeTM to Transla-tionTable needs no extra arguments
invalidParent	xtCopyFromParent	CopyFromParent must have non-NULL parent
invalidPopup	unsupportedOperation	Pop-up menu creation is only supported on ButtonPress or Enter-Notify events.
invalidPopup	unsupportedOperation	Pop-up menu creation is only supported on ButtonPress or Enter-Notify events.
invalidProcedure	deleteChild	null delete_child pro-cedure in XtDestroy
invalidProcedure	inputHandler	XtRemoveInput: Input handler not found
invalidProcedure	set_values_almost	set_values_almost pro-cedure shouldn't be NULL
invalidResourceCount	getResources	resource count > 0 on NULL resource list
invalidResourceName	computeArgs	Cannot find resource name %s as argument to conversion
invalidShell	xtTranslateCoords	Widget has no shell ancestor
invalidSizeOverride	xtDependencies	Representation size %d must match super-class's to override %s
invalidTypeOverride	xtDependencies	Representation type %s must match super-class's to override %s

Name	Type	Default Message
invalidWidget	removePopupFromParent	RemovePopupFrom-Parent, widget not on parent list
noColormap	cvtStringToPixel	Cannot allocate color-map entry for "%s"
registerWindowError	xtRegisterWindow	Attempt to change already registered window.
registerWindowError	xtUnregisterWindow	Attempt to unregister invalid window.
translation error	nullTable	Can't remove accelerators from NULL table
translation error	nullTable	Tried to remove non-existant accelerators
translationError	ambigiousActions	Overriding earlier translation manager actions.
translationError	mergingNullTable	Old translation table was null, cannot modify.
translationError	nullTable	Can't translate event thorugh NULL table
translationError	unboundActions	Actions not found: %s
translationError	xtTranslateInitialize	Intializing Translation manager twice.
translationParseError	showLine	... found while parsing '%s'
translationParseError	parseError	translation table syntax error: %s
translationParseError	parseString	Missing '\'.
typeConversionError	noConverter	No type converter registered for '%s' to '%s' conversion.
versionMismatch	widget	Widget class %s version mismatch: widget %d vs. intrinsics %d.
wrongParameters	cvtIntToBool	Integer to Bool conversion needs no extra arguments

Name	*Type*	*Default Message*
wrongParameters	cvtIntToBoolean	Integer to Boolean conversion needs no extra arguments
wrongParameters	cvtIntToFont	Integer to Font conversion needs no extra arguments
wrongParameters	cvtIntToPixel	Integer to Pixel conversion needs no extra arguments
wrongParameters	cvtIntToPixmap	Integer to Pixmap conversion needs no extra arguments
wrongParameters	cvtIntToShort	Integer to Short conversion needs no extra arguments
wrongParameters	cvtStringToBool	String to Bool conversion needs no extra arguments
wrongParameters	cvtStringToBoolean	String to Boolean conversion needs no extra arguments
wrongParameters	cvtStringToDisplay	String to Display conversion needs no extra arguments
wrongParameters	cvtStringToFile	String to File conversion needs no extra arguments
wrongParameters	cvtStringToInt	String to Integer conversion needs no extra arguments
wrongParameters	cvtStringToShort	String to Integer conversion needs no extra arguments
wrongParameters	cvtStringToUnsignedChar	String to Integer conversion needs no extra arguments
wrongParameters	cvtXColorToPixel	Color to Pixel conversion needs no extra arguments

Appendix E

StringDefs.h
Header File

```
/* Resource names */

#define XtNaccelerators "accelerators"
#define XtNallowHoriz "allowHoriz"
#define XtNallowVert "allowVert"
#define XtNancestorSensitive "ancestorSensitive"
#define XtNbackground "background"
#define XtNbackgroundPixmap "backgroundPixmap"
#define XtNbitmap "bitmap"
#define XtNborderColor "borderColor"
#define XtNborder "borderColor"
#define XtNborderPixmap "borderPixmap"
#define XtNborderWidth "borderWidth"
#define XtNcallback "callback"
#define XtNchildren "children"
#define XtNcolormap "colormap"
#define XtNdepth "depth"
#define XtNdestroyCallback "destroyCallback"
#define XtNeditType "editType"
#define XtNfile "file"
#define XtNfont "font"
```

* This appendix is part of the formal Intrinsics Specification.

```
#define XtNforceBars "forceBars"
#define XtNforeground "foreground"
#define XtNfunction "function"
#define XtNheight "height"
#define XtNhighlight "highlight"
#define XtNhSpace "hSpace"
#define XtNindex "index"
#define XtNinitialResourcesPersistent "initialResourcesPersistent"
#define XtNinnerHeight "innerHeight"
#define XtNinnerWidth "innerWidth"
#define XtNinnerWindow "innerWindow"
#define XtNinsertPosition "insertPosition"
#define XtNinternalHeight "internalHeight"
#define XtNinternalWidth "internalWidth"
#define XtNjumpProc "jumpProc"
#define XtNjustify "justify"
#define XtNknobHeight "knobHeight"
#define XtNknobIndent "knobIndent"
#define XtNknobPixel "knobPixel"
#define XtNknobWidth "knobWidth"
#define XtNlabel "label"
#define XtNlength "length"
#define XtNlowerRight "lowerRight"
#define XtNmappedWhenManaged "mappedWhenManaged"
#define XtNmenuEntry "menuEntry"
#define XtNname "name"
#define XtNnotify "notify"
#define XtNnumChildren "numChildren"
#define XtNorientation "orientation"
#define XtNparameter "parameter"
#define XtNpixmap "pixmap"
#define XtNpopupCallback "popupCallback"
#define XtNpopdownCallback "popdownCallback"
#define XtNresize "resize"
#define XtNreverseVideo "reverseVideo"
#define XtNscreen "screen"
```

```
#define XtNscrollProc "scrollProc"
#define XtNscrollDCursor "scrollDCursor"
#define XtNscrollHCursor "scrollHCursor"
#define XtNscrollLCursor "scrollLCursor"
#define XtNscrollRCursor "scrollRCursor"
#define XtNscrollUCursor "scrollUCursor"
#define XtNscrollVCursor "scrollVCursor"
#define XtNselection "selection"
#define XtNselectionArray "selectionArray"
#define XtNsensitive "sensitive"
#define XtNshown "shown"
#define XtNspace "space"
#define XtNstring "string"
#define XtNtextOptions "textOptions"
#define XtNtextSink "textSink"
#define XtNtextSource "textSource"
#define XtNthickness "thickness"
#define XtNthumb "thumb"
#define XtNthumbProc "thumbProc"
#define XtNtop "top"
#define XtNtranslations "translations"
#define XtNunrealizeCallback "unrealizeCallback"
#define XtNupdate "update"
#define XtNuseBottom "useBottom"
#define XtNuseRight "useRight"
#define XtNvalue "value"
#define XtNvSpace "vSpace"
#define XtNwidth "width"
#define XtNwindow "window"
#define XtNx "x"
#define XtNy "y"

/* Class types */
#define XtCAccelerators "Accelerators"
#define XtCBackground "Background"
#define XtCBitmap "Bitmap"
```

```
#define XtCBoolean "Boolean"
#define XtCBorderColor "BorderColor"
#define XtCBorderWidth "BorderWidth"
#define XtCCallback "Callback"
#define XtCColormap "Colormap"
#define XtCColor "Color"
#define XtCCursor "Cursor"
#define XtCDepth "Depth"
#define XtCEditType "EditType"
#define XtCEventBindings "EventBindings"
#define XtCFile "File"
#define XtCFont "Font"
#define XtCForeground "Foreground"
#define XtCFraction "Fraction"
#define XtCFunction "Function"
#define XtCHeight "Height"
#define XtCHSpace "HSpace"
#define XtCIndex "Index"
#define XtCInitialResourcesPersistent "InitialResourcesPersistent"
#define XtCInsertPosition "InsertPosition"
#define XtCInterval "Interval"
#define XtCJustify "Justify"
#define XtCKnobIndent "KnobIndent"
#define XtCKnobPixel "KnobPixel"
#define XtCLabel "Label"
#define XtCLength "Length"
#define XtCMappedWhenManaged "MappedWhenManaged"
#define XtCMargin "Margin"
#define XtCMenuEntry "MenuEntry"
#define XtCNotify "Notify"
#define XtCOrientation "Orientation"
#define XtCParameter "Parameter"
#define XtCPixmap "Pixmap"
#define XtCPosition "Position"
#define XtCReadOnly "ReadOnly"
#define XtCResize "Resize"
```

```
#define XtCReverseVideo "ReverseVideo"
#define XtCScreen "Screen"
#define XtCScrollProc "ScrollProc"
#define XtCScrollDCursor "ScrollDCursor"
#define XtCScrollHCursor "ScrollHCursor"
#define XtCScrollLCursor "ScrollLCursor"
#define XtCScrollRCursor "ScrollRCursor"
#define XtCScrollUCursor "ScrollUCursor"
#define XtCScrollVCursor "ScrollVCursor"
#define XtCSelection "Selection"
#define XtCSensitive "Sensitive"
#define XtCSelectionArray "SelectionArray"
#define XtCSpace "Space"
#define XtCString "String"
#define XtCTextOptions "TextOptions"
#define XtCTextPosition "TextPosition"
#define XtCTextSink "TextSink"
#define XtCTextSource "TextSource"
#define XtCThickness "Thickness"
#define XtCThumb "Thumb"
#define XtCTranslations "Translations"
#define XtCValue "Value"
#define XtCVSpace "VSpace"
#define XtCWidth "Width"
#define XtCWindow "Window"
#define XtCX "X"
#define XtCY "Y"


/* Representation types */

#define XtRAcceleratorTable "AcceleratorTable"
#define XtRAtom "Atom"
#define XtRBitmap "Bitmap"
#define XtRBool "Bool"
#define XtRBoolean "Boolean"
#define XtRCallback "Callback"
```

```
#define XtRCallProc "CallProc"
#define XtRCardinal "Cardinal"
#define XtRColor "Color"
#define XtRColormap "Colormap"
#define XtRCursor "Cursor"
#define XtRDimension "Dimension"
#define XtRDisplay "Display"
#define XtREditMode "EditMode"
#define XtREnum "Enum"
#define XtRFile "File"
#define XtRFloat "Float"
#define XtRFont "Font"
#define XtRFontStruct "FontStruct"
#define XtRFunction "Function"
#define XtRGeometry "Geometry"
#define XtRImmediate "Immediate"
#define XtRInitialState "InitialState"
#define XtRInt "Int"
#define XtRJustify "Justify"
#define XtRLongBoolean XtRBool
#define XtRObject "Object"
#define XtROrientation "Orientation"
#define XtRPixel "Pixel"
#define XtRPixmap "Pixmap"
#define XtRPointer "Pointer"
#define XtRPosition "Position"
#define XtRScreen "Screen"
#define XtRShort "Short"
#define XtRString "String"
#define XtRStringArray "StringArray"
#define XtRStringTable "StringTable"
#define XtRUnsignedChar "UnsignedChar"
#define XtRTranslationTable "TranslationTable"
#define XtRVisual "Visual"
#define XtRWidget "Widget"
#define XtRWidgetClass "WidgetClass"
```

```
#define XtRWidgetList "WidgetList"
#define XtRWindow "Window"


/* Boolean enumeration constants */

#define XtEoff "off"
#define XtEfalse "false"
#define XtEno "no"
#define XtEon "on"
#define XtEtrue "true"
#define XtEyes "yes"

/* Orientation enumeration constants */

#define XtEvertical "vertical"
#define XtEhorizontal "horizontal"

/* text edit enumeration constants */

#define XtEtextRead "read"
#define XtEtextAppend "append"
#define XtEtextEdit "edit"

/* color enumeration constants */

#define XtExtdefaultbackground "xtdefaultbackground"
#define XtExtdefaultforeground "xtdefaultforeground"

/* font constant */

#define XtExtdefaultfont "xtdefaultfont"
```

Appendix F

Parameter and Return Types

The following table lists all Intrinsics routines that have Widget or WidgetList parameters or Widget return values and gives the restrictions on the parameters or return values. If the type is followed by an asterisk, a note at the end of the table discusses that procedure.

Procedure	Parameter Type	Return Type
XtAddCallback	Object	
XtAddCallbacks	Object	
XtAddEventHandler	Widget	
XtAddGrab	Widget	
XtAddRawEventHandler	Widget	
XtAppCreateShell		Shell
XtAppInitialize		Shell
XtAugmentTranslations	Widget	
XtBuildEventMask	Widget	
XtCallAcceptFocus	Widget	
XtCallActionProc	Widget	
XtCallCallbackList	Object	
XtCallCallbacks	Object	
XtCallbackExclusive	Shell	
XtCallbackNone	Shell	
XtCallbackNonexclusive	Shell	
XtCallbackPopdown	Shell	
XtCallbackReleaseCacheRef	Object	
XtCallbackReleaseCacheRefList	Object	

Procedure	Parameter Type	Return Type
XtCheckSubclass	Object	
XtClass	Object	
XtConfigureWidget	RectObj	
XtConvert	Object	
XtConvertAndStore	Object	
XtCreateManagedWidget	Widget	RectObj
XtCreatePopupShell	Widget	Shell
XtCreateWidget	Object	Object
XtCreateWindow	Widget	
XtDestroyWidget	Object	
XtDisownSelection	Widget	
XtDisplay	Widget	
XtDisplayOfObject	Object	
XtGetApplicationResources	Object	
XtGetGC	Object	
XtGetSelectionRequest	Widget	
XtGetSelectionValue	Widget	
XtGetSelectionValueIncremental	Widget	
XtGetSelectionValues	Widget	
XtGetSelectionValuesIncremental	Widget	
XtGetSubresources	Object	
XtGetValues	Object	
XtGrabButton	Widget	
XtGrabKey	Widget	
XtGrabKeyboard	Widget	
XtGrabPointer	Widget	
XtHasCallbacks	Object	
XtInitialize		Shell
XtInsertEventHandler	Widget	
XtInsertRawEventHandler	Widget	
XtInstallAccelerators	Widget*	
XtInstallAllAccelerators	Widget*	
XtIsApplicationShell	Object	
XtIsComposite	Object	
XtIsConstraint	Object	
XtIsManaged	Object*	
XtIsOverrideShell	Object	
XtIsRealized	Object*	
XtIsSensitive	Object*	

Procedure	Parameter Type	Return Type
XtIsShell	Object	
XtIsSubclass	Object	
XtIsTopLevelShell	Object	
XtIsTransientShell	Object	
XtIsVendorShell	Object	
XtIsWMShell	Object	
XtIsWidget	Object	
XtMakeGeometryRequest	RectObj	
XtMakeResizeRequest	RectObj	
XtManageChild	RectObj	
XtManageChildren	RectObj	
XtMapWidget	Widget	
XtMoveWidget	RectObj	
XtName	Object	
XtNameToWidget	Object	Object
XtOverrideTranslations	Widget	
XtOwnSelection	Widget	
XtOwnSelectionIncremental	Widget	
XtParent	Object	
XtPopdown	Shell	
XtPopup	Shell	
XtPopupSpringLoaded	Shell	
XtQueryGeometry	RectObj	
XtRealizeWidget	Widget	
XtReleaseGC	Object	
XtRemoveAllCallbacks	Object	
XtRemoveCallback	Object	
XtRemoveCallbacks	Object	
XtRemoveEventHandler	Widget	
XtRemoveGrab	Widget	
XtRemoveRawEventHandler	Widget	
XtResizeWidget	RectObj	
XtResizeWindow	Widget	
XtScreen	Widget	
XtScreenOfObject	Object	
XtSetKeyboardFocus	*	
XtSetMappedWhenManaged	Widget	
XtSetSensitive	RectObj	
XtSetValues	Object	

Procedure	Parameter Type	Return Type
XtSetWMColormapWindows	Widget*	
XtSuperclass	Object	
XtTranslateCoords	RectObj	
XtUngrabButton	Widget	
XtUngrabKey	Widget	
XtUngrabKeyboard	Widget	
XtUngrabPointer	Widget	
XtUninstallTranslations	Widget	
XtUnmanageChild	RectObj	
XtUnmanageChildren	RectObj	
XtUnmapWidget	Widget	
XtUnrealizeWidget	Widget	
XtVaAppCreateShell		Shell
XtVaCreateManagedWidget	Widget	RectObj
XtVaCreatePopupShell	Widget	Shell
XtVaCreateWidget	Object	Object
XtVaGetApplicationResources	Object	
XtVaGetSubresources	Object	
XtVaGetValues	Object	
XtVaSetValues	Object	
XtWidgetToApplicationContext	Object	
XtWindow	Widget	
XtWindowOfObject	Object	
XtWindowToWidget		Widget

Notes

For `XtInstallAccelerators` and `XtInstallAllAccelerators`, both arguments must be of class Widget.

For `XtIsManaged` and `XtIsSensitive`, the return value is FALSE if the argument is not a subclass of RectObj.

For `XtIsRealized`, the test will be applied to the parent if the argument is not of class Widget.

For `XtSetKeyboardFocus`, the subtree argument must be of class Widget and the destination argument must be of class Object. If the destination is not of class Widget, the Intrinsics will deliver the events to the destination's parent.

For `XtSetWMColormapWindows`, both the widget argument and the elements of the list argument must be of class Widget.

The following table lists the restrictions for routines with parameters of type WidgetClass:

Procedure	Parameter Type
XtAppCreateShell	ShellClass
XtCheckSubclass	ObjectClass
XtCreateManagedWidget	RectObjClass
XtCreatePopupShell	ShellClass
XtCreateWidget	ObjectClass
XtGetConstraintResourceList	ObjectClass
XtGetResourceList	ObjectClass
XtInitializeWidgetClass	ObjectClass
XtIsSubclass	ObjectClass
XtVaAppCreateShell	ShellClass
XtVaCreateManagedWidget	RectObjectClass
XtVaCreatePopupShell	ShellClass
XtVaCreateWidget	ObjectClass

Appendix G

Naming
Conventions

This appendix lists the conventions used by various toolkit components and gives examples from the Pushbutton and GraphDisplay classes presented in the programmer's guide. Most of these conventions are specific to the C language. The term *mixed capitalization* means that the name is in mixed upper- and lower-case with capital letters indicating word divisions, beginning with a capital letter in most cases.

These naming conventions simplify the job of a programmer using, maintaining, or subclassing widgets by providing a uniform name space.

G.1 File Name Conventions

Each widget class provides a public header file for applications, named with the class name in mixed capitalization starting with a capital letter, and with ".h" as the suffix. If the resulting file name would be more than twelve characters, the class name is truncated to its first ten characters.

Each widget class provides a private header file for its implementation and for the implementations of subclasses, named with the class name in mixed capitalization starting with a capital letter, and with "P.h" as the suffix. If the resulting file name would be more than twelve characters, the class name is truncated to its first nine characters.

Widget implementations are normally in files named with the class name in mixed capitalization starting with a capital letter, and with ".c" as the suffix. If the resulting file name would be more than twelve characters, the class name is truncated to its first ten characters.

If a widget implementation is divided among several files, any internal header files are named with the class name in mixed capitalization starting with a capital letter, and with "I.h" as the suffix. If the resulting file name would be more than twelve characters, the class name is truncated to its first nine characters.

To provide portability to operating systems without capitalization distinctions in file names, you should not count on different capitalization to distinguish between file names.

	Pushbutton Class	*GraphDisplay Class*
Public header file	`Pushbutton.h`	`GraphDispl.h`
Private header file	`PushbuttoP.h`	`GraphDispP.h`
Widget implementation	`Pushbutton.c`	`GraphDispl.c`
Optional internal header file	`PushbuttoI.h`	`GraphDispI.h`

G.2 Widget Name Conventions

Each widget class provides a type definition for widgets of that class named with the class name in mixed capitalization starting with a capital letter and ending with the suffix "Widget", "Gadget", or "Object".

Each widget class provides an external class variable named with the class name in mixed capitalization starting with a lower-case letter and ending with the suffix "WidgetClass", "GadgetClass", or "ObjectClass".

	Pushbutton Class	*GraphDisplay Class*
Type definition	PushbuttonWidget	GraphDisplayObject
Class variable	*pushbuttonWidgetClass*	*graphDisplayObjectClass*

The remainder of the widget name conventions are important only to widget writers.

The widget instance part structure type is named with the class name in mixed capitalization starting with a capital letter and ending with the suffix "Part". Fields in this structure are all lower-case and use an underscore to separate words.

The full widget instance structure type is named with the class name in mixed capitalization starting with a capital letter and ending with the suffix

"Rec". The structure name is the same, but preceded with an underscore. Each field in this structure is a widget instance part structure named with the corresponding class name in mixed capitalization starting with a lower-case letter. The type definition for widgets of this class is defined to be a pointer to this structure type.

The widget class part structure type is named with the class name in mixed capitalization starting with a capital letter and ending with the suffix "ClassPart". Fields in this structure are all lower-case and use an underscore to separate words.

The full widget class structure type is named with the class name in mixed capitalization starting with a capital letter and ending with the suffix "ClassRec". The structure name is the same, but preceded with an underscore. Each field in this structure is a widget class part structure named with the corresponding class name in mixed capitalization starting with a lower-case letter and ending with the suffix "_class". A pointer type to this structure is named with the class name in mixed capitalization starting with a capital letter and ending with the suffix "WidgetClass", "GadgetClass", or "ObjectClass".

The static widget class structure is named with the class name in mixed capitalization starting with a lower-case letter and ending with the suffix "ClassRec". The external class variable is a pointer to this structure.

	Pushbutton Class	*GraphDisplay Class*
Instance part type	PushbuttonPart	GraphDisplayPart
Instance type	PushbuttonRec	GraphDisplayRec
Instance structure name	_PushbuttonRec	_GraphDisplayRec
Class part type	PushbuttonClassPart	GraphDisplayClassPart
Class type	PushbuttonClassRec	GraphDisplayClassRec
Class pointer type	PushbuttonWidgetClass	GraphDisplayObjectClass
Class structure name	_PushbuttonClassRec	_GraphDisplayClassRec
Static class structure	pushbuttonClassRec	graphDisplayClassRec

The declarations for the Pushbutton example are

In the public header file:

```
/* Instance type */
typedef struct _PushbuttonRec *PushbuttonWidget;

/* Widget class pointer */
extern WidgetClass pushbuttonWidgetClass;
```

In the private header file:
```
/* Instance part */
typedef struct {
    ...instance part fields, all lower case with _'s ...
} PushbuttonPart;

/* Full instance record */
typedef struct _PushbuttonRec {
    CorePart        core;
    LabelPart       label;
    PushbuttonPart  pushbutton;
} PushbuttonRec;

/* Class part structure */
typedef struct {
    ...class part fields, all lower case with _'s ...
} PushbuttonClassPart;

/* Full class record */
typedef struct _PushbuttonClassRec {
    CoreClassPart        core_class;
    LabelClassPart       label_class;
    PushbuttonClassPart  pushbutton_class;
} PushbuttonClassRec, *PushbuttonWidgetClass;

/* External definition for class record */
extern PushbuttonClassRec pushbuttonClassRec;
```

In the widget implementation:
```
/* Class record declaration */
PushbuttonClassRec pushbuttonClassRec = {
    ...static class record declaration...
};

/* Class record pointer */
WidgetClass pushbuttonWidgetClass =
    (WidgetClass) &pushbuttonClassRec;
```

G.3   Resource Name Conventions

Each resource name is a string in mixed capitalization starting with a lower-case letter.

Each resource name identifier is the same as the resource name string with the prefix "XtN".

The field corresponding to a resource name is in lower-case with underscores separating the words.

Each resource class is a string in mixed capitalization starting with a capital letter.

Each resource class identifier is the same as the resource class string with the prefix "XtC".

Each resource type is a string in mixed capitalization starting with a capital letter. The string is often, but not always, the same as the corresponding C language type.

Each resource type identifier is the same as the resource type string with the prefix "XtR".

	Border Width Resource	*Foreground Resource Class*	*Widget Resource Type*
Name	"borderWidth"	"Foreground"	"Widget"
Identifier	XtNborderWidth	XtCForeground	XtRWidget
Field name	*border_width*		
C language type			Widget

G.4   Constraint Name Conventions

These conventions are important only to widget writers.

A widget class that is a subclass of Constraint uses the additional conventions in this section when naming its constraint record. They are similar to the conventions used for widget instances.

The constraint part structure type is named with the class name in mixed capitalization starting with a capital letter and ending with the suffix "ConstraintPart".

The full constraint structure type is named with the class name in mixed capitalization starting with a capital letter and ending with the suffix "ConstraintRec". Each field in this structure is a constraint part structure named with the corresponding class name in mixed capitalization starting with a lower-case letter.

A pointer type to the full constraint structure is named with the class name in mixed capitalization starting with a capital letter and ending with the suffix "Constraint".

The example Pushbutton and GraphDisplay classes are not subclasses of Constraint, but MinMax is.

	MinMax Class
Constraint part structure type	MinMaxConstraintPart
Constraint structure type	MinMaxConstraintRec
Constraint pointer type	MinMaxConstraint

G.5   Extension Name Conventions

These conventions are important only to widget writers.

If a widget class provides a standard extension to itself, it uses the conventions in this section to name the extension record.

The extension structure type is named with the class name in mixed capitalization starting with a capital letter and ending with the suffix "ClassExtensionRec".

The type for a pointer to the extension record is named with the class name in mixed capitalization starting with a capital letter and ending with the suffix "ClassExtension".

The extension version constant is named with the class name in mixed capitalization starting with a capital letter and ending with the suffix "ExtensionVersion". If the class is an Intrinsics class, the constant begins with the prefix "Xt".

The example Pushbutton and GraphDisplay classes do not define extensions, but Composite does.

	Composite Class
Extension structure type	CompositeClassExtensionRec
Extension structure pointer type	CompositeClassExtension
Extension version constant	XtCompositeExtensionVersion

Appendix H

The X Registry and the Examples

H.1 The X Registry

There are places in the X Toolkit, in applications, in other standard libraries, and in the X protocol that define and use string names. In some of these places the names are used in a context that is visible across libraries, applications, or even systems, and conflicts are possible if different components use the same name for different things.

The MIT X consortium maintains a registry of names in various domains to avoid unintentional conflicts among programs. It is not necessary to register a name to use it, but registration provides a central name clearinghouse that developers can consult to find which names are already in use.

The categories of name registry most relevant to toolkit programmers are

Organization names
These should generally be used as prefixes for other registered names. Examples are "MIT" and "X3D".

Selection names
Applications that use private selection names should register them to avoid other applications inadvertently using the same name. A name clash could result in an application that requested a selection receiving one with a different semantic meaning than the requested one. In general, private selection names should start with a leading underscore, followed by the organizational prefix, followed by another underscore.

Selection targets
A name clash between selection targets could result in an application's receiving a requested selection in a different format than the expected one. In general, private selection targets should

start with a leading underscore, followed by the organizational prefix, followed by another underscore.

Resource types
: The actual C data type corresponding to the resource type should be registered to avoid conflicts among different widgets.

Application classes
: The application defaults file name depends upon the application class name, so two different applications with the same class name cannot have their defaults files installed on the same system at the same time. Only classes may be registered; application names may not be.

Class extension record types
: Registering these makes it less likely that two independent extensions will choose the same extension record type.

There are other categories in other domains as well, but they are less directly applicable to toolkit programmers. The current contents of the X name registry and a complete list of the domains is in the directory `mit/doc/Registry` in the Release 4 distribution from MIT.

The following information about the X Registry is taken from the Release 4 X software distribution and is accurate at the date of publication.

Requests to register names or questions about registration should be addressed to

`xregistry@expo.lcs.mit.edu`

or to

Bob Scheifler, Director MIT X Consortium
Laboratory for Computer Science
545 Technology Square
Cambridge, MA 02139

Electronic mail will be acknowledged upon receipt. Please allow up to four weeks for a formal response to registration requests and inquiries.

All registered items must have the postal address of someone responsible for the item, or a reference to a document describing the item and the postal address of where to write to obtain the document.

H.2   Getting the Example Programs

For readers with Internet access, a compressed `tar` image containing the widgets and applications in the programmer's guide is available for anonymous `ftp` under the name `asente-swick.examples.tar.Z` on the machines `gatekeeper.dec.com` and `expo.lcs.mit.edu`. The file may also appear on other machines that offer the X distribution.

Machine Name	Internet Address	Directory
gatekeeper.dec.com	16.1.0.2	pub/X11/contrib
expo.lcs.mit.edu	18.30.0.212	contrib

The sources should also be available in the Usenet comp.sources.x archive; however, the list of archive sites and even the instructions on how to get the list change frequently. One site that is likely to remain stable is uunet; if you send a mail message to netlib@uunet with "help" as the subject line, you should receive instructions by return mail on how to retrieve files from the archive. You can also contact postmaster@uunet for information on getting the sources in other ways.

Index